TECHNOLOGY OF HERBAL COSMETICS AND TOILETRIES PRODUCTS WITH FORMULAE

TECHNOLOGY OF HERBAL COSMETICS AND TOILETRIES PRODUCTS WITH FORMULAE

Written By :
EIRI Board of Consultants & Engineer

ENGINEERS INDIA RESEARCH INSTITUTE
4449, Nai Sarak, Main Road, Delhi-110 006 (India)
Ph.: 91-11-23918117, 23916431, 23840361, 9811437895
Fax :91-11-23916431, 23918117
* **E-Mail**: eirisidi@bol.net.in
* **Website**: www.eiriindia.org
Also at : 4/54 Roop Nagar, opp. Kamla Nagar, Delhi—110007

Printed and Published by :

ENGINEERS INDIA RESEARCH INSTITUTE

4449, Nai Sarak, Main Road, Delhi-110 006 (India)

Ph.: 91-11-23918117, 23916431, 23840361, 9811437895

Fax :91-11-23916431, 23918117

★ **E-Mail**: eirisidi@bol.net.in

★ **Website**: www.eiriindia.org

ISBN : 978-81-89765-13-2

Printed in New Delhi (India)

Rs. 1100

Printed and Published by Sudhir Gupta for "Engineers India Research Institute", 4449, Nai Sarak, Main Road, New Delhi-110 006 and Printed at Swastik Offset, Delhi

Preface

'Herbal Cosmetics and Toiletries Products' have got tremendous demand throughout the world. As herbal cosmetics have got wide acceptability in all age group people. India is also known for herbs of many kinds. Herbal based cosmetics have been used by almost all age groups from many years.

Herbal Cosmetics Industry set up in India is a profitable business as all the required herbs are fluently available in India. India is also exporting herbal based Cosmetics in the World.

We are presenting this book which includes various products which can be produced from herbs. The major chapters of this book are Herbal Cosmetics, Skin Purification, Hair Conditioning, Regulatory provisions Relating to Manufacture of Cosmetics, Ultra Violet Protection Sunscreen Cream, Glow Pack (All Purpose Face Mask), Hair Oil with Vitamin-E, Lanolin & Protein, Herbal Cream (All Purpose), Jojoba Body Scrub, Face Wash, Liquid Bindi (Kum Kum) or Body Spot, Tooth Paste (Gel Type), Nail Polish Or Nail Enamel with Pearlescent Pigments, Face Pack (Anti-Wrinkle), Herbal Hair Vitaliser (Anti-Dandruff), Shaving Gel, Moisturizer with Aloe Vera and Coconut oil, Mosquito Repellent Cream, Nail Polish Remover, Cucumber Lemon Face Pack, Henna Conditioning Shampoo, Ayurvedic Hair Oil (Like Banphool), Herbal Shaving Cream, Aromatherapy Liquid Soap, Herbal Fairness Cream, Hair Removing Cream (Depilatories), Nail Polish (Nail Enamel), Mud Pack (Face Pack), Herbal Shampoo, Herbal Amla Hair Oil, Acne-No Pimple Cream, Kali Mehandi (Herbal Hair Dye Powder—Black), Herbal Cold Cream, Amla Shikakai Reetha Herbal Shampoo, Fairness Vanishing Cream, Hair Styling Gel, Eye Liner (Liquid), Moisturizing Cream with Aloe vera, Aloe Pack, Herbal Brahmi Amla *Hair Oil, Haldi* (Turmeric) Chandan (Sandal) Fairness Cream, After Shave

Lotion, Peppermint Mouth Wash, Herbal Henna Powder, Toilet Powders, Beauty Preparations, Lipstics, Rouges and Eye Cosmetics, Baby Care, Afro Products, Important Details for Setting up, Regulatory Provisions Relating to Manufacture of Cosmetics, Requirements of Factory Premisses for Manufacture of Cosmetics, Suppliers of Raw Materials, Machineries and Packaging Materials.

The book has been written for the benefit and to prove an asset and a handy reference guide in the hands of new entrepreneurs & well established industrialists.

ENGINEERS INDIA RESEARCH INSTITUTE

4449, Nai Sarak, Main Road, Delhi-110 006 (INDIA)
E-mail : eirisidi@bol.net.in

Contents Cum Subject Index

1

Herbal Cosmetics

Cosmetic

Any substance, preparation, or treatment, applied to the person (a) to cleanse, (b) to alter the appearance, (c) to promote the attractiveness of the person. The term thus includes all creams, powders, lotions, and colouring agents applied to the face, scalp, hair, and hands, and many borderline products, such as deodorants, depilatories, and oral and suntan preparations.

According to the broad definitions in the preceding section, the various kinds, of cosmetic products are best grouped in three principal classes: (1) for the skin, (2) for the hair, and (3} for the nails. In form they may be dry powders, pastes, solid or liquid emulsions, or aqueous, alcoholic, or oily solutions. The methods of manufacturing are essentially those employed for the manufacture of other commercial products of similar form. In the following pages, therefore, specific information will be given only for those products that require special techniques, or notes on other points of special interest.

Cosmetology

A branch of applied science that deals with the external embellishment of the person through the use of cosmetic products and treatments. As specified in most state laws, the regions of the body that may be treated in cosmetology are the head, neck, upper chest and back, arms, and hands (now extended to include lower legs and feet). The permitted treatments are hairdressing, haircutting, temporary and permanent waving, hair bleaching and coloring, and corrective and preventive care, by massage or otherwise, of scalp and skin on face, chest, back, arms, and hands. Related branches are body massage, electrolysis, and chiropody. electrolysis, and chiropody.

INGREDIENTS OF HERBAL COSMETICS

Both organic and inorganic natural materials are used in the manufacture of herbal cosmetic products; the former have undergone a gradual shifting from natural vegetable and animal substances, through metallic compounds, to the synthetic organic. As only certain substances of a class may have the properties desired for a certain cosmetic product, the range of possible ingredients is usually limited.

Among the types of organic substances used in cosmetics are: natural and synthetic oils, fats, and waxes; liquid, semisolid, and solid hydrocarbons; soaps and synthetic surface-active agents; starches, gums, and resins; dyes and pigments; acids, alcohols, and esters; alkyl- and alkanolamines; and many others. The inorganic substances include water and hydrogen peroxide; metallic salts and oxides; acids, ammonia, fixed alkalies; and many others.

Cosmetic Emulsions

Cosmetic lotions and creams are emulsions of water-based and oil-based phases. An emulsion is a two-phase system consisting of two incompletely miscible liquids, the internal, or discontinuous, phase dispersed as finite globules in the other. Special designations have been devised for oil and water emulsions to indicate which is the dispersed and which the continuous phase. Oil-in-water (o/w) emulsions have oil as the dispersed phase in water as the continuous phase. In water-in-oil (w/o) emulsions, water is dispersed in oil, which is the external (continuous) phase (8-9).

Properties of Emulsions

The properties that are most apparent, and thus are usually most important, are: case of dilution, viscosity, color, and stability. For a given type of emulsification equipment, these properties depend upon: (1) the properties of the continuous phase, (2) the ratio of the external to the internal phase, (31 the particle size of the emulsion, (4) the relationship of the continuous phase to the particles (including ionic charges), and (5) the properties of the discontinuous phase. In any given emulsion, the properties depend upon which liquid constitutes the external phase, i.e, whether the emulsion is o/w or w/o. The resulting emulsion type is controlled by: (1) the emulsifier: type, and amount, (2) the ratio of ingredients, and (3) the order of addition of ingredients during mixing.

The dispersibility (solubility) of an emulsion is determined by the continuous phase; thus if the continuous phase is water-soluble; the emulsion can be diluted with water; conversely, if the continuous phase is oil-soluble, the emulsion can be diluted with oil.

The ease with which an emulsion can be diluted, increased by decreasing the viscosity of the emulsion. The viscosity of an emulsion when the continuous phase is in excess is essentially the viscosity of the continuous phase. As the proportion of internal phase increases, the viscosity of the emulsion increases to the point that the emulsion is no longer fluid. When the volume of the internal phase exceeds the volume of the external phase, the emulsion particles become crowded and the apparent viscosity is partially structural viscosity.

An emulsion is stable as long as the particles of the internal phase do not coalesce. The stability of emulsion depends upon: (1) the particle size; (2) the difference in density of the two phase; (3) the viscosity of the continuous phase and of the completed emulsion; (4) the charges on the particles; (5) the nature, effectiveness, and amount of the emulsifier used; and (6) conditions of storage, including temperature variation, agitation and vibration, and dilution or evaporation during storage or use. The stability of an emulsion is affected by almost all factors involved in its formulation and preparation. In formulas containing sizable amounts of emulsifier, stability is predominantly a function of the type and concentration of emulsifier.

Emulsifiers

Emulsifiers can be classified as ionic or nonionic according to their behaviour. An ionic emulsifier is composed of an organic lipophilic group (L) and a hydrophilic group (H). The hydrophilic- lipophilic balance (HLB) is often used to characterize emulsifiers and related surfactant materials. The ionic types may be further divided into anionic and cationic, depending upon the nature of the ion-active group. The lipophilic portion of the molecule is usually considered to be the surface-active portion.

Nonionic emulsifiers are completely covalent and show no apparent tendency to ionize. They can, therefore, be combined with other nonionic surface-active agents and with either anionic or cationic agents as well. The nonionic emulsifiers are likewise less susceptible to the action of electrolytes than the anionic surface-active agents. The solubility of an emulsifier is of the greatest importance in the preparation of emulsifiable concentrates.

Emulsifiers, being surface-active agents, lower surface and interfacial tensions and increase the tendency of their solution to spread.

O/w emulsifying agents produce emulsions in which the continuous phase is hydrophilic; hence, such emulsions are generally dispersible in water and will conduct electricity. The surfactants that are capable of producing such emulsions usually have an HLB of more than 6.0 (preferably 7), the hydrophilic portion of their molecules being predominant. (Between HLB 5 and 7 many surfactants will function as either w/o or o/w emulsifiers, depending on how they are used).

O/w emulsifiers		HLB
P.E.G. 300 distearate	nonionic	7.3
sorbitan monolaurate	nonionic	8.6
P.E.G. 400 distearate	nonionic	9.3
triethanolamine stearate	anionic	12.0
P.E.G. 6000 monolaurate	nonionic	19.2

W/o emulsifiers produce emulsions in which the continuous phase is lipophilic in character (oil, wax, fat, etc). Such emulsions are not generally dispersible in water and do not conduct electricity. The surfactants capable of producing such emulsions usually have an HLB of less than 6.0 and preferably below 5. The lipophilic portion of their molecules is predominant.

W/o emulsifiers		HLB
lanolin alcohols	nonionic	ca 1.0
ethylene glycol monostearate S/E	nonionic	2.0
propylene glycol monostearate S/E	anionic	3.2
sorbitan monooleate	nonionic	4.3
P.E.G. 200 dilaurate	nonionic	6.0

COSMETICS FOR THE SKIN

Under cosmetics for the skin may be included all preparations used for conditioning or embellishment—creams, lotions, masks, powders, colorings and products used for personal hygiene—toilet soaps, accessories for the bath, deodorants, and hair removers.

CREAMS

Creams constitute the largest class of cosmetic preparations used on the skin. Although the variety may seem bewildering, every true cream consists basically of an emulsion of oily and watery substances in solid or liquid form. According to their function, creams fall into three principal groups: cleansers, emollients, and finishers. Most cleansing creams and all emollient creams are water-in-oil emulsions; most of the finishing creams are oil-in-water emulsions. The Toilet Goods Association has published standards for most of the raw materials used in the making of cosmetic creams.

Cleansing creams are of three types: cold creams, "quick-liquefying" creams, and liquid cleaners. A satisfactory cleansing cream is a water-in-oil emulsion that melts at the temperature of the body and spreads readily over the skin. The oily ingredients should be light enough to penetrate a little to clear the skin of impurities, and flow away. It should not contain any appreciable amounts of substances that might be retained by the skin. The product should not be sticky; after it is removed, the skin should feel smooth, clean but not greasy, and relaxed.

The product known as *cold cream* is of historical interest because the original recipe for a cream of this kind dates from the *Ceratum refrigerans Galeni,* introduced by Galen, a physician of ancient Rome (A.D. 130-200). It consisted of almond oil, bees-wax, and rose water; the designation It was undoubtedly applied to it because of the sensation produced on the skin as the water evaporated. An early modification of the recipe, long official in some pharmacopeias, contained spermaceti and a small amount of borax as an auxiliary emulsifying agent; still later, varying amounts of mineral oil, paraffin, and other related substances were included. This type of cleanser is satisfactory for the normal skin as well as for a skin that tends to dryness. Some typical compositions for cold cream are given in Table 1.I (3, 4, 6, 9, 13). Among other fatty and waxy materials occasionally incorporated in cold creams are; carnauba wax, castor oil, ceresin. cocoabutter, olive oil, oleic acid, peanut oil, sesame oil, stearic acid (triple pressed, XXX), and certain synthetic fats and waxes. Among many newer emulsifying agents are: aminoglycol, alkanolamines, and esters of polyhydric alcohols. Distilled or de-ionized water is now used instead of rose water: practically all cleansing creams are delicately perfumed.

Table 1.I. Compositions of Cleansing Creams.

	Typical recipe, % by wt. in					
Ingredient	1	2	3	4	5	6
Almond oil	34	50	35	-	-	-
Beeswax	16	12	12	8	13	5
Lanolin	-	-	15	-	-	20
Mineral oil	-	-	-	50	45	-
Paraffin wax	-		-	-	-	-
35						
Spermaceti	-	12	8	12	6	55
Borax	1	1	-	1	1	-
Distilled water	-	-	-	-	35	35
Stronger rose water	49	25	28	29	-	-
Total	100	100	100	100	100	100

The so-called *quick-liquefying creams* as originally prepared were not really creams, that is, emulsions, but simply mixtures of liquid and solid hydrocarbons, melted together and perfumed. The principal purpose of this type of product is to melt and spread rapidly, but it is not equally effective in removing all kinds of dirt. As the long continued use of petroleum hydrocarbons is admittedly drying, cleansers of this type are more satisfactory for skins that tend toward oiliness. To meet this criticism, some compositions have been modified to contain animal and vegetable fats and waxes, and even to produce them as emulsions. For some typical compositions, see Table 1.II.

Table 1.II. Compositions of Quick-Liquefying Creams.

Ingredient	Typical recipe, % by wt. in: 1	2	3	4	5
Beeswax	16	-	9	-	7
Ceresin	-	12	-	-	12
Mineral oil	74	88	50	50	43
Ozokerite	5	-	-	-	
Paraffin wax	5	-	18	30	
Petrolatum	-	-	23	20	38
Total	100	100	100	100	100

Emollient creams are those intended for the special purpose of softening the skin, and are usually employed as lubricants or while resting. They were formerly designated "skin foods," "rejuvenating creams," "nourishing creams," etc., and are now recognizable as "night creams," or "massage creams," etc.

In physical properties, emollient creams often are of a heavier consistency than cleansing creams; because of the presence of lanolin, they are often yellowish and appreciably tacky. As lanolin, itself, is entirely too viscous to permit free motion over the skin, emollient creams contain varying percentages of vegetable and mineral oils. To avoid the yellowish tinge, mixtures of sterols with inert hydrocarbons—the so-called absorption bases—are often substituted for lanolin.

Other ingredients of emollient creams may be: benzoinated land, cocoa butter, beeswax, spermaceti; almond, corn, castor, and olive oils; hydrogenated vegetable oils; cetyl and stearyl alcohols, glycerol, glycol, and derivatives; lecithin, vitamins and estrogenic substances. Because of the relative case with which lanolin creams seem to penetrate the skin, they serve as vehicles for products with specifically intended properties; that is, bleaching, astringent, and medicated creams. The effectiveness of organotherapeutic agents, as applied externally in cosmetic creams, has been the subject of intensive research and is still a subject of controversy despite steadily encouraging reports on research. Some typical compositions for emollient creams are given in Table 1.III.

Table 1.III. Compositions of Emollient Creams.

Ingredient	Typical recipe, % wt. in: 1	2	3	4	5
Almond oil	-	-	10	10	-
Beeswax	20	8	4	10	-
Borax	1	-	-	0.5	-
Cetyl alcohol	2	2	-	-	-
Cholesterol	2.5	2	-	-	3
Cocoa butter	7	6	-	10	-
Lanolin (anhydrous)	-	10	10	5	50
Olive oil	-	50	10	-	-
Lecithin	-	1	-	-	-
Petrolatum (solid or liquid)	45.5	-	20	40	-
Stearic acid (XXX)	-	-	-	-	10
Spermaceti	-	-	4.5	5	-
Triethanolamine	-	-	-	-	8
Perfume	1	1	0.5	0.5	1
Preservative	0.5	1	0.2	0.5	1
Water, to make	100.0	100.0	100.0	100.0	100.0

Products that are high in lanolin content are specifically good as lubricants for massage of a dry skin. For the oily skin, a composition containing little or no lanolin is more satisfactory; many operators find a cleansing cream satisfactory for this purpose.

Finishing creams are those used after the skin is cleansed (and in facial treatments, after the massage) as a foundation for make-up. They are of two types: vanishing creams and pigmented foundations.

Vanishing creams is essentially an oil-in-water emulsion of stearic acid and water in which a small amount of a suitable emulsifier serves as the binder. The latter may be formed *in situ* by first mixing a portion of the stearic acid with sodium or potassium hydroxide, triethanolamine, aminoglycol, etc. This type of product is readily recognizable by its pearly luster. Sodium stearate produces a relatively harder, and potassium stearate a relatively softer, cream; the latter is usually preferable.

The so-called vanishing creams do not actually disappear into the skin, but simply spread a thin smooth film over it, which temporarily conceals roughness and enhances the effect of face powder. Because some skins are appreciably dry, modifying substances are usually added to the basic emulsion; glycerol is often present as a humectant. Among the substances used to vary the properties of vanishing creams are: cocoa butter, lanolin, cetyl alcohol, benzoinated lard, mineral oil (for superficial oiliness) and certain synthetic waxes.

The proportion of glycerol present is a most important factor. Many of the objections to vanishing creams in the early days were due to an inadequate understanding of the properties and effects of glycerol. As it can combine with water in all proportions, it may serve as a humectant and be beneficial to the skin; if used in excess, it may extract water from the tissues causing a drying or burning sensation. In humid weather it also absorbs moisture from the atmosphere, causing stickiness and spotting in face powder. In the past, certain imported creams of this type were found to contain as high as 50% of glycerol; American products are uniformly lower in content. Some typical compositions for vanishing creams are given in Table 1.IV.

Table 1.IV. Compositions of Vanishing Foundation Creams

Ingredient	Typical recipe, % by wt.in: 1	2	3	4	5
Cetyl alcohol	-	-	0.5	0.5	-
Glycerol	10	10	5	8	6
Lanolin	-	1	5	-	4
Mineral oil	-	2	5	-	-
Potassium hydroxide	1	0.5	-	-	2
Sodium hydroxide	-	0.5	-	0.4	-
Stearic acid (XXX)	25	22	20	20	15
Triethanolanine	-	-	2	1.2	-
Perfume	0.5	1	0.5	-	-
Water, to make	100.0	100.0	100.0	100.0	100.0

Pigmented foundations are modifications of the heavy creams used as theatrical make-up. Any good recipe for vanishing cream can serve as the base, the opacity being supplied by incorporating a good powder composition in appropriate shades. Some of these products are applied like vanishing cream, directly from the tube or jar, and are carefully spread over the skin a little at a time. Others, in the form of a compressed cake of cream or paste, are applied with water and a sponge, and allowed to dry. Depending upon the composition, the effect of one of these foundations may or may not be satisfactory without the application of face powder over it.

If properly compounded, these pigmented foundations (also called *cake make-up* and *powder base)* may be used on any type of skin. They are especially effective on skin that tends to oiliness because they give a smooth finish and effectively conceal the conspicuous pores and other blemishes commonly found in oily skin.

Special creams comprise all those whose composition is modified to effect some definite purpose, such as bleaching or tightening the skin, or clearing it of minor lesions.

A stringent creams are used during facial treatments for the massage of an oily skin, and for overnight use at home. Almost any good emollient cream can serve as a basis; substances added for the astringent effect are alum, zine phenolsulfonate, zinc sulfate, and the like. The exact nature of the mechanism by which an astringent cream functions is not definitely understood. As the so-called pores (actually the pilosebaceous openings) cannot be reduced in size, it is believed that the appearance of reduction results from varying degrees of swelling in the tissue surrounding the lumen of the pore. In practice the use of an astringent cream is usually supplemented by application of an astringent lotion.

Bleaching creams contain a variety of ingredients, selected either for lightening the color of the skin or for covering it with an opaque white film. Any good composition for emollient cream can serve as the basis, and the product is used both in beauty shops and at home, either as a step in a facial treament or overnight. Stronger bleaching agents incorporated in these creams are mercury compounds (chiefly ammoniated mercury, permissible to 5%); among the milder compounds commonly used are peroxides of hydrogen, magnesium, and zinc, and mild (weak) acids, such as dilute acetic, citric, and lactic. As they act slowly, these creams are supplemented by the use of bleaching lotions. The whitening creams contain titanium dioxide or zinc oxide (occasionally bismuth "subnitrate") and simply spread white pigment over the face. Older products of this type appear as thick pastes, compounded with water instead of in a cream base, or as powders, to be mixed with water.

Acne creams, intended to help in clearing the complexion of pustules and other minor lesions, are more properly classed as drugs than as cosmetics. A good emollient cream should serve as the base, preferably one very soft in consistency so that the product can be spread easily without irritating the skin. Among the active ingredients commonly employed for treatment of acne are: benzoin, B-naphthol, cade oil, camphor, boric and salicylic acids, phenol, sulfur, zinc carbonate (calamine), and zinc oxide. The composition of such a cream should be based on sound dermatological principles.

"All-purpose" creams are actually misnamed. From the foregoing discussion of the desired properties and the functions of various standard types of cosmetic creams, it should be clear that no single product can serve the purpose of all of them equally well. A cleansing cream, for example, which is intended to act superficially and leave the skin relaxed and receptive, cannot also carry effective substances into the skin, constringe it, and serve as a basis for make-up. The composition that most nearly meets multiple demands could be a well-compounded cold cream containing additional lanolin, which both softens the skin and leaves sufficient residue to serve as a foundation for powder and makeup.

Miscellaneous special creams (for example, *eye creams* or *throat* creams) are generally emollients with a base of lanolin, stiffened with natural or synthetic waxes, and containing compounds intended specifically to make wrinkles and fine lines less conspicuous.

Estrogenic Creams, The possibility of improving the condition and appearance of the skin by the external application of estrogenic substances has been for several years a subject of controversy between medical authorities and scientific investigators. Intensive research, however, undertaken independently by several reputable manufacturers, has yielded results that substantiate the claims made for estrogenic creams. According to one published report (3a), topical application of a well-compounded estrogenic cream causes considerable improvement in the skin of older women (deficient in estrogenic substance), without evidence of systemic effects or any indication of malignancy.

Protective creams, also called *industrial creams,* came into long-delayed recognition during World War II through the need for protecting the hands from injury—or merely soiling—in the prosecution of many industrial processes. The widespread adoption of these products and their admitted success should insure for them a permanent place in industrial plants.

The wide diversity of chemical irritants might seem to call for almost as many protective agents. The ideal product must spread easily and if possible penetrate into the hair folicles; it must remain stable in contact with most chemical agents, providing an oily film of low surface tension; it must not dehydrate the skin; and it must be readily removable with any good soap.

Protective creams are of four types: mixtures of fats and oils; jellies containing physical barriers; emulsions; and soap bases. Each type offers certain advantages and disadvantages, but the best all-around product seems to be an emulsion of fats and waxes with water, made with triethanolamine, and incorporating magnesium stearate or talc as the physical and chemical barrier (13).

The advantages of these protective creams in preventing industrial dermatoses are inestimable. The success of similar products, applied by women to protect their hands while doing their daily household chores, should stimulate research for better protectin of the hands in chemical and other industrial plants.

Liquid Creams

Practically any of the creams described here can be made in fluid form. Some manufacturers offer an entire line of liquid cleansing, emollient, and finishing creams (occasionally called "milks"); for advantages and disadvantages, these must be tested and judged on individual properties and personal preference. The compositions may contain up to 90% of water.

The most popular use of liquid creams is as so—called *hand lotions,* of which the long established "honey-and-almond cream" is typical. They are usually oil in-water emulsions, much improved in recent years by the use of the newer emulsifying agents, notably triethanolamine, polyhydric alcohol fatty acid esters, etc. As the stability of such emulsions is of paramount importance, the methods of manufacture frequently depend upon the nature of the emulsifying agents used, and are usually more complicated than those suitable for solid creams.

Manufacture of Creams

For the manufacture of most *creams in emulsion, form,* the following equipment should be available: mixing kettle, with thermometer (or thermostat) and agitator; source of heat—steam or water in jacket of kettle (direct heating is usually not advisable); melting container for fats, or immersion heater for removing small amounts of solid fats from drums. For fatty mixtures, pastes, and ointments, a colloid mill or some form of homogenizer is also required. The actual pieces to be used depend upon the nature of the ingredients, occasionally upon the type of emulsifying agent employed. For making small batches of cream, some items of household equipment, such as a double boiler, an egg beater, a meat chopper, and many of the modern mechanical mixing and emulsifying devices have proved satisfactory.

The oils, waxes, emulsifiers, and other oilsoluble components are heated to 75°C in a steam-jacketed kettle. The water-soluble components (alkalis, alkanolamines, polyhydric alcohols, and preservatives) are dissolved in the aqueous phase and heated to 75°C in another steam-jacketed kettle. To allow for evaporation of water during the heating and emulsification, about 3-5% excess water (based on formula weight) is added.

The procedure for preparing o/w and w/o emulsions is to add the warmed inner phase very slowly to the outer phase (also at 75°C), stirring constantly and homogenizing to assure efficient emulsification. Finely dispersed o/w emulsions can also be prepared by adding the aqueous phase to the oils. Initially the low concentration of water forms a w/o emulsion according to the phase-volume relationship. The slow addition and emulsification of the water increases the viscosity of the system while the oil phase expands to a maximum. At this point, the continuous oil phase breaks up into minute droplets as emulsion inversion occurs, characterized by a sudden decrease in viscosity. This emulsification technique proceeds smoothly at the critical inversion point in a well-balanced, low oilwax system, but it frequently causes coagulation in high oilwax emulsions. The conventional procedure of adding the inner phase to the outer is preferable for creams and lotions.

The rates of addition and mechanical agitation of the dispersed phase are critically important in determining the efficiency of emulsification. The product formed may vary from a completely dispersed inner phase in a well emulsified system, to a mixed emulsion in a poorly emulsified system, the latter owing to excessive rate of addition of inner phase and to inadequate stirring. This in turn affects the consistency, viscosity, and stability of creams and lotions.

Total stirring times and cooling rates are important to lotion viscosity, cream consistency, and emulsion stability. Experimental formulas are often developed in vessels that are not equipped with a heating and cooling jacket. Under these air-cooled conditions, longer stirring times are necessary. The transition to full scale production in jacketed equipment introduces a variable in the physical factors contributing to emulsion preparation. If cooling is started too soon after emulsification is complete, crystallization of the higher melting waxes may occur.

The temperature at which the perfume oils are added to the cream or lotion is another factor contributing to emulsion instability. The addition of perfume to a w/o emulsion proceeds smoothly owing to its solubility in the external phase. In o/w systems, the oils must break through the continuous aqueous phase to the emulsified.

If the cream is to be hot-poured, it is stirred to 5°C above the congealing point, any required color solutions are added, and the cream held at that temperature with occasional stirring during the filling procedure. If cold-filling is preferred, the cream is stirred to 35°C, any color solutions are added, and filling proceeds at room temperature.

In the packaging of creams they are transferred to containers either while they are still warm enough to be fluid, or after they are cooled. Most cold creams, cleansing creams, and emollient creams are filled warm; vanishing creams, pastes, and ointments are usually filled while cold. Apparatus includes gravity-and vacuum-operated devices. Precautions to be observed are the avoidance of air pockets in the tubes or jars, effecting of a neat smooth surface on the cream, and complete cooling of the jars before capping.

In any modern, well-equipped factory, manufacturing proceeds in an efficient manner through continuous successive operations from the mixing kettles to filling, labeling, packing in boxes or cartons, and optional steps such as the enclosing of inserts, outer wrapping, and sealing. Equipment is available, or can be devised, to meet the needs of the most exacting packaging problem.

The manufacture of *liquid creams* is more complicated because of the possibility of breaking the emulsion. As stated earlier, the method of manufacture may vary considerably with the nature of the emulsifying agent, but the proportions and purity of ingredients, the manner and speed of mixing, and other factors are highly important. All creams should be perfected in small batches before any attempt is made to make them on a large scale.

Liquid creams may be filled by gravity from large tanks, handfilled with multiple nozzles, or filled entirely automatically by vacuum apparatus. The manner of closing the bottles varies depending upon whether the closure is a cork with a decorative top, a glass stopper, a threaded metal or plastic cap, etc.

All jars, bottles, and closures must be perfectly clean before they are filled, and kept free from all contamination during the entire manufacturing process.

Cosmetic Lotions

The oils and waxes in lotions are identical to those of an emollient cream but they are present in lower concentration. An o/w emollient lotion usually contains more water than the corresponding cream; a w/ o type may have the same water content, with oily components replacing part of the wax like materials. These lotions are preferred for use during the day because they produce a lighter or less oily emollient film. However, they can be formulated to contain the same concentration of oil phase ordinarily used in creams. The sales appeal of emollient lotions derives partly from their convenience and partly from the greater variety of package design possible for liquid emulsions.

The formulation of lotions of all emulsifier and emulsion types is similar to that of emollient creams. The emulsion must be stable at elevated temperatures (45-50°C) for whatever period is deemed necessary and at room temperatures for a minimum of one year. In the freeze-thaw test of emulsion stability, the lotion is subjected to a temperature of-5°C for 24 h and is then allowed to return to room temperature, at which time it should be stable and pourable.

An example of an all-purpose hand, face, and body lotion prepared with an anionic emulsifier is: 4.00% stearic and (triple-pressed), 1.50%

lanolin anhydrous, 1.50% mineral oil, 1.00% cetyl alcohol, 0.80% triethanolamine, 0.25% preservative [methyl and propyl paraben (5:1)], 90.60% distilled or deionized water, and 0.35% perfume.

A representative all-purpose hand, face, and body lotion, prepared with cationic emulsifiers is: 1.00% cetyl alcohol, 0.50% stearyl alcohol, 1.00% lanolin anhydrous, 4.00% mineral oil, 0.10% *N*-(colaminoformylmethyl) pyridinium chloride, 0.80% *N*-(colaminoformylmethyl) pyridinium chloride stearate, 0.25% preservative (methyl and propyl paraben (5:1)], 6.00%propylene glycol, 64.80% distilled or deionized water, 0.125% sodium chloride, 0.125% sodium benzoate, 11.00% distilled or deionized water, 0.30% perfume, and 10.00% denatured alcohol no. 40.

In composition, the lotions used in cosmetic treatments vary according to the purpose for which they are intended; that is, they may be astringent, bleaching, cleansing, emollient, medicated, or refreshing lotins; still others are especially compounded for the eyes and for after shaving.

Table 1.V. Compositions of Astringent Lotions

Ingredient	Typical recipe, % by wt. in: 1	2	3	4
Alcohol	10	16	50	10
Alum	1.5	4	-	1
Boric acid	3	-	-	-
Glycerol	5	2	-	10
Zinc phenolsulfonate	-	2	2	-
Zinc sulfate	-	-	-	1
Water, to make	100.0	100	100	100

Astringent lotions are generally used in the treatment of oily skin and conspicuous pores. For an immediate degreasing effect, some recipes contain as much as 50% of alchol (ethyl or isopropyl), but results seem to be more satisfactory with less alcohol and a good selection of salts or other compounds of aluminium, magnesium, and zinc. Mild acids, for example, acetic, boric, citric, and salicylic, extract of witch hazel, b-naphthol, and resoreinol, are also used. In planning an astringent lotion it must be remembered that many compounds that might seem suitable because of their property of coagulating proteins will be incompatible with certain other substances and compounds in solution. The properties of all proposed ingredients should be studied before any decision is made.

Bleaching lotions are not so much in demand now as they were formerly, undoubtedly because of the vogue for tanning. At best the merits of such preparations are questionable. As the pigment-forming mechanism of the skin is situated at the base of the epidermis, any true bleaching agent strong enough to penetrate to the site of pigment and actually lighten the color of it could readily harm the epidermis itself.

Melanin, the pigment in skin and hair, can be bleached to a lighter color by hydrogen peroxide (at least 5%, 17-volume). A clear bleaching solution may be made of hydrogen peroxide and rose water or orange-flower water. Other suggestions are for mild acids (acetic, citric, lactic, tartaric) in scented water, with or without the addition of glycerol (to 10%). Potassium chlorate, sodium perborate, and other oxidizing chemicals are also included occasionally in bleaching lotions.

Cloudy lotions or those containing a sediment, which are to be shaken before application, may contain bismuth subnitrate, ammoniated mercury (maximum allowed, 5%), or metallic peroxides (zinc, magnesium). Lotions recommended especially for lightening freekles usually contain ammoniated mercury, which causes exfoliation of the pigment and may irritate the epidermis.

Another type of so-called bleaching lotion actually masks, rather than lightens, the color of the skin. Like the whitening creams, these lotins usually contain zinc oxide or titanium dioxide with various proportions of alcohol, glycerol, and water. As delicate flesh tints may also be added, such products often serve more properly as liquid powders.

In cosmetic treatments, as given professionally in the beauty shop, bleaching lotions are applied to supplement the usually stronger action of bleaching creams and pastes; at home they are generally used instead of these products.

Cleansing lotions are used to supplement the action of cleansing creams, and at any time for quick cleansing or for more thorough cleansing than is afforded by soap and water; they are of several types.

Lotions intended for cleansing the *dry skin* should contain relatively little alcohol or mineral oil, and only small percentages of alkaline salts or synthetic surface-active agents because all of these ingredients can only aggravate a tendency toward dryness. Borax and triethanolamine may be present to the extent of 1%; glycerol (or glycol compounds) to 5-10%; ethyl or isopropyl alcohol to 5-10%. Tincture of benzion is occasionally included; magnesium carbonate is also added to some mixtures to serve as a mechanical aid to cleansing. Such lotions must bewell shaken before they are applied, because the white powder settles on standing.

Cleansing lotions for *oily skin* many contain up to 50% of alcohol. Although the primary purpose of these lotions is to remove oil and shine from the face, many of them are so compounded that continual use may have an astringent effect and thus counter act the oily condition. Among the compounds included are synthetic detergents, mild acids (boric, salicylic), acetone, camphor, and witch hazel.

Freshening lotions (formerly called *skin toning lotions)* are used for mild stimulation of the skin, and for the complete removal of creams before the application of make—up. Alcohol may or may not be present; rose water or orange-flower water is often used as the base. Preservatives are usually required. Menthol, when used for cooling effect, must be kept to the minimum, as its secondary reaction is an occasionally unpleasant overstimulation of the skin. Glycerol is includeu for its humectant properties. Other common ingredients of skin fresheners are alum, camphor, witch hazel, and mild organic acids (3, 6, 9, 10, 13).

Medicated lotions, although used for their cosmetic effect in certain treatments, are on the borderline, if not actually over the line, into the category of drugs. It is not permissible to recommend any true cosmetic lotion for the cure of any lesion or eruption in the skin. All such claims require proof of accomplishment, and a declaration of the active ingredients of the product on the label.

Lotions commonly used for the alleviation of minor blemishes may contain antiseptics, such as alcohol, phenol, hexylresorcinol; also camphor, sulfur, resorcinol; and various zinc compounds (phenolsulfonate, carbonate, sulfate, oxide). For indirect alleviation of minor conditions by thorough cleansing of the skin, triethanolamine, either alone or in compounds with fatty acids, is used; certain synthetic detergents of the class of fatty acid sulfonates or alkyl sulfates are also used in some of the newer products.

Shaving lotions are offered for either before or after shaving. *Before-shaving preparations* may be of two types: (1) Those intended primarily to soften the beard usually have as active ingredient a wetting agent, in a base of water and glycerol, perfumed and tinted. Those to be applied before using an electic razor act like strong astringents, contracting the skin to make the hair stand up more straight. *After shaving lotions* are usually similar in composition to astringent lotions, with a higher percentage of alcohol, which serves to cool, the skin and to counteract any irritation. The alcohol also acts as a mild antiseptic to aid against infection of any abrasions. As many of the suggested ingredients may deteriorate, lotions of this type should contain preservatives.

Special Lotions

In addition to the various types of lotions used as washes for the skin of the face, at least two other types have become popular and have been the subjects of considerable sound research.

Eye lotions, used to cleanse, soothe, and brighten the eyes, should be so compounded that in pH and osmotic pressure they approximate the natural fluid, tears. Many older, compendia gave recipes for eyewashes, based on herbal extracts (camphor, cherry laurel, eupharasia or "eyebright," fennel, fleabane, snakewort, witch hazel), which could well serve the same purpose in modern preparations. In practice, herbal extracts are usually combined with boric acid, ammonium, potassium, or sodium chloride, sodium borate or salicylate, zinc salts or other suitable compounds. If any natural organic substances are used, a preservative must be added; for obvious reasons this should be selected with great care. Claims for eye lotions should be most conservative. Nothing of this kind should be recommended for the treatment of abnormal or pathological conditions; otherwise the product falls automatically into the class of drugs.

Hand lotions are of two principal types; (J) creamy fluids ("honey and-almond" type). (2) thin mucilages. They deserve to be even more widely used than they are at present because of the protection they afford to the skin of hands and arms (and legs) in cold weather, and, at any time, to hands that are exposed to soap and water or any other cause of defatting.

About the oldest of the preparations still in use is a mixture of glycerol and rose water. It was made formerly with 50% of glycerol, but the quantify has been cut to an average of 25%; in commercial production, a preservative should be added. Sorbitol is also used in place of some of the glycerol.

The familiar translucent, gelatinous or mucilaginous hand lotions consist of one or more gums (acacia, chondrus, karaya, tragacanth) with varying percentages of alcohol, glycerol (or glycols), boric acid, camphor, or benzoin; benzoic acid or one of the newer benzoic acid esters to used as the preservative.The gums,are occasionally also added to the emulsion type of hand cream. Other thickening agents used in hand lotions are agar, marsh-mallow root, starch, pectin, and the extracts from seeds of flax, psyllium, and quince.

Manufacture of Lotions

To have the proper esthetic appeal, a lotion that is intended to be clear should have the brilliance and clarity of a jewel, whether water-white or colored. Clouding can be prevented by careful study of all the ingredients of the product, in relation to their mutual interactions and compatibility. Stability at various temperatures is also important; otherwise, certain ingredients may precipitate out of the solution under varying climatic conditions. Time should always be allowed for possible changes during storage; "shelf tests" should preferably be of the full duration, rather than accelerated.

Most solutions of these types improve if they are allowed to stand for a while before they are filtered and bottled. Whenever possible, filtration by gravity is preferable *to* the application of vacuum *or* pressure. As a mechanical aid in clarification, fuller's earth, asbestos, magnesia, talc, or other substances that are inert to the solution may be distributed over the filtering medium.

As insurance against deterioration, all bottles, caps, and filing apparatus should be cleaned, and the atmosphere of the room should be kept as free as possible from all sources of contamination. The filling and capping of bottles by available standard equipment presents no difficulties.

For mucilaginous lotions, the gum-producing substances must be soaked in water, and some must be forced through sieves or fabrics to prepare them for combination with the other ingredients. General information cannot be given for all conditions; successful preparation of any product requires carefully attention to all steps in the manufacturing process outlined for it.

Deodorants and Antiperspirants

Deodorant and antiperspirant products are marketed as aerosols, creams, gels, lotions, powders, soaps,and sticks.

The FDA product and ingredient review panel for over-the-counter antiperspirants (OTC panel) has assigned three classifications to antiperspirants: category 1, safe to use; category 2, does not meet requirements, remove offending materials; category 3, may be marketed while testing continues.

The initial proposal states that color and fragrance apparently have no effect on safety; buffers do not apparently make a product more effective; a product, to remain on the market, must be at least 20% effective on at least one half of the persons tested. With a confidence rate of 95%, special tests will be set up to evaluate claims of extra effectiveness (30% or more); products aimed at combatting problem and emotional perspiration will require special tests; if a new ingredient is used tests are required for skin irritation and compatibility with normal flora.

Active Ingredients

Aluminium chloride, once commonly used in deodorants and antiperspirants, may cause fabric damage and skin irritation because of its low pH. This has led *to* the development of various basic aluminium compounds. The most widely used compound is aluminum chlorhydroxide (ACH). Other compounds that have been or are now used are: basic aluminum bromide, iodide, and nitrate, and basic aluminium hydroxychloride-zirconyl hydroxy oxychloride, with the without glycine. Zirconium salts, formerly used in antiperspirants, were banned for use in aerosol in 1977.

An example of an antiperspirant rollon is: 33.60-40.60% methyl cellulose 65 HG (high gain), 400 mPa.s (=cP), 3% solution [96.9% distilled or deionized water, 3.0% methyl cellulose 65 HG, 400 mPa.s (=cP), 0.1% methyl paraben]; 30.00-36.0% aluminum chlorhydroxide complex, 50% solution; 16.25-29.25% alcohol SDA no. 40; 4.65% propylene glycol; and 2.50% solubilized perfume [solubilizer and perfume oil (4:1)].

Deodorant-Antiperspirant Sticks

Sodium stearate, the primary gelling agent for deodorant sticks, constitutes about 7-9 wt% of these products. The grade employed depends on the fatty acid used in making the stearate. Derivatives such as acetylated sucrose distearates also can be used but are more common in antiperspirant sticks to gel cetyl alcohol-based formulations (typical use level, 28%).

There are three main types of stick formulations for antiperspirants: hydroxyethyl stearamide, which produces clear-melting, homogeneous sticks; stearamides and cetyl alcohol dry-powder dispersions of ACH; and stearamides coupled with propoxylated alcohol. The stearamide wax content is 26-29%; the active concentration, 20-25%.

Volatile silicones, the siloxanes, are employed in the newer antiperspirant sticks at levels as high as 40-50%. They function as a processing aid, reducing cracking and crumbling of the stick. The tetrameric and pentameric cyclic silicones are preferred because of their volatility. When the stick is applied to the skin, the silicones evaporate, leaving the ingredients on the skin in a nonsticky film. The silicones are useful in pump antiperspirants, acting as a lubricant for valves and a suspending agent for the active material. The compounds also act as skin lubricants and emollients.

A typical deodorant stick formula is: 75.35 wt % alcohol SDA no. 40; 17.00 wt % propylene glycol; 6.00 wt % sodium stearate, purified USP; 1.50 wt % perfume; and 0.15 wt % trichlorocarbanilide.

A typical antiperspirant stick formula is: 27.5 wt % stearic acid monoethanolamide; 240 wt % poly (dimethylsiloxane) (low viscosity, volatile); 20.0 wt % rehydrol powder: 15.0 wt % propoxylated myristyl alcohol; 9.0 wt % propylene glycol; 3.0 wt % distilled or deionized water; 1.0 wt % perfume; and 0.5 wt % myristyl lactate.

A typical dry compressed antiperspirant stick formula is: 65.75 wt % microcystalline cellulose; 25.00 wt % ultrafine powdered aluminum chlorohydrate; 9.00 wt % talc; and 0.25 wt % magnesium stearate.

Deodorizers merely prevent the emanation of an odor from the sweat, or substitute a pleasant odor for an unpleasant one. These products pass as true cosmetics and therefore require no statement of ingredients on the label. They may be prepared as powders, creams, or liquids; as used under the arms, on palms or soles, and on sanitary napkins, the first two types predominate. Common ingredients are: boric, benzoic, and salicylic acids; zinc oxide and peroxide; magnesium carbonate, talc and hydroxyquinoline sulfate. A few typical recipes are given in Table 1.VI.

Table. VI. Compositions of Deodorizers.

	Typical recipe, % by wt. in:								
	Powders			Creams			Liquids		
Ingredient	**1**	**2**	**3**	**1**	**2**	**3**	**1**	**2**	**3**
Alcohol	-	-	-	-	-	-	50	-	-
Boric acid	30	-	40	10	10	15	3	-	-
Colloodial clay	-	-	-	4	-	-	-	-	-
Glycerol	-	-	-	16	-	-	15	-	-
Hydroxyquinoline sulfate	-	10	-	-	-	-	-	2	-
Petrolatum	-	-	-	-	65	62	-	-	-
Salicylic acid	-	-	2	-	-	3	4	-	-
Talc	38	90	48	8	-	-	-	-	-
Water	-	-	-	40	25	15	28	98	95
Zinc peroxide	32	-	-	-	-	-	-	-	-
Zinc phenolsulfonate	-	-	-	2	-	5	-	-	5
Zinc stearate	-	-	10	20	-	-	-	-	-
Total	100	100	100	100	100	100	100	100	100

Antiperspiratns are strong astringents that are believed to coagulate and precipitate proteins in the skin at the site of application; the sweat is thus deflected to other regions. Products that thus "affect a function of the body" are considered drugs rather than cosmetics, and all active ingredients must be listed on the label.

Antiperspirants are usually prepared as liquids, creams, and paste in sticks. The active ingredients of first choice are salts of aluminum and zinc, of which many organic and inorganic salts are available; those most commonly used are the chloride, sulfate, chlorohydroxide complex, and acetate of aluminum (also potassium alum), and the chloride, sulfate, and phenolsulfonate of zinc. Other ingredients are formalin, hexamethylenetetramine, tannic acid and tannin, and hydroxyquinoline sulfate.

The compounding of these products calls for considerable care to keep within limits of solubility of the salts, but especially to avoid irritation of the skin and damage to clothing. The liquid preparations have most commonly been the more serious offenders on the last point.

The simplest antiperspirant is a 16-20% solution of aluminum chloride in distilled water; this may be modified by adding alum, hydroxyquinoline sulfate, glycerol, and other organic compounds. As a base for the creams, the vanishing type seems to be the most generally satisfactory, using glycerol monostearate as the principal ingredient. A few typical recipes are given in Table 1.VII.

Table 1.VII. Compositions of Antiperspirants.

	Typical recipe, % by wt. in:						
	Liquid		Cream			Stick	
Ingredient	1	2	1	2	3	1	2
Alcohol	-	6	-	10	-	-	-
Alum	8	22	-	-	10	5	-
Aluminum chloride	10	10	-	5	-	-	-
Beeswax	-	-	-	-	-	25	-
Boric acid	10	-	-	-	-	-	-
Formalin	-	-	-	1	-	-	-
Glycerol monostearate	-	-	25	15	25	-	20
Glycerol	-	-	-	-	-	-	10
Hexamethylenetetramine	-	-	-	-	-	-	3
Lanolin	-	-	-	-	-	6	-
Hydroxyquinoline sulfate	-	22	2	3	-	2	-
Petrolatium	-	-	8	4	-	30	-
Mineral oil	-	-	-	-	-	10	-
Titanium dioxide	-	-	4	-	2	2	-
Talc	-	-	-	-	-	15	-
Water	72	80	61	62	58	-	67
Zinc phenolsulfonate	-	-	-	-	5	5	-
Total	100	100	100	100	100	100	100

Manufacture of Deodorants. A few points should be observed in the making of various deodorants. Perfumes should be selected with care in order to avoid any that may be incompatible with the ingredients of the products, or that may be irritating. Hydroxyquinoline sulfate is readily contaminated and discolored by contact with iron or other metals; therefore, if it is not handled properly it may impart color to the finished product after it has stood for some time.

Deodorizers and antiperspirants are packaged in many ways: the powders, in carton, plastic, or metal containers with a sifter top; the liquids (1) in small bottles with a glass or plastic applicator and a small rubber sponge, (2) on saturated pads, packed closely in air-tight jars, and (3) most recently in flexible plastic bottles, which can be squeezed to spray the fluid through an atomizer. The creams must be in jars of convenient size with good closures; sticks are mounted in holders of wood, plastic, or coated metal.

Definitions : A sunscreen *sunburn preventive agent* is an active ingredient that absorbs 95% or *more* of light in the uv range of 290-320 *nm.* A sunscreen *suntanning agent* is an active ingredient that absorbs up to 85% of light in the uv range of 290-320 nm but transmits light at wavelengths longer than 320 nm. A sunscreen *opaque sunblock agent* is an opaque agent that reflects or scatters light in the uv and visible range at wavelengths of 290-777 nm.

Recommendations

The panel recommended the product designations based on SPF factors in Table 1.VIII.

Table 1.VIII. Sunscreen Product Designations Bases on SPF Factors

Skin type	Sunburn and tanning history	Recommended SPF factor product category designation
1	burns easily, never tans	8 or more (max)
2	burns easily, minimal tan	6-7 (extra)
3	bunrs moderately, normal tan	4-5 (moderate)
4	burns minimally, tans well	23 (min)
5	burns rarely, tans profusely	2 (min)
6	never burns, deep pigment	none indicated

Safe and effective sunscreen ingredients are listed in Table IX.

For significant residual protection, PABA must be applied at least two hours prior.

Table 1.IX. Safe and Effective Sunscreen Ingredients

Ingredient	Trade or generic name
aminobenzoic acid	
2-ethoxyethyl p-methoxycinnamate	Cinoxate
hydroxyethylaminoethyl p-methoxycinnamate	
digalloyl trioleate	
2, 2'—dihydroxy—4-methoxybenzophenone	dioxybenzone
ethyl4 [bis(2-hydroxypropyl) amino] benzoate	
2-ethylhexyl 2-cyano—3, 3-diphenylacrylate	
2ethylhexyl p-methoxycinnamate	
2-ethylhexyl salicylate	
3,3,5-trimethylcyclohexyl salicylate	Homosalate
glyceryl aminobenzoate	
2-hydroxy, 4-naphthoquinone	Lawsone
methyl anthranilate	
2-hydroxy-4-methoxybenzophenone	oxybenzone
pentyl 4-dimethylaminobenzoate	Padimate A
2-ethylhexyl 4-dimethylaminobenzoate	Padimate O
2-phenylbenzimidazole-5-sulfonic acid	
red petrolatum	
2-hydroxy-4-methoxybenzophenone-5-sulfonic acid	sulisobenzone
titanium dioxide	
2- [bis (2-hydroxyethyl) amino] ethyl salicylate	

Sunscreens

The sun emits energy in a continuous band throughout the electomagnetic spectrum. The shorter wavelengths are absorbed in the upper atmosphere so that at sea level the radiation extends from a cutoff near 290 nm through the near ultraviolet to the conventional end of the ultraviolet range, which is near 400 nm. The intensity of the radiation varies nonlinearly throughout this range.

The production of erythema and the subsequent production of melanin pigment are both maximum with 296.7 nm radiation. As the wavelength increases, both responses fall rapidly, so that 10 *u* W/cm^2 of 307 nm radiation, 100 u W/cm^2 of 314 nm. 1000 u W of 330 nm, and 10,000 u W of 340 nm radiation are required to equal the effect of 1 u W/cm^2 of 296.7 nm radiation in the production of erythema.

A unit of erythemal flux, the E-viton, is equivalent to the erythema induced by 10 u W/cm^2 of 296.7 nm radiation. The response of the skin to an E-viton (or viton) is constant: irradiation by *10* vitons for one hour produces the same erythemal response as 5 vitons for two hours. The effects owing to irradiation by different wavelengths are additive. About twenty minutes exposure to midsummer sunlight (or 40 viton min) needed to produce a minimum perceptible erythema (MPE) on normal Caucasian skin. Thus 1 E-viton acting for 40 min produces an MPE. 10 E-vitons acting 4 min or 40 E-vitons acting for 1 min will produce the same MPE.

With the realization that prolonged exposure to sunlight produces most of the ageing effects on skin and the clear implication of exposure in at least three types of skin cancer (basal cell cancer, squamous cell cancer, melanoma), use of products that protect the skin from excessive exposure has become increasingly widespread.

Sunscreens are of two types: physical and chemical. Physical screening agents, such as titanium dioxide and zinc oxide, are opaque materials that block and scatter light, and thus act as mechanical barriers. Their action is nonselective over all wavelengths. Chemical screening agents, which act by absorbing uv light, offer selective protection against certain uv wave bands, depending on their absorption spectrum. Anthranilates, cinnamates, benzyl and homomenthyl salicylate, and p-aminobenzoic acid (PABA) and its ester derivatives belong in this category and have maximal absorption in the sunburn region. A useful sunscreen resists wash-off from swimming or sweating and does not come off during exercise or rubbing. Maintenance of significant protection following swimming or sweating would suggest that the chemical is substantive or can diffuse into the horny skin layer. PABA and its esters are moderately substantive and give appreciable protection after intensive sweating and brief periods of immersion in water (5 to 10 min).

OTC *Report*

Sunscreen products for over-the-counter (OTC) human use are reviewed in a report on recommendations to the FDA by the OTC panel on Topical Analgesics. Definitions and recommendations made by the panel are reviewed below.

Sun Protection Factor (SPF)

The panel defined the ratio of the amount of energy required to produce a minimum erythemal dose (MED) to the amount of energy to produce the same MED without any treatment by the SPF. Examples given are: SPF to immersion. This probably reflects the time required for penetration into the stratum corneum. It is highly important, especially during the first few days of exposure to the sun, to reapply PABA-type sunscreens after swimming. With repeated daily applications increased protection.

Sunscreens with much greater resistance to swimming can be formulated with acrylate polymers, which leave flexible films on the surface. A chemical sunscreen incorporated in the formulation will tend to be bound in the film and remain in place despite sweating and bathing.

Table 1.X lists some effective physical and chemical sunscreens; information on various sunscreens is included in patents (17-18).

Table 1.X. Sunscreens

Chemical sunscreens	*Trade name*
2 ethoxyethyl p-methoxycinnamate	Giv-tan F (Givaudan)
menthyl anthranilate	
homomenthyl salicylate	
glyceryl p-aminobenzoate	Escalol 106 (Van Dyk)
isobutyl p-aminobenzoate	Cycloform (RSA Corp.)
isoamyl-p-dimethylaminobenzoate	Escalol 506 (Van Dyk)
2-hydroxy-4-methyxybenzophenone-5 sulfonic acid	Uvinul MS-40 (GAF)
2,2'-dihydroxy-4methoxybenzophenone	Uvinul D-49 (GAF)
2-hydroxy-4methoxybenzophenone	Uvinul M-40 (GAF)
p-aminobenzoic acid	
4-mono-and 4-bis (3-hydroxypropyl) aminoisomers of ethyl benzoate	Amerscreen P (Amerchol)
2-ethylhexyl p-dimethylaminobenzoate	Escalol 507 (Van Dyk)
Natural oils (in order of effectiveness)	
(1) mink oil	(6) safflower oil
(2) avocado oil	(7) peanut oil
(3) sweet almond oil	(8) jojoba oil
(4) sesame oil	(9) coconut oil
(5) persic oil	(10) olive oil
Physical sunscreens (opaque)	
titanum dioxide	
zinc oxide	

Examples of sunscreen formulations are the following:

Clear *Sunscreen Lotion:* 74.50 wt % poly (alkylene glycol) (Ucon LB-625, Union Carbide); 20.00 wt % alcohol denatured no. 40; 5.00 wt % PABA (sunscreen); and 0.50 wt % perfume.

Opaque Sunscreen Lotion: 67.60 wt % distilled or deionized water; 10.00 wt % sesame oil (preserved, contains antioxidant); 10.00 wt % mineral oil (Saybolt viscosity at 37.8°C is 65/75); 5.00 wt % PABA (sunscreen); 3.00 wt % stearic acid, triple pressed; 2.90 wt % propylene glycol; 0.50 wt % cetyl alcohol; 0.50 wt % triethanolamine, 98 wt % solution; 0.25 wt % preservative [methyl and propyl paraben (5:1)]; and 0.25 wt % perfume.

Because of the extent of sunscreen application to skin, any perfume used must be chosen with attention to its potential to irritate. Careful testing of its stability to heat and sunlight are also required.

Aerosols

Such cosmetic products as having creams, hair sprays, deodorants and anti-perspirants, colognes, and sunscreens are now commonly packaged as aerosol sprays. In a bulletin released in 1966 *the* Aerosol Scientific Committee of the Chemical Specialities Manufacturers Association defined an aerosol product as a liquid, solid, gas, or a mixture that is discharged by a propellant force of liquified and/or nonliquified compressed gas, usually from a disposable-type container and through a valve.

The three main components of aerosol products are the propellants, solvents and the active ingredients. Previously, the liquified gas propellants have primarily been the chloroflurocarbons (eg, Freons by DuPont) but these were banned in 1978 for use in all personal and household aerosol products, except for pharmaceuticals sucn as asthma spray.

Compressed gases (N_2, Co_2) and liquified hydrocarbons have become the primary propellants *in* revised formulations.

Make-up

The term *make-up,* originally applied to cosmetics used in the theater, now comprises products used by anyone to enhance the coloring of the face or to accentuate facial features. It thus includes face powder, rouge for cheeks and lips, and colorings for use around the eyes.

Colour

Straight colourants are referred to in the trade as primary colours, primary dyes, and primaries. The principal primary colours are red, blue and yellow. Practically every hue can be produced by blending red, yellow and blue in proper proportions. Hue, in color, is a quality whereby one color differs from another. Brightness is a measure of the reflectance value of a dye. Strength is a measure of the tinting or coloring value of a dye.

Straight colorants include both primaries and lakes of such primary colorants made by extending the primary colorant on a substratum such as aluminum hydroxide, barium sulfate, a mixture of aluminum hydroxide and barium sulfate, aluminum benzoate, or zinc oxide. These lakes vary in pure dye content strength from 2-80%. The primaries contain over 80% pure dye. Primary colorants are frequently used in diluted forms. Mixtures of two or more primary colorants are sometimes referred to as primary mixtures. Mixtures of two primary colorants are referred to as secondary colorants, and mixtures of three primary colorants, as tertiary colorants.

The initials, FD&C, D&C, and external D&C, which are part of the name of straight colorants, indicate for what use the colorant has been certified. Colorants designated FD&C may be used for foods, drugs, and cosmetics. The name of a mixture usually tells nothing of its permitted use, but if there is a restriction in the use of the colorant, a statement to that effect is required on the product lable.

For safety, colorants that have been certified for cosmetic use must contain not more than 0.002% of lead, not more than 0.0002% of arsenic, and not more than 0.003% of heavy metals other than lead and arsenic.

Most cosmetic colorants are certified coal-tar colorants. However, a few natural dyes are used in limited amounts to color foods, drugs, and cosmetics. The more important are alkanet, annatto, carotene, chlorophyll, cochineal, saffron, and henna.

Inorganic Colourants

Except for the white pigments, such as titanium dioxide, zinc oxide and talcum, the inorganic colorants are used in a number of cosmetic products. They usually have excellent light fastness and complete insolubility in solvents and aqueous solutions.

The naturally occurring colored minerals that depend for their color upon the presence of oxide of iron are known by such names as ochre, umber, sienna, etc. Because they are naturally occurring products, they possess certain inherent disadvantages. They show greater variation in color and tinting power than do manufactured pigments. The nature and amount of impurities they contain varies and may, form time to time, exclude their use in a domestic product.

The most important inorganic colorants or pigments are the iron oxides, chrome oxide greens, ultramarine pigment blues and pinks, and the carbon blacks. Iron oxide is sold in the form of yellow hydrated iron oxide, or ochre; brown iron oxide, red iron oxide, and black iron oxide. The yellow iron oxide is made by an alkaline precipitation from a ferrous salt, followed by an oxidation the product is ca 85% Fe_2O_3, and is supplied in shades from light lemon yellow to a deep orange.

The brown iron oxides, umber, are made by treating a mixture of red, yellow and black iron salt with alkali and partially oxidizing the precipitate. The brown oxide is a mixture of Fe_2O_3 and Fe_3O_4. The red iron oxides, sienna, are usually made by heating the precipitated yellow iron oxides. Light to dark red can be obtained depending on heating conditions, and the product is 96-98% Fe_2O_3.

The black iron oxide is formed by precipitation of Fe_3O_4 under carefully controlled conditions. The chromium oxide green is pure Cr_2O_3. The anhydrous pigment has a dull green shade; the hydrated pigment shows a bluish tint. This type of pigment is used in eye makeup.

Carbon blacks are of vegetable or natural gas origin. These blacks find wide cosmetic application, particularly in eye makeup.

The ultramarine blues and pinks are made from a mixture containing sulfur, sodium carbonate, charcoal, pitch or rosin, and several other ingredients carefully heated for a lengthy period. The finely pulverized pigment gives shades of ultramarine blue from the pink to the green, depending on its silica content.

Dye *Stability*

If is well known that many dyes are pH indicators. Such dyes change in hue with pH variations. Those that do not change much in hue can be affected in other important properties. It is, therefore, important to consider the pH conditions in a cosmetic product. In general, the inorganic colors are not as much affected by pH conditions as are the coal-tar dyes.

The hue of some dyes varies with the percentage of moisture present. The term bleeding is used to refer to the strengthening of the hue of a color in the presence of moisture, particularly in moist powders that are stored for a long period of time.

All water or organo-soluble dyes and most insoluble dyes and pigments are destroyed or chemically changed by the photochemical action of ultraviolet, visual light, infrared, and other short wavelength radiations. The degree of sensitivity varies with the dye and with the conditions.

The dyes change in tinctorial strength and hue, becoming progressive weaker, and usually duller, as the destruction of the dyestuff progresses. This is considered normal fading. The ability of the certified dyes to resist this chemical change owing to photochemical action has been charted for a number of the dyes and is available in tabular form.

The absence of moisture greatly retards photolytic effects. Absence of air, oxygen, hydrogen, and other oxidizing or reducing reagents also retards fading. The presence of titanium dioxide greatly accelerates it.

Judging Color Effects

Many factors affect the judgment of color, including the nature of the light source, the degree of transparency or opacity of the color, and eye strain or color memory.

Face Powders

Formulation

Face powders, both the loose the now - popular cake or pressed, is a blend of white pigments, tinted and perfumed . The function of a face powder is *to* impart a smooth, matte finish *to* the skin by masking any shine owing to the secretions of the sebaceous and sweat glands. To obtain this effect, the powder must be neither too transparent to mask the shine, nor too opaque, lest it give a masklike appearance. In addition, it must posses reasonable lasting properties; it must adhere to the skin and be reasonably resistant to the mixed secretions of the skin. Finally, through intimate contact of its perfume - laden particles over a warm and relatively large area, it should disseminate a pleasing odor, the psychological value of which is often underestimated.

No single substance possesses all the desired properties; covering power, slip, absorbency, adhesiveness, and bloom. Therefore; a modern face powder is a blend of several constituents, each one chosen for some specific quality. The materials most commonly used can be grouped in the following manner.

Covering power. To cover skin defects, such as enlarged pores and skin shine. Examples: Titanium dioxide, zinc oxide, kaolin, and magnesium oxide.

Slip. To assist in spreading and to give the characteristic smooth feeling. Examples: talc, zinc stearate, magnesium stearate, and starch.

Absorbency. To absorb sebaceous or oily secretions and perspiration, and thus reduce shine. Examples: precipitated chalk, magnesium carbonate, starch, and kaolin.

Adherence. To improve clinging to the face. Examples: Metallic Soaps, such as magnesium and zinc stearates, and small quantities of oil or fatty materials in the powder base.

Bloom. To give a smooth, velvetlike appearance to the skin. A matte effect, Examples: chalk and starch.

Representative formulas for loose and pressed powders are:

Loose face powder	***Wt %***
kaolin	3.0
talc (Italian)	64.0
talc (Sierra)	
magnesium stearate	1.5 base
magnesium carbonate	0.5
zinc oxide	15,0
corn starch	10.0
D&C red # 2 (lake) 20% in talc	
D&C red # 3 (lake) 10% in talc	

D&C orange # 4 (lake) 10% in talc	5.0	colourant dilutions
yellow iron oxide 20% in talc		
brown iron oxide 20% in talc		
perfume	1.0	
Cake or pressed powder	Wt %	
kaolin	10.0	
zinc stearate	5,0	
zinc oxide	10.0	base
magnesium stearate	5.0	
talc (French)	61.4	
mineral oil light	2.0	
cetyl alcohol	1.0	binding agent
lanolin	0.3	
D&C orange # 4 (lake) 10% in talc	2.7	
D&C red # 2 (lake) 20% *in talc*	*0.8*	colourant dilutions
brown iron oxide 20% in talc	1.0	
perfume	0.8	

The function of face powder is to conceal shine and endow the skin with a new and better looking color or tint. The finer the particle size of face powder, the greater the diffusion of light and the better the bloom, with correspondingly less shine. The reason for this is that the light is reflected in many different angles, somewhat like reflection from the frosted surface of glass. Within certain limits, the smaller the powder particles, the higher the covering power and the better the tinting. Titanium dioxide, with its extremely fine particle size, provides especially good covering power. The percentage used is generally in the range of 5-8%. A common method of determining fineness of particles is the bite test, which consists of grating the ingredients between the teeth. The gritty threshold on grating chalk powder between the teeth has been placed at ca 12 um. The materials used in a face powder should, therefore, be passed through at least a 50um (300-mesh) sieve, or, more properly, through a micronizing or micropulverizing machine.

The designation, light, medium, heavy, applied to a face powder denotes not weight, but covering power. A dry skin requires, in the absence of exceptional skin defects, a light powder; but since such a skin is lacking in grease, either the powder must possess increased powders of adherence, or a powder base must be used. A greasy skin, on the other hand, requires a powder of high opacity and grease resistance. Adherence is supplied by the skin itself, and in this case a powder containing sufficient grease-resistant constituents such as kaolin, together with a drying agent such as zinc oxide, may be used. The latter powder would be termed a heavy powder. Most women prefer a light to medium weight powder, since both are suitable to dry or normal skin.

Manufacture

The following is a procedure commonly used in manufacturing loose face powder: (1) All basic materials are screened into a Day spiral (ribbon) mixer, and blended. (2) The inorganic colourants and lakes or toners are diluted with either some of the mixed base material or with a portion of the talcum and screened. These diluted colorants are then added to the base. (3) The perfume, diuted and thoroughly mixed with a portion of the mixed base material or the talcum and screened, is added to the mixer. (4) The mixture is well blended and then transferred to a 50-um (300-mesh) silk or stainless steel screen where it is screened several times and checked for color. An efficient and rapid method of screening consists of passing the material through a micronizer, using a suitable screen. (5) If the color check indicates that adjustments are necessary, the estimated amount of colorant dilutions are added and extra base and perfume to compensate for the additions are blended in. *(6)* When the color corresponds closely with the standard, the batch should again be thoroughly mixed in the spiral mixer and the entire batch passed through the 50um (300-mesh) screen or the Fitzpatrick comminuter or a micronizer. (7) The screened material can now be stored in a cool, dry place, or can be sent to the packaging room.

The manufacturing procedure for compact powder closely parallels that for loose powder, except that the moistening agent must be added slowly and mixed well in the base materials. If water is used to moisten the base materials, the water content of the mixed powder should be reduced by drying to ca 2.5-3%. Few manufacturers use water to moisten the powder because drying lengthens the process considerably and because water may cause some bleeding. The finished powder, having been passed by the control laboratory for shade, can be stored in the same way that the loose powder is stored.

Before the powder is placed in the pans for pressing it must be agitated because the inclusion of air, introducting during the mixing and screening process, may cause breakage of the compact powder unless it is vibrated before pressing.

Because vibration does not necessarily remove all included air, the process known as prepress is a part of the manufacturing procedure for compact powder. Prepress consists of applying moderate pressure to the material placed in the pans, and then releasing the pressure before passing the cakes on to the hydraulic press. At the hydraulic press sufficient pressure is applied to make a hard, compact powder cake.

Breakage of the compact cake is a very important factor for rejection. One firm tests the cake of compressed powder by dropping it from a height of ca 0.3 m onto a thin metal plate, cushioned by a few sheets of paper. The cake of compressed powder has to withstand more than ten drops from this height to pass the control test.

Product Stability

The most common reason that loose face powder loses its saleability is loss of perfume. The stability of the perfume in a particular face powder can be readily checked by using the method of minimum quantity to discover whether perfume and powder are reacting with each other. For this test one uses not more than 0.1% of perfume. A good perfume and suitable powder should maintain a slight but agreeable perfumed note for at least two days in a vessel open to the air. The usual failure is the disappearance of all of the perfume, or the appearance of a phenolic or medicated odor.

The stability of the pigment used is of great concern to every manufacturer of face powder.Not all shades can be produced with earth colors exclusively, and it is necessary to use some organic lakes and toners. These should be used sparingly, because they are not light stable for any length of time. A simple check of light stability is to place a puff on the smoothened surface of loose face powder and then put the sample into bright sunlight for about thirty minutes. Any appreciable bleaching of the unprotected area indicates possible trouble.

Zinc stearate may develop an odor on ageing, and it is necessary to use a good grade of zinc stearate for face powder. Kaolin may develop a clalike odor when moistened, and magnesium carbonate may have a deleterious effect on the perfume. All materials used in the preparation of face powders must be carefully tested to prevent the inclusion of impurties. The same precautionary measures taken in preparing loose face powder must be observed in the manufacture of compact or pressed face powder. Additional care must be taken in the choice of ingredients since the compact face powders usually contain moistening ingredients. Off odors may also be introduced by the glues used in powder boxes, puffs or in gluing compressed powder to the metal pan.

Lipstick

Lipstick is a solid fatty-base product containing dissolved and suspended colorant materials. A good lipstick must possess a certain maximum and minimum of thixotropy; ie, it must soften enough a yield a smooth, even application with the minimum of pressure. It should not be necessary to apply a lipstick more often than every 4 to 6 hours. The applied film, no matter how thin, should to some extent be impervious to the mild abrasion encountered during eating, drinking, or smoking. The lipstick should be of such composition as to color only that portion of the lip to which it is applied, and not to bleed, streak or feather into the surrounding tissue of the mouth. It should be of a consistency that can be quickly and easily applied, and the perfume (usually present at 12%) should be carefully compounded so that it does not have an unpleasant taste. The colorants used in lipsticks are either insoluble lakes or oil-soluble dyes of the Eosin group, or both.

The bromo acids, bromo derivatives of fluoroescein, are used to produce indelibility in the applied film. Two are most generally used, dibromo and tetrabromofluorescein. Dibromofluorescein produces a yellow-red color; the tetra compound gives a more purple stain. Usually the two are used in combination, as neither produces desired results separately. From 1 -5% of these dyes are used in lipsticks; but ordinarily, 2 or 3% is adequate. Other pigments are used in concentrations of 5-15%, 10% is an average.

A highly refined grade of castor oil (qv) is one of the most common ingredients in lipstick. It is used primarily to impart viscosity to the molded stick and, secondly, because it has a small solvent action on the bromo acids. Castor oil dissolves less than 0.3% of the bromo acids. Its solvent action is owing to the presence of free hydroxyl groups in the glycerides of ricinoleic acid, which make up a large percentage of castor oil.

In the so-called high-stain sticks, a solvent such as polyethylene glycol 400 is used. The polyethylene glycol is not soluble in castor oil. A mutual solvent or coupling agent is, therefore, necessary; propylene glycol monoricinoleate is used for this purpose. Isopropyl myristate, isopropyl palmitate, butyl stearate, and some of the higher esters of the mono-and dihydric alcohols are commonly used in lipsticks, both for their solvent action on the bromo acids, and to reduce the thickness of the castor oil film.

Lanolin and various derivatives are used for their emollient properties and for a degree of tackiness and drag. Acetylated lanolinis more soluble in castor oil than lanolin itself. Lanolin oils, solvent extractions of lanolin, eliminate much of the tack of lanolin. Lanolin helps hold the lipstick mass in a uniform homogenous mixture. Lanolin, used in the proper ratio, helps to prevent sweating of the solvent oils and confers some protection against abrupt temperature changes.

Various waxes are used to impact different characteristics, such as hardness, thixotropy, melting point, and ease of application. These waxes are used in amounts regulated by the nature of the other components making up the finished stick.

Carnauba wax is responsible for stiffening the stick. If used in the proper proportions, it imparts to the stick exactly the right degree of thixotropy. Its melting point is very high, much higher than any of the other natural waxes. Candelilla wax is used for the same reason, but a lesser extent. Too much carnauba will cause a granular texture in the finished lipstick, and it is best to keep its concentration as low as possible, usually less than 5%.

Ceresin and ozokerite are both also good stiffening agents, with ceresin exhibiting the greater stiffening action. Since ceresin is merely a mixture of ozokerite and paraffin, the same effect can be obtained by using these two waxes in combination. Ceresin can have a variety of melting points, depending upon the ratio of ozokerite to paraffin, thus affecting the melting point of the lipstick. Ozokerite is used more often to raise the melting point. A combination of ozokerite and carnauba is most efficient.

Beeswax can be used to raise the melting point. It is a good binder, helping to produce a homogenous mass. In large amounts it causes granulation and a dulling effect. A typical lipstick base formulation is: 49.6 wt % castor oil; 26.3 wt % hydro-genated vegetable oil, a cocoa butter substitute; 11.6 wt % ozokerite 160; 5.0 wt % lanolin anhydrous; 4.5 wt % carnauba wax; 1.7 wt % cetyl alcohol; 1.0 wt % perfume; 0.2 qt % antioxidant; 0.1 wt % preservative, plus the necessary pigment pastes.

Manufacture

In manufacturing lipsticks, the colorants are mixed with part of the oil, usually in a Day Pony mixer, then passed through a 3 roll mill. The color and oil are ground a sufficient number of times to achieve a colorant distribution or better on a grind gage.

Gas that is absorbed on the surface of pigment particles diffuses slowly into the surrounding lipstick mass. A marked improvement is noticed in a pigment dispersion that is placed under vacuum. Dispersion of pigment involves a complicated combination of surface phenomena, eg, absorption, wetting, surface tension, interfacial tension, and formation of phase boundaries. Electrical charges must also be considered. Mechanical force alone cannot produce a satisfactory dispersion.

The base material is heated in a steam-jacketed kettle to 90°C and the ground colorants are added to the base material in the kettle. The batch is stirred with a high speed mixer for several hours. Any adjustment in shade is made by using the ground colorants. Base material is added in proportion to the amount of colorant used in the correction to keep the consistency approximately equal to that in the original formulation.

When the color match is satisfactory, the lipstick mass is drawn from the kettle and passed through a 74-um (200-mesh) stainless steel screen. It is collected in a molding pan and slabbed for future molding. Prior to molding, the mass is melted with slow agitation in a melting kettle to remove entrapped air.

Temperature control is important throughout processing, with care being taken to avoid excessive temperature in the kettle. The warmed lipstick mass is poured into warm molds, and the molds are passed through a cooling chamber. When cool, the lipsticks are removed from the molds, inserted in the lipstick holders, and flamed by passing them rapidly through a bunsen gas flame. They are then ready for packaging and distribution.

Control Methods

Manufacturing control begins with a thorough check of raw materials. A test of heat resistance of the finished product is made by holding it for 24 h in a constant temperature box at a temperature of 55°C, to determine any tendency to droop or distort. Hardness may be tested using a penetrometer.

The tendency for the stick to sweat or bleed can be checked by putting filled lipstick containers in a desiccator containing water and kept at a constant temperature of 45°C.

Shade and intensity of stain are best judged on the skin by comparison with the standard. Skin tone and undertone are also checked on the skin. Mass tone is judged by comparison with a standard.

Lipsticks

Dow corning describes lipsticks containing alkylmethylsiloxanes, in addition to castor oil, as an emollient, a wax, a suspending agent, a coloring agent and an organsilicone compound (Formula 1).

Shiseido describes a water-in-oil lipstick formulation containing a swellable clay mineral treated with a quaternary ammonium cationic surfactant. The product covers the lips smoothly and provides a long-lasting moisturizing effect as well as long-lasting color. A modified clay dispersion is first prepared by treating magnesium aluminium silicate with benzyl -dimethylstearyl ammonium chloride and adding hydrogenated lecithin, water (aqua) and glycerin. This mixture is then added to a typical lipstick mass to form a w/o emulsion stick (Formula 2).

Improved transfer resistance: A European patent application assigned to Revlon Consumer Products discloses a method of preparing makeup products with improved transfer resistance. The compositions comprise 1-70% of a volatile solvent, 0.1-15% of a silicone resin, 10-45% wax, 5-5o% powder and 1-30% oil. The compositions show better transfer resistance than previous cosmetics, which have a tendency to blot or transfer from the skin onto other surfaces, such as glassware or clothing. The compositions are prepared by grinding some of the dry components with the solvent and resin, then adding the wax and oil, followed by the remainder of the dry components.

When filled into suitable receptacles, the compositions may be used as a concealer, blush, eye shadow, foundation, lipstick or the like. An example of a transfer-resistant lipstick composition is shown in Formula 3.

Unilever discloses lipsticks containing polymeric thickening agents. Formula 4 shows a lipstick containing about 10% water (aqua) that uses polybutene and gelatin.

Lipstick overcoat: Nippon Shikizai Kogyo Kenkyush describes a simple lipstick overcoat composition containing perfluoro compounds and powders with a particle size of 0.1 -20.0 um. In an example, a lipstick overcoat contains 73% perfluoropoly-methylisopropyl ether, 25% poly (methyl methacrylate) and 2% glycerin. "*I* presume the poly (methyl methacrylate) represents the dispersed, small-particulate solid the patent specifies. Applying the composition after lipstick application prevents the lipsticks from coming off".

Smooth-spreading lipsticks: A Shiseido patent discloses another lipstick formulated as a w/o emulsion (Formula 12). The emulsion uses alkyl-ether-based emulsifying agents and contains 0.1-10% of a water-soluble polymer, such as polyvinyl alcohol. The resulting lipsticks are said to show smooth-spreading properties and to have long-lasting wearability.

Another Shiseido lipstick patent uses oil-soluble polymers, such as Escorez 1291 (an aliphatic hydrocarbon polymer from Exxon, Japan) to improve spreading and lasting properties.

Sansho Kaken discloses a hydrogel sheet consisting of polyvinyl alcohol, water (aqua) and sodium chloride for removing lipstick color marks left on the skin after being kissed. The sheet, which is pressed against the lipstick marks to remove the stain, may also contain an antibacterial agent/preservative, urea and abrasive powders.

Formula 1. Lipsticks

Octyldodecanol	10.00%
Candelilla (Euphorbia cerifera) wax	7.00
Ozokerite	4.00
Carnauba (Copernicia cerifera) wax	2.50
Acetulan	2.50
Bentone	0.60
Propylparaben	0.10
BHA	0.05
Castor (ricincus communis) oil	28.25
Pigment concentrate 7% pigment, 23% castor oil	30.00
Alkyldimethyl siloxane	15.00
	100.00

Formula 2. Water-in-oil lipstick emulsion

Polyethylene wax	7.00 Parts
Ceresin wax	4.00

Candelilla (Euphorbia cerifera) wax	7.00
Carnauba (Copernicia cerifera) wax	1.00
Castor (ricincus communis) oil	1.00
Mineral oil (paraffinum liquidum)	20.00
Glycerin bis (2-heptylundecanoate)	20.00
Pigments	9.20
Magnesium aluminum silicate (Veegum, RT Vanderbilt)	0.15
Benzyldimethylstearylammonium chloride	0.05
Hydrogenated lecithin	0.05
Water (aqua)	3.00
Glycerin	2.00

Formula 3. Transfer-Resistant Lipstick

Synthetic wax	6.00%
Ceresin	4.00
Paraffin	3.00
Isododecane	10.00
Cetyl stearate/acetylated lanolin, 90:10	5.00
Methylparaben	0.30
Propylparaben	0.10
BHA	0.10
Cyclomethicone	41.50
Isostearyltrimethylolpropane siloxysilicate	5.00
Colors	qs 100.00

Formula 4. Lipstick with polymeric Thickener

Candelilla (Euphorbia cerifera) wax	6.40 parts
Ozokerite wax	3.20
Carnauba (Copernicia cerifera) wax	0.40
Lanolin	4-80
Caprylic/capric triglyceride	6.00
Propylene glycol myristyl ether acetate	6.00
Lanolin oil	2.40
Polybutene	0.80
bis-Diglyceryl caprylate/caprate/ Isostearate / hydroxystearate adipate (Softisan 649, Huls)	9.20
Isopropyl palmitate	12.00
Soy lecithin	1.00
Sunflower oil monoglyceride	4.00
Gelatin, 270 bloom strength	0.36
Water (aqua)	9.64

Formula 5. Oil-in Water Lipstick Emulsion

Microcrystallin wax (cera microcristallina)	3.00%
Ceresin	10.00
Carnauba (Copernicia cerifera) wax	2.00
Lanolin oil	5.00
Jojoba (Buxus chinensis) oil	20.00
Castor (Ricinus communis) oil	10.00
Glyceryl tri-2-ethylhexanoate	31.80
Alkyl-ether-based surfactants	2.00
Pigments	10.00
Water (aqua)	5.00
Glycerin	100
Polyvinyl alcohol	0.20
	100.00

Foundations

Procter & Gamble describes an invisible foundation composition containing spherical inorganic components. The foundation, which is invisible on the skin, contains a light-scattering agent, such as silica, having a spherical shape and diameter of up to 30m. Coloring agents are purposely not included to accent the invisibility of the preparation.

Pola Kasei Kogyo described translucent makeup-base cosmetics with fine-pore-covering properties. Cosmetics such as the product shown in Formula 13 resist water and sebum, are translucent and cover fine pores.

Kanebo describes w/o makeup foundations containing 10-35% cyclosiloxanes, 0.5-3% sorbitan monoisostearate and/or diglycerin monoisostearate, and 0.5-3% silicon copolyols (Formula 8). The emulsions have excellent stability, do not discolor and spread easily on the skin.

Procter & Gamble discloses cosmetic tinted gels containing polymer-treated pigments and a hydrophilic gelling agent (Formula 9). This looks like a way of dispersing iron oxide pigments in a carbomer gel. The pigments are treated with water-dispersible polyester or polyester-amide polymers. The gellants may be a cellulose ether, PVP, PVA or carbomers.

Nippon Shikizai Kenkyusho discusses o/w emulsion as foundation bases. Formula 10 may interest makeup formulators.

There appears to be a continuing trend toward the development and use of hollow microspheres for makeup products, perhaps for a feeling of lightness on application, L'Oreal provides the latest example in a patent disclosing a non-compacted powder makeup containing hollow microspheres of a synthetic-thermoplastic material with a specific mass less than 0.1 g/cm^3 (Formula 11).

Elizabeth Arden describes cosmetic compositions, such as facial foundations, said to help minimize fine lines and wrinkles without irritating the skin. The compositions contain C_2-C_{28} a-hydroxy carboxylic acids and rosmarinic acid as well as their salts. A liquid eyeliner containing these materials is shown in Formula 12.

Mascara

Because of the proximity of these products to the eye, the law imposes strict limitations on the ingredients they may contain. The colorants are limited to natural dyes and inorganic and carbon pigments. The commercially available pigments used are the varying shades of the iron oxides, carbon blacks, and ultramarine blues.

Mascara, used to emphasize lashes, makes them appear longer since the ends of the lashes tend to be rather blondish, as compared to the rest of the hair length. The film applied should show good resistance to moisture and to gentle abrasion.

Cream Mascaras

In cream mascara the water has already been incorporated to provide a mascara ready for use without previous trituration. There are some advantages in this type of preparation since a much higher concentration of pigment can be incorporated than in possible in a cake. In addition, the optimum amount of water may be added rather than leaving this to the discretion of the consumer.

A typical cream mascara base is: 46.50 wt.% hydrocarbon solvent (Soltrol no. 130); 33.25 wt% distilled or deionized water; 8.25 wt% caranuba wax no.l refined; 7.50 wt% beeswax, white; 4.00wt%glyceryl monostearate S.E. (Arlacel C); 0.40 wt % poly-oxyethlene (20) sorbitan stearate (Tween 60); 0.40 wt % borax.5H_2O; 0.10 wt % propyl p-hydroxybenzoate; and 0.05 wt % methyl p-hydroxybenzoate.

The pigments used in cream mascara are ground into the base material, and the fine grind is then mixed with the necessary water and humectants to form the cream.

Eye Shadows

The colors used in eye shadows are carbon blacks, ultramarine blue, and the various yellows, browns, and reds of the iron oxide pigments. There is usually a higher concentration of pigments in eye shadows than mascaras, sometimes as high as 25%. The base into which the colorants are ground usually consists of beeswax, ozokerite, mineral oil, lanolin, and petrolatum. The method of manufacture consists of melting the waxes and oils together, adding the colorants and titanium dioxide used to impart the desired opacity, and grinding in a three-roll mill.

Eye shadows that have a metallic luster are made by incorporating finely ground aluminum, bronze, silver, or gold powders. The completed formula is heated and stirred slowly to remove occluded air and is then poured into the container.

From time to time power-shadow products, called Kohl, have appeared on the market. These are principally talcum-based with various inorganic colorants.

A prototype formula for an eye shadow is: 40.0 wt % mineral oil 65/75; 24.0 wt % ozokerite 80°C; 20.0 wt % chromic oxide hydrated (40% in petrolatum) 14.0 wt % petrolatum 45-50°C; 1.7 wt % paraffin; and 0.3 wt % propyl para-hydroxybenzoate.

Eye Makeup

L'Oreal describes eye makeup compositions containing a fine wax microdispersion. The waxes, dispersed in water (aqua) using ethoxylated glyceryl monostearate as the dispersing agent, have an average particle size of 184 nm (Formula 13).

Anhydrous eye-makeup compositions having excellent water, perspiration, sebum and oil-resistance are prepared with an oil-soluble resin. An example from a Shiseido patent uses polyisobutylene (Formula 14).

Kao describes makeup containing anionic-polymer emulsion with high film-forming ability for waterproof qualities. The anionic-polymer emulsions can also add gloss and help keep sunscreens in place. Formula 15 is an example of a cream eye shadow containing a 30% acrylic acid/butyl acrylate/methyl methacrylate copolymer emulsion in water (aqua).

L'Oreal discloses a surfactant-free eyelash and/or eyebrow makeup consisting of a wax dispersion in an aqueous phase containing water-soluble polymers (Formula 16).

Kanebo describes an emulsion-type mascara that contains a water soluble fibroin peptide (molecular-weight range of 300-3,500), an oily base having a melting point range of 60-110°C, water, a surfactant and, optionally, a hair-setting vinyl polymer. The mascara curls fine eyelashes, impart water resistance and durability, and enhance eyelash luster (Formula 17).

L'Oreal discloses a water-resistant mascara for coating the eyelashes (Formula 18).

Kanebo describes eye-makeup removers containing low-boiling (160-180°C) isoparaffins and polyoxyalkylene alkyl ether surfactants (Formula 19). The resultant products remove both oily, film-forming eye-makeup products and powdery eye shadows.

Formula 6. Eyebrow Cake

Silicone-treated talc	50.00%
Silicone-treated sericite	20.00
Magnesium stearate	2.00
Amino-acid-treated sericite	2.00
Titanium dioxide	1.20
Spherical poly (methyl methacrylate) powder	9.00
Titanium-coated mica	2.00
Titanium carbide/Titanium nitride (30:70) nano powder	8.00
Dimethylsiloxane	3.00
Octyldodecyl dimethyloctanoate	1.40
Octyldodecyl myristate	1.40
	100.00

Formula 7. Pore-covering Makeup

Stearic acid	1.00%
Mocrocrystalline (Cera Microcristallina) wax	1.00
Beeswax (cera alba)	2.00
Sucrose fatty acid ester	3.00
Squalane	2.00
Cyclomethicone	8.00
Glyceryl monostearate	3.00
Polyethyleneglycol monostearate	2.00
Titanium dioxide	3.00
Xanthan gum	0.10
Methylparaben	0.10
Triethanolamine	0.30
1, 3-Butylene glycol	6.00
Water (aqua)	qs 100.00

Formula 8. Water-in-oil Makeup Foundation

Octamethylcyclotetrasiloxane	20.00%
Sorbitan monoisostearate	1.00
Silicone copolyol	1.00
Mineral oil (paraffinum liquidum)	5.00
Petrolatum	1.00
Titanium dioxide	10.00
Iron oxide	0.50
Talc	4.50
Water (aqua)	qs 100.00

Formula 9. Tinted Makeup Gel

Glycerin	5.00%
Carbomer (Carbopol, 950, Goodrich)	0.50
Sodium hydroxide	0.25
Methylparaben	0.20
Methyldibromoglutaronitrile (and) phenoxyethanol (Euxyl K400, S&M)	0.10
Polymer-treated red iron oxide	0.20
Polymer-treated yellow iron oxide	0.40
Polymer-treated black iron oxide	0.05
Water (aqua)	qs 100.00

Formula 10. Foundation Makeup Base

Dimethylsiloxane, 10 cSt	32.90%
Mineral oil (paraffinum liquidum)	10.00
Polybutene	2.00
Paraffin	2.00
1, 3-Butylene glycol	5.00
Neopentyl glycol dioctanoate, HLB 1,3	1.00
Polyether-modified silicones, HLB 4.5	2.00
Diglyceryl disostearate, HLB 6.0	2.00
Methylparaben	0.10
Silicone-treated titanium dioxide	8.00
Silicone-treated talc	5.00
Silicone-treated sericite	3.00
Silicone-treated iron oxides	2.00
Water (aqua)	qs 100.00

Formula 11. Non-compacted Makeup Powder

Mica	23.42%
Kaolin	0.84%
Zinc stearate	0.84
Yellow iron oxide	0.12
Brown iron oxide	0.08
Nylon powder	14.70
Mineral oil (paraffinum liquidum)	49.20
Aroma	0.80
Hollow microspheres based on vinylidene chloride-acrylonitrile polymer (Expancel 551 DE, supplier)	10.0
	100.00

Formula 12. Liquid Eye-liner

Sodium lactate	2.00%
Rosmarinic acid	1.00

Sodium CMC	1.50
Hectorite	0.50
Propylene glycol	5.00
Triethanolamine shellac	5.00
Iron oxide	4.00
Methylparaben	0.10
Diazolidinyl urea (Germall II, Sutton)	0.25
Water (aqua)	qs 100.00

Formula 13. Eye-liner

Carnauba (Copernica cerifera) wax	37.500%
Ethoxylated glyceryl monostearate	9.375
Methylparben	0.200
Black iron oxide	6.000
Hydroxyethyl cellulose	0.250
Water (aqua)	qs 100.000

Formula 14. Water and Oil-resistant Mascara

Carnauba (Copernica cerifera) wax	7.00%
Beeswax (Cera alba)	2.00
Microcrystalline wax (cera microscristallina)	20.00
Lanolin	0.40
Polyisobutylene	57.60
Bentonite	3.00
Pigment	10.00
	100.00

Formula 15. Waterproof Cream Eye Shadow

Microcrystalline wax (cera microcristallina)	3.00%
Stearic acid	3.00
Mineral oil (paraffinum liquidum)	8.50
Lanolin	I .00
Sorbitan monostearate	1.50
Glycerin	5.50
Triethanolamine	1.50
Methyl hydroxypropyl cellulose	0.50
Acrylic acid/butyl acrylate/methyl methacrylate copolymer, 30% emulsion	10.00
Pearl colorant	10.00
Ultramarine blue	2.00
Aroma, preservative	qs
Water (aqua)	qs 100. 00

Formula 16. Eyelash Makeup

Paraffin wax	10.00%
Starch	5.00
Polyethylene	5.00
Black iron oxide	7.00
Carbomer (Carbopol, BF Goodrich)	0.50
Hydroxyethylcellulose	0.50
Panthenol	2.00
Water (aqua)	qs 100.00

Formula 17. Mascara Emulsion

Beeswax (cera alba)	5.00%
Ceresin	4.00
Stearic acid	8.00
Dipropylene glycol	16.00
Tert-Butanol amine	0.80
Fibroin peptide, 7% aq. sol	20.00
Acrylic polymer emulsion	16.00
Alcohol	2.00
Methylparaben	0.10
Butylparaben	0.10
Black iron oxide	12.00
Water (aqua)	qs 100.00

Formula 18. Water-Resistant Mascara

Paraffin wax	12.00%
Lanolin alcohol	15.00
Starch	2.00
Iron oxide	5.00
Isoparaffin	45.00
Montmorillonite clay	8.00
Panthenol	3.00
Chitosan Pyrrolidonecarboxylate (Kytamer PC/Amerchol)	3.00
Water (aqua)	7.00
	100.00

Formula 19. Eye-Makeup Remover

Isoparaffin, b.p. 200-280°C	70.00%
Polyoxyethylene cetyl ether	2.50
Polyoxyethylene behenyl ether	1.00
Polyoxyethiene sorbitan tristearate	1.00
Methylparaben	0.30
Propylene glycol	3.00
Water (aqua)	qs 100.00

Nail Lacquers

Advanced Genetic Technologies describes nail-polish compositions with increased adhesiveness and durability. The products contain protein-adherent polymers with hydroxyl-substituted aromatic groups, such as poly (4-hydroxystyrene). In an example, 150 mg poly (4-hyseozyaryrene). In an example, 150 mg poly (4-hydroxystyrene) was dissolved in ethyl alcohol containing 0.01 M magnesium chloride and coated onto the finger-nails. The resulting finish dried within 2 minutes to a clear, hard, glossy film that could not be scraped or peeled off the nails. The nails could be trimmed clipped or filed without cracking or chipping the finish.

Shinetsu Chem Ind discloses nail lacquers containing polyacetylenes, for products that do not discolor the nails (Formula 20).

International Beauty Design discloses nail-polish compositions that produce hard and durable coatings. A method for strengthening finger nails or toenails comprises three steps:

- Cleaning the nail surface.
- Applying one or more layers of a nail-polish composition consisting of aliphatic urethane acrylate, tripropylene glycol diacrylate, trimethylpropane ethoxylate triacrylate, methacrylic acid, l-hydroxycyclohexylphenyl ketone, butyl acetate and colorants.
- Subjecting the layers to UV treatment for curing.

Pola Chemical Industries describes nail lacquers containing selenium compounds that prevent yellow discoloration of the nails. Formula 21 is an example of a nail lacquer containing 0.01% sodium selenite. No yellow discoloration was noted after using this formula for three months, whereas, severe nail yellowing occurred using products without the sodium selenite.

Unilever discloses nail-polish remover compositions containing gelatin suspension stabilized glycerin and diglycerin. In one example a nail-polish remover contained 85% acetone, 1.0% glycerin, 1.0% diglycerin, 0.2% color, 0.2% aroma, 0.0001% gelating and water (aqua) to 100%. No explanation is given for including gelatin.

NAIL PRODUCTS

Nail Lacquer

Nail lacquer or nail polish usually consists of a resin, plasticizer, solvents, and pigment (30-32). The resins can be nitrocellulose or dinitrocellulose, also known as pyroxylin. Nitrocellulos films tend to shrink, so that their surface adhesion may be only moderate. Other resins are, therefore, added to impart adhesion. Gloss and plasticizers are added to reduce shrinkage and make the film flexible.

The solvents used influence the ease of application of the licquer, its rate of drying and hardening and the final characteristics of the film. The preferred solvents for nail lacquers are mixtures of low and medium boiling point alcohols, aromatic hydrocarbons, and aliphantic hydrocarbons.

Plasticizers may be added singly or in combinations of two or more, depending on the formulation. High molecular weight esters are used as well as castor oil. The esters can be dibutyl and dioctyl phthalate, triethyl citrate, and acetyl tributyl citrate.

The pigments used in nail lacquer formulations are carbon black, iron oxides, chromium oxides, ultramarines, metallic powders (gold, bronze, aluminum, copper), titanium dioxide. Transparent systems require the use of solvent-soluble colourants such as D&C red, green, yellow, and violet.

Pearl pigment in nail lacquer may be the natural pearl essence, guanine (2-amino-6-hydroxypurine), or a synthetic pearl that is usually a bismuth salt.

A typical nail lacquer formulation is: 30.5% wt % toluence; 12.8 wt % n-butyl acetate; 11.1 wt % n-amyl acetate; 11.1 wt % ethyl acetate; 10.0 wt % nitrocellulose; 10.0 wt % aryl sulfonamide-formaldehyde resin; 5.0 wt % isopropanol; 3.0 wt % bentonite; 2.5 wt % camphor (plasticizer); 2.5 wt % dibutyl phthalate; and 1.5 wt % ethanol.

Formula 20. Non-disclouring Nail Lacquer

Poly (1 -trimethylsilylpropylene)	0.30%
Nitrocellulose	12.00
Alkyd resin	10.00
Dibutyl phthalate	4.00
Camphor	2.00
Butyl acetate	49.70
Toluene	20.00
Pigment	1.00
Quaternary bentonite	1.00
	100.00

Formula 21. Non-yellowing Nail Lacquer

Sodium selenite	0.01%
Ethyl acetate	20.00
Isobutyl acetate	26.99
Isopropyl alcohol	2.00
Toluene	20.00
Nitrocellulose	17.00
Sucrose acetate isobutyrate	8.00
Di butyl phthalate	3.80

1, 3-Butylene glycol	0.20
Colorant	1.00
Stearalkonium hectorite	1.00
	100.00

Lacquer Removers

Lacquer removers may be made from any of a number of solvents. In most cases, any of the solvents used in the formulation of the enamels can be used as removers. The fastest acting seems to be acetone, but because of its high volatility, ethyl acetate has come into favor as well. Many of the lacquer removers contain an additive designed to leave a film on the nail, since the solvent itself has so high a degreasing tendency. Various oils and emollient compounds are added to the lacquer removers such as castor oil, lanolins, and lanolin derivatives.

A typical nail polish remover formula is: 40.0 wt % ethyl acetate; 30.0 wt % acetone; 19.0 wt % carbitol; 10.0 wt % dibutyl phthalate; 1.0 wt % sesame oil; and *qs* perfume

Cuticle Removers and Softeners

Cuticle removers and cuticle softeners usually consist of a dilute solution of alkali in water with some glycerol or other humectant added to keep the water from evaporating too easily. Potassium hydroxide, the alkali most often used, results in a somewhat harsh preparation but is effective. Trisodium phosphate, triethanolamine, and some of the quaternary ammonium salts have been used as replacements for potassium hydroxides. These are not as effective as the alkali but do a fair job of softening the cuticle.

Rouge

The term rouge (literally, red), although it properly includes all products intended to impart a glow to cheeks and lips, has gradually become limited to colorings applied to the cheeks. Rouge for the lips (except in theatrical cosmetics) originally was dispensed in little jars or pots, but it is now made in the form of crayons or sticks, and it will be considers here under a separate heading.

Rouge is available in several forms: *(1)* creams, (2) pastes, *(3)* compact powder, and (4) liquid. Choice is related to the condition of the skin and should be associated with the choice of face powder.

(I) *Cream rouge* is recommended for skin that tends toward dryness, because it can be rubbed well over the skin and blended well into the surrounding areas. To enhance the natural effect, light weight powder should be applied over it.

In cream rouge the pigment is dispersed in an emulsion that conforms in type to any of several of the creams described in the earlier section—

cold cream, emollient, or vanishing cream. The ingredients are selected from those used in various types of creams, combined to insure case of application, lasting effect, good body, and consistency during changes in temperature. White petrolatum (short fiber), white mineral oil, white beeswax, spermaceti, absorption bases, stearic acid, and cocoa butter are among the oily components used; borax and triethanolamine are used as emulsifying agents; glycerol and glycols are included as humectants.

Table 1.XI. Compositions of Cream and Paste Rouges.

	Typical recipe, % by wt. in:					
Ingredient	Cold creams		Emollient	Vanishing Cream	Pastes	
Beeswax	20	10	10	-	4	-
Borax	2	1	1	1	-	-
Ceresin	-	-	-	-	-	21
Cetyl alcohol	-	-	-	4	4	-
Cocoa butter	-	-	-	-	4	-
Glycerol	-	2	-	10	-	-
Lanolin	-	-	5	-	-	-
Mineral oil	-	35	24	-	23	53
Oleic acid	15	-	-	-	-	-
Petrolatum	25	25	40	-	60	23
Spermaceti	-	-	12	-	5	3
Stearic acid	-	2	-	25	-	-
Triethanolamine	4	1	-	-	-	-
Water	34	24	8	60	-	-
Total	100	100	100	100	100	100

The colors of preference for cream rouge are insoluble lakes, although some oil-soluble dyes are occasionally used. Dyes soluble in one or the other of the two phases of the emulsion would cause mottling darkening due to evaporation of water might also cause unevenness in the product itself and in the effect of it.

(2) *Paste rouge* is made from various fats and waxes, incorporating appropriate colors and perfume, but no water. It is used in the same manner as cream rouge; therefore, the ease of spreading, melting point and stability are important factors. Recipes for several types of cream and paste rouges are suggested in Table 1.XI (4, 5,9,13}. The

compositions suggested are best prepared as white bases, to be used in proportional amounts with the chosen colors. Perfume, and also a preservative, are also to be added.

(3) Powder rouge is usually recommended for the skin that tends toward oiliness, though many women who use the cream or paste also apply a touch of powdered rouge for repairing their make-up at odd times. For regular use on an oily skin, the powdered rouge should be applied over a heavy weight of face powder.

Because of the delicate effect desired, the composition of powder rouge resembles that of lighter-weight face powders. Talc may be present to 80%; starch, stearin, and gums may be used as the binding agent; the remaining ingredients are zinc oxide, zinc stearate, kaolin, precipitated chalk, and titanium dioxide. Many manufacturers use their prepared powder bases, adding what may be required to insure the formation of a good compact product.

(4) *Liquid rouge* is not so popular now as it was formerly, but it still appears occasionally as a novelty. It is usually a dilute solution of appropriate and approved water-soluble colors in a mixture of water, alcohol, and glycerol. Good lasting effect can be obtained by careful adjustment of the amount of cosin present; the addition of a small amount of a wetting agent assists spreading. Recipes for liquid rouge are given in various handbooks.

As *novelties,* rouge also has been offered on leaves of tissue paper in small books or envelopes, and as a white product containing alloxan, which turns red as it is rubbed over the skin.

Colors for rouge are limited by the range of tints and shades that would be normal for the natural tones in the skin, and the color of the blood as seen through it. Many manufactures offer three basic variations—clear red, orange-red, and bluish or purplishred. The merchandising of these products takes advantages of seasonal changes in the basic tone of the skin, and also of the need for slightly different shades of make-up in daylight and under certain types of artificial lighting.

Manufacture of Rouge and Lipstick. Many manufacturers in the field consider the making of rouge and lipstick so difficult and complicated that they consign their recipes to others who specialize in the production of these items. It is true that with older equipment it was inevitable that entire rooms soom became covered with various shades of red deposit; but with the newer equipment and reasonable care this waste can be almost entirely avoided.

For *paste rouge* the fats are melted and well mixed; the finely divided certified colors are added; and the mass is allowed to cool under continuous agitation. When it is about 20°F. above the solidification point, the mass is run through an ointment mill and poured into the containers.

For *cream rouge* the colors are first mixed with a portion of the petrolatum or mineral oil. Water-in oil emulsions are prepared as described under "Creams". After emulsification is complete the colored portion (and perfume) is added, and the whole mass is run through an ointment mill, if necessary, to insure thorough mixing. Oil-in-water emulsions are completely prepared without color; this is added after the mixture is cool, and the whole mass is milled before filling.

Compact powder rouge is prepared as described under face powders; the method of dry compression is preferred.

In the making of *lipsticks* that contain bromo acid this dye is incorporated in the castor oil, n-butyl stearate, or other solvent warmed in a jacketed kettle, while the fats, waxes and lakes are melted and thoroughly mixed in another vessel. The second mixture is then added to the first; the whole mass in kept under continuous agitation, and finally run through a steam-jacketed mill to insure uniform dispersion of the colors. The mixture is allowed to cool, and when it is 5-10° above the solidification point it is poured into molds and chilled quickly. The sticks are at once placed in their holders, passed through a gas flame or under an infrared lamp to smooth the surface, and covered for packaging.

Skin Pigmentation

Henkel discloses the use of indolines as tanning agents for human skin. These compounds are applied to the skin as o/w emulsions to impart a brown color to the skin without exposure to the sun (Formula 22).

Shiseido discloses the use of chaulmoogra (Taraktogenos kurzii) oil for the treatment of hypopigmentation (Formula 23). Chaulmoogra (Taraktogenos kurii) oil and its salts and esters induced pigmentation in hypomelanotic spots on the skin by causing an expansion of already pigmented areas.

A patent assigned to Estee Lauder described self-tanning cosmetic compositions dispensed as a spray. The compositions are alchol-and-oil-free and dry quickly on the skin (Formula 24).

Richardson-Vicks (now part of Procter & Gamble) has patented stabilized compositions for imparting an artificial tan to human skin. The improved stability emulsions comprise 0.120% dihydroxyacetone, 0.15% of an alkyl phosphate. such as diethanolamine cetyl phosphate, and 0.025-2.5% of a carboxylic acid copolymer, such as acrylates $C_{10}C_{30}$ alkyl acrylate crosspolymer (Formula 25).

Stiefel Laboratories describes suntanning agents containing a pseudocatalase. Suntanning is enhanced by

L'Oreal describes the use of 4-thiroesorcin derivatives in skin-whitening cosmetics. In an example, 0.01 M 4-mthyl thiroesorcin inhibited tyrosinase activity by 90% (Formula 26).

Kanebo discloses skin-lightening preparations containing cinnamic acid derivatives, which prevent melanin formation and are not irritating to the skin (Formula 27). One of the preferred compounds is 3-[2-(b-glucopyranosyloxy) phenyl]-2-cinnamic acid. At 0.1%, this compound inhibited 97.2% tyrosinase activity.

Kao discloses skin-lightening compositions containing a combination of ascorbic acid and tea-leaf extracts (Formula 28).

Sansei Seiyaku described skin preparations containing oligopeptides for inhibiting melanin formation. A cream containing anserine as the oligopeptide is shown in Formula 29.

Unilever describes topical, retinol-containing cosmetic compositions used to promote the repair of photo-damaged skin and/or to reduce or prevent the damaging effects of UV light on skin and/or to lighten the skin (Formula 30).

A Japanese patent assigned to Nonogawa Shoji YK discloses skin-lightening cosmetics containing proteogylcans and ascorbates. The proteoglycans are extracted from animal tissue. The lotion shown in Formula 31 inhibited malanin formation in vitro tests.

A Mikimoto Seiyaku patent describes cosmetics containing cholesteric liquid crystals and licorice extracts. The licorice extract is used in Japan to lighten skin; the liquid crystals, which may have a skin-moisturizing effect, also enhance the product's appearance (Formula 32).

Kojic acid has been used for many years as a skin-lightening compound in Japan. In the past few years, the use of glabridin, licorice extract, as a skin lightener has increased. Kanebo discloses the latest (Formula 33).

A patent assigned to Kose discloses the use of superoxide dismutase to enhance the effectiveness of skin-lightening agents (Formula 34).

Formula 22. *Skin-Colouring Formulation*

Zinc stearate	2.00%
Aluminium stearate	0.50
Isopropyl isostearate	13.00
Wheat germ (Triticum vulgare) oil	3.00
Methylglucose dioleate	2.00
PEG-45/dodecyl glycol copolymer	2.00
Beeswax (Cera alba)	3.00
1, 2-Dodecanediol	1.00
Propylparaben	0.20
Lactic acid	0.50
Sodium hydroxide	0.15
Methylparaben	0.20

Magnesium sulfate 7 H_2O	0.70
Glycerin	2.00
5, 6-Dihydroxyindole hydrobromide	0.9 mmole
Water (aqua)	qs 100.00

Formula 23. Treatment Cream for Hypopigmentation

Carbomer 940 (Carbopol 940, BF Goodrich)	0.20%
Triethanolamine	0.25
Buylene glycol	4.00
Glyceryl stearate	3.00
Chaulmoogra (Takaktogenos kurzii) oil	2.00
Myristyl myristate	2.50
Acetylated lanolin	3.00
PEG-20 Stearate	3.00
Cetostearyl octanoate	2.00
Mineral oil (paraffinum liquidum)	1.00
Lanolin alcohol	0.50
Octyl methoxycinnamate	3.00
Methychloroisothiazolinone (and) methylisothiazolinone (Kathon CG, Rohm & Hass)	0.10
Allantion	0.10
Water (aqua)	qs 100.00

Formula 24. Self-Tanning *Spray*

Dihydroxyacetone	5.00%
1. 3-Butylene glycol	3.00
PPG-12-buteth-16 (Ucon 50 HB660, Union Carbide)	0.50
Hydrolyzed wheat protein (and) hydrolyzed wheat starch (Cropeptide W, Croda)	0.20
Dimethyl isosorbide (Arlasolve DMI, ICI)	10.00
PEG-10 laurate (Protomate 600-ML, Protameen)	1.50
Methyldibromoglutaronitrile (and) phenoxyethanol (Euxyl K-400, Calgon)	0.20
Ethoxydiglycol (Transcutol, Gattefosee)	10.00
Glycereth-7 triacetate (Dermol GL-7A, Alzo)	5.00
PEG-40 castor oil (Surfactol 365, Cas Chem)	1.00
Water (aqua), deionized	qs 100.00

Formula 25. Artificial Tanning Lotion

Carbomer 934	0.20%
Carbomer 980	0.15
Acrylates C_{10}-C_{30} alkyl acrylate crosspolymer (Pemulin TR1, BE Goodrich)	0.15
PPG-20 Methyl glucose ether distearate	2.00
Tocopheryl acetate	1.20
Mineral Oil (paraffinum liquidum)	2.00
Stearyl alcohol	1.00
Shea (Butyrosermum perkii) butter	1.00
Cetyl alcohol	1.00
Ceteareth20	1.00
Ceteth-2	1.00
Ceteth 10	1.00
Diethanolamine cetyl phosphate	0.75
Dihydroxyacetone	3.00
DMDM hydantoin (and) iodopropylbutylcarbamate	0.25
Aroma	1.00
Cyclomethicone	2.0
Water (aqua)	qs 100.00

Formula 26. Skin-whitening Composition

4-Methyl thioresorcin	2.80%
Ethyl alcohol	50.00
PEG-40	30.00
Ethoxydiglycol	5.00
Glycerin	5.00
Water (aqua)	qs 100.00

Formula 27. Skin-lightening Composition

3- [2 - (b-glucopyranosyloxy) phenyl]-2-cinnamic acid	0.10%
Olive (Olea europaea) oil	15.00
Isopropyl myristate	5.00
Polyoxyethylene nonyl phenyl ether	0.50
Glycerin	5,00
Methylparaben	0.10
Alcohol	7.00
Water (aqua)	qs 100.00

Formula 28. Skin-lightening Composition

Glyceryl stearate	5.00%
Polyethyleneglycol monostearate	2.00

Squalane	8.00
Glyceryl trioctanoate	8.00
Stearyl alcohol	5.50
Dimethylpolysiloxane	0.20
Propylene glycol	5.00
Disodium edetate	0.10
L-Ascorbic acid phosphate magnesium salt	3.00
Tea leaf (Camillia sinensis) extract	3.00
Citric acid	0.50
Sodium citrate	0.50
Preservatives, aroma, color	qs
Water (aqua)	qs 100. 00

Formula 29. Skin-lightening Cream

PEG-40 stearate	2.00%
Glyceryl stearate SE	5.00
Stearic acid	5.00
Behenyl alcohol	1.00
Mineral oil (paraffinum liquidum)	10.00
Glyceryi trioctanoate	10.00
Glycerin	5.00
Ethylparaben	0.10
Anserine	4.00
Water (aqua)	qs 100.00

Formula 30. Photodamaged skin/lightening Treatment Oil

Retinol	0.20%
Cysteaminophenol	1.00
Isopropanol	10.00
Volatile silicone	80.00
Ethylhexyl palmitate	8.70
Antioxidant	0.10
	100.00

Formula 31. Skin-lightening Lotion

Alcohol	8.00%
PEG hydrogenated castor oil	0.40
Glycerin	5.00
1, 3-Butylene glycol	3.00
Proteoglycan extracts	10.00
L-Ascorbic acid phosphoric acid magnesium salt	3.00
Citric acid	0.50

Sodium citrate	1.00
Aroma	qs
Water (aqua)	qs 100.00

Formula 32. Skin Lightener

Cholesteryl 12-hydroxystearate	3.00%
Cholesteryl heptanoate	3.00
Cholesteryl oleate	2.00
Cholesteryl butyrate	1.00
Licorice (Glycyrrhiza glabra) extract	1.00
Neutralized carboxyvinyl polymer	0.30
Water (aqua)	qs 100.00

Formula 33. Skin Lightener

Alcohol	10.00%
Polysorbate 20	0.50
BHT	0.01
Aroma	0.05
Potassium 2-phenylbenzimidazole 5-sulfonate	0.50
Glabridin	0.10
Glycerin	5.00
Xanthan gum	0.10
Water (aqua)	qs 100.00

Formula 34. Skin-lightening Preparation

Superoxide dismutase	3.12×10^{-5} nM
Kojic acid	1.00%
1, 3-Butylene glycol	20.00
Polyoxyethylene hydrogenated castor oil monoisostearate	1.00
Lactic acid	0.05
Sodium lactate	0.03
Water (aqua)	qs 100.00

Hair

Glycolipids and siloxanes: Kao describes hair dyes containing glycolipids and siloxanes, to provide long lasting colours without damaging the hair. The siloxanes are selected from dinethyl siloxanes, methyl phenyl siloxanes, amino-modified silicones, fatty-acid-modified silicones, alcohol-modified silicones, cyclic silicones, polyether -modified silicones, fluorine-modified silicones and alkyl-modified silicones (Formula 1). Of course, this is the first step; and oxidize must be added to develop the colour in the hair.

Tyroisinase *activators and pantothenic acid:* A patent assigned to Lion discloses the use of tyrosinase activators and pantothenic acid (and derivaties) to prevent hair from graying. Culturing human melanocytes with both 0.025% of the 2-amino-2-methyl-l, 3-propanediol salt of 8-methyxy-c AMP and 0.05% calcium pantothenate increase tyrosinase activity 240%, compared to a 193% increase without the pantothenate salt. However, Lion's patent gives to date for hair treated with this combination.

Dopa: Unilever cosmetic describes compositions containing dihydroxyphenylalanine (DOPA) derivatives for darkening hair. An analog of DOPA, dihydroxyphenyl serine, can be absorbed by skin or by hair follicles and metabolized in vivo. This leads to melanin formation in skin or the growth of melanin-pigmented hair. Consequently, the composition gives controlled skin darkening that mimics sun-induced tanning or brings about the growth of dark hair in place of gray or white hair (Formula 2). After two days in the presence of 0.1 mm dihydroxyphenylserine, cultured hair follicles were observed to darken. The hair shaft that grew from the follicles showed dark color.

Permanent dyes: Shiseido discloses a unique non-oxidative permanent-dye formulation for hair and synthetic fibres. By mixing a gelling agent, water (aqua), a mercaptan-based reducing agent and a certified FD&C or D&C dye, Shiseido produces a highly effective, easily employed permanent-dye gel composition that imparts a desired color into both natural and synthetic fibres. In the preferred compositions, the user adds the mercaptan-based reducing agent to the composition immediately before applying the gel composition to the fibres. Merely rubbing the gel onto the fibres permanently embeds the desired color into the fibres.

Temporary dyes: Bristol-Myers Squibb discloses compositions and methods for temporarily coloring hair using chemically synthesized or biosynthetic water-soluble melanins. The compositions comprise, in addition to the melanin compound, water-dispersible cationic compounds. The cationic material, which forms a complex with most of the water-soluble melanin, can be a surfactant, such as dicetyldimmonium chloride, or a cationic polymer, such as polyquaternium-6, 11 or -39. The patent procedure dissolves 40 mg solubilized melanin in 5 ml water (aqua) for solution 1 and adds 40 mg dicetyldimmonium chloride to 5 ml water (aqua) to make solution 2. A mixture of solutions 1 and 2 at pH 7.1 is used to treat hair.

Non-oxidative dyes: A recent European patent application discloses an interesting two-step, non-oxidative hair-dye system. The user first applies a composition containing 2—hydroxyl-1,4-naphthoquinone to the hair. This remain in place for about 30 minutes. In the second step, the user applies a preparation containing 5, 6-dihydroxyindole, which remains on the hair for an additional 10 minutes before being rinsed off. The treatment gives the processed hair a blond color (Formula 3).

Shampoo dyes: Kao describes shampoo containing direct hair dyes that have excellent dyeing and cleansing properties (Formula 4).

Henkel discloses a one-step product for simultaneously washing and coloring the hair that uses a coupler-developer oxidation coloring agent, a cationic polymer, an anionic surfactant and an amphoteric surfactant. Formula 5 gives a medium-blond hair dye.

Clairol discloses direct hair dyes having a quaternary center with a long aliphatic chain. The dyes have a high affinity for hair, are shampoo-stable and impart uniform dyeing. A hair dye comprises 0.2% dimethylhexadecyl-2 (2-nitroanilion) ethyl ammonium iodide, 65% ethyl alcohol and water (aqua) to 100%.

Bleaching agents: Hoyu describes bleaching agents containing sulfite salts, benzyl alcohol and cationic surfactants (pH 7-9) to bleach dyed hair without damaging the hair or changing the native hair color. A gel-type composition containing 4% sodium sulfite, 5% benzyl alcohol and 3% cetyltrimethylammonium chloride effectively bleaching the dyed hair colour without bleaching the native, black color. This almost sounds like a stripping agent for previously used non-oxidative hair dyes.

A Takara Belmont patent describes hair bleaches containing bicarbonates, hydrogen peroxide and persulfates at pH 5-8. These are said to show less damage to hair and a low incidence of irritation to the skin. The product formula describes three mixtures, apparently mixed before use. The first mixture is a 3% water (aqua) solution of ammonium bicarbonate; the second mixture is a 17% water (aqua) solution of 35% hydrogen peroxide. To produce the bleach, Takara Belmont mixes 60 g each of solutions 1 and 2 with 1 g of ammonium persulfate powder. A bundle of hair coated with this mixture, kept at 50°C for 15 minutes, washed and dried, and bleached brightly showed to damage.

A Poly Chemical Industries patent describes hair preparations containing 0.0001% sodium selenite that prevent UV-induced yellowing of hair.

Natural pigments: Kashiwa Chemical discloses hair dyes containing natural pigments extracted from Dactylspius coccus, Monascus purpureus, Coccus lacca and Polygonus tinctrium, including capsaicin, ceraminic acid and laccaic acid (Formula 6).

A German patent describes the enhancement of cosmetic hair coloration via exposure to light. The chemical coloration of hair is enhanced, yielding brighter and stronger colors, by subsequent exposure of the hair to light, especially coherent light in the wavelength range 600-1, 200 nm, preferably 780 nm. This treatment alters the a-helical structure of the hair macrofibrils, particularly the enzyme coordination and redox potential. Researchers irradiated hair by placing a hood with laser diodes set into the inner surface over the head.

E.C. DeWitt and Co. disclose hair-darkening compositions containing thiosulfates and bismuth acetate derivatives. A hair dye was prepared using bismuth citrate, disodium EDTA, glycerine, alcohol, sodium thiosulfate, polysorbate 80 and aroma in an aqueous base.

Bristol-Myers Squibb discloses other melanin-forming hair dyes. A hair-dying kit comprises three items:

- An aqueous solution of DOPA compound
- A water-soluble oxidant
- A buffering agent to maintain a pH of 6-10.

When the DOPA compound reacts with the oxidant in an aqueous environment, it provides a high concentration of a nitrogenous phenolic melanin precursor, which converts to melanin while in the hair. Combining a DOPA (0.15 g DOPA, 7.5 ml 0.1 M HC1) and an oxidant (0.9 g $K_3Fe(CN)_6$, 1.15 g disodium phosphate, 0.3 g hydrated trisodium phosphate and 7.5 ml water (qua) solution provides the aqueous reaction medium, with an initial pH of 7.2. Exposing a swatch of virgin gray hair to the aqueous reaction medium for 30 minutes, rinsing with water (aqua), shampooing and drying leaves the hair several shades darker.

Chlorotrichosis: An article by M. Sticherling et al briefly reviews why hair turns green. The problem of green discoloration, sometimes referred to as chlorotrichosis, often results from deposition of exogenous copper through both occupational and vacation activities.

These days, a common source of exogenous copper is tap water or swimming-pool water. The metal is released from copper fittings by the acidic pH of the water and, according to one report, after flurodiation of drinking water. It is also released after the addition of copper-based algaechides to, or chlorination of, swimming-pool water. In most cases, the problem affects patients with light-blond hair.

Predisposing factors that must be present as well for green discoloration to occur include previous hair damage (either mechanically, by sun or by peroxide bleaching), dyeing, frequent contant with chlorinated water or use of an alkaline shampoo. However, reported causes of green hair other than exogenous copper deposition include use of tar shampoo and industrial exposures to cobalt, chromium and nickel. You may wish to obtain a reprint of this short but through review for your files because it contains almost 40 valuable references on this subject.

Formula 1. *Hair Dye*

p-Phenylenediamine	1.00%
Oleic acid	10.00

Oleic acid diethanolamide	8.00
Oleyl alcohol	2.00
Polyoxyethylene octyldodecyl ether	10.00
Ethyl alcohol	15.00
Propylene glycol	10.00
Polyether modifies *silicone*	1.00
Glycolipid hydroxypropyl either	1.00
Ammonia to pH 10.00	qs

Formula *2. Anhydrous Hair Darkener*

Dihydroxyphenylserine	5.00%
Isopropyl alcohol	10.00
Ethylhexylpalmitate	8.70
Antioxidant	0.10
Volatile silicone	qs 100.00

Formula 3. Two-step Non-oxidative Hair Dye

First Application

2-Hydroxyl-1, 4-naphthoquinone	0.50%
Carob gum	3.00
Citric acid	4.00
Milk powder	qs 100.00

Dilute with 3 times its weight of water (aqua) and apply to hair for 30 minutes.

Second Application

5, 6-Dihyrdoxyindole	0.50%
Alcohol	10.00
Hydroxypropyl cellulose	1.06
Capryl caprylglucosides (Triton CG 110, Rohm & Haas)	2.00
Triethanolamine	0.75
Tartaric acid	0.30
Preservative	qs
Water (aqua)	qs 100.00

Apply for 10 minutes and rinse from the hair.

Formula 4. *Direct Hair-Dye Shampoo*

Disodium lauryl ether sulsosuccinate, 30%	27.00%
Sodium lauryl sarcosinate, (30%)	7.50
C_{9-11} Alkylpolyglucoside, (35%)	19.00
Dimenthyllaurylamine oxide, (35%)	6.00
Laurylhydroxysulfobetaine, 30%	3.50
PEG160- sorbitan stearate	1.00

Polysorbate 60	1.00
Preservative	0.30
EDTA	0 50
Polydimethyldiallylammonium chloride	0.50
Citric acid	1.00
Henna (Lawsonia inermis) extract	0.10
Basic yellow no. 57	0.01
Basic red no. 76	0.08
Basic blue no. 99	0.01
Water (aqua)	qs 100.00

Formula 5. Hair-coloring/conditioning Shampoo

C_{12-18} Fatty alcohol	10.50%
Sodium laureth sulfate	5.00
Cocoalkyldimethylammonium betaine	3.00
Polyquaternium-10 (Polymer JR 400, Amerchol)	1.00
a-Naphthol	0.40
1, *3-bis* (2, 4-diaminophenoxy) proper	0.10
Resorcinol	0.15
p-Toluylene-diamine sulfate	0.21
EDTA	0.20
Sodium sulfate	1.00
Ammonia solution, 25%	6.00
Water (aqua)	qs 100.00

Formula 6. Hair Dye Containing Natural Pigments

Glyceryl monolinoleate	1.80%
Polyoxyethylene polyoxypropylene glycol	1.20
Polyethylene glycol	4.00
Berberine chloride	0.80
Copper/sodium chlorophyll	0.70
Hematin	0.50
Cochineal	1.50
Citric acid	0.20
Aroma	0.30
Water (aqua)	qs 100.00

Hair Preparations

Shampoos

Present day shampoos usually contain a primary detergent which can be a fatty alcohol sulfate, ether sulfate, sarcosinate, or one of many other anionics. The primary detergent can also be amphoteric or nonionic.

The secondary, or auxiliary, detergent is usually an alkanolamide, which controls the viscosity of the product and increases the quality and volume of the foam (33-39).

Soap Shampoo

Soap shampoos do not cleanse well in hard water areas. They are primarily aqueous solutions of soft soap combined with preservatives, sequestrants, color, and perfume.

Soapless Shampoo

Soapless shampoos are primarily based on aqueous solutions of sulfonated oils such as sulfonated castor oil and sulfonated olive oil combined with preservatives, color, and perfume.

Low pH Shampoos

Unlike many of the propertiees ascribed to shampoos, such as foaming, cleansing, luster, and manageability, pH is an intangible in that it cannot be observed or demonstrated during product usage, and the effects of low pH are not obvious to the user. It has been reported that mild aqueous acids cause antiswelling action on the cuticle scales of the hair. As the cuticle tightens, the hair gains luster because light is more efficiently reflected from the surface of the hair shaft. In the absence of external charges hair shows its highest strength and resiliency at pH 4.0-6.0. Some surfactants do not perform will in an acid medium. Fatty alcohol sulfates hydrolyze rapidly and decompose below pH 4.0. Alkanolamides generally react in a similar manner. However, combinations of triethanolamine, and sodium and ammonium lauryl sulfates with amine oxides can be adjusted to low pH with good stability. Examples of clear, stable shampoo formulations adjusts to pH 4.0 are: 54.0 wt % water; 40.0 wt % ammonium lauryl sulfate (30% solution); 6.0 wt % cocamidoopropylamine oxide (30% solution); and *qs* (as needed) preservative, color, perfume, acid, etc.

Amphoteric Shampoos

Amphoteric surfactants are generally assumed to be less irritating to the eyes than other detergent or soap reprations. They are usually low foam materials, and it is customary to combine them with anionic surfactants. Amphoteric shampoos are based on the use of imidazoline, betaine, and sulfobetaine surfactants. Amphoteric-base shampoos are difficult to thicken and difficult to opacity. Amphoterics can be blendedess with equal parts of either high foaming anionic lauryl sulfates or the sulfo-succinate half esters. Amine oxides can also be used instead of the more irritating alkanolamides. The keratin substantivity of the betaine amphoterics is greatest at pH 5.5-6.5. The following shampoo formula, which has been adjusted to a pH of 5.8, illustrates the use of amphoterics:

17.0 wt % ammonium lauryl sulfate; 6.0wt%Monomate CPA-40 (sulfo-sauccinate half ester); 2.0wt%MonatericISA-35(isostearic imidazoline); and *qs* perfume, preservative, color, and water.

Dandruff Shampoos

Dandruff is the product of hyperkeratinization. The rate of keratinization has increased to the point that the scales become more visible. There are not known differences in the incidence of dandruff in men and women or among races. Dandruff shampoos contain ingredients that effectively control dandruff by allowing a normal turnover rate of epidermal cells. Ingredients used in some anti-dandruff shampoos are coal tar, quaternary ammonium compounds, resorcinol, salicylic acid, selenium sulfide, sulfur, undecylenic acid and derivatives and zinc pyrithoine (zinc 2-mercaptopyridine 1-oxide; zinc moadine). Selenium sulfide and zinc pyrithione are cytostatic (reduce epidermal cell turnover rate). Zinc pyrithione is strongly absorbed by the hair, with absorption related to concentration, pH, temperature, product formulation, and time of exposure. Since these are medicated shampoos, formulations should be nonirritating and nonsensitizing.

A typical lotion cream shampoo is: 47.0 wt % distilled or deionized water; 42.1 wt % sodium lauryl sulfate, 28% active; 4.0 wt % ethylene glycol monostearate; 3.0 wt % coconut fatty acid diethanolamide; 3.0 wt % propylene glycol; 0.5 wt % perfume; and 0.4 wt % preservative.

A typical clear liquid shampoo is: 50.0 wt % triethanolamine lauryl sulfate, 65% active; 27.6% wt % distilled or deionized water; 10.0 wt % propylene glycol; 5.0 wt % lauric acid diethanolamide; 4.0 wt % myristic acid; 2.0 wt % oleyl alcohol; 0.8 wt % perfume; 0.4 wt % preservative; 0.1 wt % citric acid; and 0.1 qt % sequesterant Na_2.

A typical viscous liquid shampoo is: 60.0 wt % triethanolamine lauryl sulfate, 38% active; 21.1. wt % distilled or deionized water; 3 0 wt % myristicacid; 2.0 wt % oleyl alcohol; 2.0 wt % propylene glycol; 1.0 wt % perfume; 0.5 wt % poly (vinylpyrroliddionone) K-30; and 0.4 wt % preservative.

A typical antidandruff shampoo is: 65.3 wt % water; 25.5 wt % sodium lauryl sulfate; 5.0 wt % stearic acid; 2.1 wt % lauramine oxide; 1.0 wt % zinc pyrithione powder; 0.7 wt % sodium hydroxide pellets; 0.4 wt % sodium chloride; plus preservative, color, and perfume.

Shampoo Additives

Foam builders are principally fatty acid alkanolamides. Conditioning agents are amine oxides, fatty alcohols, lanolin derivatives, esters of fatty acids, silicones, cationic materials, and polyacrylamides. Opacifying agents are higher fatty alcohols, such as stearyl and cetyl, and glycol and glycerol esters of fatty acids. Sequestering agents prevent formation of insoluble calcium and magnesium soaps and prevent discoloration owing to iron contamination. Citric acid, tartaric acid and salts of EDTA are commonly used sequestrants. Viscosity builders are cellulose derivatives, alkanolamides, and carboxy-vinyl polymers. Preservatives are usually the hydroxybenzoates, formaldehyde, imidazolidinyl-urea compounds (Germall), sorbates, and 1 (3-chloroallyl) 3, 5, 7—triazo-l azoniaadamantane chloride (Dowicil).

Hair *Straighteners*

Though the thioglycolate straighteners are essentially the same as products used for hair waving, they differ in that the straighteners are appreciably more viscous to help keep the hair straight while it is being softened. After application, the hair is repeatedly combed, which may be a factor in scalp irritation. Since curly hair is quite resistant, the softening process takes a rather long time and the danger of hair damage and scalp irritation proportionately increases. When it reaches the desired straightness, the hair is rinsed and treated with a conventional neutralizer such as sodium bromate. A typical formula for a thioglycolate straightener is: 52.00-53.00 wt % distilled or deionized water; 22.00 wt % glyceryl monostearate, pure; 17.50 wt % ammonium thioglycolate (50% solution, 8.75% thio acid); ca 4.50 wt % ammonium hydroxide (28% solution, sufficient to product pH 9.2-9-4); 1.75wt% Brij 35; 1.00 wt% mineral oil; 0.50-1.00 wt%perfume; and 0.15 wt % preservative [methyl p-hydroxybenzoate and propyl *p*-hydroxybenzoate (3:1)].

The Gant and Hersh patent relates to compositions and methods for straightening kinky hair or for curling straight hair.

Depilatories

Products used for the removal of unwanted hair by chemical agents are commonly called depilatories. The requirements of a depilatory are that is should be (I) nonirritaring and innocuous, (2) efficient in action, removing hair within a 10 min period, and (3) be without odor or have the pleasant odor of the perfume.

The activity of the depilatory substance depends upon (1) the nature of the depilating or denaturing agent, (2) the duration of the action, (3) the pH of the cosmetic medium, and (4) the temperature of the reaction.

The depilatory most widely used today is based on calcium thioglycolate in a strongly alkaline medium, pH ca 12.3. It also contains a small amount of a wetting agent, a filler, enough slaked lime to attain the required pH, and alkali stable perfume. The commercial products are sold either as thin or very thick pastes, packaged in a jar or collapsible tube.

A typical formula for a depilatory is: 69.0 wt% base cream [60.10 wt % distilled water (solvent); 32.00 wt % calcium carbonate (filler); 6.15 wt % cetyl alcohol (bodying agent for cream); and 1.75 wt % product G—2135 (wetting agent and emulsifier)]; 15.0 wt % distilled water; 6.8 wt % calcium hydroxide (pH control); 5.4 wt % calcium thio-glycolate (depilating agent); 3.4 wt % strontium hydroxide (pH control); and 0.4 wt % perfumePerfumes used for depilatories have to be specially formulated to overcome the intense product sulfide odor and be stable in the high pH medium of 12.3.

In manufacture the following precautions must be observed: (1) avoidance of metal contamination from iron or copper or other heavy metals, pure stainless steel is satisfactory; (2) avoidance of unnecessary exposure to air as oxidation reduces product strength; (3) pH control at ca 12.3, which should be checked before packaging; (4) choice of proper packaging, pure tin is best, wax-lined lead tubes, glass, and polyethylene packaging are satisfactory.

Waxing

A very old method for removal of hair makes use of a material known as epilating wax. This wax is a mixture of rosin and beeswax, which is melted, applied to the area to be treated, and allowed to solidify, after which the wax mixture is peeled from the skin. During this peeling action, the hair is actually pulled out and removed from the skin along with the wax mixture.

BATH PRODUCTS

When bathing, dirt, perspiration, and microorganisms are initially removed from the surface of the skin by the water and soap. The water also causes the outermost layers of the epidermis to swell slightly so that they are shed more rapidly. If the bath contains suitable additives, it also can show effects that extend beyond the hygienic aim and contribute cosmetically.

Bath Oils

The subjective response to the use of any bath oil is generally favorable. This is to be expected since bathing itself imparts a feeling of softness to the stratum corneum, and even the slightest deposition of an emollient adds to this effect The addition of fragrances and fragant oils to baths was recorded as early as the Roman era.

Bath oils fall into one of two major categoreis: (l) spreading or floating bath oils and (2) dispersible bath oils. Spreading bath oil is usually an anhydrous system that is oleaginous. The hydrophobic system floats on the surface of the bath water. The spreading action is facilitated by inclusion of small amounts (usually ca 5%) of an oil soluble surfactant. The lowering of the surface tension of bath water by the surfactant permits the oil to form a continuous film, rather than existing as individual droplets. Ideal surfactatns should demonstrate a reasonably high hydrophilic-lipophilic balance (HLB) (ca 9) yet remain soluble in the oleaginous composition.

From a functional standpoint the floating layer of perfumed oil affords a pleasant fragrance and a desirable feel to the skin. The oleaginous film adheres to the body surface and imparts a hydrophobic barrier to the keratin.

The oleaginous composition may consist of one or more of the commonly accepted hydrophobic components; natural vegetable oils, animal-derived lipids, such as lanolin and mink oil, low melting fatty alcohols, such as oleyl and hexadecyl, low melting synthetic glycerides, such as glyceryl mono-oleate and glyceryl monolaurate, and mineral oils.

Dispersible bath oils contain a sufficient concentration of surface active agents to solubilize the oleaginous components through micellar solubilization, or to disperse them as the internal phase of an oil-in-water emuslion. The addition of either system to the bath water disperses oil throughout the bath water. Unlike the spreading bath oil, which maintains its oleaginous character in water, the dispersible bath oil loses some of its oleaginous character as the result of oil-in-water dispersibility. Dispersible bath oils leave a layer of dilute oil in a water dispersion on the skin. As the water evaporates from this, a hydrophobic residue remains, providing a moisture barrier on the skin surface.

The nature (HLB) and concentration of the surfactant component also dictates whether the dispersible bath oil turns milky on addition to water (blooming bath oil), whether it remains clear on dispersing in water, or whether the bath oil generates any foam (foaming bath oil). Surfactants with lower HLBs, such as polyoxyethylene oleyl ether (HLB 4.9), are oil soluble and yield oils that produce the characteristic blooming. Perfume is generally employed in a concentration of 3-20%, obviously depending *on the nature and* quantity *of* surfactant.

The dispersible bath oils are usually preferred by the consumer over the floating type because they are water dispersible (washable) whereas the latter may leave an oil slick in the tub and may create drain clogging problems.

Foaming Bath Oils and Foam Baths

These are based on suitable surfactants, either liquid or powder, which are blended with color, perfume, and foam stabilizers. Addition of warm or hot running water produces a fragrant foam.

Bath Salts

Two types of bath salts are available. The first is formulated with crystalline salts such as rock salt and epsom salt to which color and perfume are added. These are not water softeners. The second type is the water softening type based on sesquicarbonates, phosphates, and borates. Color and perfume are added and in some products, small percentages of fatty acid ester are included for nondrying effects.

Bubble baths contain sulfated fatty alcohols or their derivatives, sometimes mixed with saponin, water-softening agents, and sodium alginate, which helps to preserve the foam. These products may be made in powdered (granulated) or liquid form. To be most effective in producing bubbles. The material should be added directly *to* a vigorous steam of water as it flows from the faueet. They serve to disperse perfume, remove curd from hard water, and insure thorough cleansing of the skin. Some of them, however, are sometimes incompatible with soap, and the wetting agents employed may be drying *to the* skin.

Bath powders, usually designated as *talcum, after-bath, body, or dusting powders,* may consist entirely of talc, but they usually contain also some variable percentage of precipitated chalk, colloidal clay, and magnesium or zinc stearate. The first two additives serve as absorbents for any moisture that may remain on the skin after drying with a towel; the third makes the powder adhere better. Titanium dioxide or zinc oxide may be added to lighten the color of the mixture.

With the exception of the powders used by men after shaving, most powders of this class are not tinted. The perfume should be prefixed, *to* insure that the earthy odor of talc is well covered.

Baby powders are usually only lightly perfumed, and they may contain a small proportion of boric acid. The so-called antiseptic baby powders usually contain hydroxyquinoline ("oxyquinoline") sulfate.

Manufacture of Bath Products. Bath salts serve just as well without either color or perfume, though for esthetic appeal they are usually both tinted and scented. The appropriate color is dissolved in a saturated solution of the compound used (for example, sodium sesquicarbonate). If alcohol soluble dyes are used, a small amount of a gum or resin should be added as a fixative. The solution of dye is then sprayed over the mass of salt, which is under *constant* agitation in order to distribute the tint evenly and prevent the crystals from clumping.

The perfume for bath salts must be stable to alkalies; it is first combined with a resinous fixative and sprayed over the salts.

For efferverscent bath salts, all the ingredients except the acids must be dried separately and then carefully mixed until thoroughly blended. Bath salts may be prepared in several delicate tints, using the appropriate certified colors, and in many different scents, of which pine seems to be preferred.

Two products, formerly used for the bath but now practically superseded by bath salts, are *violet ammonia,* a strongly perfumed, 30%

solution of ammonia, with or without green soap, which effectively softens bath water; and *toilet vinegar,* a solution of various aromatic oils with acetic acid or ethyl acetate and 75-90% of alcohol, which served only to perfume the bath.

Bath oils, for perfuming the bath, are usually mixtures of sulfonated castor or olive oil, or other liquid dispersing agents, and some form of natural or synthetic perfume oil. They disperse quickly throughout the water and are compatible with soap, but they are extremely drying to the skin. The principal advantage offered by these products is that they combine with any hard-water elements and prevent the formation of a ring of curd around the tub. Other subtances suggested for bath oils that do not disperse in water contain solvents such as diethyleneglycol monoethyl ether as perfume vehicle. Creamy bath oils, sometimes called *bath milks,* are liquid emulsions of stearic acid or stearates, with glycerol or glycols, and mineral oil, usually emulsified with organic amines.

SOAPS

Although soaps as a class are not included among the products that come within the purview of the Federal Food, Drug and Cosmetic Act, toilet soaps, in so far as they cleanse, alter the appearance, or promote the attractiveness of the person, may be considered as cosmetics.

It is generally conceded that the best soaps for the skin are those made substantially from olive oil. For various economic reasons, and an unwarranted belief in the merits of copious lathering, coconut oil has been used in increasing amount. Coconut oil soap furnishes abundant lather, but it is admitted to be harsh and irritating to the skin; according, it is commonly used as an addition to soaps made of tallow and palm oil. Good bases for toilet soaps are available in flakes or chips, either as mechanical mixtures of different soaps or combinations made from mixtures of olive, coconut, and other vegetable oils with tallow.

All that should be claimed for a toilet soap is that it cleanse efficiently. In the choice of soap as a cosmetic cleanser, it must be remembered that purity of the ingredients is not so important as the nature of the ingredients. Soap-and-water cleansing is specifically recommended for the oily skin, but not just any soap should be used. A favorite product may actually be 100% a chemically pure soap in itself, but if it is made entirely or largely from coconut oil it may be quite unsatisfactory or unsuitable for cosmetic purposes.

Equal in importance to the oils, fats, and fatty acids used in the making of soap are the alkalies, and the water that assists in cleansing. Sodium and potassium hydroxides and carbonates has been commonly employed, and more recently several of the organic amino compounds, for example, triethanolamine, have come into use. The prevalence of hard water presents a complication in the satisfactory use of soap because it causes the precipitation of an insoluble soap as an interfering and unsightly curd or secum on whatever is being washed. It is recognized that this can be circumvented by using sufficient soap to insure complete precipitation and then continuing with more. This practice is easier on the skin than the use of soaps that include harsh water softeners, but it is not always practical.

Special Soaps. Practically all good toilet soaps are milled (often designated "French. They are delicately scented, if not similarly to other products in a manufacturer's line, at least with an odor that does not interfere with that of other cosmetics. Cakes are available in all sizes from 1-lb. pieces for the bath to dainty "guest size" tablets, and still smaller pellets or wafers used for individual manicures.

(1) *"Castile soap",* a term used for centuries (and still commonly believed) to designate a soap made exclusively from olive oil, has been applied to "any nice white soap" since a ruling of the Federal Trade Commission in 1926. Many soaps so designated now consist wholly or largely of coconut oil, with or without other fats and oils.

(2) *Floating soaps,* popular for the bath, result from beating air into the product during manufacturing.

(3) *Green soap* (officially soap mollis, or soft soap), formerly made of linseed oil, now of olive oil, and potash, is the basis of the following tincture.

(4) *Tincture of green soap* (35% alcohol) is often recommended in cosmetology for the treatment of excessively oily skin (and hair), and as an aid in the removal of comedones (blackheads). It is too drying for continued use on normal or dry skin.

(5) *Hard-water soaps* for toilet and bath are usually made of coconut oil, and contain some percentage of sodium carbonate, trisodium phosphate, or other compound that precipitates the calcuim and magnesium salts before they can interfere with the soap. They may be used for the bath, but preferably not on the face.

(6) *Transparent glycerin soaps,* which vary in popularity, are made from tallow, castor oil, and coconut oil, with about 10% of glycerol, 10% of sugar, and usually some alcohol. They seem to have a strong esthetic appeal, but are often found to be drying to the average skin.

(7) *Superfatted soaps,* designed to counteract the drying effect of alkali or other ingredients in plain soap, are supposed to leave an emollient film on the skin after washing. Many of these are practically useless with hard water. If the superfatting principle is wholly or largely lanolin (similar to sebum in the skin), the lathering of the soap is not inhibited to the same extent as it is with the so-called cold-cream soaps, which contain an excess of mineral oil. Moreover, the addition of lanolin

seems to benefit the skin, whereas the mineral oil merely leaves it greasy without correcting the drying action of the plain soap.

(8) *Medicated soaps* may contain sulfur, phenol, iodine, or other antiseptic compounds, which may have some effect on certain conditions in the skin. Often the actual effect is more psychological than physical, although some modern antiseptic soaps display a demonstrable capacity of reducing the bacterial flora of the skin.

Although they are used more in shampoos *(q. v.),* so-called "soapless" compounds (synthetic surface-active agents with various properties) have been added also to some toilet soaps. Some of these substances do improve the action of soaps in hard water but, because many of them are extremely drying to the skin, the indiscriminate addition of these compounds to formerly acceptable recipes for toilet soap is not to be recommended without further research.

Specifications for all kinds of toilet soaps have been published by the National Bureau of Standards, the American Society for Testing Materials (1), and other organizations dedicated to protecting both the public and the industry.

Manufacture

Soap manufacture is generally by one of three methods. In the boilded process, the fats, oils, and alkalies are all boiled together until saponification is complete. The soap is salted out with or without varying percentages of glycerol left in the soap. This is the most widely used process. In the semiboiled process, exact chemical amounts of the fats, oils, and alkalis are mixed and heated to start the saponification, after which the reaction is allowed to complete itself. In the cold process, the fats, oils, and a calculated quantity (less than needed for complete saponification) of alkali are placed in a crutcher and gently heated and mixed. When saponification is underway the material is poured into soap frames where the reaction completes itself spontaneously. The glycerol which is the by-product is left in the soap.

Transparent soaps are prepared with sugar, alcohol and glycerol or a combination of these materials in the approximate proportions: sugar, 10-15 wt % of the soap; alcohol, 50% of the fatty acid present in the soap; glycerol, 50% of the fatty acid present in the soap.

Detergency or cleaning ability is usually determined by soiling cloth with a standard smudge or soiling mixture made according to the following formula: lamp or carbon black, 2.0 g; heavy mineral oil, 5.0 g; tallow, 3.0 g; carbon tetrachloride, 2000.0 ml.

It is well known that soaps and detergents remove the natural oil secretions (sebaceous matter) as well as the dirt. This drying effect can be partially overcome by superfatting the soap or detergent bar. The presence of superfatting agents reduces the cleansing efficiency thereby preventing complete degreasing of the skin surface. From a dermatological aspect, the superfatting of soaps should be advantageous. Apart from the dermatological aspect, the addition of superfatting agents to soap also makes the process of milling and plodding easier because the soap is rendered more plastic, it contributes to the quality of the final product by reducing the tendency of the soap cake to split or crack in use. Superfatted soaps have a superior velvety feel and produce an especially smooth lather.

Superfatting agents are: lecithin (qv) (softens and moisturizes skin); amine oxides and fatty acid amides (improve soap texture and lathering properties); lanolin (improves texture of soap); casein (improves lather and skin feel); and cocoa butter (emollient and moisturizer).

Deodourant Soaps

About half the soap market is claimed for deodourant soaps. These are usually quality soap bars containing either Irgasan DP-300 (Triclosan) or 3, 4, 4'-trichlorocarbanilide (Triclocarban). A patent was issued in 1972 for a germicidal detergent bar that contains poly (vinylpyrrolidinone)-iodine complex.

Shaving Preparations

Dry hair in the beard is usually quite compact and is resistant to cutting by a razor blade. Preliminary treatment with hot water and soap removes the sebum, a complex mixture of lipids secreted by the sebaceous glands, and absorbed by the beard, that presents a barrier to water and impedes hair softening. The use of a shaving soap or shaving cream provides a wet, lubricatig blanket of water that reduces friction between the razor blade and the skin.

Shave Soap

Shaving soaps or shaving sticks are hard soaps, sodium salts of primarily saturate fatty acids, that are usually applied with a shaving brush.

Lather Shave Cream

Shave creams are formulated as lather shave and brushless shave. Lather shave creams are soft soaps formulated with potassium hydroxide salts of saturated and unsaturated fatty acids, and containing a small percentage of sodium hydroxide to regulate viscosity, body and consistency. Added to the basic product are humerctants such as glycerol and propylene glycol, emollients such as lanolin and lanolin derivatives, boric acid in small percentage to neutralize any excess alkali, and menthol for its cooling effect. The water content of a lather shave is about 35 to 40%, and the pH of the lather is about 10.

A typical formula for shaving cream is: 41.52 wt % water: 30.8 wt % stearic acid; 10.0 wt % glyceol; 7.7 wt % coconut fatty acids; 7.0 wt % potassium hydroxide; 1.0 wt % lonolin; 1.0 wt % boric acid; 0.57 wt % sodium hydroxide; 0.5 wt % sodium silicate; and *qs* perfume.

Brushless Shave Cream

Brushless shave creams are similar to vanishing creams, with an excess of free fatty acid, usually stearic, emulsified into a nonalkaline base of suitable viscosity or consistency. Its softening effect is not so rapid as that obtained with a lather shave.Brushless shave creams have a water content higher than that of lather shaves, and a pH of 6.0-6.5. Additives are similar to those used in lather shave formulations. A typical formulation is: 70.8 wt % water; 17.0 wt % stearic acid; 4.0 wt % glycerol; 4.0 wt % glyceryl monostearate; 2.0 wt % mineral oil; 1.2 wt % triethanolamine; 1.0 wt % lanolin; qs preservative; and qs perfume. All formulations contain preservatives and usually fragrance to cover the base odor of the soap and additives.

Aerosol Shave Creams

Aerosol shave creams in pressurized containers are convenient to use because the lather is easily obtained in a ready to use form from the can and is easily rinsed off the face. Formulations are either aqueous soap solutions or soap emulsions that are pressurized with a mixture of propane and isobutane. The product is expelled from the container through a valve. The expelled liquid expands to a foam as the propellant is released. Aerosol shave creams contain additives similar to those used in lather shave formulas.

Self-Heating Shave Creams

Self-heating shave creams are formed from an exothermic reaction that occurs when two components, one containing an oxidizing agent and the other a reductant, are expelled together from a dual compartment container.

Gel Shave Creams

Gel Shave creams are emollient aqueous gels that are soap based and contain a volatile solvent such as pentane. Expelled as a soft gel from a pressure container, the shave cream is rubbed on the face, and the solvent is released. The released solvent expands as it volatilizes, and the gel becomes a foam.

ORAL PRODUCTS

Toothpastes

Toothpastes are suspensions of polishing agents and detergents in a suitable binder, generally packaged in a collapsible tube. The Council on Dental Therapeutics of the American Dental Association has established define criteria for approval of dentifrices. Some of the requirements are based on the degree of hardness, degree of abrasiveness. and particle size of the polishing agent. The use of medicinals or of drugs that should be used only under the supervision of a dentist are not approved by the Council for over-the-counter purchase by the consumer.

The principal ingredients in toothpastes or powders are: polishing agents (calcium carbonate, magensium carbonate, di-or tricalcium phosphate, talc etc); detergents (soap, anionic surface active agents); binders (ecipients) and humectants (glycerol, propylene glycol, sorbitol, mucilages or gums, etc); sweeteners (saccharin, sorbitol); preservatives (benzolic acid, hydroxybenzoates); flavors (essential oils, etc.) and water.

Cellulose derivatives, such as methyl cellulose, are sometimes used to maintain satisfactory consistency and stannous fluoride or sodium monoflurophosphate may be added as anticaries agents.

A prototype formula of toothpase is: 32.200 wt % glycerol; 27.00 wt% calcium phosphate, dibasic 36.675wt%water; 2.000 wt% sodium N-lauroyl sarcosinate; 1.00 wt % carrageenan TP-4; 0.500-1.000 wt % flavor; 0.400 wt % sodium monofluro-phosphate; 0.125 *wt* % saccharin sodium USP; 0.100 wt % sodium benzoate USP.

A recently developed dentifrice contains synthetic, amorphous, porous silica xerogel as the polishing and cleansing ingredient. A formula example is: 39.0 wt % water; 34.76 wt % glycerol; 12.0 wt % silica Xerogel V; 6.0 wt % sodium lauryl sulfate (21% in glycerol); 5.0 wt % silica Aerogel 1; 1.5 wt % hydroxyethyl cellulose; 1.1 wt % flavour; 0.41 wt % stannous fluoride; 0.2 wt % saccharin; and 0.03 wt % FD&C Blue no. 1 (1% solution).

Preservatives

Changes and deterioration in cosmetic products can be brought about by changes in acidity or alkalinity, or as a result of hydrolysis, oxidation, heat and light, and bacterial or fungal contamination. The source of bacterial or fungal contamination of cosmetic products can be the raw materials, water from dirty ion exchangers, contaminated equipment, or dirty bottles and cap liners. Even cosmetic products that are properly prepared require addition of preservatives to ensure adequate shelf life. In addition to all other quality assurance tests run by the laboratory, suitable microbiological tests should also be run on the finished product.

Characteristics of the ideal preservative or mixture of preservatives are: (I) activity of low concentration; (2) physical and chemical compatibility and effectiveness over a wide range of pH; (3) effectiveness against a wide range of microorganisms; (4) ready solubility and stability to heat and storage, and limited tendency to migrate into the nonaqueous phase; (5) lack of odor, color, toxicity, and irritation in the concentrations used.

Preservatives frequently used in cosmetic products are: p-hydroxybenzoates (parabens) (most effective in acid pH); dehydroacetic acid (active against fungi); sorbic acid and sorbates (active against fungi, pH-dependent); imidazolidinylurae (Germall (115) (synergistic with other preservatives); 2-bromo-2-nitro-l, 3-propanediol (broopol) (active against gram-negative bacteria, releases formalydehyde): formaldehyde (strong antibacterial); and l-(3-chloroallyl)-3, 5, 7-triaza-l-azoniaadamantane chloride (Dowicil 200 as cosmetic preservative) (formaldehyde donor).

Cosmetic formulations and packaging may interact with some preservatives. The nonionic emulsifiers commonly used in cosmetic formulations do not significantly interfere with preservative action when used in a concentration below 1%. In higher concentrations the emulsifier can form aggregates that extract preservatives from the oil-water phases, leaving a low concentration of preservative; Lipid-soluble preservatives may migrate into plastic container walls and into plastic cap liners. Some components of a cosmetic formulation can enhance preservative action. The ingredients of many perfume oils, eg, have antimicrobial properties. Synergisms of preservative mixtures are also possible. Mixtures of parabens are more effective than individual parabens, and mixtures of parabens and imidazolidinylurea and significantly more active and widen the range of microorganisms against which the cosmetic product is protected. Whatever preservative system is chosen should undergo microbial challenge testing in the final product.

Antioxidants

An antiodixant is a substance capable of slowing the rate of oxidation of autoxidizable materials. It should be soluble in both water and oil; be odorless, nontoxic, nonallergenic, and effective in low concentration; and be stable under conditions of use. Phenolic antioxidants are usually soluble in oil and generally insoluble in water. Propyl gallate has a solubility of about 1.8% in water. The addition of propyl gallate requires a chelating agent to prevent reactions with iron contaminants which will cause color changes. Calcium disodium EDTA is slightly soluble in oil. The most widely used antioxidants are butylated hydroxyanisole (BHA), butylated hydroxytoluene (BHT), PG and nordihydroguaiaretic acid (NDGA). A widely used antioxidant mixture contains 20% BHA, 6% PG, 4% citric acid, and 70% propylene glycol.

Toxicity and Test Methods

Animal Studies

Even though true sensitization does not occur equally in animals and humans, the animal test provides some measure of protection by serving as a screen. Sensitization of animals makes a material suspect, and so great caution is exercised before using the material on humans. On the other hand, a negative sensitizing result on animals indicates that the material is probably not a strong sensitizer and further tests on humans offers little risk. The final tests must, however, be clinical trials on human subjects.

Preliminary animal tests are performed to determine whether the material has an acute or chronic toxicity, and, if so, the MLD_{50}. These tests involve feeding the material to the animals which are subsequently sacrificed for close examination of the organs, glands, and brain.

Percutaneous toxicity is determined by the application of the material to cleanly shaven necks and backs of animals over a regularly scheduled period. The condition of the skin is carefully checked and the animals are observed for any signs of systemic toxicity and their tissues are examined for pathological changes. The final tests must, however, be clinical trials on human subjects.

Human Safety Testing

Irrespective of the completeness of the program carried out with the animals, initial trails on humans must be on a limited number of individuals. Evaluation of sensitizing potential should begin with 10 or 12 panelists. Full-scale tests must then be carried out before the product is released to market. Although 60 panelists are generally adequate as precursors to large-scale studies, forthcoming regulations are expected to require tests on 200.

In human safety trials of topically applied materials the principal concern in most cases is induced cutaneous reactions. If, however, animal studies indicate significant absorption of components of the formulaion, clinical trials must also monitor such absorption by testing blood and urine which may reflect subclinical systemic toxic effects.

The cutaneous reactions that may result from application of cosmetics are of three types: primary irritation, contact, sensitization, and reactions that develop following exposure to the sun. The potential of topically-applied materials to induce these reactions is evaluated by means of patch tests.

Sensitization Potential

One of the most critical evaluations is the determination of sensitizing potential. Two basic procedures have been most frequently employed, and numerous variatios of these have been used. One of the basic procedures has limited value since it detects only very strong sensitizers. Present consideration of the human patch test will primarily be limited to the repeated insult procedure and its various modifications. Two variations were originally developed—one byShelanski and Shelanski and the other by Draize. Both of these procedures employ repeated applications made over a period of four or five weeks. They differ in that ten sensitizing applications are made in the Draize procedure and fifteen are made in the Shelanski procedure. They differ also in that challenge applications are made only to the original tests sites in the Draize procedure, but are made to previously unpatched sites as well as the original test site in the Shelanski procedure.

A short review of these and other procedures involving human panelists has been presented by Kligman, who suggested the maximization procedure as an alternative. Various methods for achieving the objective of Kligman's maximization procedure have been employed, an interesting one being a Hill Top Research procedure in which the skin is abraded prior to sample application. The test materials are applied to abraded sites on the upper arm under patches. Reactions top the test applications are scored on Wednesday, Friday, and Monday following applications on the preceding Monday, Wednesday, and Friday. The patches are removed by the panelists 24 h after application. Nine applications are made in three successive weeks, and the challenge application is made on Monday of the sixth week. The challenge applications are made to previously unpatched sites. Abrasions of the test sites are made just prior to sample applications on test days, 1, 4, 7, and 11, or preferably, prior to each application. This more frequent scheduling of abrading can be done when up to four materials are evaluated on abraded skin only. The abrasions, in the form of two concentric circles with diameters of 1.25 cm and 1 cm, are inficted by a specially constructed apparatus. The skin areas are cleansed with isopropyl alcohol just prior to abrading. A separate sterile abrader is used for each panelist. All adhesive patches and absorbent pads applied over abraded areas are sterilized by exposure to ethylene oxide prior to use. The usual grading scale is utilized.

Patch test reaction scoring scale

0 no evidence of irritation
1 slight erythema
2 marked erythema
3 erythema and papules
4 edema, erythema may or may not be present
5 erythema, edema, and papules
6 vesicular eruption

7 strong reaction spreading beyond test site min reaction meets minimal requirements for grade assigned

Effect on superficial layers of skin

A slight glazed appearance
B marked glazing
C glazing with peeling arid cracking
D glazing with fissures
E film of dried serious exudate covering all or portions of the patch site
F small petechial erosions and/or scabs

Another procedure employed is to strip the skin by repeated application and removal of adhesive tape from the test sites prior to sample applications.

Regardless of the procedure employed in tests on human panelists, mimimal reactions, frequently evoked during the serial applications and at challenge, require expert judgment as to whether the material is a sensitizer or not. It is frequently necessary to conduct rechallenges in order to assess the significance of the observed reactions.

When properly applied, the repeated insult test is a severe test for the sensitizing potential of products. Many products that induce sensitization in a low percentage of panelists tests by this procedure can be used without untoward reactions. The proposed use must be considered. For example, a product that shows minimal sensitization potential and is to be used on the feet should not be marketed. On the other hand, a product that would be used infrequently under nonconclusive conditions could probably be safely marketed.

In addition to its value as predictor of sensitizing potential, the repeated insult patch test furnishes valuable information on the primary irritant characteristics and cumulative primary irritant properties of test materials. The latter property is descriptively referred to freutently as skin fatigue.

Some assurance that products found to be minimal sensitizers can safely marketed may be obtained by conducting product-use challenges of panelists who have been sensitized in the patch test procedure. If these reactive individuals do not respond to use applications, it is most unlikely that senitization would be induced by normal use of the product. However, this reasoning cannot be applied to products used for whole-body applications. Whole-body exposures by sensitized panelists cannot be safely done, and limited area applications may be misleading.

2

Skin Purification

Skin purification or cleansing involves removal of dead cells *and* toxins generated within the skin, dirt, grime, makeup, chemical pollutants, allergens and infectious material, if any adhering to the skin.

Taking a daily bath in the morning using an antiseptic soap or any other body cleanser could be sufficient as far as body in general is concerned as they are most of the times remains covered with clothes, but not good enough for your face which is most of the times remains exposed to the external environment and faces the vagaries of environment. Special attention, therefore should be given to face so that it could counter the effect of environment, stress, infection and aging process.

Skin Purification Routine

A general and very much functional skin purification routine which you could follow at home without spending to much on beauty aids is described below:-

- Wash your facewith freshwater three to four times a day.
- Purify your face with a natural or mild foaming face wash or cleanser once or twice a day.
- Purify your face with a skin purifying or cleansing lotion twice a day and always before going to bed.
- Exfoliate the skin of dead cells once a week.
- Use a deep cleansing face mask once a week.
- Use a facial steam once in a fortnight.

To follow the above skin purification routine you need following four types of produts;

(i) Powder Cleansers/Face Washes
(ii) Cleansing Lotion
(iii) Exfoliating Lotion or Scrubs,
(iv) Face Masks.

(i) Face Washes

Face washes are foaming/non-foaming cleansers which cleanse the skin thoroughly and neutralizes the effect of toxins & allergens on skin. Foaming face washes are effective in removing all the dirts and pollutants but they sometimes disturb the acid mantle of the skin because of their alkaline nature. They also makes the skin dry by removing the natural moisture from the skin. Therefore, a foaming face wash should be selected carefully. It should be pH balanced, free from soaps, mild on skin and should not disturb the acid mantle of the skin & dermal water balance.

(ii) Cleansing Lotion

Cleansing lotions are spread on the face and then wiped off to carry away grime, dirt, toxins, infection etc. The ingredients of a lotion enter the derm pores and help in removing dirt or toxins to come out.

(iii) Exfoliating Lotion or Scrubs

Exfoliating preparations remove dead skin cells either physically or chemically. Scrubs are highly effective deep cleansing treatments. Its derma abrasive action help in removal of skin impurities, improves dull complexion, removes blackheads and tightens the skin, leaving the skin smooth and elastic.

(iv) Face Masks

Face masks are meant for deep cleansing, hydrating and stimulating the skin. These masks clears the skin of dirt and pollutants, improves blood circulation by increasing the temperature and gives a feeling of tightness to skin.

Natural Face Washes

Natural face wash for Dry Skin

Base Ingredients

Gram flour	2 table spoon
Milk or Milk Cream	1/4 table spoon
Water(luke warm)	5 table spoon

Active Ingredients

Almond oil	2-4 drops
Aloe vera gel	1/4 table spoon
Chamomile powder	1/4 table spoon
Rose petal powder	1 /4 table spoon
Linseed powder	1/4 table spoon

Method of Preparation

Mix gram flour, milk or milk cream (in case your skin is extremely dry and flaky) in warm water and beat to make a smooth paste. Add to this 2 to 4 drops of almond oil, 1/4 table spoon aloe vera gel, 1/4 table spoon Chamomile powder, 1/4 table spoon Rose petals and 1/4 table spoon Linseed powder. Keep the cleanser paste mixed with active ingredients for 15 minutes to diffuse the active principles of herbs into the paste.

Application of paste

Apply paste gently all over face and neck and massage into skin for two minutes. Wash your face with fresh or luke warm water.

The above cleansing preparation when applied on the face regularly will give you soft and silky feeling with no stretching of skin which you often feel after washing the face with soaps.

In the above preparation gramflour and milk or milkcream is used as base material with water as gramflour makes a very smooth paste with water which has extraordinary spreadability, also it do not extracts too much of the natural oils from the skin. Milk or milk cream provides desired emolliency to the skin and removes the stretchy feeling of the skin.

Linseed are mucilaginous and provide necessary moisture to the skin. Aloe has remarkable antiaging and soothing effect on the skin. Chamomile is a strong antiseptic agent and cleanse the skin of infectious material. Rose is cooling and soothing to skin and give aroma to cleansing preparation. Almond oil is a rich source of Vitamin A and improves the skin's dry condition.

Natural Face Wash for Normal Skin

Base Ingredients

Gram flour/Wheat flour	2 table spoon
Milk	1 table spoon
Water	5 table spoon

Active Ingredients

Aloe vera gel	1/4 table spoon
Cucumber juice	1/2 table spoon
Chironji seed powder	1/4 table spoon
Honey	1/4 table spoon
Turmeric	1/4 table spoon

Method of Preparation

Mix gramflour/wheat flour, milk and water to prepare smooth paste. Add to it active ingredients one by one with simultaneous mixing to make a smooth paste.

Application of Paste

Apply the paste on your face and neck with gentle massage and leave it on your face for two minutes, wash your face with fresh water.

Normal skin is the best type of skin among all the skin types and requires least care to maintain its normal health. The above cleansing preparation for normal skin is a mild cleansing preparation containing a mild antiseptic and healing agent (Turmeric), a depigmenting agent

(Cucumber), a moisturiser (Honey), an antiaging agent (Aloe) and a scar eraser (Chironji) to preserve the good health of the skin.

Natural Face Wash for Oily Skin

Base Ingredients

Bajara flour ,	2 table spoon
Reetha powder	1/4 table spoon
Water	5 table spoon or more
Milk	1 table spoon

Active ingredients

Tulsi leaf powder	1/2 table spoon
Lemon juice	10 drops
Neem leaf powder	1/4 table spoon
Revandhchini	1/4 table spoon
Aloe vera gel	1/4 table spoon

Method of Preparation

Heat the water in a container and allow the temperature to reach near boiling. Take off the container from flame and add to it bajra flour and reetha powder with mixing to extract essential glycolipids and saponins from Bajra and Reetha respectively.

Add other ingredients one after the other with mixing to make a smooth paste of ingredients. Keep it as such till the temperature reaches to room temperature.

Application of Paste

Apply paste with gentle massage on your wet face and neck and leave it on your face for 2 - 3 minutes. Wash your face with fresh or luke warm water.

The above cleanser for oily skin is formulated considering all the flaws of an oily skin. Reetha is incorporated to remove excess of oil from skin surface through its mild foaming action. Bajra is used as a main base ingredient because of its ability to absorb excessive oil from the skin. It is also a good source of glycolipids which are identical to natural ceramides and keep the skin firm and elastic.

Oily skin is prone to get infected with bacteria causing acne, therefore an effective antibacterial agent has to be incorporated in the cleansing preparation to control acne problem. Both Tulsi and Neem are very effective antibacterial agents, particularly Tulsi which is claimed to have a strong antiacne activity even in very low concentrations.

Lemon juice and Revandhchini (rhubharb) provide astringency to close large derm pores which is a visible feature of the oily skin and helps in controlling sebum production from the skin. Aloe vera gel is incorporated to maintain the skin moisture and to ward off the wrinkles from face.

Face Wash for Sensitive or Combination Skin

Base Ingredients

Kolanut powder	2 table spoon
Milk	1 table spoon
Water	3 table spoon

Active Ingredients

Tulsi leaf powder	1/2 table spoon
Methi seed powder	1/4 table spoon
Aloe seed powder	1/4 table spoon
Pangar (Horse chestnut) seed powder	1/4 table spoon
Muletthi (liquorice) root powder	1/4 table spoon

Method of Preparation

Mix Kolanut powder, milk and water to make a smooth paste, add to it finely ground active ingredients one after other with simultaneous mixing.

Application of Paste

Apply the paste on your face and neck with gentle massage. Keep it on your face for atleast 2 minutes and then wash with fresh or luke warm water.

It is really difficult to manage the good health of sensitive/combination skins. The skin get damaged due to frequent occurrence of acne, blackheads or white heads. The behaviour of skin is vary erratic. Cleansing of such skins with soaps will further damage the skin and make the skin flaky in dry patches of the skin. Using common astringents like lemon juice and tannins on sensitive skin to control oil will further irritate the skin. The cleansing preparation mentioned above has been formulated with great care with no irritating and damaging effect on the skin.

The cleanser for the sensitive/combination skin contains Kolanut powder as a base ingredient. Kola nut is well known for its remarkable anti-irritant and soothing properties. Milk is added to provide necessary emolliency to the drier patches of the skin. Tulsi is a strong antibacterial agent and effectively controls the acne porblem.

Pangar (Horse chestnut) is an astringent, mild foaming and stimulatory herb and helps in controlling oil production and cleanses the skin with very mild foaming action.

Liquorice powder is helpful in controlling the sebum production from oil glands of the skin and regulates the oil secretion on to skin surface. Methi seeds are cleansing and softening in action and maintain the dermal water balance on the skin. Aloe is a rejuvenating and soothing herb which stimulates collagen synthesis in skin and keeps the skin firm and elastic.

Natural Cleansing Lotion

Natural Lotion Cleansers are easy to prepare and are convenient to apply on your face. The only demerit is that these can not be preserved for long time. They will last long only for one week if preserved under refrigerated conditions.

Natural Cleansing Lotion for Dry Skin

Base Ingredients

Milk	4 table spoon
Almond Oil	2-4 drops
Water	3/4 Cup.

Active Ingredients

Aloe vera gel	1/4 table spoon
Chamomile powder	1/4 table spoon
Linseed powder	1/4 table spoon
Rose water	1/4 table spoon

Method of Preparation

Boil Chamomile powder, Linseed powder in water for 5-10 minutes, cool and filter through a double muslin cloth. Add Milk, Rose water, Almond Oil and Aloe vera gel. Mix and filter again.Store in a clean dry container under refrigerated conditions. Apply twice a day to cleanse your face.

Natural Cleansing Lotion for Oily Skin

Base Ingredients

Honey	1 table spoon
Water	3/4th Cup.

Active Ingredients

Ocimum(Tulsi) leaf powder	1/4 table spoon
Lemon juice	5-10 drops
Neem leaf powder	1/4 table spoon
Revandhchini root powder	1/4 table spoon
Aloe vera gel	1/4 table spoon

Method of Preparation

Boil Tulsi leaf powder, Neem leaf powder, Revandhchini powder in 3/4 cup of water for 5 to 10 minutes, cool and filter through double muslin cloth. Mix Lemon juice, Honey and Aloe vera gel and preserve in a clean dry container under refrigerated condition.

Natural Cleansing Lotion for Normal Skin

Base Ingredients

Honey	1/2 table spoon
Milk	1 table spoon
Water	3/4 Cup

Active Ingredients

Aloe vera gel	1/4 table spoon
Cucumber extract	1/4 table spoon
Chironji powder	1/4 table spoon
Turmeric powder	A pinch

Method of Preparation

Boil Turmeric powder and Chironji powder in 3/4 cup of water for 5 to 10 minutes, cool and filter through double muslin cloth and add to it Honey Milk, Aloe vera gel and Cucumber extract. Filter again and store under refrigerated condition.

Natural Cleansing Lotion for Sensitive/ Combination Skin

Base Ingredients

Honey	1/2 table spoon
Rose water	1 table spoon
Water	3/4th cup.

Active Ingredients

Tulsi leaf powder	1/2 table spoon
Methi seed powder	1/4 table spoon
Aloe vera gel	1/4 table spoon
Pangar seed powder	1/4 table spoon
Muletthi root powder	1/4 table spoon

Method of preparation

Boil Tulsi leaf powder, Methi seed powder, Pangar seed powder and Muletthi root powder in 3/4 cup of water for 5 to 10 minutes, cool and filter through a double muslin cloth. Add Honey, Rose water, Aloevera gel and mix. Store in a clean dry container and preserve under refrigerated condition.

FACIAL SCRUBS

Facial scrubs are used to remove mechanically the top layer of skin which is mainly composed of dead cells. The scrubs consists of abrasive particles incorporated in a cleansing preparation. They makes the skin scrupulously clean and smooth. The most common abrasive particles used in facial scrubs are walnut shells, apricot seed shells, groundnut kernels, almond meal etc.

The face is rinsed with water and the scrub is then massaged over the entire face and neck avoiding the eyes and nostrils for few minutes and left for half a minutes or so. Finally the facial scrub is washed off with fresh or luke warm water. They are generally used once or twice of week.

Natural Facial Scrubs

Facial Scrub for Dry Skin

Cleanser Base

Gram Flour	1/2 table spoon
Milk Cream	1/4 table spoon
Milk/Water	3 table spoon or more

Scrubs

Almond or Groundnut meal	1 table spoon

Other Active Ingredients

Linseed	1/2 table spoon
Chamomile powder	1/4 table spoon

Method of Preparation

Mix all the ingredients of cleanser base to form a smooth paste. Add to it Almond/Peanut Kernel meal and beat to make a homogenous mass. Add other herbal ingredients and leave it for sometime.

Application of Facial Scrub

Apply the scrub on wet face and massage for 2 to 3 minutes and then wash with lukewarm/fresh water.

Groundnut meal or Almond meal is an oily granular mass and an effective abrasive which scrubs off the dead skin cells from skin without producing any dryness to skin. Linseed powder produces a mucilaginous mass which eases the application of scrub on to the face.

Facial scrub for Normal Skin

Cleanser base

Gram flour	2 tablespoon
Water	3 tablespoon
Milk	1 tablespoon

Scrub

Wallnut/Apricot shell powder	l/4 tablespoon

Active Ingredients

Aloevera gel	2 tablespoon
Turmeric	a pinch

Method of Preparation

Mix all the ingredient of a cleanser base to make a smooth paste in luke warm water. Add to it finely ground wallnut shell powder or Apricot seed shell powder and beat to make a homogenous paste. Add Aloe vera gel and Turmeric to paste and mix again.

Application of Facial Scrub

Apply the scrub with gentle massage on face and neck for 2 to 3 minutes 'and leaves it on the face for 30 seconds. Wash off the face with fresh or luke warm water.

The hard ground rounded Apricot seed shell or walnut shell powder are particular good for healthy and undamaged skin which is characteristic of a normal skin type.

Facial Scrub for Oily Skin

Cleanser Base

Barley flour	2 table spoon
Reetha powder	1/4 table spoon
Water	3 parts

Active Ingredients

Tulsi leaf powder	1/4 table spoon
Revandhchini powder	1/4 table spoon
Honey	1/4 table spoon

Scrub

Walnut shell powder	1 table spoon

Method of Preparation

Mix all the cleanser base ingredients in hot water and add to it walnut shell powder. Mix active ingredients & beat to make a smooth paste. Allow to cool to room temperature.

Application of Facial Scrub

Apply the facial scrub on wet face and massage for 2 to 3 minutes and then wash the face with fresh or luke warm water.

Walnut shell powder has a strong abrasive action and helps in cleansing skin of dead cells where it is difficult remove as in case of oily skins. Tulsi and Revandhchini helps in controlling acne and excessive oil production on skin respectively.

Facial Scrub for Sensitive/Combination Skin

Cleanser Base

Kolanut powder	2 tablespoon
Milk	1 tablespoon
Water	3 tablespoon or more

Active ingredients

Tulsi	1/4 table spoon
Pangar seed powder	1/4 table spoon

Scrub

Mango seed powder	1/4 tablespoon

Method of Preparation

Mix all the cleanser ingredient in warm water and beat to make a smooth paste. Add to it Mango seed powder, Tulsi leaf powder and Pangar seed powder and mix again to make a homogenous paste.

Application of Facial Scrub

Apply the scrub with gentle massage on face and neck for 2 to 3 minutes and leave it on the face for 30 seconds. Wash the face with fresh or luke warm water.

Mango seed powder is very gentle scrub and do not irritate the damaged skin. It is a good source of calcium, magnesium, silica and phosphorus with good astringent properties. These minerals are important to maintain the dermal water balance of the skin and keep the skin firm and elastic.

FACE MASKS

The use of face mask by women to enhance her beauty dates back to early antiquity when some of the earths were used to cleanse and heal the skin. Basic use of face pack/mask is to cleanse skin of the face thoroughly from grease, dirt, dead cells, blackheads etc. and giving the skin a feeling of cleansing and tightening. As the face mask is left over on the face for a considerable period of time, therefore a number of active ingredients are added to improve the various skin conditions. Face masks should be applied once in a fortnight.

Face Mask for Dry Skin

Base Ingredients

Oat Meal	3 table spoon
Kaolin	1 table spoon
Milk	2 table spoon
Water	l/4thcup.

Active Ingredients

Almond Oil	2 drops
Aloe vera gel	1/4 table spoon
Chamomile powder	1/4 table spoon
Rose water	1/4 table spoon
Linseed powder	1/4 table spoon

Method of Preparation

Mix all the base and active ingredients and beat to produce a smooth paste.

Application of Mask

Apply the paste on your face and spread it to form a uniform layer. Leave it on your face for 15 to 30 minutes to draw out dirt, grime, blackheads etc. and to stimulate & condition the skin through active ingredients.

Oatmeal is a sand coloured fine grain obtained from oat grains. It has a good calming and cleansing effect on the skin. Oatmeal with other ingredients has a stimulating, soothing and rejuvenating effect on the skin and bring back vital moisture and oils to the skin.

Face Mask For Oily Skin

Base Ingredients

Oat meal	2 table spoon
Fuller's Earth	2 table spoon
Reetha powder	1 /4 table spoon
Water	1/4 cup.

Active Ingredients

Tulsi leaf powder	1/4 table spoon
Neem leaf powder	1/A table spoon
Revandhchini root powder	1/A table spoon
Aloe vera gel	1/4 table spoon
Lemon juice	10-15 drops.

Method of Preparation

Mix the base ingredients in water to produce a smooth paste. Add to the paste active ingredients and mix well till a homogenous paste is produced.

Application of Mask

Fuller's Earth with Oatmeal forms an effective absorbent of dirt, toxins, allergens etc. On drying it form a firm layer on the face and therefore, has a transient tightening effect on the skin. The face mask in overall has a good deep cleansing, antiseptic, astringent, rejuventing and stimulating effect on skin, and controls sebum production.

Face Mask For Normal Skin

Base Ingredients

Oatmeal	3 table spoon
Milk	2 table spoon
Water	1/4 cup

Active Ingredients

Honey	1/4 table spoon
Aloe vera gel	1/4 table spoon
Cucumber juice	1 table spoon
Chironji seed powder	1/4 tablespoon

Method of Preparation

Mix all the base ingredients and active ingredients to produce a smooth paste.

Application of Face Mask

Apply the pack/mask on your face in a uniform layer. Leave it on your face for 15 to 30 minutes and then wash with fresh or luke warm water.

The Oatmeal in combination of other active ingredients cleanse the skin thoroughly. It also helps in removing minor blemishes and improve complexion. For better tightening effect replace one part of Oatmeal with Fuller's Earth or China day.

Face Mask for Sensitive/Combination skin

Base Ingredients

Oat meal	1 table spoon
Kolanut powder	2 table spoon
Fuller's Earth	1 table spoon
Water	1/4 cup.

Active Ingredients

Pangar seed powder	1/4 table spoon
Methi seed powder	1/4 table spoon
Muletthi powder	1/A table spoon
Tulsi leaf powder	1/4 table spoon
Aloe vera gel	1/4 table spoon

Method of Preparation

Mix base ingredients and active ingredients to make a smooth paste.

Application of face Mask

Apply the mask on your face to form a uniform layer. Leave it on your face for 15 to 30 minutes and then wash with fresh or luke warm water.

The Oatmeal in combination with Kolanut powder and Fuller's Earth form an effective absorbent,soothing and irritation alleviating face mask which cleanse the face of infection and dirt. It also helps in controlling oil production in oily patches.

3

Hair Conditioning

The origin of conditioning of hair is the outcome of the need of women or soft, silky, resilient and healthy looking hair. Though the modern onditioning products appears *to* be recent in origin but the use of onditioner dates back to antiquity. Infact present conditioners are the nodern sophisticated expression of the old crude conditioning recipes repared from natural products like milk, yolk, oils, herbs etc.

Need of Conditioning

Conditioning is needed to bring the disturbed or weakened hair which have resulted from interaction with the environment like dust, wind, sunlight, ultraviolet light etc. or due to chemical treatment such as bleaching, permanant waving, frequent shampooing, blow drying, perming etc. Such disturbed hair appears dry, lifeless, tend to look dull, harsh, porous and brittle.

The conditioning of hair gives hair life, bounce, softness, volume, body, sheen, a silky touch, controls fly away and makes hair styling easy by making up natural deficiency of sebum, restoring the protective sheath, filling the gaps, flattening or tightening the cuticle scales and alleviating the senstivity.

A conditioner is applied on the hair to promote the following properties.

(1) Smooth, easy combing in both wet and dry hair.
(2) Enhancement of the lustre of the hair.
(3) Should give body or volume to the hair in case of thin hair.
(4) Carryout the structural repair of the hair e.g. sebum deficiency, protein deficiency and cuticle repair.
(5) Control fly away by reducing the static electricity caused by the combing and brushing.

The conditioning is based on the concept of absorption of adequate ingredients to modify the hair texture and its surface properties. A variety of hair conditioners could be developed depending on the need of hair or to produce a variety of effect on hair. Among various conditioners protein conditioners are most popular as hair composed mainly of proteins. These protein conditioners contain proteinaceous materials like digested proteins polypeptides etc. and have restorative and healing effect on the hair shaft. Other types of conditioners include oily materials like silicone fluids, vegetable oils, lanolins etc. to reduce fibre frictior and abrasive effects. Moisturising materials are used to remoisturis the hair and reduce the dry brittle feeling. Oil controlling materials a added to control the sebum production in scalp.

Modern hair conditioning agents contains synthetic chemicals a conditioning agent which are good in improving the condition of the ha but the only demerit of these conditioners is their tendency to build u on scalp.

Some natural hair conditioning preparations are described below:

HENNA CONDITIONER FOR ALL HAIR TYPES

Ingredients

Henna leaf powder	100 grams
Hibiscus flower powder	2 table spoon
Methi seed powder	1 table spoon
Costus root	1 table spoon
Water	quantity sufficient to make paste

Method of Preparation & Use

Make a smooth paste by mixing finely ground herbal ingredients wit water (luke warm). Apply the paste on your hair and scalp and leave it for 1 to 30 minutes. Wash hairs with fresh or luke warm water and dry the hair.

Henna is one of the most popular herb used for its conditionin properties on hair. It has a variety of effect on hair like conditioning antidandruff, dyeing and UV-protectant. Hibiscus or jasut is well-know for its growth promoting and antidandruff properties. It also darkens th colour of hair. Methi seeds are mucilaginous cleansing and hair softenin herb, and improves the dull looking hair. Costus or Kustha root is stimulant herb and impart blackness and shine to the hair.

The protein conditioner for Dry & Damaged Hair

Ingredients

Methi seed powder	4 table spoons
Warm water	1 cup
Egg albumin	egg white from 1 egg

Method of Preparation & Use

Stirr the Methi seed powder in warm water and allow to thicken the water to a shampoo like consistency. Cool and add to it egg albumir and mix well. Apply the paste on your hair and scalp for 15 to 30 minutes

Methi seed powder is a traditional component of hair care products mainly for its cleansing and softening activity & bring back normal health for dull hair. Egg albumin is a rich source of animal albumin protein and make up the protein deficiency of damaged hairs.

onditioning Oils for Dry Hair

Jojoba Oil	1 table spoon
Olive Oil	1 table spoon
Lecithin powder	1 pinch

1ethod of Preparation & Use

Dissolve lecithin in a mixture of Jojoba oil and Olive oil by warming. .pply the luke warm oil on hair and scalp and leave the conditioning oil n your hair & scalp for 1 to 2 hours. Wash your hair with a mild foaming air cleanser.

Jojoba oil is a natural emollient and hair conditioning agent. Lecithin ; known to have local stimulatory properties and stimulate the circulation f blood to hair. This brings vital nutrients to the hair follicle thus helps in reventing dryness and damage to hair due to nutrient deficiency. Olive il is a general emollient of the hair and scalp. Use this preparation once week.

;onditioning Lotion for Oily Hair

Mulhetthi decoction(Liquorice)	4 table spoon
Lemon juice	1 table spoon
Honey	1/2 table spoon

1ethod of Preparation & Use

Boil 2 tablespoon full of Mulhetthi root powder in water *for 10 to 15* ninutes, over a low flame of a gas burner. Cool and filter through double nuslin cloth.

Mix Mulhetthi decoction, Lemon juice and Honey. Apply on scalp ind hair and leave the lotion on hair for 15-30 minutes. Wash the hair vith luke warm water and dry. Use this lotion once a week.

Liquorice Mulhetthi is a claimed to have sebum controlling properties. t in combination with lemon juice (astringent) has good oil controlling properties on hair and scalp. Honey is a good moisturiser of hair and scalp.

4

Regulatory Provisions Relating to Manufacture of Cosmetics

A licence is required under the Drugs & Cosmetics Rules fo manufacture of cosmetics for sale / distribution. This licence is issued by the state regulatory authorities (State Drugs Control Department o State Food and Drug Administration).

How to Obtain Licence

An application in prescribed form (Form 31) along with fee together with following documents is made to the office of the State Drugs Controller or Commissioner, Food & Drug Administration (FDA) :

Layout plan of the factory premises;

A list of equipment and machinery installed;

A document about the constitution of the firm i.e., and affidavit of proprietorship in case of sole-proprietorship, a copy of partnership deed, in case of partnership firm, a copy of memorandum and articles of association in case of a private limited or public limited company;

A document showing possession of the applicant on the proposed premises for factory e.g. rent agreement, rent receipt etc.

Usually the application forms are got printed by the State Drugs Control Dept./ FDA and are available from their office. Apart from the documents mentioned above State Drugs Control Department /FDA may also require certain affidavits or some other relevant information. Before grant of licence (which is issued in Form 32) the factory premises are inspected by the officer(s) of the State regulatory agency. During inspection, the officer finds out whether :

The applicant has provided adequate space for manufacturing operations, quality control and storage of raw materials, packaging materials and finished products.

The applicant has provided adequate equipment and machinery for manufacture of cosmetics which he intends to manufacture.

The applicant has provided adequate testing facilities for raw materials & finished form of cosmetics or has made arrangements for testing with an approved testing laboratory. State regulatory agency together with federal agency approves testing laboratories where manufacturers of drugs and or cosmetics can get their products and raw materials tested.

The applicant has whole time services of a person who has either of the qualifications :

Diploma in Pharmacy (D. Pharm.),

Registered Pharmacist,

Intermediate in science with chemistry as one of the subjects.

Minimum requirements of space, equipment and machinery for manufacture of cosmetics have been prescribed under Schedule M-II to the Drugs & Cosmetics Rules.

DESIGNING OF PLANT LAYOUT:-

There are many points which have to be considered while designing a layout for cosmetics factory, Salient features are specified as follow.

1. Total area of land available for construction.
2. Percentage of area that can be covered under local laws.
3. Cosmetics to be manufactured, i.e., type of products, creams / lotions, lipsticks, shampoos, etc.
4. Scale of operation, i.e., small scale, medium scale, large scale.
5. Type of equipment and machinery proposed to be used, i.e., manual, semi-automatic, automatic.
6. Logical flow of materials, i.e., goods in -stores -production - quarantine and assembly - goods out.
7. Provisions of national and local laws governing factories, i.e., Factories Act and rules made thereunder, Environment Protection Act and rule made thereunder.
8. Segregation of manufacturing areas as per Schedule M (II) to the Drugs & Cosmetics Rules.
9. Segregation of raw material storage area into quarantine area, approved raw material area and rejected raw material area.
10. Provision for storage areas for packaging materials, finished product under quarantine and finished products.
11. Provision for change or gowning room before entry into production area.
12. Placement of water supply lines and drainages system. (Readers may refer to IS : 1172 -1983).
13. Segregation of rest and refreshment rooms.
14. Provisions of the Excise Act in relation to storage of alcohol, if cosmetic preparations contain alcohol.
15. Segregation of hazardous materials, e.g., solvents for manufacture of nail enamels.
16. Provision of air-locks prior to production areas for eye make up preparation.
17. Provision for areas for testing laboratory, i.e., segregation of chemical, instrumental & microbiological laboratories.

18. If there is provision for maintenance work shops, these should be separated from production areas.
19. Provision for boiler, cold water plant, if these are to be installed.
20. Provision for water storage.
21. Provision for water treatment plant.

Requirements of Factory Premises For Manufacture of Cosmetics

1. General Requirements

(A) **Location and Surroundings** - The factory shall be located in a sanitary place and hygienic conditions shall be maintained in the premises. Premises shall not be used for residence or be interconnected with residential areas.

(B) **Buildings** - The buildings used for the factory shall be constructed so as to permit production under hygienic conditions and not to permit entry of insects, rodents, flies etc.

The walls of the room in which manufacturing operation are carried out, shall be up to a height of six feet from the floor, be smooth, even and washable and shall be such as not to permit retention or accumulation of dust.

(C) **Water Supply** - The water used in manufacture shall be of potable quality.

(D) **Disposal of Water** - Suitable arrangement shall be made for disposal of waste water.

(E) **Health, clothing and sanitary requirement of the staff** - All workers shall be free from contagious or infectious diseases. They shall be provided with clean uniforms, masks, headgears and gloves wherever required. Washing facilities shall also be provided.

(F) **Medical Services** - Adequate facilities for first-aid shall be provided.

(G) Working benches shall be provided for carrying out operations such as filling, labeling, packing etc. Such benches shall be fitted smooth, impervious tops capable of being washed.

Conditions of Licence :

Licenced cosmetics manufacturer has to comply with certain conditions. These conditions in brief are :

Manufacturer should continue to provide and maintain the premises, equipment and staff as at the time of grant of licence.

Manufacturer should test each batch or lot of raw materials before its use in the manufacture of cosmetics.

Manufacturer should test each batch of finished cosmetics. Cosmetics appearing under Schedule S should conform to the Indian Standards framed by the Bureau of Indian Standards.

Manufacturer should maintain records of raw materials, manufacture of each batch of cosmetic(s) and their testing. In the raw material and manufacturing record, atleast the particulars those given under Schedule U (I) to the Drugs and Cosmetics Rules should be shown. For convenience of the readers Schedule U (I) is reproduced here.

Schedule U (I)

Particulars to be shown in the Manufacturing Records

1. Serial number
2. Name of the product
3. Lot / Batch size.
4. Lot / Batch number.
5. Date of commencement of manufacture and date when manufacture was completed.
6. Names of all ingredients, quantities required for the lot / batch size. Quantities actually used.
7. Control reference numbers in respect of raw materials used in formulation.
8. Reference to analytical report numbers.
9. Actual production and packing particulars indicating the size and quantity of finished packings.
10. Date of release of finished packing for distribution or sale.
11. Signature of the expert staff responsible for the manufacture.

Manner of Labelling - Subject to other provisions of the rules, a cosmetic shall carry.

1. On both the inner and outer labels :
   (a) the name of the cosmetics.
   (b) the name and the principal place of business of the manufacturer.
2. On the outer label -
   (a) A declaration of the net contents expressed in terms of weight for solids, fluid measure for liquids, weights for semi-solids, combined with numerical count if the content is sub-divided : Provided that this statement need not appear in case of a package of perfume, toilet water or the like, the net content of which does not exceed 60ml or any package of solid or semi-solid cosmetic the net content of which does not exceed 30 grams.
3. On the inner label ; where a hazard exists :
   (a) Adequate direction for safe use,
   (b) Any warning, caution or special direction required to be observed by the consumer,
   (c) A statement of the names and quantities of the ingredients that are hazardous or poisonous.

4. A distinctive batch number, that is to say, the number by reference to which details of manufacture of the particular batch from which the substance in the container is taken are recorded and are available for inspection, the figures representing the batch number being preceded by the letter "B" : Provided that this clause shall not apply to any cosmetic containing 10 grams or less if the cosmetic is in solid or semi-solid state, and 25 milliliters or less if the cosmetic is in a liquid state :
   Provided further that in the case of soaps, instead of the batch number, the month & year of manufacture of soap shall be given on the label.
5. Manufacturing licence number, the number being preceded by the latter 'M'.
6. Where a package of a cosmetic has only one label such label contain all the information required to be shown on both the inner and the outer labels, under rules.

List of Dyes, Colours and Pigments permitted to be used in Cosmetics and Soaps :- as given under IS : 4707 (Part I) - as specified by the Bureau of Indian Standards.

Common name of the Colour	***Colour Index Number***	***Chemical name of the colour***
Guinea Green B	42085	Monosodium salt of 4-N-ethyl-p-sulfobenzylaminodipheny-lmethylone- (1 -(N~ethyl-N-p-sulfoniumbenzyl) 2,5 cyclohexadienimine).
Light Green SF Yellowish	42095	Disodium salt of 4-[4-(N-ethyl-p-sulfobenzyl-amino)-phenyl)-4-sulfoniumphenyl) methylene]-2(-(-N-ethyl-N- sulfobenzyl) 2,5-Cyclo-hexadienimine.
Tartrazine	19140	Trisodium salt of 3-carboxy-5-hydroxy-1-p-sulfophenyl-4-p-sulfophenylazo-pyrazole.
Sunset yellow FCF	15985	Disodium salt of 1-p-sulfophenyl-azo-2-naphthol-6-sulfonic acid.
Ponceau 3R	16155	Disodium salts of a mixture of 1-alkyl-phenyl-azo-2- naphthol-3, 6-disulfonic acid.
Amaranth	16185	Trisodium salt of 1-(4-sulfo-1-napthyl-azo) 2-naphthol 3,6-disulfonic acid.

Erythrosine	45430	Disodium salt of 9-0-carboxyphenyl-6 hydroxy-2, 4, 5, 7-tetrauidi-3-isoxanthone.
Ponceau SX	14700	Disodium salt of 2-(5-sulfo-2, 4-xylyl-azo)-1-naphthol-4sulfonic acid.
Brilliant Blue FCF1	42090	Disodium salt of 4-(9-4-(N-ethyl-p-su!fobenzylamino-phenyl)-(2-sulfonium-phenyl)-methylene)-(1-(N-ethyl-N-p-sulfobenzyl)- " 2,5-cyclohexadienimine).
Indigo carmine	73015	Disodium salt of 5,5'-indigotin-disulfonic acid.
Wool Violet 5 BN	42640	Monosodium salt of 4-(N-ethyl-p-sulfo- (Acid violet 6B) benzylamino)-phenyl)-(4-(N-ethyl-p-(sulfonium-benzylamine)-phenyl) methylene)-(N,N- dimethyl-" 2,5-cyclohexadienimine.
Light Green SF Yellowish	42095	Calcium salt of 4-(4-N-ethyl-p-sulfobenzyl) (monophenyl) (4-sulfonium-phenyl)-methylene), (1(N-ethyl-N-p-sulfobenzyl-) " 2,5-cyclohexadienimine.
Alizarin cyanine	61570	Disodium salt of 1,4-bis(O-sulfo-p-toluino) Green F.anthraquinone.
Quinazarine Green SS	61565	1,4-bis-(p-Toluino)-anthraquinone.
Fast Green FCF	42053	Disodium salt of 4-(4-(-ethyl-p-sulfobenzyl-amino)-phenyl)(4-hydroxy-2 sulphonium-phenyl) methylene)-(1-N-ethyl-N-p-sulfo-benzyl)- "2,5-cyclohexadienimine).
Acid Fast Green	42100	Monosodium salt of (4-(4-(-ethyl-p-sulfo-benzylamino) phenyl)-(O-chlorophenyl)-methylene)-1-(N-ethyl-N-p-sulfonium-benzyl-" 2,5-cyclohexadientienimine.
Pyranine Concentrated	59040	Trisodium salt of 10-hydroxy-3, 5, 8-pyrene-trisulfonic acid.
		Disodium salt of disulfonic acid of 2-(2-Quinolyl)-1,3- indandione.

Quinoline Yellow SS	47000	2-(2-quinolyl)-1, 3-indandione.
Poneceau 2 R	16150	Disodium salt of 1-xylyl-azo-2-naphthol-3, 6-disulfonic acid.
Lithol Rubin B	15850	Monosodium salt of 4-(o-sulfo-p-tolyl-azo) 3-hydroxy-2-naphtholic acid.
Lithol Rubin BCA	15850	Calcium salt of 4-(o-sulfo-p-tolyl-azo) 3-hydroxy-2-naphthoic acid.
Lake Red D	15500	Monosodium salt of 1-0 carboxy-phenylazo-2-naphthol.
Lake Red DBA	15500	Barium salt of 1-0-carboxypheny-lazo-2-naphthol.
Lake Red DCA	15500	Calcium salt of 1-0-carboxypheny-lazo-2-naphthol.
Toney Red	26100	l-p-phenylazophenylazo-2-naphthol.
Oil Red OS	26125	1-Xylylazomylyl-azo-2-naphthol.
Tetrabromo-Fluorescein	45380	2, 4, 5, 7Tetrabromo-3, 6-fluorandiol.
Eosin TS	45380	Disodium salt of 2, 4, 5, 7-tetrabromo-9-0-carboxyphenyl-6—hydroxy-3-isoxanthone.
Eosin YSK	45380	Disodium salt of 2, 4, 5, 7-tetrabromo-9-0-carboxyphenyl-6-hydroxy-3-isoxanthone.
Tetrachloroflu-Orescein NA	45366	2, 4, 5, 7-Tetrachloro-S, 6-fluorandiol.
Tetrachloroflo-urscein K	45366	Disodium salt of - 9-0-Carboxyphen L-2, 4, 5, 7-tetrachloro-6-hydroxy-3-isoxanthone.
Tetrachloro Tetra	45410	2, 4, 5, 7-Tetrabromo-12, 13, 14, 15-tetrachloro-3, 6-fluorandiol.
Phloxine B	45410	Disodium salt of - 2, 4, 5, 7-Tetrabromo-9-(3, 4, 5, 6-tetrachloro-o-carboxyphenyl)-6-hydroxy-3-isoxanthone.
Bluish Orange TR	45457	1, 4, 5, 8, 15-Pentabromo-2, 7-dicarboxy-3, 6-fluorandiol.
Helindone Pink CN	73360	5, 5-Dichloro-3,3i-dimethyl-thioindigo.
Brilliant Lake R	15800	Calcium salt of 3-hydroxy-4-phenylazo-Red-2-naphthoic acid.
Deep Maroon	15880	Calcium salt of 4-(a-sulfo-2-naphthylazo)-3-(Fanchon) hydroxy-2-naphthoic acid.

Toluidine Red	12120	1-(0-Nitro-p-tolylazo)-2-naphthol.
Flaming Red	12085	1-(0-Chloro-p-nitrophenylazo)-2-naphthol.
Deep Red (Maroon)	12350	3-Hydroxy-N-(m-nitrophenyl)-4-(o-nitro-p-tolylazo)-2-naphthamide.
Alba Red	13058	o-(p-B, B'-Dihydroxy-diethylamino)-phenyl-azo)-benzoic acid.
Orange G	16230	Disodium salt of 1-phenylazo-2-naphthol-6-8-disulfonic acid.
Orange II	15510	Monosodium salt of 1-p-sulfophenylazo-2-naphthol.
Dichlorofluo	45365	4, 5-Dichloro-3, 6 fluorandiol rescein
Dichlorofluo rescein NA	45365	Disodium salt of 9-o-Carboxyphenyl-1-4, 5-dichloro-6 hydroxy-3-isoxanthone.
Diiodofluo	45425	4, 5 Diiodo-3, 6-fluorandiol. rescein
Erythrosine Yellowish NA	45425	Disodium salt of 9-o-Carboxyphenyl-6-hydroxy-4, 5 diiodo-3-isoxanthone.
Erythrosine Yellowish K	45425	Disodium salt of 9-o-Carboxyphenyl-6-hydroxy-4, 5 diiodo-3-isoxanthone.
Erythrosine Yellowish NH	45425	Disodium salt of 9-o-Carboxyphenyl-6-hydroxy-4, 5 diiodo-3-isoxanthone.
Orange TR	45456	4, 5, 15-Tribromo-2, 7-dicarboxy-3, 6-fluorandiol.
Alizarin	58000	1, 2-Anthraquinonediol.
Dibromodiiodo-fluorescein	45371	4, 5-Dibromo-2, 7-diiodo-3, 6-fluorandiol.
Resorcin Brown	20170	Monosodium salt of 4-p-sulfophenylazo-2-(2, 4, xylylazo)-1, 3-resorcinal.
Alphazuring FG	42090	Diammonium salt of 4-(-N-ethyl-p-sulfoben -zylamino)-phenyl)-(2-sulfoniumphenyl)-methylene)-(1-(N-5- cyclohexadienimine).
Alizarin Astrol B	61530	Monosodium salt of 1-methylamino-4-(o-sulfo-p-toluino)- anthraquinone.
Indigo	73000	Indigotin.
Patent Blue NA	42052	Monosodium salt of 4-(4-(N-ethyl-benzyl-amino)-phenyl)-(5-hydroxy-4-sulfo-sulfonium-phenyl-methylene) (N-ethyl-N-Benzyl-" 2-5 cyclohex-adienimine).

Patent Blue CA	42052	Calcium salt of 4-(4-(N-ethyl-benzylamino-phenyl)-(5-hydroxy-4-sulfo-methylene)(N-ethyl-N-Benzyl-" 2-5-cyclohexadienimine.
Carbanthrene	69825	3, 3-Dichloroindanthrene. Blue
Naphthol Blue Black	20470	Disodium salt of 8-amino-7-p-nitrophenylazo-3-phenylazo-1-naphthol-3, 6-disulfonic acid.
Alizurol Purple SS	60725	1-hydroxy-4-p-toluino-anthraquinone.
Acid Red 89	23910	
Acid Red 97	22890	
Acid Blue 1	42045	
Food Blue 3	42045	
Natural Orange 6	75480	
Solvent Blue 4	44045	
Solvent Yellow 18	12740	
Food Yellow 12	12740	
Solvent Red 1	12740	
Solvent Yellow 32	48045	
Fanchon Yellow	11680	(a)-(o-Nitro-p-tolylazo) acetoacetanilide.

INDIAN STANDARDS FOR COSMETICS

1.	After Shave Lotion	IS : 9255-1979
2.	Bindi (Liquid)	IS : 10998-1984
3.	Cologne	IS : 8482-1977
4.	Cosmetic pencils	IS : 9832-1981
5.	Depilatories, chemicals	IS : 9636-1988
6.	Hair Cream (First revision)	IS : 7679-1978
7.	Hair oils (Second revision)	IS : 7123-1993
8.	Henna powder	IS : 11142-1964
9.	Kum Kum powder	IS : 10999-1964
10.	Lip salve	IS : 10284-1982
11.	Lipstick	IS : 9875-1990
12.	Nail Polish (Nail enamel)	IS : 9245-1975
13.	Oxidation, hair dyes, liquid (with amendment No. !)	IS : 8481-1977
14.	Pomades & brilliantines (first revision)	IS : 9339-1988
15.	Powder hair dyes	IS : 10350-1982
16.	Shampoo, synthetic detergent based (first revision)	IS : 7884-1992
17.	Shampoo, soap based (first revision)	IS : 7669-1990
18.	Shaving cream	IS : 9740-1981
19.	Skin Cream (first revision)	IS : 6608-1978
20.	Skin powder for infants (first revision)	IS : 5339-1978

21. Skin powder (first revision) IS : 3959-1978
22. Tooth paste (second revision) IS : 6356-1993
23.. Tooth powder (first revision) IS : 5383-1976
24. Toilet soap IS : 2888-1983
25. Antibacterial Toilet Soap IS : 11479-1985
26. Shaving Soap IS : 5784.-1970
27. Transparent soap IS : 11303-1985

Indian Standards For Cosmetics Raw Materials

1. Ammonium chloride for cosmetic industry IS : 11015-1984
2. Bees wax, bleached for cosmetic industry (second revision) IS : 4028-1992
3. Borax for cosmetic industry IS : 11023-1984
4. Boric Acid for cosmetic industry (fifth revision) IS : 263-1990
5. Butyl p-hydroxy benzoate for cosmetic industry (second revision) IS : 6334-1987
6. Calcium Carbonate, precipitated for cosmetic industry (second revision) IS : 918-1985
7. Calcium stearate for cosmetic industry {second revision) IS : 2519-1983
8. Castor oil for cosmetic industry IS : 11486-1985
9. Coconut diethanolamide (first revision) IS : 7101-1983
10. Coconut oil for cosmetic industry IS : 11470-1985
11. Di-calcium phosphate for dentifrice (second revision) IS : 1767-1980
12. Ethyl acetate for cosmetic industry IS: 10283-1982
13. Ethyl p-hydroxy benzoate for cosmetic industry (second revision) IS : 4652-1987
14. Glycerine for cosmetic industry IS ; 12590-1988
15. Glyceryl monostearate for cosmetic IS : 4236-1985
16. Groundnut oil for cosmetic industry IS : 11375-1985
17. Isopropyl alcohol for cosmetic industry IS : 10301-1982
18. Isopropyl myristate for cosmetic industry (second revision) IS : 5356-1983
19. Kaolin for cosmetic industry (third revision) IS : 1463-1983
20. Lanolin, anhydrous for cosmetic industry (first revision) IS : 5340-1981
21. Magnesium Carbonate for cosmetic industry (third revision) IS : 2528-1984
22. Magnesium Oxide for cosmetic industry IS : 2529-1983

(second revision)

23.	Magnesium Stearate for cosmetic industry (second revision)	IS : 2521-1984
24.	Methyl p- hydroxybenzoate for cosmetic industry (second revision)	IS : 4653-1985
25.	Mineral oil for cosmetic industry (first revision with amendment No. 3)	IS : 7299-1974
26.	p-Phenylene diamine	IS : 10377-1982
27.	Petroleum Jelly for cosmetic industry (first revision)	IS : 4887-1980
28.	Propyl p-hydroxy benzoate for cosmetics industry (second revision)	IS : 6333-1985
29.	Sesame oil for cosmetic industry	IS : 11376-1985
30.	Sodium hydroxide for cosmetic industry (first revision)	IS : 9831-1987
31.	Sodium Lauryl Ether Sulphate	IS : 11487-1985
32.	Sodium Lauryl Sulphate for cosmetic industry (third revision)	IS : 3986-1988
33.	Sodium Silicate for cosmetic industry (with amendment No. 1)	IS : 9601-1980
34.	Sorbitol solution (70%) (second revision with amendment No.1)	IS : 3987-1983
35.	Stearic Acid for cosmetic industry	IS : 9681-1980
36.	Talc for cosmetic industry (third revision)	IS : 1462-1985
37.	Titanium Dioxide for cosmetic industry (second revision)	IS : 2851-1983
38.	Water soluble sodium carboxymethyl cellulose for cosmetic industry	IS : 9830-1988
39.	Zinc Oxide for cosmetic industry (second revision)	IS : 2850-1983
40.	Zinc Stearate for cosmetic industry (second revision)	IS : 2520-1984

5

Ultra Violet Protection Sunscreen Cream

Introduction :-

Ultra Violet Protection Sunscreen Cream is one of the important skin care cosmetic product having worldwide demand. The cream helps to protect skin of people from harmful effect of UitraViolet radiations which causes erythema (reddening) on the skin. The intensity of the erythema produced on the skin with the amount of UV energy absorbed by the skin. Erythema usually starts to develop after a latent period of 2-3 hours and reaches its maximum intensity within 10-24 hours after exposure.

The studies by scientists have indicated that chronic exposure to intense sunlight may cause serious hazards. It may also produce degenerative changes in the connective tissue of the corium and result in the so-called premature aging of the skin. This is evidenced by the thickening of the skin, the loss of natural elasticity and the appearance of wrinkles, all resulting from the loss of the skin's water binding tendency to form skin blemishes.

It has been seen that exposure to sunlight vary with season and the time of the day. At sea level the UV energy of Sunlight is greatest between 10A.M. and 2 P.M. In mid summer, with a maximum of UV-B energy falling on the skin at noon. In the early morning or late after noon, when sunlight falls on the skin at a lower angle, the intensity of the solar evergy is considerably lower and sunburn is unlikely to occur. The scientific studies shows that UV-A radiation ranges in Wavelength from 320 nm-400 nm, which cause a preliminary inflammation. The UV-B radiation ranges 290nm-320nm, which cause sunburn as well as irritating reactions. The UV-C radiation ranges 200nm-290nm wavelength, which cause erythema and also damages to the tissues.

The sunscreen agents absorb 95 per cent or more of UV radiation within the wavelength of 290-320nm and prevents sunburn. Opaque sunblock agent reflects and scatters all radiation in the UV and visible range, thereby preventing or minimizing both sunburn and suntan.

The Sunscreen Cream is one of the most important and useful skin care cosmetic product, which help people to work longer in the sunlight.

The product is demanded all over the world. The demand of this product is rising at a rapid pace day by day both in domestic as well as in international market. A new entrepreneur or industrialist can earn excellent profit by adding this product in their cosmetic range.

Properties of Good Quality Ultra Violet Protection Sunscreen Cream :-

1. It is effective in absorbing erythmogenic radiation in 290-320 nm range without breakdown which could reduce its efficiency or give rise to toxic or irritant compound.
2. It allows full transmission in 300-400 nm range to permit the maximum tanning effect.
3. It is non-volatile, resistant to water and perspiration.
4. It possess suitable solubility characteristics to allow Sunscreen Cream to accommodate the requisite amount of sun screening.
5. It is mild and odourless.
6. It is non-toxic, non-irritant and non-sensitizing.
7. It is capable of retaining its protective capacity for several hours.
8. It is stable under conditions of use.
9. It does not stain clothing.

Uses and Applications :-

1. Ultra Violet Protection Sunscreen Cream is unique as cosmetics in that the manner of use may involve multiple and extensive daily applications to large areas of the body surface and, in addition, it may be applied to skin already damaged by sunburn.
2. It is used by people of all age groups and in varying conditions of health.
3. Ultra Violet Protection Sunscreen Cream is used by teenagers, girls, ladies, women and men who are moving in the sun in day times.
4. it is used in summer season to protect the skin from sunburn.

B.I.S. Specification:-

There is no such B.I.S. Specification available on "Ultra Violet Protection Sunscreen Cream" with Bureau of Indian Standards. But it can be tested as per the cosmetic norms prior to selling in the market.

Government Regulation :-

"Ultra Violet Protection Sunscreen Cream" is a cosmetic product which come under Drug & cosmetic Rules 1945.

To manufacture "Ultra Violet Protection Sunscreen Cream", the manufacturers have to apply to the licensing authority appointed by the state Government in Form-31 (if the manufacturer wants to manufacture products for sale or distribution).

Raw Materials Require and its Availability :-

To manufacture a standard quality Ultra Violet Sunscreen Cream the raw materials require, are named as Mineral Oil, Oleic Acid, Oxy Methyl Cinnamate, Emulsifying Wax, Isopropyl Palmitate, Silicon Oil, Cetyl Alcohol, Glycerine, Titanium Dioxide, Zinc Oxide, Triethanol amine, Purified Water, Vitamin A, Preservative, Propylene Glycol, Perfumes, Colour, Herbal Extracts and Laboratory testing chemicals.

The packaging materials require are HDPE/PET Jars, Laminated Plastic Collapsible Tubes, Aluminium foil Laminated Seal, Printed Mini Outer Cartons, Corrugated Cardboard Boxes, Labels, Self adhesive tapes, Box straps etc. These raw materials and packaging materials are indigenously available and can be procured from nearby local available sources.

Ultra Violet Protection Sunscreen Cream

Formulation:-

Ingredients		*Parts by Weight*
Mineral Oil	-	4-6
Oleic Acid	-	7-8
Oxy Methyl Cinnamate	-	1-2.5
Emulsifying Wax	-	4-5
Isopropyl Palmitate	-	1-3
Silicon Oil	-	0.5 - 1
Cetyl Alcohol	-	1.5-2
Glycerine	-	3-4
Titanium Dioxide	-	1-2
Zinc Oxide	-	0.5 - 1
Purified Water	-	to make 100
Vitamin A	-	0.2-0.75
Preservative	-	0.3-0.7
Propylene Glycol	-	2-3
Perfumes	-	0.1-0.5
Colour	-	q.s.
		100

Manufacturing Process :-

To manufacture best quality Ultra Violet Protection Sunscreen Cream, It is suggested to proceed the following processing steps.

1. Procure all the raw materials from good reputed dealers or suppliers.
2. Analyse and test all the raw materials for purity and good quality.

3. Weigh all the raw materials as specified in the formulation.
4. In a stainless steel vessel fitted with S. S. Stirrer, heat Mineral Oil, Oleic Acid, Oxy methyl Cinnamate, Emulsifying Wax, Isopropyl Palmitate, Silicon Oil, Cetyl Alcohol together at 70°C with melting and stirring to prepare an uniform fatty mass.
5. In a S. S. planetary mixer, heat Glycerine, Titanium Dioxide, Zinc Oxide, Triethanol Amine, Purified Water together at 70^{0}0 till it become uniform.
6. Now, add step-4 preparations to step-5 preparations with uniform mixing and stirring till an uniform emulsion is formed.
7. In another stainless steel vessel, dissolve Vitamin-A and Preservative in Propylene Glycol with warming and mixing uniformly.
8. Now, add step-7 preparations to step-6 preparations at 35°C with stirring and mixing thoroughly.
9. Then add perfumes or fragrances to step-8 preparations, mix thoroughly with stirring.
10. Add the colour solutions to the cream and mix thoroughly.
11. The final UV protection Sunscreen Cream is quality tested and standardized.
12. The finished product is now filled in jars. The jars are sealed by aluminium foil, then capped. The labels are pasted and batch coded. The finished jars are now placed in mini outer cartons and these mini cartons are now packed in corrugated master cartons. The cartons are strapped.
13. The finished Cartons are placed in store and marketed to the desired customers, dealers or distributors.

Process Flow Sheet For Manufacturing of Ultra Violet Protection Sunscreen Cream

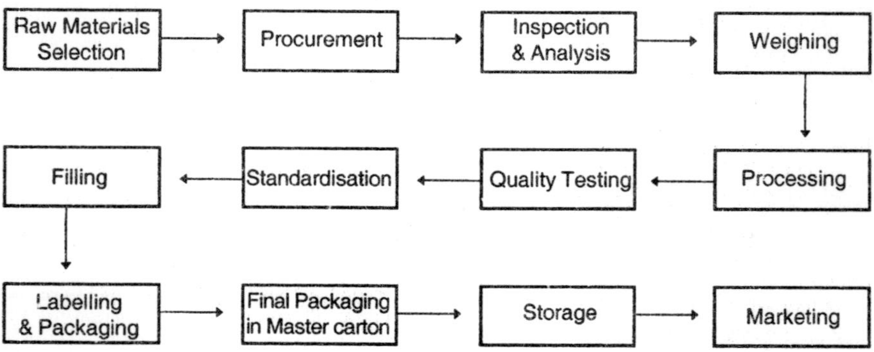

Plant & Machineries Require :-

1. Planetary Mixer with Stainless Steel body and stirrer.
2. Mixing Vessel (S.S. made) with stirrer fitted with electric heating system.
3. Water de-ionisation unit.
4. Stainless steel melting vessel.
5. Automatic or semi-automatic tube weighing, filling and sealing machine.
6. Automatic or semi-automatic jar weighing, filling and sealing machine.
7. Semi-automatic labeling machine .
8. Semi-automatic Carton sealing and strapping machine.
9. Laboratory Testing equipments and Glasswares.
10. Weighing balance, weights & others.

PROJECT FINANCIAL ANALYSIS :-

1.	Production Capacity	-	100 Kgs. Per Day / Per Shift. Ultra Violet Protection Sun Screen Cream
2.	Land & Building	-	On Rent.
3.	Covered Area Require	-	300 Sq.mts.
4.	Plant & Machinery Cost	-	Rs. 3.80 lacs.
5.	Other Fixed Capital	-	Rs. 1.20 lacs.
6.	Total Fixed Capital Require	-	Rs. 5.00 lacs.
7.	Working Capital Require Per Month	-	Rs. 6.00 lacs.
8.	Margin Money	-	Rs. 1.50 lacs.
9.	Total Project Cost	-	Rs. 6.50 lacs.
10.	Total Capital Require	-	Rs. 11.00 lacs.
11.	Cost of Production Per Month	-	Rs. 6.20 lacs.
12.	Turnover Per Month	-	Rs. 8-50 lacs.
13.	Gross Profit Per Month	-	Rs. 2.30 lacs.
14.	Rate of Return Per Annum	-	251 %
15.	Manpower Requirement	-	5 Nos.
16.	Electric Power Load	-	10KWs
17.	Water Requirement Per Month	-	100 KLs.

FINANCIAL RESOURCES FOR PROJECT ESTABLISHMENT :-

1.	Term Loan (65% of Fixed Capital) From Financial Institution	Rs.	3.25 lacs.
2.	Working Capital Loan (75% of Working Capital) From Bank	Rs.	4.50 lacs.
3.	Promoter's Capital Raised By Main Promoter.	Rs.	3.25 lacs.
		Rs.	11.00 lacs.

6

Glow Pack (All Purpose Face Mask)

Introduction :-

Glow Pack is a type of face pack also known as "ALL PURPOSE FACE MASK". It is highly used by girls & women of all age group. It is applied over face skin for 1-2 hours. It is applied in the viscous paste or cream form. It cleanse the skin, removes the dead skin or skin debris & black heads. It tightens the skin pores, removes some wrinkles from aged skin layers, make the skin shining and glowing. It removes dead cells, infection & impurities of skin, reduces freckles, blemishes and pigmentation. Nourishes dull & dehydrated skin.

Now a days, there are lot of research going on over the skin care products. The best products which are scientifically tested & medically passed over several tests, are sent for marketing all over the world. That's why, cosmetic industry is growing day by day. Everyday new cosmetic products are coming in the market with new innovative approach. The products are highly consumed in every country of the world.

The market demand is rising at a faster pace all over the world.

Properties of a Good Quality Glow Pack :-

1. Glow Pack is available in highly viscous paste form.
2. The product is applicable on all types of skins, having non-irritating and non-toxic nature.
3. The product is biologically and ecologically safe.
4. The product can be used by human being in any climatic conditions, in any part of the world.
5. The product is washed by water after application on skin.
6. The product does not dry. Its quality does not change during its storage and shelf life period.

Uses and Applications:-

1. Glow Pack is formulated with natural ingredients and components, it is accepted by every women and men of all age catagories.
2. The product is used by women and girls in home or houses and used in almost all the beauty conscious high profile societies.

3. The major consumers are beauty parlours, Spa clubs, Five star hotels, deluxe & super deluxe star hotels etc.
4. All the film stars, actors & actresses, models and others are using it regularly.

B.I.S. Specification :-

There is no B.I.S. Specification available on "Glow Pack (All purpose face mask)" with Bureau of Indian standards. But this product is quality tested as per the cosmetic norms prior to selling in the market. The quality norms should be strictly considered and adopted by all the manufacturers.

Government Regulations :-

"Glow Pack (All purpose face mask)" is a cosmetic product which come under Drug & cosmetic Rules 1945.

To manufacture "Glow Pack (All purpose face mask)", the manufacturers have to apply to the licensing authority appointed by the state Government in Form-31 (if the manufacturer wants to manufacture products for sale or distribution).

Raw Materials Require and its Availability :-

To manufacture a standard good quality Glow Pack (All Purpose Face Mask), the raw materials require, are named as Kaolin, Bentonite, Calamin, Cetyl Alcohol, Sodium Lauryl Sulphate, Guar Gum Powder, Purified Water, Glycerine, Preservative, Perfumes, Herbal Extracts and Laboratory chemicals.

The packaging materials viz. jars, outer mini cartons, corrugated cartons, adhesive tapes, HDPE box straps, stickers, labels etc. are required for processing and packaging of cosmetics products. All the raw materials and packaging materials are indigenously available. It can be procured from nearby available local sources.

Glow Pack (All Purpose Face Mask)

Formulations

Ingredients		*Parts by weight*
Kaolin	-	20-24
Bentonite	-	4-8
Calamin	-	8-12
Cetyl Alcohol	-	1-4
Sodium Lauryl Sulphate	-	0.2-1
Guar Gum Powder	-	1-3
Purified Water	-	Q.S to make 100
Glycerine	-	8-12
Preservative	-	0.2-0.75
Perfumes	-	0.5-2
		100

Manufacturing Process :-

To manufacture the Glow Pack (All purpose face mask), it is suggested to adopt the following steps as described in details :-

1. First of all, purchase all the raw materials from reputed suppliers.
2. Analyse and test all the ingredients for quality assessment.
3. Weigh all the raw materials as specified in the formulation.
4. Now, in a stainless steel vessel fitted with S.S. Stirrer, pour Sodium Lauryl Sulphate, Guar Gum and Purified Water. Heat the vessel on low flame of a gas burner with continuous stirring of materials.
5. In another vessel, pour Glycerine and Preservative and dissolve the preservative with mild heating.
6. In another vessel, pour Cetyl Alcohol and heat till it starts melting.
7. Now, mix (step- 4) preparations with the (step-6) Cetyl Alcohol liquid with continuous stirring. This will result in the formation of a white emulsion cream.
8. Add to (step-7) white emulsion, the Kaolin Powder, Bentonite powder & Calamin powder, mix with gentle stirring to avoid any air entrapment, so that a smooth paste may be produced.
9. Now, cool the mixture to 40°C and mix (step-5) Preservative & Glycerine solution to it with uniform mixing.
10. Then add the perfume to (step-9) preparations at room temperature and mix again. The All purpose face mask or Glow Pack is now ready.
11. The Glow Pack is quality tested, standardised and packed in cosmetic grade plastic jars. The jars are labelled and marked with batch No, MRP, Date of manufacturing etc.
12. These jars are packed in corrugated cardboard cartons. The cartons are sealed with adhesive tapes and then strapped.
13. These cartons are now placed in store and sent to desired customers for marketing.

Process Flowsheet For Manufacturing of Glow Pack (ALL Purpose Face Mask)

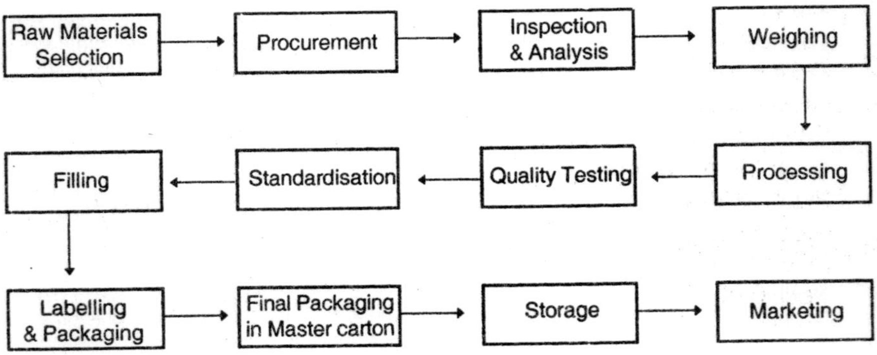

Plant & Machineries Require :-

1. Stainless steel mixing vessel with stirrer.
2. Weighing balance.
3. Gas burner with cylinders.
4. Laboratory equipment & Glasswares.
5. Semi-automatic or manual weighing filling and jar sealing machine.
6. Labeling & coding machine.
7. Box strapping machine.
8. Water purification unit.

PROJECT FINANCIAL ANALYSIS :-

1.	Production Capacity	- 200 Kgs. Per Day / Per Shift. Glow Pack (All Purpose Face Mask)
2.	Land & Building	- On Rent.
3.	Covered Area Require	- 250 Sq.mts.
4.	Plant & Machinery Cost	- Rs. 2.90 lacs.
5.	Others Fixed Capital	- Rs. 1.20 lacs.
6.	Total Fixed Capital Require	- Rs. 4.10 lacs.
7.	Working Capital Require Per Month	- Rs. 4.60 lacs.
8.	Margin Money	- Rs. 1.15 lacs.
9.	Total Project Cost	- Rs. 5.25 lacs.
10.	Total Capital Require	- Rs. 8.70 lacs.
11.	Cost of Production Per Month	- Rs. 4.80 lacs.
12.	Turnover Per Month	- Rs. 6.50 lacs.
13.	Gross Profit Per Month	- Rs. 1.70 lacs.
14.	Rate of Return Per Annum	- 235%
15.	Manpower Requirement	- 5Nos.
16.	Electric Power Load	- 10 KWs
17.	Water Requirement Per Month	- 100 KLs.

7

Hair Oil With Vitamin-E, Lanolin & Protein

Introduction :-

Hair Oil with Vitamin-E, Lanolin and Protein plays a vital role in hair root nourishment, rejuvenation and emollient action to the skin of scalp. The product is coming in the haircare categories. Now a days, with rise in pollution level, improper food habits, social tensions, family tensions, exposure to different climatic conditions from time to time, the hair loses its strength, shining and texture. Which results in premature hair graying, hair falling and ultimately leads to baldness. These condition arises due to shortage of protein, vitamin and water in the root of hair follicles. To strengthen the hair roots and hair strands, the hair oil helps to the large extent. It provides natural protein, vitamin to keep scalp skin and hair root healthy. Due to its emollient action it do not allow dandruff formation on the scalp. It helps to retain moisture in the scalp skin.

The hair oil also provides energy with its ingredients content and keep the hair follicle beautiful and shining for longer period. Besides, it also provides energy to brain cells, raises blood circulation in the nerves with sensational feeling on application.

The hair oil is considered to be an energy product. The demand of this product is rising day by day all over the world. The product helps to reduce nutrition deficiency in hair and scalp. So the beauty conscious people are finding this product most suitable.

A new entrepreneur with good marketing strategy can enter into the market to earn excellent profit.

Properties of Good Quality Hair Oil with Vitamin-E, Lanolin and Protein :-

1 The hair oil may be both greasy and non-greasy type.
2 It keeps the hair lustrous, shiny, beautiful and smooth in texture.
3 It helps to remove the dandruff and check further dandruff formation on the scalp.
4 It provides essential nutritions to hair root, hair follicle as well as scalp skin.
5 It does not causes any side effect.
6 The product maintains long term vitality of hair follicle and keeps the hair shiny for longer period.

Uses and Applications :-

1. Hair Oil with Vitamin-E, Lanolin and Protein is used by both men and women of all age group all over the world.
2. It is used by every people in our country due to its effectiveness over human scalp and hair roots.
3. It is used to emolliate and maintain moisture balance of the hair.
4. The hair oil is also used for a number of hair and scalp disorders like dandruff, hair fall, hair graying etc.

B.I.S. Specification :-

Depending upon the ingredients used in the preparation of Hair oil the B.I.S. specification for Hair oils (IS-7123) have been divided into following three types-

Type - 1 :- Hair oil based on Vegetable oils.

Type - 2 :- Hair oil based on Mineral oil (light liquid paraffins).

Type - 3 :- Hair oil based on a mixture of Vegetable oil and Mineral oil.

Government Regulation:-

"Hair Oil with Vitamin-E, Lanolin and Protein" is a Cosmetic product which come under Drug & Cosmetic Rules 1945.

To manufacture "Hair Oil with Vitamin-E, Lanolin and Protein" the manufacturer has to apply to the licensing authority appointed by the State Government in Form-31 (if the manufacturer wants to manufacture products for sale or distribution) or Form-31 A, (if the manufacture wants loan license to manufacture cosmetic product.).

Market Status:-

The Indian Hair Oil market is a very big market and worth over Rs. 800 crores. The last one decade has shown tremendous growth in the Hair oil market and the demand is growing at a rate of 20 % per Annum in the rural areas and 7-8 % in the urban areas. It has been estimated that with rise in population growth, the demand of Hair Oil with Vitamin-E, Lanolin and Protein will grow at a rapid pace.

Raw Materials Require and its Availability :-

The raw materials require to manufacture Hair Oil with Vitamin-E, Lanolin and Protein are named as Refined Coconut Oil, Mineral Oil, Lanolin (Wool fat), Isopropyl Myristate, Vitamin E Oil, Protein Hydrolysate, Preservative, Perfume or Fragrance, colour (Oil soluble), Herbal Extracts and Laboratory testing chemicals.

The packaging materials require are HDPE/PET Bottles, Flip Top Caps, Labels, shrink wrap, mini outer cartons, Corrugated card board boxes, self adhesive tapes, box straps etc. These raw materials and packaging materials are indigenously available and can be procured from nearby available local sources.

Hair Oil With Vitamin-E, Lanolin and Protein

Formulation :-

Ingredients		*Parts by Weight*
Refined Coconut Oil	-	40-42
Mineral Oil	-	to make 100
Lanolin (wool fat)	-	2-3
Isopropyl Myristate	-	3-4
Vitamin - E Oil	-	1-2
Protein Hydrolysate	-	4-5
Preservative	-	0.3
Perfume or Fragrance	-	0.1-0.5
Colour (oil soluble)	-	q.s.
		100

Manufacturing Process :-

To manufacture good standard quality Hair Oil with Vitamin-E, Lanolin and Protein the manufacturers are suggested to proceed the following processing steps.

1. Procure all the raw materials from good reputed dealers or suppliers.
2. Analyse and test all the raw materials for purity and good quality.
3. Weigh all raw materials as specified in the formulation.
4. In a jacketed stainless steel vessel fitted with S. S. Stirrer, heat Refined Coconut Oil, Mineral Oil, Lanolin, Isopropyl Myristate at 70°C with Stirring thoroughly in order to melt and mix all the ingredients uniformly. Cool the oil to 40°C.
5. Now, take a portion of oil step-4 Preparations and dissolve Vitamin-E, Protein hydrolysate and Preservative by mixing it uniformly.
6. Then add step-5 preparations to step-4 preparations with mixing thoroughly to prepare a homogeneous product.
7. Now, add colour and perfume / fragrance one by one with thorough mixing.
8. The final hair oil is quality tested and standardized.
9. The finished oil is packed in HDPE or PET bottles. The bottles are capped, labeled and batch marked.
10. The bottles are packed in corrugated cartons.
11. The cartons are sealed with adhesive tapes and box strapped.
12. The finished cartons are placed in store and marketed to the desired dealers, distributors or customers.

Process Flowsheet For Manufacturing of Hair Oil with Vitamin-E, Lanolin and Protein

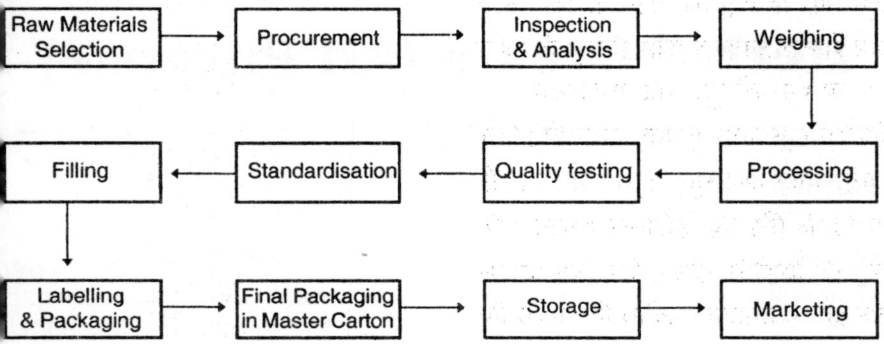

Plant & Machineries Require :-

1. Mixing vessel (S.S.Made) fitted with S.S. Stirrer.
2. Reaction vessel fitted with S.S. Stirrer.
3. Weighing balance.
4. Laboratory analytical equipment.
5. Laboratory Glassware.
6. Filtration unit or filter press.
7. Filling tank.
8. Semi-automatic weighing filling sealing machine.
9. Labeling machine.
10. Other equipments.

PROJECT FINANCIAL ANALYSIS :-

1.	Production Capacity	-	100 Kgs. Per Day / Per Shift. Hair oil with Vitamin-E. Lanolin and Protein
2.	Land & Building	-	On Rent.
3.	Covered Area Require	-	300 Sq.mts.
4.	Plant & Machinery Cost	-	Rs. 3.60 lacs.
5.	Others Fixed Capital	-	Rs. 1.20 lacs.
6.	Total Fixed Capital Require	-	Rs. 4.80 lacs.
7.	Working Capital Require Per Month	-	Rs. 6.25 lacs.
8.	Margin Money	-	Rs. 1.56 lacs.
9.	Total Project Cost	-	Rs. 6.36 lacs.
10.	Total Capital Require	-	Rs. 11.05 lacs.
11.	Cost of Production Per Month	-	Rs. 6.40 lacs.
12.	Turnover Per Month	-	Rs. 8.50 lacs.
13.	Gross Profit Per Month	-	Rs. 2.10 lacs.
14.	Rate of Return Per Annum	-	228 %
15.	Manpower Requirement	-	5 Nos.
16	Electric Power Load	-	10 KWs
17.	Water Requirement Per Month	-	100 KLs.

8

Herbal Cream (All Purpose)

Introduction:-

All Purpose Herbal Cream is one of the important cosmetic preparations coming under the Skin Care category. Though the terminology "All purpose" indicates that this cream can be used for various applications. It can be used as foundation cream, cleansing cream, hand cream, protective cream or as an emollient cream. The all purpose cream is sometime referred to as "sports cream" . The single product can serve various purposes in beautification of human being specially women, girls, ladies of all age group. The product is highly in demand all over the country. It is mostly consumed in beauty parlours, men's beauty parlours, houses, homes, star hotels and almost by every economic class societies. The cream is somewhat oily, but non-greasy in use. It is being water-in-oil type emulsion thus spreads readily on skin and make a protective film.

Requirement of Good Herbal All Purpose Cream :-

A good Herbal All Purpose Cream should comply the following Requirements.

1. It can be used as a foundation cream. It must provide a satisfactory foundation base for make-up without being too greasy.
2. As a cleansing cream it should liquefy readily, be of an oily nature but should be free from "drag". It should not be readily absorbed by the skin.
3. As a hand cream it should be emollient yet not leave a greasy or sticky film on the skin.
4. As a protective cream and as an emollient cream it should leave a continuous but non-occlusive oil film on the skin.

Properties of a Good Herbal All Purpose Cream :-

1. The Herbal All Purpose Cream is non-irritating, non-toxic, biologically & environmentally safe for all types of skin.
2. The product is smooth in application over the skin.
3. The product has sufficient shelf life.
4. The product has uniform texture.
5. It can nourish, rejuvenate the skin.

Uses and Applications :-

1. Herbal All Purpose Cream is one of the important variety of cream, which serves multipurpose application. It is mostly used by economic class people who generally can not afford to purchase different types of creams for their different applications.
2. It is used in beauty parlours & men's beauty parlours to beautify both women and men.
3. It is mostly used in rural segments and popularised among mass population of our Country.
4. The product is used by almost every female, girls, women or men of all age group.

B. I. S. Specification :-

There is no specific B. I. S. Specification on "Herbal All Purpose Cream" available with Bureau of Indian standards. But prior to sellding this cream in market, it is suggested to check all the cosmetics norms as specified in the IS-6608 : Skin Cream as published by Bureau of Indian standards.

Government Regulation :-

"Herbal All Purpose Cream" is a cosmetic product which come under Drug & Cosmetic Rules 1945

To manufacture "Herbal All Purpose Cream", the manufacturers have to apply to the licensing authority appointed by the state Government in Form-31 (if the manufacturer wants to manufacture products for sale or distribution).

Raw Materials Require and its Availability:-

To formulate a good quality Herbal All Purpose Cream, there are various cosmetic grade chemicals require viz. Stearic Acid, Lanolin, Bees wax, Mineral oil, Polysorbate-80, Sorbitan trioleate, sorbitol, purified water perfumes, preservatives, herbal extracts, Aloe vera gel, laboratory chemicals and packaging materials require all these raw materials are indigenously available and can be procured from nearby local available sources

Herbal All Purpose Cream

Formulation:-

Ingredients		*Part by weight*
Stearic Acid	-	13-16
Lanolin	-	2-4
BeesWax	-	1-2
Mineral oil	-	22-24
Polysorbate-80	-	0.5 - 1

Sorbitan trioleate	-	0.5-1
Sorbitol	-	8-12
Purified water	-	to make 100
Perfumes	-	0.1-0.2
Preservatives	-	0.2 -0.75
Herbal Extract(Tulsi, Sandal, Methi seed)	-	0.3-2
Aloe vera gel	-	2
		100

Manufacturing Process:-

To prepare a good standard quality herbal all purpose cream, the production charge can adopt the following processing steps

1 Purchase all the raw materials from good reliable reputed dealers or traders

2 Analyse or test all the raw materials for its quality assessment.

3. Weigh all the raw materials as mentioned in the formulation.

4. Now, in a stainless steel vessel fitted with S. S. Stirrer, motor and accessories, feed Stearic Acid, Lanolin, Bees wax, Mineral oil, Polysorbate-80, Sorbitan trioleate and heat it to 70° to 80°C to melt all the solid fatty matter and mix it to obtain uniform liquid.

5. In another stainless steel vessel fitted with S. S. Stirrer, pour sorbitol and preservative and heat it to dissolve the preservative completely. Then to it add the purified water with uniform mixing in heating condition at 60-70°C.

6. Now, add step-5 preparations to step-4 preparations slowly with uniform stirring till it is completely mixed to form a creamy mass with continuous stirring.

7. Cool the creamy mass preparations to 40°-45°C and to it add the perfumes, herbal extracts, Aloe vera gel and again mix it uniformly to homogenise the final preparations.

8. The final preparations is tested and standardised as per the norms of cosmetics.

9. Now, fill it in plastic collapsible tubes or jars, seal it and cap it to avoid aerial contacts. These are now labelled and packed in outer cartons and then in master cartons.

10. The master cartons are now sealed with adhesive tapes and strapped.

11. The cartons are placed in store and marketed to the desired customers.

Process Flowsheet For Manufacturing of Herbal Cream (All Purpose)

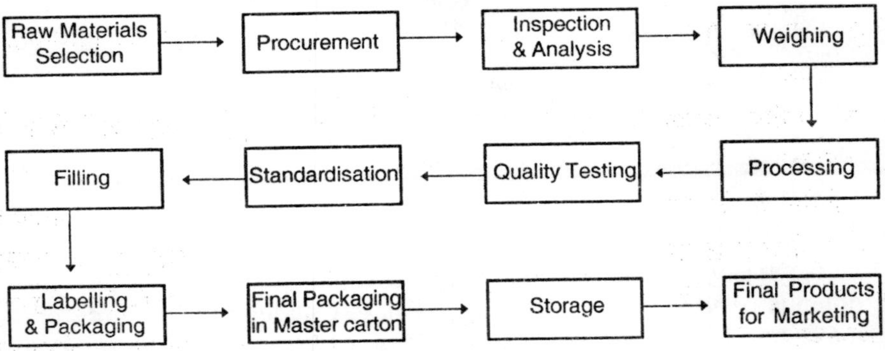

Plant & Machineries Require :-

1. Planetary Mixer with Stainless Steel body and stirrer.
2. Mixing Vessel (S.S.made) with stirrer fitted with electric heating system.
3. Water de-ionisation unit.
4. Stainless steel melting vessel.
5. Automatic or semi-automatic tube weighing, filling and sealing machine.
6. Automatic or semi-automatic jar weighing filling and sealing machine.
7. Semi-automatic labeling machine .
8. Semi-automatic Carton sealing and strapping machine.
9. Laboratory Testing equipments.
10. Weighing balance, weights & others.

9

Jojoba Body Scrub

Introduction :-

Jojoba Body Scrub is a nutrient rich skincare cosmetic product. This product is used to cleanse the body skin, to cleanse the pores of skin, remove dead skin, skin flakes, blemishes, wrinkles etc. It rejuvenates the skin, soothes, moisturizes and softens the skin textures. When it is applied and rubbed on the skin it removes the skin debris, refresh the skin, cause tightening sensations to the body skin. The skin becomes smooth and soften. The product has natural skin nourishing component which energize, rejuvenate and refresh the skin by giving it a young look. The jojoba seed powder provides good abrasive action, whereas jojoba oil soothes, moisturizes and soften the skin by maintaining its natural flexibility. The product has very good cosmetic as well as ayurvedic therapeutic value. It contains bees wax which also act as emollient. Jojoba Body Scrub is rich in protein which enters in the skin layer and removes the nutrition deficiency.

The product is gaining momentum in the international market. The demand of natural product is rising day by day both in domestic as well as overseas market.

The publicity and advertisement in TV channels, cable networks, national and internal newspapers, magazines, journals, beauty news and in other news papers is raising its demand all over the world.

A new entrepreneur or industrialist can manufacture and market the product with good brand name, excelient packaging and strategic marketing network to earn good profit.

The quality product and beautiful packaging is the main criteria to market the product all over the world.

Properties of a Good Quality Jojoba Body Scrub :-

A good quality Jojoba Body Scrub has following properties.

1. It is smooth in texture, non-irritating, non-allergenic, non-toxic in nature.
2. It is ecologically and biologically safe for human application.
3. It rejuvenates and refresh the skin of face and body.
4. It removes skin debris, dirts, dusts, black heads from face and body skin.

5. Its ingredients soothens and retain moisture of the skin to maintain glow and flexibility.

Uses and Applications:-

1. The Jojoba Body Scrub is used to shine the face skin and body skin.
2. It is used by women, ladies, girls to look beautiful and cute.
3. It is used in beauty parlours, men's parlours, Spa clubs etc.
4. It is used by girls, ladies on special occasion for beautiful look and appearance.
5. It give pleasant skin tightening sensation to women in between 30-50 years age.
6. The product is used by every female, housewife, office going ladies and other beauty conscious women, fashionable models, film actresses and others.

B.I.S. Specification:-

There is no such B.I.S. specification available on "Jojoba Body Scrub" with Bureau of Indian standards. But the product can be tested as per the cosmetics norms prior to selling in the market.

Government Regulations :-

"Jojoba Body Scrub" is a Cosmetic product which come under Drug & Cosmetic Rules 1945.

To manufacture "Jojoba Body Scrub" the manufacturer has to apply to the licensing authority appointed by the State Government in Form 31 (if the manufacturer wants to manufacture products for sale or distribution) or Form -31A (if the manufacture wants loan license to manufacture cosmetic product).

Raw Materials Require and its Availability :-

To manufacture the Jojoba Body Scrub, the raw materials require are named as Stearic Acid, Cetyl Alcohol, Bees Wax, Emulsifying Wax, Sorbitol, Triethanol amine, Purified Water, Jojoba Seed Powder, Preservative, Jojoba Oil, Colour, Perfume, Herbal Extracts and Laboratory testing chemicals. All raw materials are awailable in India.

The packaging materials require are HDPE/PET Jars, Laminated Aluminium Seals, Caps, Labels, Printed Mini paper Cartons, Corrugated card board boxes, Self adhesive tapes, Box straps etc.

These raw materials and packaging materials are indigenously available and can be procured from near by available local sources.

Jojoba Body Scrub

Formulation :-

Ingredients	-	*Parts by Weight*
Stearic Acid	-	3-4
Cetyl Alcohol	-	1-2

Bees Wax	-	4-5
Emulsifying Wax	-	0.5-1
Sorbitol	-	4-5
Triethanol amine	-	0.5-1
Purified Water	-	to make 100
Jojoba Seed Powder	-	2-3
Preservative	-	0.3-0.5
Jojoba Oil	-	1-2
Colour	-	q.s.
Perfume	-	0.1-0.5
		100

Manufacturing Process :-

To manufacture good standard quality Jojoba Body Scrub, the manufacturers are suggested to proceed the following processing steps.

1. Procure all the raw materials from good reputed dealer or suppliers.
2. Analyse and test all the raw materials for purity and good quality.
3. Weigh all the raw materials as specified in the formulation.
4. In a stainless steel vessel fitted with S. S. Stirrer, heat and melt Stearic acid, Cetyl alcohol, Bees wax, Emulsifying wax at 70°C with stirring and mixing thoroughly to a homogenize fatty phase.
5. In a stainless steel planetary mixer heat Sorbitol, Triethanolamine, Purified Water at 70°C with mixing and dissolving thoroughly.
6. Now, add the step-4 preparations to step-5 preparations and mix thoroughly till an uniform emulsion is obtained.
7. Then add jojoba seed powder (coarse) to the step-6 preparations. Mix it till uniform for 10-15 minutes.
8. In another stainless steel vessel add preservative in a little portion of purified water, warm it to dissolve the preservative completely.
9. Add the step-8 preparations to step-7 preparations with mixing thoroughly till uniform.
10. Then at 35°C add the jojoba oil, perfume and colour solution one by one till a final uniform product is obtained.
11. The final jojoba body scrub is quality tested and standardized.
12. The finished product is now packed in jars, sealed, capped, labelled and batch coded.
13. The finished jars are now packed in mini printed cartons and then packed in corrugated cartons. It is sealed with adhesive tapes and box strapped.
14. The cartons are stored and marketed to the desired distributors or dealers.

Process Flowsheet For Manufacturing of Jojoba Body Scrub

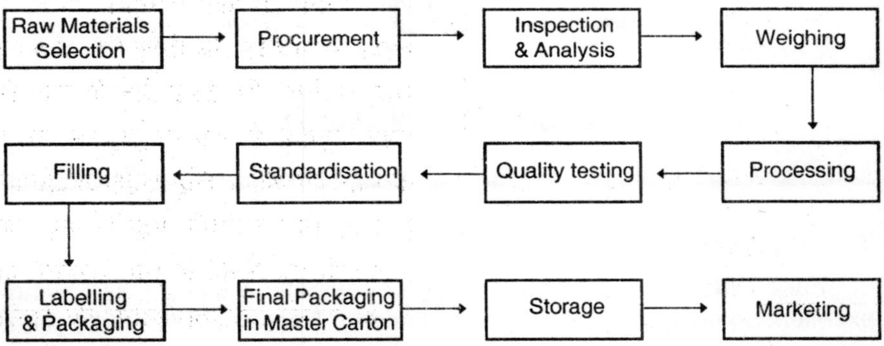

Plant & Machineries Requirement :-

1. Powder mixing unit or blender.
2. Stainless steel vessel fitted with S.S. Stirrer, motor etc.
3. Stainless steel vessels.
4. Planetary mixer with S. S. bowls.
5. Weighing balance.
6. Water heater.
7. Paste filling machine for jars.
8. Mouth Sealing machine.
9. Labeling and batch coding machine.
10. Box strapping machines.
11. Laboratory equipments, Glasswares and accessories.

10

Face Wash

Introduction:-

Face Wash is one of the important cosmetic preparations having excellent domestic and international demand. The product is mostly used in the middle and upper segments of society. Face wash is a mild product and is used to cleanse the face skin without any irritation or allergy. The product removes the dirt, dust, grease, oils, skin debris and cleanse the face with mild action by imparting fresh feeling to the user. The product is used by people of all categories. It is now used in every star hotels, restaurants, Spa-clubs, beauty parlours, houses, homes in large quantities. The beauty conscious male and female, fashionable models, actors and actresses, film stars, business men, high class executives, high profile ladies, girls mostly use it.

The product is now manufactured and marketed by a number companies in India as well as in other Countries. The product is gaining rapid demand all over the world. To add a new range in their cosmetics category, an existing or new industrialists and entrepreneurs can proceed to manufacture this product with different fragrance and in different colours.

Properties of Good Quality Face Wash:-

The Face Wash of good standard quality has following properties and characteristics.

1. It is mild towards skin and have good foam stability.
2. It is free from bacteria or pathogenic micro-organisms.
3. It is ecologically safe and biodegradable.
4. It is harmless, non-toxic and non- irritating in nature.
5. It has very mild perfumes, and mild in action.
6. It passes through all cosmetic norms before marketing the products.

Uses and Applications :-

1. Face Wash is used in every family who can afford to purchase it.
2. It is used to cleanse the face to remove dirt, dead skins, black heads, dusts, oil from face skin.
3. It is used by almost all the family who are health and beauty conscious.

4. It is used in five star hotels, Spa-clubs, beauty parlours by every females and males for fresh feeling.

B. I. S. Specification:-

There is no B.I.S. specification available on "Face Wash" with Bureau of Indian standards. However it should pass through cosmetic quality testing norms to obtain good quality product.

Government Regulations :-

Face Wash is a cosmetic product which come under Drug & cosmetic Rules 1945.

To manufacture Face Wash, the manufacturers have to apply to the licensing authority appointed by the State Government in Form-31 (if the manufacturer wants to manufacture products for sale or distribution).

Raw Materials Require and its Availability :-

The major raw materials require for manufacturing of Face wash are named as Sodium Lauryl Ether Sulphate, Cocodiethanolamide, Cocobetaine, Propylene Glycol, Citric acid, Sodium chloride, Laboratory chemicals. packaging materials etc.

These raw materials and packaging materials are indigenously available and can be procured from nearbylocal available sources.

FACE WASH (Transparent Clear)

Formulation :-

Ingredients		Parts by weight
Sodium Lauryl Ether Sulphate	-	30-34
Cocodiethanolamide	-	2-5
Cocobetaine	-	3-5
Propylene Glycol	-	2-4
Citric Acid	-	0.2-0.75
Sodium Chloride	-	1-3
Purified Water	-	to make 100
Preservative	-	0.2-0.75
Colour (Water Soluble dye)	-	q.s.
Perfumes or Fragrances	-	q.s.
		100

Manufacturing Process :-

For manufacturing good quality Face Wash the processing steps are required to be operated as follow:-

1. The raw materials are procured from good reputed suppliers.
2. All the raw materials are inspected and quality tested in laboratory.

3. The raw materials are now weighed in the specified quantity as mentioned in the formulation.
4 Now, in a jacketed stainless steel vessel fitted with stirrer, pour SLES, Cocodiethanolamide, Cocobetaine and purified water. Stir well to dissolve all the ingredients homogeneously.
5 In another stainless steel vessel pour Propylene Glycol and preservative. Heat it to 70-80°C on a gas burner to dissolve the preservative in the propylene Glycol.
6 Now, add this preservative solution (step-5) to the (step-4) solution with continuous stirring to homogenize the product.
7 In another Vessel dissolve Citric acid in little quantity of water and add dropwise to (step-6) liquid with continuous stirring till its pH is obtained in between 6-7.
8 Now, in another vessel dissolve Sodium chloride in water to prepare the salt solution. This salt solution is now added dropwise with stirring to the (step-7) liquid. It will start to thicken. The addition is carried on till desired viscosity is obtained.
9 Now, add mild perfume in little quantity to the finished product of (step-8) with homogeneous stirring and mixing to obtain final Face Wash.
10 The final Face Wash is quality tested and standardized.
11 The Face Wash is now filled in the desired size bottles of 50ml, 100ml, 200ml, 500ml etc. and mouth is sealed by semi-automatic sealing machine.
12 The bottles are now labelled and sealed with heat shrink film by heat shrink sealing machine.
13 These bottles are now packed in corrugated cartons of desired number and size as per customers demand.
14 The cartons are now sealed by adhesive tapes and then box strapped.
15 The final packed Face Wash is now placed in store and marketed to the desired customers.

Process Flowsheet For Manufacturing of Face Wash

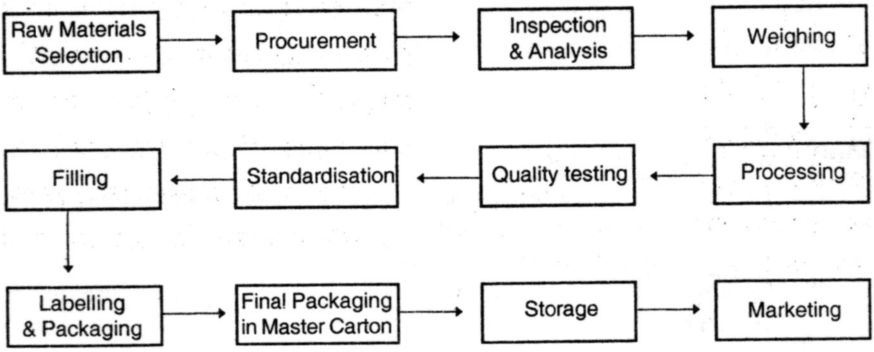

Plant and Machineries Require :-

1. Weighing balance.
2. Stainless steel jacketed vessel with S.S. Stirrer.
3. Stainless steel vessel with stirrer.
4. Gas burner with cylinders.
5. Laboratory equipment and Glasswares.
6. Bottle Filling & sealing Unit.
7. Labelling machine.
8. Shrink wrapping machine.
9. Cartons sealing & box strapping machine.
10. Miscellaneous equipments.

Note : All above plant and equipments are available in India. For getting these, the suppliers addresses are provided at the end of the book.

11

Liquid Bindi (Kum Kum) or Body Spot

Introduction :-

Liquid Bindi (Kum Kum) is an important variety of colour cosmetics coming under decorative colour cosmetics category. The product does not have any sorts of direct benefit on the body. But it is exclusively used on the forehead by married women to indicate that they are married. The red coloured liquid Bindi is mostly used by Indian married women. Which indicates the religious purity and symbolizes their social obligation towards married life. The married woman find the liquid bindi as the symbol of their husband living in this world, whatever their cast or their religion may be. But, in foreign Countries the Liquid Bindi (kum kum) does not have any such social or moral value, rather it is considered as a simple decorative cosmetics. The foreign ladies use various different coloured liquid bindi by matching with their dresses or garments. They do not have any social importance, religious considerations, moral obligations or any sorts of social boundations. In India different coloured Liquid Bindi (Kum Kum) are used by unmarried or virgin girls, college going girls or office going females. But the married ladies use only red coloured liquid bindi to maintain their chastity, social value in Indian Society.

The market demand of this product is rising day by day with social consciousness, beauty consciousness among women of every societies. The domestic market demand is rising at a rapid pace with rise in population and moral consciousness.

A new small entrepreneur can manufacture and market this product in every part of our country to earn excellent profit.

There are several manufacturers, who are manufacturing and marketing this product in unorganised tiny scale sector. But, there exists a huge demand potential in every part of our country.

(Properties of a Good Quality Liquid Bindi (Kum Kum) or Body Spots :-

1. The liquid bindi is non-toxic, non-irritating, non-allergenic in characteristics.
2. It dries quickly after application.
3. It is washable with water.
4. It does not leave any stains on the forehead after washing.

5. It is formulated in different shades in different colours.
6. The product does not react with any type of skin.

Uses and Applications :-

1. Liquid Bindi (Kum Kum) in red colour is used by every married Indian lady, whose husband is alive.
2. Different coloured liquid Bindi is used by unmarried girls to look beautiful. They are using the liquid bindi by matching with their sarees or dresses to decorate themselves.
3. It is used by females, whether housewives or working ladies.

B.I. S. Specification :-

There is no B. I.S. Specification available on "Liquid Bindi (Kum Kum)" with Bureau of Indian Standards. But it can be tested by Cosmetics norms.

Government Regulation :-

"Liquid Bindi (Kum Kum)" is a Cosmetic product which come under Drug & Cosmetic Rules 1945.

To manufacture "Liquid Bindi (Kum Kum)" the manufacturer has to apply to the licensing authority appointed by the State Government in Form-31 (if the manufacturer wants to manufacture products for sale or distribution) or Form -31 A, (if the manufacture wants loan license to manufacture cosmetic product.).

Raw Materials Require and its Availability :-

To manufacture a Liquid Bindi (Kum Kum) the raw materials require are named as Veegum (Magnesium Aluminium Silicate), PolyVinyl Pyrollidone (PVP K-30), Pigments (Non Toxic), Purified water, Preservative and laboratory testing Chemicals.

The packaging materials require are glass or plastic bottles with plastic brush fitted caps, corrugated small boxes, corrugated master cartons, self adhesive tapes, box straps. The raw materials and packaging materials are indigenously available and can be procured from nearby available sources.

Liquid Bindi (Kum Kum) or Liquid Body Spots

Formulation :-

Ingredients		Parts by Weight
Veegum (Magnesium Aluminium Silicate)	-	1-2
Polyvinyl Pyrollidone (PVP K-30)	-	1-2
Pigments (Non toxic)	-	9-10
Purified Water	-	to make 100
Preservative	-	0.2-0.5
		100

Manufacturing Process :-

To manufacture good standard quality Liquid Bindi (Kum Kum), the manufacturers are suggested to proceed the following processing steps.

1. Procure good quality raw materials from reputed dealers/ suppliers.
2. Weigh all the ingredients as specified in the formulation.
3. In a stainless steel vessel fitted with S.S. Stirrer add veegum and water with constant stirring to dissolve the veegum completely until smooth and free of visible particle.
4. Dissolve Polyvinyl Pyrollidone in little quantity of water in another S. S. Vessel with mild heating.
5. Add PVP solution to veegum solution and mix until uniform.
6. Then add pigment into the solution and mix homogeneously.
7. Now, add preservative and mix till homogeneous.
8. The final product is quality tested and standardised.
9. The liquid Bindi is now filled in plastic bottles of size 10ml, 15ml or 20ml size bottles.
10. The bottles are then packed in small cartons and then in big cartons.
11. It is now placed in store and marketed.

Process Flowsheet for`Manufacturing of Liquid Bindi (Kum Kum) or Body Spot

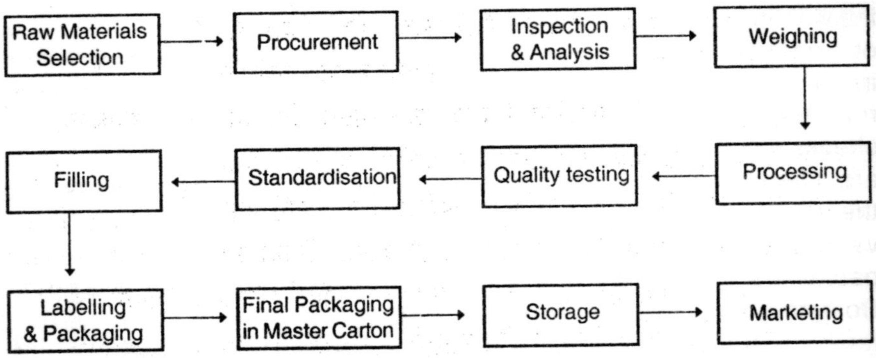

Plant & Machineries Require :-

1. Stainless Steel Vessel fitted with S.S. Stirrer, motor and accessories.
2. Stainless steel tank.
3. Tripple roller mill.
4. Bottle filling tanks.
5. Laboratory equipments & Glasswares.
6. Miscellaneous tools, jigs, fixtures.

12

Tooth Paste (Gel Type)

Introduction :-

Tooth Paste (Gel Type) is a type of dentifrice product categorised into oral care cosmetics product. It is used to clean the teeth by removing adherent soiling matter from the hard teeth surface with minimal damage to that surface. The mild surface active agent present in the tooth paste aid in the penetration and removal of the adherent film and helps to suspend removed soiling matter. The foam produced also effect in making tooth cleaning more pleasurable. The gel type tooth paste has aesthetic appeal in the mouth due to its flavouring and sweetening ingredients. This tooth paste is now formulated with various modern ingredients which not only helps cleaning of food debris but also makes the teeth free from bacteria, bad smells and make feel pleasant by cooling effect. The teeth becomes white and shiny due to cleaning as well as bleaching action of surface active agents and oxidising agents. It enhance the whitening effect on the teeth . This gel type tooth paste helps removal of fermentable debris from the mouth, reduce bacterial activity, increase in the resistance to tooth attack. This tooth paste plays an important role in prevention of oral diseases by providing good oral hygiene. It checks formation of plaque, inflammation of gums, foul smelling. There are different types of transparent gel type tooth pastes now available in the market in different colours viz. Red, blue, green, lemon yellow with various flavours and provides cooling to the mouth. These types of tooth pastes are now manufactured and marketed by Hindustan Lever ltd, Colgate and others. The gel type tooth paste market is growing at a rapid pace all over the world due to aesthetic appeal it provides to the teeth. The teeth becomes white and shiny. It is a life time asset for every human being. So people should use good tooth paste to maintain the oral hygiene throughout their life.

Requirement of Good Quality Gel Type Transparent Tooth Paste :-

1. When used properly, it clean the teeth adequately by removing food debris, plaque and stains.
2. It leave the mouth with fresh, clean sensation.
3. Its cost is moderate to encourage regular and frequent use by all.
4. It is harmless pleasant and convenient to use.

5. It is packed economically and is stable during its commercial shelf life.
6. It conform to ISI standards.
7. If prophylactic claims are made, these should be substantiated by properly conducted clinical trials.
8. It is easily dispensable though plastic collapsible tubes.

Properties of Good Quality Gel Type Tooth Paste :-

1. The gel type tooth paste has sufficient teeth cleansing power.
2. The product has good mouth feel during and after its application.
3. It is harmless, non-irritating and non-toxic in nature.
4. It do not contain any sorts of abrasive.
5. The product has good flavour, cooling effect and anti-bacterial action.

Uses and Applications :-

1. It is used to cleanse the teeth, to remove fouling smeli from mouth.
2. It can be used by men, women and children.

B.I.S. Specification :-

This Gel Type Tooth Paste is passed through the testing norms as mentioned in IS-6356-Tooth paste.

Government Regulation :-

"Gel Type Tooth Paste" is a cosmetic product which come under Drug & cosmetic Rules. 1945.

To manufacture, "Gel type Tooth Paste" the manufacturers have to apply to the licensing authority appointed by the State Government in Form-31 (if the manufacturer wants to manufacture products for sale or distribution).

Tooth Paste (Transparent Gel type)

Formulation-

Ingredients		*Parts by weight*
Carbopol-940	-	0.2 - 0.25
Glycerine	-	10-12
Purified water	-	q. s. to make 100
Sodium Saccharine	-	0.2-0.5
Sodium Lauryl Sulphate	-	8-12
Sodium Hydroxide (10% Solution)	-	5-7
Flavour (Lemon or other)	-	0.2-0.5
Colour (Red, Blue, Lemon Yellow, Green)	-	0.1-0.5
Peppermint oil	-	0.5 - 1
		100

Manufacturing Process :-

To manufacture good quality transparent gel type Tooth Paste the manufacturers should proceed the following processing steps.

1. Procure all the raw materials from market or from reputed dealer.
2. Analyse and test all the raw materials before sending into process.
3. Weigh all the ingredients as specified in the formulation.
4. In a stainless steel closed tank fitted with S.S. Stirrer and vacuum pump pour glycerine, Carbopol-940, Purified water and heat it to 60-70°C with constant stirring.
5. In another S.S. Vessel prepare the colour solution by mixing the colour with little water till an uniform solution is produced. Now, add this colour solution to step-4 preparations with constant stirring.
6. In another S.S.vessel prepare sodium saccharine solution by dissolving sodium saccharine in purified water. Now, add this sodium saccharine solution to the step-5 preparations.
7. Now, cool step-6 preparations to 40°C then add the Sodium Lauryl Sulphate and Sodium Hydroxide solution one by one with slow stiring to avoid any formation of air bubble inside the product. The product is mixed and deaerated by vaccum pump to expel out all the bubbles from it.
8. To this deaerated product add peppermint oil and flavour with slow stirring to obtain the uniform product.
9. This final gel type tooth paste is quality tested, packed in tubes and outer cartons and then in the master carton.
10. The final product is placed in store and marketed to the desired customers.

Process Flowsheet For Manufacturing of Tooth Paste (Gel Type)

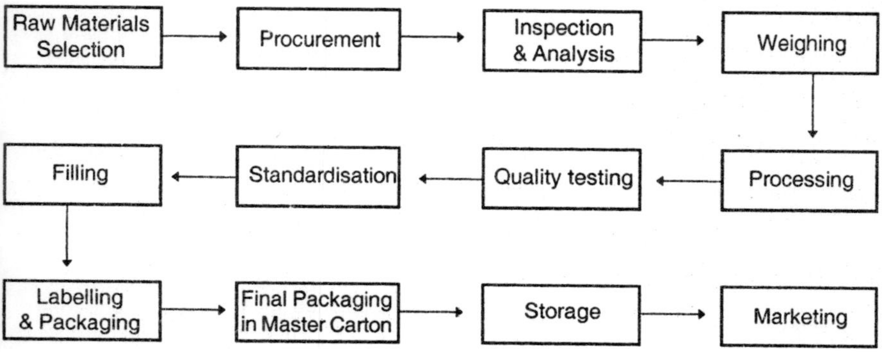

Plant & Machineries Require :-

1. Stainless steel tanks fitted with S.S.Stirrer, heating jacket, vacuum pump, motor, accessories.
2. Stainless steel tank with stirrer.
3. Weighing scale.
4. Tube filling and sealing machine.
5. Cardboard packaging machine.
6. Batch coding machine.
7. Carton strapping machine.
8. Laboratory equipments & Glasswares.
9. Tools, Jigs, fixtures etc.

Note : Capacity and size of the project may vary according to the entrepreneur requirements. Entrepreneur may contact 'EIRI' office for further details of this project.

13

Nail Polish Or Nail Enamel With Pearlescent Pigments

Introduction

Nail Enamels or Nail Polish are commonly used terminology for nail lacquer. The largest and most important group of manicure preparations is that of nail enamel or nail lacquer. Nail enamel with pearlescent pigment is innovation in the nail enamel formulations and preparations. The pearlescent pigments suspensions available in the market are procured and mixed in the formulation along with colour pigments or dyes dispersions to prepare the nail enamel into various desired shades with glossy shiny effect. The product raises the beauty and glamour of the famale multi folded.

It has been found that, in addition to the general conventional pigments, nail enamel can be incorporated with iridescent materials pearlessence pigment which is Guanine (2-Amino-6-hydroxy purine) a crystalline substances isolated from the scales or body or various fish. In its pure form it is non toxic. It has a high refractive index-1.8. Its pearly lustre and brilliance are due to the simultaneous reflection of light both from the upper layers of its transparent crystals and from the crystal planes at different depths, secondly to the alignment of crystals in the same direction, made possible by their shape and depend on the degree of dispersions of the crystals in the lacquer. Natural pearl essence is commercially available in the form of the suspension in a nitrocellulose-butyl acetate lacquer at a level of about 11 per cent and is used in clear or pigmented nail enamel at a concentration of between 8 and 10 percent. Besides, there are synthetic pearl pigments available in the market which are chemically known as Bismuth oxychloride, another one is mica coated with titanium dioxide. The nail enamel with pearlescent pigments provides lustrous shiny coating on nails and decorate the nails beautiful.

The various lustrous shades of nail polishes are manufactured and marketed by a number of companies for the global female customers to make them more beautiful and gorgeous. At present, international cosmetics brand leaders L'oreal, Revlon, Lakme and others have revolutionised world cosmetics markets with various innovative nail enamels with their continuous R & D efforts to prepare the worldclass products. The high profile fashion and beauty conscious girls, ladies, women are prefering their products more and more due to the best quality and best packaging materials they are using in their products for global markets. The market is expanding day by day, new products are immediately finding places among the females. A new entrepreneur with sound technology, good quality finished products and in descent packaging can enter in the market without any trouble to earn good profit.

Requirement of Good Nail Enamel with Pearlescent Pigments :-

A good Nail Enamels or Nail Polish fulfil the following requirements.

1. It is easy and convenient to apply.
2. It is innocuous to the skin and nails.
3. It is stable on storage as regards homogeneity, separation, sedimentation, Colour and interaction of ingredients.
4. It give a film of satisfactory characteristics.
5. It is non-toxic, non-irritating in nature and ecologically safe.

The Characteristics of Good Nail Enamel with Pearlescent Pigments :-

1. The Nail Enamels or Nail Polish film is even in thickness.
2. The Nail Enamels or Nail Polish film is uniform in colour means pigments uniformly dispersed in the medium.
3. The enamel film has good gloss, it implies a smooth uniform shiny film over nail.
4. It has good adhesion to the nail.
5. It has sufficient flexibility to avoid brittleness and cracking.
6. It is hard, non-tacky surface, resistant to impact and scratching.
7. The nail enamel film dry in 1-2 minutes without development of bloom in humid atmosphere.

Uses and Applications :-

1. Nail Enamels or Nail Polish are available in various shades depending on the choice of females and matching with their dresses or sarees. It is used to decorate their nails of hands and foots.
2. The fashionable beauty conscious girls, ladies, women use nail enamel during all the social function.
3. It is one of the largest and most important manicure preparations.
4. This products is highly used in beauty parlours, beauty salons, to decorate the nails.

B.I.S. Specification :-

There is no such B.I.S. Specification available on "Nail Enamels or Nail Polish" but the product is tested as per the cosmetics norms.

Government Regulations :-

"Nail Enamels or Nail Polish" is a cosmetic product which come under Drug & cosmetic Rules. 1945.

To manufacture, "Nail Enamels or Nail Polish" the manufacturers have to apply to the licensing authority appointed by the State Government in Form-31 (if the manufacturer wants to manufacture products for sale or distribution).

Raw Materials Reguirement and its Availability :-

The major raw materials require are Nitro Cellulose, Resin, Plasticisers, Solvents, Pigment or dyes dispersions, diluents etc. Besides, there are packaging materials such as glass bottles or vials, caps fitted with small brush, corrugated small boxes, corrugated cartons etc.

Nail Enamel with Pearlessence Pigment

Formulation ;-

Ingredients		***Parts by weight***
Part A:-		
Nitrocellulose ((1/2) second viscosity)	-	8-10
Aryl Sulfonamide - Formaldehyde Resin (Santolite MHP)	-	8-10
Plasticiser (Santiciser S or 160)(Dibutyl Phthalate)	-	3-5
Ethyl Alcohol	-	4-5
Ethyl Acetate	-	18-20
Butyl Acetate	-	15-17
Toluene	-	to make 100
		100
Part B :-		
Pigments or Dyes dispersions (D & C Red 6, 30, 36; FD & C Yellow 5, 6 etc.)	-	4-5
Pearlessence Pigment Suspension	-	8-10

Manufacturing Process :-

To prepare a standard quality Nail Enamel with Pearlessence Pigment, a manufacturer should proceed following processing steps.

1. Procure all the raw materials from reputed suppliers.
2. Analyse all the ingredients as per cosmetic grades specification.
3. Weigh all the ingredients as specified in the formulation.
4. In a closed stainless steel vessel fitted with S.S. Stirrer and flameproof motor, feed the Nitrocellulose and solvent mixture of Ethyl Alcohol, Ethyl Acetate, Butyl Acetate, Toluene and keep on slow stirring for 3-5 days till Nitrocellulose is completely dissolved in solvent.

5. The Nitrocellulose solution is filtered and to it add the Santolite MHP resin and again mix homogeneously with slow stirring. Then to this resin liquid, add the DiButyl Phthalate plasticizer with slow stirring for 2-3 hours till a homogeneous lacquer is formed.
6. To this transparent lacquer add the pigment dispersion or dye dispersion as per desired shades required to be sent in the market. The product is stirred for 4-6 hours till completely mixed and no particles are seen in the final product.
7. The final Nail Enamel is now quality tested and standardized to the requisite viscosity.
8. The final Nail Enamel is now packed in small glass bottle of sizes 5ml, 10ml, 15ml, 20ml as desired by customers.
9. The bottles are packed in small boxes of 12 Nos, 24 Nos. The boxes are now further packed in the outer corrugated cartons and strapped.
10. The cartons are placed in store and marketed to the desired customers.

Process Flowsheet For Manufacturing of Nail Polish or Nail Enamel with Pearlescent Pigment

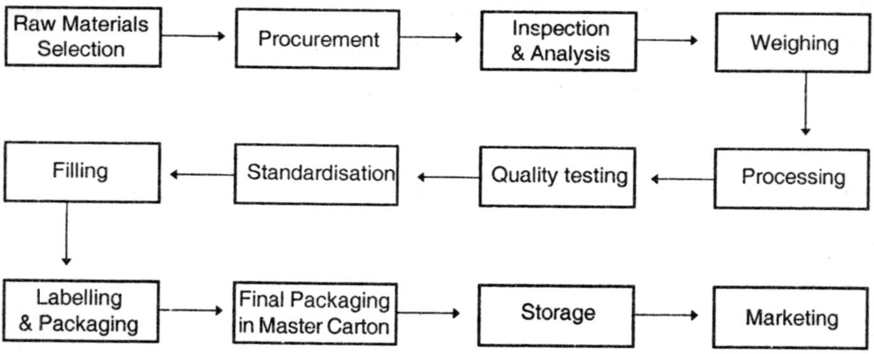

Plant & Machineries Require :-

1. Stainless steel closed top tank fitted with S.S. Stirrer, flame proof motor and accessories.
2. Weighing balance.
3. Stainless steel tanks.
4. Filling tanks (S.S. - 316 Made).
5. Laboratory Equipments and glasswares.
6. Tools & fire safety equipments.

14

Face Pack (Anti-Wrinkle)

Introduction :-

Face Pack (antiwrinkle) is a Cosmetic product coming in skincare category. The product after prolong application reduces and eliminates wrinkle from the face skin.

The face packs are basically applied on the face in the form of liquids or pastes. They are allowed to dry or to set with the object of improving the appearance of the skin by producing a transient tightening effect as well as by cleansing the skin. The warmth and tightening effect resulting from their application produce the stimulating sensation of rejuvenated face, while the colloidal and absorptive clays and earth present in some packs will absorb grease and dirt from the facial skin. When they are eventually removed from the face, skin debris and black heads may be removed simultaneously.

Now a days, number of active ingredients are added to have a variety of effect on the skin such as deep cleansing, Stimulation, Astringency, Hydration, Rejuvenation etc. The product has high demand all over the world.

Properties of A Good Quality Anti-Wrinkle Face Pack :-

1. It should be a smooth paste without gritty particles and without an earthy or objectionable odour.
2. Applied to the face it should dry out rapidly to form an adherent coating on the skin, but this coating should be capable of subsequently being removed either by peeling off the face or by gentle washing without any pain.
3. It should produce a definite sensation of tightening of the skin after application.
4. It should produce a significant cleansing of the skin.
5. It must be dermatologically innocuous and non-toxic.
6. The pH of final preparation is maintained within 5-7 range.

Uses and Applications :-

1. The Anti-Wrinkle Face Pack is used to eliminate wrinkle, control wrinkle formation and check the wrinkles to appear on regular uses on the face.

2. It is used by both women and men to rejuvenate and make the skin texture smooth, wrinkle free.
3. The product is used in beauty parlours, houses, homes by every women to maintain their beauty and look.
4. The product is used to remove skin debris, dead cells, black heads and refresh it by maintaining the flexibility of the skin.

B.I.S. Specification :-

There is no such B.I.S. Specification available on "Anti-Wrinkle Face Pack" with Bureau of Indian standards. But the product should pass through cosmetics permitted standards applicable over human skins.

Government Regulation :-

Anti-Wrinkle Face Pack is a Cosmetic product which falls under Drug & Cosmetic Rules, 1945.

To manufacture Anti-Wrinkle Face Pack the manufacturer has to apply to the licensing authority appointed by the State Government in Form-31 (if the manufacturer wants to manufacture product for sale or distribution) or Form -31A, (if the manufacture wants loan license to manufacture cosmetic product.).

Raw Materials Require & its Availability :-

The raw materials require to manufacture the Anti-Wrinkle Face Pack are named as Sodium Carboxy Methyl Cellulose, Glycerine, Isopropyl Myristate, Triethanolamine, Glycollic Acid, Purified Water, Polyethylene Glycol-400, Propylene Glycol, Unitrienol T-27, Preservative, Perfume, Colour, Herbal Extracts and Laboratory testing chemicals.

The packaging materials require are HDPE/PET Jars, Laminated Aluminium Seals, Caps, Labels, Shrink wrap films, Mini paper cartons, Corrugated cardboard boxes, Self adhesive tapes, Box straps etc. The raw materials and packaging materials are indigenously available and can be procured from nearby available local sources.

Anti-Wrinkle Face Pack

Formulation :-

Ingredients		*Parts by Weight*
Sodium Carboxy Methyl Cellulose	-	2-3
Glycerine	-	2-3
Isopropyl Myristate	-	4-5
Triethanolamine	-	0.5-1
Glycollic Acid	-	0.1-0.4
Purified Water	-	to make 100
Polyethylene Glycol-400	-	3-4

Propylene Glycol	-	2-3
UNITRIENO LT-27	-	2-3
Preservative	-	0.3-0.7
Perfume	-	0.1-0.5
Colour	-	q.s.
		100

Manufacturing Process :-

To manufacture good standard quality Anti-Wrinkle Face Pack, it is suggested to proceed the following processing steps.

1 Procure all the raw materials from good reputed dealers or suppliers.
2. Analyse and test all the raw materials for purity and good quality.
3. Weigh all the raw materials specified in the formulation.
4. In a stainless steel vessel mix Sodium Carboxy Methyl Cellulose in a portion of purified water and stire to mix thoroughly.
5. In another stainless steel planetary mixer heat Glycerine, Isopropyl Myristate, Triethanolamine, Glycollic Acid, Purified Water at 70°C and mix it thoroughly till uniform.
6. In a stainless steel vessel heat PEG-400, Propylene Glycol, UNITRIENOL T-27 at 70°C with mixing and stirring thoroughly.
7. Now, add step-6 preparations to step-5 preparations with mixing thoroughly till the complete emulsified mass is cooled to 45°C.
8. In another stainless steel vessel dissolve Preservative in a little portion of water with warming and mixing thoroughly.
9. Add the step-8 Preservative solution to step-7 preparations and mix it thoroughly. Then add the step-4 preparations to it with uniform mixing and stirring thoroughly.
10. Add perfumes and colour solutions one by one to step-9 preparations and mix it thoroughly.
11. The final Anti-Wrinkle Face Pack is now quality tested and standardized.
12. The product is now packed in HDPE Jars, sealed by laminated Aluminium seals, capped, labelled, batch coded. It is then packed in printed mini cartons and then further packed in Corrugated cardboard boxes.
13. The Cartons are sealed and box strapped. Then it is placed in store and marketed to the desired customers, dealers and distributors.

Process Flowsheet For Manufacturing of Herbal Anti-Wrinkle Face Pack

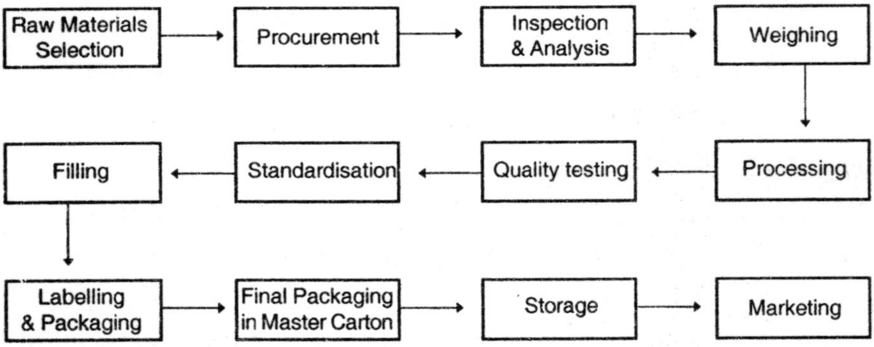

Plant & Machineries Requirement :-

1. Weighing balance & weights
2. S. S. Vessels
3. Planetary Mixer.
4. Stainless steel Jacketed mixing Vessel fitted whit S. S. Stirrer.
5. Semi-automatic Jars weighing, filling and sealing machines.
6. Labelling machine.
7. Water de-ionisation unit.
8. Carton sealing or strapping machines.
9. Laboratory testing equipments.

Note : All above plant and equipments are available in India. For getting these, the suppliers addresses are provided at the end of the book.

15

Herbal Hair Vitaliser (Anti-Dandruff)

Introduction :-

Herbal Hair Vitalizer (Anti-Dandruff) is coming under haircare category of cosmetic products. This product eliminates dandruff from the scalp and also protects the formation of dandruff further. Dandruff is basically caused by microorganism P. Ovale. Dandruff is a condition of the scalp characterized by the massive disquamation of small flakes of stratum corneum. It has been mentioned as a scaling disorder. The cause of dandruff is due to the physiological, traumatic and infective factors. Some study indicates the possible roles of hormones, metabolic faults, diet and nervous tensions, as well as inflammatory reactions to topical medicaments and cosmetics. It has found that the yeast like microorganisms P.Ovale and P.Orbiculare are common members of the scalp flora. They cause dandruff in the scalp. Dandruff results from excessive scaling of scalp, without clinical signs of inflammation. It reaches a peak in winter and eases off in summer.

The Anti-Dandruff agents added to the cosmetics preparations fulfill the following requirements.

A. It is antimicrobial, to prevent proliferation, an aggravating factor of the local disorders.

B. Keratolytic or exfoliative, to cleanse the scalp by promoting the elimination of dead skin.

The Anti-Dandruff Hair Vitalizer meet these requirements. The Anti-Dandruff Cosmetic products are highly demanded all over the world. The demand of this product is rising day by day due to rise in the dandruff problem among both women and men.

A new entrepreneur or industrialists can manufacture this product and add it to their cosmetics range to earn huge profits.

Properties of A Good Quality Anti-Dandruff Hair Vitaliser :-

1. The Anti-Dandruff Hair Vitaliser is a cosmetic preparation which keeps scalp dandruff free.
2. It is non-irritating, non-toxic, non-allergenic.
3. It do not cause any side effect on the scalp.
4. It is biologically, Clinically and environmentally safe.

5. It removes dandruff and also stops dandruff formation by causing hair healthy, shiny and lustrous.
6. It is available in both non-greasy as well as greasy form.

Uses and Applications :-

1. The Anti-Dandruff Hair Vitaliser is used by almost every people all over the world due to its medicinal, antimicrobial properties. It is effective over human scalp and hair roots.
2. It is used for a number of hair or scalp disorders.
3. It is used by women and men of all age group. It is used by young boys, girls, ladies and gents who are suffering from dandruff problem.

B. I. S. Specification :-

There is no B.I.S. specification available on "Anti-Dandruff Hair Vitaliser" with Bureau of Indian standard. However it should pass through cosmetics quality testing norms to obtain good quality product.

Government Regulation :-

Anti-Dandruff Hair Vitaliser is a cosmetfc product which falls under Drug & cosmetic Rules 1945.

To manufacture Anti-Dandruff Hair Vitaliser, the manufacturers have to apply to the licensing authority appointed by the State Government in Form-31 (if the manufacturer wants to manufacture products for sale or distribution).

Raw Materials Require & its Availability :-

The raw materials require to manufacture Anti-Dandruff Hair Vitaliser are named as Bis (2-Pyridyl-1-oxide) disulphide Soluble magnesium sulphate Complex, Camphor, Menthol, Isopropyl Alcohol (IPA), Purified Water and Laboratory testing chemicals.

The packaging materials require are HDPE or PET bottles, fliptop caps, labels, Printed Mini Cartons, Corrugated Cardboard boxes, Self adhesive tapes, Box straps.

The raw materials and packaging materials are indigenously available and can be procured from nearby available local sources.

Anti-Dandruff Hair Vitaliser

Formulation :-

Ingredients		*Parts by Weight*
Bis (2-Pyridyl-1-oxide) disulphide		
Soluble magnesium sulphate Complex	-	0.10-0.20
Camphor	-	0.05-0.15
Menthol	-	0.05-0.10
Isopropyl Alcohol (IPA)	-	40-55
Purified Water	-	to make 100
		100

Manufacturing Process :-

To manufacture a good standard quality Anti-Dandruff Hair Vitaliser, it is suggested to proceed the following processing steps.

1. Procure all the raw materials from good reputed dealers or suppliers.
2. Analyse and test all the raw materials for purity and good quality.
3. Weigh all the raw materials as specified in the formulation.
4. In a Closed stainless steel vessel fitted with S. S. Stirrer add Isopropyl Alcohol, Menthol, Camphor and dissolve it thoroughly by mixing continuously. Then add Soluble Magnesium Sulphate Complex of Bis(2-pyridyl-1-oxide) and mix it till it is dissolved in alcohol.
5. Now, add purified water to the step-4 preparations and mix it thoroughly.
6. Test the finished Anti-Dandruff Hair Vitaliser for quality and then standardize it.
7. The finished product is now packed in brown coloured bottles and seal it by stoppers and caps
8. The bottles are labelled and batch coded. These bottles are now packed in printed mini paper cartons and then further packed in corrugated cardboard boxes.
9. The Corrugated cardboard boxes are sealed with adhesive tapes and strapped with PP/HDPE straps.
10. The finished cartons are now placed in store and marketed to the desired customers, dealers and distributors.

Process Flowsheet for Manufacturing of Anti-Dandruff Hair Vitalizer

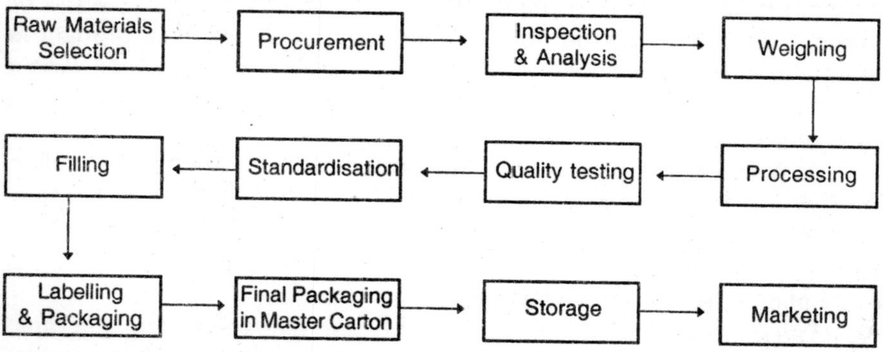

Plant & Machineries Requirement :-

1. Closed top stainless steel vessel fitted with S. S. Stirrer and flameproof motor and other accessories.
2. Weighing balance.
3. Bottles weighing filling and sealing unit.
4. Labelling and batch coding machine.
5. Laboratory equipments and glasswares.
6. Cartons strapping machine.
7. Miscellaneous tools.

16

Shaving Gel

Introduction :-

Shaving Gel is an innovative cosmetic preparations coming in the range of skincare cosmetic category. It is used for wet shaving purposes. It is used to soften the hair of beard and moustache. So that the hair can be cut easily with razor. The shaving gel can be applied on the face skin with or without brush. The product is coming in the premium range of Men's Cosmetics.

It has been seen that man tends to regard the removal each day of 20000-25000 terminal hairs protruding 300-500 micro metre from the skin at angles of 30-60°C and covering a facial area of 250cm2, as something of a chore. A wide range of preparations are now available that prepare beard and face for shaving, increase speed and comfort during the shave and confer a feeling of well being after shaving.

Now a days, this product is accepted worldwide in the premium segments of middle and upper class of societies. The rich people or executives prefer this product in their daily shavings. This product is highly consumed in houses, homes, star hotels, deluxe hotels, men's parlours, salons etc. It is preferred by every executives in metro and sub metro cities.

At present this product is manufactured and marketed by Indian Shaving Product company in the brand name Gillete. It has totally revolutionized Indian men's cosmetics market. The performance of this product is excellent. It moisturizes, lubricates the face skin giving a sensational feeling after shaving.

The domestic as well as international market is expanding at a rapid pace. It's major outlets are all the departmental stores, shopping malls, medical stores and almost every standard shops who are selling cosmetic goods.

A new entrepreneur or industrialists can launch this product with top quality packaging and excellent marketing network to earn high profit. The media publicity will create huge demand of this product all over the world.

Properties of A Good Quality Shaving Gel :-

1. Shaving Gel should be non-irritating to the skin.
2. It should retain moisture during the period it remains on the face.

3. It should soften the hair of beard and moustache to easily cut by razor.
4. It should provide sufficient lubricity so that razor glides along the face.
5. It should be stable over a wide range of temperature.
6. It should not corrode the containers in which it is packed.
7. It should be easily washed down without creating clogging problems.
8. It should be ecologically safe and should be biodegradable in nature.
9 It should be harmless, non-toxic and properly pH balanced product.

Uses and Applications :-

1. Shaving Gel is used by men while shaving to soften the beard.
2. It is used in houses, homes, star hotels, salons, men's beauty parlours by every grown up man to shave the beard.
3. It is used by almost every man who are shaving their beard and moustache.

B.I.S. Specification :-

There is no such B.I.S. Specification available on "Shaving Gel" with Bureau of Indian standards. But the product is tested as per cosmetic norms prior to selling in the market.

Government Regulation :-

Shaving Gel is a cosmetic product which falls under Drug & Cosmetic Rules, 1945

To manufacture this product, the manufacturers have to apply to the licensing authority appointed by the State Government in Form -31 (If the manufacturer wants to manufacture products for sale or distribution).

Raw Materials Require & its Availability :-

The raw materials require to manufacture a good standard quality Shaving Gel are named as Mineral Oil, Lanolin, Potassium Stearate, Glycerine, Borax, Sodium Lauryl Sulphate, Purified Water, Carbopol-934, Preservative, Propylene Glycol, Perfume or Fragrance, Colour (water soluble) and Laboratory testing chemicals.

The packaging materials require are plastic collapsible tubes, caps, printed mini paper cartons, Corrugated Cardboard boxes, Self adhesive tapes, Box straps. The raw materials and packaging materials are indigenously available and can be procured from nearby available local sources.

Shaving Gel

Formulation :-

Ingredients	-	Parts by Weight
Mineral Oil	-	1-2
Lanolin	-	0.5-1
Potassium Stearate	-	14-16
Glycerine	-	6-8
Borax	-	0.3-0.7
Sodium Lauryl Sulphate	-	1-2
Purified Water	-	to make 100
Carbopol-934	-	0.5-0.7
Preservative	-	0.3-0.7
Propylene Glycol	-	4-6
Perfume or Fragrance	-	0.1-0.5
Colour (Water Soluble)	-	q.s.
		100

Manufacturing Process :-

To manufacture good standard quality Shaving Gel, manufacturers are suggested to proceed the following processing steps.

1. Procure all the raw materials from good reputed dealers or suppliers.
2. Analyse and test all the raw materials for purity and good quality.
3. Weigh all the raw materials specified in the formulation.
4. In a stainless steel vessel dissolve carbopol-934 in a portion of purified water with mixing and stirring to prepare a homogeneous gel.
5. In another stainless steel vessel fitted with S. S. Stirrer dissolve Potassium Stearate, Glycerine, Borax, Sodium Lauryl Sulphate in purified water by mixing it thoroughly.
6. Now, add step-4 preparations to step-5 preparations in a planetary mixer and heat it to 70°C with mixing thoroughly to prepare uniform mass.
7. In another stainless steel vessel heat Mineral oil and Lanolin together at 70°C by mixing and stirring uniformly.
8. Add the step-7 preparations to step-6 preparations by mixing it thoroughly at 70°C. Then continue mixing till its temperature is reduced to 35°C.
9. In a separate stainless steel vessel dissolve preservative in Propylene Glycol by warming and mixing it thoroughly.
10. Add step-9 preservative solution to step-8 preparations and mix it uniformly.

11. Then add perfumes or fragrances and colour solutions one by one with mixing and stirring thoroughly.
12. The final shaving gel is quality tested and standardized.
13. The finished shaving gel is now filled in laminated plastic collapsible tubes. The tubes are sealed, batch coded and packed in printed mini paper cartons. These mini paper cartons are packed in corrugated master cartons. The cartons are sealed and box strapped.
14. The finished cartons are placed in store and marketed to the desired dealers, distributors or shop keepers.

Process Flow Sheet For Manufacturing of Shaving Gel

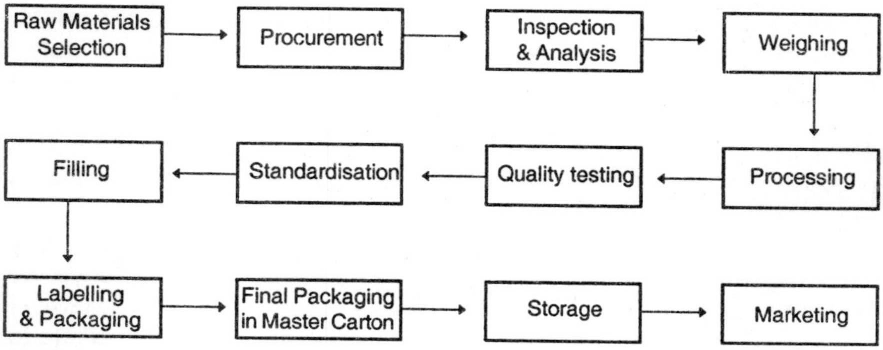

Plant & Machineries Requirement :-

1. Planetary Mixer with Stainless Steel body and stirrer.
2. Mixing Vessel (S.S.made) with stirrer fitted with electric heating system,
3. Water de-ionisation unit.
4. Stainless steel melting vessel.
5. Automatic or semi-automatic tube weighing, filling and sealing machine.
6. Semi-automatic batch coding machine.
7. Semi-automatic Carton sealing and strapping machine.
8. Laboratory Testing equipments and Glasswares.
9. Weighing balance, weights & others.

17

Moisturizer With Aloe Vera and Coconut Oil

Introduction :-

Moisturizer with Aloe Vera and Coconut oil is one of the good variety of skincare cosmetic product. The product is having medium oil content. This moisturizer is easily spreadable. It contains higher quantity of water. It is considered to be an after bath emollient. It is applied to the body with the object of replacing natural skin liquids removed during bathing. Their function is basically to prevent the occurrence of dry skin. This product is a type of oil-in-water emulsions. Generally the moisturizers are sold in lotion form and are usually formulated to give good "rub-in" and feel properties. The coconut oil serves as a good natural emollient where as Aloe Vera helps to retain and restore moisture level inside the layers of the skin.

The drying of skin take place due to two reasons. The first is due to prolonged exposure to low humidity and air movement, which modifies the normal hydration gradient of the stratum corneum. The second is due to physical or chemical changes in the skin due to processes such as aging, continual degreasing etc.

The moisturizer with Aloe Vera and Coconut oil helps to retain moisture in the skin layer due to Aloe Vera extract, where as coconut oil form an emollient film on the skin, which do not allow the moisture to escape from the skin by providing a protective film over the skin. The skin become smooth, shiny, lustrous, soft and refresh. Aloe Vera is considered to be having antiaging properties. Which cause soothing, healing and when externally applied it helps to keep the skin healthy. Oil-in-water extracts of Aloe Vera when used externally claimed to significantly increase the soluble collagen level suggesting to tropical antiaging effect. The skin looks healthy, smooth with natural beautiful appearance and texture.

This product is demanded by almost every women and men of all age group. The international demand as well as domestic demand is rising day by day at a rapid pace with rise in population and growing media publicity in every part of the world. There are very few manufacturers of this product.

A new entrepreneur or industrialist can manufacture and market this product along with other range of cosmetics with good packaging and marketing skill to earn excellent profit.

Properties of A Good Quality Moisturizer with Aloe Vera and Coconut Oil :-

1. The Moisturizer with Aloe Vera and Coconut oil is formulated with low oil content and should have high moisture retention power.
2. It should be non-irritating and non-Allergic to any type of skin.
3. It should have soothing effect over dry skin.
4. It should have appropriate water and oil balance.
5. It should be ecologically safe and biodegradable in nature.
6. The product should be formulated witn good mild fragrance and pleasant in application.
7. The product should have good viscosity and can be packed in various standard containers viz. Jars and tubes.

Uses and Applications :-

1. The Moisturizer with Aloe vera is highly used in Summer season or in winter season to retain and to restore moisture balance in the layer of the human skin.
2. It is used by both men and women of all age categories.
3. It is a mass product and is used by almost every age group male and female.
4. The aged people find it most suitable to maintain their skin texture and flexibility.
5. It is used in almost every home or houses by girls, ladies, gents, youngsters to look beautiful and healthy.

B.I.S. Specification:-

There is no such B.I.S. Specification available on "Moisturizer with Aloe Vera and Coconut oil" with Bureau of Indian standards. But, the product can be tested as per the IS-6608 - Skin Cream, norms prior to selling it in the market.

Government Regulation :-

Moisturizer with Aloe Vera and Coconut oil is a cosmetic product which falls under Drug & Cosmetic Rules, 1945.

To manufacture this product, the manufacturers have to apply to the licensing authority appointed by the State Government in Form -31 (If the manufacturer wants to manufacture products for sale or distribution).

Raw Materials Require & its Availability :-

The major raw materials require to manufacture the Moisturizer with Aloe Vera and Coconut oil are named as Coconut Oil, Stearic Acid, Isopropyl Palmitate, Propylene Glycol Monostearate, Lanolin, Triethanolamine, Glycerine, Sodium Lauryl Sulphate (SLS), Purified

Water, Aloe Vera Extract (1:1), Preservative, Perfumes or Fragrances, Colour and Laboratory testing chemicals.

The packaging materials require are HDPE Bottles, Laminated Plastic Collapsible tubes, Caps, Labels, Printed Mini outer Cartons, Corrugated Cartons, Self adhesive tapes, Box straps etc. The raw materials and packaging materials are indigenously available and can be procured from nearby available local sources.

Moisturizer with Aloe Vera and Coconut Oil

Formulation :-

Ingredients		*Parts by Weight*
Coconut Oil	-	5-6
Stearic Acid	-	4-5
Isopropyl Palmitate	-	1-2
Propylene Glycol Monostearate	-	1-2
Lanolin	-	1-2
Triethanolamine	-	1-2
Glycerine	-	1-2
Sodium Lauryl Sulphate (SLS)	-	0.1-0.4
Purified Water	-	to make 100
Aloe Vera Extract (1:1)	-	3-5
Preservative	-	0.2-0.5
Perfumes or Fragrances	-	0.1-0.5
Colour	-	q.s.
		100

Manufacturing Process :-

To manufacture good standard quality Moisturizer with Aloe Vera and Coconut Oil, it is suggested to proceed the following processing steps.

1. Procure all the raw materials from good reputed dealers or suppliers.
2. Analyse and test all the raw materials for purity and good quality.
3. Weigh all the raw materials as specified in the formulation.
4. In astainless steel vessel fitted with S. S. Stirrer heat Coconut oil, Stearic Acid, Isopropyl Palmitate, Propylene Glycol Monostearate and Lanolin to 70°C with mixing and stirring thoroughly.
5. In a stainless steel planetary mixer heat Triethanolamine, Glycerine, Sodium Lauryl Sulphate, a portion of purified water to 70°C with mixing till all the ingredients are dissolved completely.
6. Now, add step-4 preparations to step-5 preparations at 70°C till it is mixed and emulsified perfectly.

7. In another stainless steel vessel mix preservative in other portion of purified water with warming and mixing thoroughly. Add Aloe Vera extract to preservative solution and mix it thoroughly.
8. Add the step-7 preparations to the step-6 preparations at 35°C and mix it thoroughly till uniform.
9. Then add perfumes or fragrances and colour solutions one by one to Step-8 preparations till uniformly mixed.
10. Test the final moisturizer and standardize it.
11. The final moisturizer is now packed in HDPE plastic Bottles or laminated plastic collapsible tubes. The containers are sealed, batch coded and packed in printed mini cartons.
12. The mini cartons are packed in corrugated master cartons. The cartons are further sealed by self adhesive tapes and strapped.
13. The final cartons are now placed in store and marketed to the desired customers.

Process Flow Sheet For Manufacturing of Moisturizer with Aloe Vera & Coconut Oil

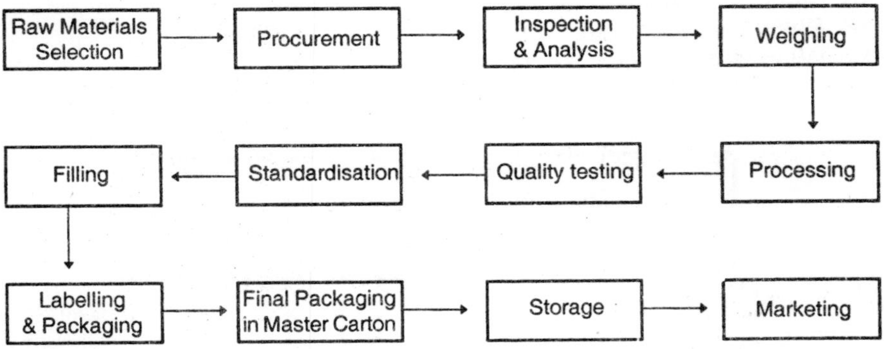

Plant & Machineries Require .:-

1. Planetary Mixer with Stainless Steel body and stirrer.
2. Mixing Vessel (S.S.made) with stirrer fitted with electric heating system.
3. Water de-ionisation unit.
4. Stainless steel melting vessel.
5. Automatic or semi-automatic tube weighing, filling and sealing machine.
6. Automatic or semi-automatic bottle weighing filling and sealing machine.
7 Semi-automatic labelling machine .
8. Semi-automatic Carton sealing and strapping machine.
9. Laboratory Testing equipments and Glasswares.
10. Weighing balance, weights & others.

PROJECT FINANCIAL ANALYSIS :-

1.	Production Capacity	-	100 Kgs. Per Day / Per Shift. Moisturizer with Aloe Vera and Coconut Oil
2	Land & Building	-	On Rent.
3	Covered Area Require	-	300 Sq.mts.
4	Plant & Machinery Cost	-	Rs.4.50 lacs.
5	Others Fixed Capital	-	Rs.1.20 lacs
6.	Total Fixed Capital Require	-	Rs.5.70 lacs
7	Working Capital Require Per Month	-	Rs.5.00 tacs
8	Margin Money	-	Rs.1.25 lacs
9	Total Project Cost	-	Rs.6.95 lacs
10.	Total Capital Requirement	-	Rs.10.70 lacs
11	Cost of Production Per Month	-	Rs.5.20 lacs
12.	Turnover Per Month	-	Rs.7.50 lacs
13.	Gross Profit Per Month	-	Rs.2.30 lacs
14	Rate of Return Per Annum	-	258 %
15.	Manpower Requirement	-	5 Nos
16.	Electric Power Load	-	15 KWs
17.	Water Requirement Per Month	-	100 KLs

Note : The project cost may vary according to the production capacity.

18

Mosquito Repellent Cream

Introduction :-

Mosquito Repellent Cream is legitimately considered to be a cosmetic preparations, as it is presented in cosmetic form or even in combination with other functional attributes. Mosquito is considered as a disease vectors in man. A study reported that the relative attractiveness of man's skin to the mosquito depends upon a balance between the attractiveness of certain elements of sweat and the repellency of skin lipids. The best mosquito repellent chemical compound is Diethyltoluamide. Chemically it is called as N, N-diethyl-m-toluamide, other names are DET, Detamide, Delphene or Metadelphene (the trade mark compounds of Hercules powder cO.).

Diethyltoluamide or N, N-Diethyl-m-toluamide is a colourless liquid with a faint pleasant odour, almost insoluble in water and Glycerine, but miscible with alcohol or Isopropyl alcohol. The commercial material contains a minimum of 95 per cent of the meta-isomers. Diethyltoluamide is an effective mosquito repellent for 18-20 hours compared with other agents. It is the most effective repellent against mosquito, as well as blackflies, chiggers, ticks, and fleas. The minimum effective dose for protection against mosquito (Aedes aegypti) ranged from 50 - 77 microgram per square centimeter of skin. Moreover its great persistence, resistance to wiping action, resistance to sweating and its non-oily nature has broaden its application.

The rising in diseases like malaria, dengue and other sorts of fever is transmitted by mosquito bitting. To protect the person from mosquito bitting, this cream helps to large extent by repelling mosquitoes as well as other insects. This product is now manufactured and marketed by Godrej, Good knight group and few other manufacturers. The domestic and international demand is rising day by day.

A new entrepreneur or industrialist can manufacture and market this product with good packaging and good marketing strategies to earn excellent profit.

Properties of A Good Quality Mosquito Repellent Cream :-

1. The mosquito repellent cream should be non-toxic, non-irritating, non-allergenic in nature.

2. It should be biologically and environmentally safe for all types of skin.
3. The product should be smooth in application over the skin.
4. The cream should have sufficient shelf life.
5. The product should be uniform in texture.
6. It is resistant to wiping action, resistant to sweating. It repells mosquitoes as well as other insects.
7. It is safe and has very very low toxicity as approved by US FDA norms.

Uses and Applications :-

1. The cream is used by everybody.
2. It is useful during tours and travels to protect from mosquito bittings.
3. It is used in houses, homes and almost every places to protect the persons from mosquito bittings.
4. It is useful for all the people to protect and repel mosquitoes causing fever, diseases like malaria, dengue, typhoid etc.

B. 1. S. Specification :-

There is no B. 1. S. Specification on "Mosquito Repellent Cream" is available with Bureau of Indian standards. But prior to selling this cream in the market, it is suggested to check all the cosmetics norms as specified in the IS-6608-skin cream published by Bureau of Indian standards.

Government Regulations :-

Mosquito Repellent Cream is a cosmetic product which falls under Drug & Cosmetic Rules, 1945.

To manufacture Mosquito Repellent Cream, the manufacturers have to apply to the licensing authority appointed by the State Government in Form-31 (if the manufacturer wants to manufacture products for sale or distribution).

Raw Materials Require & its Availability :-

The raw materials require to manufacture the Mosquito Repellent Cream are named as Stearic Acid, Isopropyl Myristate, Diethyltoluamide, Triethanolamine (TEA), Glycerine, Purified Water, Neem Oil, Basil Oil, Eucalyptus Oil, Preservative, Propylene Glycol, Colour, Perfume and Laboratory testing chemicals.

The packaging materials require are Laminated Plastic Collapsible tubes, Caps, Printed outer Mini Cartons, Corrugated Cartons, Self adhesive tapes, Box straps etc.The raw materials and packaging materials are indigenously available and can be procured from nearby available local sources.

Mosquito Repellent Cream

Formulation :-

Ingredients		*Parts bv Weiqht*
Stearic Acid	-	10-12
Isopropyl Myristate	-	2-3
Diethyl toluamide	-	15
Triethanolamine (TEA)	-	2-3
Glycerine	-	4-6
Purified Water	-	to make 100
Neem Oil	-	0.2-0.5
Basil Oil	-	0.2-0.5
Eucalyptus Oil	-	0.2-1
Preservative	-	0.2-0.5
Propylene Glycol	-	2-4
Colour	-	q.s.
Perfume	-	0.1-0.3
		100

Manufacturing Process :-

To manufacture good quality Mosquito Repellent Cream, it is suggested to proceed the following processing steps.

1. Procure all the raw materials from good reputed dealers or suppliers.
2. Analyse and test all the raw materials for purity and good quality.
3. Weigh all the raw materials as specified in the formulation.
4. In a stainless steel vessel fitted with S. S. Stirrer heat Stearic Acid, Isopropyl Myristate and Diethyl toluamide at 70°C with mixing and stirring thoroughly.
5. In a stainless steel planetary mixer heat Triethanolamine, Glycerine and Purified Water at 70°C with mixing and stirring thoroughly.
6. Now, add step-4 preparations to step-5 preparations with thorough mixing and stirring at 70°C. Stire well for 15-20 minutes till temperature is reduced to 40-45°C.
7. In another stainless steel vessel mix Neem oil, Basil oil, Eucalyptus oil uniformly and add to step- 6 preparations.
8. In a separate stainless steel vessel dissolve Preservative in Propylene Glycol with little warming upto 40°C and mixing it uniformly.
9. Add step-8 preparations to step-6 preparations with thorough mixing.

10. Then add perfumes or fragrances and colour solution one by one with uniform mixing and stirring.
11. Test the final mosquito repellent cream for quality and standardize it.
12. Now fill and pack the cream in laminated plastic collapsible tubes.
13. The cream filled tubes are batch coded, packed in printed mini outer cartons. It is further packed in corrugated cardboard cartons. The cartons are sealed and strapped.
14. The final cartons are now placed in store and marketed to the desired customers.

Process Flow Sheet For Manufacturing of Mosquito Repellent Cream

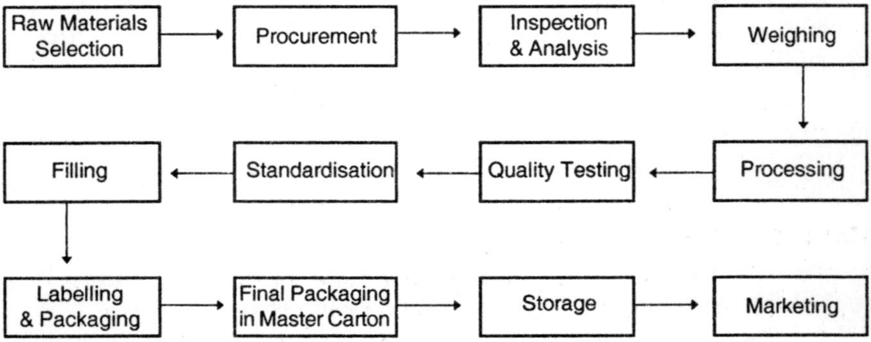

Plant & Machineries Requirement :-

1. Planetary Mixer with Stainless Steel body and stirrer.
2. Mixing Vessel (S.S.made) with stirrer fitted with electric heating system.
3. Water de-ionisation unit.
4. Stainless steel melting vessel.
5. Automatic or semi-automatic tube weighing, filling and sealing machine.
6. Automatic or semi-automatic jar weighing filling and sealing machine.
7. Semi-automatic labelling machine.
8. Semi-automatic Carton sealing and strapping machine.
9. Laboratory Testing equipments and Glasswares.
10. Weighing balance, weights & others.

19

Nail Polish Remover

Introduction :-

Nail polish Remover is basically a simple solvent mixture of organic solvents which may contain small amounts of fatty material to counteract any excessive drying action of the solvents on the nails. Now a days, esters such as Butyl stearate or fatty alcohol or soaps may be used for the same purpose. These products should be non-irritating to the skin. Now, another type of nail polish remover is available in the market. This is so-called "non-smeary" remover which claim to remove the nail lacquer without smearing the nails or the adjoining skin. These products consist of a mixture of water and water-miscible solvents such as Ethyl Acetate in which the water content is only of the order of 8-9 %.

Today the media publicity, fashion show, beauty show, advertisement in magazines, Newspaper, FM-Radio, Cinemas have made such wide publicity that even the girls, ladies from rural areas are becoming more and more beauty conscious. The high profile ladies, young girls, school college going girls, models, film actresses and other beauty conscious women are changing their nail lacquer daily by matching with their dresses, sarees, garments etc. To remove the old nail lacquer, nail polish remover plays a major role. It not only softens the enamel film, but also loosens the film from nail either by dissolving or by wetting of the film to make it easy to remove. The nail polish can be dissolved in remover and can be wiped out by cotton or cloth without any scratches on the nails.

The demand of nail polish remover is parallel to the demand of the nail polish. The demand of the colour cosmetics is rising at a rapid pace all over the world. Due to growth in female population and growth in media publicity the demand of this nail polish remover is also rising. A new entrepreneur can add this product in their cosmetics range to earn excellent profit.

Properties of A Good Quality Nail Polish Remover :-

1. The Nail polish removers are mixture of organic solvents, which dissolves or softens the nail lacquer and make it easy to wipe out or to remove by cloth.
2. The product should have low evaporation rate.

3. The product should have good wetting power to dissolve the enamel.
4. The product should have low boiling point.
5. It should not cause any irritation to skin.
6. It should have good perfume or fragrances. So that it can be accepted by everybody.
7. The product comprises organic solvents, so it should be kept away from flame contact. It should be placed out of children's reach.

Uses and Applications :-

1. The Nail polish remover is used to remove the film of enamel either by dissolving or by wetting the film. The old nail enamel film is wiped out by clean cloth or cotton.
2. The product is packed in glass bottle and sealed air tight to protect from evaporation. It should not be packed in plastic bottle, otherwise it will dissolve the wall of the plastic bottle and product will be leaked and evaporated.
3. It is used by every beauty parlors, every ladies, girls, models, actresses and others.

B.I.S.Specification :-

There is no B.I.S. Specification available with Bureau of Indian standards on "Nail Polish Remover". But the finished product can be tested as per cosmetic norms.

Government Regulation :-

Nail polish Remover is a Cosmetic product which falls under Drug & Cosmetic Rules, 1945.

To manufacture Nail Polish Remover the manufacturer has to apply to the licensing authority appointed by the State Government in Form-31 (if the manufacturer wants to manufacture products for sale or distribution) or Form -31 A, (if the manufacture wants loan license to manufacture cosmetic product.).

Raw Materials Availability :-

All the Raw materials are available indigenously and can be procured from local suppliers or dealers.

Nail Polish Remover

Formulation - 1

Ingredients		Parts by weight
Amyl Acetate	-	49
Acetone	-	49
Perfumes	-	2
		100

Formulation - 2

Ingredients		Parts by weight
Ethyl Alcohol	-	33
Petroleum Ether	-	33
Acetone	-	33
Perfumes	-	1
		100

Formulation - 3

Ingredients		Parts by weight
Butyl stearate	-	4-7
Diethylene Glycol Monoethyl Ether	-	8-12
Acetone	-	84-85
		100

Formulation - 4

Ingredients		Parts by weight
Butyl stearate	-	1-4
Ethyl Acetate	-	12-16
Butyl Acetate	-	22-27
Acetone	-	25-30
Toluene	-	Q S to make 100
Perfume	-	1-2
		100

Manufacturing Process :-

Nail polish remover can be prepared by proceeding the following points stepwise by manufacturers :-

1. Procure.all the ingredients from reputed wholesale dealers or traders.
2. Analyse or test the quality of each components in laboratory.
3. Weigh all the ingredients as specified in the formulation.
4. Pour all the ingredients one by one in a closed top stainless steel vessel fitted with flame proof motor and S.S. Stirrer.
5. Mix all the ingredients for 10-15 minutes at room temperature.
6. Test the final product and standardise as per cosmetic norms.
7. Fill the product in glass bottle of size 25 ml, 50ml, 100ml, 100ml, 20 ml.
8. Label the bottles with all precuations,
9. Pack these bottles in double layered corrugated cartons and strap it.

10. Store the cartons in fire proof storage and send it to desired dealers/distributors for marketing.

Process Flowsheet for Manufacturing of Nail Polish Remover

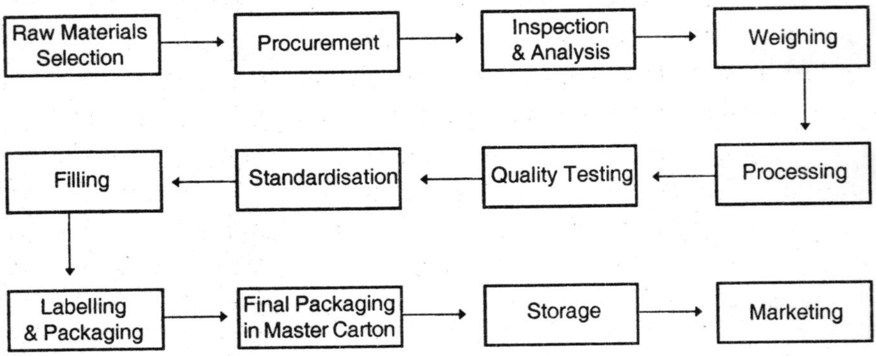

Plant & Machineries Reguirement :-

1. Weighing Balance.
2. Stainless Steel Vessel (closed top) fitted with S.S. Stirrer and flame proof motor.
3. Semi automatic glass bottle weighing filling and cap sealing machine.
4. Labelling machine and batch coding machine.
5. Cartons sealing and strapping machine.
6. Laboratory equipments and Glasswares.

Note : Detialed project report on above project is available with EIRI. Contact 'EIRI' office for more details.

20

Cucumber Lemon Face Pack

Introduction :-

Cucumber Lemon Face Pack is the innovation in herbal skin care cosmetics ranges. The vegetative ingredients are now gaining importance and acceptance in our day to day life. The modern researches reveal the facts of application of vegetables, herbs, fruits and other natural ingredients in formulation and manufacturing of different skin care cosmetics. The people are now finding these products more suitable for their natural beauty and long lasting good look. The natural ingredients present in the face pack imparts stimulating sensation of rejuvenation. This face pack is applied over face and allowed to dry in 30-120 minutes. With drying, the skin tightening effect and warmth is experienced. This cucumber lemon face pack removes dead skin, skin debris, black heads after application and rinsing with water. It cause the face skin more glowing, shining and rejuvenate the skin texture. Besides, its ingredients cucumber restores skins moisture, re-energize and refresh the skin. The other ingredient lemon oil leaves natural radiance over the skin and create aromatherapy effect to refresh the feelings and rejuvenate the mood. Now, there are very few manufacturers who are manufacturing and marketing this product.

Properties of Good Quality Cucumber Lemon Face Pack :-

A good quality Cucumber Lemon Face Pack has following properties to maximize its effect over human skin

1. Cucumber Lemon-Face Pack is non-irritating, non-toxic in nature.
2. It is biologically, ecologically safe on application over human skin.
3. It do not cause any harsh effect or excessive dryness on skin after application.
4. It rejuvenate the skin by removing all impurities from skin. So that skin will glow and look younger than its actual age.

Uses and Applications :-

1. Cucumber Lemon Face Pack is used by girls, women, ladies, office going female executive, housewives, fashionable models, actors and actresses, TV artists and almost all the women who are beauty conscious.

2 It is used in beauty parlours, Men's parlours, Spa clubs, beauty institutes etc.
3 It is used by women all over the world to beautify their appearance.

B.I. S. Specification :-

There is no such B.I.S. Specification available on "Cucumber Lemon Face Pack" with Bureau of Indian standards.

But the product is passed through cosmetics permitted standards applicable over human skin.

Government Regulation :-

"Cucumber Lemon Face Pack" is a Cosmetic product which come under Drug & Cosmetic Rules, 1945.

To manufacture "Cucumber Lemon Face Pack" the manufacturer has to apply to the licensing authority appointed by the State Government in Form-31 (if the manufacturer wants to manufacture products for sale or distribution) or Form -31A, (if the manufacturer wants loan license to manufacture cosmetic product.).

Raw Materials Require and its Availability :-

The major raw materials require to formulate and manufacture cucumber iemon face pack are Cetyl Alcohol, Glycerine, Sodium Lauryl Sulphate (SLS), Emulsifying Wax, Purified Water, Kaolin, Bentonite, Lemon oil, Cucumber Extract, Preservative, Purified Water, Perfume or Fragrance, Colour, Herbal Extracts and Laboratory testing chemicals.

The packaging materials require are HDPE/PET Jars, aluminium seals, caps, labels, outer cartons, corrugated master cartons, self adhesive tapes, box straps etc. These are indigenously available and can be procured from nearby local available sources.

Cucumber Lemon Face Pack

Formulation :-

Ingredients		*Parts by Weight*
Cetyl Alcohol	-	3 - 5
Glycerine	-	10-12
Sodium Lauryl Sulphate (SLS)	-	0.2 - 0.3
Emulsifying Wax	-	0.4-0.6
Purified Water	-	to make 100
Kaolin	-	30 - 35
Bentonite	-	5-6
Lemon oil	-	4-5

Cucumber Extract (1 : 1)	-	4-5
Preservative	-	0.3 - 0.5
Purified Water	-	5-6
Perfume or Fragrance	-	q.s.
Colour	-	0.1-0.4
		100

Manufacturing Process :-

To manufacture a good quality Cucumber Lemon Face Pack, it is Suggested to proceed the following processing steps.

1. Procure all the ingredients from good suppliers or traders.
2. Analyse and test each ingredients for best quality cosmetics.
3. Weigh each ingredients separately as specified in the formulation.
4. In a stainless steel vessel fitted with S. S. Stirrer heat Cetyl Alcohol at 70°C to melt it completely.
5. In another stainless steel vessel fitted with S.S. Stirrer, heat Glycerine, Sodium Lauryl Sulphate, Emulsifying Wax, Purified water at 70°C to melt and mix ingredients homogeneously.
6. Now, add step-4 preparations to step-5 preparations and stire uniformly till it is cooled to 50°C.
7. In a planetary mixer pour step-6 preparations and dry mixture of Kaolin, Bentonite powder and mix it thoroughly to bring it to paste form.
8. To the step-7 preparations add lemon oil and cucumber extract with uniform mixing at 40°C.
9. In another stainless steel vessel dissolve preservative in little quantity of water with warming to prepare solution. This preservative solution is added to step-8 preparations with continuous mixing.
10. Then to the step-9 preparations add colour solution and perfumes with mixing homogeneously.
11. The final face pack is now tested & standardized.
12. This final Cucumber lemon face pack is now packed in plastic jars, sealed with Aluminium foil and capped the jars.
13. The jars are now labelled, packed in outer carton and then in corrugated master cartons. The cartons are sealed with adhesive tapes and strapped.

Process Flowsheet For Manufacturing of Cucumber Lemon Face Pack

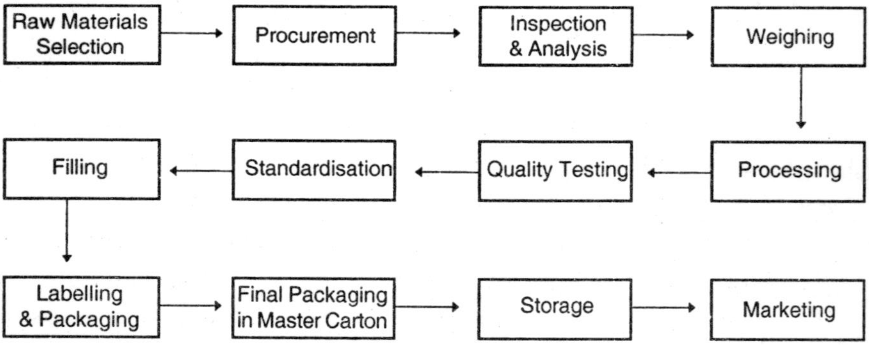

Plant & Machineries Require :-

1. Sieving machine.
2. Electric Oven.
3. Weighing balance & weights.
4. Ribbon blender with S.S.body.
5. Planetary Mixer.
6. Stainless steel mixing Vessel fitted with Stirrer.
7. Jars weighing, filling and sealing machines.
8. Labeling machine.
9. Water de-ionisation unit.
10. Carton sealing or strapping machines.
11. Laboratory testing equipments.

21

Henna Conditioning Shampoo

Introduction :-

Henna Conditioning Shampoo is one of the good variety of shampoo which has natural conditioning effect over hair. It imparts shining, silky effect and makes the hair beautiful. Henna conditioning shampoo is accepted by everybody. It is available in both pearly and clear transparent form. The product is formulated and manufactured as per the customer's requirement. It's ingredients quantity may be adjusted considering the application on dry hair, oily hair or normal hair. The natural ingredient henna plays vital role. It also do not have any side effect on the hair as well as on scalp. This product is now highly demanded all over the world. The girls, women who are highly beauty conscious, they find this product as a boon for them.

Now a days, the herbal cosmetics market is growing at a rapid pace all over the world. The growth rate is increasing with people's continuous inclination towards herbal cosmetics

Properties of Good Quality Henna Conditioning Shampoo :-

The Henna conditioning shampoo has following properties to meet the international acceptance m every climatic conditions.

1 The shampoo is easily spread over hair.

2 It is efficient in removing grime, excess oil and scalp debris in soft and hard water

3 It is easily rinsed away very quickly.

4 The wet hair are easily combed after shampooing the hair

5 The shampoo has shining effect over hair.

6 The hair is easily dried after application and rinsing of shampoo

7 The shampoo is of good variety. After shampooing, the dry hair can easily be combed and set it out in desired style.

8 The shampoo is safe on the scalp and no irritation, reddening or other discomfort is caused by its use.

Uses and Applications :-

1 Henna conditioning shampoo is used by both men and women of all age group
2 It is used in houses, hotels, five star hotels, deluxe hotels, Spa-clubs, beauty parlours, Hair salons etc.
3 It is used to cleanse the hair, scalp debris and excess oils from scalp
4 It is used by models, actors, actresses, film stars and others

B.I.S Specifications :-

There is no B.I.S Specifications available on "Henna Conditioning Shampoo' with Bureau of Indian standards. But this shampoo is tested as per IS-7884 or IS-7669, as per the permissible cosmetics norms

Government Regulations :-

"Henna Conditioning Shampoo" is a cosmetic product which come under Drug & Cosmetic Rules 1945

To manufacture, "Henna Conditioning Shampoo" the manufacturers have to apply to the licensing authority appointed by the state Government in Form-31 (if the manufacturer wants to manufacture products for sale or distribution).

Raw Materials Require :-

The shampoo can be formulated with following types of ingredients.

1 Surfactants.
2 Foam boosters and stabilizers.
3 Conditioning Agents.
4 Special additives.
5 Preservatives.
6. Sequestering Agents.
7. Viscosity modifiers.
8. Opacifying or clarifying agents.
9. Fragrances
10. Colour.
11. Stabilizers.
12. Herbal Extracts.

Besides these raw materiais, packaging materials of good quality plastic should be procured like HDPE/ PET Bottles, labels, Aluminium seals, caps, corrugated boxes, adhesive tapes, box straps etc.

Henna Conditioning Shampoo (Clear)

Formulation:-

Ingredients		*Parts by Weight*
Sodium Lauryi Ether Sulphate	-	30-37
Coconut Diethanolamide	-	3-5
Cocobetaine	-	2-5
Propylene Glycol	-	2-4
Citric Acid solution	-	0.3-0.7
Sodium chloride	-	1-2
Preservative	-	0.25-0.75
Colour (water soluble)	-	Q.S.
Conditioner	-	0.5 - 1.50
Fragrance or Perfume	-	0.3 - 1
Henna Extract	-	0.1-2
Purified water	-	to make 100
		100

Manufacturing Process :-

The Henna Conditioning Shampoo of good quality can be manufactured by adopting following stepwise manufacturing process :-

1. First of all, procure all the raw materials from good reputed suppliers.
2. Analyze and test all the raw materials for suitability.
3. Weigh all the ingredients as specified in the formulation.
4. In a stainless steel vessel fitted with S.S.Stirrer, pour SLES, Cocodiethanolamide, Cocobetaine and Purified water, stire well to dissolve all the ingredients.
5. Now, in another stainless steel vessel pour Propylene Glycol and Preservative. Heat the vessel to 70-80°C on a gas burner to dissolve the preservative in Propylene Glycol.
6. Now, mix step-5 preparations to step-4 preparations with continuous stirring.
7. Add conditioner to the step-6 preparations and mix again.
8. Now, dissolve Citric acid in purified water in another stainless steel vessel. Add this solution to step-7 preparations dropwise to reduce the pH of the above preparations to near neutral in between 6-7.
9. Now, dissolve the colour in water in a small vessel and add dropwise with stirring to step-8 preparations.

10. Dissolve Sodium chloride in water in another vessel and add dropwise with stirring till the desired consistency is obtained.
11. Add the fragrance and henna extract with continuous stirring till final uniform shampoo is obtained.
12. The shampoo is now quality tested, standardized and then filled in plastic bottles in desired sizes.
13. The bottles are labelled and sealed. These are further packed in corrugated cardboard boxes. The corrugated boxes are sealed and strapped.
14. The boxes are placed in store and marketed to the desired customers.

Process Flowsheet For Manufacturing of Henna Conditioning Shampoo

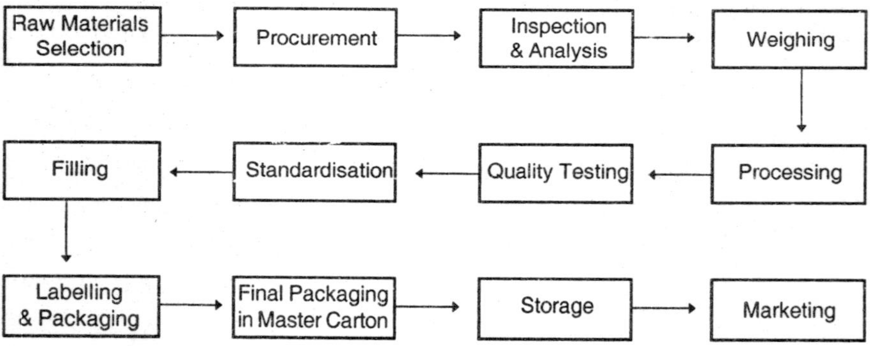

Note : The project cost may very according to the production capacity.

22

Ayurvedic Hair Oil (Like Banphool)

Introduction :-

Ayurvedic Hair Oil (Like Banphool) is one of the important product having therapeutic value to cure headache, to cool the brain and scalp, to relief from tension, to arrest hair fall and other various specific properties. It nourishes hair roots, helps to induce better sleep, by making calm to the tense nerves. The product is highly in demand in Uttar Pradesh, Bihar, Jharkhand, Orissa, West Bengal, Assam along with other states of our country. This hair oil is finding a prominent position in the mass market. This hair oil is cheaper in price in comparison to other hair oils. Again due to its good herbal contents, it is also popular among the middle segments of our society. This hair oil is highly accepted due to its medical value without any side effects. So its demand is rising day by day all over the country.

This Ayurvedic Hair Oil is formulated by using all the natural ingredients available in the market. It replaces the coconut oil demand upto some extent, all over the country. It energises the brain nerves, stops dandruff formation, makes the hair smooth and shiny. Considering its importance and market demand, there are some new products in new Brand names have come up in the market. The ayurvedic hair oil brand names are viz. Navratna Hair Oil, Himtaj Hair Oil, Maha Bhringraj Hair Oil, Sesa Hair Oil and other brands available in the market. Only high quality products with best ayurvedic effect, are accepted by everybody. The market of ayurvedic hair oil is expanding at a rapid pace and has captured the rural segments extensively by the potential manufacturers. The people are becoming aware with media publicity over TV, cables, news papers, posters, banners etc. about the products soon. The marketing aspects are covered within no time by the manufacturers. There is tremendous market demand of this ayurvedic hair oil, all over the country.

Properties of Good Quality Ayurvedic Hair Oil (Like Banphool Oil) :-

1. The Ayurvedic Hair Oil is safe on scalp, hair root.
2. It do not have any side effect, means it do not cause irritation, etching on the scalp.

3. The product's shelf life is sufficient.
4 This hair oil is ecologically and biologically safe.
5. This hair oil do not solidify during winter.
6. It do not give any off smell during its shelf life.
7. It do not have any toxic element in its content.
8. The oil gives cooling effect on the scalp.

Uses and Applications :-

1. The ayurvedic hair oil (like banphool) is used to tone up the scalp, hair roots.
2. It is used to energise and nourish the brain nerves by its active herbal constituents.
3. It is used to cool and calm the excited or tense nerves and induce good night sleep.
4. This ayurvedic hair oil is used by both men and women of all age group.
5. This oil is used by almost every people, those who understand the therapeutic value of this oil.
6. This ayurvedic hair oil is used to nourish hair roots, strengthen the hair follicle and make the hair healthy and shiny in appearance.

B. I. S. Specification :-

There is no such B.I.S. Specification available on "Ayurvedic Hair Oil (like Banphool)" with Bureau of Indian standards. But this product can be tested as per the cosmetics norms prior to sending for marketing of the products.

Government Regulations :-

"Ayurvedic Hair Oil" is a Cosmetic product which come under Drug & Cosmetic Rules, 1945.

To manufacture "Ayurvedic Hair Oil" the manufacturer has to apply to the licensing authority appointed by the State Government in Form-31 (if the manufacturer wants to manufacture products for sale or distribution) or Form -31A, (if the manufacturer wants loan license to manufacture cosmetic product.).

Raw Materials Require and its Availability :-

The ayurvedic / herbal hair oil (Like Banphool oil) contains major ingredients as refined sesame oil, alongwith other minor ingredients like essential oils, herbal extracts. The packaging materials, stickers, labels, cardboard boxes, cartons, tapes, straps etc. are used.

These raw materials and packaging materials are indigenously available and can be procured from nearby sources.

Ayurvedic Hair Oil (Banphool type)

Formulation 1:-

Ingredients		*Parts by Weight*
Refined Sesame Oil (Til oil)	-	96 - 98.35
Camphor Oil	-	0.25 - 0.50
Clove Oil	-	0.10 - 0.25
Sandal Oil	-	0.10 - 0.25
Amla Extract	-	0.44 - 1.00
Baheda Extract	-	0.03 - 0.1
Hartago Extract	-	0.03 - 0.1
Jatamansi Extract	-	0.10 - 0.25
Kewra Extract	-	0.10 - 0.25
Pudina Extract (Mint Leave Extract)	-	0.25 - 0.65
Preservative	-	0.25 - 0.75
Colour (Oil soluble cosmetic red colour)	-	q.s.
		100

Formulation 2 :-

Ingredients		*Parts by Weight*
Refined Sesame Oil (Til oil)	-	36 - 38.35
Light Liquid Paraffin	-	30-40
Camphor Oil	-	0.25 - 0.50
Refined Groundnut oil	-	20 - 30
Clove Oil	-	0.10 - 0.25
Sandal Oil	-	0.10 - 0.25
Amla Extract	-	0.44 - 1.00
Baheda Extract	-	0.03 - 0.1
Hartago Extract	-	0.03 - 0.1
Jatamansi Extract	-	0.1 - 0.25
Kewra Extract	-	0.1 - 0.25
Pudina Extract (Mint Extract)	-	0.25 - 0.65
Preservative	-	0.25 - 0.75
Colour (Oil soluble cosmetic red colour)	-	q.s.
		100

Manufacturing Process:-

To prepare good quality Ayurvedic Hair Oil like Banphool, it is suggested to proceed the following processing steps.

1. First of all, Purchase all the raw materials from good reputed suppliers.
2 Analyse and test all the raw materials in the laboratory.

3. Weigh the ingredients as specified in the formulation.
4. In a stainless steel vessel fitted with stainless steel stirrer, motor and accessories, pour a part of refined Sesame oil and heat it to 70-80°C on a gas burner with constant stirring. To the hot oil add preservative and stir tiil it is completely dissolved. Then to it add the cosmetic grade oil soluble red colour and mix it homogeneously.
5. Add this dye mixed oil to the reșt of sesame oil and stir it completely. Then to this oil add essential oils and herbs extracts one by one and mix it thoroughly to homogenize it.
6. This product is now tested in the lab and standardised.
7 This is now packed in glass bottles. The caps are sealed by manual or semi-automatic sealing machine and labelled as per the choice of customer.
8. The final bottles are now packed in the carton. The cartons are sealed with adhesive tapes and strapped.
9. The cartons are then placed in store and marketed to the desired traders.

Process Flowsheet For Manufacturing of Ayurvedic Hair Oil (Like Banphool)

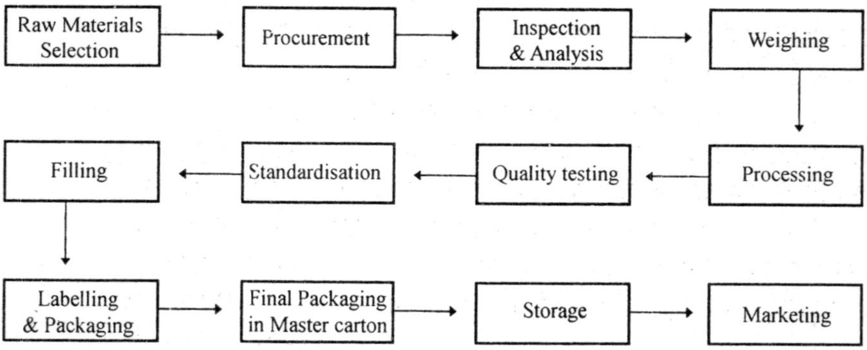

Note : Detialed project report on above project is available with EIRI. Contact 'EIRI' office for more details.

23

Herbal Shaving Cream

Introduction :-

Herbal shaving Cream comes under the category of wet shaving preparations. To minimize the trauma of shaving, the herbal shaving cream is now made available, that prepare the beard and face for shaving, increase speed and comfort during the shave and confer a feeling of well being after shaving. The choice of shaving preparation is highly individualistic. The main functional requirements of a wet shaving preparation, are to soften the beard, to lubricate the passage of razor over the face and to support the beard hair. The product should be non-irritating to the skin. It should assist in removing shaving debris from the face. It should be stable over wide range of temperatures. It should be resistant to rapid drying out and collapse. It should be non-corrosive to the razor blade and easily rinsed from the razor and face. The shaving cream helps in skin lubrication to the comfort, closeness and speed of wet shaving. The herbal shaving cream should be economical and maintain the hair in a fully water saturated condition. The product is now highly demanded by every man all over the world.

Requirement of Good Quality Herbal Shaving Cream :-

A good herbal shaving cream meet the following requirement.

1. It produce a rich copious leather composed of small bubbles.
2. It has good wetting properties.
3. It is smooth, soft and free from lumps.
4. It adhere readily to both face and brush. It is easily removed on rinsing.
5. It retain a satisfactory consistency and texture in all temperature conditions like to be encountered in use.

Characteristics of a Good Herbal Shaving Cream :-

The Herbal Shaving Cream has following properties.

1. It is easy to transfer to the face.
2. It is easy to spread on the face.
3. It has wetting and drainage properties of the foam.
4. It has comfort and closeness of shave.
5. It has sufficient foam stability.

6. It has ease of removal of lather and shaving debris from razor and basin.
7. It is formulated with acceptable and compatible perfume.

Uses and Applications :-

1. The herbal shaving cream is used by every people who have beard and moustache.
2. It is used by males from 16 years onwards who used to shave their beard.
3. It is used in salons, barber shops, home, house, star deluxe hotels to shave the people.
4. It is an essential commodity of daily life of male.

B.I.S. Specification :-

There is no such B.I.S. Specification available on "Herbal Shaving Cream" with Bureau of Indian standards. The product is tested as per the cosmetics norms prior to selling in market.

Government Regulations :-

"Herbal Shaving Cream" is a Cosmetic product which come under Drug & Cosmetic Rules, 1945.

To manufacture "Herbal Shaving Cream" the manufacturer has to apply to the licensing authority appointed by the State Government in Form-31 (if the manufacturer wants to manufacture products for sale *or* distribution) or Form -31A, (if the manufacturer wants loan license to manufacture cosmetic product.).

The major brands of shaving cream available in Indian market are listed as follow.

- Gillette
- Godrej
- Old Spice
- Dettol
- Nivea
- Park Avenue
- Premium
- Vi-John
- Denim
- Other brands

Raw Materials Require and its Availability :-

The major raw materials require are Potassium Stearate, Stearic Acid, Glyceryl Monostearate, Ethoxylated Lanolin, Sorbitol, Sodium Lauryl sulphate, Cocobetaine, Purified water, Propylene Glycol, Menthol, Preservative, Basil Oil, Lavender oil, Sandalwood oil, Colour, Perfume or Fragrance, Herbal Extracts and Laboratory testing chemicals.

The major packaging materials require are plastic collapsible tubes, lami tubes or Aluminium Collapsible tubes, caps, outer paper Cartons, corrugated master cartons, adhesive tapes, box straps. These raw materials and packaging materials are indigenously available and can be procured from nearby local available sources.

Herbal Shaving Cream

Formulation :-

Ingredients		*Parts by weight*
Potassium Stearate	-	28-30
Stearic Acid	-	5-7
Glyceryl Monostearate	-	3-4
Ethoxylated Lanolin	-	2-3
Sorbitol	-	3-4
Sodium Lauryl sulphate	-	3-4
Cocobetaine	-	0.5-1
Purified water	-	to make 100
Propylene Glycol	-	10-12
Menthol	-	0.5-1
Preservative	-	0.2 - 0.5
Basil Oil	-	0.1-1
Lavender oil	-	01-1
Sandalwood oil	-	0.1-1
Colour	-	q.s
Perfume or Fragrance	-	0.1-0.5
		100

Manufacturing Process :-

To manufacture a good quality Herbal Shaving Cream, it is suggested to proceed the following processing steps

1 Procure all the ingredients from good suppliers.
2 Analyse and test each ingredients for best quality products
3 Weigh each ingredients separately as specied in the formulation
4 In a planetary mixer fitted with S. S. bowl and stirrer, heat & melt Potassium Stearate, Stearic Acid, Glyceryl Monostearate and Ethoxylated Lanolin together and mix uniformly
5 In another S. S. Vessel fitted with S. S. Stirrer pour Sorbitol, Sodium Lauryl Sulphate, Cocobetame. Water and heat it to 70 in ^{0}C with stirring till uniform.
6 Now, mix the step-5 preparations to step-4 preparations with stirring
7 Now, in another stainless steel vessel heat Propylene Glycol, Menthol and preservative with heating at 40^{0}C. Now, add this preparations to step-6 preparations with uniform mixing
8 Now, in a separate stainless steel Vessel mix Basil oil. Lavender oil, Sandal Wood oil to homogenise.
9 Add the step-8 essential oil mixture to step-7 preparations with continuous thorough mixing.

10. Add the colour solution to step-9 preparations with thorough mixing.
11. Test the final Herbal Shaving Cream and standardize it
12. Now, fill it in printed laminated plastic collapsible tubes *or* printed aluminium tubes. Seal the tubes and place it in outer paper cartons. Then, pack it in final corrugated master cartons
13. Seal the master cartons by adhesive tapes and strap the final cartons
14. Now, place the cartons in storage and send it for marketing.

Process Flowsheet For Manufacturing of Herbal Shaving Cream

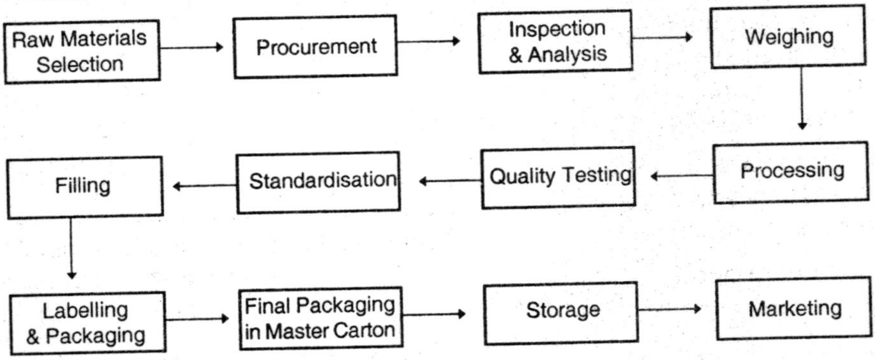

> **Note :** Capacity and size of the project may vary according to the entrepreneur requirements. Entrepreneur may contact 'EIRI' office for further details of this project.

24

Aromatherapy Liquid Soap

Introduction :-

Aromatherapy Liquid Soap is one type of bath preparations having aromatherapy effect on the user during and after bath. The product is easy to apply in place of toilet soap cake. A little quantity of this liquid soap creates a rich foam, moisturizes the body skin and leaves a mood freshening effect over the human being. This product removes dirt, grime, skin oils, debris and off smell or fouling smell of sweat from the body, armpit and neck portions. In addition to this, it condition the skin, deodorize, perfume the body and bathroom, stimulates the sensation and rejuvenate the feeling by its aromatic essential oils. The product is gaining importance all over the world. Even the common people are finding its importance all over the world.

The product is available in various colour and various aromas from floral (Rose, lavender, Ylang-Ylang, Patchouli, Neroli, Jasmin etc.), Vegetative (Mandarin, lemon, ginger and others), fruity (strawberry, banana, green apple, mango, orange flavours) to other various range of fragrances and flavours.

There are very few manufacturers of this product in India and in Internationa! Countries.

The people are finding this product as magical to reduce depression, anxieties, tension, uneasy feeling in their day to day life. This product helps them to relax, freshen up their feelings, rejuvenate their moods and help them to feel better in every aspects.

The demand of this product is growing day by day all over the country as well as all over world.

A new entrepreneur with quality product and in beautiful packaging can enter into the market in all segments from premium urban segments to the rural segments to earn excellent profit.

In our country with rise in population growth and changing in living pattern, beauty consciousness, fashion orientation of society, the acceptance of this product is gradually increasing and will be multifolded in the coming future.

A new entrepreneur can add this product in their cosmetics range and create a supply chain all over the country.

Properties of Good Quality Aromatherapy Liquid Soap :-

1. It provide copious foam at minimal concentration.
2. It's pH is properly balanced.
3. It remove dirts, grimes, skin oils, fouling smells of sweat.
4. It is mild, non-irritating, non-toxic, non-allergenic to body skin.
5. It has adequate cleansing power.
6. It is biologically safe and environmentally acceptable.
7. Its aroma is compatible and pleasant to refresh the feeling.

Uses and Applications :-

1. Aromatherapy liquid soap is an essential cosmetics preparations used by almost everybody in their bath and in hand washing.
2. It is used in every home, houses, restaurants, five star hotels, offices, air ports, waiting halls and in all the corporate offices to wash the hands.
3. It is used by every body both women and men during their bath in middle and upper class of society.
4. This is used by people of all age group.

B.I.S. Specification :-

There is no such B.I.S. Specification available on "Aromatherapy Liquid Soap" with Bureau of Indian Standards. But the product is required to be tested as per the Cosmetics norms prior to selling in the market.

Government Regulations :-

"Aromatherapy Liquid Soap" is a Cosmetic product which come under Drug & Cosmetic Rules, 1945.

To manufacture "Aromatherapy Liquid Soap" the manufacturer has to apply to the licensing authority appointed by the State Government in Form-31 (if the manufacturer wants to manufacture products for sale or distribution or Form -31A, (if the manufacturer wants loan license to manufacture cosmetic product.).

Raw Materials Require & its Availability :-

The major raw materials require in its manufacturing are Sodium Lauryl Sulphate, Cocobetaine, Sodium Stearate, Propylene Glycol, Purified Water, Glycol Distearate, Sodium Chloride, Preservative, Lemon Oil, Neroli Oil, Rosemary Oil, Perfumes or Fragrance, Colour (water soluble), Herbal Extracts and Laboratory testing chemicals.

The packaging materials required are PET or HDPE plastic Bottles, Fliptop Caps, Labels, Corrugated Cartons, Pressure sensitive self adhesive tapes, box straps etc. These are indigenously available and can be procured from nearby local available sources.

Aromatherapy Liquid Soap

Formulation :-

Ingredients		*Parts by weight*
Sodium Lauryl Sulphate	-	15-17
Cocobetaine	-	3 - 5
Sodium Stearate	-	8-10
Propylene Glycol	-	1 - 2
Purified Water	-	to make 100
Glycol Distearate	-	1-2
Sodium Chloride	-	1-1.5
Preservative	-	0.2 - 0.7
Lemon Oil	.	0.5 - 0.8
Neroli Oil	-	0.5 -0.8
Rosemary Oil	-	0-5 - 0.8
Perfume or Fragrance	-	0.1 - 0.5
Colour (Water soluble)	-	q.s.
		100

Manufacturing Process :-

To prepare a good quality Aromatherapy Liquid Soap, it is suggested to proceed the following processing steps.

1. First of all, Procure all the ingredients from the good reputed suppliers.
2. Analyse and test each ingredients for best quality product.
3. Weigh each ingredients separately as specified in the formulation.
4. In a stainless steel vessel fitted with S. S. Stirrer, pour Sodium Lauryl Sulphate, Cocobetaine, Sodium Stearate, Propylene Glycol and Purified water. Heat it together at 70°C till all the ingredients melt and mix to prepare an uniform preparations.
5. In another stainless steel vessel heat Glycol Distearate at 70°C with stirring.
6. Now, add step-5 compound to step-4 preparations with uniform mixing and stirring to cool to 40°C.
7. Add sodium choride solution to step-6 preparations dropwise with stirring.
8. In another vessel dissolve preservative in little purified water and add to the step-7 preparations with mixing at 35°C.
9. In a separate stainless steel vessel mix Lemon oil, Neroli oil, Rosemary oil together with stirring and add to step-8 preparations.

10. Then add the perfume and colour solution one by one and mix uniformly till homogeneous.
11. The final aromatherapy liquid soap is now quality tested and standardized.
12. The liquid soap is now packed in PET or HDPE plastic bottles and bottles are capped. The bottles are now labelled and packed in corrugated master cartons. The cartons are sealed with self adhesive tapes and strapped.
13. The cartons are now stored and marketed to the desired customers, dealers or distributors.

Process Flowsheet For Manufacturing of Aromatherapy Liquid Soap

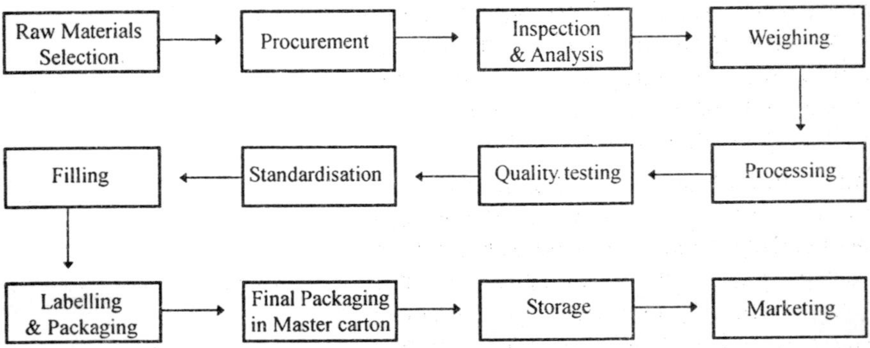

> **Note :** All above plant and equipments are available in India. For getting these, the suppliers addresses are provided at the end of the book.

25

Herbal Fairness Cream

Introduction :-

Herbal Fairness Cream is one of the excellent Skincare Cosmetics product having international acceptance.It is now popular among the Indian people mostly in girls, women to look fair and beautiful. The product is gaining importance all over the country. This fairness cream is a type of vanishing cream. When it is applied on the face skin and rubbed, it penetrates in the skin. After continuous uses, it reduces the pigment of skin and make the skin fairer and beautiful.

Now a days, the fairness cream market demand is growing at a rapid pace in domestic as well as in international market. The two major market player Hindustan Lever Ltd. and Cavin Care Ltd.,with their brand "Fair & Lovely" and "Fair Ever" are selling the large Quantity of fairness cream all over India. The girls, teen agers, house wives, office going women, female executives, models, actresses, TV artists, TV news readers, fashionable models and almost every beauty conscious women are buying and using this product to look beautiful and glamorous. It is becoming a necessary in their skincare cosmetic range. Its persistent use gradually reduces the pigmentations from the skin. The skin becomes fair day by day.The natural herbal extracts present in the cream imparts shining beauty to the females. The publicity in the television, cable TV and news paper has popularized this product and has created the excellent demand from every part of the country. This cream is now available in every shops, General stores, departmental stores, medicine shops, medical stores and in other places in market. This product is demanded by almost everybody. A new entrepreneur or cosmetics manufacturer can add this product in their cosmetic range and earn high profit.

Properties of Good Quality Herbal Fairness Cream :-

1. Herbal Fairness Cream is applicable on all types of skins.
2. It is applied on the skin, It do not cause any side effects.
3. It is compatible with human body as well as with environment.
4. The product has appropriate viscosity for filling in tubes and jars. It is easy for dispensing from Jars or tubes.
5. It is easily washable and removable from face with water.

Uses and Applications :-

1. Herbal Fairness Cream is generally considered as ayurvedic / Herbal cosmetics preparation. So it is widely accepted by all age group of people.
2. The beauty Consciousness and glamour has raised its demand muitifolded among youngsters, teenager, young married women, girls going to marry, new brides, grooms, office going male and female executives and among almost every body.
3. It is used in homes, houses, five star hotels, beauty parlours, spa-clubs, modelling institution etc.

B. I. S. Specification :-

There is no such B. I. S. Specification available on "Herbal Fairness Cream" with Bureau of Indian standards. But prior to selling this cream into market, it is suggested to check all the cosmetics norms as specified in the IS-6608-skin cream published by Bureau of Indian standards.

Government Regulations:-

"Herbal Fairness Cream" is a cosmetic product which come under Drug & Cosmetic Rules, 1945.

To manufacture, "Herbal Fairness Cream" the manufacturers have to apply to the licensing authority appointed by the State Government in Form-31 (if the manufacturer wants to manufacture products for sale or distribution).

Raw Materials Require and its Availability :-

To formulate and manufacture a good quality Herbal Fairness Cream, the raw materials required are listed viz. Mineral oil, Stearic Acid, Emulsifying wax, Silicon oil, Ethylene Glycol Monostearate (EGMS), Isopropyl Palmitate (IPP), Glycerine, Sodium Lauryl sulphate, Triethanolamine, Zinc oxide, Titanium dioxide, Purified water, Preservative, Propylene Glycol, Methi seed extract, Basil oil, Sandal wood oil, Lactic acid (Alpha Hydroxy Acid), Perfume or Fragrance, Colour (Water soluble), Herbal Extracts and Laboratory testing chemicals.

The packaging materials required are plastic Collapsible tubes, jars, aluminium seals, labels, outer cartons, corrugated master cartons, adhesive tapes, box straps etc.

These are indigenously available and can be procured from nearby available local sources.

Herbal Fairness Cream

Formulation :-

Ingredients		*Parts by weight*
Mineral oil	-	5 - 6
Stearic Acid	-	4-5
Emulsifying wax	-	1-3
Silicon oil	-	0.5-2
Ethylene Glycol Monostearate (EGMS)	-	0.5-1
Isopropyl Palmitate (IPP)	-	1-2
Glycerine	-	2-3
Sodium Lauryl sulphate	-	0.5 - 1
Triethanolamine	-	1-2
Zinc oxide	-	0.5 - 1
Titanium dioxide	-	0-5 - 1
Purified water	-	to make 100
Preservative	-	0.2-0.7
Propylene Glycol	-	2-3
Methi seed extract	-	1-1.5
Basil oil	-	1-1.5
Sandal wood oil	-	1-1.5
Lactic acid (Alpha Hydroxy Acid)	-	1-1.5
Perfume or Fragrance	-	0.1 - 0.5
Colour (Water soluble)	-	q.s.
		100

Manufacturing Process :-

To prepare a good standard quality Herbal Fairness Cream, it is suggested to proceed the following processing steps.

1. Procure all the ingredients from good suppliers or dealers.
2. Analyse and test each ingredients for best quality products.
3. Weigh each ingredient separately as specified in the formulation.
4. In a stainless steel vessel fitted with S. S. Stirrer, pour Mineral Oil, Stearic Acid, Emulsifying Wax, Silicon Oil, Ethylene Glycol Monostearate and Isopropyl Palmitate. Heat these compounds together at 70°C with uniform stirring.
5. In a stainless steel planetary mixer fitted with S. S. Stirrer pour Glycerine, Sodium Lauryl Sulphate, Triethanolarnine, Zinc Oxide, Titanium Dioxide and purified water. Mix and heat together at 70°C to homogenize the product.
6. Now, add step-4 preparations to step-5 preparations with continuous stirring till temperature is reached to 40°C.

7. In another stainless steel vessel dissolve the preservative in Propylene Glycol with heating to 40°-50°C. Cool it to 35°C and add to step-6 preparations.
8. Add Lactic Acid, Methi seed extract to step-7 preparations with uniform mixing. Then, add the Basil oil, Sandal wood oil with mixing homogeneously.
9. Add the perfume or fragrance and colour solution to the step-8 preparations.
10. Now, test and standardize the final Herbal Fairness Cream.
11. Fill the cream in tubes or jars as per customers choice. Seal it and pack in outer carton and then in corrugated master cartons.
12. The cartons are now sealed with adhesive tapes and strapped.
13. The final cartons are now placed in store and marketed to the desired customers, dealers or distributors.

Process Flowsheet For Manufacturing of Herbal Fairness Cream

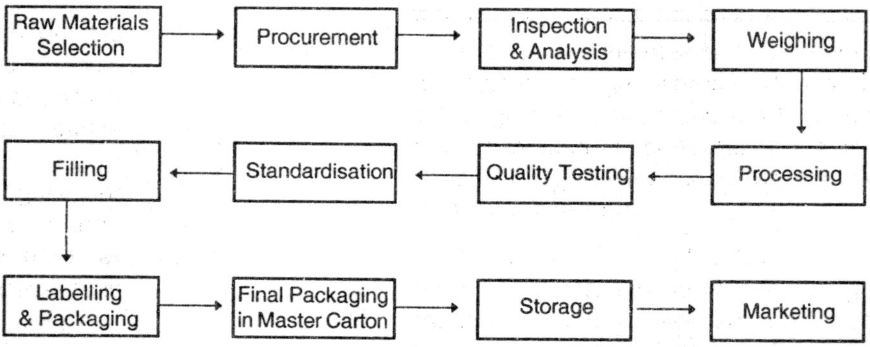

Note : The project cost may very according to the production capacity.

26

Hair Removing Cream (Depilatories)

Introduction :-

Hair Removing Cream is also called as depilatory. It is one of the cosmetics product falling in the segment of skin care cosmetics. Though it is not a skin care cream, but it comes in contact with skin on the area of application. It helps in removing unwanted hair over the skin. It is used by both men and women.

Hair Removing Cream (Depilatories) have been used for centuries to remove superfluous hair. Many women though prefer to razor shave but the depilatory has the advantage that it removes the hair at the neck of the hair follicle. Depilation is different from epilation. In case of epilation the hair is removed permanently by plucking the hair out and removing the root or using the processes known as electrolysis or diathermy. In this treatment the hair root is destroyed by high frequency current which is passed through a tiny needle inserted into the hair follicle. This is the most costly way of removing hair, but if the treatment is carried out successfully the hair does not grow again. But hair removing cream plays a vital role in removing out undesired hairs from any part of human body. The cream is easy to apply on the human body and also easy to remove. The product is gaining momentum all over the world. The product is now available with different fragrances, like Rose, Sandal, Lemon, Floral, fruit, herbal with Aloe Vera and other ingredients based. New entrepreneur can launch new products for acceptance all over the world.

Properties of Good Quality Hair Removing Cream :-

1. The Hair Removing Cream has skin soothing effect.
2. it is easily applied over the skin to remove the hair.
3. It do not cause any irritation, redness or allergy to the skin.
4. The product is spread easily during the application but firm enough to remain localized and in close contact with the hair.
5. The cream is left on the skin for 10-15 minutes according to the strength of the hair growth and then removed by scraping and finally washing.

6. The product do not give rise to erythema, skin irritation or dermatitis due to incorrect alkali / thioglycollate balance.
7. The product is non-toxic and non-irritant to the skin.
8. It is efficient in action, removing hair rapidly, preferably in 4-6 minutes.
9. It is preferably odourless.
10. It is stable on storage.
11. It is harmless to clothing.
12. It is preferably cosmetically elegant.

Uses and Applications :-

1. It is used to remove the superfluous hair without injury to the skin from legs, hands etc.
2. This cream preparation has advantage that they avoid any danger of cutting or abrading the skin in regions such as the underarms, where it is difficult to see the area clearly and even more difficult to guide a razor over the complicated contours.
3. This product has apparent advantage that they discourage the regrowth of hair if they are applied regularly.

B.I.S. Specification :-

There is no such B.I.S. Specification available on "Hair Removing Cream", But the product is tested as per the cosmetics norms.

Government Regulation :-

"Hair Removing Cream" is a cosmetic product which come under Drug & Cosmetic Rules. 1945.

To manufacture, "Hair Removing Cream", the manufacturers have to apply to the licensing authority appointed by the State Government in Form-31 (if the manufacturer wants to manufacture products for sale or distribution).

Raw Materials Require and its Availability :-

All the raw materials are available indigenously and can be procured from local available sources.

Hair Removing Cream

Formulation :-

Ingredients		*Parts by weight*
Calcium Thioglycollate trihydrate	-	5 - 7
Calcium Carbonate	-	15 - 18
Mineral oil (Cosmetic Grade)	-	4-6
Cetyl Alcohol	-	4 - 7

Sodium Lauryl Sulphate (Powder or needle)	-	0.3 - 0-7
Glycerine	-	3 - 5
Purified Water	-	q.s. to make 10
Perfumes	-	0.2-0.4
Calcium Hydroxide	-	Sufficient to adjust pH
Colour	-	q.s.
		100

Manufacturing Process :-

To prepare a good quality Hair Removing Cream, the production incharge has to proceed the following steps.

1 Procure all the raw materials from good reputed dealers or traders.

2 Analyse and test the ingredients in laboratory for good quality product.

3 Weigh all the ingredients in quantity as specified in the formulation.

4. In a stainless steel vessel fitted with stirrer, pour Mineral Oil and Cetyl Alcohol. Heat the vessel at 70-80°C to melt Cetyl Alcohol and mix with Mineral Oil.

5. In another vessel dissolve Sodium Lauryl Sulphate in a part of water by mild heating and stirring

6 Now, add the Sodium Lauryl Sulphate Solution to the step-4 liquid mixture of Cetyl Alcohol and Mineral Oil to prepare a cream base.

7 Now, prepare a mixture of Glycerine, Calcium Thioglycollate and Calcium Carbonate mix to a paste form with sufficient water.

8 Then add this paste (step-7) to the cream base (step-6) with homogeneously mixing in a planetary mixer. Add perfume to it and mix uniformly.

9 In another vessel mix the Calcium Hydroxide in purified water with stirring uniformly.

10 Add the Calcium Hydroxide Solution to (Step-8) cream and adjust the pH of the cream to around 11.5-12.5. Finally mix the cream in the planetary mixer for 15-20 minutes to obtain an uniform final Hair Removing Cream.

11 The final cream is quality tested and filled in glass jars or plastic jars of size 25gms. 50gms. 100gms etc.

12 The glass jars are now sealed, capped, labeled and placed in the outer cartons and then in the corrugated cardboard boxes.

13 The cartons are now placed in store and marketed to the desired customers.

Plant & Machineries Require :-

1 Stainless steel vessel with stirrer
2 Planetary mixer with accessories
3 Gas burner with LPG cylinders
4 Filling machine for glass jars.
5 Sealing machine.
6. Labelling machine.
7. Cartons sealing and box strapping machine.
8. Laboratory testing equipments & glasswares.
9. Other tools and accessories.

Process Flowsheet For Manufacturing of Hair Removing Cream

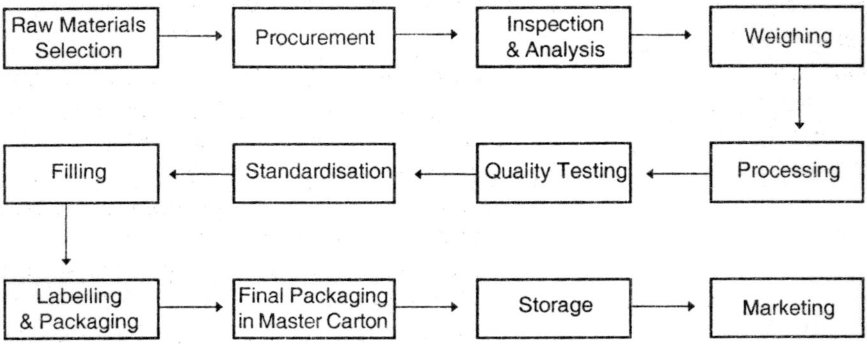

> **Note :** Detialed project report on above project is available with EIRI. Contact 'EIRI' office for more details.

27

Nail Polish (Nail Enamel)

Introduction :-

Nail polish is the general term used for nail enamel or nail lacquer or nail varnish . Though nail polish terminology is totally different from nail enamel. As it contains powder abrasives whereas nail enamel is formulated differently with cellulose lacquer, aryl sulfonamide formaldehyde resin, plasticizers, solvent mixtures and with D & C or FD & C pigments dispersion. The product provides lustrous shiny coating on nails and decorate the nails beautiful. The modern beauty conscious girls, ladies or women or high fashionable models decorate their nails by matching with their sarees or dresses to express their glamorous, gorgeous, beautiful appearance during fashion shows, social functions and various other special occasions. The various colour shades of nail enamels are coming in the market and manufactured by different manufacturers considering the economic status of the people in our country as well as in other countries. At present the international cosmetics leaders L'oreal, Revlon, Lakme, and others have launched the nail lacquer with most ultramodern touch for global women users. Their products are unbeatable and economically high priced meant for high class society and have very premium segment products. Besides, there are a number of small manufacturers who are manufacturing the nail lacquer for medium and below medium class society. Their marketing demand is growing day by day all over the country. A new entrepreneur can take the opportunity for manufacturing and marketing of good nail enamel for sub urban and rural segments.

Requirements of Good Quality Nail Enamel or Nail Polish :-

A good Nail Enamel fulfil the following requirements.

1. It is easy and convenient to apply.
2. It is innocuous to the skin and nails.
3. It is stable on storage as regards homogeneity, separation, sedimentation, Colour and interaction of ingredients.
4. It give a film of satisfactory characteristics.
5. It is non-toxic, non-irritating in nature and is ecologically safe.

The Characteristics of a Good Nail Enamel Film:-

1. The Nail Enamel Film is even in thickness.
2. The Nail Enamel Film is uniform in colour means pigment is uniformly dispersed in the medium.
3. The enamel film has good gloss, it implies a smooth uniform shiny film over nail.
4. It has good adhesion to the nail.
5. It has sufficient flexibility to avoid brittleness and cracking.
6. It is hard, non-tacky film surface, resistant to impact and scratching.
7. The nail enamel film dry in 1-2 minutes without development of bloom in humid atmosphere.

Uses and Applications :-

1. The Nail Enamels are available in various shades depending on the choice of females and matching with their dresses or sarees. It is used to decorate their nails of hands and feet.
2. The fashionable beauty conscious curls, ladies, women use nail enamel during all the social function.
3. It is one of the largest and most important manicure preparations.
4. This products is highly used in beauty parlours, beauty salons, to decorate the nails.

B.I.S. Specification :-

There is no such B.I.S. Specification available on "Nail Polish" But the product is tested as per the cosmetic-norms.

Government Regulations :

"Nail Polish" is a cosmetic product which come under Drug & Cosmetic Rules. 1945.

To manufacture, "Nail Polish", the manufacturers have to apply to the licensing authority appointed bv the State Government in Form-31 (if the manufacturer wants to manufacture products for sale or distribution

Raw Materials Require and its Availability :-

The major raw materials require are Nitro Cellulose, Resin, Plasticisers, Solvents, Pigment or dyes dispersions, diluents etc. Besides, there are packaging materials such as glass bottles or vials, caps fitted with small brush, corrugated small boxes, corrugated cartons etc.

Nail Enamel (Nail Lacquer)

Formulation :-

Ingredients		*Parts by weight*
PartA:-		
Nitrocellu.lose ((1/2) second viscosity)	-	8 - 10
Aryl Sulfonamide - Formaldehyde Resin (Santolite MHP)	-	8 - 10

Plasticiser (Santiciser S or 160. DiButyl Phthalate)	-	3 - 5
Ethyl Alcohol	-	4 - 5
Ethyl Acetate	-	18-20
Butyl Acetate	-	15-17
Toluene	-	to make 100
		100

Part B :-

Pigments or Dyes dispersions (D & C Red 6, 30, 36. FD & C Yellow 5, 6, 7.)	-	4-5

Manufacturing Process :-

To prepare a standard quality Nail Enamel (Nail Lacquer), the manufacturer should proceed following processing steps.

1. Procure all the raw materials from reputed suppliers.
2. Analyse all the ingredients as per cosmetics grades specification.
3. Weigh all the ingredients as mentioned in the formulation.
4. In a closed stainless steel vessel fitted with S.S. Stirrer and flameproof motor, feed the Nitrocellulose and solvent mixture of Ethyl Alcohol, Ethyl Acetate, Butyl Acetate, Toluene and keep on slow stirring for 3-5 days till Nitrocellulose completely dissolved in solvent.
5. The Nitrocellulose solution is filtered and to it add the Santolite MHP resin and again mix homogeneously with slow stirring. Then to this resin liquid add the DiButyl phthalate plasticizer with slow stirring for 2-3 hours till a homogeneous lacquer is formed.
6. To the transparent lacquer add the pigment dispersion or dye dispersion as per desired shades required. The product is stirred for 4-6 hours till completely mixed and no particles are seen in the final product.
7. The final laquer is now quality tested and standardized to the requisite viscosity.
8. The final nail enamel is now packed in small glass bottle of sizes 5ml, 10ml, 15ml, 20ml as desired by customers.
9. The bottles are now packed in the small boxes of 12 Nos, 20 Nos or any suitable quantity. The boxes are now further packed in corrugated master cartons and strapped.
10. The cartons are now placed in store and marketed to the desired customers.

Process Flowsheet For Manufacturing of Nail Polish or Nail Enamel

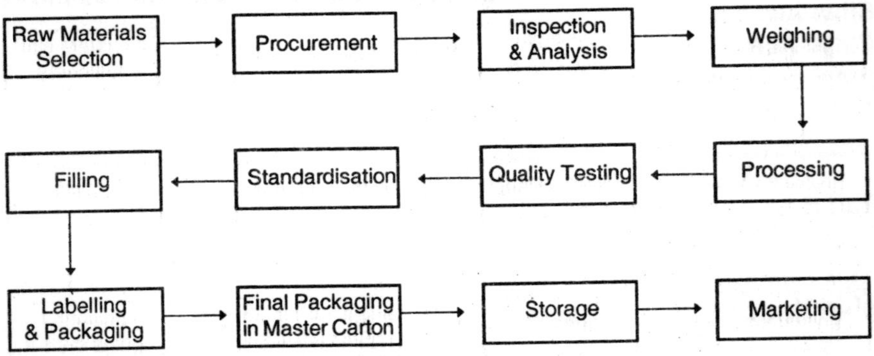

Plant & Machineries Require :-

1. Stainless steel closed top tank fitted with S.S. Stirrer, flame proof motor and accessories.
2. Weighing balance.
3. Stainless steel tanks.
4. Filling tanks (S.S. Made).
5. Laboratory Equipment and glasswares.
6. Tools & fire safety equipments.

> **Note:** Capacity and size of the project may vary according to the entrepreneur requirements. Entrepreneur may contact 'EIRI' office for further details of this project.

28

Mud Pack (Face Pack)

Introduction:-

Mud Packs (Face Packs) have been used by women from very ancient age. In antiquity, some earths believed to be possessing miraculous healing power were used on the face. Now a days, Mud Packs are applied either in the form of liquid or paste over face and are allowed to dry for 30-120 minutes. With drying, the tightening effect and Warmth is experienced. This produces stimulating sensation of rejuvenation. Some of the Mud Packs contain absorptive clays. As such, when these are removed, skin debris and black heads may be removed along with them. Which cause the face more glowing, shining and make women feel beautiful and youth.

Properties of Good Quality Mud Packs (Face Packs) :-

1. They should form a smooth paste (free from gritty particles) and should have pleasant odour.
2. When applied to the face, they should dry out rapidly to form an adherent coating on face. However, the coating should be such which can be removed either by peeling off the face or by gentle washing without causing pain.
3. They should produce a sensation of tightening of the skin after application.
4. They should capable of producing significant cleansing of the skin.
5. They should be non-toxic to the skin.

Uses and Applications :-

1. Mud Pack is one of the important variety of cosmetic product which is used by women in all the developing or developed countries considering the natural ingredients as main components.
2. It is used in beauty parlours, houses, in modern high profile societies due to beauty consciousness by women, girls and today even by men who are highly conscious about their facial appearance.

Types of Mud Pack (Face Pack):-

There are two types of mud packs available in the market. These are classified as :-

(A) Dry powder Mud Pack .

(B) Ready to use paste Mud Pack.

These mud packs are formulated and marketed all over the world considering the choice and acceptance of people from every categories and every part of the world.

Varieties of Mud Packs Available in Market :-

1. Herbal Mud Pack.
2. Vegetable Mud Pack.
3. Rose Mud Pack.
4. Sandal Mud Pack.
5. Neem Mud Pack.
6. Lemon Mud Pack.
7. Orange Mud Pack.
8. Cucumber Mud Pack.
9. Tulsi Mud Pack.
10. Yeast Mud Pack.
11. Anti - pimple Mud Pack.
12. Fruit Mud Pack.
13. Egg Mud Pack.
14. Anti-Wrinkle Mud Pack
15. Anti - Blemishes Mud Pack
16. Almond Mud Pack.
17. Peppermint Mud Pack.
18. Pudina Mud Pack.
19. Cream Mud Pack.
20. Milk Mud Pack,
21. Apple Mud Pack.
22. Strawberry Mud Pack.
23. Bride tone Mud Pack.
24. Apricot Mud Pack.

B.I.S. Specification :-

There is no such B.I.S. Specification available on "Mud Pack" with Bureau of Indian standards. But the products should pass through cosmetics permitted standards applicable over human skins.

Government Regulation:-

"Mud Pack (Face Pack)" is a Cosmetic product which falls under Drug & Cosmetic Rules, 1945.

To manufacture "Mud Pack (Face Pack)" the manufacturer has to apply to the licensing authority appointed by the State Government in Form-31 (if the manufacturer wants to manufacture products for sale or distribution) or Form -31A, (if the manufacturer wants loan license to manufacture cosmetic product.).

Raw Materials Require and its Availability:-

The major raw materials require to manufacture the Mud Pack (Face Pack) are Kaolin (Cosmetic Grade), Bentonite, Calamine, Sodium Lauryl Sulphate, Purified Water, Glycerine, Preservative, Perfumes, Colours etc.

The packaging materials require are named as HDPE/PET Jars, Aluminium Seals, Caps, Labels, Shrink Wraps, Printed outer cartons, Corrugated master cartons, Self adhesive tapes, Box straps etc.

The raw materials and packaging materials are indigenously available and can be procured from nearby available local sources.

Mud Based Face Pack (Mud Pack)

Formulation :-

Ingredients		*Parts by weight*
Kaolin (Cosmetic grade)	-	10-16
Bentonite	-	2-8
Calamine	-	6-14
Sodium Lauryl Sulphate	-	0.1-1.0
Purified water	-	50-60
Glycerine	-	6-12
Preservatives	-	0.25-1.00
Perfumes	-	q.s
Cosmetics colour	-	q.s

Manufacturing Process:-

Mud or earth based face packs contain high percentage of solids. Mud which are used in face pack preparation include china clay, colloidal kaolin, Fuller's earth, Bentonite etc. Mud pack may be prepared either in powder form or paste form.

If Mud pack is marketed in power form then it is mixed with water before application. This pack, on drying, harden on skin and contract giving a sensation of mechanical astringency.

Before preparation of Mud Pack, it is advisable to decontaminate the Earth, Bentonite, Kaolin by heating it in oven for appropriate time to kill all the micro-organisms. The detail steps are described as follow:-

1. Procure all the raw materials from good reliable suppliers.
2. Analyze all the raw materials for quality product.

3. Weigh the required quantity of dry ingredients and transfer to a dry blender (usually ribbon blender). Blend all the ingredients homogeneously.
4. This material is then transferred to a planetary mixer.
5. In another stainless steel vessel fitted with stirrer, add water and other liquid ingredients or water soluble ingredients then mix homogeneously to a uniform solution.
6. Now, this liquid phase solution is added in small additions to the dry solids in planetary mixer with continuous agitation. Initially these additions produce very high viscous dough. Subsequently, with more additions viscosity gradually decreases. Towards end of the process, additions may be made at the shorter time intervals.
7. The final Mud Pack is standardized and filled in jars (wide mouth bottles) by semi automatic weighing, filling and sealing macnine.
8. The bottles or jars are labelled by semi automatic labelling machine.
9. These final jars are now packed in corrugated cartons and the cartons are sealed by adhesive tapes.
10. The cartons are stored and marketed to the desired customers.

Process Flowsheet For Manufacturing of Mud Pack (Face Pack)

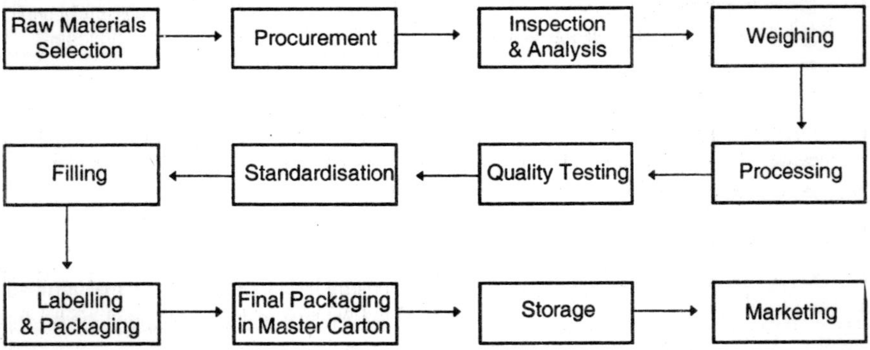

Plant & Machineries Require :-

1. Sieving machine.
2. Electric Oven.
3. Weighing balance & weights.
4. Ribbon blender with S.S.body.
5. Planetary Mixer.
6. Stainless steel mixing vessel fitted with S. S. Stirrer.
7. Jars weighing, filling and sealing machines.
8. Labelling machine.

9. Water de-ionisation unit.
10. Carton sealing and strapping machines.
11. Laboratory testing equipments, Glasswares.

PROJECT FINANCIAL ANALYSIS :-

1.	Production Capacity	-	100 Kgs Per Day / Per Shift Mud Pack (Face Pack) in Paste Form
2.	Land & Building	-	On Rent.
3.	Covered Area Require	-	250 Sq.mts
4.	Plant & Machinery Cost	-	Rs. 2.90 Lacs.
5.	Others Fixed Capital	-	Rs. 1.20 lacs.
6.	Total Fixed Capital Require	-	Rs. 4.10 lacs.
7.	Working Capital Require Per Month	-	Rs. 4.50 lacs.
8.	Margin Money	-	Rs. 1.13 lacs.
9.	Total Project Cost	-	Rs. 5.23 lacs.
10.	Total Capital Requirement	-	Rs. 9.60 lacs
11.	Cost of Production Per Month	-	Rs. 4.70 lacs.
12.	Turn Over Per Month	-	Rs. 7.00 lacs.
13.	Gross Profit Per Month	-	Rs. 2.30 lacs.
14.	Rate of Return Per Annum	-	288%
15.	Manpower Requirement	-	5 Nos.
16.	Electric Power Load	-	10 KW.
17.	Water Requirement Per Month	-	100 KLs.

Note : Detialed project report on above project is available with EIRI. Contact 'EIRI' office for more details.

29

Herbal Shampoo

Introduction:-

Herbal Shampoos are basically one of the prime cosmetic product used by all strata of the population all over the world. Shampoo is mainly used to clean scalp and hair to make hair smooth, shining, lustrous and easy to comb and set. There are two types of shampoo available in the market. One is modern shampoo and another is Herbal Shampoo. These shampoos are formulated from different ingredients as per the choice of customers. Now a days, the importance of herbs has been considered by formulators, scientists, chemists, doctors and almost by every body in the world, due to beneficial effects on human body with no-side effect on the human being. The application of easily available herbs, natural products, fruits, vegetables and other ingredients are used to formulate various types of Herbal Shampoos which are found and considered as eco-friendly, human friendly, bio-friendly and compatible to almost every types of human skins, human hairs

There are two types of shampoo available in the market.

(a) Clear transparent Gel type shampoo.

(b) Pearly translucent or opaque shampoo.

Both types of shampoos are formulated in modern as well as herbal varieties considering the end users requirement. These shampoos are prepared for oily hair, dry hair or normal hair as per the structure of human hair. Now a days, Herbal Shampoos for normal hairs are marketed in almost every part of our country. Due to continuous growth in population, as well as social beauty awareness, rise in fashion and advertisement in television, news paper, magazine, the consumption of Herbal Shampoo and other cosmetics is gaining momentum at a faster pace. The market demand is rising almost every where in the world. Similarly our domestic as well as export demand is increasing day by day. A new entrepreneur will consider it profitable to earn excellent profit.

Properties of Good Quality Herbal Shampoo :-

1 A good shampoo should be prepared with perfectly pH balanced.

2 It should clean hair and scalp thoroughly without stinging or irritation and should not remove too much of natural oil from the scalp.

3 The successful preparation of Herbal Shampoo must leave the hair fragrant, lustrous, soft, shiny and must do a satisfactory cleaning without removing an excessive amount of oil from scalp.
4 The Herbal Shampoo should be effective in removing dandruff.
5 It should have good foaming power. It should be active and effective in hard water like normal water.

Uses and Applications :-

1. Herbal Shampoos are used to wash and cleanse the hair and scalp.
2. It is used by everybody, children, men, women of all age group to make their hair Shiny, lustrous and beautiful.
3. It is used in houses, star hotels, tourist centers and almost everywhere by men and women to cleanse their scalp and hair.

B.I.S. Specification:-

There is no B.I.S. Specification available on "Herbal Shampoo" but it is available on "Modern Shampoo" with Bureau of Indian standards tc standardize the finished products before selling in the market.

Government Regulation :-

"Herbal Shampoo" is a Cosmetic product which falls under Drug & Cosmetic Rules, 1945.

To manufacture "Herbal Shampoo" the manufacturer has to apply to the licensing authority appointed by the State Government in Form-31 (if the manufacturer wants to manufacture products for sale or distribution) or Form -31A, (if the manufacturer wants loan license to manufacture cosmetic product.).

Raw Materials Require :-

A Herbal Shampoo consists of ingredients or raw materials which are chemically classified in the following categories-

1. Surfactants-Cleaning and foaming agents.
2. Foam boosters and stabilizers.
3. Conditioning Agents.
4. Special additives.
5. Preservatives.
6. Sequestering Agents.
7. Viscosity modifiers (viscosity improvers or viscosity reducers)
8. Opacifying or cleaning agents.
9. Fragrances or perfumes.
10. Stabilizers.
11. Cosmetic permitted colour/dye
12. Diluents (De-ionized water).

13. Herbal Extracts.
14. Other special ingredients.

Packaging Materials :-

1. Bottles (HDPE, PET or Glass bottles)
2. Caps & stopper.
3. Stickers, labels.
4. Paper inner box.
5. Corrugated cartons.
6. Adhesive tapes.
7. HDPE /PP Straps.
8. Others.

HERBAL SHAMPOO

Formulation:-

Ingredient		*Parts by weight*
Sodium Lauryl Ether Sulphate (SLES)	-	32-40
Cocodiethanolamide	-	3-5
Cocobetaine (Additive)	-	3-5
Propylene Glycol (PG)	-	1-4
Citric Acid	-	0.1-1
Sodium Chloride	-	1-2
Quaternary Ammonium Compound	-	1-3
Preservative	-	0.2-0.5
Conditioner	-	0.2-1
De-ionised water	-	48-55
Colour (water soluble cosmetic colour)	-	q.s
Perfume (water soluble)	-	q.s
Herbal Extract (Amla, Shikakai, Reetha, Brahmi, Jatamansi & others)	-	0-5.2

Manufacturing Process:-

Herbal shampoo is prepared by following processing steps one by one to obtain good quality final product. Details of processing steps are described as follow :-

1. First of all purchase all the ingredients from good quality suppliers.
2. Analyse and Test all the ingredients to find its suitability for preparation of good quality herbal shampoo.
3. Now, weigh all the ingredients as specified in the formulation.
4. In a stainless steel vessel fitted with stirrer, pour SLES, Cocodiethanolamide, Cocobetaine and Demineralised water. Dissolve and mix homogeneously all the ingredients in the water with the help of stirrer.

5. Now in another vessel pour the preservative and Propylene Glycol. Heat the vessel to 70- 80° C by gas burner or by electric heating system to dissolve preservative in Propylene Glycol completely.
6. Now, mix the above preservative solution (Step-5) to solution in (Step-4) with stirring homogeneously.
7. To the above solution in (Step-6), add the conditioner and mix again.
8. Now, dissolve citric acid in water in another vessel and add dropwise to (Step-7) solution to obtain neutral pH of (Step-7) solution. Check the solution continuously to see neutral pH by pH paper strip.
9. Now, dissolve the colour in water and add this colour solution to (Step-8) solution dropwise to obtain the desired colour.
10. To this (Step-9) solution, add the quaternary ammonium compound and stire homogeneously.
11. Now, dissolve sodium chloride in water in another vessel. This sodium chloride solution is added dropwise with stirring to (Step-10) solution. The preparation will start to thicken till the desired final consistency or viscosity is obtained.
12. Add perfume, herbal extracts to the (Step-11) solution and mix uniformly. This finished herbal shampoo is now standardized, tested & stored in a clean dry stainless steel tank .
13. This shampoo is now filled in the plastic bottles by semi-automatic or automatic weighing, filling & sealing machine.
14. The filled bottfes are now labelled and packed in the corrugated cartons.
15. The cartons are now placed in store and sent to customers for marketing.

Process Flow Sheet For Manufacturing of Herbal Shampoo

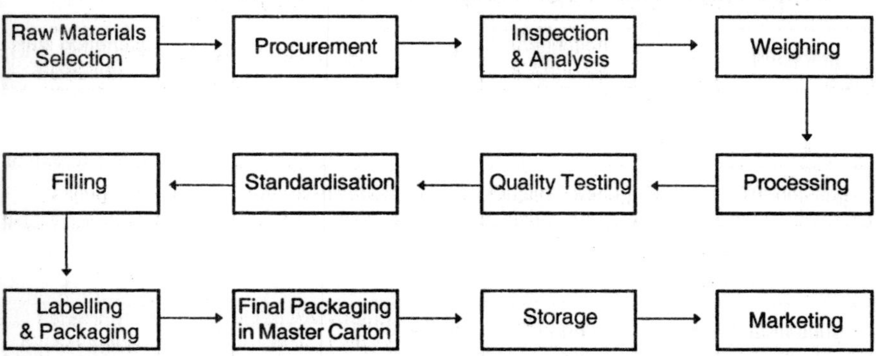

Plant and Machineries Require :-

1. Reaction vessel (Stainless steel - 316 made), fitted with S.S Stirrer, M.S. Jacket & heating electrodes and other accessories.
2. Stainless steel tanks with stirrer.
3. Gas burner.
4. Semi-automatic weighing, filiing and sealing machine.
5. Labeling machine.
6. Heat shrink wrap machine.
7. Carton sealing machine.
8. Laboratory equipment.
9. Electrical equipment and others.

PROJECT FINANCIAL ANALYSIS :-

1.	Production Capacity	-	200 Kgs Per Day / Per shift Herbal Shampoo
2.	Land & Building	-	(On Rent)
3.	Covered Area Require	-	300 Sq.mts.
4.	Plant & Machinery Cost	-	Rs. 4.50 lacs.
5.	Others Fixed Capital	-	Rs. 1.30 lacs.
6.	Total Fixed Capital Require	-	Rs. 5.80 lacs.
7.	Working Capital Require Per Month	-	Rs. 5.60 lacs.
8.	Margin Money	-	Rs. 1.40 lacs.
9.	Total Project Cost	-	Rs. 7.20 lacs.
10.	Total Capital Requirement	-	Rs. 11.40 lacs.
11.	Cost of Production Per Month	-	Rs. 5.80 lacs.
12.	Turn Over Per Month	-	Rs. 8.00 lacs.
13.	Gross Profit Per Month	-	Rs. 2.20 lacs.
14.	Rate of Return Per Annum	-	228%
15.	Manpower Requirement	-	5 Nos.
16.	Electric Power Load	-	18 KW.
17.	Water Requirement Per Month	-	150 KLs.

30

Herbal Amla Hair Oil

Introduction :-

Herbal Amla Hair Oil is one of the most popular hair care Cosmetic Product in India. The use of Herbal Amla Hair Oil to treat common hair problems like- dandruff, headache, hair failing etc. are common in India since ancient times. A large number of ayurvedic preparations like Amla oil, Bhringraj oil, Japakusum oil, Chameli oil and others are still popular in India and used for a variety of purposes like anti-dandruff, hair blackening, brain stimulations, mood freshening etc.

Now, there are broadly two kinds of hair oils available in the market. These are classified as :-

1. Pre-wash Hair Oils :- Which are applied before shampooing the hair to massage the scalp and stimulate the hair growth.
2. Post-wash Hair Oils :- Which are applied after shampooing. These are non-greasy hair oils containing a large proportions of light liquid paraffin to give a non greasy feel to the hair and the hair could be combed in a desired style.

Properties of Vegetable Oils used in the Preparations of Herbal Amla Hair Oil :-

1. Vegetable oil should be liquid at room temperature at 25° C.
2. When pure they are colourless, odourless and tasteless. The characteristic colour, odours and flavours associated with natural oil are imparted to them by foreign substances.
3. They are lighter than and insoluble in water and therefore form the upper layer when mixed with it. They are readily soluble in organic solvents.
4. They readily form emulsions when agitated with water in the presence of soap, gelatin or other emulsifiers.

Properties of Light Liquid Paraffin Oils :-

Light Liquid Paraffin Oil is a petroleum product. It is transparent, colourless, oily liquid having applications in hair care and personal care cosmetics. It is extensively used in hair oils in combination of vegetable oils in varying proportions to reduce the excessive greasiness of the vegetable oils in the hair oil.

Properties of Good Quality Herbal Amla Hair Oil :-

1. Herbal Amla Hair Oil may be both greasy type and non-greasy type.
2. It keeps scalp dandruff free.
3. It keeps the head cool, due to medicinal effect of amla on the scalp of human being.
4. It do not cause any sorts of side effect on the scalp.
5. It cause the hair lustrous, shining, beautiful on both men and women of all age group.
6. It has mood freshening effect on human being.

Uses and Applications :-

1. Herbal Amla Hair Oil is used by men and women of all age group all over the world.
2. It is used by almost every people in our country due to its ayurvedic effect over human scalp and hair roots.
3. It is used to emolliate and moisturize the hair.
4. It is also used for a number of hair and scalp disorders like dandruff, hair fall, hair greying etc.

B.I.S Specification :-

Depending upon the ingredients used in the preparation of Hair oil, the B.I.S. specification for Hair oils (IS-7123) have been divided into following three types-

Type - 1 :- Hair oil based on Vegetable oils.

Type - 2 :- Hair oil based on Mineral oil (light liquid paraffins).

Type - 3 :- Hair oil based on a mixture of vegetable oil and mineral oil.

Government Regulation:-

Herbal Amla Hair Oil is a Cosmetic product which falls under Drug & Cosmetic Rules, 1945. .

To manufacture Herbal Amla Hair Oil the manufacturer has to apply to the licensing authority appointed by the State Government in Form-31 (if the manufacturer wants to manufacture products for sale or distribution) or Form -31A, (if the manufacturer wants loan license to manufacture cosmetic product.).

Market Status:-

The Indian Hair Oil market is a very big market and worth over Rs. 700 crores. The last one decade has shown tremendous growth in the Hair oil market and the market is growing at a rate of 20 % per Annum in the rural areas and 7-8 % in the urban areas. It has been estimated that with rise in population growth rate the demand of Herbal Amla Hair Oil will grow positively at a rapid pace in coming future.

Amla:-

Amla is botanically named as Emblica officinalis. It is one of the rich source of vitamin C. It is mostly used in hair care cosmetics like hair oil, hair dyes, herbal shampoos and others. Its ayurvedic effect is mostly helpful for toning and treatment of hair and scalp disorders.

Formulation of Herbal Amla Hair Oil

Ingredients		***Parts by weight***
Sunflower oil	-	30-60
Light liquid Paraffin oil	-	70-39
Amla extract	-	0.2-1
Preservative	-	0.01-0.75
Colour	-	q.s
Perfume	-	q.S

Manufacturing process :-

The Herbal Amla hair oil is prepared by following detail processing steps :-

1. First of all, procure good quality raw materials from good reputed suppliers.
2. Test ail the ingredients for their application in manufacturing of hair oil.
3. Weigh all the raw materials as specified in the formulation.
4. Now, take sunflower oil and light liquid Paraffin oil in a clean and dry stainless steel vessel fitted with S.S.Stirrer. Mix it thoroughly.
5. Now, preservative is dissolved in small quantity of above oil separately by mild heating on a gas burner and then added to the rest of the mixed oil and then mix again.
6. Take out 20 liters of the above base oil and add to it the Amla in powder form in another small kettle (50 liter. Capacity). Heat the kettle at 60-70° C for 3 to 4 hours. Switch off the kettle and allow to cool the extract.
7. Mix the extract in base oil and stire the oil.
8. Dissolve colour in 200ml. of the above preparations separately and then add it dropwise with stirring to the base oil to produce desired colour.
9. Add perfume in the last.
10. Filter the oil through a filter press to have a sparkling clean hair oil.
11. The oil is now quality tested as per B.I.S specification.

12. It is filled in the plastic or glass bottles of desired sizes by automatic or semi-automatic weighing, filling and bottle sealing machines.
13. The bottles are now labelled by semi-automatic machine or by manual method.

Process Flowsheet For Manufacturing of Herbal Amla Hair Oil

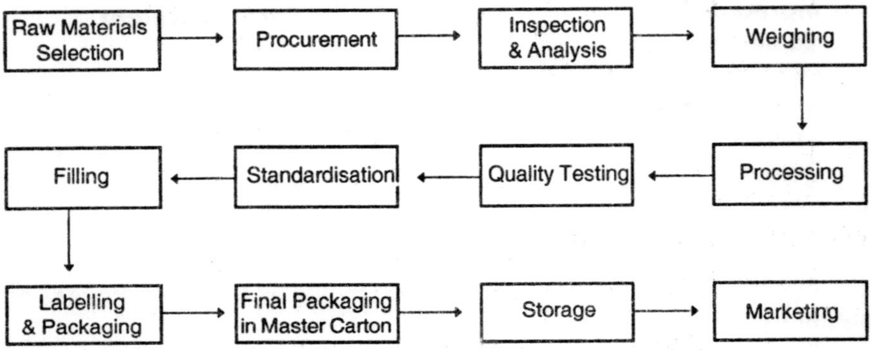

14. The products are now packed in final corrugated cartons and sealed by adhesive tapes.
15. It is now placed in store and marketed to the desired customers.

Plant & Machineries Require :-

1. Mixing vessel (S.S.-316 Made) fitted with S.S.Stirrer.
2. Reaction vessel fitted with S.S.Stirrer.
3. Weighing balance.
4. Laboratory analytical equipment.
5. Powder grinding unit.
6. Filtration unit or filter press.
7. Stainless Steel Filling tank.
8. Semi-automatic weighing filling sealing machine.
9. Labeling machine.
10. Other equipments.

Availability of Raw Materials :-

All the Raw materials are indigenously available and can be procured from nearby available sources.

PROJECT FINANCIAL ANALYSIS :-

1.	Production Capacity	-	100 Ltrs. Per Day / Per Shift Herbal Amla Hair Oil
2.	Land & Building	-	On Rent.
3.	Covered Area Require	-	200 Sq.mts..
4.	Plant & Machinery Cost	-	Rs. 2.60 lacs.
5.	Others Fixed Capital	-	Rs. 0.80 lacs.
6.	Total Fixed Capital Require	-	Rs. 3.40 lacs.
7.	Working Capital Require Per Month	-	Rs. 3.00 lacs.
8.	Margin Money	-	Rs. 0.75 lacs.
9.	Total Project Cost	-	Rs. 4.15 lacs.
10.	Total Capital Requirement	-	Rs. 6.40 lacs.
11.	Cost of Production Per Month	-	Rs. 3.20 lacs.
12.	Turn Over Per Month	-	Rs. 4.50 lacs.
13.	Gross Profit Per Month	-	Rs. 1.30 lacs.
14.	Rate of Return Per Annum	-	265 %
15.	Manpower Requirement	-	4 Nos.
16.	Electric Power Load	-	10 KW.
17.	Water Requirement Per Month	-	100 KLs.

Note : Capacity and size of the project may vary according to the entrepreneur requirements. Entrepreneur may contact 'EIRI' office for further details of this project.

31

Acne - No Pimple Cream

Introduction :-

Acne-No Pimple Cream is a variety of cosmetic product having importance among the young generation, specially for female. The acne or pimples develop on the face due to the various reasons, which reduce their beauty. To protect the face from pimples and to purify the skin or to protect from any external effect, this cream serves as good medium. It leaves long term effect on the skin and makes their skin oil free and smooth. It protects pimple growth by penetrating inside the skin layers. This cream, though it is not a medicine, but it imparts its medicinal effect more as well as its cosmetics effect. Now a days, there are several manufacturers, who are manufacturing this product, but the good quality product with long lasting effect is only surviving in the market.

Properties of Good Quality Acne-No Pimple Cream :-

1. This cream has pimple curing, skin purifying and bacteria resistance quality.
2. It absorb the oil, which is secreted by glands and cause the pimples to grow.
3. It also cause the skin to become smooth and rejuvenate, so that appearance of female face will be good looking.
4. It do not cause any side effect or allergy on the face skin.

Uses and Applications :-

1. The Acne-no pimple cream is used by almost every young girls or women in India as well as other countries.
2. It stops pimple growth, removes pimples from face with regular application over face skin.
3. This cream is suitable for everybody.

B.I.S. Specification:-

There is no such B.I.S. Specification available on "Acne-No Pimple Cream" with Bureau of Indian standards. But this product is quality tested under strict norms of Cosmetics and Drug legislations before sending for sell in the market.

Government Regulation :-

"Acne-No Pimple Cream" is a Cosmetic product which come under Drug & Cosmetic Rules, 1945.

To manufacture "Acne-No Pimple Cream" the manufacturer has to apply to the licensing authority appointed by the State Government in Form-31 (if the manufacturer wants to manufacture products for sale or distribution) or Form -31A, (if the manufacturer wants loan license to manufacture cosmetic product.).

Market Potentiality:-

The market potentiality and demand of Acne-No Pimple Cream is growing day by day due to rise in pimple problem among young generations all over the country. So demand is existing and also growing at rapid pace.

ACNE -NO PIMPLE CREAM

Formulation :-

Ingredients		*Parts by weight*
Mineral oil	-	2-5
StearicAcid	-	12-15
Preservative	-	0.2-1
Potassium Hydroxide	-	0.5-1.5
Purified water	-	69.50 -72.50
Sorbitol	-	2-5
Cetyl Alcohol	-	0.2-2
Silicon oil	-	0.5-2
Perfume	-	q.s.
		100

Manufacturing Process :-

To prepare Acne-no pimple cream of good quality the following processing steps have to be followed step by step to prepare final product.

1. Procure all the raw materials from good reputed suppliers.
2. Analyse and test the quality of raw materials to obtain good finished product.
3. Weigh all the ingredients as specified in the formulation.
4. Now, in a Jacketed stainless steel vessel pour Mineral Oil, Cetyl Alcohol, Stearic Acid and Silicone Oil. Heat it at 70-80° C to melt the Stearic Acid and is mixed with other ingredients homogeneously by stirrer.
5. In another stainless steel vessel add Water, Preservative, Potassium Hydroxide, Sorbitol and mix with slight heating to obtain uniform solution.

6. This preservative solution of (Step-5) is added slowly to (step-4) oil phase mixture with continuous stirring and cooling slowly to obtain an uniform emulsion of cream.
7. To this cream, add perfume with continuous stirring to obtain the finished product.
8. This cream is now quality tested and standardized as per International standard norms.
9. The finished Acne-no pimple cream is now packed in plastic or glass jars of various sizes from 25 ml to 500 ml size jars.
10. The jars faces are sealed by laminated aluminum foils, capped and labelled as per market requirements.
11. The finished labelled cream jars are printed with batch No., MRP., Manufacturing date, Expiry date and with other informations.
12. The jars are now packed in outer cartons and then in corrugated cartons. The cartons are sealed with adhesive tapes and strapped.
13. The Cartons are now placed in store and sent for marketing.

Process Flowsheet For Manufacturing of Acne-No Pimple Cream

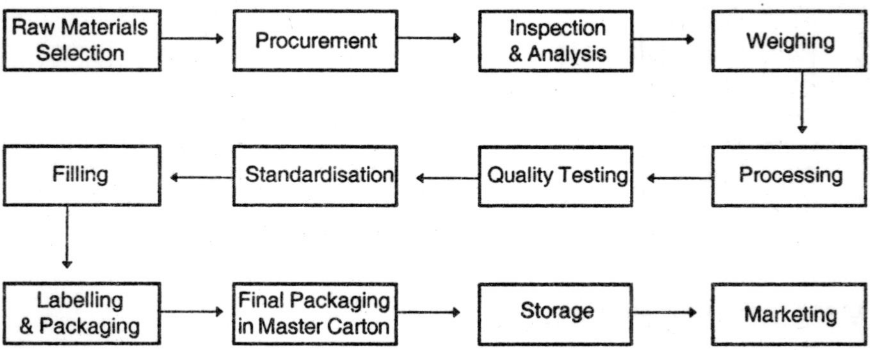

Plant & Machineries Require :-

1. Stainless steel jacketed vessel fitted with S.S.Stirrer, oil heating system with complete accessories.
2. Stainless steel vessel with S. S. Stirrer.
3. Weighing Balance.
4. Laboratory equipments, process control equipments and others.
5. Jar weighing, filling and sealing machine.
6. Labeling machine.
7. Batch marking machine.
8. Carton sealing and box strapping machine.
9. Other tools, jigs & devices.

Raw Materials Availability:-

All the raw materials are indigenously available and can be procured from nearby local available sources.

PROJECT FINANCIAL ANALYSIS :-

1.	Production Capacity	-	100 Kgs. Per Day / Per Shift Acne-No Pimple Cream
2.	Land & Building	-	On Rent.
3.	Covered Area Require	-	200 Sq.mts..
4.	Plant & Machinery Cost	-	Rs. 3.80 Lacs.
5.	Others Fixed Capital	-	Rs. 0.80 lacs.
6.	Total Fixed Capital Require	-	Rs. 4.60 lacs.
7.	Working Capital Require Per Month	-	Rs. 4.50 lacs.
8.	Margin Money	-	Rs. 1.13 lacs.
9.	Total Project Cost	-	Rs. 5.73 lacs.
10.	Total Capital Requirement	-	Rs. 9.10 lacs.
11.	Cost of Production Per Month	-	Rs. 4.70 lacs.
12.	Turn Over Per Month	-	Rs. 7.00 lacs.
13.	Gross Profit Per Month	-	Rs. 2.30 lacs.
14.	Rate of Return Per Annum	-	303 %
15.	Manpower Requirement	-	5 Nos.
16.	Electric Power Load	-	12 KW.
17.	Water Requirement Per Month	-	100 KLs.

Note : The project cost may vary according to the production capacity.

32

Kali Mehandi (Herbal Hair Dye Powder-Black)

Introduction :-

Now a days, Herbal Hair Dye Powder is one of the prominent cosmetic product having worldwide demand to dye white hair or grey hair to black or in various shades. With rise in fashion awareness and publicity in Television and other various media, the people are demanding more and more to this product. Due to safety permissible limit of various ingredients in its formulation, it is worldwide accepted by users from the age 18 years onwards of male and female.

The Herbal Hair Dye is one of the important segment of Cosmetic industry which is gaining market demand potentiality at a rapid pace. The reason is simple to look young and beautiful. To colour the hair in various shades, different ingredients in different proportions are mixed together to prepare various coloured hair dyes, which are used by men and women all over the world. There are approximately more than 30 shades of powder herbal hair dyes available in the market. But, the most prominent acceptable colours are black brown, chestnuts, burgundy, blonde colours.

Categories of Hair Dyes Available in the Market :-

Modern hair colourings are best classified on the basis of saturation of lastingness of the colour effect on the human hair. Major categories can thus be classified as temporary, semi-permanent and permanent hair colorants.

Temporary Hair Colorants :-

Temporary Hair Colorants are defined as products, which produce colour on the hair which is removed by single shampoo.

Semi-Permanent Hair Colorants :-

Semi-Permanent Hair Colorants have been marked for more than 25 years. These dyes are of low enough molecular weight to penetrate into cuticle and partially into the cortex of hair. Most result, they are somewhat resistant to shampooing. In general, manufacturer specify that semi-permanent colorants produce an effect which will withstand between six and twelve shampoo wash.

Permanent Hair Colorants :-

Permanent Hair Colorants represent the major segment of the hair coloring market in the United States. Reasons for their popularity include the facts, that is possible to go lighter, darker or stay on the shade and that the result is resistant to frequent shampooing. Permanent hair colorants contain colourless precursors which will react with oxidizing agents inside the hair tile to produce colour molecules and stay over hair for longer period.

Properties of Good Quality Herbal Hair Dyes :-

Herbal Hair Dye (Kali Mehandi) has following properties to prove itself as best product -

1. It Is toxicologically safe.
2. The colouration achievable minimum time at ambient temperature is 10-30 minutes.
3. The hair dye impart a natural appearance to the hair under variety of lighting conditions.
4. It produce minimum scalp staining.
5. It is convenient to use.
6. The sunlight fastening is good.
7. The colour after dyeing of the hair is uniform from the root to the tip.
8. It effects hair as a hair conditioner.
9. It is economical & inexpensive.

Uses and Applications :-

1. Herbal Hair Dyes are used by almost every people whose hair have become white or grey.
2. It is used by fashionable models, film actor and actresses to colour their hair.
3. It is now used by common people all over the world to look young and beautiful.

B.I.S. Specification :-

Bureau of Indian standards has published following IS specification to test the Powder Hair Dyes as per their norms before selling it in the market.

IS-10350 :- Powder Hair Dyes.

Government Regulation :-

Powder Herbal hair dye is a cosmetic product which come under Drug & Cosmetic Rules, 1945.

To manufacture, "Herbal Hair Dye Powder" the manufacturers have to apply to the licensing authority appointed by the State Government in Form-31 (if the manufacturer wants to manufacture products for sale or distribution) or Form-31A, (if the manufacturer wants loan license to manufacture cosmetic product).

Raw Materials :-

Herbal Hair Dyes are basically prepared from Henna as a major ingredients, which is chemically & biologically safe on human application. Besides, there are other ingredients like Amla, Reetha, Shikakai which are considered as adjuncts. There are some colouring chemicals which are added to develop various shades on hair without any side effects.

Herbal Hair Dye Powder (Kali Mehandi)

Formulations

Ingredients		*Parts by weight*
Henna Powder	-	43-70.50
Citric Acid	-	5-15
Magnesium Carbonate	-	1-5
Barium Peroxide	-	15-25
P-Phenylene diamine	-	8-10
Sodium sulfite	-	0.5-2
Amla powder	-	5
Shikakai powder	-	5
		100

Manufacturing Process :-

To manufacture good quality herbal hair dye the following processing steps have to be adopted.

1. Procure all the raw materials from good reputed suppliers.
2. Dry all the raw materials in tray dryer or drum dryer to reduce the moisture level to 0.5-2 % for longer shelf life.
3. Check all the raw materials for good quality.
4. Weigh all the raw materials as specified in formulation to obtain standard quality finished product.
5. Now, grind all the materials Henna, Amla, Shikakai into powder form of very fine size. Strict vigilance should be kept that no larger particles or bigger lumps should remain inside the powdered material.
6. This powder material is now fed to the Ribbon blender. To this, the rest ingredients are added and mixed thoroughly and homogeneously to obtain finished product.
7. This herbal hair dye powder is now quality tested and standardized to obtain good quality product.
8. The finished powder is packed in the printed pouches by fully automatic weighing filling and pouch sealing machine.

9. The finished pouches are now packed in inner paper cartons in 5,10 pcs. per pack. Then, these inner cartons are packed in corrugated cardboard boxes and sealed by adhesive tapes and box strapping.
10. The cartons are now placed in store and marketed to the desired customers or distributors.

Process Flowsheet For Manufacturing of Herbal Hair Dye Powder - Black (Kali Mehandi)

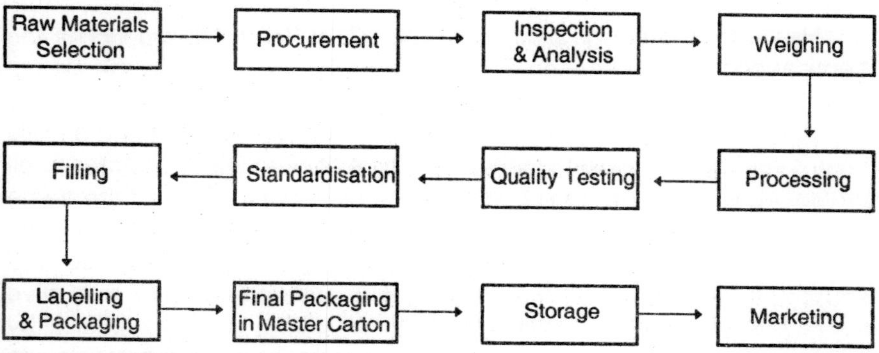

Plant & Machineries Require :-

1. Weighing balance with weights.
2. Oven or Tray Dryer.
3. Pulveriser with complete accessories.
4. Ribbon blender or mixer.
5. Automatic weighing, filling & pouch sealing machine.
6. Laboratory equipment & all accessories.
7. Box strapping machine.
8. Miscellaneous equipments.

Note : Detailed project report on above project is available with EIRI. Contact 'EIRI' office for more details.

33

Herbal Cold Cream

Introduction:-

Herbal Cold Cream is an important skin Care Cosmetics product having application in winter season in our country. In winter season the skin of people become brittle, dry and flaky. This cream helps to maintain the moisture, flexibility and restore its natural texture by providing an oily layer over the skin. Scientifically, it is a type of oil-in-water or water-in-oil emulsion. It is difficult to rub in over the skin. "Cold Cream" the name stems from cooling effect of such product on the skin. In the second century emulsions were composed primerily of natural waxes and vegetable oils. Natural wax was bees wax and vegetable oil was olive oil. At the turn of the twentieth century, vegetable oil was replaced by mineral oil due to unstable characteristics of unsaturated vegetable oils which prone to aerial oxidation and cause off smell in the cream. Now a days, the modern cold cream is formulated with mineral oil, petroleum jelly and several other herbal ingredients which reduces the vitamins, proteins deficiency of human skin by restoring its moisture balance and other essential components to maintain the texture and look of skin as beautiful. The skin becomes smooth, flexible wrinkle free and shiny due to the effect of natural oils.

The demand of this Herbal Cold Cream is growing day by day all over the world due to good effect in the winter season. In India winter season prevails from November to March. During this period the demand rises to multifold. But, in cold country or cold region it is demanded round the year by the people to maintain their beautiful appearance and natural look. In India, this product is manufactured in the brand name of Ayur, Ponds, Lakme and by other several brands by other companies. Still there is excellent rising demand for good quality products. So, a new entrepreneur can add this product in their cosmetic range for domestic as well as international market to earn good profit.

Properties of Good Quality Herbal Cold Cream :-

The Herbal Cold Cream has following important properties.

1. The Herbal Cold Cream is non-irritating, non-toxic, non-allergenic, biologically and environmentally safe for all types of skin.

2. The product is smooth in application over the skin.
3. The product has sufficient shelf life.
4. The product is uniform in texture.
5 It nourish and rejuvenate the skin.
6 It has protective oily film over the skin after application.

Uses & Applications :-

1. The Herbal Cold Cream is an essential cream for everybody during winter season. It is used by almost everybody to maintain their beautiful skin structure.
2. It is used by girls, ladies, women and men of all age group. In winter season the skin contracts and loses their flexibility. The Herbal Cold Cream reduces brittleness, flaky and other defects of the skin.
3. It is used in Urban, Sub-urban and rural segment by every people who are generally beauty conscious.
4. This cream is also used in Beauty parlours, Spa- Clubs, hotels etc.

B. I. S. Specification :-

There is no specific B. I. S. Specification on “Herbal Cold Cream” available with Bureau of Indian standards. But prior to selling this cream in market, it is suggested to check all the cosmetics norms as specified in the IS-6608-skin cream published by Bureau of Indian standards.

Government Regulations :-

“Herbal Cold Cream” is a cosmetic product which come under Drug & Cosmetic Rules. 1945.

To manufacture, “Herbal Cold Cream” the manufacturers have to apply to the licensing authority appointed by the State Government in Form-31 (if the manufacturer wants to manufacture products for safe or distribution).

Raw Materials Require and its Availability :-

To formulate a good standard quality Herbal Cold Cream there are following chemicals ingredients required, which are named as viz. Petroleum Jelly, Liquid paraffin oil, Oleic Acid, Cetyl Alcohol, Cetostearyl Alcohol, Emulsifying Wax, Triethanol amine, Sorbitol, Purified water, Preservative, Propylene Glycol, Silicon oil, Almond oil, Lavender oil, Neem oil, Carrot seed oil. Colour, perfumes and Laboratory Chemicals.

Besides, there are packaging materials viz. Plastic Jar, Caps, Laminated aluminium seal, Printed outer Cartons, Corrugated Cardboard boxes, adhesive tapes, box straps. The raw materials and packaging materials are indigenously available and can be procured from nearby local available sources.

Herbal Cold Cream

Formulation :-

Ingredients		*Parts by Weight*
Petroleum Jelly	-	4-6
Liquid Paraffin	-	3-5
Oleic Acid	-	8-10
Cetyl Alcohol	-	7-9
Cetostearyl Alcohol	-	2-4
Emulsifying Wax	-	2-3
Triethanol amine	-	1-2
Sorbitol	-	1-2
Purified water	-	to make 100
Preservative	-	0.3 - 0.7
Propylene Glycol	-	5-6
Silicon oil	-	1-2
Almond oil	-	0.5-1
Lavender oil	-	0.5 - 1
Neem oil	-	2-3
Carrot seed oil	-	1-2
Colour	-	0.1 -0.5
Perfumes	-	q.s.
		100

Manufacturing Process :-

To prepare a best quality Herbal Cold Cream, it is suggested to adopt the following manufacturing steps one by one.

1 First of all, purchase all the ingredients from good quality suppliers.

2 Analyse and test all the ingredients to find its suitability for preparation of good quality Herbal Cold Cream.

3 Now, weigh all the ingredients as specified in the formulation.

4 In a stainless steel vessel fitted with S. S. Stirrer, add Petroleum Jelly, Liquid Paraffin, OleicAcid, Cetyl Alcohol, Cetostearyl Alcohol & Emulsifying wax. Heat it to 70-80°C and mix thoroughly to obtain an uniform mix.

5 In another Stainless Steel Vessel fitted with S. S. Stirrer, pour Triethanol amine, Sorbitol and purified water, heat it to 70-80°C to dissolve it completely.

6 Now, add the step-4 preparations to step-5 preparations with uniform continuous stirring.

7 In another S.S. vessel dissolve preservative in Propylene Glycol with heating to 40-50°C and stirring.

8 Add step-7 solution to step-6 preparations at 35°C with uniform mixing.

9 In another stainless steel vessel, mix Silicon oil, Aimond oil, Lavender oil, Neem oil. Carrot seed oil uniformly. Now, add it to step-8 preparations with continuous thorough mixing
10 Then prepare colour solution by dissolving colour in little water and add to the step-9 preparations.
11 To the Step-10 preparations, add the perfume or fragrance and mix uniformly
12 The final product is quality tested and standardized.
13 The final Herbal Cold Cream is now filled in Plastic Jars of desired size with mouth sealing by laminated aluminium foil. The jars are now capped.
14 The final jars are now labelled, batch coded and packed in outer cartons and then further packed in corrugated master cartons. The cartons are sealed by adhesive tapes and strapped
15 It is now placed in and marketed to the desired customers.

Process Flowsheet For Manufacturing of Herbal Cold Cream

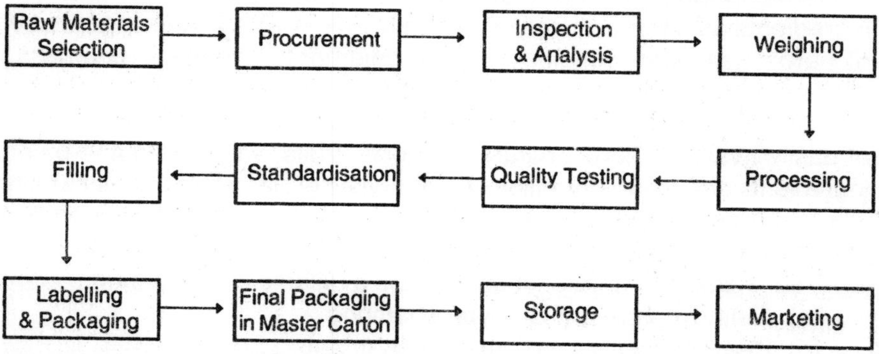

Plant & Machineries Require :-

1. Planetary Mixer with Stainless Steel body and stirrer
2 Mixing Vessel (S.S. - 316 made) with stirrer fitted with electric heating system
3. Water de-ionisation unit.
4. Stainless steel melting vessel.
5. Automatic or semi-automatic tube weighing, filling and sealing machine.
6. Automatic or semi-automatic jar weighing filling and sealing machine.
7. Semi-automatic labeling machine.
8. Semi-automatic carton sealing and strapping machine.
9. Laboratory Testing equipments.
10. Weighing balance, weights & others.

34

Amla Shikakai Reetha Herbal Shampoo

Introduction:-

Amla Shikakai Reetha Herbal Shampoos are basically one of the prime cosmetics product used by all strata of the population all over the world. Shampoo is mainly used to clean scalp and hair to make hair smooth, shining, lustrous and easy to comb and set. There are two types of shampoo available in the market. One is modern shampoo and another is Herbal Shampoo. These shampoos are formulated from different ingredients as per the choice of customers. Now a days, the importance of herbs has been considered by formulators, scientists, chemists, doctors and almost by everybody in the world, due to benificial effects on human body with no-side effect on the human being. The application of easily available herbs, natural products, fruits, vegetables and other ingredients are used to formulate various types of Herbal Shampoos which are found and considered as eco-friendly, human friendly, bio-friendly and compatible to almost every types of human skins, human hairs.

There are two types of shampoo are available in the market.

(a) Clear transparent Gel type shampoo.

(b) Pearly translucent of opaque shampoo.

Both types of shampoos are formulated in modern as well as herbal varieties considering the end users requirement. These shampoos are prepared for oily hair, dry hair or normal hair as per the structure of human hair. Now a days, Herbal Shampoos for normal hairs are marketed in almost every part of our country. Due to continuous growth in population, as well as social beauty awareness, rise in fashion and advertisement in television, news paper, magazine, the consumption of Herbal Shampoo and other cosmetics is gaining momentum at a faster pace. The market demand is rising almost every where in the world. Similarly our country's domestic as well as export demand is increasing day by day. A new entrepreneur will consider it profitable to earn excellent profit.

Properties of Good Quality Amla Shikakai Ritha Herbal Shampoos :-

1 A good shampoo is prepared with perfectly pH balance.

2 It clean hair and scalp thoroughly without stinging or irritation and remove too much of natural oil from the scalp.

3 The successful preparation of Amla Shikakai Reetha Herbal Shampoo leave the hair fragrant, lustrous, soft, shiny and do a satisfactory cleaning without removing an excessive amount of oil from scalp.

4 The Amla Shikakai Reetha Herbal Shampoo is effective in removing dandruff.

5 It has good foaming power. It is active and effective in hard water like normal water.

Uses and Applications :-

1. Amla Shikakai Reetha Herbal Shampoos are used to wash and cleanse the hair and scalp.
2. It is used by everybody, children, men, women of all age group to make their hair Shiny, lustrous and beautiful.
3. It is used in houses, star hotels, tourist centers and almost everywhere by men and women to cleanse there scalp and hair.

B.I.S. Specification :-

There is no B.I.S, Specification available on "Amla Shikakai Reetha Herbal Shampoo" but it is available on Modern Shampoo with Bureau of Indian standards to standardize the finish products before selling in the market.

Government Regulation :-

"Amla Shikakai Reetha Herbal Shampoo" is a Cosmetic product which come under Drug & Cosmetic Rules, 1945.

To manufacture "Amla Shikakai Reetha Herbal Shampoo" the manufacturer has to apply to the licensing authority appointed by the State Government in Form-31 (if the manufacturer wants to manufacture products for sale or distribution) *or* Form -31A, (if the manufacturer wants loan license to manufacture cosmetic product.).

Raw Materials Require:-

Amla Shikakai Reetha Herbal Shampoo consists of ingredients or raw materials which are chemically classified in the following categories-

1. Surfactants-Cleaning and foaming agents.
2. Foam boosters and stabilizers.
3. Conditioning Agents.
4. Special additives.
5. Preservatives.
6. Sequestering Agents.
7. Viscosity modifiers (viscosity improvers or viscosity reducers).
8. Opacifying or cleaning agents.

9. Fragrances or perfumes.
10. Stabilizers.
11. Cosmetic permitted colour/dye.
12. Diluents (De-ionized water).
13. Herbal Extracts.
14. Other special ingredients.

Packaging Materials:-

1. Bottles (HDPE, PET or Glass bottles)
2. Caps & stopper.
3. Stickers, labels.
4. Paper inner box.
5. Corrugated cartons
6. Adhesive tapes.
7. HDPE /PP Straps
8. Others.

Amla Shikakai Ritha Herbal Shampoo

Formulation:-

Ingredients		*Parts by Weight*
Sodium Lauryl Ether Sulphate (SLES)	-	32-40
Cocodiethanolamide	-	3-5
Cocobetaine (Additive)	-	3-5
Propylene Glycol (PG)	-	1-4
Citric Acid	-	0.1-1
Sodium Chloride	-	1-2
Quaternary Ammonium Compound	-	1-3
Preservative	-	0.2 - 0.5
Conditioner	-	0.2-1
De-ionised water	-	48-55
Colour (water soluble Cosmetic colour)	-	q.s
Perfume (water soluble)	-	q.s
Herbal Extract (Amla, Shikakai, Reetha, Brahmi, Jatamansi & others)	-	0.5-2
		100

Manufacturing Process:-

Amla Shikakai Ritha Herbal Shampoo is prepared by following processing steps one by one to obtain good quality final product. Details of processing steps are described as follow :-

1. First of all, purchase all the ingredients from good quality suppliers.
2. Analyse and Test all the ingredients to find its suitability for preparation of good quality shampoo.
3. Now, weigh all the ingredients as specified in the formulation.
4. In a stainless steel vessel fitted with stirrer, pour SLES, Cocodiethanolamide, cocobetaine and demineralised water. Dissolve and mix homogeneously all the ingredients in the water with the help of stirrer.
5. Now, in another vessel pour the Preservative and Propylene Glycol. Heat the vessel to 70-80° C by gas burner or electric heating system to dissolve preservative in Propylene Glycol completely.
6. Now, mix the above preservative solution Step-5 to solution in Steps-4 with stirring homogeneously.
7. To the above solution in Step-6, add the conditioner and mix again.
8. Now, dissolve Citric Acid in water in another vessel and add dropwise to Step-7 solution to obtain neutral pH of Step-7 solution. Check the solution continuously to see neutral pH by pH paper strip.
9 Now, dissolve the colour in water and add this colour solution to Step-8 solution dropwise to obtain the desired colour.
10 To this Step-9 solution add the quaternary ammonium compound and mix homogeneously.
11. Now, dissolve sodium chloride in water in another vessel. This sodium chloride solution is added dropwise with stirring to Step-10 solution. The preparation will start to thicken till the desired final consistency or viscosity is obtained.
12 Add perfume, herbal extracts to the Step-11 solution and mix uniformly. This finished herbal shampoo is now standardised, tested and stored in a clean dry stainless steel tank
13. The shampoo is now filled-in the plastic bottle by semi-automatic or automatic weighing filling sealing machine.
14. The packed bottles are now labelled and filled in the corrugated cartons.
15. The cartons are now placed in store and sent to customers for marketing.

Process Flowsheet For Manufacturing of Amla Shikakai Reetha Herbal Shampoo

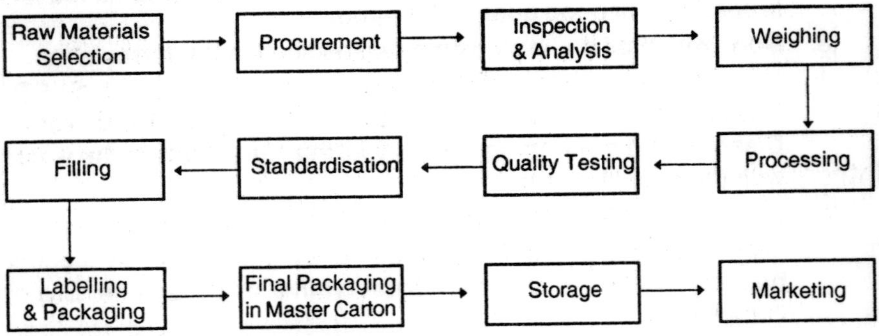

Plant and Machineries Require :-

1. Reaction vessel (Stainless steel-316 made), fitted with S.S Stirrer, M.S. Jacket & heating electrodes and other accessories.
2. Stainless steel tanks with stirrer
3. Gas burner.
4. Semi-automatic weighing, filling and sealing machine
5. Labeling machine.
6. Heat shrink wrap machine
7. Carton sealing machine
8. Laboratory equipment
9. Electrical equipment and others

PROJECT FINANCIAL ANALYSIS :-

1. Production Capacity - 200 Kgs Per Day / Per shift Amla Shikakai Reetha Herbal Shampoo
2. Land & Building - (On Rent)
3. Covered Area Require - 300 Sq.mts.
4. Plant & Machinery Cost - Rs. 4.50 lacs.
5. Others Fixed Capital - Rs. 1.30 lacs.
6. Total Fixed Capital Require - Rs. 5.80 lacs.
7. Working Capital Require Per Month - Rs. 5.60 lacs.
8. Margin Money - Rs. 1.40 lacs.
9. Total Project Cost - Rs. 7.20 lacs.
10. Total Capital Requirement - Rs. 11.40 lacs.
11. Cost of Production Per Month - Rs. 5.80 lacs.
12. Turn Over Per Month - Rs. 8.00 lacs.
13. Gross Profit Per Month - Rs. 2.20 lacs.
14. Rate of Return Per Annum - 228 %
15. Manpower Requirement - 5 Nos.
16. Electric Power Load - 18 KW.
17. Water Requirement Per Month - 150 KLs.

35

Fairness Vanishing Cream

Introduction :-

Fairness Vanishing Cream is a type of oil-in-water emulsion. The high percentage of stearic acid in this cream gives a snow like appearance to the cream, therefore, vanishing creams are also known as snow cream.This cream contains some ingredients having good effect on the skin by reducing black pigment formation inside layer of the skin and gradual reduction of accumulation of black pigment. So, the persons who are applying this cream on their face feel that they are becoming whiter and whiter after continuous prolonged applications. This cream is now widely accepted all over the world. This is used by both women and men of all age group. The beauty conscious girls and ladies are mostly preferring this product in every part of our country. So the market consumption and demand is excellent. The growth of cosmetics consumption is rising in our country day by day due to rapid awareness created by TV Publicity, News paper, Magazines, Beauty Magazines, Film Magazines, Internet communication and other advertising methods.

Properties of Good Quality Fairness Vanishing Cream :-

1. Fairness Vanishing cream is applicable on all types of skins.
2. It is applied on the skin. It do not cause any side effects.
3. It is compatible with human body as well as with environment.
4. The product has appropriate viscosity for filling in tubes and jars. It is easy for dispensing from Jars or tubes.
5. It is easily washable and removable from face with water.

Uses and Applications :-

1. Fairness Vanishing Cream is used by girls, ladies, men & women of all age group.
2. It is also used in beauty parlours, Salons, Five Star Hotels, Spa-Clubs, beauty institutes, beauty schools for application on the customers.
3. It is used in any climate, in any seasons, in any places by every people without any hassles.
4. The product is applicable by all types of people as it is economical and less expensive.

B.I.S. Specification :-

There is no B.I.S. Specification available on "Fairness Vanishing Cream" with Bureau of Indian Standards But, IS-6608 :- Skin Cream, Specify all the detail testing methods for standard quality finished products.

Government Regulations :-

"Fairness Vanishing Cream" is a cosmetic product which come under Drug & Cosmetic Rules. 1945.

To manufacture, "Fairness Vanishing Cream" the manufacturers have to apply to the licensing authority appointed by the State Government in Form-31 (if the manufacturer wants to manufacture products for sale or distribution).

Raw Materials Require and its Availability :-

Stearic Acid, Cetyl alcohol, Light liquid paraffin, Glycerol, Preservative, Triethanol amine, Perfumes, Herbal extract, Purified water etc. are the major raw materials for manufacturing of fairness vanishing cream. The packaging materials are tubes, jars, labels, stickers, mouth seals, adhesive tapes, inner boxes, outer cartons, box straps etc. which are available indigenously.

Fairness Vanishing Cream

Formulation :-

Ingredients		Parts by weight
Stearic Acid	-	18-24
Cetyl Alcohol	-	0.5-2
Light Liquid Paraffin	-	4-7
Glycerol	-	4 - 7
Preservative	-	0.2 - 0.75
Triethanol amine	-	1-3
Perfumes	-	0.5 - 1.5
Herbal Extract	-	0.1 - 0.5
Purified Water	-	Q.S to make 100
		100

Manufacturing Process :-

To manufacture good quality Fairness Vanishing Cream the production incharge has to follow detail manufacturing process step by step : -

1. First of all, procure all the raw materials from good reputed suppliers.
2. Analyze and test all the ingredients for good quality product.

3. Weigh all the ingredients in appropriate quantity as specified in the formulation.
4. Pour Triethanolamine in a stainless steel vessel fitted with stirrer. Add purified water and stire well. Heat the vessel on a low flame of a gas burner at 70-80°C.
5. Now, in another vessel heat the Glycerine and Preservative mixture at 70-80°C on a gas burner to dissolve the preservative in Glycerine.
6. In a stainless steel jacketed vessel feed Stearic Acid, Cetyl Alcohol and Light Liquid Paraffin and heat it to 70-80°C, so that all the solid fats get dissolved.
7. Now, mix step-5 preservative solution to step-6 fatty acid phase with continuous stirring and add this to step-4 preparations with stirring. This will result in the formation of a white emulsion (cream).
8. To the cream, add herbal extract and perfumes at 40°C mix it again. The vanishing cream is ready now.
9. The final fairness Vanishing Cream is quality tested and standardized.
10. The cream is now packed in tubes or jars in desired quantity of 25 ml, 40 ml, 50ml, 100ml Size etc.
11. The product is now labelled, sealed and packed in corrugated cartons.
12. The cartons are now placed in store and marketed to the desired customers.

Process Flowsheet For Manufacturing of Fairness Vanishing Cream

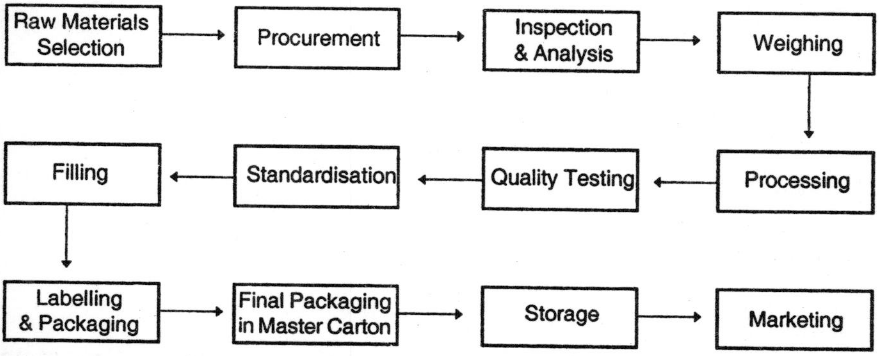

Plant & Machineries Require :-

1. Stainless steel vessel with stirrer.
2. Jacketed S.S.Vessel with stirrer.
3. Gas burners.
4. Laboratory testing equipments and Glasswares.

5. Tube weighing, filling and sealing machine.
6. Jars weighing, filling and sealing machine.
7. Cartons sealing and box strapping machine.
8. Labeling machine (semi-automatic).
9. Other equipments

PROJECT FINANCIAL ANALYSIS :-

1. Production Capacity	-	100 Kgs Per Day / Per shift Fairness Vanishing Cream
2. Land & Building	-	(On Rent)
3. Covered Area Require	-	350 Sq.mts.
4. Plant & Machinery Cost	-	Rs. 3.80 lacs.
5. Others Fixed Capital	-	Rs. 1.20 lacs.
6. Total Fixed Capital Require	-	Rs. 5.00 lacs.
7. Working Capital Require Per Month	-	R,s. 4.00 lacs.
8. Margin Money	-	Rs. 1.00 lacs.
9. Total Project Cost	-	Rs. 6.00 lacs.
10. Total Capital Requirement	-	Rs. 9.00 lacs.
11. Cost of Production Per Month	-	Rs. 4.20 lacs.
12. Turn Over Per Month	-	Rs. 6.25 lacs.
13. Gross Profit Per Month	-	Rs. 2.05 lacs
14 Rate of Return Per Annum	-	273 %
15 Manpower Requirement	-	5 Nos
16 Electric Power Load	-	15 KW
17 Water Requirement Per Month	-	150 KLs

36

Hair Styling Gel

Introduction:-

Hair Styling Gel is a type of Hair dressing preparations coming under the hair care Cosmetics Category. This product is basically used to maintain the hair styles with the help of a very fine binding agent to hold the hair in their respective styling position. This product is useful for both men and women. This product helps to improve the control and manageability of hair, to impart some lustre and to maintain a hair style in spite of the movement involved in daily activities and despite the various environment conditions to which hair is submitted (wind, dryness, humidity, heat, cold, sun etc.). The relative importance of these factors varies from one place to another, from one country to another, from one climatic conditions to another climatic condition, from age to age and according to the state of the hair. It also differs notably between men and women users. Men generally consider adequate control for a hair styling gel with gloss as secondary consideration. Whereas women first look for products that give a pleasing appearance and fragrance to the hair, but at the same time they require good hold. They do not want products which render hair heavy and which tend to make it lank or greasy.

The trend in Women's fashion for softer and freer styles and the increasing use of the brushing techniques have led to an increase in the demand for products that enhance disentangling and a greater need for the products that protect, strengthen and /or improve the conditions of the hair. Besides it, some new products which have been developed to impart set, manageability, sheen to hair having combed in different styles. Hair styling gel is available in different colour viz. Pink, Blue, Green, White transparent without Colour and in various fragrances. They form clear, non-greasy and quite glossy films while considerably improving the set retention of the hair. They tend to form a plastic sheath round each individual hair. So that the setting effect is not completely lost on combing out the hair. The film formed on the hair has to withstand without breaking or flaking repetitive combing and brushing while maintaining good adhesion in order to preserve the set.

Now a days, there are various manufacturers who are manufacturing the hair styling gels for various market. But the entrepreneurs with good quality product and good marketing strategy, can earn good profit.

Properties of Good Quality Hair Styling Gel :-

1. The Hair Styling Gel is compatible with the wetness of the hair at the time of application and waterproof, after drying, while remaining flexible.
2 It is easily shampooed out and is not sticky.
3 It is washed with clean water.
4 It is non-toxic, non-irritating and maintain good adhesion.
5 It is used to help the hair for softness, sheen, disentangling

Uses and Applications :-

1 It is used by men and women to set the hair style in the desired shape
2 It is used in beauty parlours, men's salon to maintain the hair style.
3 It is used by young girls, boys, fashion conscious ladies and gents to look beautiful
4 It is used to maintain the hair styles by film actors, actresses, models and artists

B. I. S. Specification :-

There is no such B. I. S. specification published on "Hair Styling Gel" by Bureau of Indain Standards but it is tested according to the cosmetics norms prior to selling in the market.

Government Regulation :-

"Hair Styling Gel" is a Cosmetic product which come under Drug & Cosmetic Rules, 1945.

To manufacture "Hair Styling Gel" the manufacturer has to apply to the licensing authority appointed by the State Government in Form-31 (if the manufacturer wants to manufacture products for sale or distribution) or Form -31A, (if the manufacturer wants loan license to manufacture cosmetic product.).

Raw Materials Requirement and its Availability :-

The Hair Styling Gel is formulated with film forming polymers, plasticiser, perfumes, colorants, additives, pure water etc. and is packed with packaging materials, tapes, straps, cartons, labels etc. These are indigenously available and can be procured from near by local sources.

Hair Styling Gels

Formulations -1

Ingredients		***Parts by Weight***
Polyvinyl Pyrollidone (K-30)	-	0.8-1
Polyethylene Glycol	-	1.5-2
Carbopol-940	-	1-1.5

Triethanol amine	-	1.5-2
Purified water	-	to make 100
Colour (water soluble cosmetic colour)	-	0.1 - 0.2
Perfume or fragrance	-	0.2 - 0.5
		100

Formulation -2

Ingredients		***Part by weight***
Polyvinyl Pyrollidone (K-30)	-	2-3
Polyethylene Glycol	-	9-12
Carbopol-940	-	0.5-1
Triethanol amine	-	0.5-1
Ethoxylated oleyl Alcohol	-	2 - 4
Purified water	-	to make 100
Ethyl Alcohol or Isopropyl Alcohol	-	25-30
Colour (Water Soluble Colour)	-	0.1-0.2
Perfume or fragrances	-	0.2-0.5
		100

Manufacturing Process :-

To prepare a good quality hair styling gel, it is suggested to follow the processing steps described here.

1. Purchase all the cosmetics grade raw materials from reputed dealers or traders.
2. Analyse all the raw materials for purity and good quality in the laboratory.
3. Weigh all the ingredients as specified in the formulation.
4. In stainless steel tanks, dissolve PVP resin in water and carbopol in water separately with stirring for 4-6 hours.
5. Now, in a stainless steel planetary mixer (closed top) feed the PVP resin liquid and carbopol liquid and mix to homogenise the product. Now, to it add the polyethylene glycol slowly with stirring. Then add Triethanol amine with slow stirring till homogenise. Care should be taken to avoid bubble formation and entrapment in the gel.
6. Now, in another stainless steel vessel add little water and water soluble colour, mix it homogeneously.
7. Now, add this colour solution to the step -5 preparations and mix it slowly till homogenize
8. Then add the perfume or fragrance to the step-7 preparation with slow mixing.
9. The final product is filled in the plastic jars, sealed and labelled as per the customers choice.

10. The product is now packed in corrugated cartons. Cartons are sealed and strapped.
11 The cartons are placed in store and marketed to the desired customers.

Process Flowsheet For Manufacturing of Hair Styling Gel

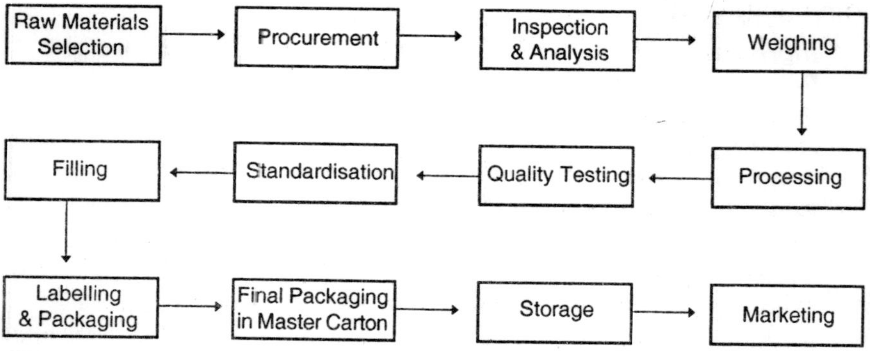

Plant & Machineries Require:-

1. Stainless steel tank fitted with S. S. Stirrer.
2. Planetary mixer with motor and accessories.
3. Weighing scale.
4. Laboratory Equipments & Glasswares.
5. Jar Filling machine.
6. Tools, tackles and accessories.

PROJECT FINANCIAL ANALYSIS :-

1. Production Capacity - 100 Kgs Per Day / Per Shift Hair Styling Gel
2. Land & Building - (On Rent)
3. Covered Area Require - 300 Sq.mts.
4. Plant & Machinery Cost - Rs. 2.40 lacs.
5. Others Fixed Capital - Rs. 1.20 lacs.
6. Total Fixed Capital Require - Rs. 3.60 lacs.
7. Working Capital Require Per Month - Rs. 3.00 lacs.
8. Margin Money - Rs. 0.75 lacs.
9. Total Project Cost - Rs. 4.35 lacs.
10. Total Capital Investment - Rs. 6.60 lacs.
11. Cost of Production Per Month - Rs. 3.15 lacs.
12. Turn Over Per Month - Rs. 4.50 lacs.
13. Gross Profit Per Month - Rs. 1.35 lacs.
14. Rate of Return Per Annum - 245 %
15. Manpower Requirement - 5 Nos.
16. Electric Power Load - 10 KW.
17. Water Requirement Per Month - 100 KLs.

37

Eye Liner (Liquid)

Introduction :-

Eye Liner (Liquid) is preparations for use on eyelids, particularly the upper eyefids, close to the eyelashes, to help to accentuate the expressiveness of eyes. Eye liners are used after the eye shadow. It has been applied to give the eyes a more striking appearance. The desired effect is obtained by using either in liquid form or in pencil form. Now a days, eye liners are avaifable in liquid, cake and pencil form.

The products are made in a wide range of shades from white through pastel shades to blue, black blue, violet, green and black.

The product is gaining market excessively in beauty related displays. The models, film actresses, house ladies, high profile fashionable ladies, girls are using this product to raise their beauty and glamour during special occasions, festivals, marriage ceremonies, social functions, tea parties etc. This product makes special attraction to their youthness and decorate their aopearance beautiful. It is accepted worldwide by women.

The product is a type of cosmetic coming under colour cosmetic segment.

Properties of Good Quality Liquid Eye Liner :-

1. The Eye Liner glide on without tugging or pulling on the eyelid.
2. The colour coverage is good and blend easily.
3. The formulation is such that the depth of colour can be controlled during application.
4. The line last all day without smudging or smearing.
5. The eye liner spread easily and smoothing and dry out fairly rapidly.
6. It do not cause any irritation *or* allergy to eye.

Uses and Applications :-

1. Eye liner is used on the edge of eye lids to look the eyes beautiful.
2. Liquid eye liners may be used to apply colour to the tissue around the eyes. Usually a brown colour, black colour or blue colour is considered good for appearance and fashion.
3. Eye liners are available in liquid, powder, compact, pencil or semiviscous paste form as per the convenience in application by the customers.
4. The major consumers are ladies, girls or women of all age group.

B.I. S. Specification :-

There is no B. I.S. Specification available on "Eye Liner (Liquid)" with Bureau of Indian Standards. But, it is tested as per the cosmetics norms.

Government Regulation :-

"Eye Liner (Liquid)" is a Cosmetic product which come under Drug & Cosmetic Rules, 1945.

To manufacture, "Eye Liner (Liquid)" the manufacturer has to apply to the licensing authority appointed by the State Government in Form-31 (if the manufacturer wants to manufacture products for sale or distribution) or Form -31 A, (if the manufacturer wants loan license to manufacture cosmetic product.).

Raw Materials Requirement :-

The Eye Liner (Liquid form) can be formulated by using following cosmetics grade chemicals viz. Magnesium Aluminium Silicate (Veegum), Water Soluble Polymer (Polyvinyl Pyrollidone), Pigments (black, blue, blue black, green, brown etc.), Preservatives, Purified de-ionized water etc.

Besides this, the packaging materials are also required to pack it suitably.

Eye Liner (Liquid)

Formulation -1

Ingredients		*Parts by Weight*
Charcoal Powder (>400mesh size)	-	18-22
Propylene Glycol	-	1 - 3
Castor oil	-	13-17
Purified Water	-	to make 100
Preservative	-	0.2 - 0.5
		100

Manufacturing Process :-

To manufacture good quality Eye Liner (Liquid), it is suggested to go through the following steps.

1. Procure all the ingredients from good reputed Suppliers.
2. Analyse for good quality products.
3. Weigh all ingredients as per the formulation.
4. In a planetary mixture or colloid mill, add castor oil and charcoal Powder (400-500 mesh size) mix it together.
5. In another stainless steel vessel fitted with S. S. Stirrer, pour Propylene Glycol and Preservative and heat the vessel to 70-

80°C to dissolve the preservative completely. Now add purified water into it and mix uniformly.

6. Now, add the step-5 solution to step-4 paste slowly with continuous mixing till a homogeneous finished product is obtained.
7. Test the quality of finished product and standardise it for final packaging.
8. Pack the product in small 10ml, 15ml, 20ml size glass bottles, having plastic applicator fitted within the cap. The bottles are sealed and packed in small corrugated boxes of 12 or 24 pieces
9. These bottles are now packed in big corrugated boxes of size 10kgs, 15kgs or 20kgs.
10. The cartons are now strapped, placed in store and send for marketing.

Formulation - 2

Ingredients		***Parts by Weight***
Veegum (Magnesium Aluminium Silicate)	-	1-3
Polyvinyl Pyrollidone (PVP K-30)	-	1-2
Iron Oxide Black Pigment (Cosmetic Grade)	-	8-10
Purified Water	-	to make 100
Preservative	-	0.2-0.5
		100

Manufacturing Process:-

To manufacture good quality Eye Liner (Liquid), it is suggested to go through the following steps.

1. Procure good quality raw materials from reputed dealers/ suppliers.
2. Weigh all the ingredients as specified in the formulation.
3. In a stainless steel vessel fitted with stirrer, add veegum and water with constant stirring. In order to dissolve the veegum completely continue mixing until it becomes smooth and free of visible particle.
4. Dissolve Polyvinyl Pyrollidone in little water in another S. S. Vessel with mild heating.
5. Add PVP solution to Veegum solution and mix until uniform.
6. Then, add Iron Oxide pigment into the solution and mix homogeneously.
7. Now, add the preservative and mix until fully smooth uniform product is obtained.
8. The final product is now quality tested and standardised.

9. This liquid eye liner is now filled in glass bottles of size 10ml, 15ml or 20 ml size bottles.
10. The bottles are then packed in small cartons and then in big cartons.
11. It is now placed in store and marketed.

Process Flowsheet For Manufacturing of Eye Liner (Liquid)

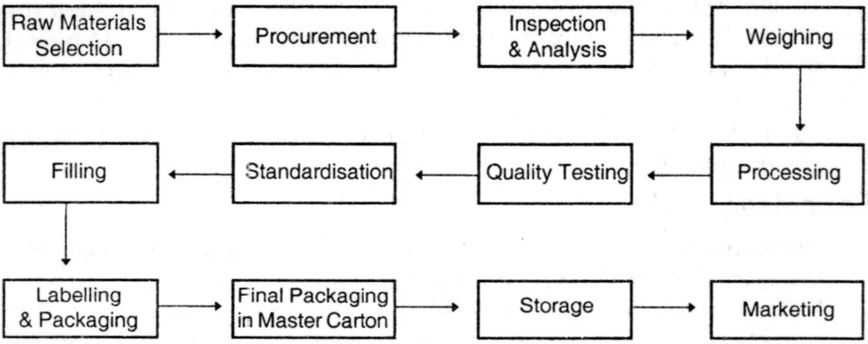

Plant & Machineries Require :-

1. Weighing Balance.
2. Stainless Steel Vessel (closed top) fitted with S.S.Stirrer and flame proof motor.
3. Semi automatic glass bottle weighing, filling and cap sealing machine.
4. Labeling machine.
5. Cartons sealing and strapping machine
6. Laboratory equipments, Glassswares.

38

Moisturizing Cream With Aloe Vera

Introduction :-

Moisturizing Cream with Aloe Vera is an important type of Cosmetic product coming in Skin Care Cosmetic Category. It is basically having low oil content. This Cream is easily spreadable and "rub in" quickly. It contains higher quantity of water which plasticizes the outer dead layers of epidermis of skin to give the much desired attribute, appearance as soft, smooth and healthy skin. It has been found that if water is lost more rapidly from lower layer of the skin, the skin becomes dehydrated and loses its flexibility. The skin loses it sheen and texture gradually. The oil alone can not restore its flexibility. There are three different routes to restore water to dry skin. These routes are occlusion, humectancy and restoration of deficient materials, which may be (and often are) Combined.

The major function of moisturizing cream is to restore water in the skin layer by presence of water in the cream and protection of water loss from the skin by oily film created by oil or fat ingredients. The cream becomes more effective in retaining moisture or water content of the skin. The skin become healthy and flexible. Its texture becomes smooth and give the beautiful feeling and appearance to the user.

Now a days, there are several manufacturer who are manufacturing this cream using different compositions and ingredients. But Aloe Vera is playing a complete role to maintain water balance in the skin layer. The moisturizing cream based on Aloe Vera, is gaining worldwide acceptance by the people of almost every countries. But there are very few manufacturers who are manufacturing this product fulfilling all the norms. A new entrepreneur can manufacture and market this product to earn excellent profit.

Properties of Good Quality Moisturizing Cream with Aloe Vera :-

1. The moisturizing cream is formulated with low oil content and has high moisture retention power.
2. The cream is non-irritating and non-allergenic to any type of skin.
3. It has soothing effect over dry skin.

4. It has appropriate water and oil balance.
5. It is ecologically safe and biodegradable in nature.
6. The product is formulated with good mild fragrance and pleasant in application.
7. The product has good viscosity and can be packed in various standard containers viz. Jars and tubes.

Uses and Applications :-

1. The Moisturizing Cream with Aloe Vera is highly used in Summer season or in winter season to retain and to restore moisture balance in the layer of the human skin.
2. It is used by both men and women of all age group.
3. It is a mass product and is used by almost every male and female.
4. The aged people find it most suitable to maintain their skin texture and flexibility.
5. It is used in almost every home or houses by girls, ladies, gents, youngsters to look beautiful and healthy.

B.I.S. Specification:-

There is no such B.I.S. Specification available on "Moisturizing Cream with Aloe Vera" with Bureau of Indian standards. But, the products can be tested as per the IS-6608 - Skin Cream, norms prior to sending it to the market.

Government Regulation :-

"Moisturizing Cream with Aloe Vera" is a cosmetic product which come under Drug & Cosmetic Rules, 1945.

To manufacture this product, the manufacturers have to apply to the licensing authority appointed by the State Government in Form -31 (If the manufacturer wants to manufacture products for sale or distribution).

Raw Materials Require and Availability :-

The Moisturizing Cream with Aloe Vera can be formulated with various cosmetic grade chemicals, laboratory grade chemicals etc. Besides these, there are packaging materials such as jars, tubes, outer cartons, master cartons, labels, adhesives tapes, straps etc. required. These are indigenously available and can be procured from nearby local available sources.

Moisturizing Cream with Aloe Vera

Formulation :-

Ingredients		*Parts by Weight*
Cetyl Alcohol	-	0.5-1
Mineral oil	-	5-7
Isopropyl Myristate	-	0.5-1

Stearic Acid	-	2-5
Giyceryl Monostearate	-	0.5-1
Sorbitol (70%)	-	1-2
Glycerine	-	1-2
Triethanol amine	-	1-2
Aloe Vera Gel	-	5-6
Purified water	-	to make 100
Preservative	-	0.3-0.75
Perfumes or Fragrances	-	q.s.
Colour (Cosmetic Grade)	-	q.s.
		100

Manufacturing Process :-

To manufacture a good quality Moisturizing cream with Aloe Vera, it is suggested to adopt the following processing steps.

1. First of all, procure all the raw materials from reputed suppliers or dealers.
2. Analyze and test all the ingredients as specified in the formulation.
3. Weigh all the ingredients as mentioned in the formulation.
4. In a jacketed stainless steel vessel fitted with S.S. Stirrer, pour Cetyl Alcohol, Mineral oil, Isopropyl Myristate, Stearic Acid and Glycery! Monostearate. Heat at 70°-80° C to melt and mix all the ingredients uniformly.
5. In another stainless steel vessel fitted with S. S. Stirrer, Pour Sorbitol (70%) solution, Glycerine, Triethanol amine (TEA), purified water and Aloe Vera gel. Heat it at 70°C-80°C with continuous slow stirring till uniform.
6. Now, add step-6 preparation to step-5 preparation at 70°C with continuous stirring till uniform. Cool it to 40°C.
7. In another Stainless steel vessel dissolve the Preservative in water completely with stirring. Then add this Preservative solution to step-6 preparations with slow stirring till uniform.
8. Now, add perfumes or fragrances and colour solution (prepared by mixing colour in little quantity of water) to the step-7 preparation and mix uniformly.
9. Test the quality of final product, standardize it as desired by customers.
10. Fill this moisturizing cream in tubes or jars in desired quantity. Then seal it.
11. Affix Labels on the jars and pack it in outer cartons. The outer cartons are further packed in corrugated cartons and sealed by adhesive tapes and strapped.
12. It is placed in store and marketed to the desired customers.

Process Flowsheet For Manufacturing of Moisturizing Cream With Aloe Vera

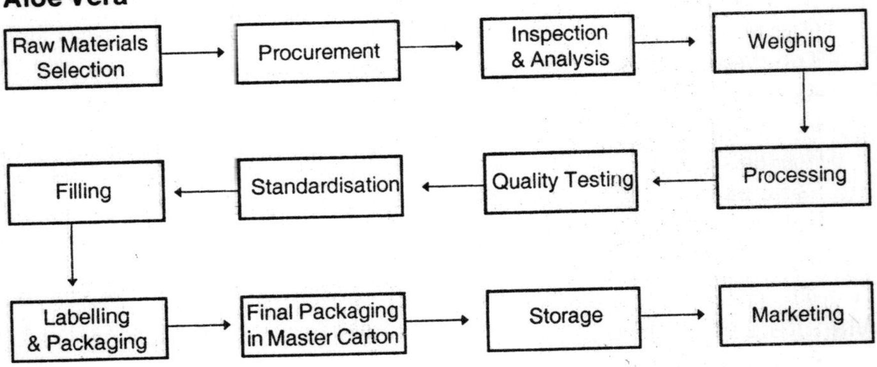

Note : Detailed project report on above project is available with EIRI. Contact 'EIRI' office for more details.

39

Aloe Pack

Introduction :-

Aloe Pack is one of the important Cosmetics product coming under the Skin Care category of Cosmetics. This is different from Mud Pack. It is a type of Hydro-Colloid based system. It contains Aloe Vera extract which retains moisture on the face skin and rejuvenate the skin by maintaining its flexibility. The Aloe Pack is applied to the face skin in the form of paste. This is allowed to dry or to set with the object of improving the appearance of the skin, by producing a transient tightening effect as well as by cleansing the skin. The warmth and tightening effect resulting from its application produce the stimulating sensation of a rejuvenated face. Aloe Pack has specific excellent properties to remove dirt, grease from the facial skin. When it is removed from the face, skin debris and blackheads may be removed simultaneously with moisture retaining in the layer of skin.

The product is gaining international importance among women & girls of all age group.

This product is highly in demand in beauty parlours, body care centres all over the world. A new entrepreneur or industrialist can add this product in their Cosmetics range to earn excellent profit.

Properties of Good Quality Aloe Pack :-

The good quality Aloe Pack has following properties and passes through all cosmetic norms.

1. Aloe Pack is a smooth paste without gritty particles and without an earthy or other objectionable odour.
2. It dry out rapidly to form and adherent coating on the skin. It is easily removed or peeled off by gentle washing without producing any pain.
3. It produce a definite sensation of tightening of the skin after its application over faces.
4. It produce good cleansing of the skin.
5. It is dermatologically innocuous and non-toxic.
6. It is bio-degradable and environmentally safe.
7. The product has pleasant feeling fragrance for easy acceptance.

Characteristics of Aloe Pack :-

Aloe Pack is a type of hydro-colloid product and can be presented as high-viscosity sols which after application lose water and form a flexible gel film.

The sensation of tightness is produced by the eventual shrinking of the gel on loss of further moisture. The film may be plasticised by the inclusion of humectants such as glycerol, propylene Glycol or Sorbitol. The Aloe Pack contains Aloe Vera extract which retains moisture in the layer of skin. Which helps to maintain flexibility of skin.

Uses and Applications :-

1. Aloe Pack is used by females, ladies, models, actresses, high profile fashionable ladies to maintain texture and smooth appearance of the skin.
2. It is mostly used in beauty parlours to apply to brides to beautify their appearance.
3. It is used by housewives, office going ladies, college girls to look beautiful.
4. It is used to treat the facial skin and to rejuvenate it to look healthy.

B.I.S. Specification :-

There is no such B.I.S. Specification published by Bureau of Indian standard on "Aloe Pack'; But it can be tested as per the Cosmetics norms prior to selling in the market.

Government Regulations :-

Aloe Pack is a cosmetic product which come under Drug & Cosmetic Rules, 1945.

To manufacture this product, the manufacturers have to apply to the licensing authority appointed by the State Government in Form -31 (If the manufacturer wants to manufacture products for sale or distribution).

Raw Materials Require and Availability :-

The major raw materials require to formulate Aloe Packs, are specified as Polyvinyl Pyrrolidone, Purified Water, Glycerine, Propylene Glycol, Isopropyl Myristate, Aloe Vera extract, preservatives, fragrance, Colour, laboratory chemicals etc. Besides, the packaging materials, jars, outer cartons, master cartons, adhesive tapes, box straps etc. are required. These are indigenously available and can be procured from nearby available sources.

Aloe Pack

Formulation :-

Ingredients		*Parts by Weight*
Poly Vinyl Pyrollidone (K-15)	-	2-3
Purified Water	-	to make 100
Glycerine	-	7-10
Propylene Glycol	-	0.5-2
Isopropyl Myristate	-	0.5-2
Aloe Vera Extract (1:1)	-	4-6
Preservative	-	0.2-0.7
Perfumes or Fragrances	-	q.s.
Colour (Cosmetic Grade)	-	q.s.
		100

Manufacturing Process :-

To manufacture a good standard quality Aloe Pack, the manufacturing incharge should take care to follow the specified processing steps.

1. Purchase all the cosmetic grade raw materials from good reputed dealers or traders.
2. Analyse all the raw materials in laboratory prior to sending for manufacturing
3. Weigh all the raw materials as specified in the formulation.
4. In a stainless steel vessel fitted with S. S. Stirrer, motor and accessories, add Polyvinyl Pyrollidone resin and purified water. Mix it slowly with stirring to obtain uniform gel.
5. In another stainless steel vessel, pour Glycerine, Propylene Glycol and Isopropyl Myristate and then mix it.
6. Now, add the step-5 preparations to step-4 preparations and mix it uniformly.
7. Prepare Aloe Vera extract by cold processing from inner gel of Aloe Vera leaf in water and Propylene Glycol mixture (1:9) till extract is obtained. Add this extract to step-6 preparations and mix it uniformly.
8. In another stainless steel vessel, dissolve preservative in water by heating and stirring to prepare uniform solution. Then add this solution to step-7 preparations.
9. Add perfume or fragrance and colour solution (Colour is mixed in water uniformly) to the step -8 preparations with continuous stirring.
10. Test the final preparations and standardize it.
11. The final Aloe Pack is now packed in jars or tubes and labelled as per customers acceptance.

12. It is then packed in printed inner carton and these inner cartons are further packed in corrugated master cartons. These cartons are sealed, strapped and placed in store. Then marketed to the desired customers/dealers/distributors.

Process Flowsheet For Manufacturing of Aloe Pack

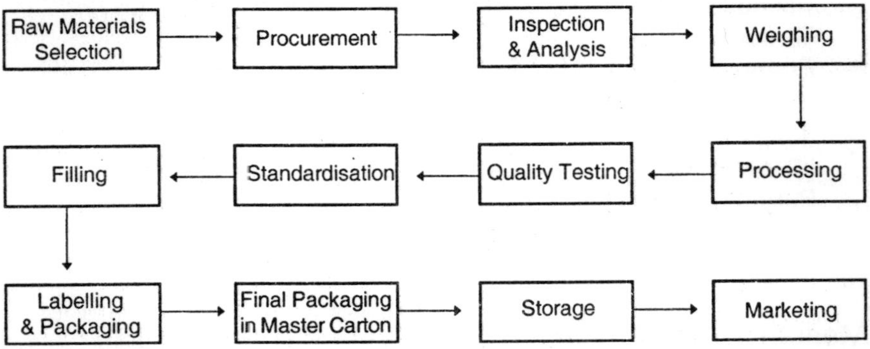

Plant & Machineries Require :-

1. Stainless Steel vessel fitted with S. S. Stirrer, motor and accessories.
2. Stainless steel planetary mixer with accessories.
3. Weighing balance.
4. Water de-ionisation unit.
5. Water heater.
6. Tube or Jars filling, sealing machine.
7. Semi-automatic labeling machine.
8. Batch coding machine.
9. Laboratory equipments and Glasswares.

> **Note :** Capacity and size of the project may vary according to the entrepreneur requirements. Entrepreneur may contact 'EIRI' office for further details of this project.

40

Herbal Brahmi Amla Hair Oil

Introduction :-

Herbal Brahmi Amla Hair Oil is one of the most popular hair care in India. Use of Brahmi Amla hair oil to treat common hair problems like-dandruff, headache, head cooling, hair falling etc. are common in India since ancient times. A large number of ayurvedic preparations like Amla oil, Bhringraj oil, Japakusum oil, Chameli oil and others are still popular in India and used for a variety of purposes like anti-dandruff, hair blackening, Brain stimulations, mood freshening and many other reasons.

Now, there are broadly two kinds of hair oils available in the market. These are classified as :-

1. Pre-wash Hair Oils :- Which are applied before shampooing the hair to massage the scalp and stimulate the hair growth.
2. Post-wash Hair Oils :- Which are applied after shampooing. These are non-greasy hair oils containing a large proportions of light liquid paraffin to give a non greasy feel to the hair and hair could be combed in a desired style.

Properties of Good Quality Herbal Brahmi Amla Hair Oils :-

1. Herbal Brahmi Amla Hair Oil is both greasy type and non-greasy type.
2. It keeps scalp dandruff free.
3. It keeps the head cool, due to medicinal effect of brahmi and amia on the human being.
4. It do not cause any sorts of side effect on the scalp.
5. It cause the hair lustrous, shining, beautiful *on* both men and women of all age group.
6. It has mood freshening effect on human being.

Uses and Applications :-

1. Herbal Brahmi Amla Hair Oil is used by men and women of all age group all over the world.
2. It is used by almost every people in our country due to its ayurvedic effect over human scalp and hair roots.
3. It is used to emolliate and moisturize the hair,
4. It is also used for a number of hair and scalp disorders like dandruff, hair fall, hair greying etc.

B.I.S. Specification :-

Depending upon the ingredients used in the preparation of Hair oil, the B.I.S. specification for Hair oils (IS-7123) have been divided into following three types-

Type - 1 :- Hair oil based on Vegetable oils.

Type - 2 :- Hair oil based on Mineral oil (light liquid paraffins).

Type - 3 :- Hair oil based on a mixture of vegetable oil and mineral oil.

Government Regulation :-

Herbal Brahmi Amla Hair Oil is a Cosmetic product which come under Drug & Cosmetic Rules, 1945.

To manufacture Herbal Brahmi Amla Hair Oil the manufacturer has to apply to the licensing authority appointed by the State Government in Form-31 (if the manufacturer wants to manufacture products for sale or distribution) or Form -31 A, (if the manufacturer wants loan license to manufacture cosmetic product.).

Market Status:-

The Indian Hair oil market is a very big market and worth over Rs. 700 crores. The last one decade has shown tremendous growth in the Hair oil market and the market is growing at a rate of 20 % per annum in the rural areas and 7-8 % in the urban areas. It has been estimated that with rise in population growth, the demand of Herbal Brahmi amla hair oil will grow at a rapid pace.

Amla:-

Amla is botanically named as Emblica officinalis. It is one of the rich sources of vitamin C. It contains natural vitamins. It is mostly used in hair care cosmetics like hair oil, hair dyes, herbal shampoos and others. Its ayurvedic effect is mostly helpful for toning and treatment of hair and scalp disorders.

Brahmi :-

Brahmi is botanically known as Bacopa monnieri. It is a glabrous, succulent, small, Prostrate or creeping annual herb, found through out India in wet and damp places. Brahmi is a creeper plant commonly found along the marshes and pond edges.

In India, it is found in Uttar Pradesh, Punjab, Haryana, Bihar, West-Bengal, Tamil Nadu, Kerala, Karnataka, foot hills of Himachal Pradesh & Uttaranchal.

The entire plant constitutes the well-known drug Brahmi. It is astringent, bitter and cooling and is reported to improve the intellect.

It promotes mental calm & clarity and assists in the practice of Yoga and meditation.

It is frequently used in Indian and Japanese Medicines. It is primarily used as a nerve tonic to treat insomnia and nervous tension, with secondary applications as diuretic.

Herbal Brahmi Amla Hair Oil

Formulation :-

Ingredients		*Parts by weight*
Sunflower oil	-	30-60
Light liquid Paraffin oil	-	70-38
Amla Extract	-	0.2-1
Brahmi Extract	-	0.5-1
Preservative	-	0.01-0.75
Colour (Cosmetic grade oil soluble)	-	q.s.
Perfume	-	0.1-1
		100

Manufacturing Process :-

The Herbal Brahmi Amla hair oil is prepared by following detail processing steps :-

1. First of all, procure good quality raw materials from good reputed suppliers.
2. Test all the ingredients used in manufacturing of hair oil.
3. Weigh all the raw materials as specified in the formulation.
4. Now, take sunflower oil and Light liquid Paraffin oil in a clean and dry stainless steel vessel fitted with S.S.Stirrer. Mix it thoroughly .
5. Now, preservative is dissolved in small quantity of above oil separately by mild heating on a gas burner and then added to the rest of the mixed oil and then mix uniformly.
6. Take 20 liters of the above base oil and add to it the Brahmi and Amla in powder form in another small kettle (50 liter. Capacity). Heat the kettle at 60-70° C for 3 to 4 hours. Switch off the kettle and allow to cool the extract.
7. Mix the extract in base oil and stire the oil.
8. Dissolve the colour in 200mi. of the above preparation separately and then add it dropwise with stirring to the base oil to produce desired colour.
9. Add perfume in the last.
10. Filter the oil through a filter press to have a sparkling clean hair oil.
11. The oil is now tested as per B.I.S specification.

12. It is now filled in the plastic or glass bottles of desired sizes by automatic or semi-automatic weighing filling and bottle sealing machines.
13. The bottles are now labeled by semi-automatic machine or by manual method.
14. The products are now packed in final corrugated cartons and sealed by adhesive tapes.
15. The cartons are now placed in store and marketed to the desired customers.

Process Flowsheet For Manufacturing of Herbal Brahmi Amla Hair Oil

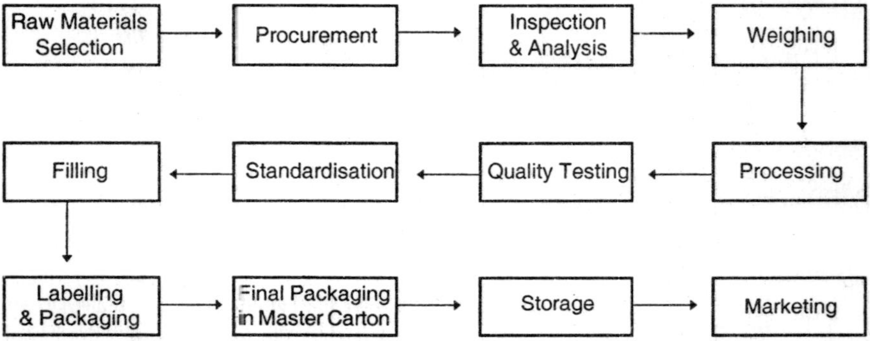

41

Haldi (Turmeric) Chandan (Sandal) Fairness Cream

Introduction :-

Haldi Chandan Fairness Cream is an important Cosmetic preparation coming under skin care category. The Cream is termed as herbal or ayurvedic cream. The Haldi Chandan Fairness Cream is a type of Vanishing Cream. Which when applied over face skin it reduces the skin pigments gradually and after prolong uses the skin becomes fairer and formation of black pigment inside the skin layer is gradually reduced. The fairness cream is now highly in demand all over the world. In India, there are very few manufacturers who are selling the fairness cream in large quantities. The few branded products available in the market are Fair & Lovely, Fair Ever, Lamour, Vicco-turmeric, Hue, Vi-John and others. The market demand is rising at a rapid pace in every part of our country. The young girls, house wives, office going ladies, models, actresses and almost every women demand this cream to look fair and beautiful. It is becoming a necessary to their personal care Cosmetic range. Due to its positive effect even men are also using it to look fair and smart. The product is now available in Consumer pack plastic collapsible tubes and jars of different sizes.

The media publicity has created a large domestic as well as international market demand that everybody are aware to purchase it for their family members. The product is gaining momentum in skin care Cosmetic range. A new entrepreneur with best quality product and high quality packaging design can create a huge demand for domestic and international consumers to earn excellent profit.

Properties of Good Quality Haldi Chandan Fairness Cream :-

A good quality Haldi Chandan Fairness Cream comply following requirements.

1. Haldi Chandan Fairness Cream is applicable on all types of skins.
2. It is applied on the skin. It do not cause any side effects.
3. It is compatible with human body as well as with environment.
4. The product has appropriate viscosity for filling in tubes and jars. It is easy for dispensing from Jars or tubes.
5. It is easily washable and removable from face with water.

Uses and Applications :-

1. Haldi Chandan Fairness Cream is generally considered as ayurvedic / herbal cosmetics preparation. It is widely accepted by all age group of people.
2. The beauty Consciousness and glamour has raised its demand multifolded among youngsters, teenagers, young married women, girls going to marry, new brides, grooms, office going male and female executives and among almost every body.
3. It is used in homes, houses, five star hotels, beauty parlours, spa-clubs, modelling institution etc.

B. I. S. Specifications :-

There is no specific B. I. S. Specification on "Haldi Chandan Fairness Cream" available with Bureau of Indian standards. But prior to selling this cream into market, it is suggested to check all the cosmetics norms as specified in the IS-6608-skin cream published by Bureau of Indian standards.

Government Regulations :-

"HaldJ Chandan Fairness Cream" is a cosmetic product which come under Drug & Cosmetic Rules. 1945.

To manufacture "Haldi Chandan Fairness Cream" the manufacturers have to apply to the licensing authority appointed by the State Government in Form-31 (if the manufacturer wants to manufacture products for sale or distribution).

Raw Material Require and its Availability :-

To formulate and manufacture a good standard quality Haldi Chandan Fairness Cream the Listed Cosmetic grade raw materials and laboratory chemicals are require viz. Stearic Acid, Glyceryl Monostearate, Mineral oil, Triethanol amine, Titanium Dioxide, Zinc oxide, Sodium Lauryl Sulphate, purified water, preservative, perfumes, fragrance, colour, Turmeric extract, chandan extract, laboratory chemicals etc.

The packaging materials required are laminated plastic collapsible tubes, jars, aluminium seals, labels, outer cartons, corrugated master cartons, adhesive tapes, box straps etc. These raw materials and packaging materials are indigenously available and can be procured from nearby available local sources.

Haldi (Turmeric) Chandan (Sandal) Fairness Cream

Formulation :-

Ingredients		*Parts by weight*
Stearic Acid	-	8-10
Glyceryl Monostearate (GMS)	-	5-6

Mineral oil	-	7-9
Triethanol amine	-	0.5-2
Titanium Dioxide	-	0.5-1
Zinc Oxide	-	1-2
Sodium Lauryl Sulphate	-	0.5-0.75
Purified Water	-	to make 100
Preservative	-	0.3-0.7
Perfumes or Fragrance	-	0.2-0.5
Colour	-	q.s.
Turmeric	-	0.5-2
Chandan (Sandal Extract)	-	0.5-2
		100

Manufacturing Process :-

To prepare a good quality Turmeric and Sandal Fairness Cream, it is suggested to all manufacturers to adopt the following processing steps.

1. Purchase all the raw materials from good reliable reputed dealers or traders.
2. Analyse or test all the raw materials for its quality assessment.
3. Weigh all the raw materials as mentioned in the formulation.
4. Now, in a Stainless Steel Vessel, Fitted with S. S. Stirrer, pour Mineral oil, GMS and Stearic Acid. Heat all the ingredients to 70-80°C to melt and mix uniformly.
5. In another stainless steel vessel fitted with S. S. Stirrer, heat purified water to 70-80°C, to it add Sodium Lauryl Sulphate, Triethanol amine, Zinc oxide, Titainum Dioxide and mix it thoroughly.
6. Now, add Step-4 preparations to step-5 preparations with continuous stirring at 70°C.
7. In another S. S. Vessel dissolve preservative in a little quantity of purified water with slight warming and stirring. Then add this preservative solution to step-6 preparations slowly with mixing uniformly.
8. To the step-7 preparations add colour solution and mix homogeneously.
9. Cool the step-8 preparations to 40°C and add the fragrance, turmeric extract and sandal extract with uniform mixing.
10. The final product is now quality tested and standardized as per desired cosmetic norms.
11. The cream is now packed in jars of desired quantity (25gm, 50gm, 100gm, 200gms etc.) and sealed to keep away from aerial contacts.

12. The filled jars are now labelled and packed in printed outer paper boxes. These paper boxes are now placed in corrugated master cartons.
13. The master cartons are sealed by self adhesive tapes and strapped.
14. These boxes are placed in store and marketed to the desired customers.

Process Flowsheet For Manufacturing of Haldi (Turmeric) Chandan (Sandal) Fairness Cream

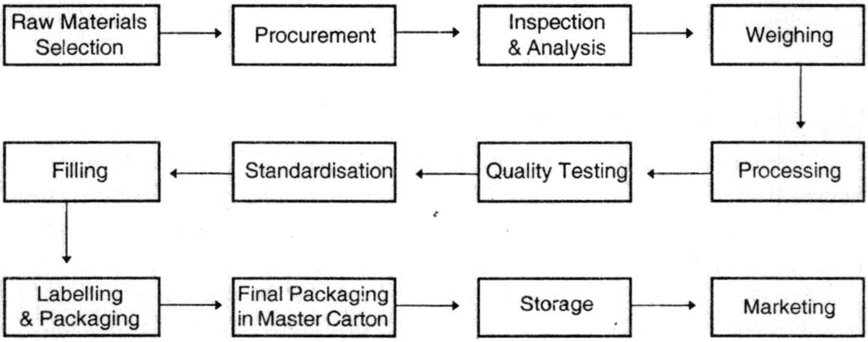

Plant & Machineries Require :-

1. Planetary Mixer with Stainless Steel body and stirrer.
2. Mixing Vessel (S.S. - 316 made) with stirrer fitted with electric heating system.
3. Water de-ionisation unit.
4. Stainless steel melting vessel.
5. Automatic or semi-automatic tube weighing, filling and sealing machine.
6. Automatic or semi-automatic jar weighing filling and sealing machine.
7. Semi-automatic labeling machine .
8. Semi-automatic Carton sealing and strapping machine.
9. Laboratory Testing equipments.
10. Weighing balance, weights & others.

42

After Shave Lotion

Introduction:-

After Shave Lotion is a type of cosmetics product coming under men's cosmetics category. It is basically used after shaving to feel cool and to impart antiseptic action over the shaving areas. It is basically formulated to sooth and cool the skin, to tighten it, to close the pores, to sterilise and stem the flow of bold from any inadvertent nicks or cuts.

The purpose of an after shave preparations is to relieve the slight irritation or "after glow" and confer a pleasant feeling of comfort and well being after shaving. This is achieved by giving a slight coolness, anaesthesia, mild astringency or emolliency to the skin. At the same time, the preparations should be antiseptic and help to keep the skin free from bacterial infection during the sort time it take to recover from the slight degree of injury inflicting during the shaving operation. The extent to which these properties are emphasised depends on the type of formulation.

Simply, an After Shave Lotion is a clear aqueous ethyl alcohol solution containing a perfume and colour. The desired balance of mild astringency and coolness is achieved by controlling the ratio of ethyl alcohol to water. 3 Analysis of popular UK brands of after shave lotion shows that they contain 50-70% by weight ethyl alcohol, whereas in USA 40-60% by volume of alcohol to obtain the balance of properties.

The commercial success of an after shave lotion is largely dependent on the perfume and the way in which the product is marketed. Many different perfume types, for example Spicy, Chypre, Sandal wood, floral, leather and tobacco have been successful. The creation of a stable balanced perfume, which is free from components likely to cause skin irritation or sensitisation, is the province of the perfumer.

Now a days, the major after shave lotion manufacturers who are marketing their products in brands - Gillete, Old Spice, Emami, Godrej and others.

Properties of Good Quality After-Shave Lotion :-

1. After Shave Lotion has anti-septic properties.
2. It do not cause any skin irritation, etching etc.

3. It is non-toxic, ecologically and biologically safe.
4. It provides soothing and cooling effect over skin.
5. The perfume of the product is appealling to the users.

Uses & Applications :-

1. The after-shave lotion is used by almost everybody those who are shaving their beard and moustache.
2. It is used in houses, salons, beauty parlours, where shaving is done by razor to remove hair from the skins, from face, arm pits etc.
3. It is having a very good sensational masculine feeling after its application. The people are using it in their everyday life.
4. It's floral or fragrantic and cooling effect appeals everybody.

B.I.S. Specification :-

There is no B.I.S. Specifications available on "After Shave Lotion" with Bureau of Indian standards

Government Regulation :-

"After Shave Lotion" is a Cosmetic product which come under Drug & Cosmetic Rules, 1945.

To manufacture "After Shave Lotion" the manufacturer has to apply to the licensing authority appointed by the State Government in Form-31 (if the manufacturer wants to manufacture products for sale or distribution) or Form-31A (if the manufacturer wants loan iicense to manufacture cosmetic product.).

Raw Materials Availability :-

All the raw materials & packaging materials are indigenously available and can be procured from nearby local sources.

After Shave Lotion

Formulation- 1

Ingredients		*Parts by Weight*
Alcohol (Absolute Ethyl Alcohol)	-	40 - 45
Purified water	-	52.5 - 57.75
Glycerine	-	1- 3
Quarternium- 19	-	0.25 - 0.50
Perfume	-	0.01 - 0.5
Colour	-	Q.S.
Preservative	-	0.1-0.3
		100

Formulation - 2

Ingredients		*Parts by Weight*
Alcohol (Absolute Ethyl Alcohol)	-	40 - 45
Sorbitol	-	4-6
Purified water	-	to make 100
Lactic Acid	-	0.5-1
Menthol	-	0.1-0.5
Perfume	-	0.01-0.5
Colour	-	Q.S.
Preservative		0.1-0.3
		100

Manufacturing process

To prepare after shave lotion based on above formulation the following steps have to be adopted in manufacturing of the product.

1. The raw materials are required to be purchased from good suppliers or dealers.
2. After procurement, all the raw materials are analysed and tested in the laboratory.
3. The materials are weighed in desired quantity as specified in the formulation.
4. In a stainless steel vessel fitted with S.S.Stirrer, pour Glycerine and Preservative. Heat the vessel over gas burner to dissolve the preservative completely.
5. In another closed top vessel (S.S. Vessel) fitted with stirrer and flame proof motor, pour Alcohol, Quarterium-19 and a part of purified water and mix it thoroughly.
6. To the step-5 preparations, add the step-4 preparations with slow mixing till uniform.
7. In another vessel prepare colour solution by mixing colour & balance purified water the with slow stirring.
8. Now, add this colour solution to the step-6 preparations with stirring till uniform. Then *to* it add the perfume and mix thoroughly.
9. The final product is now quality tested, standardised and packed in bottles of desired size. The bottles are labelled and batch coded.
10. The bottles are now packed in outer cartons and in the final master cartons. The cartons are now strapped.
11. The final cartons are placed in store and marketed to the desired customers.

Process Flowsheet For Manufacturing of After Shave Lotion

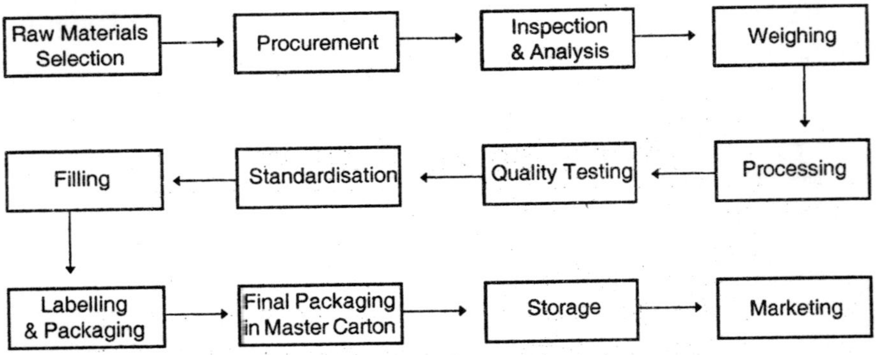

Plant & Machineries Require :-

1. Mixing tank (Stainless Steel Made), closed top fitted with stirrer and flame proof motor,
2. Stainless steel tank with stirrer.
3. Gas burner & cylinder.
4. Filling tank.
5. Laboratory equipments and Glasswares.
6. Tools, fixtures etc.

43

Peppermint Mouth Wash

Introduction :-

Peppermint Mouth Wash is a type of mouth cleanser cum refreshing liquid having antibacterial action in the mouth. It is a type of oral care product, which is used to refresh the mouth after each meal. It is available in ready to use form or in concentrate form, which can be diluted with clean water prior to use as per direction. The mouth wash performs various functions in oral hygiene. It has been found that there are various types of mouthwashes formulated all over the world. "

1. Mouthwashes containing anti-bacterial agents.
2. Mouthwashes containing fluoride.
3. Mouthwashes containing minerals (Astringent agents).
4. Mouthwash containing flavours.

The anti-bacterial mouthwash helps reduce bacterial population in the mouth. The fluoride mouthwash helps to reinforce the fluoride layer on the enamel of the teeth. The mineralising mouthwash (astringent mouthwash) helps to repair early carious lesions disease. Mouthwash containing flavours will refresh the mouth as well breath. It has been considered that mouthwash plays vital role in rinsing food debris from the mouth, helps in reduction of bacterial population, imparting flavour to mouth cavity and thereby imparting flavour to breath. At present there are few manufacturers, who are manufacturing this product in India. So a new entrepreneur can take opportunity to launch new products in domestic as well as international market.

Properties of Good Quality Mouthwash :-

1. Mouthwash preparations meet all the oral hygienic considerations.
2. It is properly pH balanced to fulfil all the international norms or FDA regulations.
3. The product is formulated with cosmetic grade raw materials.

Uses and Applications :-

1. Mouthwash in ready to use liquid form is basically used to rinse the food debris, reduce bacterial population and refresh breath in the mouth.

2. It is used by both male and female of all age group.
3. It can be used after each meal, lunch or dinner to refresh mouth feelings and refresh breath.

Different Types of Mouth Wash Available :-

There are following varieties of mouthwashes available in international market. The names are specified as follows:-

Alkaline Mouthwash.
Analgesic Mouthwash.
Antiseptic Mouthwash.
Aromatic Mouthwash.
Astringent Mouthwash.
Chlorophenol Mouthwash.
Lactic acid Mouthwash.
Mentholated Mouthwash.
Peppermint Mouthwash.
Peroxide Mouthwash.
Phenol Mouthwash.
Quinosol Mouthwash.
Resorcin Mouthwash.
Salol Mouthwash.
Salol-Thymol Mouthwash.
Thymol Mouthwash.
Glycerine Thymol Mouthwash.
Zinc chloride Mouthwash.
Aerosol Mouthwash cum mouth freshener.

B.I.S. Specification:-

There is no such B.I.S. Specification available on "Mouth Wash" with Bureau of India Standards, but materials is tested as per FDA norms on the oral hygiene products.

Government Regulation :-

"Mouth Wash" is a Cosmetic product which come under Drug & Cosmetic Rules, 1945.

To manufacture "Mouth Wash" the manufacturer has to apply to the licensing authority appointed by the State Government in Form-31 (if the manufacturer wants to manufacture products for sale *or* distribution) or Form -31A, (if the manufacturer wants loan license to manufacture cosmetic product.).

Raw Materials Require and its Availability :-

There are various raw materials require to formulate the mouth wash. The major raw materials are antibacterial agent, preservative, essential oils or flavours, solvents, Purified water, water soluble colour, Glycerine etc. along with packaging materials, labels, card board boxes, corrugated cartons etc. These materials are available indigenously and can be procured from nearby local sources.

Peppermint Mouthwash

Formulation- 1

Ingredients		*Parts by weight.*
Thymol	-	0.01 - 0.03
Absolute Ethyl Alcohol	-	3 - 5
Borax	-	1 - 2
Sodium Bicarbonate	-	0.5 - 1
Glycerine (purified)	-	6-8
Purified water	-	to make 100
Flavour (Peppermint oil)	-	0.1 - 0.2
Colour (Water Soluble)	-	Q.S.
		100

Manufacturing Process :-

To manufacture good quality Mouth wash the production incharge should take care to proceed following processing steps.

1. Purchase all the ingredients from standard reputed dealers or traders.
2. Analyse and test all the raw material as per standard testing norms.
3. Weigh ali the ingredients as mentioned in the formulation.
4. In a stainless steel tank fitted with S.S. Stirrer, Pour Ethyl Alcohol absolute, Thymol, Glycerine, Peppermint oil and mix it thoroughly with stirrer to homogenise it.
5. In another vessel add Sodium Bicarbonate, Borax in purified water and mix uniformly with mild heating.
6. Now, add step-5 preparations to the step-4 preparations and stire to mix uniformly.
7. Now, in another vessel prepare colour solution by dissolving the colour in little quantity Purified water.
8. This colour solution is added to the step-6 preparations by mixing slowly till uniform.
9. The final product is filtered and quality tested. Then, it is filled and sealed in plastic(PET) bottles. The labels are pasted.
10. The bottles are packed in outer cartons and corrugated master cartons.
11. The final cartons are strapped, placed in store and then sent for marketing to the desired customers.

Process Flowsheet For Manufacturing of Peppermint Mouth Wash

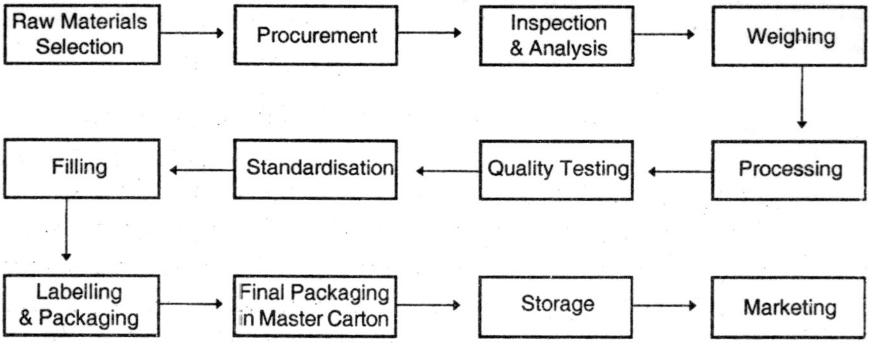

Plant & Machineries Require :-

1. Stainless Steel vessel (closed top) fitted with flame proof motor and stirrer.
2. Mixing vessel of stainless steel made, fitted with S.S. Stirrer.
3. Filling tank (S.S.made)
4. Label pasting machine.
5. Box strapping machine.
6. Laboratory equipments.
7. Tools, fixtures and accessories.

44

Herbal Henna Powder

Introduction :-

Herbal Henna Powder is a type of natural preparations used on the hair to dye white hair naturally without any chemical contents. It not only covers the grey hair but also makes hair smooth and shiny.

It does not cause any harm to human hair and scalp. It do not cause irritations or any types of etching on the scalp. It exerts its herbal effects over hair or scalp. This product can be useful with every type of hair from ages of 18 years onwards.

Now a days, people are becoming more health and beauty conscious. People are purchasing and using only biologically safe natural cosmetics products for personal adornment. So natural cosmetics are gaining market demand potential all over the world. The acceptance of natural cosmetics is rising day by day among both men and women all over the world for long lasting lusts and glamour over human being. So, its domestic as well as export demand is rising proportionately with rise in population growth in every part of the world.

Properties of Good Quality Herbal Henna Powder :-

Herbal Henna Powder itself indicates that it is a herbal product. It has following properties.

1. It do not contain any moisture.
2. It is non-irritating and non-toxic in characteristics.
3. It is biologically safe and ecologically compatible on application over human hair.
4. It causes no side effect over scalp or hair.
5. Its dye is safe for regular application.

Uses and Applications :-

1. Herbal Henna Powder is a direct substitute of all the available Hair dyes (Herbal & Modern) in the market. It is applied on the hair by both men and women to obtain natural black or brown hair colours.
2. It can be applied by anybody with no side effect over hair. As it does not contain any chemical.
3. It can be applied at any climate, in any country without any problem.

B.I.S. Specification :-

There is no B.I.S. Specification available with Bureau of Indian Standards on "Herbal Henna Powder". But this product is tested as per the cosmetics norms prior to marketing.

Government Regulation :-

"Herbal Henna Powder" is a cosmetic product which come under Drug & Cosmetic Rules, 1945.

To manufacture this product, the manufacturers have to apply to the licensing authority appointed by the State Government in Form-31 (If the manufacturer wants to manufacture products for sale or distribution).

Raw Materials Require and its Availability :-

Herbal Henna Powder is basically prepared from the major ingredients Henna, Amla, Shikakai, Neem leaves, Lemon Peels and other natural ingredients. There is no scarcity of any of these raw materials in our country. So there is no trouble in production of Herbal Henna Powder round the year.

All the herbs, raw materials are available indigenously. These can be procured from nearby local sources.

Herbal Henna Powder

Formulation:-

Ingredients		*Parts by weight*
Starch powder	-	0.2-2
Henna powder	-	Q.S to make 100
Dry Amla fruit powder	-	3-6
Shikakai seed powder	-	1 - 4
Kathha Powder	-	1-4
Lemon peel powder	-	0.5 - 2
Neem leaf powder	-	0.5-2
		100

Manufacturing Process :-

To manufacture good quality Herbal Henna Powder the specified manufacturing steps have to be followed by the manufacturers :-

1. First of all, purchase all the raw materials from genuine suppliers, dealers or traders.
2. Test its quality, moisture content and other details.
3. Weigh all the raw materials as specified in the formulation.
4. Mix all the raw materials and pulverize it in a pulverser to very fine particle size.
5. Then, Sieve it through a wire mesh to remove larger particles if any.

6. The product is now quality tested and standardized.
7. These Herbal Henna powder is now packed in moistureproof air tight pouches by automatic or semi-automatic pouch packing machine.
8. These pouches are now packed in the outer cardboard paper cartons of 5, 10 Pcs each.
9. These small cartons are packed in corrugated cardboard boxes. Then, corrugated boxes are sealed with adhesive tapes and strapped.
10. The cartons are now placed in store and marketed to the desired distributors, dealers or traders.

Process Flowsheet For Manufacturing of Herbal Henna Powder

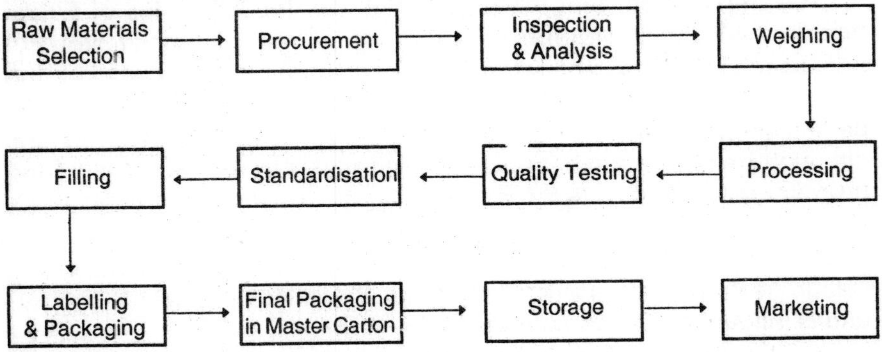

Plant & Machinery Require :-

1. Weighing Balance.
2. Drying oven.
3. Pulveriser with all accessories.
4. Sieving machine.
5. Automatic Pouch weighing, filling & sealing machine.
6. Laboratory equipment & Glassware.
7. Carton strapping machine.

45

Toilet Powders

Face powders constitute an indispensable article of my lady's toilet. She is able to find a powder of whatever quality may suit her purse, and the first thing that attracts her is perfume. This is, however, by no means the only feature which appeals to the discerning woman; she is interested also in colour, texture and adherence to the skin.

Assuming, then, that the perfume makes the first sales of a face powder, will an intriguing odour produce repeat sales? No, not necessarily; it is the appearance and finish given to the skin by the powder which induces the majority of women to buy, repeatedly, any particular make. This characteristic may almost be described as 'texture' although generally ladies apply the term rather to the 'fineness' of the powder - that is to say, to the dimensions of the silk sieve through which the powder passes in the course of its manufacture, thus producing fineness of sub—division and even distribution of all ingredients including colour. Texture, then, is a most important characteristic of a face powder, and is influenced by the following considerations;

(1) the powder must have good covering power and so hide skin blemishes;
(2) it must adhere perfectly to the skin and not blow off easily;
(3) it must not be completely dissipated in a few minutes and so make re-powdering continually necessary;
(4) the finish given to the skin must be preferable of a matt or peach-like character;
(5) shine on or around the nose must be completely eliminated. The powder must be absorbent;
(6) there must be sufficient 'slip' to enable the powder to spread on the skin by the puff without producing a blotchy effect;
(7) the constituents of the powder must be such that a clown-like effect is impossible. The preference should be rather towards one of transparency.

Raw Materials

The main substances used to impart all these good qualities are as follows: Light kaolin, zinc oxide, titanium dioxide, light calcium carbonate (precipitated calcium carbonate), purified talc (talcum), light magnesium carbonate, stearates of zinc and magnesium.

Other materials which have been commonly used as ingredients of face powders but are now only used when indicated either by reasons of ease of availability or cost include the following: Zinc carbonate, barium carbonate, kieselguhr, and the salts of bismuth. Starch is an economical material included in some powders, but is not often used in modern formulations, barium sulphate and calcium sulphate are often used in compacts because they help to prevent and compacts breaking.

Covering Power

Covering power is obtained by the use of light kaolin, zinc oxide, or titanium dioxide. These materials give degress of covering power in the order mentioned. Kaolin is light in use and has the greatest grease-resisting properties, being excelllent therefore for oily skins; zinc oxide is heavier and titanim dioxide the heaviest. Using these materials face powders can thus be prepared with differing covering properties. Titanium dioxide is, however, often the material chosen to provide the covering properties of a face powder, a suitable proportion being used in perference to the higher proportion of zinc oxide and kaolin, which are required to obtain the same effect.

Zinc oxide may be used on economical grounds and for this reason is often preferred in talcum powder where less covering power is required. Only the finest qualities of zinc oxide should not be used, since lower grades contain gritty particles. Zinc oxide also has a tendency to form balled particles and it is a good plan to sieve the material separately before mixing wilth any of the other ingredients of a particular formula. Only the finest B.P.quality of light kaolin should also be used again to ensure that the material is free from grilttilness.

Adhesiveness

Adhesiveness is obtainted primarily with the stearates of zinc and magnesium; zinc stearate is commonly used. Magnesium stearate has a slightly better covering power and is considered more adhesive than the zinc salt. Magnesium stearate is thus often preferred for high quality face powders, whereas zinc stearate is used extensively in talcum powders. Both materials are obtainable from high grade stearic acids and superfine qualities now prepared specially for the cosmetic industry are available with excellent colour and texture, and a minimum of odour. Both are light and fluffy products and when used in suitable proportions give to the powder an attractive velvety softness. Moreover they are 'water-proof, and tend to maintain the complexion in inclement weather. Stearates of lithium and calcium are also available and used with similar effect to zinc and magnesium stearate. Lithium stearate in particular has good covering properties, and a fluffy texture.

Magnesium and calcium salts of myristic acid are also available as specially materials for use in high quality products. Magneisum myristate has a better texture than magnesium stearate, and a higher specific volume. It also has a more oily or greasy feel and is correspondingly more adhesive to the skin. Because of these properties very good effects can be obtained by using only small proportions of the material.

Complete dissipation on the skin in a short time is very noticeable in those powders which are prepared with an exceptionally large proportion of talcum. Talc is used, however, as the main ingredient of many face powders. Talc of cosmetic quality is purified hydrated magnesium silicate. It is obtained from several countries, the best known available being of Italian of Indian origin. The Italian variety is by far the best quality and recommended both for face powders and talcum powders. It is much whiter in colour and finer in texture than the Indian. Italian talc is also much less liable to be contaminated with micro-ogranisms, an important factor when considering manufacture of talcum powder for baby use. Talc is, however, often sterilized before use which overcomes this particular problem. Talc imparts the property of silkiness and provides slip to a product and these properties can be demonstrated by rubbing between the fingers or on the back of the hand. This test also illustrates the degree of fineness and a sample should not show many particles of a crystalline character when reviewed obliquely after spreading finely in this manner. Special grades of micronized talc are available, and are of even texturer and bulk, and used in compacted products. They are also essential for aerosol products.

Peach-Life Finish

The peach-like finish given to the skin by face powders can be achieved by use of rice starch. Other starches are used in cheaper powders, maize starch being often employed. As is well known, however, the particles of rice starch are much finer than those of any other cereal and a distinct preference is, in consequence, shown for it. Rice starch is prone to absorb moisture and should be placed in a drying oven for two to three hours before use.

Potato starch should be avoided. The question of a shiny nose, is, incidentally closely associated with starches. This particular part of the anatomy is inclined to perspire and powders which are absorbent, such as starch or kaolin, more readily rectify this blemish. Rice starch is particularly absorbent and thus favoured for this additional reason. The objection taken to its use is centred in the belief that as starch absorbs moisture so it swells and distends the pores. In modern types, therefore, it is seldom found, and the peach finish is obtained instead with light precipitated calcium carbonate.

Occasionally speciality materials such as silica or powdered silk are included in face powders. Silica is available in a very finely divided form of a very fluffy nature, and used to increase the bulk. It also has very good adhesion properties and is used to prepare powders of a light transparent type.

Powdered silk is obtained by a partial hydrolysis of silk protein and the hydrolysate is then ground to an impalpable powder, and special grades are available to the cosmetic industry which are light and bulky and of a good white colour. It should not be used in excess of 30 per cent. Light magnesium carbonate is also used for the same purpose, but at a lower concentration. Both materials are used to absorb perfume which then helps to disperse the perfume throughout the remaining ingredients of a formulation:

	(per cent)
Light kaolin	20-50
Zinc oxide or carbonate	5-30
Titanium dioxide	1-5
Rice starch	20-50
Light magnesium carbonate	5-10
Light calcium carbonate	5-30
Magnesium stearate	1-5
Zinc stearate	1-10
Talcum	50-75
Magnesium myristate	1-5

The process of shifting and mixing is important. Several raw materials, particularly starch, chalk, and talcum, are bought in sacks, and although frequently lined, it is amazing how much extraneous matter seems to find its way inside during transit. This matter is, however, readily eliminated by means of a 120-mesh sieve, and silk is unquestionably the finest material for this purpose. Substances such as zinc oxide do not sift readily; they clog the sieve, particularly if it is a metal one. Silk does not possess this disadvantage, and is almost universally employed, for small operations the raw materials may be brushed through twice, but for quantity production machines are indispensable. The powders are emptied into a hopper on the floor level and carried by cup-conveyor to be deposited on the end of an inclined revolving silk drum. This has a small 'knocker[1] which prevents clogging. The extranesous matter falls from the lower and of the drum, while the fine ingredients pass through in the course of its revolutions. Below is a rapidly rotating shaft having bent arms, which ensure perfect mixing.

Face Powder Bases

The most popular face powders consist of any of the above substances, judiciosly combined, but all should contain either some zinc oxide or titanium dioxide as the material to impart a degree of covering power. The proportion of ingredients used can be altered to give slight variation in the properties of the powder, but, as a rule, powders are classified as being of a light, medium, or heavy type, although they must not be either too light or too heavy. A selection of formulae for face powder bases follow:

(Light type)

Zinc stearate	70
Zinc oxide	100
Light calcium carbonate	200
Talc	630
	1000

(Medium type)

Zinc stearate	70
Zinc oxide	100
Titanium dioxide	20
Light calcium carbonate	200
Talc	610
	1000

(Heavy type)

Magnesium stearate	50
Light kaolin	200
Zinc oxide	150
Light calcium carbonate	400
Talc	200
	1000

(Heavy type)

Titanium dioxide	50
Zinc oxide	150
Magnesium stearate	50
Light calcium carbonate	150
Light kaolin	250
Talc	350
	1000

(Medium type)

Zinc stearate	150
Zinc oxide	175
Light calcium carbonate	200
Talc	475
	1000

Colours

The colouring of a face powder is designed to produce a wide range of shades suitable to blend with and enhance the natural complexion, and to do this a long programme of experimental work must be undertaken. A suitable range is thus based on shades designed for the blonde and fair skinned, the brunette and dark skinned user, and those who require a face powder to tone down a naturally florid type complexion. The so-called 'natural' range originally consisting of pinkish shades was designed for use by the fair skinned, but these are now required to be of a more subtle character to avoid an artificial appearance. Similarly the original cream or rachel shades based on high proportions of ochres are modified to give more subtle tones. Blue, green and brown and even black pigments are used to achieve the desired effects which are essentially designed to blend with and enhance the natural complexion.

The names ascribed to modern shades are consequently more often selected for their sale and psychological appeal rather than a connection with the actual colours used. The exceptions to this fashion are shades such as tan or olive which are always acceptable for dark or suntanned skins.

Colours used for face powder must have good dispersing properties. A concentrated pigment invariably contains hard aggregates which are formed during the drying proceeds of manufacture, and these are not broken down by subsequent milling. Consequently if a concentrated pigment is used it must first by milled, not only to reduce the particle size but as a means of removing all hard aggregates which occur in concentrated pigments. Colours specially prepared for face powder are available from manufacturers. These are reduced colours prepared during the manufacture of the pigment itself when the pigment is reduced on based used in the face powder compositions. Experimental work on blending must therefore be carried out using pigments which have either been specially milled to remove agglomerates or preferably using the specially manufactured semi-prepared colours.

For experimental work a further dilution of the pigment should be made using one part of the pigment mixed with nine parts of calcium carbonate. This mixture will not require any further milling, but should be mixed in a small sifter and mixing machine specially reserved for this purpose. A similar procedure of dilution should be carried out when the process is transferred to the manufacturing scale, that is before the addition of colours to the bulk powder used for the powder base. Careful attention to this procedure ensures even dispersion of the pigments and reduces the limit of error both in experimental work and on the manufacturing scale.

The colours for face powder, rouges and eye make-up powders are mainly based on inorganic earths, oxides, and ultramarines. All these naturally occurring materials are suitable for use in powder based products. Iron oxide pigments for example, vary in colour through red, yellow and brown, including ochres, ambers, and siennas. These materials, however, occur in various degrees of purity and generally contain high levels of lead and arsenic. They are now manufactured synthetically by a wet oxidation process and by variations in the process a complete range of colour shades is obtained. Generally known as 'synthetic inorganics" or 'cosmetic oxides' they contain low levels of impurities, are of small particle size, and high colour strength. Most important they can be manfactured to agreed colour standards and an adequate range of colours from greenish yellow through ranges to purple, reds, browns, and blacks can be obtained by judicious blending of selected batches of the manufactured synthetics. Some indication of these is given below:

Cosmetic yellow ochre
Cosmetic red oxide
Cosmetic umber
Cosmetic brown oxide
Cosmetic black oxide
Cosmetic hydrated chromium oxide (blue/green)
Cosmetic oxide (yellow/green)
Ultramarines are also available as for example:
Cosmetic ultramarine blue
Cosmetic ultramarine violet

extending similarly through a range of shades. These colours are available in a reduced form specially prepared for use in coloured powder products. This helps to obtain good consistent dispersions in the product and also reduced variations of supplies to a minimum. Nevertheless manufacturers are advised to prepare standard dispersions in a medium such as talc or light calcium carbonate in order to compare the tinctorial properties of individual batches of colour as received from the supplier. Small variations in batches of colour can cause trouble and checks against a standard avoid adjustments having to be made to the end product. Use of reduced colours also minimizes bleeding effects which can be troublesome in powder products and occurs particularly with the concentrated forms. Resistance to bleeding is one of the most imporatant factors required for a face powder colour. This is the result of a solvent effect and is caused mainly by perfume. Any perfumes to be used in a face powder should be checked to see that no solubilization takes places. A test should also be made to check for bleeding in the presence of water which can be present in use as skin preparation.

Pigments which bleed cause the product to change colour on the skin or powder puff and are responsible for streaky effects in use. It is for this reason that water-soluble dye-stuffs should never be used in powder used for face or eye make-up. Similarly any organic pigments which are sometimes considered for their brightening effect should be carefully screened before use.

Another type of inorganic pigment used for colouring powder products is the range of metallic colourants used to give gold, silver, and similar metallic effects. Aluminium powders are used to obtain silver effects and gold or bronze colours are obtained using copper and copper alloys which have also been reduced to fine powders by milling.

Other coloured metallic shades such as blues and greens are prepared from powdered alumnium by treating the powder with a solution of a basic dyestuff. In addition to the normal range of powder colours, special shades are prepared which are designed to give a luminous and translucent effect on the skin. The luminous or transluscent and shimmer effect is obtained by using the following materials:

(1) natural pearl essence (guanine);
(2) bismuth oxychloride;
(3} synthetic pearl pigments.

Natural pearl essence (guanine) is obtained from fish scales and is generally available as a dispersion in castor-oil. It occurs as thin narrow platelets and produces excellent shimmering silver effects as a result of light reflection from the crystals as they occur *in* depth through a dispersing medium. The high cost of the material does, however, restrict its use.

Bismuth oxychloride is used as a substitute for natural pearl essence and although it gives a good pearl effect does not have the brilliant lustre of the natural product. It is now prepared in special grades for cosmetic use and is also available as bismuth pearl pigments.

Synthetic pearl pigments can be obtained in various shades including white, gold, and pink. They are based on mica Hakes coated with titanium dioxide. Several grades are available and these vary in their brilliance or lustre effect according to the particle size of the platelets.

To prepare face powders incorporating one or more of the pearlized colourants, reduce the content of the cosmetic earths and oxides so that the base colour is less opaque. This permits maximum effect.of the pearlized material and the natural complexion is enhanced by the translucent lustre or frosted effect. Sometimes a pearlized or frosted powder is dusted over the more dense normal face powder to produce highlights. Similarly when formulating, reduce the proportion of heavy opaque materials which tend to diminish the lustre. On the other hand the proportion of talc, which itself has a faint lustre, can be increased.

A basic light type formula (No. 2535) can be modified to prepare a pearlized or frosted face powder as follows:

Magnesium stearate	70
Zinc oxide	80
Light calcium carbonate	100
Inorganic pigments	50
Pearl pigment	100
Talc	600
	1000

Perfume

A face powder will never achieve large sales unless the odour is pleasing. This must not be 'thin' that is to say, the odour must be 'round' and have 'body', and yet possess an elusive flowery freshness. The value of any particular perfume type is largely a matter of opinion, but there is at the present time a distinct inclination towards a sweet, flowery fragrance which must be persistent without becoming cloying. The strong, pungent Eastern type of perfume is seldom perferred by the lady of good breeding and taste. From the maker's point of view the perfume should be complex, and thus difficult to duplicate.

With a view to making this question quite clear, it will be best to consider two well-defined examples of perfumes suitable for face powders and the modifications in price which are possible by the choice of different raw materials. Two apt examples may be cited in rose and a light bouquet odour based upon jasmin. In the case of rose, the alcohols having basic rose odours are rhodinol, nerol, citronellol, geraniol, and linalol. Rhodinal of finest quality is obtained by fractionating Bourbon geranium oil, and the price is a standard one depending upon the market price of the raw material. Nerol is obtained in standard quality either from petitgrain oil or by synthesis from geraniol. Citronellol is obtained from citronellal by reduction and also from geranium oil. It is probably isomeric with rhodino, but the odour has a. slightly higher note. Geraniol occurs in the market in three grades-the finest from palmarosa oil, the medium grade from Java citronella oil, and the lowest grade from Ceylon citronella oil. Linalol occurs in linaloe oil and in shiu oil. The former is the superior product. In deciding which of these bases to employ, the perfumer is naturally guided by the quality of his finished product. For the best results he would employ a mixture of rhodinol, nerol, citronellol, and palmarosa geraniol. For a cheaper product he would use mainly Java citronella geraniol with touches of rhodinol and citronellol. Nerol would be quite out of the question, because it is the most expensive of the rosaceous alcohols. Another indispensable and also comparatively inexpensive, base is phenylethyl alcohol. This would enter both expensive and cheap products. The esters of this alcohol are also very valuable, especially phenylethyl propionate, which has an odour closely associated with that of the red rose. This ester is about double the price of the alcohol, and would therefore only enter the better grade perfume. Ionone is a very useful synthetic for imparing freshness to any rose compound. The best product is alpha ionone, which varies in odour with the skill of the manufacturer in eliminating impurities occurring in the lemon-grass oil used in its synthesis. The alternative is the so-called 100 per cent ionone, which is usually a mixture of the alpha and beta isomers, together with the residual impurities already referred to. This product would therefore go into the cheaper rose compounds. There is also a wide range of esters of the alcohols geraniol and citronellol. Gernyl acetate is not expensive, and could be used in cheaper compounds. Patchouli and vetivert oils are used in traces for giving body to some rose compounds. In both these oils there is a choice in price according to the source of the raw material. For imparting intensity of odour nonylaldeyhde in traces is much employed. The quantity used, although the product is expensive, would not preclude its employment in cheaper compounds. Ethyl cinnamate also, in traces, is useful for this purpose, and the same remarks as to price apply. To come finally to the crux of the whole matter-the natural product-there is a choice between rose otto and rose absolute, but the cost is far too high in either case to receive consideration in the cheaper product. For very cheap roses traces of diphenyl methane or oxide may be employed to fortify the usaul bases. With regard to fixation, substances, which may be used in both qualities are benzoin, styrax, santal, artificial musks, benzyl iso-Eugenol, and vanillin. Their prices and the quantities used are so small as to make it needless to consider their omission. In the finest compounds it is customary to use the above-mentioned substances, but to use also the natural fixative extracts, such as musk and civet. To illustrate the above notes it will be well to give three concrete examples capable of endless modification to suit the taste of the perfumer and also the price he has to consider.

Table 45.1: Rose compounds

Raw material	Grade I	Grade II	Grade III
Rhodinal	100	120	—
Nerol	20	—	—
Citronellol	100	40	—
Linalol	—	50	100
Geraniol 1 (Palmarosa)	120	200	—
Geraniol 2 (Java citronella)	—	70	250
Geraniol 33 (ceylon citronella)	—	—	100
Phenylethyl alcohol	120	300	250

Phenylethyl propionate	200		
Citronellyl butyrate	1	—	—
Geranyl acetate	3	60	8
Alpha ionone	120	50	—
100 per cent ionone	—	30	80
Patchouli oil	1	1	1
Vetivert oil	—	1	2
Nonyl aldehyde	1	1	1
Ethyl cinnamate	—	1	2
Rose otto	60	10	—
Rose absolute	30	—	—
Diphenyl methane	—	—	10
Sandalwood oil	—	10	70
Musk ketone	3	5	5
Vanillin	1	1	1
Benzyl benzoate	70	50	120
Musk extract, 3 per cent	20	—	—
Civet extract, 3 per cent	30	—	—
Total	**1000**	**1000**	**1000**

It should be noted that there are also many other raw materials which may be used, but which have not been mentioned above. Among these are the various geranium oils-particularly French geranium distilled over roses, eugenol, cinnamic alcohol, heliotropin, coriander oil, etc.

When experiments are commenced upon a bouquet compound there are no definite limits as to the possible raw mterials which may be used, and in consequence the creation takes upon itself a much more difficult aspect than that of the flower compound already dealt with. In the case of a jasmin bouquet, substances outside the usual straightforward jasmin compound constients have to be tried and blended for several weeks to gauge the odour of the finished creation. The ultimate object is to produce something having a jasmin odour note, but an underlying fragrance of an intangible natural background of numerous flowers as it were, with the fragrance of jasmin flowers predominanting. With no price to consider, the perfumer has the whole gamut of odours to experiment with regardless of cost. In a low-priced article, however, considerable reliance has to be placed on the crystalline synthetics for the background, and oils of the jasmin type, plus benzyl acetate as the principal odour note. For the purpose of these notes we will assume that the perfumer has already available in his laboratory a good-quality artificial jasmin compound made without natural jasmin; then it can be used in both the expensive and cheap perfume. Using this as a base, the fresh flowering note may be improved and modified with bergamot and ylang-ylang oils.

Table 45.2: Jasmin bouquet

Raw material	Grade I	Grade II
Jasmin compound	100	100
Bergamot oil	100	100
Ylang-ylang oil, Manilla	90	
Ylang-ylang oil, Bourbon		120
Neroli oil, Bigarade	10	
French petitgran oil		30
Orange blossom absolute	15	—
Rose otto	15	—
Rose compound	—	30
Rhidinol	—	70
Concrete orris oil	25	—
Beta ionone	—	5
Methyl ionone	130	—
Alpha ionone	—	100
Carnation compound	120	—
iso-Eugenol	—	100
Acetyl iso-Eugenol	—	20
Amber synthetic	100	100
Heliotropin	60	60
Vanillin	10	10
Coumarin	40	40
Musk ketone	30	30
Benzoin resinoid, Siam	25	25
Peru balsam	10	10
Jasmin chassis absolute	50	—
Benzyl acetate	—	48
Amyl cinnamic aldehyde	—	2
Civet extract, 3 per cent	50	—
Ambergris extract, 3 per cent	20	—
Total	**1000**	**1000**

In the latter case there are three qualities available, the Manila, Bourbon, and the commoner cananga oil. The quality of odour, as usual, bears a direct ratio to the cost price. These oils may be further modified with the neroli oil, orange blossom absolute, rose otto, concrete orris, methyl ionone and artificial carnation. Body and fixative value may be given to these oils by the use of amber synthetic, heliotropin, vanillin, coumarin, artificial musks, benzoin and Peru balsam. Finally, the jasmin flowery note is imparted by additons of natural jasmin chassis absolute. In the example below the cheaper substitutes are placed immediately below each ingredient.

When using a well-blended compound in either face powders or compacts, it is best to employ about 2 per cent of perfume. This is first rubbed down with an absorbent powder, such as light magnesium carbonate or calcium carbonate and added to the other powders before shifting and mixing. In the case of compacts it is well to remember that the perfume does have a slight influence on the final colour and tends to darken it. When compacts dry out after 2 or 3 days, it will be noticed that the shade of colour is slightly lighter than when first pressed. In general, about one-quarter the weight of colours is necessary to give the same shade to a finished compact as is already standardized in the existing loose face powder.

Compact Powders

Compact powders have enjoyed many years of popularity chiefly on account of their convenience, for they can be carried in the handbag and deftly used without any danger of soiling clothing. They consist of an ordinary lace powder mixed with a suitable blending agent and the mix is compressed either by hand operation or machine into cake form. The composition of the mix must be such that the compacted powder must come off easily when rubbed with a powder puff, and the addition of binding agent must be so controlled that the compact must not break under normal conditions of use and storage. There are three distinct processes of production, i.e. damp, wet, and dry. As a rule the bases for the first type contain a fairly large percentage of talcum, but are never overloaded with starch as this makes the compact too hard, and when rubbed with a puff it becomes shiny and 'slate-like'. On the other hand, the presence of some starch is desirable because of its binding properties which prevents the tablet disintegrating to powder. When only a small proportion of starch is included in the powder base another binding agent must be included in the formula, and materials such as light magnesium carbonate, acacia or tragacanth gums are used for this purpose. Gum resins such as benzoin or tolu and styrax are also useful. Compact powders prepared in this way are comparatively hard, although correct formulation and manufacturing technique does ensure that the powder is readily transferred to the puff, a distinction should clearly be made between the compact powder and the modern type of 'cream' compact or compressed powder which contains fatty materials as part of the binding material and produces a softer product which although when correctly made maintains its compressed form and is more readily transferred to the puff. It is probably true to say that the original type of compact powder is now only used for the manufacturer of rouge and eye make-up preparations.

Cake Make-up

Cake make-up is in some ways a type of powder compact, but in this case the normal constituents of a face powder are mixed with both oil and water miscible materials to a stiff paste-like consistency sometimes compared to a powder cream. This is dried, finely ground by milling and compressed into a cake. They generally contain a higher proportion of pigments than loose face powder. The cake is used by moistening with a wet application sponge which reconstitutes a power cream in situ. This is applied in wet form and allowed to dry on the skin as a fairly thick film. Consequently its use and popularity is governed to a large extent by the tastes of a market or a fashion vogue which requires a heavy type of make-up. As a heavy type make-up it is acceptable for use in artificial lighting and is also useful to hide skin blemishes. A patent issued in 1937 (British Patent No. 501732) prescribes the composition of a cake make-up as follows:

(1) Pigments and colours	12-50 per cent
(2) Oily and Waxy constituents	0.8-24 per cent
(3) Water-soluble (water miscible dispersing agents)	1.0-13 per cent
(4) Fillers	35-80 per cent

Two types of formulae are given for the powder base as follows:

Zinc oxide	150
Light calcium carbonate	300
Talc	430
Pigments	120
	1000

Light calcium carbonate	100
Calcium sulphate	120
Rice starch	40
Light kaolin	300
Talc	320
Pigments	120
	1000

Use either of the following formulae to prepare the cream base used as a binder. The second formula is more fatty and forms a thicker cream when the end product is applied to the skin.

A	White petroleum jelly	100
	Lanolin	50
	Glyceryl monostearate (self-emulsifying type)	100
B	Propylene glycol	100
	Water (softened or distilled)	650
		1000

	Methyl parahydroxybenzoate	0.2 per cent
A	Petroleum jelly	100
	Lanolin	30
	Mineral oil	100
	Glyceryl monostearate (self-emulsifying type)	75
B	Glycerin	100
	Sodium lauryl sulphate (powder or needles)	20
	Water (softened or distilled)	575
		1000
	Methyl parahydroxybenzoate	0.2 per cent

First prepare the coloured powder by miling the pigments with a suitable proportion of calcium carbonate as a diluent. Disperse the perfume (2 per cent) in the remaining calcium carbonate. Mix the remaining power ingredients in a sifter mixer and add the pigment mixture and perfume mixture. Set aside until required.

To prepare the cream base melt together the ingredients of A to a temperature of about 70°C. Heat ingredients of B to about 75°C. Add the preservative and add B to A with slow continuous stirring until a smooth cream is formed. Now mix the powder base with the cream base in a dough type mixer using 2 parts of powder base to 1 part of cream base. Mixing is best carried out by placing about one third of the cream base into the mixer and adding sufficient of the powders to form a paste. Following this by adding more cream base followed by powder base and so on until the whole has been added. This process takes some time and stirring is continued until a perfectly smooth and even coloured paste is obtained. It is permissible to add a small amount of additional water if the mass does not appear sufficiently smooth. Care should be taken not be add too much water in an attempt to reduce mixing time, since this will openly add to the length of drying process later.

The mass is the removed and broken into suitably sized pieces which are spread on to trays lined with grease proof paper, ready for drying. Drying is carried out by racking the trays and placing in a current of warm (not hot) air. Fierce heat not only destroys the perfume but also causes alteration to the colour on the edges of the mass. Drying is best carried out in two stages. At the half way period the mass is removed and then crumpled to a relatively fine powder and drying is continued until the mass is dry enough to be sieved. When completely dry the powder is sieved, re-mixed, and pressed into cakes using either a hand or machine operated press.

Compressed Powders

The modern type of compact powder is that known as compressed powder, also known as cream powder, or simply pressed powder, and although it cannot be said to have replaced loose face powder it has certainly reduced the demand. This, in like manner to the original compact powders is due, no doubt, to convenience in use, and also because it contains fatty materials which help adherence to the skin, and gives good covering power without the necessity of applying a foundation cream.

Both in composition and behaviour the compressed powder can be regarded as intermediate between the original compact and the cake makeup. Compressed powders are also made with suitable colours for use as eye-shadow powders. They are made by using either a wet mix and drying process in a somewhat similar fashion to a cake make-up or by a dry compression method. With either process it is essential to control the pressure of the compressing machine so that the product is neither too hard, and thus resembles a compact or cake make-up, nor is to too soft so that it crumbles to the touch. The finished product can be varied and modified to specific requirements depending upon the following factors.

1. Composition of the dry powder base.
2. The composition and proportion of fatty material used.
3. Mixing and sieving techniques.
4. The pressure control of the pressing machine during compression of the prrepared base.Care must be maintained to ensure that neither the pressure nor the weight of the mix used in each stamping varies, otherwise this will result in variable and faulty products.

Manufacture of compressed powder products, therefore, requires considerable technique, and experimental batches should always be made to vary the fatty content, and to judge its effect using a certain degree of compression per standard weight of powder. Then adjust the content of fatty material and again observe the effect of the same degree of compression. By followng this rather laborious technique the correct coditions for a specific mix, fat content, and pressure will be estalished to obtain a satisfactory product. The ideal product should not be too hard, not to soft. It should rub off easily on to the puff and contain sufficient fatty material to make it adhere to the skin. Suitable powder bases can be prepared as follows:

Titanium dioxide	75
Kaolin	300
Zinc stearate	100
Talc	525
	1000

Zinc oxide	100
Titanium dioxide	50
Magnesium stearate	100
Kaolin	200
Talc	550
	1000

Zinc oxide	100
Titanium dioxide	50
Zinc stearate	100
Kaolin	250
Talc	500
	1000

The powder base usually contains a higher proportion of zinc and/ or titanium oxides than that used in loose face powder, and consequently it is also necessary to use a higher percentage of pigments. Use about 2 per cent of perfume. From 3 to 4 per cent of fatty material is added by spraying onto the powder base. The fatty material can be lanolin (anhydrous) used alone or mixed with suitable oily materials to break up the stickiness and consequent difficulty in handling, or a lanolin derivative such as acetylated lanolin alcohols (Acetulan-American Cholesterol Products, Ltd.). Suitable blends are as follows:

Acetylated lanolin alcohols	900
Petroleum jelly	100
	1000

Lanolin anhydrous	800
iso-Propyl myristate	200
	1000

Lanolin	700
Cetyl alcohol	150
iso-Propyl myristate	150
	1000

Acetylated lanolin alcohols	700
Cetyl alcohol	150
Petroleum jelly	150
	1000

Melt the fat-wax mixture and spray onto the powder base. Adequate mixing with the base is best obtained by first makiig a concentrated mix with part of the powders, adding and mixing with the bulk and milling with a Kek type pin mill. Finally, pass the mix through a sifter-mixer machine and compress.

The alternative method of manufacture is to prepare the fatty material into an oil-in-water emulsion before mixing with the powder base. If this method is used about 10-15 per cent of the emulsion is mixed with the powder, depending on the fat concentration to give a concentration of 35 per cent fatty material in the finished dried product. The method of mixing is the same as for the non-aqueous additive. If the emulsion is used the mix must be spread out on trays for 2 or 3 days to dry out before compressing, formulae for emulsion bases are as follows:

A	Lanolin	150
	iso-Propyl myristate	25
	Petroleum jelly	50
	Glyceryl monostearate (self-emulsifying type)	100
B	Water (softened or distilled)	675
		1000
Methyl parahydroxybenzoate		0.02 per cent

A	Lanolin	100
	Cetyl alcohol	25
	Stearic acid	200
	Mineral oil	50
B	Glycerin	80
	Borax	15
	Water (softened or distlled)	630
		1000
Methyl parahydroxybenzoate		0.02 per cent

It will be seen from these formulae that the composition of the fatty additive can be varied considerably and each formulation can easily be made in small quantities and used to check the adhesive properties by pressing between the figures or stamping in a hand operated press.

Having obtained a satisfactory powder product the adjustments to pressure must then be made with the compressing machine to obtain the correct pressure combined with the most suitable amount of takeoff of the finished compressed powder.

Talcum Powder

Talcum powder continues to enjoy a very wide sale. It is used to absorb moisture after bathing and especially in warmer countries to absorb perspiration. It acts as an efficient lubricant and preventive and tends to allay any irritation of the skin due to chafing. In view of the fact that this type of powder contains a very large proportion of talc, some remarks regarding standards of purity are given.

1. The primary physical charactreristic is that of colour. Best quality materials are white, second quality products are greyish-white, and others which should be avoided, are distinctly grey.

2. The next important point to notice is that of 'slip'. This peculiar characterisitc is best illustrated in talc of good quality. Inferior qualities do not exhibit the requisite amount of 'slip', and since the lubricating action is most essential for good quality products, only good quality talc with adequate 'slip' properties should be used.
3. The last physical characteristic worthy of mention is that of lustre. A good sample should be lustrous without exhibiting any undue amount of glitter when examined in a fine film. Unusual radiance or glitter is often due to insufficient grinding or sifting of the pow dered material and such samples should not be used.

The physical characteristics of talc vary according to their country of origin and it is generally acknowledged that the finest talc of good white colour, high lustre, and adequate slip properties is that of Italian origin. Indian talc of good quality is also available. Samples of talc, do, however, vary and in addition to careful examination of physical characteristics a bacteriological examination is desirable since certain qualities have been found to be heavily contaminated with bacteria. In such cases the talc should be sterilized before use.

Talcum should also be submitted to a chemical examination. This consists of estimating the percentage of acid soluble matter. Absolutely pure talc is not obtainable since the mineral deposits contain varying amounts of impurities, consisting chiefly of iron. Any sample containing over 4 per cent of matter soluble in hydrochloric acid should be rejected. Much has been said regarding the comparative values of Italian and American talcs, but the examined numerous specimens and has found the externally superior. The average sample has given the following figures:

Italian talc   1 to 2 per cent soluble in HC1

American talc   3 to 4 per cent soluble in HC1

The absence of a large quantity of impurity is desirable, largely on account of its deleterious influence on the perfume, and to some extent owing to the irritation it may cause to the skin. In the former case, it will not only tend to alter the odour, but it often affects the colour of certain perfume ingredients. From these hints, the reader will readily appreciate the importance of the high degree of chemical purity required in a good talcum.

Many of the talcum powders sold are nothing more nor less than French chalk which has been suitably perfumed. Better quality products contain a metalic stearate to give additional lubricating properties. Zinc stearate is considered to have beneficial dermatological properties being soothing and mildly antiseptic and is preferred to magnesium stearate.

Zinc oxide is also used in talcum powders. This is a mild astringent for the skin and is also soothing and has some healing effect to skin chafing or minor abrasions. It is also useful to relieve the prickling and irritation which occurs in prickly heat.

Light magnesium carbonate or light calcium carbonate are included to increase fluffiness and also for their value as absorbing materials to aid the addition of perfume during the manufacturing procedure, as described under face powders. The following are typical formulae for talcum powders:

Zinc stearate	50
Light calcium carbonate	250
Talc	700
	1000
Perfume	q.s.

For all talcum powders mix the perfume with the light calcium carbonate and allow to stand, preferably overnight, before mixing with the other ingredients. A concentration of 0.5 per cent of perfume is generally adequate. Concentrations higher than this are often overpowering in their effect.

Zinc stearate	50
Zinc oxide	50
Light magnesium carbonate	150
Talc	750
	1000

After-shave talcum is smoothed into the skin after drying the face to give a clean matt appearance. Its alternative name is invisible talc and it is made by adding a light suntan pigment to an ordinary talcum formulation. The content of talc should be high, however, as the powder is not required to have noticeable covering properties.

Zinc oxide	40
Light calcium carbonate	80
Talc	880
	1000
Perfume	0.2 per cent
Cosmetic oxide pigment	Sufficient

Deodorant Powders

To prepare a deodorant powder include zinc oxide and zinc stearate for their mild astringent effect, and a suitable bacteriacide, such as chlorhexidine diacetate or bithioinal, to suppress proliferation of the micro-organisms responsible for development of perspiration odour. Suitable formulae are as follows:

Zinc oxide	50
Zinc stearate	50

Chlorhexidine diacetate	3
Light calcium carbonate	100
Talc	797
	1000
Perfume	0.2-0.5 per cent
Zinc oxide	100
Zinc stearate	50
Bithional	5
Light calcium carbonate	50
Talc	795
	1000
Perfume	0.2-0.5 per cent

Baby Powders

Baby powders closely resemble talcum powders, having similar composition but they usually contain an antiseptic material. Boric acid has been used for this purpose for many years. It is known, however, that boric acid accumulates in the body when administered orally and similarly when it is applied as a powder it can be absorbed by broken skin tissue or mucous membrane. Because infants and young children are particularly susceptible to boric acid poisoning it is only recommended to be used in powders at concentrations up to 5 per cent, and even so, such powders at concentrations up to 5 per cent, and even so, such powders should not be applied freely to any broken areas of skin. Formulae for zinc, starch, and boric powders used unperfumed for their absorbent and antiseptic properties are prepared as follows:

Powdered boric acid	30
Zinc oxide	100
Rice starch	870
	1000

Alternative antiseptic materials are now preferred to boric acid and modern baby powers are, therefore, often similar in composition to deodorant powders. Zinc or magnesium stearate are used as adhesives and give a soft velvery feel to the finished product. Starch powder is used as a moisture absorbent. A suitable absorbent dusting powder or baby powder is made simply using zinc oxide, starch, and talc, as follows:

Zinc oxide	150
Rice starch	200
Talc	650
	1000

Alternative formulae are given:

Chlorhexidine diacetate	3
Zinc Oxide	100

Light magnesium carbonate	120
Talc	777
	1000
Chlorhexidine diacetate	3
Zinc stearate	50
Zinc oxide	100
Light magnesium carbonate	150
Talc	697
	1000
Cetrimide (B.P.)	2
Magnesium stearate	70
Light magnesium carbonate	120
Zinc oxide	150
Talc	658
	1000

For baby powder use a rose or light floral bouquet perfume at a concentration of from 0.2 to 0.3 per cent. Preferable the perfume should be one which has been tested and shown to be non-irritant and non-sensitizing. Perfumes used for baby powders or deodorant powders should also be tested for discolouration by exposing the final product to sunlight. This is because antiseptic materials of a phenolic nature react with certain perfumery materials to form colour complexes.

Talcum powders containing antiseptic materials are also used for prickly heat and fungus infections of the skin. Undecylenic acid and/ or zinc undecylenate are also used specifically for treatment or athelete's foot and other similar infections. A suitable powder is prepared as follows:

Zinc stearate	20
Calcium carbonate	50
Methol	2.5
Undecylenic acid	20
Zinc undecylenate	100
Talc	807.5
	1000.0

Procedure: Mix the menthol by grinding with part of the calcium carbonate and mix with the remaining ingredients, and finally sieve and mix.

To prepare an aerosol talc use a grade of micronized talc which will pass through a 300 or 325 mesh sieve or preferably one with a maximum particle size of 2 microns. Fine quality grades of metallic stearates are also required and a small proportion of a low viscosity fatty acid ester is included as a lubricant which helps to prevent the powder from clogging the-value. A suitable formula is given:

Talc base

A	Micronized talc	910
	Magnesium myristate	60
B	iso-Propyl myristate	30
		1000
	Perfume	1.0-2.0 per cent

Procedure: Mix the micronized talc and magnesium myristate (A) and prepare separately a mixture of perfume and iso-Propyl myristate, (B). Weight A and B separately into the aerosol container. Container charge.

Container charge	13
Talc base	87
Propellant	12
	100

A high pressure propellant is used to reduce the cold wet effect experienced by using low pressure propellents.

Container: Plain tin plate or lacquered or plain aluminium 2 piece or monobloc. Valve: Special powder valve which allos solid particles to pass without clogging.

A deodorant talc suitable for use on the body or as a foot spray is made on similar lines by including a suitable bactericide.

Deodorant base

Micronized talc	905
Magnesium myristate	60
Chlorhexidene diacetate	5
iso-Propyl myristate	30
	1000
Perfume	1.0-2.0 per cent

Procedure: Prepare a trituration of Chlorhexidene diacetate with part of the talc and add to the remaining powders and mix well. Proceed as for the previous formula.

Container: Internally lacquered aluminium. Valve: Special powder valve which allows solid particles to pass without clogging.

46

Beauty Preparations

MASCARA-EYEBROW PENCILS-EYE SHADOWS

Eye shadow is an important item in make up. The three popular colours are blue, brown, and green. This preparation is applied on the eyelids and around the eyes to accentuate their brilliance.

Eyebrow pencil are hard crayons, usually black, and are used for darkening the eyebrows and for simulating eyebrow growth when none is evident.

Mascara is used for the eyelashes and as a rule is applied with a brush. Mascara is popular in makeup cosmetics, and will be discussed in detail.

In making mascara, care must be exercised in selecting the colour and the other basic constituents. The colour must be harmless and intense in shade. A number of types of lampblack may be used for black. For brown shades, burnt umber or synthetic ochre with or without the addition of a trace of lampblack will give suitable shades. Such colors are sometimes offered to the trade in paste form.

There are three types of mascara: liquid, cream and cake. Liquid mascara must be a permanent suspension of coloring matter, usually in a light mucilaginous vehicle. Gum acacia, tragacanth, karaya, and gelatin are useful for the mucilage. Gelatin increase the ability of the mascara to cling to the lashes.

An emulsion of glyceryl monostearate and water, combined with color, is effective. Methyl cellulose is also useful.

Cream mascara usually consist of an emulsion of glyceryl monostearate and water, stiffened to the proper consistency by the use of waxes or gums. Another type consist of pigment milled into a mixture of vegetable or mineral oil and wax.

The most popular type of mascara is the cake form. Sometimes this was made of mild toiler soap, sometimes with beeswax and petrolatum added. This type has the disadvantage of smarting type eyes if not carefully used.

One of the best mascara bases is glyceryl monostearate. But mascara made only of glyceryl monostearate and pigment is unsuitable because no coloring will adhere to the moist brush when it is rubbed on the cake. To avoid this, the surface tension of the material must be lowered with triethanolamine. Triethanolamine can be combined with cetyl alcohol, stearic acid or other fatty acids such as oleic or ricinoleic. About 50% of the base should consist of triethanolmine soaps, the rest of petrolatum and waxes.

NO. 1 Mascara

Mild toilet soap base	100 lbs.
Zinc oxide	1 lb.
Petrolatum (cream	2 lbs.
Gum tragacanth solution	
(1 1/4 lbs. gum to 25 lbs. hot water)	24 lbs.
Black shade	20 lbs. D & C
Black # 1	
	20 lbs. Logwood Ext.
Brown shade	20 lbs. D&C
Brown #1	
	1 lb. D&C Black #1
	10 lbs. Logwood Ext.
Blonde shade	24 lbs. D&C
Brown # 1	

Mill, plod and shape in same manner as toilet soap is made.

No. 2 Mascara

Glyceryl monostearate	10.0%
Triethanolamine	3.0
Stearic acid	15.0
Petrolatum	20.0
Gelatin	2.0
Water	17.0
Beeswax	25.0
Prepared lampblack	8.0
	100

Soak the gelatin in hot water. Melt beeswax, stearic acid, petrolatum and glyceryl monostearate, stir in the lampblack thoroughly. Add the trietanolamine to the gelatin suspension and then add the mixture to the melted mass. Stir well. Any type of mascara can be made from this base, the beeswax being the regulator by varying which any degree of consistency can be obtained.

No. 3 Eye Shadow

Eye shadow Base

White petrolatum, short fibre, soft	70.75%
Cetyl alchol	3.0
Lanolin	10.5
White beeswax	5.25
Spermaceti	10.5
	100.0

No. 4 Eye Shadow Blue

White beeswax	2.25%
Spermaceti	4.5
Lanolin	4.5
White petrolatum, short fibre soft	42.65
Ultramarine	15.28
Zince oxide	30.57
Perfume	0.25
	100.0

Mix the colour with the zinc oxide, add the petrolatum to make a mass and grind it through an ointment mil. Melt the beeswax, spermaceti and lanolin. Add the colour base and the perfume.

No. 5 Make-up Preparations

Brown

Beeswax	2.25%
Spermaceti	4.5
Lanolin	4.5
White petrolatum, short fibre, soft	41.5
Zinc oxide	26.9
Burnt umber	20.0
Perfume	0.5
	100.0

Mix the green pigment with the zinc oxide; add burnt umber and run it through an ointment mill. Melt the other ingredients; add the color base and perfume.

No. 6 Green

Beeswaxi	3.36%
Spermaceti	6.72
Lanolin	6.72
Petrolatum, short fibre, soft	43.75
Chrome oxide	15.0
Zinc oxide	24.2
Perfume	0.25
	100.0

No. 3 Eye Shadow

Mix the green pigment with the zinc oxide; add the petrolatum and run it through an ointment mill. Melt the other ingredients: add: the colour base, perfume and mix.

No. 7 Eyelash and Eyebrown Pomade

Peach Kernel oil	18.0%
Parafifn	11.0
Petrolatum	70.3
Menthyl p-hydroxybenzoate	0.2
Perfume	0.5
	100.0

No. 8 Eyelashlux

Benzoinated lard	50 parts
Stearic acid XXX	20 parts
Beeswax	5 parts
Liquid petrolatum	30 parts
Castor oil	5 parts
	100.0

Make base by melting together.

For black add 10 oz. lampblack per 25 lbs. of base.

For brown add 8 oz. burnt umber per 25 lbs. of base.

To incorporate colors melt the base and rub color very smooth with sufficient molten base to wet color well. Add slowly to molten base, pour into molds. If packaged in tubes thin to proper consistency with castor oil.

No. 9 Eyebrow Pencil

Yellow wax	10.0%
Paraffin	30.0
Cocoa butter	30.0
Petrolatum	20.0
Carbon black	10.0
	100.0

No. 10 Eyebrow Pencil Base

Soft parafifn	40.0%
Hard parafifn	42.0
Colour, as desired	18.0
	100.0

SHAVING CREAMS

The equipment required to make no-lather cream is quite simple. It consists of a steam-jacketed kettle made either from tinned copper, aluminium, glass-lined steel or stainless steel. This is required to hold and heat the stearic acid and other oils. A lye tank made from either black iron or stainless steel is required for the lye. The agitating kettle consists preferably of a stainless steel, steam-jacketed kettle equipped with a slow moving agitator. There is furthermore required the necessary measuring vessels and scales to measure and weight out the ingredients. Laboratory testing equipment should be available and, of course, collapsible tube or jar filling and closing equipment is necessary for packaging the product. In cases where large quantities are produced, cartoning machinery is desirable.

A few comments should be made regarding the steam-jacketed agitator kettle. While stainless steel is best, tinned copper or glass-lined steel may be used to prevent discoloration of the cream. The kettle should be so built that the bottom outlet of the kettle is flush with the inside, or just slightly above the bottom of the dome or cone if the bottom is conical or dome shaped. This opening should not be smaller than 2 1/2 inches. The agitator should move slowly, not over 10 R.P.M. It should be of strong, stout construction, be made of the same materials as the kettle itself and be of such design as to mix the cream well when it is stiff and to difficult consistency to stir. If it is desired to accelerate the cooling of the batch, the jacket of the kettle may be equipped to circulate cold water, which should enter from the bottom and flow out at the top. This arrangement makes it possible to cool a lot of cream over night while stirring and fill it the day after it is made. In this regard it is again to be emphasized that the agitator should be of the slow motion type, for long time rapid mixing is apt to aerate the cream.

As was indicated above many combinations of the ingredients mentioned are possible to make brushless shaving creams. These may varied to suit the chemist's ideas and to give advertising materials to sell the finished products. It is not possible to set forth all the formulas which may be devised. Of these combinations, therefore, we will consider only a few typical ones.

The brushless shaving of the earlier type is made by the following formula:

Stearic acid (triple pressed)	13 lbs.
Coconut oil (cochin)	2 lbs. 13 oz.
Caustic potash lye 38° B	3 lbs. 6 oz.
Glycerin	12 lbs. 8 oz.
Boric acid (crystals)	2 lbs.
Water (soft or distilled)	60 lbs.
Perfume	3 oz.

The method of procedure in manufacturing brushless shaving cream by this formula is first to break the stearic acid into pieces and mele it together with the coconut oil by indirect heat in a separate kettle.

The boric acid is dissolved in about a gallon of water, heated to near the boiling point. When the solution is clear, the glycerin is added.

The rest of the water and the caustic potash lye are poured into the mixing kettle and heated to 140° to 150° F. The hot boric acid solution is poured in on top of the water and temperature is maintained at around 150°.

The stearic acid-coconut oil mixture is now run into the kettle on top of the water-lye-glycerin solution through a strainer with the agitator runing. After all of the stearic acid is added, the agitation continues untill the mass is smooth.

Continue the stirring for several hours or a better procedure is to turn the cold water into the jacket of the cream mixing kettle and stir over night untill the cream is cold, then the perfume is added and stirring is continued to distribute it properly. When the cream is completely cold it should be examined for consistency, after which it may be filled into jars or tubes as desired.

A brushless shaving cream made with lanolin has the following composition.

Stearic acid (triple pressed	25 lbs.
Anhydrous lanolin	3 lbs.
Alcohol (S.D.3A)	2 lbs.
Triethanolamine	3/4 lb.
Borax	1/2 lbs,
Glycerin	3 lbs.
Water (distilled or softened)	70 lbs.
Perfume	4 oz.

The modus operandi for this formula is first to melt the stearic acid and lanolin by indirect heat in the melting kettle. Pour the water into the mixing kettle and when heated dissolve the borax in a portion thereof. Add the borax solution and the triethanolamine to the hot water in the mixer. This has been heated to about 150° F.

With the agitator runing pour the stearic acid-lanolin mixture slowly into the mixing kettle; stir untill smooth and the white emulsion has formed. Continue the stirring until the mass cools, then add the glycerin, alcohol and perfume.

Another brushless shaving cream made with triethanolamine is formulated as follows;

Strearic acid (triple pressed)	240 lbs.
Beeswax	80 lbs.
Mineral oil	40 lbs.

Melt these ingredients in a separate kettle at about 160° F.

Triethanolamine	15 lbs.
Water (distilled or software)	1210 lbs.
Borax	8 lbs.
Sulfonated castor oil	4 lbs.
Glycerin	48 lbs.

Pour these together in the mixing kettle and heat to 150° F., being sure that the borax is all dissolved by agitating the liquid well.

With the cream is of the proper consistency, turn the cold water into the jacket and agitate over night. In the morning add about 5 pounds of suitable perfume continue mixing untill the perfume is uniformly distributed.

It is advisable in making up this formula that a close check of all weights to made. If the cream is too stiff hot water may be added in the mixer to thin to the proper consistency.

No. 3 Brushless Shaving Cream

Stearic acid	13 lbs.
Coconut oil	2 lbs. 13 oz.
Water distilled	7 gals.
Potash lye 38° B	3 lbs. oz.
Borax	6 oz.
Carbitol	6 1 /2 pints
Glycerin USP	2 lbs.
Perfume	3 oz.

Melt the stearic acid and coconut oil and strain through cloth into a clean kettle. Dissolve boric acid, potassium carbonate, borax, glycerin and carbitol in water. Have both solutions at 85° C. Pour the water solution in the mixer first. Then add the stearic acid very slowly while stirring- Start the mixer in a low speed and when the cream starts to get (hick, put in high speed untill the cream is white, smooth and cool. Then add perfume and mix for a moment.

No. 4 Brushless Shaving Cream

Strearic acid	15 lbs.
Beeswax	5 lbs.
Mineral oil	2 1/4 lbs.
Sulfonated castor oil	4 oz.
Triethanolamine	15 oz.
Water	78 lbs.
Borax	8 oz.
Glycerin	3 lbs.

Brushless shaving creams are apt to undergo changes as they age. As has already been indicated, atmospheric conditions, especially extreme heat and extreme cold contribute greatly to these variations. For these reasons it is advisable to take samples of the filled tubes from batch. These should be kept under extreme heat and extreme cold in the laboratory for a period of weeks and then checked for consistency at room temperature. While the creams hold up more satisfactorily on the acid side, it frequently happens in the cream as it ages. Constant, careful investigation is necessary to produce a completely satisfactory product.

While the formula referred to above are merely types, it is possible to alter them in many directions. This may be done, for example, by using olive oil instead of coconut oil, glyceryl monostearate instead of lanolin, other amines, like amines, like amino methyl propanol, instead of triethanolamine. solubilized mineral oil instead of the regular cold cream type, of mineral oil. Then too, a wetting agent may be added to increase the spreading power of the cream on the face, and possibly its rinsing qualities. Or cer Lain germicidal substance may be partly replaced by which hazel. These are just a few of the many suggestions for giving these creams distinctive properties and characteristic. These additions and variations may samples which are made up shoulc' be carefully studied in the laboratory before going into actual production.

The popularity of brushless shaving creams, or no-lather shaving creams is still increasing. For this reasons they deserve close attention and study of those interested in producing shaving products.

MOUTH WASHES

The raw malerials used in various mouth washes are numerous. Among the more common antiseptic substances that find their use in these products are thymol, benzoic acid, chlorthymol, sodium perborate, boric acid, formaldehyde, the phenol sulfonates especially zinc, menthol, salol eucalyptol and certain essential oils or their isolates, phenol resorcinol, beta napthol and potassium chlorate. Alcohol in sufficient concentration increase the antiseptic property. More recently the quaternary ammonium compounds are being used in certain directions. Certain of these ingredients like the chlorates and borates are now considered dangerous to use especially by children. Others like chlorthymol cause an unpleasant bite if used even in small quantities and the peroxides are not very stable. It must also be remembered that if bactericidal properties are assigned to combinations containing these substances their antiseptic action can be confined under conditions of use. If these products are diluted as is the case at times, before use, the diluted product must be efficacious. Such preparations may come under two Federal laws, the Insecticide Act of 1910 and the Food, Drug and Cosmetic Act of 1938, depending upon how the claims are expressed.

Other raw materials used in mouth washes consist of flavors, astringents, colours and solvent. The flavoring oils most generally used are peppermint, methyl salicylate, cassia, anise, thyme, caraway, cloves, myrrh, spearmint, geranium, otto of rose and many others. Sugar, astringent is zinc chloride though alum and tannin have also been used in limited amounts. In colouring mouth washes only F.D. & C. Colours should be used. These should be stable toward the rest of the ingredients. As solvents water, alcohol, glycerin and propylene glycol are used. It is permissible in U.S. to use tax-free specially denatured alcohol. This usually contains some of the flavoring ingredients of the preparation as denaturing agents.

The equipment required to make these liquids is quite simple. Suitable tanks, mixers, chilling coils if used and filters are required. The solutions are not usually difficult to make though it should be remembered it is good practice to dissolve the water insoluble ingredients in the alcohol or glycerin rather than in the water- alcohol medium. Clarification of these solutions at times is a difficult operation. The procedure outlined under the chapter "Clarification of Liquids" should be followed closely in such cases.

The following formulas are typical of the numerous types used. At the very outset as Number I we present that well-known National Formulary preparation "Liquor Antisepticus."

No.1

Boric acid	1.5%
Thymol	0.1
Eucalyptol	0,5
Methyl salicylate	0.1
Oil of thyme	0.03
Menthol	0.1
Alcohol	30.0
Water	67.67

Dissolve boric acid in 60% of the water and other ingredients in 60% of the alcohol. Pour water solution into alcoholic solution, add 2% of purified talc and allow mixture to stand with occasional stirring for forty-eight hours. Filter. Add rest of alcohol and water, and add caramel colouring if darker colour is desired. An interesting variation of this follows:

No.2

Benzoic acid	1.0%
Boric acid	2.0
Alcohol	8.5
Eucalyptol	0.05
Oil of thyme	0.1
Oil of wintergreen	0.3
Water	88.0
Caramel colouring	0.05
	100.0

The boric acid is added to part of water and boiled untill completely dissolved; add this solution to the rest of the water and allow to cool. Dissolve benzoic acid in part of the alcohol. The oils are added to rest of the alcohol. Add these solutions to the water mix rapidly and add caramel colour. Mix again for four hours. Chill in a cooling tank and filter. Or mix with 2% of purified talc, and allow to stand for 48 hours and filter.

No. 3 Alkaline Mouth Wash

Potassium bicarbonate	2.1%
Borax	2.0
Oil of sassafras	0.1
Thymol	0.05
Eucalyptol	0.1
Methyl salicylate	0.05
Cudbear, tr. of	0.2
Alcohol	5.0
Glycerin	9.0
Water distilled	81.4
	100.0

Dissolve the potassium bicarbonate and sodium borax in 50% of the water. Dissolve the oils in alcohol, add the alkaline solution, the tincture of cudbear, and the rest of the water. Mix thoroughly for two hours. Allow to stand for 48 hours. Chill and filter. Two per cent of purified talc may be used to acid clarification.

No. 4 Chloro-Phenol Mouth wash

Benzoic acid	1.0%
Cinnamon oil	2.0
Phenol	1.5
Chloroform	1.5
Alcohol	37.5
Oil of peppermint	0.5
Glycerin	56.0
	100

Dissolve the benzoic acid in the chloroform, add the glycerin and mix. Dissolve the cinnamon, peppermint and phenol in alcohol and mix two solutions together. Mix for two hours, chill and filter.

No.5 Resorcin Mouth Wash

Resorcinol	5.0
Zinc chloride	0.03
Menthol	0.5
Thymol	0.2
Eucalyptol	0.03
Camphor	0.03
Oil of peppermint	0.05
Alcohol	25.0
Glycerin	10.0
Water	59.16
	100.0

Dissolve resorcinol and zinc chloride in water, and the thymol, eucalyptol, wintergreen, menthol and camphor in the alcohol. Mix the two solutions together and add glycerin. Mix one hour, chill and filter.

FACIAL MASKS

Masks are often called "astringents." In a chemical sense astringents refer to that class of materials, such as tannic acid and alum, which precipitate protein from solution. Temporarily masks act like astringents but not a chemical sense.

Albumen, in itself, has most of the properties for a good liquid mask, but some people are sensitive to albumen and it decomposes readily. Dextrin, casein, starch, althea and the various gums, such as acacia, tragacanth, quince seed, Tra-gum and karaya are good substitutes for, albumen. Acacia gum appears to be best. It is soluble enough to make a flowing solution, and it forms a uniform layer as it dries on the face. Tragacanth base makes the mask too pasty, and desides it does not flow readily, Karaya and quince seed mucilages alone are much too stringy. Accordingly, acacia gum seems the best base for liquid mask. The gum is soluble in water and is not injured by a fairly high concentration of alcohol, which enables the mask to dry rapidly. Acacia mucilge is easy to preserve and in addition has no disgreeable odor.

If, however, acacia gum mucilage is employed solely as the base of the mask, it is apt to shrink and break up too rapidly in drying. This condition may be overcome by the addition of a small amount of glycerin. It must not be forgotten, however, that a certain contraction of the gum is necessary, for this property gives the masks its drawing power. But the directions should emphasize that the face must be covered at all times by a uniform layer of the preparation. Only then can it exert maximum contracting action.

Dextrine and starch, added to the acacia gum mucilage are said to enhance the drawing qualities of the gum. Some masks also utilize gelatine, either by itself of dissolved with other gums.

The consistency of a good mask should be about that of molasses at room temperature. Is must flow easily when brushed on the skin. No mask should take longer than five minutes to dry completely. Varying the concentration of the alcohol will provide the desired drying time.

Acacia masks do not have the absorptive properties of the clay types because clay masks absorb and absorb many impurities. Acacia does this also to limited extent, but not as effectively as the clay types. However, a small amount of colloidal clay suspended in the acacia gum solution, will make a gum mask more "absorptive."

A few masks contain irritants for the purpose of imparting a tingling sensation. This effect is supposed to stimulate the sebaceous glands and sluggish pores, but the real value of local irritants is to bring the blood to the surface of the skin.

A good mask does not require irritants to stimulate the glands. A product containing acacia gum, a small amount of dextrin, alcohol, glycerin, a non-irritating preservative like the methyl ester of para-hydroxybenzoic acid, a trace of cetyl alcohol, boric acid, and perfumed with camphor, menthol, and lavender, makes a refreshing and cooling mask. If a tingle is desired, increase the menthol a trifle untill the proper effect is obtained.

No. 1 Acacia Mask

Part I	
Acacia gum (best grade)	37.0%
Dextrin (best grade)	2.0
Boric acid	0.5
distilled water	47.7
Part II	
Alcohol	9.0
Glycerin	1.0
Cetyl alcohol	2.0
p-hydroxy-methyl-benzoate	0.15
Camphor	0.2
Oil of lavender	0.3
Menthol	0.15
	100.0

A small amount of tincture of benzoin may be added if a more opaque product is wished. In manufacturing this product the ingredients comprising Part I and Part II are mixed separately and then Part II is poured slowly, and with constant stirring, into the liquid portion. The use of a colloid, if possible, ensures a better product.

Using this formula and varying the different ingredients, a commercial product of any desired consistency may be made. The above preparation is removed after use on the face by water.

A formula for a facial mask in dry form which the user makes up herself by mixing water is viz.

No.2

Althea (marshmallow root)-(ground)	50%
Corn starch	25
Orris root powdered	24
Calcium perborate	1
Perfume	Q.S.
	100.0

This type of mask was referred to as a rejuvenator in the past but such a name is no longer permitted under existing U.S. statues. Due to the presence of a perborate it is presumed to have some skin whitening properties.

Facial clays enjoy a fluctuating popularity. A few years ago their popularity was national in scope, but there is as yet no evidence that demand will again become nation wide.

Facial clays are pastes consisting of inert materials, water and glycerin. Sometimes rubber latex and casein are included. The following formulas are representative.

No.3

Purified kaolin	32.0%
Kieselguhr	10.0
Glycerin	15.0
Alcohol	20.0
2% acacia mucilage	10.0
Water	12.0
Perfume	1.0
	100.0

Heat the water and glycerin to 170° F. Run it into a mass mixer; add the dry materials and mix for about two hours. Then add the mucilage and the perfume dissolved in alcohol. Greater fluidity can be obtained by increasing the water content.

No.4

Purified zinc peroxide	10.0%
Purified kaolin (colloidal clay)	24.0
Kieselguhr	5.0
Glycerin	15.0
2% acacia mucilage	10.0
Water	25.0
Alcohol	10.0
Perfume	1.0
	100.0

Use same process as for No.I.

No.5

Bentonite	10.0%
Alcohol	10.0
Purified kaolin	35.0
Glycerin	13.0
Tragacanth mucilage 2%	20.0
Water	10.9
Perfume	1.0
Methyl p-hydroxy-benzoate	0.1
	100.0

Same process as for No.1.

47

Lipsticks

Lipsticks have gained popularity during the past ten years to such an extent that they are now probably used more than any other single cosmetic product. This increase in popularity is undoubtedly influenced by the widening choice of colours available. Originally the function of the lipstick was to give a positive bright red colour to the lips and this was eventually modified to include blue-reds for brunettes and orange-reds for blondes. These early shades were all designed to give dramatic effects which at one time were considered an essential part of the allure and glamour attributed to make-up. Modern lipsticks still include several shades which are variations of true red, but no manufacturer would consider his range complete without including several pastel shades of rose, pink, or coral type. These soft toned colours appeal equally to the sophisticated and to the teenager making discreet experiments in the art of make-up.The modern range of colours is devised to meet various demands controlled by such factors as skin and hair colouring, fashion requirements, and the age of the user.

The lipstick is a product which illustrates a true cosmetic designed to beautify or improve natural beauty. Use of a brush is advocated to give a smooth outline, and its cosmetic application may be utilized in many ways. A thin mouth maybe corrected by extending the lipstick above the upper lipline, or the mouth can be made to appear smaller by applying the lipstick well within the natural lipline. After application it is usual to remove any excessive grease or oil by blotting the lips with tissue.This practice favours the formulation of an emollient stick which is smooth and easy to apply rather than a stick which is smooth and easy to apply rather than a stick which gives a matt appearance and drags on the lips when it is being applied.

In addition to ease of application the lipstick should also have the following characteristics:

(1) a good degree of indelibility.
(2) high retention of colour intensity,
(3) complete freedom from grittiness and be non-drying,
(4) a desirable degree of plasticity,
(5) a pleasant odour and flavour.

A lipstick should also have the following storage characteristics;

(1) a smooth and shiny appearance,

(2) freedom from 'bloom' or sweating,

(3) a suitable degree of firmness during reasonable variations of climatic temperature,

(4) retain plasticity without any tendency to dry-out or crumble.

The stick consists of colouring materials dispersed and suspended in a base prepared from a blend of oils and waxes adjusted to yield the desired melting point and viscosity. The temperature of the body varies between 36° and 38°C, the mouth exhibiting the higher figure. The lipstick must have a melting-point higher than this and appreciably higher if the product is expected to withstand exposure to hot climates.The most appreciated melting point is about 62°C, but from 55° to 75°C represent quite satisfactory products.

Composition

To consider the formulation of lipsticks the basic raw materials are conveniently classified as follows:

(1) wax mixture

(2) oil mixture

(3) bromo mixture

(4) colours

(5) preservatives and other additives

Waxes and Oils

The composition of the wax mixture is of prime importance. Best results are obtained by using a mixture of waxes of different melting pointsand adjusting the final melting point of the stick by adding a sufficient quantity of a high melting point wax. Sticks formulated on these lines do not have marked thixotropic properties but have a more cream-like or plastic consistency. Formulations which contain a high concentration of a single high melting point wax should be avoided. The following notes indicate the behaviour of some of the more important waxes used in lipsticks:

WHITE BEESWAX m.p. 62-64°C Use from 3-10 per cent.

A useful material to bind oils and higher melting point waxes. The molten wax shrinks slightly on cooling and thus helps preparation of moulded products. Higher concentratioins give a dull waxy appearance and cause the stick to crumble during use.

CANDELILLA WAX m.p. 65-69°C Use from 5-10 per cent.

This material has a melting point of similar range to that of beeswax and gives a smooth and glossy appearance to a lipstick if used at a slightly higher dosage concentration than the proportion of beeswax. A mixture of candelilla wax and beeswax is suitable to use as the principle wax content of the product.

OZOKERITE WAX m.p. 60-80°C Use from 3-10 per cent.

The wax is useful to increase the melting point of the stick. Stick containing more than 10 per cent ozokerite tend to crumble during application.

CERESIN WAX m.p. 60-75°C

This is sometimes referred to as mineral wax and is also used to denote a form of ozokerite purified with sulphuric acid. The name ceresin wax is now generally used to describe commercial products consisting of a mixture of purified ozokerite with other solid hydrocarbons to give waxes of various melting points. It is used to increase the melting point of the product in a similar manner to ozokerite.

CETYL ALCOHOL m.p. 45-50°C Use from 2 to 3 percent

CETOSTEARYL ALCOHOL m.p. about 43°C

These materials have good emollient properties on the skin and are often included in lipstick formulations in an attempt to obtain similar effects. Only small proportions should be used, however, as concentrations higher than 5 per cent give the stick a dull appearance which develops to a 'bloom' on storage. High concentations have also been known to be the cause of minute crystals forming on the surface of a stick after storage.

The oil mixture is required to blend intimately with the waxes to provide a suitable film when the stick is applied to the lips. It also functions as a solvent of eosin dyestuffs and as a dispersing agent for insoluble pigments. A suitable mixture is one which when incorporated in the formula enables the product to spread easily and at the same time give a thin film with good covering power. A thick or greasy film is not desirable.

Castor oil is used in many formulations on account of its unique properties. Suitable refined grades are of good colour and are odourless and tasteless. The oil is not as prone to rancidity as is olive oil or almond oil, but nevertheless it should not be used without the addition of a suitable antioxidant. Both olive oil and almond oil are unsuitable for use in lipsticks. The high viscoity of castor oil makes it an ideal vehicle to prepare dispersions of pigments, and these remain suspended during the mixing and moulding stages of manufacture. The oil was originally used as a solvent for bromo acids and although not more than 0.5 per cent bromo acid will dissolve in the oil, any undissolved dyestuff is finely dispersed in the finished product. Many solvents for bromo acids have been suggested for use in lipsticks, but with few exceptions these are unsuitable, either because of the volatility, odour or taste, or toxicity. A suitable product can still be prepared using castor oil as the only eosin solvent. The eosin should be dissolved by heating in the castor oil and any excess allowed to settle and removed by straining. This is a useful precautionary measure since the straining process removes gritty particles which are occasionally present and these can scratch and irritate the lips. As a general guide, about 40 to 50 per cent of castor oil is used in a stick. Higher proportion can be used but in these cases the waxes must be adjusted to give a high melting point otherwise the stick gives a thick greasy film.

Liquid parafffin or white mineral oils are used to give a glossy appearance after application. No more than 5 per cent should be used in the formula. Lipsticks containing a higher proportion than this come off the lips easily and also run or bleed around the lips. An equally effective gloss can be obtained with 2 or 3 per cent of isopropyl myristate or isopropyl myristate or isopropyl palmitate, and this concentration does not affect the permanency of the film.

Oleyl alcohol is used in some formulations as a replacement for castor oil. Refined grades only are used since commercial grades have an unpleasant fatty odour and taste. The material is a better eosin solvent than castor oil and is useful to prepare sticks with high staining properties. A stick based on oleyl alcohol spreads smoothly and evenly, but gives an oily film unless the waxes are adjusted to give the product a high melting point. An antioxidant should always be used with oleyl alcohol.

A lipstick composition can be prepared by mixing suitable proportions of the materials already mentioned. It is more usual to add materials of a fatty nature, such as lanolin or one of the lanolin derivatives to act as blending agents of the liquid and solid ingredients.

These materials are considered to have a plasticizing effect.They improve spreading properties and increase the thickness and stability of the film. They also prevent separation and migration of liquid ingredients from the solids, factors which cause sweating or bloom characteristics in the finished product. They also prevent brittleness and help to disperse the pigments and prevent them from settling out. In the composition of a formula these materials are considered as part of the oil mixture, being distinct from the solid ingredients.

Anhydrous lanolin (wool fat) is commonly used as a blender and the amount used can vary from 2 to 20 per cent. A high proportion of lanolin is useful to provide a particular emollient effect, or when fashion requires a thick unctuous film. Sticks containing a high concentration of lanolin may be greasy or sticky and the odour becomes noticeable particularly during storage. It is now more usual to have a stick which gives effective colour coverage with only a thin film of lipstick on the skin. In this type of formulation 5 to 7 per cent of lanolin is quite sufficient.

Lanolin absorption bases are often recommended as a replacement for lanolin to reduce stickness. These are mainly proprietary mixtures of lanolin and hydrocarbons such as petroleum jelly or wax, and consequently have a corresponding lower plasticizing effect than an equal proportion of lanolin.

Lanolin derivatives are also used, but are often less effective than lanolin as a plasticizer.

Iso-Propyl linoleate is a useful material to include in lipsticks as an additional emollient and protective against the drying effects and possible irritation caused by pigments and bromo acids.

Acetoglycerides

Acetoglycerides have certain unique properties whereby they act as blending agents and modify the rheological properties of mixture of oils, fats and waxes. Used in a lipstick they make the composition more plastic so that a suitable blend remains firm under warm conditions retaining its mobility and good spreading properties at low temperatures. They are non-drying and cause the lipstick to impart a non-greasy emollient film on the lips. These properties, together with their ability to give plasticity and prevent brittleness, make them suitable materials for stick products. The acetoglycerides may be prepared by acetylation of fats which have been previously modified by reaction with glycerin. Several commercial products are now available and these vary in compositiion depending upon the basic starting material and the method of manufacture. They are essentially mixture of mono and digiycerides which are either completely or partially acetylated. For purposes of formulation they are best considered in 2 main groups, the liquid and the solid forms. Their behaviour may be explained by considering the liquid acetoglycerides as having a plasticizing effect on the oily constituents, and the solid acetoglycerides as having a similar effect on the waxes. For this reason a mixture of 2 parts of a solid acetoglyceride with 1 part of a liquid acetoglyceride will give a better result than that obtained by using them singly. Theoretically such a mixture should have all the desirable features of lanolin, but in practice this is found not be so.The ideal blend is a mixture of liquid and solid acetoglycerides, with some lanolin. With such a blend of acetoglycerides the proportions of lanolin and other ingredients are adjusted to obtain a lipstick with the desired physical characteristics.

Bromo Mixture

There are a number of other fatty materials which are sometimes included in a lipstick blend. Some of these mentioned in the general list of lipstick raw materials which follow are best used only in small proportions to obtain slight modifications of texture or type of film required. In other cases, certain fatty materials have a specific function as a constituent of the bromo mixture. This term is used to denote that portion of the product which imparts an indelible stain as distinct from the opaque film of colour given by insoluble pigments. The modern trend often calls for a product with high staining qualities rather than one which covers the lips with a thick film of a vividly coloured material.The indelible type of stick has obvious advantages for, not only does the make-up appear more natural, but there is less pigment transfer during application and little need for constant touching up. Some degree of stain is always desirable and the composition of the bromo mixture is important whether it is used in a high stain product or in formulations containing low proportions of stain and lake colours. Essentially the bromo mixture is a solution of the staining dyestuff blended with suitable materials to enable the dyestuff to remain either wholly or partially in solution or intimately dispersed in the oil/wax base. The dyestuffs generally referred to as bromo acids consist of fluoresceins, halogenated fluoresceins and related water-insoluble dyes. When applied to the skin they form an indelible stain which is a slightly different shade than the acid. The bromo acids available as D and C colours fall broadly into two groups, those which are red and give a red or reddish-blue stain, and those which are orange-red and give a pink to yellowish-pink stain. Thus the stain used must be of the right colour for the finished product; blue staining dyestuffs, for example, should not be used in a pink or coral coloured stick. The degree of staining is a function of the amount of dissolved dyestuff, and it follows that this depends on the solvent used.

For general lipstick formulations which are not regarded as of the high staining type about 2 or 3 per cent of bromo acid is used. This amount is not completely dissolved if castor oil is the only solvent present in the formula and even if the undissolved dyestuff is finely dispersed it remains suspended in the oil/wax film. This does not penetrate or have the same affinity for the skin as the dissolved material and thus does not contribute much to the staining properties. It also happens that undissolved bromo acids often remain as small hard agglominates in the mass even after passing through a roller mill. If these are not detected and are present in the finished product they have a slight abrasive action and although this is not necessarily detected by the user they are considered to cause iritation with the possibility of allergenic effects. Becuase of the low solubility of bromo acids in castor oil and since a high degree of staining is desirable several materials have been examined for their potential use as solvents for bromo acids. Such a solvent should not be of too high a volatility. It should not have either a disagreeable odour or taste, or cause iritatioin, and should be compatible with the oil and wax mixture.

Butyl stearate is a useful material used in conjunction with castor oil. It acts as a partial solvent and has wetting properties which promote fine dispersion of undissolved dyestuff.

Tetrahydrofuryl alcohol and esters such as the acetate, stearate, and benzoate are effective bromo acid solvents, although some of the esters, particularly the acetate, have penetrating odours and require masking with suitable perfumes. Formulations containing solvents of this type tend to have a drying effect on the skin and can also cause dermatitis, but as they dissolve up to 25 per cent of bromo acids only small amounts are required to give good staining properties. To offset any drying effect the content of emollient ingredients of the lanolin type should be increased. Proprietary mixtures of esters of tetrahydrofuryl alcohol are available commercially as bromo acid solvents and it is claimed that these do not cause irritation.

When plastic containers are being considered for the end product tests should be carried out to determine whether the amount of solvent present is sufficient to attack the plastic.

Glyceryl derivatives, such as glyceryl monostearate, glyceryl monolaurate and diethylene glycol monostearate, are also useful to include with bromo acids. Of these, monostearate compound are preferred since they have a better odour than monolaurates. Standard formulations can be modified to increase the staining properties by including a glyceryl derivative to partly replace waxes of similar melting point.

Propylene glycol, triethylene glycol and polyethylene glycol are also suitable eosin solvents. The latter, also known as macrogols, are mixtures of condensation polymers of ethylene oxide and water. Those with an average molecular weight of 200 to 700 are liquids, and those with a molecular weight of more than 1000 vary in consistency from a soft plastic texture to solid waxes resembling hard paraffin. A number is used in the name, for example, Macrogol 1500 indicates the average molecular weight of the polymer. If a high stain product is required the best effects are obtained by using a polyol. These materials are strongly hydrophilic and have some affinity for the moist surface of the lips. Dissolved dyestuff is transferred to the lips and becomes fixed as a stain. When incorporated in an existing formulation, however, they show tendency to bleed out if they are incompatible with the remaining ingredients of the base.This can be overcome by including one of the following materials:

propylene glycol monoricinoleate,
propylene glycol monolaurate,
propylene glycol monomyristate.

The myristate derivative has a better odour than the ricinoleate or laurate compounds.These materials act as co-solvents or coupling agents of the bromo acids solution and the oil/wax mixtures. The system can be demonstrated by preparing the following mixture:

Bromo acid	15
Propylene glycol	200
	215

A clear solution is obtained. To this solution add propylene glycol monomyristate as follows:

Bromo acid	15
Propylene glycol	200
Propylene glycol monomyristate	100
	315

This blend gives a solution of bromo acid which mixes with mineral oil and castor oil and produces a homogenous mass with waxes. By regulating the amount of bromo acids and solvent the dyestuff solution is dispersed evenly throughout the mass. This is the bais of the high stain lipstick known as the two-phase system. In the so-called three-phase system bromo acid is used in excess of its solubility and undissolved dyestuff is finely dispersed in the blend. In this case the phases consist of:

(1) liquid phase containing dissolved bromo acid,
(2) dispersed phase containing bromo acid in co-solvent or coupling agent,
(3) solid wax phase.

Good staining is obtained in both types of system by transfer of bromo acid to the lips via the hydrophilic solvent.

Lipsticks containing a glycol or glycol derivative should be checked for their effect on plastics before being packaged in plastic containers.

Insoluble Dyestuffs and Lake Colours

Insoluble dyestuffs and lake colours are the main colouring ingredients as distinct from the staining materials. They consist of calcium, barium, and aluminium lakes. Calcium and barium lakes prepared from azo type dyestuffs are also used. These are known as lake toners or simply toners. The amount used in a lipstick varies between 10 and 15 per cent depending upon the shade and opacity of the film. To accommodate the varying amounts of pigments used in a range of shades it is sometimes necessary to make adjustments to the composition of the base. Regulations for assuring the safety of colours used in lipsticks are under consideration and it seems likely that in due course of time all the colours used will require certification as a provision of the Food & Drugs Act. Manufacturers of dyestuffs are aware of impending lesgislation and can be relied on to supply 'safe' or 'permitted' colours at the present time, or such 'certified colours' as may result from new regulations. Thus although the cosmetic manufacturer assumes responsibility for the safety of the finished product in this particular instance he may rely on the supplier to a large extent.

In addition to the safety factor, there are a number of variables which occur with currently used permitted colours. These relate to certain physical characteristics and affect formulation and the behaviour of the mass during the manufacture and moulding procedures. When formulating to prepare a range of shades it is essential to examine all colour samples to determine whether they are suitable and with a view to fixing standards for subsequent supplies. Colours must be of a fine and even particle size to ensure smooth application. They must be of good opacity with adequate colouring and covering power. The behaviour characteristics of colours with oil are also of importance since this affects the final consistency of the mass. The mass becomes thicker if colours with high oil absorption values are used, and when preparing a range of shades it becomes necessary in some cases to modify the formulation of the base owing to the varying behaviour of a particular blend of colours. Data obtained from these tests is useful in preparing a balanced formulation and also for correcting difficulties which may occur during manufacture. As a result of heating during processing, colours having a high oil absorption cause the mass to become gel-like and thixotropic, particularly if excessive heat is used, or when a batch is constantly being reheated for moulding. This problem also occurs if the colour contains an unduly high moisture content or when occluded air is present as a result of the grinding process. It is clear, that preliminary tests are an important factor contributing to successful formulation and manufacture, and each supply of colours should be examined to ensure that they do not deviate from established standards.

Additives

It is essential to include a preservative in the product, and for this purpose 0.1 per cent of propyl-p-hydroxybenzoate is used. Concentrations of 0.2 per cent may cause a slightly burning sensation, and occasionally on sensitive skins this can trigger-off an eosin allergy reaction.

Titanium dioxide is frequently used as an additive to modify the shade of the basic pigments. The compound has a very high degree of brightness and has the greatest covering power of all other white pigments. In this respect it is superior to and is preferred to zinc oxide for use in lipsticks and other cosmetic products where covering power is required. It was used originally to obtain vivid effects with high proportions of colours, but is now frequently used with low proportions of colours to obtain delicate pastel shades, whilst at the same time retaining the necessary degree of opacity. Only grades of the Anatase form of tianium dioxide are suitable for cosmetic work.These are available with a low content of soluble salts and are specially milled to eliminate oversize particles. Material prepared to this high standard by the manufacturer a more readily dispersed to a paste during processing. For lipstick work the paste is prepared by first milling the material with a suitable quantity of castor oil. This is milled through a triple roll mill until smooth before adding to the colours or other ingredients of the mass. Titanium dioxide for use in oil/wax mixtures must also be dry, since moisture prevents adequate wetting with oil. This results in difficulties in handling and moulding owing to the formulation of white streaks of the pigments which float persistently on the surface of the mass.

Several materials have been suggested for use as additives with the conventional lipstick to enhance the value of the make-up. These include an oil-soluble sunscreen to filter the sun's rays and prevent the lips from sun blisters. A silicone fluid can be used as a fixative and to prevent colours from bleeding on the lips. Polyvinyl pyrrolidone is considered to form a film on the lips and also reduce any tendency towards allergenic reactions. Used at a concentration of 0.5 to 1.0 per cent it is also used as a binding agent for the dyestuffs in high stain products, iso-Propyl linoleate is used to prevent drying effects and reduce the possibility of irritation by dyestuffs.

The perfume used in lipsticks must not contain any ingredients which are likely to be irritating or toxic. It should have a pleasant taste and cover any fatty odour of the base. Generally 1.0 per cent gives satisfactory results and at this concenration the risks of irritation are reduced to a minimum.

It is advisable to include antioxidants in all lipstick formulations to prevent rancidity developing on storage and a suitable synergistic mixture is prepared as follows:

Propyl gallate	60
Citric acid	40
Butylated hydroxy anisole	200
Propylene glycol	700
	1000

Use o.l per cent of this mixture calculated on the finished product.

In the following table a number of raw materials used in lipstick formulation are given, together with an indication of the quantities used. This varies between fairly wide limits as indicated:

	(per cent)
Acetylated monoglyceride (liquid type)	5-15
Acetylated monoglyceride (solid form)	5-15
Antioxidant	0.1-0.2
Candelilla wax	5-10
Carnauba wax	1-3
Castor oil	30-65
Ceresine	5-20
Cetyl alcohol	2-5
Cholesterine absorption base	5-20
Glyceryl monostearate	5-10
Hard paraffin	1-5
iso-Propyl myristate	2-5
tso-Propyl linoleate	1-5
Lanolin absorption bases	5-10
Lanolin, anhydrous	5-15
Lanolin derivatives	5-10
Liquid paraffin	1-5
Oleyl alcohol	1-10
Ozokerite	1-10
Propylene glycol monoricinoleate	5-15
Soft paraffin	1-5
Spermaceti	5-15
Stearic acid	1-5
Stearyl alcohol	5-10
White beeswax	5-20
Bromo acids	0.5-3
Solvent	5-10
Colours	5-15
Perfume	0.1-2
Preservative	0.1-0.2

Lipstick Formulae

A selection of typical lipstick formulae follows. Each formula can be modified by light alteration to the proportions of oils and waxes to adjust the melting point, spreadability, and amount of film on the lips according to the particular characteristics required, The first selection of formulae include typical proportions of lake colours and bromo acids. Titanium is not included, but all the formuale gives are suitable for use with titanium dioxide. When this material is used it should be Included as part of the total given as lake colour content. Perfume, preservative, and antioxidant should be added to all formulae as already indicated.

(Non-greasy type with good staining properties)

Castor oil	270
Beeswax	200
Mineral oil	30
Lanolin	50
Cetyl alcohol	20
tso-Propyl myristate	30
Ozokerite wax	100
Carnauba wax	35
Propylene glycol	110
Propylene glycol monoricinoleate	40
Lake colours	100
Bromo acids	25
	1000

Castor oil	390
Beeswax	50
Lanolin	30
iso-Propyl myristate	20
Ozokerite wax	50
Carnauba wax	40
Candelilla wax	70
Propylene glycol	60
Glyceryl monostearate (S.E.)	30
Acetylated monoglyceride (solid type)	70
Acetylated monoglyceride (liquid type)	50
Lake colours	120
Bromo acids	20
	1000

(Non-greasy type)

Castor oil	360
Beeswax	120
Mineral oil	20
Lanolin	30
iso-Propyl myristate	20
Ozokerite wax	50
Carnauba wax	20
Candelilla wax	20
Propylene glycol	100 Gl
Glyceryl monostearate (self-emulsifying type)	50
Acetylated monoglyceride (solid type)	50
Acetylated monoglyceride,(liquid type)	20
Lake colours	120
Bromo acids	20
	1000

Castor oil	400
Acetylated monoglyceride (solid type)	50
Acetylated monoglyceride (liquid type)	25
Lanolin	20
iso-Propyl myristate	20
Propylene glycol monomyristate	100
Propylene glycol	20
Beeswax	75
Candelilla wax	70
Ozokerite	50
Carnauba wax	50
Lake colours	100
Bromo acids	20
	1000

The formulae which follow show the oil, wax, and bromo acid mixtures separately. The formulae are given as bases and lake colours can be added in the usual proportions as required.The proportions of bromo acids indicated are for normal or high stain sticks and are reduced for special sticks where low stain properties are required.

Oleyl alcohol is used in the following formula for an emollient stick with high stain properties.The high degree of staining is not obtained if the bromo acids are first dispersed in the castor oil instead of the mixture of oleyl alcohol and propylene glycol. Good staining is only obtained when the bromo acid mixture is prepared separately as shown in the formula.

Oil mixture	
Castor oil	390
Bromo acid mixture	
Bromo acids	30
Oleyl alcohol	200
Propylene glycol monomyristate	100
Wax mixture	
Candelilla wax	100
Ozokerite wax	80
Carnauba wax	100
	1000

A well-balanced base with medium staining and good storage properties in varying temperature conditions is as follows:

Oil mixture

Acetylated monoglyceride (liquid type)	60
Acetylated monoglyceride (solid type)	25
Castor oil	450
iso-Propyl linoleate	10

Lanolin	20
iso-Propyl myristate	20
Bromo acid mixture	
Propylene glycol monomyristate	120
Propylene glycol	30
Bromo acids	20
Wax mixture	
Beeswax	75
Candelilla wax	70
Ozokerite wax	50
Carnauba wax	50
	1000

Successful preparation of lipstick shades depends to a large extent upon adequate dispersion of the lake colours in the lipstick mass. For convenience it is advisable to prepare dispersions of the lake colours in castor oil and use these for both experimental work and also duing the manufacturing procedure. Dispersions are prepared by milling, generally as 25 per cent concentrations in castor oil and this can either be prepared as required or conveniently obtained from the manufacturer of cosmetic colours. It is also convenient to prepare or obtain similar dispersions *of* bromo acids and titanium dioxide. Use of these dispersions ensures consistency of the results obtained during laboratory experimental work and satisfactory reproduction of laboratory results when these are altered to manufacturing scale.

When using oil dispersions the castor oil is omitted from the basic formula and the balance of the amount required is added after the proportions of lake colours, bromo acids, and titanium dioxide dispersions have been determined by experiment.

A modification of the previous formula (No. 2214), convenient for use in experimental work, is made as follows:

(Lipstick base)

Oil mixture	
Acetylated monoglyceride (liquid type)	60
Acetylated monoglyceride (solid type)	25
Lanolin	30
iso-Propyl myristate	20
'Bromo acid mixture'	
Propylene glycol monomyristate	120
Propylene glycol	30
Wax mixture	
Beeswax	75
Candelilla wax.	80

Ozokerite wax	50
Carnauba wax	60
	550

Details of lake colours, bromo acids and titanium dioxide required to obtain typical lipstick shades are given below using lipstic base formula No. 2215. The additives given are in 'paste' form consisting of 25 per cent dispersions of the material in castor oil. Modifications to the shades are easily made by varying the proportions given or by using alternative dispersions. In all examples the formulae are prepared to contain the correct proportion of castor oil (i.e. 450 parts per 1000) corresponding to formula No. 2214

Details of colours and additives are given for strong positive coloured sticks, soft toned pastel shades, and iridescent or pearly types.

Basic shades

1. Basic red

Lipstick base No. 2215	550
Orange paste (bromo acid)[1]	40
Orange paste (bromo acid)[2]	40
Red paste (lake colour)[3]	120
Orange paste (lake colour)[4]	120
Titanium dioxide paste	130
	1000

2. Pink

Lipstick base No. 2215	550
Orange paste (bromo acid)[1]	40
Red paste (lake colour)[3]	40
Orange paste (lake colour)[4]	40
Titanium dioxide paste	320
Castor oil	10
	1000

3. Orange

Lipstick base No. 2215	550
Orange paste (bromo acid)[1]	40
Orange paste (bromo acid)[2]	40
Orange paste (lake colour)[4]	60
Titanium dioxide paste	300
Yellow paste (cosmetic oxide)[5]	10
	1000

For soft toned pastel shades the proportions of bromo acids and lake colours are reduced.

1. Pastel Rose

Lipstick base No. 2215	550
Orange pasle (bromo acid)[1]	20

Red paste (lake colour)[3]	24
Orange paste (lake colour)[4]	16
Titanium dioxide paste	360
Castor oil	30
	1000

2. Pastel Peach

Lipstick base No. 2215	550
Orange paste (bromo acid)[2]	20
Orange paste (lake colour)[4]	25

2. Pastel Peach *(continued)*

Yellow paste (cosmetic oxide)[5]	10
Titanium dioxide paste	355
Castor oil	40
	1000

[1]Orange paste 25595
[2]Orange paste 25592
[3]Red paste 2561 D.F. Anstead Ltd.
[4]Orange paste 25119
[5]Cosmetic oxide paste 25717

Iridescent or pearlescent lipsticks are made using natural pearl essence or a synthetic pearlescent pigment.The synthetic material can be of the crystalline bismuth oxychloride type or of platelets of mica coated with titanium dioxide or bismuth oxychloride. Crystalline bismuth oxychloride is available in several grades and they produce different effects of brilliance, sheen, and opacity depending on the crystal size.The coated micas also give effects of sheen and brilliance when used on their own and they are also used at low concentrations with bismuch oxychlorides for special sparkle and speckle effects.

The bismuth oxychlorides are available in powder form or as 70 per cent dispersions in castor oil which like paste colours, are more convenient for use in lipstick work. These are used in the formulae which follow and the quantity of castor oil added is adjusted as with previous formulae.Titanium dioxide is not used because it masks the translucent brilliance of pigments based on bismuth oxychlorides and bromo acids are either used in small proportions or omitted from this type of lipstick.

1 .Pearlescent rose

Lipstick base No. 2215	550
Red paste (lake colour)[1]	22
Orange paste (lake colour)[2]	18
Pearlescent pigment paste[3]	200
Castor oil	210
	1000

2. Pearlescent peach

Lipstick base No. 2215	550
Orange paste (lake colour)[2]	25
Pearlescent pigment paste[3]	200
Castor oil	225
	1000

[1]Red paste 2561-D.F. Anstead Ltd.

[2]Orange paste 25119—D.F. Anstead Ltd.

[3]Iriodin WR 70—E. Merk. Darmstadt or Bismuth Oxychloride NLY Rona Pearl Co.

Coloured lustre pigments are prepared with titanium coated micas and used to obtain special effects. An attractive range of golden tones with brilliance and sparkle is made by adding varying proportions of from 5 to 10 per cent of a gold lustre pigment to a rose or peach type lipstick. Lustre pigments are generally supplied in powder form and should be made into a paste with sufficient castor oil before mixing with the lipstick mass.

Lipstick base No. 2215	550
Orange paste (lake colour)[1]	20
Yellow paste (cosmetic oxide)[2]	15
Lustre pigment powder[3]	50
Castor oil	365
	1000

'Orange paste 25119-D.F. Anstead Ltd.

[2]Cosmetic oxide paste 25717-D.F. Anslead Ltd.

[3]MP23 Sparkling gold pearl powder—Rona Pearl Co.

Attractive shades are also made by adding a pearlescent pigment to deeper and more intense colour. As an example a reddish blue or plum coloured lipstick is made as follows:

Lipstick base No. 2215	550
Red paste (lake colour)[1]	60
Blue paste (lake colour)[2]	10
Pearlescent pigment paste[3]	150
Castor oil	230
	1000

[1]Red paste 2561-D.F. Anstead Ltd.

[2]Blue paste 25670-D.F. Anstead Ltd.

[3]Iriodin WR 70—E. Merk, Darmstadt or Bismuth Oxychloride NLY-L- Rona Pearl Co.

A shimmer stick is made with a natural or synthetic pearl essence. It is applied to the lips as a second application over a more conventional lipstick colour to give highlights, gloss, and brilliance.

The sticks should spread easily and smoothly and are generally slightly softer than the normal lipstick. They are also used as part of the make-up of face and eyes to obtain special highlight effects.

There is increasing interest in the use of cosmetic products and make-up preparations by men. Many of the products used follow conventional lines and in certain cases a product is equally suitable for use by men and women. A typical example is a lipstick of low pigment content and covering properties which can be used both by men and women to enhance the appearance, lubricate the lips and prevent, dryness. A suitable product is made using the basic lipstick formula already given by adding bromo acid and a suitable oil-soluble red dyestuff. In the following formula the proportion of oil soluble dyestuff can be increased to suit individual tastes.

Lipstick base (No.2215)	860
Oil-soluble red dyestuff	2
Bromo acid[1]	20
	882

[1]Use a 25 per cent dispersion of D and C Red 21 in castor oil.

If an oil-soluble sunscreen agent is included in the oil phase of this stick, the product can be used by both men and women for sunbathing or skiing.

A formula is as follows:

Natural pearl essence[1]	200
Castor oil	338
iso-Propyl myristate	20
Coconut oil	160
Lanolin	55
Red paste (lake colour)[2]	2
Candelilla wax	70
Beeswax	50
	895

[1]20 per cent disperssion in castor oil.

[2]Red paste 2561—D.F. Anstead Ltd.

The proportion of beeswax and candelilla wax is increased if a firmer product is required, and the stick can also be made without a lake colour.

Manufacture

Manufacture of lipsticks varies only slightly according to the type of formulation, and a general procedure can be outlined. If a solvent is used for the bromo acid this solution is first prepared and set aside until required. If colour pastes are not being used the lake colours are first dispersed by mixing with a suitable quantity of oil, and the colour paste obtained is passed through a triple roll mill until smooth and free from agglomerates and gritty particles. Any titanium dioxide being used in the product is treated in a similar manner before it is added to the colour mix.

The colour mixture is then mixed with the bromo acid mixture. The lower melting point fats and waxes are next melted together and mixed with the colours and bromo mixtures at the same temperature. This mixture is re-milled until perfectly smooth. The preservative and antioxidant is dissolved in any remaining oil and added to the mix. The high melting point waxes are now melted and added to the bulk at the same temperature. The perfume is finally added and the mass stirred thoroughly but gently to avoid incorporation of air. The mass should not be milled after the high melting point waxes have been added. Gentle stirring is continued until the mass is homogenous and it is then poured into moulds.

Use of an automatic ejection mould is preferred for large quantities and split moulds are satisfactory for small production runs. The mould is lubricated before pouring either with liquid paraffin or *iso*-propyl myristate.This should be carried out carefully and efficiently without leaving any surplus lubricant on the surface. The melted mass is poured at as low a temperature as is practicable to prevent the colours from settling out. For this reason it is usual to warm, the moulds, otherwise the mass tends to set in ridges as it comes in contact with the cold surfaces. After moulding the sticks are chilled to encourage contraction of the waxes since this facilitates easy removal of the sticks.

Automatic ejection moulds are fitted with a water jacket which is used to warm or chill the mould as required.

Other Lip Products

Lip pencils are prepared in a similar manner to lipsticks but contain a higher proportion of high melting point waxes. The firmer consistency enables the product to be moulded in a long and slim form similar to a crayon. The lip pencil is generally sold as a companion product to a lipstick and is prepared in the same shade, the purpose being to use the border pencil to give a firm outline on the skin before applying the softer lipstick.

Carnauba wax is used to increase the melting point of a lipstick, but in some cases use of this wax on its own makes the stick brittle, in which case the content of all the waxes is increased proportionally until the required degree of firmness is obtained.

The following formula which is suitable for the preparation of a lipstick can be modified to prepare a lip pencil by increasing the carnauba wax content from 30 parts to 70 parts:

Castor oil	400
Acetylated monoglyceride (liquid type)	150
iso-Propyl myristate	20
Lanolin	40
Acetylated monoglyceride (solid type)	50
Beeswax	70
Ozokerite wax	50

Carnauba wax	30
Candelilla wax	70
Lake colours	100
Bromo acids	20
	1000

Fashion trends vary concerning the appearance of the lips after make-up. A lipstick is sometimes required to give a natural appearance with a matt finish and at other times a high gloss is required either with or without a strong colour effect. A light application of an oil over the lipstick application is used to obtain a high gloss. A more adhesive preparation in the form of a lip jelly or lip gloss can be made using a mixture of fatty materials.

Petroleum jelly	500
Lanolin (anhydrous)	500
	1000
Castor oil	100
Lanolin (anhydrous)	900
	1000

The product is perfumed and tinted with an oil soluble dyestuff and applied either with the finger tip or by means of a lip brush.

Lip salve or lip pomade is used to prevent the lips from becoming dry or for treatment of cracked lips. Formulae are given:

Mineral oil (cosmetic quality)	450
Beeswax	250
Spermaceti	300
	1000
Lanolin (anhydrous)	150
Petroleum jelly (white)	500
Paraffin wax	350
	1000

The following formulae give softer products with good emollient properties:

Lanolin (anhydrous)	100
Petroleum jelly (white)	600
Paraffin wax	300
	1000
Lanolin (anhydrous)	50
Petroleum jelly (white)	550
Paraffin wax	300
iso-Propyl palmitate	100
	1000
Lanolin (anhydrous)	100
Mineral oil (cosmetic quality)	400
Beeswax	500
	1000

The salve is moulded similar to a lipstick and generally has a rounded end for application.The sticks are mainly prepared without colour, but an oil-soluble dyestuff can be added to prepare a rose or pink coloured product, if required.

Liquid lipstick consists of a suspension of lipstick pigments in a suitable liquid vehicle such as ethyl alcohol. A simple mixture such as this, however, suffers from uncontrolled spreading during application, lack of adhesion and too rapid an evaporation of the vehicle. These defects are overcome by the incorporation of a gelating compound such as ethyl cellulose to increase the viscosity and allow for greater control of application to the skin. After the evaporation of the alcohol, the ethyl cellulose remains on the lips as a varnish which also acts as the binder for the colourants.To prevent embrittlement of the varnish (and subsequent flaking on the lips) a suitable plasticizer such as castor oil is incorporated, which also reduced the evaporation rate of the alcohol.

Commercially available ethyl cellulose is graded according to the viscosity of a known concentration in a solvent. A grade must therefore be selected to give a suitable viscosity at the required concentration. A basic formula for a liquid lipstick is given as follows:

Ethyl cellulose (80-105 cps)[1]	90
Ethyl alcohol	768
Bromo acids	2
Castor oil	105
Lake colours	35
	1000

[1]The viscosity is that of a 5 percent concentration by weight in 80:20 toluene: ethyl alcohol mixture, determined at 25°C

It will be noted that the concentration of bromo acids and lake colours is less than those used in the normal type of solid lipsticks.

The advantage of this product is that a good indelible gloss is obtained without producing a greasy film on the lips.

Lip varnish is intially a clear varnish which is applied over the normal lipstick. Its value is mainly an aesthetic one to make the lipstick more permanent and thereby less likely to be inadvertently transferred to drinking utensils and clothing.

Such a product can be prepared by slight modification of the liquid lipstick formula and omission of the colourants.

Ethyl cellulose (8-11 cps)	100
Ethyl alcohol	900
	1000

48

Rouges and Eye Cosmetics

Rouges can be applied either before or after powdering, depending upon the type of product being used. All types of rouge are made in numerous shades varying from the palest of pinks to the deep blue reds and the conventional rouge contains a high proportion of red or reddish brown pigments. Products containing lower proportioins of pigments are used as toners or blenders for special highlighting effects. The pigments used must be carefully chosen and checked for resistance to bleeding. Bleeding can occur as a result of the moisture and sebum present on the skin surface or as a result of the ingredients of the base used for the product. For this reason the pigments used should be checked for resistance to bleeding in the presence of water, oil, alcohol, and the perfume. A small proportion of a suitable bromo acid is often included (red or orange tone) as this gives a natural blushing effect which is particularly attractive when used in products containing low proportions of pigment.

Liquid Rouges

Liquid rouges do not have as great an appeal as the cream or powder types, but they are nevertheless attractive products and are very easily applied, if correctly formulated. A suitable product is prepared as follows:

A	Cetyl alcohol ethoxylate[1]	30
	iso-Propyl myristate	20
	Cetyl alcohol	5
	Diethylene glycol monostearate	45
B	Glycerin	200
	Water (softened or distilled)	700
		1000

Perfume	0.2 per cent
Pigment	2.0 per cent
Titanium dioxide	2-3 per cent
Methyl parahydroxybenzoate	0.15 percent
Bromo acid	0.02 per cent

[1]Lubrol type-I.C.I. Ltd.

Procedure: First prepare the emulsion base by heating together the ingredients of (A) to a temperature of 70-75°C. In a separate vessel dissolve the preservative in the glycerine by heat. Add the water and heat to 75°C. Add B to A with slow continuous stirring. Continue stirring and allow to cool adding the perfume at about 35°C. Finally add the pigment and titanium, and mix well.

The following liquid rouge contains a higher proportion of oil which contributes to even application:

A	Mineral oil	120
	Acetylated monoglyceride (liquid type)	120
	iso-Propyl myristate	120
	Oleic acid (redistilled)	80
B	Triethanolamine	40
	Water (softened or distilled)	520
	1000	
Perfume		0.3 per cent
Pigments		2-3 per cent
Methyl parahydroxybenzoate		0.15 per cent
Butylated hydroxyanisole		0.01 per cent
Bromoi acid		0.02 per cent

Procedure: Disperse the pigments and eosin in A and mill. Heat A and B independently in separate vessels to 70-75°C. And add part B to A with stirring. Cool with stirring, adding the perfume at about 35°C.

In this cream the degree of oiliness can readily be controlled by varying the ratios of mineral oil, acetylated monoglyceride, and iso-Propyl myristate. As the proportion of acetylated monoglyceride is increased the product becomes less oily and more emollient. It is advisable to include an antioxidant such as propyl gallate or butylated hydroxyanisole to prevent rancidity developing on storage.

Powder Rouges

Powder rouges are prepared as compressed powders as compacts. They consist of pigmented powders generally formulated with a high proportion of tale and containing a binding agent to enable the mix to be compressed in tablet form. Typical formulae for the powder base are as follows:

Zinc stearate	170
Rice starch	170
Tale	660
	1000
Perfume	2.0 per cent
Pigments	12-15 per cent
Light magneium carbonate	100
Prepared chalk	200
Zinc oxide	100

Rice starch	150
Tale	450
	1000
Perfume	2.0 per cent
Pigments	12-15 per cent

Zinc oxide	100
Lanolin	300
Light Magnesium carbonate	200
Tale	400
	1000
Perfume	2.0 per cent
Pigments	12-15 per cent

When the compact is to be made by the dry process the binding material is included in the mix. This can consist of 1.0 per cent of tragacanth or acacia powder. As an alternative binding material small amounts of a lanolin derivative and *iso* Propyl myristate can be used, as given in the following formula:

Kaolin	50
Calcium carbonate (precipitated)	50
Magnesium carbonate	50
Zinc stearate	50
Talc	750
Pigments	50
	1000
Perfume	2.0 per cent

Binder: iso-Propyl myristate Lanolin absorption base equal parts.

Procedure: Mix the binding materials together add the perfume and mix with the magnesium carbonate. Add to the remaining ingredients and mix well. Grind and compress into godets.

For manufacture by the damp or wet process the binding agent is prepared separately and is based on materials such as tragacanth gum, a mixture of soap and tragacanth gum and polyvinyl pyrrolidone. Formulae are given as follows:

Tragacanth	10
Alcohol	20
Water (softened or distilled)	970
	1000
Methyl parahydroxybenzoate	0.2 per cent

Procedure: First wet the tragacanth with alcohol, and then add the water in a continuous stream and stir well. Allow to stand for 24 hours stirring occasionally, and pass through muslin. This is then ready for use. Dissolve the preservative in the water, with the aid of heat before adding to the tragacanth.

Tragacanth	12
Soap chips	40
Wate. (softened or distilled)	948
	1000
Methyl parahydroxybenzoate	0.2 per cent

Procedure: Prepare a concentrated solution of the soap chips with sufficient hot water and use this to prepare a tragacanth paste. Add the remaining water in a continuous stream and mix well. Allow to stand for 24 hours stirring occasionally, and pass through muslin before use. Dissolve the preservative in the water with the aid of heat before adding to the soap tragacanth mix.

About 12 to 15 per cent of the binding agent solution is mixed with the previously prepared coloured powder mix. For the wet type process sufficient is added to prepare a fairly damp paste which is the moulded in shallow capsules of about 1/1/4 inches in diameter. The blocks are then dried at normal temperature in a current of air. If undue heat is applied during the drying time they will split, and apart from this the perfume will be damaged. During the drying time the compacts are stood on blotting paper to absorb any excess moisture. When dry they are trimmed with a special rotating knife to give a perfectly smooth finish to the surface. They are then stuck with a suitable adhesive to the base of the container. For the so-called damp process the coloured powder base is mixed thoroughly with about 5 to 10 per cent of binding agent solution. The amount of moisture required in the mix can be judged by pressing a quantity between finger and thumb when it should be sufficiently damp to hold together without crumbling. If the mix is too wet at this stage it should be broken into suitable sized pieces and allowed to dry. When the correct degree of moisture has been obtained the mix is. compressed either by automatic or hand operated machine direct into a godet. The compact are then allowed to stand in a current of air at normal temperature to dry off before being fixed into containers.

Rouge Creams

Rouge creams are often preferred to powder rouges as they are more easily applied over a foundation cream and give a suitable base for face powder. The powder type tend to leave sharply defined edges to the make-up, which look unnatural unless they are carefully applied. Rouge creams are prepared as anhydrous preparations based on thixotropic blends of waxes, oils and fatty acid esters, or as emulsions of the cold cream type. Vanishing cream type emulsions can be used also but should include up to 8 or 10 per cent of glycerin or propylene glycol. This is used as a pigment dispersing agent and also promotes even application of the product. Products made using a vanishing cream base should preferably be packaged in tubes. Formulae are given,

(Anhydrous type)

Petroleum jelly	400
Acetylated lanolin[1]	50
Acetylated monoglyceride (solid type)	100
iso-Peopyl myristate	390
Ozokerite	50
Carnauba wax	10
	1000
Perfume	2.0 per cent
Pigments	5.0 per cent

[1]Modulan type—American Cholesterol Products Inc.

Procedure: Mix the ingredients together and add the pigments and mill.

Pigments used for cream rouges should be obtained as a semi-processed colourant in one of the basic ingredients used in the product and the formula adjusted accordingly.

(Cold cream type)

A	Mineral oil	460
	iso-Propyl myristate	100
	Spermaceti	100
	Beeswax	120
B	Borax	5
	Water (softened or distilled)	215
		1000
	Perfume	1.0 per cent
	Pigments	5.0 per cent
	Methyl parahydroxybenzoate	0.15 per cent
	Propyl parahydroxybenzoate	0.02 per cent

Procedure: Disperse the pigment to a smooth paste with the iso-Propyl myristate. Heat together the remaining ingredients of A to a temperature of 70-75°C. Add the pigment dispersion. Heat ingredients of B in a separate vessel to 70-75°C. Add B to A with slow continuous stirring and allow to cool adding the perfume at about 35°C. Fill warm.

(Vanishing cream type)

A	Stearic acid	150
	Hartolan[1]	10
	iso-Propyl myristate	25
	Lanolin	25
	Beeswax	50
	Glyceryl monostearate (self emulsifying type)	70
B	Propylene	50
	Glycerin	30
	Water (softened or distilled)	590
		1000

Perfume	1.0 per cent
Pigments	5.0 per cent
Methyl parahydroxybenzoate	0.15 per cent
Propyl parahydroxybenzoate	0.01 per cent

[1]Croda Ltd.

Procedure: Melt together the ingredient of A and heat to 70°C. In a separate vessel heat B to 70-75°C and add B to A with stirring. Allow to cool and add the perfume at 35°C. Add the pigments in a semi-processed form, preferably as dispersed colourant in propylene giycol, making the necessary adjustment to the formula.

Eye Make-up

Cosmetic preparations for the eyes are now an essential feature of the facial make-up, assuming as much importance as the use of lipsticks. The basic steps of the eye make-up involve use of an eyebrow pencil to enhance the natural eyebrow or to modify the outline after plucking; use of eye shadows for the eyelid and for shadowing towards the eyebrow; use of crayons or liners to contour the eyes, and mascara to enhance the appearance of the lashes. As with all types of coloured preparations, correct choice of pigments is most important and these should only be obtained from a manufacturer able to supply the special blends of permitted cosmetic oxides and ultramarines required. Reference has already been made to the range of colours available. For eye make-up a limited number of specialized colours are also available. To facilitate dispersion wherever possible, reduced colourants should be obtained *on* bases similar to one of the ingredients in a particular formulation.

Eyebrow Pencils

Eyebrow pencils are prepared in a range of colours from black through brownish-black and brown to blue. The true pencil type made by pencil manufacturers are fairly hard and generally used to lightly accentuate the natural line and natural hair. Separate leads are also made for use in an automatic case. A softer version also made by the pencil manufacturer is of the wax or crayon type, and is more often used to improve the browline after plucking. The true cosmetic eyebrow pencil is made of similar composition to a lip-pencil wiih a higher proprotion of waxes than a lipstick to increase the melting point so that the pencil can be moulded as a thin stick and sharpened to a point. A suitable formula is as follows:

Beeswax	24
Ozokerite	24
Butyl stearate	9
Lanolin	3

Castor-oil	25
Mineral oil	15
	100
Perfume	1-2 per cent
Butylated hydroxyanisole	0.002 per cent

Procedure: Melt the ingredients together and add the dispersed colour. Stir well and strain through muslin. Add the perfume and pour into moulds.

Eyeshadow

Eyeshadow is used to give a background of colour to the eyes and there is virtually no limit to the number of shades which are used, from the more conventional blue, green, and mauve, to very light or transluscen shades of beige, grey, and white. Gold and silver colourings are used for evening wear. Eyeshadows are prepared in wax bases as creams, in stick form, as loose powders, or as compressed powders.

Wax or cream bases and sticks

Wax or cream bases and sticks must be firm enough to suspend the pigments, but sufficiently thixotropic to spread easily by gentle stroking over the eyelids. After application the residual film should not be tacky or form into 'lines'. A suitable anhydrous cream base can be made as follows:

Petroleum jelly	480
Liquid lanolin[1]	40
Microcrystalline wax (m.p. 65-70°)	80
Beeswax	40
iso-Propyl myristate	360
	1000
Perfume	0.5 per cent

Procedure: The ingredients are melted together and mixed. To prepare the finished eyeshadow up to 25 per cent of pigment is included, i.e. 25 parts of pigment mixed with 75 parts of the base. As already indicated as adjustment to the formula is necessary when dispersed pigments are used.

The pigments are included in the following formula:

Petroleum jelly	200
Liquid lanolin[1]	50
Ozokerite	150
iso-Propyl myristate	400
Pigments	200
	1000
Perfume	0.5 per cent

Procedure: Mix dispersed pigments with the petroleum jelly, liquid lanolin, and iso-Propyl myristate adjusting the formula to allow for dispersing agent. Heat to about *70-75° C* and mill. Add the ozokerite and stir until uniform. Allow to cool and add the perfume at about 30-35°C. Mix and pour into suitable containers.

To prepare a 'pearlized' or 'translucent' eye shadow include either a natural or synthetic pearl essence or a lustre pigment. The following base spreads easily and gives an even non-greasy film:

(Base only)

iso-Propyl myristate	80
Beeswax	120
Petroleum jelly	800
	1000

Translucent eye shadows are prepared from this base as follows:

Base No. 2356	700
Pigment	50
Lustre pigment[1]	200
Tale	50
	1000

The quantities given in this formula for pigment and lustre pigments refer to the dry weight and when used in this form these materials should be sieved before incorporating in the base. Adjustments to the formula are made when pigment dispersions and pearl or lustre suspensions are used. Use of talc is not essential, but gives a little more cover on the skin and does not suppress the pearlescent effect.

Pastel shade effects and increased covering properties are obtained by replacing the talc with an equal proportion of titanium dioxide. This should also be obtained as a ready milled dispersion in a suitable vehicle. 'Pearl' or 'translucent' effects arc also enhanced by using a suitable proportion of magnesium myristate, as indicated in the following formula:

Base No. 2356	700
Pigment	50
Lustre pigment	200
Magnesium myristate[1]	50
	1000

Cream eye shadows are made using a non-fatty or cream type vehicle and are suitable for lube packing. A base formula is prepared as follows:

[Cream base)

A	Lanolin	10
	Mineral oil	100
	Stearic acid	25
	Glyceryl monostearate (self-emulsifying type)	30
B	Glycerin	50

Triethanolamine	5
Water (softened or distilled)	780
	1000
Perfume	0.5 per cent
Methyl parahydroxybenzoate	0.2 per cent
Propyl parahydroxybenzoate	0.05 per cent

Procedure: Heat A and B independently to 75°C and add B to A slowly with continuous stirring. Cool with stirring, adding the perfume at about 35°C.

The finished product is prepared by adding 10 parts of pigment to 100 parts of the above base. A shimmer or pearlescent effect is made as follows:

Cream base No. 2359	1000
Pigment	100
Pearl suspension in mineral oil[1]	300
	1400

A suspension of a pearl essence in mineral oil can also be used as the additive for an anhydrous cream base, when the proportioin of oily material in the formula should be correspondingly reduced.

Eyeshadow stick performs the same function as the anhydrous cream and is prepared by moulding in similar manner to the preparation of lipsticks. The base is required to be thixotropic to give smooth and even application without being greasy or sticky. In the formulae which follow the proportions of pigment, lustre pigment, and talc refer to the dry material.

(Stick base)

Beeswax	50
iso-Propyl palmitate	160
Petroleum jelly	250
Oleyl alcohol	50
Paraffin wax	220
Cetyl alcohol	30
Lanolin	40
	800
Perfume	0.5 per cent
Propyl parahydroxybenzoate	0.01 per cent
Butylated hydroxyanisole	0.02 per cent

Procedure: Heat the iso-Propyl palmitate, petroleum jelly, oleyl alcohol, and lanolin together. Add the perservative and antioxidant.

The waxes are added during manufacture of the completed stick as follows:

Base No. 2361	820
Pigment	80
Lustre pigment	100
	1000

Procedure: Mix the pigment with the melted oils and fats of the base and mill. Add the melted waxes and lustre pigment and mix, and allow to cool before adding the perfume. Pour into moulds and allow to set.

The above formula gives a stick of good colour intensity with a 'glitter' or 'pearl' effect. Pastel shades with glitter and translucent effect are made by modifying the proportions of colour and lustre additive as follows:

Base No. 2361	720
Pigment	30
Talc	50
Lustre pigment	200
	1000

Powder Eyeshadow

Powder eyeshadow is prepared either as loose or compressed powder as an alternative to the cream or stick form, it is comparatively easy to apply and blends on to the eyebrow and does not readily form into 'lines', and for this reason is often preferred to other forms of eyeshadow. A suitable base is as follows:

Talc	400
Magnesium myristate	440
Titanium dioixide	160
	1000

Pigments-use about 7 per cent depending on the tinctoral properties of the pigment.

Procedure: Mix the pigments with a proportion of the talc and sieve. Sieve the titanium dioxide separately, and add the pigment blend followed by the remainder of the talc and magnesium myristate. Mix and sieve.

To prepare pearlized or translucent eyeshadow powders the basic formula is modified, and opaque materials such as titanium dioxide are not used as these prevent or mask the light reflecting properties of pearlescent materials. A formula for a pearlescent eye shadow powder is as follows:

Talc	350
Pigment	150
Pearlescent pigment[1]	500
	1000
Perfume	0.5 per cent

Procedure: Sieve together the sale and pigment and mix. Add the pearlizing agent, sieve and mix. The powder should not be milled, as this procedure reduces the light reflecting properties and pearlescent characteristics.

The following powder spreads smoothly and evenly and gives a transparent appearance with a good glitter effect.

Magnesium myristate	350
Pigment	150
Pearlescent pigment[1]	500
	1000
Perfume	0.5 per cent

Pearlized or pearlescent eye shadow powders are made with standard conventional colours and in a wide range of pastel shades. Pearlescent effects are obtained by using natural pearl essences, prepared from crystalline fish guanine, synthetic 'crystalline' bismth oxychloride, and pearlescent pigments prepared by deposition of bismuth oxychloride on platelets of white mica.The materials have good gloss and slip properties and also give some degree of opacity to the products. In this respect they replace titanium dioxide as an opacifier particularly as titanium dioxide tends to mask the brilliance and pearlescent effect. Zinc stearate and kaolin can be used to increase the opacity if this property is required.

Highlights effects with additional sparkle and brilliance are obtained by using lustre pigments based on a titanium dioxide coated mica. Coloured lustre pigments generally referred to as iridescent colours based on titanium coated mica reflect and transmit colour and are used for special effects. An attractive range of pearlized and translucent eye shadows, is made without using an opacifier as follows:

Pigment	150
Pearlescent pigment[1]	250
Tale	600
	1000
Pigment[1]	150
Lustre pigment	250
Talc	600
	1000

More opaque pearlescent powders are prepared as follows:

Pigment	150
Kaolin	200
Zinc stearate	75
Lustre pigment[1]	250
Talc	325
	1000

Pigment	150
Kaolin	150
Zinc stearate	75
Lustre pigment[1]	250
Pearlescent pigment[2]	50
Talc	325
	1000

The formulae given for opaque powders are suitable for processing as compressed eye shadow powders to use neat or with water and brush applicators, as shadows or eye-liners.

Compressed powder eye shadow is made following the procedure described under compressed powders using 5 to 6 per cent of a lanolin ester (iso-Propyl lanolate— Amerlate P; or acetylated lanolin alcohols--Acetulan, American Cholesterol Products Inc.) as the binding material. The lanolin ester is also used to disperse the perfume and is sprayed on the powder/pigment mix after the first sieving or milling process. The mix is re-milled or re-seived and the pearlizing agent added so that the lustre is not affected by milling. Finally, the powder is compressed into godets adjusting the pressure to ensure ease of takeoff, and application with a sponge-tipped applicator.

Eyeliners

Eyeliners are used after the eyeshadow has been applied to give the eyes a more striking appearance. The desired effect is obtained by using either a soft pencil or crayon or more usually with a product in liquid or cake form applied with a brush. The products are made in a wide range of shades from white through pastel shades to blues, greens, and black.

Liquid eye-liners consist of a suspension of pigment in a base containing a film-forming material which helps to fix the product after application and prevent smudging. The liner should also spread easily and smoothly and dry out fairly rapidly.

A small proportion of an emulsifying wax such as glyceryl monostearate or diethylene glycol monostearate is useful to help smooth application, and to increase the viscosity and suspending properties of the vehicle. A suitable proportion of a surface-active agent also assists spreading properties and even application. Glycerin is used to give a smooth film and prevent drying out and caking, but if used in too high a proportion slows down the rate of drying and causes smudging on the eye after application. The final consistency of the product depends to some extent on the specific volume or density of the pigment so that a basic formula is not necessarily suitable for all the shades required. When this occurs the volume of pigment used should be adjusted with a suitable amount, of light magnesium carbonate, or a magnesium aluminium silicate

(Veegum—R.R. Vanderbilt Company Inc.). Suspensions of these materials tend to thicken on standing, so that filial evaluation of a product should not be made until samples have been allowed to stand, to allow time for this adjustment of viscosity to take place.

Colloidal silica* (aerosil-Degussa) and magnesium aluminium silicate are also used on their own account as pigment suspending agents. Consequently formulations for liquid eye liners can vary from shade to shade according to any variations in the physical characteristics of the pigment used. Typical formulae are as follows:

Magnesium aluminium silicate[1]	25
Film-former (polyvinyl pyrrolidone)	20
Glycerin	50
Lanolin	5
Diethylene glycol monostearate	30
Sodium lauryl sulphate (needles)	10
Pigment	100
Water	760
	1000
Methyl parahydroxybenzoate	0.15 per cent
Propyl parahydroxybenzoate	0.01 per cent

If a perfume is required in this product use only 0.1 to 0.15 per cent of a tested non-sensitizing and non-irritant type.

Procedure: Disperse the silicate with sufficient water to a liquid consistency. Dissolve the P.V.P. in water. Warm gently and add to the melted stearate and lanolin. Stir to form a cream. Dissolve the preservative in the glycerin and disperse the pigment in the solution. Mill if necessary and add to the mix. Finally add the sodium lauryl sulphate, dissolve in a little water and mix.

The following formula illustrates the slight variations which are required due to variations in the characteristics of the pigment:

Magnesium aluminium silicate[1]	28
Film former (polyvinyl pyrrolidone)	20
Glycerin	24
Lanolin	5
Diethylene glycol monostearate	30
Sodium lauryl sulphate	10
Colloidal silicon dioxide[2]	5
Pigment	120
Light magnesium carbonate	30
Water	708
	1000
Methyl parahydroxybenzoate	0.15 per cent
Propyl parahydroxybenzoate	0.01 per cent

Procedure: Disperse the pigment with the colloidal silica and light magnesium carbonate and carry out the remaining procedure as already given.

Use of a carboxy vinyl polymer as a suspending and dispersing agent is illustrated in the following formula:

Carboxy vinyl polymer[1]	5
Film former (polyvinyl pyrrolidone)	15
Glycerin	50
Sodium lauryl sulphate	5
Pigment	100
Triethanolamine	5
Water	720
	900
Methyl parahydroxybenzoate	0.15 per cent
Propyl parahydroxybenzoate	0.01 per cent

Procedure: Disperse the carboxy vinyl polymer with part of the water and add the triethanolamine with stirring. Add the polyvinyl pyrrolidone dissolved in an adequate portion of the water. Dissolve the preservative in the glycerin and disperse the colours in the solution, and add to the solution and mix well.

Adjustments to the pigment dispersion using light magnesium carbonate or colloidal silica must likewise be made to this formula if necessary.

Cake eye-liners resemble cake eyeshadows but generally contain a higher proportion of pigment and sufficient binding agent to form a cream or paste, for application with a wet brush. They can be made according to the wet mix and drying procedure described for cake make-up, using a cream base as the binding material. Alternatively they can be made by following the dry-mix method described for compressed powders, using an acetylated lanolin alcohol as the binding agent. A suitable base is made as follows:

Zinc stearate	100
Precipitated calcium carbonate	60
Kaolin	50
Pigments	100
Talc	690
	1000

Titanium dioxide is only included in the base if it is required to prepare specific shades. It is not required for distinctive colours such as blacks browns, blues, and greens.

Procedure: The pigments are first milled with the calcium carbonate and the mix is added to the remaining ingredients in a shifter mixer. Add about 5.0 per cent of acetylated lanolin alcohol by spraying during the final mixing. Slow spraying and thorough mixing is essential.Use of the lanolin derivative as the binding agent gives the compressed cake a creamy consistency with good adhesive properties when it is subsequently wetted.

Mascara

Mascara or eyelash cosmetic is on of the most popular of eye make-up preparations. It is used eilher to darken to colour the lashes and to give an illusion of greater density and length. This practice has indeed been followed since the time of the early dynasties. Kohol or Kohl was used by the ladies of ancient Egypt for darkening their lashes when materials used included antimony sulphide, lead sulphide, copper oxide, and magnesium oxide. These were mixed with oil and applied with a stick along the eyebrows and under the eyelids. More recently, mascaras were prepared in 'cake' form and consisted of a mixture of lamp black and soap bound together with a little water, the mixture then being stamped out in moulds.

Cake mascara is still a convenient and popular product and is now prepared using ethanolaminc soaps as an emulsifier and binding material. Solutions of ethanolamine soaps are only mildly alkaline and consequently less likely to cause irritation than the more alkaline sodium soaps used originally. The mascara is prepared in moulded bars and applied with a little water and rubbed on to the cake .The moisture forms an emulsion with the soap and the resultant paste or cream is thus transferred to the lashes. The use of ethanolamine soaps enables oils and waxes to be included in the base and the proportion of these materials can be varied to control the required degree of hardness and water repellency. The most satisfactory results are obtained by using natural waxes such as beeswax, carnauba wax, and spermaceti, since these are more compatible with a soap base than hydrocarbon based oils or waxes. The balance between the proportions of waxes and soaps is important to maintain a moisture repellent film which is free from smudging. Of the waxes used, carnauba wax and beeswax increase the glossy appearance of the cake, whereas the soap gives it a dull appearance, and if an excessive proportion of carnauba wax is used the resultant film becomes brittle. Correct balance of materials is, therefore, essential. Hard, brittle, or flaky films can be corrected by including a small proportion of lanolin, or a fatty acid ester.

Silicone oils can also be used to increase resistance to moisture. Glyceryl monostearate is useful as a binding material which also helps to form a smooth paste when the cake is wetted before application. Hydrocolloid gums, and thickeners such as hydroxy methyl cellulose and alginates can also be used in small proportions. These increase the viscosity of the aqueous phase and make the proportions of soap and oils or waxes a little less critical in a formulation. They also help to bind the pigments onto the lashes as the emulsion dries out. Mascara is prepared in several shades with black remaining a favourite colour, followed by brownish-black and blue-black. A range of cosmetic grade carbon blacks is available for use in eye cosmetics. These are manufactured by the 'channel' process and are available in a range of particles sizes. For cosmetic uses the most suitable grades are those of particle size in the 20 micron region. For brownish-black carbon black is blended with a suitable cosmetic brown oxide, and cosmetic ultramarine blue is used with carbon black for a blue black shade. For greens and yellow-greens use chromium oxide and hydrated chromium oxide for more brilliant blue-greens. Cosmetic grades should always be used, and with all shades particular care should be taken during manufacture to ensure that the pigment is thoroughly 'wetted out' with a suitable liquid component part of the base, before being incorporated in the final mix. Titanium dioxide can be used to reduce the intensity of the colour and this material should also be thoroughly wetted in similar fashion during manufacture. Formulae for cake-mascara are as follows:

A	Carnauba wax	50
	Beeswax	150
	iso-Propyl myristate	30
	Stearic acid	350
	Glyceryl monostearate	50
B	Triethanolamine	150
C	Sodium alignate	70
	Ultramarine blue	120
	Carbon black	20
	Titanium dioxide	10
		1000

Use of perfume is not essential for mascaras, but if required use 0.1-0.15 per cent of a rose type perfume of a non-sensitizing and non-irritant type. As a preservative use:

Methyl parahydroxybenzoate	0.15 per cent
Propyl parahydroxybenzoate	0.01 per cent

It is also advisable to include 0.002 per cent of butylated hydroxyanisole as a precautionary measure to prevent oxidation and rancidity.

Procedure: Mell together the ingredients of A with the exception of the carnauba wax. Use this hot oil/wax mixture to wet-out the pigments already mentioned, and maintain at a temperature of 85°C. Heat the triethanolamine to 80°C and add with slow and continuous stirring to the melted oils/wax mixture. Mill until smooth. Finally add the carnauba wax. Remelt and mix well and pour into moulds.

In the above formula the blend of waxes and fatty acid ester provide suitable hardness, and glyceryl monostearate and triethanolamine soap form an emulsion in situ when a wet brush is rubbed on the cake. A disadvantage which is occasionally associated with the use of a cake-type mascara is the variation in the amount of water which is applied by individuals during use. In this respect, a cream-type product which is used with a dry brush is considered by some to be an improvement. The consistency can be varied from a lotion to a thick cream. A suitable formula is as follows:

(Cream)

A	Stearic acid	120
	iso-Propyl myristate	70
	Glyceryl monostearate (self-emulsifying type)	50
B	Glycerin	50
	Triethanolamine	35
	Water (softened or distilled)	575
C	Pigments	100
		1000

Use the preservatives and antioxidant system already given for cake-mascara.

Procedure: Wet-out the pigments as described for the previous formula using the melted waxes and add B with slow stirrin. Mill until smooth.

A cream lotion type can be prepared as follows:

(Cream lotion)

A	Stearic acid	105
	Microcrystalline wax	20
	Carnauba wax	65
	Paraffin wax	55
	Cosmetic mineral oil	15
B	Water (softened or distilled)	492
	Triethanolamine	48
C	Pigments	200
		1000

Use the preservative and antioxidant system above and carry out the procedure as already described.

A lotion-type cream with good lasting properties can be prepared from an emulsion based on triethanolamine stearate, containing about 5 per cent of polyvinyl alcohol, or a film-forming resin, such as polyvinyl acetate, or a film-forming co-polymer. The resin acts as a pigment dispersant, and also binds the pigments onto the lashes.

A	Stearic acid	25
	iso-Propyl myristate	40
B	Triethanolamine	10

	Polyvinyl acetate	50
	Water (softened or distilled)	775
C	Pigments	100
		1000

Use the perfume, preservative and antioxidant system. The procedure is similar to the previous formula. If there is any tendency for the pigments to settle in this lotion include about 1.0 per cent of hydrated aluminium silicate (bentonite)—prepared as a suspension using a suitable proportion of the water given in B.

Automatic mascara or mascaramatic is conveniently packaged in a tubular type container fitted with an applicator. This consists of a rod fitted either with a grooved end, or a suitable shaped spiral brush, so that the mascara can be applied in a rotating manner to the lashes. The tubular container is designed with a restriction at the opening which effectively removes excess liquid as the applicator is withdrawn for use. The distribution and depth of the grooving of the rod type applicator, and the length and arrangement of the bristles of the spiral brush applicator are most important, and play an important part in the success of the product. Attempts to design applicators using moulded plastic have been unsuccessful, because these do not distribute the mascara evenly.

The liquid mascara used is designed to have a viscosity which can be readily and evenly applied by the specifically designed applicator. It should also be quick drying and moisture proof. The product can be based on a liquid cream mascara of suitable viscosity, prepared with ethanolamine soaps or on a film-forming resin of similar composition to an eye-liner. These products, do however, tend to dry out over a period of time, particularly when the container is being constantly opened and closed in use. The best results are obtained using a suitable mixture of waxes in a non-aqueous system based on a medium to heavy grade of an isoparaffinic solvent. A low molecular weight polyethylene is used to form a gel with the solvent to act as a colour dispersant and suspending agent, and also to leave a pigmented film on the lashes after evaporation of the solvent.The success of the product, therefore, depends upon the strength of the polyethylene film, the evaporation rate of the solvent, and the proportion and type of waxes use to determine the final deposition on the lashes. A formula is given as follows:

Carnauba wax	17
Beeswax	45
Ozokerite wax	45
Microcrystalline wax	10
Polyethylene	35
Isoparaffin[1]	580

Pigments	100
	832

[1]Isopar H—Esso petroleum Company Ltd. Shellsol T—Shell Chemical Company Ltd.

Procedure: Mix the polyethylene with about half the amount of solvent using a propeller type mixer moderate agitation. Heat to about 100°C and stir. Remove the heat and add to remainder of the solvent and cool rapidly .The purpose of gelling in half the solvent is to enable 'shock' cooling to be obtained by the addition of the remaining portion. Thorough dispersion and rapid cooling are essential for the preparation of a stable gel. Wet-out the pigments in the gel, add the melted waxes and mix thoroughly.

A variation of this formula is given using a firmer gel and a lower content of waxes. First prepare the gel by the method described:

Polyethylene	120
Isoparaffin	880
	1000

The mascara is then made as to the following formula:

Pigment	300
Colloidal silicon dioxide[1]	18
Carnauba wax	160
iso-Propyl myristate	5
Gel	517
	1000

[1]Aerosil—Degussa:

Procedure: Heat the gel to 70-75°C and wet out the pigment and colloidal silicon dioxide. Add the wax and iso-Propyl myristate. As already indicated the properties of the product depend on the proportion of waxes in relation to the strength of gel used.

In addition the choice of pigment is important and samples should be evaluated to assess their functional properties in this types of product. Some samples do not wet out satisfactorily, or do not stay in suspension and as a result may cause smudging after application. Use of colloidal silicon dioxide as indicated in the above formula will help to suspend the pigment and overcome these difficulties. The exact quantity required often varies from shade to shade and can only be determined by experiment.

Eyelash lengtheners are used to make the lashes appear longer and thicker. They are made by including up to 5 per cent of nylon or rayon fibres in a mascara or mascaramatic preparation. The formulations given should be adjusted by a slight reduction in the proportion of gel or wax, to compensate for the effect on the viscosity caused by the addition of the fibres.

Eye Make-up Removes and Eye Lotions

Eye make-up removes consist of suitable low viscosity oils such a slight mineral oil used either alone or mixed with a fatty acid ester. iso-Propyl myristate is the most suitable ester for this purpose because of its low viscosity, but iso-Propyl palmitate is also satisfactory.

iso-Propyl myristate	250
Light mineral oil	750
	1000

The product is usually sold in the form of cotton pads which are saturated with the oil. If plastic containers are used these should be carefully checked to make sure that they are not affected by the fatty acid ester. More viscous blends of oils containing emollients such as lecithin, lanolin, or lanolin derivatives, are used as tissue oils to apply around the eye orto the throat, as a treatment for lines and wrinkles. Suitable formulae are as follows:

Olive-oil	100
iso-Propyl myristate (or iso-Propyl palmitate)	100
Castor-oil	800
	1000

iso-Propyl lanolate	50
Lanolin	50
Olive-oil	100
iso-Propyl palmitate	200
Castor-oil	600
	1000

In both these products use up to 0.2 per cent of a non-irritant perfume, and include 0.002 per cent of a butylated hydroxyanisole as an antioxidant.

Eye lotions are recommended as a beauty aid to keep the eyes clean and bright, and to relieve strain and irritation. Solutions should be iso-tonic with lachrymal secretion and the product should be prepared using an aseptic technique and sterilized either by autoclaving or by filtration and packed in previously sterilized containers. Boric acid and sodium borate are used as mild bactericedes and fungicides, and witch hazel water has a mild astringent and cooling effect. Zinc sulphate has a stronger astringent effect, and is also used to relieve infiammation in conjunctivitis. Formulae are as follows:

Boric acid	10
Zinc sulphate	2
Distilled water	988
	1000

Sodium chloride	5
Sodium borate	5
Glycerin	20

Witch hazel	50
Distilled water	920
	1000
Boric acid	10
Zinc sulphate	*2*
Glycerin	20
Distilled witch hazel	100
Distilled water	868
	1000

Chlorbutol can be included in any of the above lotions as a mild analgesic at a dosage of 0.1 to 0.2 per cent, and as a preservative at 0.5 per cent. Where chlorbutol is not included use 0.1 per cent of methyl parahydroxy benzoate as a preservative.

Cosmetic eye drops based on a solution of methylene blue are antiseptic and impart an attractive blue colour to the whites of the eyes.

Methylene blue	0.02
Sodium chloride	9.00
Distilled water	990.98
	1000.00
Methyl parahydroxybenzoate	0.1 per cent

49

Baby Care

Introduction

Baby cosmetics and toiletries, intended for use on new-born babies and children of up to five years old, represent a very special category indeed. They are invariably functional, rather than decorative, mainly concerned with keeping the baby or child clean, comfortable and healthy. Since babies and young children are somewhat more vulnerable than their adult counterparts, baby products must be carefully formulated to be extremely mild and gentle to skin and hair. These considerations impose a number of requirements and constraints for the design, evaluation and manufacture of baby-care products. Any person working in the area of baby care must understand these issues and adhere to them accordingly.

Finally, it is important to recognise that baby products have a significant part to play in giving an emotive benefit to the user, that is the parent. It is essential that products used on the young are safe, but the ability to leave the hair and skin feeling soft and clean, and with a pleasant smell is equally important in providing emotional support for protective parental instincts.

Specific Basic Requirements for Baby Products

The basic requirements for baby products are very similar to those for products aimed at the adult sector. However, additional factors, over and above those normally encountered, must be adhered to and, in the opinion of the author. The following list indicates the minimum requirements for any product to be sold in this market sector.

(i) Products should be functional, efficacious and demonstrably capable of delivering the benefits for which they are purchased. Functionality should not sacrifice aesthetics, and pleasantness of use is a mandatory requirement.

(ii) Products should comply with the most stringent standards of safety, such that they can be used with absolute confidence on even the youngest skin.

(iii) Products should contain the purest grades of materials available and the microbiological purity of the finished product should be tightly controlled to eliminate the risk of infection.

(iv) The levels of dyestuffs and fragrances should be kept as low as possible so as to reduce the risk of adverse skin reactions. At the present time an increasing number of fragrance-free products are appearing in the market.

(v) Preservative levels in baby products should be kept to a minimum, whilst ensuring adequate preservation to negate the risk of contamination or infection of the user.

(vi) Product packaging should be carefully designed to minimise the risk of product ingestion or other form or misuse. A number of tamper-proof of child proof enclosures and containers are available, and should be used where possible.

(vii) The platform on which the product is marketed should communicate a high degree of honesty and trust, with emphasis on the benefits of product purity and performance, rather than ephemeral marketing claims.

Product Types and their Presentation

Baby Powders

Powders are amongst the earliest and best known of all baby products, with a very high level of penetration into the target market. The primary function of a baby powder is to absorb residual moisture on the skin and to provide a degree of mild lubrication, thus reducing the possibility of post-cleansing chaffing and soreness.

The main ingredient in baby powder is normally talc, known chemically as hydrated magnesium silicate. It is chosen for its unique ability to provide a high degree of silkiness and lubricity on the skin, due to its unusual morphology. This property is conferred by the flat, hexagonal, platelet structure of the talc crystals, which exhibit a low coefficient of inter-particular friction, producing a high degree of 'slip'. Raw tale is mined from the earth, therefore must be purified before it can be safely used. A natural contaminant of the talc from some sources is asbestos, a fibrous material that can produce a fatal lung disease, known as asbestosis, in humans. Obviously, talc of this type should not be used. Bacteria, natural contaminants in talc, must be controlled. *Clostridium tetani* is the causative organism of tetanus, so the importance of an effective sterilisation process cannot be over-emphasised. Many methods of sterilisation have been tried over the years, but that utilising gamma irradiation is still amongst the most popular. A second method, now becoming far more widespread in use, is steam sterilisation. This involves heating the raw talc, under pressure, with superheated steam at temperature exceeding 120°C for periods of 30 min or more. Whilst this method is very effective, it is essential to remove any residual moisture from the raw talc after the sterilisation process, otherwise the likelihood of contamination by adventitious microorganisms will be significantly increased.

Some power products are composed simply of talc and a low level of fragrance. Many contain other additives, claimed to give the product additional benefits. Additives that possess a higher degree of moisture absorbency then talc may be included, making the baby powder more effective. Such materials include kaolin, magnesium and calcium silicates, and starch-based products. However, whilst these materials achieve extra absorbency, they compromise the lubricious feel of talc itself, impairing the feel of the finished product. This advantage can be minimised by careful selection of the physical form of the absorbent material used. Generally fine particle size with uniform spherical shape should be selected. The inclusion of low levels of mild bactericides can improve performance in terms of the prevention of nappy rash. Powdered zinc oxide, with mild bactericidal properties, is often incorporated at levels between 1 and 5% for this purpose. A typical formulation for an absorbent baby powder designed to help prevent the formation of nappy rash is illustrated below.

	Wt%
Talc	77.90
Starch	20.00
Zinc Oxide	2.00
Perfume	0.10

Perhaps the best known baby powder on the market today is that from Johnson & Johnson, which is a high purity talc-based product.

A more recent innovation in this product sector is liquid talc. Topically between 5 and 15% of talc is suspended in an oil-in-water emulsion, yielding a product which provides a convenient method of applying talc to a baby's skin. Apart from the pleasant cooling effect of the product in use, the elimination of dusting and avoidance of unintentional inhalation of airborne particles confers additional advantages. A typical formulation for a baby liquid talc, based on an oil-in-water emulsion, is illustrated below.

	Wt%
Cetearyl alcohol	0.60
Cyclomethicone (and) dimethicone	1.00
Polawax NF*	2.50
Carbomer 980	0.20
PEG7 glyceryl cocoate	0.50
Talc	12.00
Triethanolamine	to pH 7.0
Water	to 100
Perfume, preservative etc.	*q.s.*

• Polalwax NF* is a registered trade name of Croda Chemicals Limited.

When formulating a product of this type it is important to ensure that good application characteristics are combined with sufficiently high viscosity so that the talc remains homogeneously dispersed within the product, even after storage at elevated temperature for extended periods of time.

Lotions and Creams

It is impossible to cover every aspect, of baby lotions and creams in this chapter, but the products normally possess one of two primary functions, cleansing and/or protection. Products designed for cleansing are commonly lower viscosity lotions, while those intended to give a protection benefit are generally higher viscosity creams. Traditional baby-cream products were heavy water-in-oil emulsions. Their modern day counterparts are more commonly oil-in-water. Lotions, on the other hand, are nearly always oil-in-water emulsions, which are more favourable for producing the required aesthetics and cleansing function.

Classic formulations for protective baby creams were based on mineral oil or petrolatum, emulsified with an anionic emulsifier such as triethanolamine stearate. Such products generally possess a relatively high oil: water ratio, making them ideal for use in the nappy area after cleansing during nappy changes. These creams leave a protective film of oil on the surface of the baby's skin, thus reducing the chances of chaffing and soreness, and leaving the skin soft, and smooth. In addition, water-in-oil creams leaves no sensation of coldness on a baby's skin, as the evaporation of the internal water phase is retarded by the presence of the external oil phase. A traditional protective baby cream, based on mineral oil and incorporating an anionic emulsification system, is illustrated below.

	Wt%
Mineral Oil	30.00
Petrolatum	2.00
Stearic acid	1.20
Stearyl alcohol	1.00
Cetyl alcohol	0.70
Triethanolamine	0.65
Propylene glycol	1.00
Water	63.45
Perfumes, preservatives etc.	q.s.

Modern baby creams are frequently based on non-ionic emulsifier systems, and offer protective benefits combined with a high degree of emolliency and much improved aesthetics. A typical formulation is illustrated below.

	Wt%
Mineral Oil	15.00
Propylene dicaprate/dicaprylate	5.00
Cyclomethicone	3.00
POE sorbitan monostearate	1.50
Sorbitan monostearate	1.00
Glycerine	2.00
Water	72.50
Perfumes, preservatives, etc.	q.s.

A special type of protective baby cream, yet one that nevertheless constitutes a very important market sector, is that designed to help the prevention of nappy rash. Nappy rash is a painful inflammatory conditions, normally found in the anogenital area of the baby's anatomy. The aetiology of nappy rash is subject to debate but the main causative factor is widely accepted as the microbiological breakdown of urine and faecal constituents into irritant materials, principally ammonia, which are subsequently held in close contact with the baby's skin by the nappy itself. An effective nappy rash cream must therefore be formulated to provide good barrier properties and to inhibit the proliferation of bacteria and fungal micro-organisms in the occlusive nappy area. Products of this type are typically water-in-oil emulsions that are able to provide an effective barrier against moisture and chemical attack, with the inclusion of active such as zinc oxide, hexamidine and benzalkonium chloride to reduce the levels of micro-organisms present. A typical water-in-oil nappy rash cream, containing zinc oxide, is illustrated below *[2]*.

	Wt%
Petrolatum	13.00
Mineral oil	15.00
Sorbitan isostearate	2.00
Microcrystalline wax	3.50
Glycerine	4.50
Zinc Oxide	7.00
α-Bisabolol	0.20
Magnesium sulphate	0.70
Lactic acid/sodium lactate buffer	to pH 5.5
Water	to 100.00
Perfume, preservative talc.	q.s.

Baby lotions are invariably lower viscosity oil-in-water emulsions, with the internal oil phase of the product providing the cleansing property. Mineral oil, with the ability to cleanse by solubilising fats and other lipophilic substances found on the skin, is the most favoured base. Most cleansing lotions also contain emollients to leave the skin feeling soft and smooth after use. Water, present in the product as the external phase of emulsion, provides a fresh, cooling sensation during use, due to the rapid evaporation of water vapour from the skin's surface. Mixed non-ionic surfactants, frequently used for emulsification of lotion products, offer maximum degree of flexibility in formulation design. A typical formulation for a baby lotion cleanser is illustrated below.

	Wt%
Mineral Oil	12.00
Dimethicone	2.00
Isopropyl palmitate	1.50
POE sorbitan monooleate	*1.20*
Sorbitan monooleate	0.70
Propylene glycol	1.00
Water	81.60
Perfumes, preservatives etc.	*q.s.*

Soaps

Soap, one of the earliest methods of cleaning the body, is normally a mixture of alkali metal salts of long-chain fatty acids. Triglycerides, for example tallow, palm oil and coconut oil, provide the basic 'fats' from which the fatty acid mixtures used for soap are derived. The finished soap properties are primarily dependent on the mixture and ratio of triglycerides used. Tallow, for example, gives a much harder soap than coconut oil. Potassium soaps are much softer than their sodium-based counterparts, although, in practice, they are rarely used. The finished soap bar can be modified by the addition of other ingredients, such as emollients, opacifiers and chelating agents.

Although there is no evidence to suggest that soap is harmful to a baby's skin, its very alkaline pH (typically 9-10) is a disadvantage, and is implicit in the drying effect that soap is considered to have on skin. Consequently, baby soaps often contain emollients or superfatting ingredients (to help minimise the drying effect), white color and low fragrance levels.

This disadvantage of soap led to the development of a new type of cleansing bar, with mild properties and superior skin-feel, ideally suited for babies and young children. Such products, commonly known as 'syndet' bars, are made from synthetic detergents, most of which are based on isothionate or sulphosuccinate systems. Various additives, including plasticisers, binders and lather enhancers, can be added to the product to modify the properties of the finished bar.

The mildness of the syndet bar is largely attributable to its 'neutral' pH (5-7). To date, Syndet bars have not widely penetrated the market, particularly the baby-care market, for two main reasons: (i) they are much more difficult to manufacture than their soap-based equivalents;

and (ii) the production costs are between three and fives times that of soap. Syndet bars marketed as baby products should be white in colour, not discolouring with age, and should contain minimum practical levels of fragrance, thus ensuring maximal consumer perception of mildness in use.

Hair Products

In the context of baby use, hair products can be strictly limited to shampoos and conditioners, the former being far more important than the latter. The most important requirements are mildness and low eye-sting potential. The latter is particularly relevant since the blink response of babies and young children is not fully developed and gives no protection to the cornea against contact with external substances.

The low activity of a baby's sebaceous glands means that the potential for soiling of the hair is not particularly high, therefore the cleansing requirements for an effective product are not severe.

Mildness is normally achieved through the use of non-irritating surfactant systems, all of which have limited detergency properties. One of the earliest, and perhaps still the best known baby shampoos, is that from Johnson & Johnson. This product was the first to make extensive use of amphoteric imidazolines, blended in specific rations with milder types of alkyl ether sulphate. This combination was used in conjunction with selected non-ionic surfactants to give the now famous 'no more tears' claim.

In more recent years many new amphoteric surfactants have been developed, allowing much greater flexibility in the formulation of mild baby shampoos. Amphoteric betaines and anionic sulphosuccinates, in combination with alkyl ether sulphates (3 or 4 moles ethylene oxide) produce detergent systems for mild shampoos. Much attention has also been given to effective irritation mitigants which when added to already mild surfactant systems, further ameliorate the potential for adverse reactions in the eye. Classically, both sorbitan and sucrose fatty acid esters have been used for this purpose. A typical formulation for a mild baby shampoo is illustrated below.

	Wt%
Sodium lauryl ether (3.0) sulphate, 70%	6.00
Cocamidopropyl betaine, 30%	12.00
Polyoxyethylene (80) sorbitan monolaurate	6.00
Polyethylene glycol distearate	1.50
Water	74.50
Perfumes, preservative, colour, etc.	q.s.

In recent years there has been increasing concern over the potential toxicity of 1,3-dioxane, an impurity found in most ethoxylated surfactants.

Consequently, baby shampoos based on detergent systems containing only amphoteric surfactants have been developed. The perceived need for this change is largely unfounded however, as levels of dioxane found in modern ethoxylated surfactants materials are very low indeed.

With respect to hair conditioners, it must be recognised that the primary function for baby use is detangling, rather than conditioning *per se.* A baby's hair does not require conditioning in the same way as that of adult as it has not been subjected to regular combing and styling treatments. The detangling attributes are, however, extremely important, as even gentle combing after washing can result in knotting and breaking, causing discomfort and distress for the child. As a result, conditioning agents in baby conditioners are chosen for their ability to impart good wet-combing and slip characteristics, rather than to improve dry hair properties—the main aim of adult products. Relatively low levels of quaternary ammonium salts, such as distearyl dimethyl ammonium chloride are used to achieve this objective. A typical formulation for a baby hair conditioner is illustrated below.

	Wt%
Distearyl dimethyl ammonium chloride	2.00
Ethoxylated stearylamine	0.30
Cetyl alcohol	1.50
Hydroxyethyl cellulose	0.80
Water	95.40
Perfumes, preservative, colour etc.	q.s.

Whilst the potential for eye sting from a conditioner is significantly less than that for a shampoo, mildness should still be paramount in the formulators mind. Typically, quaternary ammonium salts with higher molecular weight hydrophobic chains offer the best potential for mildness on the eyes, due to their increased molecular size and distribution of the cationic charge. A material of this type which has more recently become popular is behentrimonium (C_{22}) chloride.

Bath Products

Baby bath products must provide both gentle cleansing action, and pleasant aesthetics *for* mother and baby during the bathing process. Like baby shampoos, baby bath products need not possess high activity, as the extent of soiling of a baby's skin will be low by comparison with that of an adult.

The primary requirement of a baby bath is that it should be functional, yet mild on the skin, and be as non-drying as possible. When diluted in bath water, the product is often used to shampoo a baby's hair, therefore low eye irritancy is essential. For this reason, baby bath formulations generally contain low active detergent systems composed of mild alkyl ether sulphates (3 or 4 moles ethylene oxide) combined with a relatively high ratio of imidazoline or betaine foam boosters. In this way, sufficient quantities of light, open foam for the cleansing process with no significant drying of the skin at the in-use dilution, is obtained. The viscosity of the product should be such that easy and rapid dispersion in the bath water is possible with minimum agitation. A perfume level as low as possible, but sufficient to generate a pleasant odour in use is desirable. Additional ingredients may be used to minimise any drying effect and enhance the softness and feel of the skin after use. Many materials are claimed to be beneficial. Care must be taken when selecting hydrophobic oils for this purpose, so as not to impair foaming characteristics. A popular means *of enhancing* moisturing properties is to include low levels of polyol fatty acid esters, with which a minimal effect on the foaming capability of detergent systems, and considerable enhancement of pleasant skin-feel may be achieved. The formulation shown below illustrates this:

	Wt%
Sodium lauryl ether (3.0) sulphate, 70%	5.00
Lauryl betaine, 30%	8.00
PEG-7glyceryl cocoate	2.00
Water	84.50
Electrolyte (viscosity builder)	0.50
Perfumes, preservative, colour etc.	q.s.

A second, although much less important category of bath product, is baby bath oil. Here the emphasis is *on* the mildness rather than cleansing, although the use of such products does not provide a pleasant means of removing superficial soil from the baby's skin in a bath environment. A simple baby bath oil formulation is illustrated below:

	Wt%
Caprylic/capric triglyceride	80.00
Polysorbate 85	20.00
Perfume, preservative, colour etc.	q.s.

Moussed Products

The term 'mousse' normally refers to a product that is filled into a sealed container, which is pressurized with a propellant that serves both to 'mousse' the product, and to expel it from its pressurized container. Mousses offer novel ways of improving the convenience of baby products, particularly in view of their suitability for single-handed operation. They also offer the advantage of being 'pre-foamed' at the time or dispensing, providing significant in-use benefits for baby shampoos and baby cleansing products. However, at the present time, there are very few moussed baby products on the market. The reason is unclear, but the additional cost, the historical connection with adult hair-care products, and the potential danger of pressurised containers if misused, may be significant factors. An early product was 'Care For Kids' baby shampoo mousse, launched in the US by the Revlon Group in the mid to late 1980s. Despite views that this would lead to an increased demand for similar products, the market remains largely undeveloped.

Products available in the market today are principally skin care mousses, where the functional benefit is moisturisation rather than cleansing. These formulations are normally based on low viscosity oil-in-water emulsions, utilising an oil-soluble propellant system, which provides an instantaneous creamy foam when the product is dispensed.

When formulating baby mousses, the safety considerations normally associated with baby products are paramount. In particular, the propellant system chosen must present no hazard to a baby's skin or respiratory system, even under conditions of predictable misuse.

Wipes and Tissues

Baby wipes and tissues represent one of the fastest growing sectors of the baby products market. There are essentially two types of baby wipe, categorised by function of either 'cleaning plus freshening' or 'cleansing plus moisturing'. The first type are normally 'aqueous' wipes, while the latter are referred to as 'lotion' wipes, depending on the nature of the wipe impregnant. The wipe itself is normally made from paper or fabric, the latter offering improved strength and aesthetics over the former, at higher cost. Paper substrates may be either 'wet-laid' or 'air-laid' and are manufactured in different weights, depending on the properties required. Fabric substrates come in a variety of different materials, including viscose-rayon, cotton, or various combinations of the two.

Aqueous wipe impregnants are composed largely of water, with the addition of solubilisers to improve cleansing properties and assist in the stabilisation of low levels of fragrance. Lotion wipes, normally much more effective in cleansing than their aqueous-based counterparts, are generally stable, low viscosity oil-in-water emulsions, the internal phase of which provides the cleansing and moisturing properties. Emollient esters and silicones are often added to enhance postuse skin feel. A more recent innovation is the antibacterial or 'total care' lotion wipe. These formulations contain low levels of bactericidal agents which are included to help in the prevention of nappy rash. Additionally, water-repellent materials may be added to help protect the skin in the advent of nappy soilage. The production of a safe and effect wipe product, with adequate preservation throughout the expected shelf-life, is a problem. A wipe with a high water content provides an ideal environment to support microbial growth, if contamined with adventitious micro-organisms.

Oils

Traditional oils, offering gentle and effective cleansing, particularly in the nappy area, are one of the oldest forms of baby product. The oil itself has a softening and moisturising effect on the skin, the residual layer affording some barrier protection against subsequent nappy soilage.

Historically, product design has been simple and straightforward with high purity, low viscosity mineral oil enjoying almost universal use. Additional ingredients are usually restricted to fragrance and a small quantity of solubiliser. A major disadvantage is the inevitable greasiness in use. Overcoming this problem by the use of degreasing additives, for example low levels of fumed silica, have not been successful.

Recently the design approach to baby oils, motivated by the requirement to deliver an effective cleanser with improved aesthetics and lower greasiness. has changed. Many methods have been tried, one of which is the extensive use of vegetable-based oils such as soyabean oil, jojoba oil or palm kernel oil. Although these are not such effective cleanses, they are often perceived as being less greasy. They are, however, more readily oxidised, leading to rancidity and malodour.

Contemporary baby oils use another approach to improve product aesthetics. High purity mineral oil is mixed with light esters, volatile silicone oils or mixture of the two. Esters, for example isopropyl myristate, 'dilute' the greasy effects of the mineral oil, while volatile silicones, such as cyclomethicone, evaporate rapidly from the skin's surface after application, leaving behind a thinner oil layer. A light, non-greasy babv oil may be obtained using the following formulation.

	wt%
Mineral oil	70.00
Octyl palmitate	5.00
Isopropyl myristate	10.00
Cyclomethicone	15.00
Perfumes, solubilisers, antioxidants etc.	*q.s.*

Perfumes and Colognes

The popularity of perfumes and colognes for baby use varies in different parts of the world, more so than with any other product. The prime function of a perfume is to leave a pleasant odour on the baby's skin. A cologne achieves a lesser but similar effect, while simultaneously cooling the skin.

Not surprisingly, colognes are particularly popular in hot countries, especially parts of southern Europe around the Mediterranean, where they are often applied several times a day to cool the skin and alleviate discomfort caused by heat. Most baby colognes are water-based products, containing iow levels of fragrance and a solubilizer to assist with fragrance dispersion. Other additives include plant extracts, said to impart soothing benefits to the skin. Microbiological contamination from these materials may be a hazard. The cooling effect of the cologne can be greatly enhanced by the addition of relatively low levels of ethyl alcohol. This is rarely done because of the adverse drying effects of alcohol on the skin.

When formulating baby perfumes and colognes, product safety must be the prime concern. Of all cosmetic ingredients, fragrances are most *commonly* associated with skin allergies and sensitisation reactions. It follows therefore, that any fragrance compound selected for use in this type of baby product should be subjected to the most rigorous safety assessment, before commercialisaion is contemplated.

Perfumes for babies are controversial, as the 'image-led' marketing strategy for perfumes and fine fragrances has little relevance for babies, whose social interaction is confined primarily to that of the parent-child relationship. Nevertheless, perfumes and fine fragrances for babies are currently very popular in some parts of Europe, notably in France. Obviously babies and young children are not sufficiently developed to determine their own social image through the fragrances they wear. Perhaps the perceived need for this type of product is driven largely by the parents' desire to extend their own social values to their offspring.

Raw Materials for Baby Products

The prime requirement for any baby product is absolute safety. Great care should be taken that raw materials used are not only efficacious but also innocuous, with no incidence of irregularity in their toxicological profile. Only the purest grades of material should be selected, and careful attention paid to the types and levels of any impurities that may be present. This is increasingly important with the current use of pesticides, antioxidants and preservative, with which even low levels of contamination in the raw material may be potentially harmful to a baby's delicate skin. If any doubt is encountered over raw material selection, significant confidence can be gained by the use of materials which conform to the requirements of the British Pharmacopoeia (BP), European Pharmacopoeia (EP) or the United States Pharmacopoeia (USP). Specification must encourage tight control over the quality of material used, such that confidence in the batch-to-batch consistency is high. The concentrations of raw materials must be carefully chosen to eliminate all risks, even of minor skin reactions. The comedogenic nature of any material destined for use in baby products must also be considered. The 'comedogenicity' of a material describes its potential to form comedones, or 'spots', on the skin. Use of comedogenic materials should be avoided.

Particular diligence is required in the selection of raw materials for detergent-based products, which, by their very nature, exhibit a higher propensity for irritation of the skin. Even the so-called 'mild' detergents will extract natural lipids from the skin's surface layers. The formulator's skill in selecting a synergistic blend of detergent materials that exhibits lower irritancy than its component parts is particularly valuable. Materials used should exhibit very low microbial counts, and the absence of any micro-organism that can be classified as pathogenic is mandatory. This is particularly relevant in the case of talc, starches, natural gums and plant extracts, where high levels of contamination by micro-organisms, sometimes pathogenic, are known to occur.

Of particular importance is the quality of water used. The purity of this ingredient, a major component in the vast majority of products, often overlooked, is one of the most common causes of problems in the finished product, particularly those of a microbiological nature.

Developmental Pathways

Formulation Development

Formulation starts with an evaluation of the marketing concept and accompanying brief, clearly identifying the product design. Early developmental work will focus on establishing a 'base formulation', which can be progressively modified to satisfy the product brief. This base technology can be derived from many sources, including the formulator's personal knowledge, prior technology of a similar type, or the vast quantity of guideline formulations available in raw material suppliers' literature. Product prototypes, satisfying as closely as possible the performance requirements of the original brief are then submitted for initial evaluation of product efficacy, preservative efficacy, product stability and product safety. At this stage, the manufacturing process should be studied. Optimisation of the product, and subsequent full evaluation, aids the decision as to whether or not launch the product.

Practical Requirements

Although developmental pathways can be precisely defined, practical requirements for any new product development must be observed. Aspects of safety have already been highlighted as mandatory. In addition the formulation must support the marketing concept, allow easy and convenient use of finished product, and be compatible with the chosen packaging presentation. The product should meet the defined cost targets, allowing effective marketing of the finished product, while offering the purchaser a high quality product at a realistic price.

Product Evaluation

Product evaluation is an integral step in any new product development exercise. Three main techniques are used to ensure that the product meets the defined performance criteria.

Laboratory Evaluation

Laboratory techniques are used to evaluate early development prototypes and, by screening formulations, to assist in the development process before progressing into more sophisticated and expensive evaluation exercises. The many established laboratory techniques available may be modified to suit the formulator, and to extend the range of possibilities. Viscosity, density and pH are readily determined using simple instrumental techniques, and can help to identify correct product design rapidly. In the development of detergent products the rose-Miles test is a useful means of determining the quantity and quality of foam generated by products in-use. Skin absorption characteristics for emulsion-based products can be predicted through careful selection of raw materials, combined with rheological evaluation in the laboratory. In baby products containing active ingredients, for example nappy-rash creams, the active material can often be measured spectrophotometrically to determine its availability in the product base.

Mother and Baby Panels

While useful data on product performance may be obtained with laboratory techniques, the most meaningful tests are in-use studies. Classical in-use evaluation techniques involve either panel or consumer testing, but assessment of baby products present a special problem in that the end-user, the baby or child, is frequently unable to express an opinion. For this reason, a common technique for evaluating the performance of baby products is to use mother and baby panels. These panels may be conducted with the assistance of the local health clinic. The mother uses the test product on her child for a fixed period of time and subsequently acts as the respondent for the research exercise. The mother may also use the product on herself, yielding valuable information regarding the performance of the product on adults, and providing an opinion of the suitability for the baby. This format is one of the most valuable ways of assessing product performance since it is the mother, and not the child, who will ultimately buy the product.

Clinical trials use the same methodology as mother and baby panels but are carried out with a higher degree of medical supervision, monitoring the possibility of adverse skin reactions. Such trials, which normally utilise 50 to 100 respondents, are particularly useful when assessing the performance of 'active' products, such as nappy-rash creams.

Finally, it is essential to note that adequate product safety must be obtained for the product under test before any evaluation using mother and baby panels is undertaken.

Consumer Research

For the reason outlined earlier consumer research, the final evaluation step prior to launch of the product, is not always used for baby products. It can, however, provide certain information that the mother and baby panel cannot. The most valuable data is information about the acceptability of branding for the product. In all human evaluation trials, informed consent must be sought before starting the test, and requirements for product safety must not be compromised in any way.

Product Safety Requirement

The need for the highest standards of product safety for baby-care products has been emphasised throughout this chapter. Notwithstanding, there are legal requirements for any toiletry product to be safe, for use as intended, throughout its shelf-life. There is, however, no defined evaluation programme for determining the safety of a product, and this decision is therefore left to the individual. The legal aspects must, of course, be observed but with baby products there is also a high degree of emotive importance in ensuring product safety This must always be remembered. The perception of vulnerability of babies or young children, and the need to protect them from anything harmful is very strong.

A testing programme, ensuring that the product meets these high standards of safety, is not easy. Historically, such programmes may have included a wide variety of safety tests, culminating with evaluation using animal studies. This approach is expensive and time-consuming, and intense concern has been expressed over the unnecessary use of animals in safety evaluation. Consequently, it has become increasingly feasible to devise a testing programme that avoids animal testing altogether, yet provides a high degree of confidence in product safety. When adopting this approach, careful selection of raw materials and close examination of their toxicological profiles is essential. Fragrances used must conform, as a minimum requirement, to the guidelines laid down by IFRA (International Fragrance Research Association and RIFH (Research Institue for Fragrance Materials). If sufficient toxicity data is lacking, an increasing number of in *vitro* tests are available to determine product safety. For example, cytotoxicology, using various cell cultures, has already been successfully employed to determine the irritation potential for detergent-based products such as baby shampoos.

When reasonably satisfied with toxicological safety data, studies on human volunteers are normally conducted using adults, not babies. Occlusive patch testing and arm immersion studies are often used to gain more knowledge about the safety profile of a product. Should circumstances demand, a number of more sophisticated methods are available. Human volunteer programmes should reflect the in-use situation, and be carried out over minimum period of two weeks. Testing on babies or young children may then be considered, but must only be carried out under strictly monitored conditions, such as the mother and baby panels.

Product Preservation

Product preservation is necessary for two reasons: (i) to prevent the product becoming contaminated during use; and (ii) to protect the user from possibility of harmful infection. Preservation is particularly relevant in baby-care products often used around the nappy area, where there is normally a high incidence of faecal micro-organisms such *Escherichia coli.* The potential for contamination of the product and reinfection of the user at a later date is high.

By definition, all preservatives are harmful to living organisms, therefore should be used with extreme caution. A full review of available toxicological data on any preservative used in baby product is mandatory. The preservative level should be kept as low as possible, consistent with adequate activity. Higher preservative efficacy can often be obtained by utilizing the broad spectrum and synergistic activity of preservative blends. In order to minimise the total preservative addition levels in a product, it is essential that the raw materials used are microbiologically as clean as possible. A minimum micro-biological specification of less than 100 colony forming units (cfu) per gram is recommended and absence of pathogens is essential. The practice of over-preservation of a product to compensate for poor manufacturing practice must be avoided, particularly in the case of baby-care products.

Preservative efficacy testing is essential. The microbiological quality of toiletry and personal-care products is covered by recommendations and guidelines issued by the CTPA (Cosmetics, Toiletries and Perfumes Association) in 1975. The reference to baby products specified less than 100 cfu per gram or product, and absence of pathogenic organisms.

Finally, the media often compounds the issue of product preservation. A particular preservative can become 'unfashionable' overnight, sometimes causing irreparable commercial damage to any products containing it. However, the temptation to produce 'preservativefree' products should be avoided, as the potential for harm to the user, through product contamination, far outweighs the risk of adverse skin reactions to the preservative system.

Product Stability

Before a product can be launched, the producer must ensure that it will remain in good condition, be safe to use, and fulfil its intended function throughout its envisaged shelf-life. In terms of safety, this shelf-life may be defined as three years. Consequently, product stability is an essential consideration when any *new product* is developed. Clearly, since it is not practical to wait three years before launching a product, it is necessary, as far as is reasonably practical, to predict product stability. The most common technique is an accelerated ageing study, which is similar for baby and adult products. Product parameters, such as appearance, odour, viscosity, density and active matter, are measured and the product is then stored under a wide variety of conditions, for a period of time. The minimum recommended number of storage conditions are listed below.

(i) Freeze thaw cycling (-30°C to room temperature ; six cycles)

(ii) Storage at 5°C

(iii) Storage at room temperature in darkness

(iv) Storage at room temperature in the presence of UV light

(v) Storage at 40°C

Periodically, for example one month intervals, products stored under these conditions are reassessed and changes in measured or sensory attributes checked. During this exercise, microbiolgical challenge tests are carried out on product stored under various conditions, to see if preservative efficacy has been affected. The decision determining suitability for launch is largely arbitrary; the longer the test duration, the lower the risk in the marketplace. For baby products, maximum levels of caution are advised, and successful completion of ageing studies of not less than three months, and preferably six months, should be considered mandatory.

Manufacture and Quality Control

Manufacture

The production of baby products, or indeed any cosmetic or toiletry, is normally a simple process. It involves the mixing of the required raw materials, perhaps with heating and cooling, in a variety of ways. Of paramount importance for baby products are the procedures used, general cleanliness in the production area and compliance with GMP (good manufacturing practice) guidelines.

Mixing vessels used for manufacturing baby products should conform to a number of fundamental requirements. Fabrication should be of high quality stainless steel, at least grade 304 and ideally grade 316 and should have the optimum configuration for producing a wide variety of products. Steam-jacketed vessels, with a simple impeller and some form of high-shear mixing device to produce emulsions, are a good starting point. Vessels should be maintained in a clean condition and should be sanitised regularly, according to defined procedures. Associated pipework should not contain any 'deadlegs' and must be continually cleaned and sanitised. Scoops and stirring paddles used for mixing should also be fabricated from stainless steel and should be kept clean and dry at all times. Control of raw materials and manufacturing processes must be specified according to GMP requirements, and all personnel should be adequately trained.

Finally, the quality of water used for the manufacture of baby products should be of the highest order. Water should be chemically purified using a two-stage deionisation plant, and microbiological integrity may be obtained through the use of ultra filtration and UV irradiation treatment.

Water for the manufacture of baby products should be used immediately after purification, ideally on demand and should on no account be stored in static containers prior to use. Finished bulk product should be filled immediately into the primary packaging in order to preserve product integrity. If finished bulk has to be stored for any length of time prior to filling, purpose-designed hygienic storage containers should be used.

Quality Control

Quality control, the final, extremely important process before a product is released for general sale, must ensure that all product leaving the factory meets the required specification. There is currently an increasing emphasis on quality assurance rather than quality control, the essential difference being to monitor the entire manufacturing process rather than to measure the product it produces. This is the approach of total quality management, and is nowhere more relevant than in the production of baby products.

50

Afro Products

Introduction

This chapter deals specifically with cosmetic products designed for use by people of African origin. Intensive research and development of products in this field during the 1980s has resulted in the acceptance and recognition of this class of product as a legitimate, and now established part of the general skin, and in particular hair care market. The development of such products is therefore a relatively recent consideration. It must above all take into account fashion and the different characteristics of the skin and hair of this ethnic group.

Hair Structures

The purpose here is to point out important differences that have a bearing on the approach to formulating Afro products. First impressions suggest that Caucasian and Afro hair are structured very differently. Caucasin being straight and Afro tightly curled. Under the microscope, however, the two hair types appear similar, except that Afro hair is somewhat elliptical in transverse section whereas Caucasian hair is circular. Chemical analysis reveals that the amino acid contents are very much the same. The distribution of sulphur-containing amino acids, however, is different and accounts for the structural variations that give rise to quite different appearance. In wavy, tightly curled hair there is a non-uniform distribution in that the disulphide bridges are more prevalent on one side of the hair fibre.

The principal reason why specific products are required for treatment of Afro hair lies in the widespread use of chemical treatments to restyle or straighten it. These treatments rupture the bonds that link protein fibres, and thus weaken the structure of the hair. Indeed, the more drastic treatments, which cleave peptide bonds, can cause the destruction of the fibres themselves. Consequently, formulation must be chosen with specific recognition of these facts. Products in this range can be divided into two categories; (i) less-aggressive chemical treatments than those normally designed for the straightening process; and (ii) products that will restore lustre, body and moisture content to chemically treated hair.

Skin Characteristics

In contrast to the relatively subtle chemical differences between Caucasian and Afro hair, there are more fundamental differences in the skin types. These must be considered when designing products for the care and decoration of the skin.

Colour is the most obvious difference and is due to the variation of pigments—haemoglobin, carotene and melanin—in the epidermis. The level of melanin is the crucial factor in determining the colour of skin. The greater quantity of melanin in black skin is due to the greater activity of the melanocytes that produce the grains of melanosomes. These 'mature' into melanin in the epidermis, developing from colourless to black and moving closer to the skin surface. In white skin the maturing process occurs only to a limited extent, and smaller, round melanosomes tend to clump together in bundles. In black skin the larger, oval, mature melanosomes are singly dispersed and evenly distributed throughout the epidermis giving it its characteristic colour. There is considerable variation in the quantity of melanin present in 'black' skin, and this gives rise to a much wider range of skin tones. Consequently, in order to represent the full range of skin tones found in a dark-skinned people, some 35 shades are required.

Black skin characteristically possesses a tough outer layer of the epidermis. This is prone to scarring, which can result in serious disfigurement. Black skin also contains a greater number of sebaceous glands than white skin (40-60% more). This does not, however, automatically result in more oiliness, although it often produces a shiny surface. All basic skin types (dry, sensitive, normal, oily and combination) are observed for black skin just as they are for white.

Many problems associated with black skin arise from change in pigmentation. For example, loss of colour (hypopigmentation) is common to all races and occurs in disorders such as the little-understood , vitiligo (leucoderma). This effect, unsightly in white skins, can be devastating in black skins. Darkening of the skin or hyperpigmentation, again occurring in all races, can be a particular problem for black women as a result of hormonal changes during pregnancy, or the use of the contraceptive pill. Both darkening and lightening of the skin (due to the local increased pigmentation of destruction of melanocytes) can occur as the horny layer of the skin heals after damage caused, for example, by spots and rashes. Common skin conditions such as acne can lead to serious disfigurement for those with black skin. When formulating facial care products for black skin it is therefore especially important to select raw materials shown to possess low comedogenicity so as to avoid irritation or the initiation of comedones 'acne'.

Ashy skin (xerosin) is a particular problem resulting from excessive drying of the skin. This can be caused by harsh detergents or environmental effects such extreme cold spells or excessive dry heat. The condition manifests itself as dry white patches, commonly on elbows, knees and backs of hands. In areas where conditions are extremely dry, occlusive preparations inhibiting water loss are particularly valuable, although type would be entirely inappropriate for areas of high humidity. For these conditions, light moisturising non-occlusive preparations, allowing passage of moisture to and from the skin, are required.

Hair Products

The formulations described in the following sections are examples designed to offer products suitable for restyling Afro hair using treatments which take account of the need to condition and remoisturise before, during, and after treatment. Where applicable, suppliers of formulation ingredients are given. Full details of these, and other suppliers, can be found in Appendix 1.

Relaxing and Restyling Products

Hair-straightening treatment using caustic alkaline chemicals has a severely detrimental effect on the hair shaft. Such treatment should never be used on hair in poor condition. The treatment procedure therefore comprises three stages:

(i) a preconditioning programme
(ii) a relaxer treatment (sodium, potassium or guanidine hydroxide); and
(iii) a post-conditioning treatment

Preconditioning programme A conditioning programme prior to the relaxing treatment is necessary to improve the physical state of the hair. Ideally, this should be started two weeks previously to allow buildup of sebum and protective oils on both hair and scalp. The oily buildup slows the relaxation process and lessens damage to the hair. A three-stage process is recommended.

(i) initial shampoo with protective conditioning shampoo;
(ii) moisturising with hot oil treatment; and
(iii) deep conditioning using rinse-off conditioners containing substantive actives.

Table 50.1. Protective shampoo C1454

	Wt%
Empicol AL30T (ammonium lauryl sulphate, 28%)	30.00
Crotein Q or Crodacel QM (steartrimonium hydrolysed animal protein) or (cocodimonium hydroxyl ethyl cellulose)[b]	0.50
Crodafos SG or N3N (PPG-5 ceteth-10	

phosphate) or (DEA oleth-3 phosphate)[b]	3.00
Incronam 30 (cocoamidopropyl betaine)[b]	10.00
Triethanolamine, 99%	0.30
Deionised water	to 100
Perfume, preservatives, colour	*q.s.*

[a] Albright & Wilson; [b]Croda Chemicals Ltd.

Method of manufacture: dissolve Crotein or Crodacel in water alongwith the Crodafos and triethanolamine; add Empicol followed by Incronam 30. Make final adjustment to pH 5.0-5.5

Table 50.2. Conditioning shampoo C1219

	Wt%
D-Panthenol	0.50
Crodasinic LS30 (sodium lauryl sarcosinate)[a]	20.00
Incronam 30 (cocoamidopropyl betaine)[b]	10.00
Empilan CDE (cocoamide DEA)[b]	5.00
Incroquat SDQ25 (stearalkonium chloride, 25%)[a]	0.20
Croquat L (lauryldimonium hydroxypropyl hydrolysed animal protein)[a]	1.00
EDTA	0.10
Deionised water	to 100
Lactic acid	*q.s. to pH 6.7*
Perfume, preservative, colour	q.s.

[a] Alrbight & Wilson, [b]Croda Chemicals Ltd.

Method of manufacture: warm together all components to 60-65"C. When homogenous, stir to cool.

Table 50.3. Conditioning shampoo C1343 (high concentration)

	Wt%
Incronam 30 (cocoamidopropyl betaine)[a]	13.00
Empicol ESB3 (sodium laureth sulphate, *28%)*[b]	46.00
Crodalan AWS (polysorbate (80) (and) cetyl acetate (and) acetylated lanolin alcohol)[a]	1.00
Crotein Q (steartrimonium hydrolysed animal protein)[a]	1.00
Empilan CDE (cocamide DEA)[b]	1.00
Deionised water	to 1.00
Lactic acid	to
pH 6.00	
Perfume, preservatives, colour	q.s.

[1] Croda Chemicals Ltd.;[b] Albright & Wilson
Method of manufacture: simple blend, with warming and mechanical agitation as necessary. Note this is a high concentrate shampoo; if desired, the detergent content may be reduced to make a cheaper milder product

Conditioning shampoo Conditioning shampoo contain a protective protein and are designed to clean, increase the strength of the hair and reduce the porosity of the hair fibre. They may also be used as post-relaxing conditioners.

Table 50.4. Conditioning shampoo C1571M3

	Wt%
Empicol AL30T (ammonium lauryl sulphate 28%)[a]	40.00
Incronam 30 (cocoamidopropyl betaine)[b]	6.30
Incromate SDL (stearamidopropyl dimethylamine lactate)[b]	2.00
Empilan CDE (cocamide DEA)[3]	2.25
Dow Corning 193 surfactant (dimethicone copolyol)[a]	2.25
EGMS PE3127 (glycol stearate)[b]	1.00
Croquat L (lauryldimonium hydroxypropyl hydrolysed animal protein)[b]	0 50
Crodacol CS/BP (cetostearyl alcohol)[b]	0.5O
Deionised water	to 100
Lactic acid/sodium lactate buffer	to pH 5.50-6.00 (approx. 1.0%)
Perfume, preservative colour	q.s.

Albright & Wilson: [h]Croda Chemicals Ltd.: [a] Dow Corning Ltd.
Method of manufacture: combine all ingredients with half of the quantity of water and heat to approximately 70°C. With stirring, add remaining cold water. Stir to cool

Table 50.5. Pearlised conditioning shampoo C1571M3

	Wt%
Empicol AL30T (ammonium lauryl sulphate, 28%)	40.00
Incronam 30 (cocoamidopropyl betaine)[b]	6.30
Empilan CDE (cocoamide DEA)[a]	2.25
Dow Corning 193 surfactant (dimethicone copolyol)[c]	0.50
EGMS (E 3127 (glycol stearate)[b]	1.00
Croquat L (lauryldimonium hydroxypropyl hydrolysed animal protein)[b]	0.50

Crodaco CS (cetostearyl alcohol)[b]	0.50
Deionised water	to 100
Lactic acid/sodium lactate buffer	to pH 5.00-6.00
Perfume, preservative, colour	q.s.

[a] Albright & Wilson: [b]Croda Chemicals Ltd.: [c] Dow Corning it

Method of manufacture: combine all ingredients (excluding the buffer) with half the quantity of water and heat to approximately 70°C. With stirring, add remaining cold water. Stir to cool. In addition to pretreatment, this shampoo represents an excellent conditioner shampoo for post-treatment cleansing of the hair.

Hot oil treatment This treatment (Table 50.6) can use either a traditional oil-based product, a light mineral oil alone, or an aqueous-based product, which relies on the substantive effects of a cationic material (i.e. cocotrimonium chloride and quaternary proteins or gums) combined with the moisturising effects of a humectant.

Table 50.6. Hot oil treatment C1463M1

	Wt%
White mineral oil (25cSt at 25°C)	to 100
Crodamol ICS (isocetyl stearate)[a]	15.00
Crodamol PMP (PPG-2 myristyl ether propionate)[a]	5.00
Incroquat SDQ-95 (stearalkonium chloride)	0.20
Novol(oleyl alcohol)[a]	2.50
Isopropyl alcohol	1.00
Perfume, preservative, colour	q.s.

[a] Croma Chemicals Ltd

Method of manufacture: simple mixing with gentle heat to dissolve the solid material. Cool. Add perfume

Table 50.7. Deep pre-conditioner C 5004

	Wt%
Lanolic acid (lanolin acid)[a]	2.00
Polawax NF (non-ionic emulsifying wax)[a]	3.00
Novol (oleyl alcohol)[a]	1.00
White petroleum jelly	4.00
Crdacol S95 (stearyl alcohol)[a]	4.00
Incroquat SDQ-25 (stearalkonium chloride, 25% active)[a]	10.00
Crotein O (hydrolysed animal protein)[a]	1.00

Crotein HKP/SE (hydrolysed keratin)	0.50
Croderol GA7000 (glycerine)[a]	3.50
Deionised water	to 100
Perfume, preservative	q.s.

[a] Croda Chemicals Ltd.

Methods of manufacture: melt oils and waxes together and heat to 70°C. Dissolve the protein and aminoacids in water. Heat to 70° and add oil phase. Cool with stirring.

Table 50.8. High activity deep pre-conditioner C5O19

	Wt%
Novol (oleyl alcohol)[a]	1.00
Crodacol C90 (cetyl alcohol)[a]	2.50
Incroquat SDQ-25 (stearalkonium chloride)[a]	1.80
Croquat L (lauryldimonium hydroxypropyl hydrolysed animal protein)[a]	1.00
GMS A/S ESO743 (glyceryl stearate (and) PEG-100 stearate)[a]	3.00
White mineral oil (25cSt at 25°C)	4.00
Deionised water	to 100
Perfume, preservative	q.s.

[a]Croda Chemicals Ltd.

Method of manufacture: heat oil phase at 75°C. Heat the aqueous phase to 8O°C. Add the water to oil phase slowly with stirring. Stir to cool. Fill off at 30°C.

Deep conditioning Deep conditioning treatments use creams containing a high level of quaternary (cationic) product (e.g. stearalkonium chloride), humectant, fats and oily material (Tables 50.7 and 50.8). The conditioner should be applied for 10-20 min and then rinsed off.

Relaxer treatments These consist of two types: (i) sodium/potassium hydroxide or guanidine hydroxide hair-straightening formulations; and (i) thiglycollate-based chemical relaxation treatment.

Sodium/potassium hydroxide or guanidine hydroxide hair-straightening formulations **These** formulations are effective but aggressive. In addition to the ameliorating preconditioning programme outlined, damage other hair is lessened by the inclusion of emollient oils in the products.

Sodium/potassium hydroxide based relaxers (Table 50.9) are formulated as viscous creams. The emulsificalion systems are often based on non-ionic, self-bodying emulsifying waxes, together with auxiliary emulsifiers such as ethodylated alcohols. A sodium hydroxide level of 1.9-2.4% is used in the formulation depending on the strength required. C5042MI contains a protein derivative, for its excellent conditioning effects. High levels (25-30%) of protective emollients, i.e. hydrocarbon oils and waxes, must be included in these formulations to slow down the reaction of the caustic on the hair, and to reduce burning or irritation of the Scalp. It is also important that only materials chemically stable at the high pH resulting from the NaOH are employed in this class of product.

Table 50.9. Hair relaxer creams

	wt% VM5042MI	C1624	C834M1	BW29
Polawax NF (non-ionic emulsifying wax)[a]	7.50	—	—	—
Crodacol C90 (cetyl alcohol)	1.00	—	—	—
White petroleum jelly BP	20.00	20.00	20.00	21.00
White mineral oil (25cSt at 25°C)	10.00	10.00	10.00	15.00
Crodafos N ION (DEA oleth-10 phosphate)[a]	1.50	—	—	—
Crodafos CES (cetearyl alcohol (and) ceteary phosphate)[a]	—	—	—	700
Crodacol S70 (stearyl alcohol)[a]	—	—	—	2.00
Crodacol; C 70 (cetyl alcohol)[a]	—	—	—	1.00
Volpo S10 (steareth-10)[a]	2.50	—	—	—
Solan E (PEG-75 lanolin)[a]	—	0.50	0.50	—
Polawax A32 (non-ionic emulsifying wax)[a]	—	11.00	—	—
Volpo CS15 (ceteareth-15)[a]	—	1.0	—	—
Liquid base CB3929 (mineral oil (and) lanolin alcohol)[a]	—	5.00	—	—
Polawax GP2000)non-ionic emulsifying wax)[a]	—	—	15.00	—
Crodacol S95 (stearyl alcohol)[a]	—	—	1.00	—
Volpo N15 (oleth-15)[a]	—	—	2.00	—
Polycol 5 (laneth-5[a]	—	—	—	1.00
Solan 50 (PEG60 lanolin)[a]	—	—	—	0.50
Propylene glycol	2.00	5.00	2.00	2.00
Deionised water	to 100	to 100	to 100	to 100
Croquat M (cocodimonium hydroxypropyl hydrolysed animal protein)[a]	1.00	—	—	—
Sodium hydroxide, 25% aqueous solution	6.80	8.00	8.50	8.40
Perfume, preservative, colour	*q.s.*	*q.s.*	*q.s.*	*q.s.*

[a]Croda Chemicals Ltd.

Note:

(1) For mild strength product, 7.0-7.5% of a 25% solution of sodium hydroxide is suggested.

(2) For medium strength product, 8.0-8.5% of a 25% solution of sodium hydroxide is suggested.

(3) For high strength product, 9.0-9.5% of 25% solution of sodium hydroxide is suggested.

Method of manufacture: heat oil and water phases separately to 65°C Add water to oils with stirring. Add sodium hydroxide solution at 45°C; add perfume. Continue stirring and cool to 30-35°C, homogenise by milling, cool and fill into container.

Because of the difficulty in formulating products of this class, which are effective, safe and both chemically and physically stable, various raw-material suppliers now offer pre-compounded emulsifying bases. To these bases the appropriate (prescribed) levels of protective emollients, active ingredient (Na or KOH), conditioner and water are added. The manufacturing technique involved in the preparation of these products is essentially the same as that described for the formulation illustrated in Table 50.9.

Alternative alkaline relaxer treatments use guanidine hydroxide in place of sodium hydroxide. Guandine hydroxide is created *in situ* from guanidine carbonate and calcium hydroxide, necessitating a two-component system in which the active chemicals are kept separate until required (Table 50.10 and 50.11). The guanidine relaxer is prepared by mixing four parts of the cream base (Table 50.10) with one part of the liquid activator (Table 50.11). This causes release of guanidine hydroxide to relax the hair.

Relaxation treatment using either sodium hydroxide or guanidine hydroxide systems requires applications of the cream relaxers to the hair for approximately 20 min. after which it is removed by rinsing and shampooing. Extreme caution should always be exercised both in the development of and use of these products. Appropriate trials and testsmust be performed in order to ensure the product is not over-aggressive, thus being destructive to the hair or irritating to the scalp. Following this residual alkaline material on the hair must be completely neutralised. This is accomplished by washing the hair with an acid-based shampoo (Table 50.12). In order to ensure stability of the detergent base in the acidic environment, ammonium salts (e.g. ammonium lauryl sulphate) and amphoteric products (e.g. cocamidopropyl betaine) are incorporated into the shampoo. The use of an acid-base indicator will give a change of colour in the lather when all the residual alkali has been neutralised.

Table 50.10 Guanidine hydroxide hair relaxer c5002; cream base

	Wt%
Polawax (non-ionic emulsifying wax)	15.00
Crodacol CS/BP (cetostearyl alcohol)[a]	1.00
Volpo N10 (oleth-10)[a]	2.00
White petroleum jelly	8.00
White mineral oil (25cSt at 25°C)	9.70
Deionised water	to 100
Propylene glycol	5.00
Calcium hydroxide	5.00
Perfume, preservatives	q-s.

[a]Croda Chemicals Ltd.

Method of manufacture; heat the oil phase and water separately to 60°C. Add water to the oils with efficient agitation. Continue to stir until the cream starts to thicken (around 45°C).Add calcium hydroxide and stir with scrapping to disperse.

Table 50.11. Guanidine hydroxide hair relaxer C5002 liquid activator

	Wt%
Guanidine carbonate	25.00
Keltrol F (xanthan gum)[a]	0.20
Deionised water	to 00
Preservatives	*q.s.*

[a]Kelco/AIL Ltd

Method of manufacture: dissolve the Keltrol and preservatives in the water with stirring and heat to 70°C. Cool to 45°C and add the guanidine carbonate.

Table 50.12. Neutralising shampoo C5003

	Wt%
Empicol AL30T (ammonium lauryl sulphate, 28%)[a]	20.0-40.00
Incronam 30 (cocoamidopropyl betaine)[b]	5.00
Incromine Oxide C (cocoamidopropyl amine oxide)[b]	3.00
Crodafos SG (PPG-5 ceteth-20 phosphate)[b]	3.00
Crotein HKP S F (hydrolysed keratin)[b]	1.00
Citric acid	1.00
Deionised water	to 100
Perfume, preservative, colour	*q. s.*

[a] Albright & Wilson; [b]Croda Chemicals Ltd.

Method of manufacture: add the Empicol A130T to water at 65°C. Add the Incronam 30 and the Incromine Oxide C; mix until uniform; Add the Crodafos SG. Cool to 50°C and add the Crotein HKP S F and citric acid. Cool to room temperature

Thiglycollate-based chemical relaxation treatment An alternative chemical treatment giving a waved, less curly appearance to the hair, instead of the aggressive straightening achieved with sodium hydroxide relaxer products, is based on sulphur-containing reducing agents, principally Thiglycollates. Thiglycollates disrupt sulphur-sulphur bonds in the hair protein by their reducing action; subsequent application of an oxidising agent (neutraliser) results in reformation of the protein sulphur-sulphur linkages.

Table 50.13. Ammonium thioglycollate hair-relaxed cream C 5001

	Wt%
Crodacol C90 (cetyl alcohol)[a]	2.00
Crodafos N10N (DEA oleth-10 phosphate)[a]	1.50
Volpo S2 (steareth-2)[a]	0.50
White mineral oil (25 cSt at 25°C)	13.00
White petroleum jelly BP	11.50
Crosterene SA4310 (stearic acid)[a]	8.00
Deionised water	to 100
Propylene glycol	2.00
Volpo S10 (steareth-10)[a]	2.50
EDTA	0.50
Croquat M (cocodimonium hydrolysed animal protein)[b]	1.00
Ammonium thioglycollate, 60%	9.00
Ammonium hydroxide 88	4.63
Perfume, preservative, colour	q.s.

[a]Croda Chemicals Ltd.

Method of manufacture: heat oil and water phases separately to 65-70°C. Add water phase to oils under stirrer. Add ammonium hydroxide to ammonium thioglycollate. Cool emulsion to 45°C and add ammonium thioglycollate mix. Final pH must be adjusted to 9.5±0.2 by further addition, if necessary, of ammonium hydroxide.

During the reforming of these bonds, the hair fibre is styled into a new, relaxed structure, resulting in a less rightly curled appearance. As with the more drastic caustic-based treatments, thioglycollate relaxing of the hair has an adverse drying effect on the fibres—the hair will feel rough and have a greater porosity. An elaborate, conditioning, after care programme is therefore essential to keep the treated hair in optimum condition. Note that in the US hair is straightened with caustic, a process which can result in much hair fall and if drastic, in baldness at the scalp.

Soft curls are provided using thioglycollate treatment to relax the hair and then rolling onto rods (Jerry curls).

Ammonium thioglycollate products are formulated as gels or viscous creams (Table 50.13). They are applied to the hair for up to one hour, prior to wrapping the straightened hair on curling rods to style it. A slightly weaker ammonium thioglycollate solution (often called a curl booster or charger) is also applied. This is similar to thioglycollate permanent-wave treatments for Caucasian hair.

The incorporation of a quaternised protein provides beneficial conditioning effects, but these are merely temporary and will be removed when the hair is next shampooed. A more permanent conditioning treatment (e.g. the Kerasol* process) can also be incorporated into the thioglycollate treatment. This procedure provides a conditioning action, which is effective through numerous shampooings, by covalently bonding the conditioner protein 'Kerasol' to the hair between the reduction and oxidation steps in the waving process. In addition to imparting general condition, the hair is left more receptive to moisture, thus enhancing the effect of subsequent treatments such as curl activators, and achieving maximum beneficial effect. The overall process is as follows:

Table 50.14. Clear gel perm wave C279

	wt%
Deionised water	to 100
Procetyl AWS (PPG-5 ceteth-20)	or
Solan E (PEG-75 lanolin)[a]	1.00
Carbopol941 (carbomer 941)[a]	1.86
Thioglycollate acid, 70%	7.24
Ammonium hydroxide, 28%	8.35
Sodium heptanoate dihydrate[a]	0.10
Perfume, preservative, colour	q.s.

[a]Croda Chemicals Ltd; [b]B.F. Goodrich

Method of manufacture: dissolve Procetyl AWS/Solan E in a little water. Dissolve sodium heptanoate into 5% of water. Hydrate Carbopol in rest of water; when hydrated add ammonium hydroxide solution, then Procetyl AWS Solan E solution; lastly add sodium heptanoate dihydrate solution. pH should be 9.5+0.1 Note: hydroxyethyl cellulose may be employed as the gellant in place of the carbopol if desired.

Table 50.15. Kerasol permanent conditioner C1401

	Wt%
Kerasol (soluble animal keratin)[a]	5.00-10.00
Crotein Q (steartriammonium hydrolysed animal protein)[a]	0.50

Deionised water	to 100
Perfume, preservatives, colour	q.s.

"Croda Chemicals Ltd.

Method of manufacture: simple blend of components in water

(i) Perm reduction step (Table 50.14)

(ii) Rinse

(iii) Kerasol conditioning treatment (Table 50.15)

(iv) No rinse

(v) Neutraliser oxidation step (Table 50.16)

The neutralising process, during which the sulphur linkages are reformed and the hair is 'locked' into its new shape or style, uses products based on peroxides or bromates. This is exemplified by the neutraliser shown in Table 50.16, which is based on sodium bromate.

The thioglycollate treatment is normally concluded with a conditioner, which must be light to avoid weighting down the curls. The product shown in 17 combines a fatly quaternary and a humectant to aid in conditioning and moisturising the hair. The use of a moisturising spray, combing humectant (e.g. propylene glycol) and acetamide MEA, together with protein additives, for remoisturising and improving the hair condition, is also popular.

Table 50.16. Sodium bromate neutraliser C5045/hydrogen peroxide neutraliser no. 5

	wt%	
Croduret 40 (PEG-40 hydrogenated caster oil)[a]	3.00	
Cellobond HEC5000A (hydroxy ethyl cellulose)[b]	00.0.30	—
Sodium bromate	10.00	—
Disodium phosphate	0.50	—
Deionised water	85.20	89.50
Crillet 1/perfume[a]	1.00	1.00
Hydrogen peroxide (30%)	—	6.50
Dow Corning Q2-7224[c]	—	4.00
Trimethylsilylamodimethicone (and) dimethicone and) octoxynol 40 (and) isolaureth-6 (and) glycol		
phosphoric acid	— to	pH 3.4

[a]Croda Chemicals Ltd; [b]BP Chemicals; [c]Dow Corning Ltd.

Method of manufacture C5045: dissolve HEC in water and heat to 80°C, when hydrated, add Croduret and Crillet perfume blend, at 40-45°C add disodium phosphate and sodium bromate, adjust pH to 7.00+ or -0.30. Method of manufacture no. 5: mix all ingredients in the order given. Adjust pH to 3.4 phosphoric acid.

Table 50.17. Hair conditioner C1410

	wt%
Conditioner base CB0967 (proprietary blend)[a]	4.00
Incromectant AMEA-70 (acetamide MEA)[a]	5.00
Deionised water	to 100
Lactic acid	to pH 4.00-4.50
Perfume, preservatives, colour	*q.s.*

[a]Croda Chemicals Ltd.

Method of manufacture: heat all components together to 65-70°C, except perfume and lactic acid. Stir to cool, perfuming and adjusting pH to 4.0-4.5 at 45°C. Fill off at 40°C.

Further possible treatments include curl activator products, hair-grooming creams and lotions, and moisturising and oil sheen sprays, of which can be used to impart gloss and sheen, and to enhance the lustre of the hair. Curl activators based on Carbopol (see Table 50.18), contain a high level of humectants to activate the curl. In temperate zones; where a lighter treatment is required, propylene glycol in combination with glycerine is the humectant; in hot climates a heavier, more durable, higher gloss preparation is recommended, with partial or total replacement of the glycol with glycerine. The preferred ration of glycerine to glycol is generally 2:1. Extremely hot climates require the inclusion of suitable block copolymers (e.g. Ucon 50 to HB660) to give a more lasting effect. The curl activator gel shown in Table 50.19 is based *on* a microemulsion gel, a formulation which is suitable for all climatic conditions. Again, high levels of propylene glycol/glycerine are used. These systems, are, however, sensitive to minor changes in raw materials and, due to the inherently high surfactant level, can be irritating to the eye.

Table 50.18. Curl activator gels based on Carbopol

	wt%	
	C1391	C1398
Carbopol 940 (carbomer 940)[a]	0.50	0.66
Propylene glycol/glycerine	25.00	12.00
Crillet 1 (polysorbate 20), Procetyl AWS (PPG-5 ceteth-20), or Croduret: 40 (PEG-40) hydrogeneated castor oil)[b]	6.00	5.00
Deionised water	to 100	to 100
Triethanolamine, 99%	to pH 6.0-7.0	—
Croderol GA7000 (glycerine)[b]	—	10.00
Diisopropylamine	—	to pH 6.5-7.0
Perfume, preservatives, colour	*q.s.*	*q.s.*

[a]*B.F.* Goodrich; [b]Croda Chemicals Ltd.

Method of manufacture: hydrate Carbopol in water (60-65°C). Add propylene glycol and preservatives, neutralised to ph 6.5-7.0 with amine. Combine perfume and Crillet, and add to Carbopol gel. Stir until a clear homogeneous gel is obtained. Fill off. Note: for the preparation of heavier texture improved durability, the propylene glycol may be wholly or partially replaced with glycerine.

Table 50.19. Curl Activator gel C1128

	wt%
Crodafos N3N (DBA oleth-3 phosphate)[a]	7.48
Volpo N5 (olelh-5)[a]	10.88
White mineral oil (25 cSt at. 25°C)	16.05
Incromectant AMEA (acetamide MEA)[a]	0.20
Sorbitol. 70% solution	11.00
Croderol GA7000 (glycerine)[a]	7.00
Hexylene glycol	2.00
Deionised water	to 100
Perfume, preservatives, colour	q.s.

[a]Croda Chemicals Ltd.

Method of manufacture: heat oil phase to 65-70°C. Heat water phase to similar temperature. Slowly add water to oils with stirring, and cool rapidly.

Recommended formulations for emulsion-based hair-grooming products (combining humectants and emollient oils), a moisturising spray, and a comb-out oil are shown in Tables 50.20 to 50.23. These products are used at the end of the thioglycollate treatment to help to maintain the hair in its optimum condition.

Table 50.20. Hair grooming cream/lotion C 1450

	wt%
GMS A/S ESO743 (glyceryl stearate (and) PEG-100 stearate)[a]	4.00
Crodamol MM (myristyl myristate)[a]	4.00
Liquid base CB3929 (mineral oil (and) lanolin alcohols)[a]	3.00
Crodalan LA4028 (cetyl acetic (and) acetylated lanolin alcohol)[a]	1.00
GMS GEO803 (glyceryl stearate)[a]	2.50
Volpo CS20 (ceteareth-20)[a]	1.00
Squalene	0.60
Deionised water	to 100
Croderol GA7000 (glycerine)[a]	10.00
Incromectant AMEA-70 (acetamide MEA)[a]	1.00

D-Panthenol	0.40
Incroquat SDQ25 (stearalkonium chloride)[a]	1.00
Perfume, preservatives	*q.s.*

[a]Croda Chemicals Ltd.

Method of manufacture: Combine oil phase and water phase and heat to 65- 70°C. Add water to oils with stirring. Stir to 45°C and perfume. Stir to cool.

Table 50.21. Hair-softening spray lotion C1129

	wt%
Croderol GA7000 (glycerine)[a]	10.00
Propylene glycol	20.00
Perfume	0.20
Crillet 1 (polysorbate 20)[a]	2.00
Deionised water	to 100
Preservatives, colour	q.s.

[a]Croda Chemicals Ltd.

Method of manufacture: blend Crillet and perfume, add Croderol, glycol, water and preservative. Stir till clear.

Post-conditioning treatment Post-relaxation treatment to combat the defatting nature of the relaxer includes use of a conditioner as in the preconditioning programme (Tables 50.1 to 50.5), together with a scalp grease (24) to lubricate the scalp and prevent dryness and flaking between roots.

To complete the relaxation treatment the hair can be styled in the normal way. Examples of a setting lotion and styling gels are given in Tables 25 and 26. A hair-groom cream, which is applied to provide a moisturising, glossy effect, is shown in Table 50.27.

Table 50.22. Moisturising sprays mist C5016

	wt%
Propylene glycol	7.00
Croderol GA 7000 (glycerine)[a]	1.00
Incromectant AMEA-70 (acetamide MEA)[a]	1.50
Crotein HKP/SF (hydrolysed keratin)[a]	0.50
Crodacel QM (cocodimonium hydroxy ethylcellulose)[a]	0.50
Deionised water	to 100
Perfumes, preservatives, colour	*q.s.*

[a]Croda Chemicals Ltd.

Method of manufacture: dissolve Crodacel QM in water. Add the protein and amino acids. Blend in the remainder of the ingredients. Fill off. This product designed to be dispensed from a mechanical pump applicator.

Table 50.23. Comb-out oil C5008

	wt%
Lanexol AWS (PPG-12 PEG-50 lanolin)[a]	4.00
Crotein Q (steartrimonium hydrolysed animal protein)[a]	1.00
Crodacel GA7000 (glycerine)[a]	10.00
Crodacel QM (cocodimonium hydroxy ethyl cellulose)[b]	0.10
Dow Corning 193 fluid (dimethicone copolyol)[b]	0.50
Deionised water	to 100
Perfume, preservatives, colour	q.s.

[a]Croda Chemicals Ltd.; [b]Dow Corning Ltd.

Method of manufacture: combine ingredients under good agitation.

Table 50.24. Scalp grease C5048

	wt%
Paraffin wax (140/145°C)	5.00
Crodamol IPM (isopropyl myristate)[a]	6.00
White mineral oil (25 cSt at 25°C)	30.00
Lanolin[a]	10.00
Super Hartolan (lanolin alcohol)[a]	3.00
White petroleum jelly	46.00
Perfume, preservatives, colour	q.s.

[a]Croda Chemicals Ltd.

Method of manufacture: heat all ingredients together with the exception of the perfume. Cool, stir in fragrance and fill.

Table 50.25. Setting lotion C1444

	wt%
PVP/VA S630 (PVP/VA Copolymer)[a]	1.50-3.00
Gafquat 755N (polyquaternium 11)[a]	1.50-3.00
Deionised water	to 100
Crillet 1 (polysorbate 20) or Crovol 70 series (ethoxylated vegetable oils)[b]	q.s.
Preservatives	q.s.

[a]GAF Europe, [b]Croda Chemicals Ltd.

Method of manufacture: dissolve PVP/VA in water, followed by Gafquat. Pre-dissolve perfume in Crillet or Crovol (ratio 3:1) and add to water phase with stirring. Add preservative and colour and fill off. Note: The ratio of perfume to Crillet or Crovol may have to be altered to achieve clarily depending on perfume used. One part perfume to four parts solubiliser is given as normal starting point.

Table 50.26. Hair styling gels

	wt%	
	C1123	C1465
PVP K30 (polyvinyl pyrrolidone)[a]	2.00	3.00
Carbopol 940 (carbomer 940)[b]	0.50	0.50
Volpo N20 (oleth-20)[c]	1.00	—
Triethanolamine, 99%	—	0.75
Procetyl AWS (PPG-5 ceteth 20)[c]	0.50	—
Ethanol 74 OP	—	15.00
Crotein O (hydrolysed animal protein)[c]	0.50	—
Uvinol D50 (benzophenone-2)[d]	0.10	—
Crillet 1 (polysorbate 20)[c]	—	0.50
EDTA	0.10	—
Disopropanolamine	0.30	—
Deionised water	to 100	to 100
Perfume, preservatives, colour	q.s.	*q.s.*

[a]GAF Europe; [b]B.F. Goodrich: [c]Croda Chemicals Ltd., [d]BASF (UK) Ltd

Method of manufacture:

(1) Cl 123: hydrate the carbopol in one third of the water (60-65°C). Dissolve the remaining components in the rest of the water. Mix together—the product will gel. Adjust to pH 6-7.

(2) C1465: hydrate the Carbopol in one third of the water (60-65°C) When fully hydrated, neutralise with amine to form the gel. Dissolve PVP K30 in ethanol and add to gel. Pre-dissolve perfume in Crillet, add to gel and stir to clear. Fill off.

Hair Pomades and Grooming Aids

Hair pomades—the original hair products—are examples of mild products offering modern formulations for use with a very traditional African hairstyle. 'Canerow' is the art of plaiting the hair close to the scalp in a variety of patterns, a style which has passed from generation to generation amongst African women.

Table 50.27. Hair groom cream W/OC 933

	wt%
Polawax GP200 (non-ionic emulsifying wax)[a]	5.00
White mineral oil (25 cST at 25°C)	40.00
White petroleum jelly BP	4.00
GMS N/E GEO803 (glyceryl stearate)[a]	0.50
Deionised water	to 100
Carbopol 934 (carbomer 934)[b]	0.50
Propylene glycol	5.00
Triethanolamine, 99%	to pH 6.8-7.0
Perfume, preservatives	*q.s.*

[a]Croda Chemicals Ltd.; [b]B.F. Goodrich

Method of manufacture: combine oil phase and heat to 70°C. Hydrate Carbopol in water phase, and heat to 70°C. Add oil to water with efficient agitation, add triethanolamine at 60°C followed by perfume at 50°C. Fill off at 40°C.

Traditionally, natural oils such as shea butter and coconut oil are used to keep the scalp supple while the hair is being teased and stretched into tight plaits. The modern formulation for a hair pomade, C1411 (Table 50.28), consists of a blend of oil, petroleum jelly and waxes. This pomade is also suitable for use during the 'hot-comb' procedure for temporarily straightening the hair, a treatment which runs a considerable risk of burning the scalp and also has a damaging effect on the hair shaft. The temporary straightening achieved in this way only remains until the hair comes into contact with moisture, when the crinkly appearance will re-occur.

Table 50.28. Hair pomade C1411

	wt%
Lanolin[a]	4.00
White mineral oil (25 cSt at 215°C)	to 100
Microcrystalline wax (78-82°C)	28.00
Aluminium stearate G[b]	1.20
Crodamol IPM (isopropyl myristate)[a]	2.50
BHT	0.01
Perfume, preservative, colour	q.s.

[a]Croda Chemicals Ltd.; [b]Durham Chemicals Ltd.

Method of manufacture: add aluminium stearate to cold mineral oil whilst stirring. Stir well until thoroughly dispersed. Maintain mixing and heat oil

105-110°C. adding microcrystalline wax. When the aluminium stearate has completely dissolved, a slightly gelatinous solution will form. Begin cooling, adding the rest of the ingredients, except perfume, at 90°C. Add perfume at 75°C. Fill off at 70°C

Skin Products

Dermatological problems can often arise due to the use of cheap semi-refined materials; the use of reliable suppliers, coupled with an understanding of the significance of raw materials specifications, is an important step in producing satisfactory results. Careful raw materials selection plays an important part in designing formulations for any product, but is especially significant for products designed for black skin. The cosmetic qualities of all materials must be ensured.

Raw Material Selection—Factors for Consideration

Emollient comedogenicily The skin condition of acne (or comedone formation) causes particular problems to black skin. Work on the comedogenicity of common cosmetic emollients to assess their potential to cause (or aggravate) comedones, has resulted in the grading of emollients according to low, medium or high comedogenic categories (Table 50.29 to 50.31). This provides a useful guide when formulating. Low comedogenic rated products (Table 50.29) are recommended for use in facial care products, materials with a medium rating (Table 50.30) can be used with caution, while a high comedogenic rating (Table 50.31) identifies materials that are preferably avoided or kept to a minimum.

Table 50.29. Emollient materials with a low comedogenic effect

Avocado oil	Beeswax (25% in mineral oil)	Candelilla wax
Castor oil	Glycerine	Cetyl alcohol
Cholesterol	Lanolin oil	Isocetyl stearate
Lanolin	Pentaerythritol	White mineral oil
PEG-200	tetraisostearate	Penterythritol
Spermaceti wax	Stearyl alcohol	tetracaprylate
Stearic acid	Diisopropyl adipate	Propylene glycol
Octyl palmitate (5%)	PPG-2 myristyl	Dimethicone
Cyclomethicone	propionate	

Table 50.30. Emollient materials with a medium comedogenic effect

Glyceryl monostearate	Myristyl myristate-Octyl	palmitate (50%)
Ethoxylated lanolin	White petroleum jelly	Capric caprylic triglyceride
Olive oil	Arachis oil	
Sesame oil	Lanolin alcohols	

Table 50.31. Emollient materials with a high comedogenic effect

Cocoa butter	Isopropyl myristate	Isopropyl palmitate
Acetylated lanolin	Oleyl alcohol	Crude petroleum jelly
Alcohols	Isopropyl lanolate	Sweet almond oil

Occlusivity Another important aspect of cosmetic products is the degree to which passage of water (or gaseous vapour) to and from the skin is controlled. Cosmetics that impede insensible perspiration are deemed 'occlusive', a phenomenon attributed to the emollient phase having a linear structure, which acts as a barrier on the skin. Occlusive preparation can lead to uncomfortable sensations and give rise to localised heating of the skin and prickly heat. However, if correctly manipulated, such characteristics can be used to advantage in creams designed for treatment of ultra-dry skin caused by adverse physical and environmental conditions. By preventing moisture loss, skin can be kept hydrated and moisturised from within. Materials suitable for such applications (e.g. treatment of ashy skin at elbows and knees) are high quality white mineral oils and petroleum jelly. Lanolin and certain derivatives are similarly valuable since they are capable of retaining moisture in an emulsified form at the skin's surface. Materials such as lanolin, liquid lanolin, lanolin alcohols and lanolin absorption bases are all suitable for use in preparations requiring occlusive properties. The traditional use of natural vegetable oils such as shea butter and palm oil, which applied neat to the skin, has generally been replaced by petroleum jelly and mineral oil. These achieve a similar but more comfortable effect.

The formulation of products for hot humid climatic conditions, where water loss from the skin is important, requires the use of ingredients that will operate to reduce the occlusivity of the cosmetic product. In particular, inclusion of a porositone (a branched chain ester) such as 2-ethyl hexyl palmitate (deemed non-occlusive) serves to provide low occlusive, light-textured creams and lotions. Other suitable branched chain esters are di-2-ethyl hexyl adipate, cetostearyl octanoate, 2-ethyl hexyl cocoate, 2-ethyl hexyl succinate and acetylated lanolin alcohol.

Emulsification Systems

The traditional emulsification system involves the use of soaps, the properties of which naturally confer an alkaline pH to the cosmetic product. This can theoretically damage the acid mantle of the skin-part of the skin's natural protective system—leaving it susceptible to bacterial attack and skin disorders. Despite this, many market leader products with good safety records have been used on amine soap systems, particularly the triethanolamine stearate system with a pH of 7.5-8.5. The aforementioned use of highly refined materials for cosmetic products is particularly important in the case of amines; low quality triethanolamine can contain secondary amines as impurities.

These materials are recognised for their potential for forming nitrosamines—carcinogenic chemicals resulting from the interaction of secondary amines and nitrites.

Preferred emulsification systems for more sophisticated products are non-ionic materials. These give the formulator greater flexibility in terms of the type of emulsion (oil-in-water or water-in-oil), pH and inclusion of additional materials (e.g. cationic germicides). Favoured non-ionic emulsifiers (and emulsifier combinations) involve sorbitan esters and their ethoxylated castor oil derivatives, and surface-active lanaolin derivatives.

Humectant selection Most cosmetic creams and lotions contain humectants to prevent the product drying out at the surface; the humectants also act as moisturisers on the skin. In dry climates, the occlusivity approach is a practical method for retaining skin moisture.

Table 50.32. O/W hand and body lotions

	wt%		
	C1076M1	C1282B	C1437M 1
Crodamol IPM (isopropyl myristate)[a]	5.00	—	3.00
Polawax GP200 (non-ionic self-emulsifying wax)[a]	—	2.00	2.70
Crosterene SA4310 (stearic acid)[a]	—	1.00	0.18
Crodamol CAP (cetearyl octanoate)[a]	2.00	—	—
Silicone fluid 200/100 cSt (dimethicone)[b]	2.00	—	—
Crodafos CDP (DEA ethyl phosphate)	—	0.50	—
GMS S/E GE0802 (glyceryl stearate S/E)[a]	—	—	1.50
Lanolin[a]	—	0.50	—
White mineral oil (25 cSt at 25°C)	5.00	2.00	2.10
Crodamol W (stearyl heptanoate)[a]	—	2.00	—
Crodamol OHS (octyl hydroxystearated)[a]	—	—	2.70
GMS A/S ES0743 (glyceryl stearate and) PEG-100 stearate)[a]	6.00	—	—
Refined cocoa butter	1.50	—	—
Deionised water	to 100	to 100	to 100
Propylene glycol	2.00	—	2.20
Croderol GA7000 (glycerine)[a]	—	3.00	—
Sodium lactate lactic acid buffer solution (pH 5.5)[a]	1.00	—	—
Carbopol 941 (carbomer 941)[c]	—	0.10	0.10
Triethanolamine, refined	—	0.60	0.10
Perfume, preservative, colour	*q.s.*	*q.s.*	*q.s.*

[a]Croda Chemicals Ltd; [b]'Dow Corning Ltd.; [c]B.F. Goodrich

Method of manufacture: heat oil and water phases separately to 65-70°C. Where included, Carbopol should be hydrated in the water phase first, omitting the amine. Add water to oil phase under stirrer and stir to cool. The carbopol should be neutralised with amine at 60°C. Perfume at 40-45°C and fill off at 30°C.

In the lighter preparation, the cream itself can moisturise due to the inclusion of suitable moisturing components in the formulation. Typical humectants used to achieve this are glycerine, sorbitol, polyethylene glycol, sodium pyrrolidone carboxylate, sodium lactate/ lactic acid buffers and urea. Acyl Alkanolamides have also been shown to be effective moisturisers.

Other highly successful materials for use in moisturising cosmetic products are proteins and amino acids. These have the ability to retain high levels of moisture while imparting a pleasant feel to the skin. Classically, collagen has been employed in this role, but other useful protein derivatives include hydrolysed animal and plant-derived proteins, together with the somewhat more evocative proteins derived from silk, egg and *milk. In* more up-market products, special *complexes* of proteinaceous materials, such as hyaluronic acid/protein complex and chondroitin sulphate/protein complex, have been shown to improve extensibility and elasticity of the skin. Lanolin is also particularly valuable additive in this class of moisturiser.

Other highly successful materials for use in moisturising cosmetic products are proteins and amino acids. These have the ability to retain high levels of moisture while imparting a pleasant feel to the skin.

Table 50.33. All-over body creams

	wt%		
	C1433	C1409	C1416
Liquid base CB3929 (mineral oil (and) lanolin alcohol)[a]	6.50	—	—
Crodamol OP (octyl palmitate)[a]	—	4,00	2.00
Crodamol LA (cetyl acetate (and) acetylated lanolin alcohol)[a]	3.50	—	—
Crodamol 1PM (isopropyl myristate)	—	6.00	—
White mineral oil (25 cSt at 25°C)	—	—	2.00
GMS A/S ES0743 (glyceryl stearate (and) PEG-100 stearate)[a]	4.30	6.00	—
GMS N/E ES0803 (glyceryl stearate)[a]	—	3.00	5.00
Volpo CS10 (ceteareth-10)[a]	—	1.00	—
Refined cocoa butter	—	—	2.00
Fluilan (lanolin oil)[a]	—	—	1.00
Crosterene SA4310 (stearic acid)[a]	4.30	3.00	2.00
Crodamol CAP (cetearyl octanoate)	3.00	—	—
Polawax GP200 (non-ionic self-emulsifying wax)[a]		3.00	3.00

Dt-Alpha tocopherol[a]	—	0.50	—
Silicone fluid 200/100 cSt (dimethicone)	—	—	1.00
Almond oil	—	1.00	—
Cithrol 6MS fPEG-12 *slearate)*[a]	—	—	1.00
Deionised water	to 100	to 100	to 100
Propylene glycol	1.50	—	—
Croderol GA7000 (glycerine)[a]	—	2.50	4.00
Carbopol 934 (carbomer 934)[d]	—	0.25	0.25
Triethanolamine, refined	—	0.60	0.60
Perfume, preservatives, colour	q.s.	q.s.	q.s.

[a]Croda Chemicals Ltd. [b]BASF (UK) Ltd; [c]Dow Corning Ltd.; [d]B.F. Goodrich
Where included, Carbopol should be *hydrated in the* water first, *omitting the* amine. Add water to *oil* phase under stirrer and stir to cool. The Carbopol should neutralised with amine at 60°C. Perfume at 40-45°C and fill off at 30°C.

Table 50.34. W/O general purpose creams

	wt%		
	C741	C436	C489M
Crill 6 (sorbitan isostearate)[a]	2.50	—	—
Liquid base CB3939 (mineral oil (and) lanolin alcohol)[a]	5.00	12.00	—
White microcrystalline wax (78-82°C)	9.00	5.80	3.40
Hartolite (modified lanolin alcohols)	—	3.16	—
Aluminium stearate G[b]	0.10	—	—
Satulan (hydrogenated lanolin)[a]	—	—	2.50
White mineral oil (25 cSt at 25°C)	16.50	8.70	16.00
White petroleum jelly BP	—	—	2.50
Ozokerite wax 65-70°C	—	2.20	—
Lanolin[a]	—	—	9.50
BHT	0.01	0.01	0.01
Crodacol CS/BP (cetostearyl alcohol)[a]	—	0.30	—
Croderol GA7000 (glycerine)[a]	1.50	2.50	3.50
Magnesium sulphate	0.70	0.70	0.70
Deionised water	to 100	to 100	to 100
Perfume, preservatives, colour	q.s.	q.s.	*q.s.*

Croda Chemicals Ltd. [b]Durham Chemicals Ltd.
Methods of manufacture: heal oil and water phases separately to 65-70°C. Add water to oils with stirring. Stir to cool, adding perfume at 45°C. When cool, homogenise with triple roll mill or other suitable equipment.

Table 50.35. O/W glycerine silicone hand creams

	wt% C1432M1	C1502
Silicone fluid Fl 11/200 cSt (dimethicone)[a]	3.00	3.00
Crodacol C90 (cetyl alcohol)[b]	4.00	9.00
GMS N/E GE0803 (glyceryl stearate)[b]	2.0	—
Crodex A (anionic emulsifying wax BP)[b]	7.00	10.00
Crodamol 1PM (isopropyl myristate)[b]	5.00	—
Crodamol OHS (octyl hydroxysterate)[b]	—	3.00
Deionised water	to 100	to 100
Crodroi GA7000 (glycerine)[b]	10.00	35.00
Perfume, preservatives, colour	q.s.	q.s.

[a]Dow Corning Ltd.; [b]Croda Chemicals Ltd.

Methods of manufacture: heat oil and water phases separately to 65-70°C Add water to oils with mechanical stirring. Stir to 45°C and perfume. Sir to cool and fill off.

Skin creams and lotions Skin creams and lotions fall into two categories: (i) those for use in warm humid climates; and (ii) those for use in dry climates or during the dry season. The first category comprise relatively light-textured products with low occlusivity, exemplified by all-over skin-care lotions (Table 50.32); and all over body creams (Table 50.33).

For the second category, water-in-oil emulsions are favoured. The skin-cream formulations shown in Table 50.34 include a super-emollient moisturising cream (C489M) designed for treating 'ashy skins'. The moisturising hand creams shown in Table 50.35 are characterised by high levels of glycerine and silicone incorporated into the emulsion system. These hand creams deposit a wax-like film, which gives a dry emollience and avoids excessive oiliness.

An additional product that assumes importance in the black populace is generally termed complexion or fade cream. This contains hydroquinone, a chemical product that is used to lighten the skin, and is commonly misunderstood as making black people whiter. In fact, hydroquinone creams are more often used to lighten specific darker areas of skin (the result of hyperpigmentation), thus 'evening-out' the skin tone. Formulations for hydroquinone creams are shown Table 50.36.

Table 50.36. Hydroquinone creams

	wt% C1420	C1564
Liquid base CB3929 (mineral oil (and) lanolin alcohol)[a]	7.00	7.00
Crodacol CS BP (cetostearyl alcohol)[a]	5.00	5.00
GMS A/S ES0743 (glyceryl stearate (and) PEG-100 stearate)[a]	10.00	10.00
Polycol 15 (laneth-15)[a]	3.00	
Deionised water	to 100	to 100
Croderol GA 7000 (glycerine)[a]	2.00	
PEG-1500	—	4.00
Ascorbic acid	0.20	0.20
Citric acid	to pH 4.00	—
Hydroquinone	2.00	2.00
Sodium metabisulphite	0.10	0.20
Perfume, preservatives, colour	q.s.	*q.s.*
EDTA	0.30	0.35

[a]Croda Chemicals Ltd

Method of manufacture: heat the water and oil phases to 65-70°C. Add the water phase to the oil phase with stirring. Stir until 40-45°C. Add, in order, sodium metabisulphite, ascorbic acid, hydroquinone and citric acid. Perfume at 40°C (the perfume must not react with hydroquinone or bisulphite). Adjust the pH value, if necessary, to 4.00-4.50 with citric acid.

General Practical Considerations

Many of the precautions outlined in this chapter apply to the general manufacture of make-up (colour cosmetics). The manufacture of ethnic products, however, necessitates a complete range of different colour shades that are complementary with black skin. All the normal rules for testing and evaluating product stability and safety apply but particular attention to the special market place conditions are essential. Severe conditions of humidity, heat and UV radiation occurring in parts of Africa should be carefully considered when determining test conditions and microbiological preservation.

51

Important Details for Setting up

MANUFACTURE OF COSMETIC FOR SALE [OR FOR DISTRIBUTION]

Manufacture on more than one set of premises. — If cosmetics are manufactured on more than one premises, a separate application for each such premises shall be made and a separate license obtaining for each such premises.

Application for license to manufacture cosmetics [for sale or for distribution]. —

(1) Application for grant or renewal of [license to manufacture cosmetics for sale or for distribution] [shall be made up to ten items for each category of cosmetics categorized in Schedule MI! to the Licensing Authority appointed by the State Government for the purpose of this part (hereinafter in this Part referred to as Licensing Authority) in form 31 and shall be accompanied by a license fee of rupees two thousand and five hundred and an inspection fee of rupees one thousand for every inspection thereof or for the purpose of renewal of license.]

(2) If a person applies for the renewal of license after expiry but within six months of such expiry, the fee hundred plus an additional fee at the rate of rupees one thousand.

(3) Application by a license to manufacture additional items of cosmetics shall be accompanied by a fee [rupees one hundred for each item subject to a maximum of rupees three thousand for each application].

(4) Afee of [rupees two hundred and fifty] shall be paid for duplicate copy of a license issued under sub-rule (1), if the original is defaced, damaged or lost.

Application for loan license to manufacture cosmetics. —

(1) Application for grant or renewal of a loan license for the manufacture for sale of cosmetics [shall be made up to ten items of each category of cosmetics categorized in Schedule MII in form 31A to the Licensing Authority and shall be accompanied by a license fee of rupees two thousand and five hundred and an inspection fee of rupees one thousand for every inspection thereof].

Explanation —— For the purpose of this rule a 'loan license' means a license which a licensing authority may issue to an applicant who does not have his own arrangements for manufacture but who intends to avail himself of the manufacturing facilities owned by a license in Form-32.

(2) If a persons applies for the renewal of a loan license after its expiry but within six months of such expiry, the fee payable for the renewal of such a license shall be [rupees two hundred and five hundred plus an additional fee at the rate of rupees four hundred for each months or part thereof].

(3) The licensing authority shall, before the grant of a loan license, satisfy himself that the manufacturing unit has adequate equipment, staff, capacity for manufacture and facilities to undertake the manufacture on behalf of the applicant for a loan license.

(4) The loan license shall be granted by the licensing authority to only such applicants who propose to avail of the facilities of manufacture of cosmetics in the premises of manufacturer located in the same State where the applicant is located. In case the manufacture of cosmetics which are not available in the State where the applicant is located, the licensing authority, after consulting the licensing authority where the manufacturing unit is located, may grant the loan license.

(5) Subject to the provisions of sub-rule (2), application for manufacture of additional items on a loan license shall be accompanied by a fee of [rupees one hundred for each item subject to a maximum of rupees three thousand per application],

(6) A [fee of rupees two hundred and fifty] shall be paid for a duplicate copy of license issued under sub-rule (1) if the original is defaced, damaged or lost.]

Condition for grant or renewal of a license In form 32.—Before a license in Form 32 is granted or renewed , the following conditions shall be complied with by the applicant:—

(1) The manufacture shall be conducted under the direction and personal supervision of a competent technical staff consisting of at least one person who is a whole time employee and who possesses any one of the following qualifications:—

(a) holds a Diploma in Pharmacy approved by the Pharmacy Council of India under the Pharmacy Act, 1948 (8 of 1948), or

(b) is registered under the Pharmacy Act, 1948 (8 of 1948), or

(c) has passed the Intermediate Examination with Chemistry as one of the subjects or an examination recognized by the licensing authority as equivalent to it.

[(2) The factory premises shall comply with the requirements and conditions specified in Schedule MII.]

(3) The applicant shall either -

(i) provide and maintain adequate staff, premises and laboratory equipment for testing the cosmetic manufacture, and the raw materials used in the manufacture, or

(ii) make arrangements with some institution approved by the licensing authority for such tests to be regularly carried out in this behalf by the institution.

Form of license to manufacture cosmetics for sale [or for distribution] against application in Form 31, shall be granted in Form32.

Inspection before grant or renewal of license. Before a license under this Part is granted or renewal in Form32, Form 32a or Form 33, the licensing authority shall cause the establishment, in which the manufacture is proposed to be conducted or being conducted, to be inspected by one more Inspectors appointed under the Act. The Inspector or Inspectors shall examine all portions of the premises, plant and appliances and also inspect the process of manufacture intended to be employed or being employed along with the means to be employed or being employed for standardizing and testing the substances to be manufactured and inquire into the professional qualifications of the technical staff to be employed. He shall also examine and verify the statements made in the application in regard to their correctness, and the capability of the applicant to" comply with the requirements of components technical staff, manufacturing plants, testing equipments and the requirements of plants and equipments as laid down in Schedule Mil read with the requirements of maintenance of records.

Report by Inspector. The inspector of inspector of inspectors shall forward a detailed descriptive report giving his or their findings on each aspect of inspection along with his or their recommendations after completion of his or their inspection to the licensing authority.

Grant or refusal of license. - (1) If the Licensing Authority after such further enquiry, if any, as he may consider necessary is satisfied that the requirements of the rules under the Act have been compiled with and that the conditions of the license and the rules under the act shall be observed, he shall grant or renew a license in Form 32, Form 32A or Form 33.

(2) If the licensing authority is not so satisfied, he shall reject the application and shall inform the applicant of the reasons for such rejection and of the conditions which must be satisfied before a license can be granted or renewed and shall supply the applicant with a copy of inspection report.

Further application after rejection. — If within a period of six months from the rejection of an application for license, the applicant informs the licensing authority that the conditions [aid down have been fulfilled and deposits an inspection [fee of rupees two hundred and fifty], the Licensing Authority may, if, after causing further inspection to be made, he is satisfied that the conditions for the grant of license have been complied with, issue a license in Form-32, Form-32A, Form-33.

Appeal to the State Government. Any person who is aggrieved by the other passed by the licensing authority refusing to grant or renew a license under this part may within ninety days form the date of receipt of such order, appeal to the State Government and State Government may, after such enquire in to the matter as is considered necessary and after giving the said person an opportunity for representing the case, pass such order as it think fit.

Form of loan license to manufacture cosmetics for sale [or for distribution]. — A loan license to manufacture cosmetics for sale [or for distribution] against application in Form-31A shall be granted in Form-30A.

Duration of license. — An original license or a renewed license shall unless sooner suspended or cancelled be [valid for a period of five years on and form the date on which] it is granted or renewed:

Provided that if the application for renewal of a license in force is made before its expiry or if the application is made within six months of its expiry, after payment of additional fee, the license shall continue to be in force until orders are passed on the application and the license shall be deemed to have expired, if application for its renewal is not made within six months of its expiry.

Certified or renewal. — The certificate of renewal of a license in Form-32A shall be issued in Form-33.

Certificate of renewal of loan license. — The certificate of renewal of a license in Form-32A shall be issued in Form-33A.

Duration of loan license: — An original loan license in Form-32 A or a renewed loan license in Form-33 A, unless sooner suspended or canceled shall be [valid for a period of 5 years on and from the date on which] In which it is granted or renewed:

Provided that if the application for the renewal of a license is made before its expiry, or if the application is made within six months of its expiry after the payment of the additional fee, the license shall continue to be in force until orders are passed on the application. The license shall be deemed to have expired if the application for its renewal is not made within six months of its expiry.

Conditions of license.- A license in Form-32 shall be subject to the conditions stated therein and to the following other conditions, namely :-

(a) The license shall provide and maintain staff, premises and equipment.

(b) The license shall comply with the provisions of the Act and the rules made there under and with such further requirements, if any, as may be specified in any rules to be made hereafter under Chapter IV of the Act.

(b) The license shall keep records of the details of each batch of cosmetic manufactured by him and of raw material used therein as per particulars specified in Schedule U(1) and such records shall be retained for a period of three years.]

(c) The licensee shall test each batch or lot of the raw material used by him for the manufacture of the cosmetics and also each batch of the final product and shall maintain records or registers showing the particular in respect of such tests the records or registers shall be retain for a period of three years from the date of manufacturer.

(d) The license shall allow any [inspector appointed under the Act] to enter with or without prior notice any premises where the manufacture of a substances in respect of which the license is issued is carried on, to inspect the premises and to take samples of the manufactured products under a receipt.

(e) The license shall allow an Inspector to inspect all register and records maintained under these rules and shall supply to the Inspector such information as he may required for the purpose of ascertaining whether the provisions of the Act and the rules made hereunder have been complied.

(f) The license shall maintain an Inspection Book in Form 35 to enable an Inspector to rescored his impressions and the defects noticed.

Provided that clauses (b) and (c) shall not apply to the manufacture of soap and the procedure for testing of raw material and the records to be maintain by a manufacture of soap shall be such as are approved by the licensing authority.

Additional information to be furnished by an applicant for license or a licensee to the licensing authority.— the applicant for the grant of a licensee or any person granted a licensee under this part shall, on demand, furnish to the licensing authority, before the grant of the license or during the period the license is in force, as a case may be, documentary abidance in respect of the ownership or occupation on rental or other basis of the premises, specified in the application for license or in the license granted, constitution of the firm, or any other relevant matter, which may be required for the purpose of verifying the correctness of the statements made by the applicant of the licensee while applying for or after obtaining the license as the case may be .

Condition of license in Form-32A. — (a) A license in Form-32A shall be deemed to be cancelled or suspended, if the license owned on by the licensee, in Form-32, whose manufacturing facilities, is canceled or suspended, as the case may be, under these rule.

(b) The licensee shall comply with the provision of the Act and these rules and with such of the further requirements, if any, as may be specified from time to time in chapter 4th of the Act, provided that where such for the requirements are specified in the rules, these would comes in to force lour months after publications in the Official Gazette.

(b1) The licensee shall keep records of the details of each batch of cosmetics manufactured by him and raw material used therein as per particulars specified in Schedule U1 and such records shall be retained for a period of three years.

(c) The licensee shall test each batch or lot of the raw material use by him of the manufacture of the cosmetics and also each batch of the final products and shall maintain records or register showing the particular in respect of such tests. The records or register shall be retained for a period of three years from the date of manufacture.

(d) The license shall allow an inspector appointed under the Act to enter with or without prior notice any premises where the manufacture of substance in respect of which is the license is issued is carried on, to the inspect the premises and to take samples to the manufactured products under the receipt.

(e) The licensee shall allow an Inspector to inspect all registers and records maintained under these rules and shall supply to the inspector such information as he may require for the purpose of ascertaining whether the provisions of the Act and the rules made there under have been complied.

(f) The licensee shall maintain an inspection book in Form-35 to enable an inspector to record his impression and the defect noticed.

Cancellation and suspension of license. (1) The licensing authority may, after giving the license an opportunity to show cause why such an order should not be passed, by an order in writing stating the reasons therefore, cancel a license issued under this Part or suspend it for such period as he thinks fit, either holly or in respect of some of the substance to which it related, if in his opinion, the license has failed to comply with any of the conditions of the license or with any provisions of the Act or the rules made there under.

(2) A licensee whose license has been suspended or cancelled may appeal within a period of three months from the date of the order to the State Government which shall considering the appeal, pass orders, and such orders shall be final.

Prohibition of manufacture of cosmetics containing colors other than those prescribed. (1) No cosmetics shall be manufactured which contain dyes, colors and pigments other than the one specified by the Bureau of Indian Standards (IS: 4707 Part I as amended) and Schedule Q.

The permitted synthetic organic color and natural organic colour used in the cosmetic shall not contain more than —

(i) 2 parts per million of Arsenic calculated as Arsenic Trioxide.

(ii) 20 parts per million of lead calculated as lead.

(iii) 100 parts per million of Heavy Metals other than lead calculated as the total of the respective metals.

Prohibition of manufacture of cosmetic containing Hexachlorophene. — No cosmetic containing Hexachlorophene shall be manufactured: Provided that in the case of soaps Hexachlorophene may be used in concentrations not exceeding one per cent weight by weight:

Provided further that the following cautionary note shall be printed shall appear in a conspicuous manner on the wrapper of package of each soap, namely:-

"Contains Hexachlorophene - not to be used on babies".

Use of lead and Arsenic compounds for the purpose of coloring cosmetics prohibited.—The use of lead and Arsenic compounds tor the purpose of coloring cosmetics is prohibited.

Form of intimation for purpose of taking samples of cosmetics.—Where an inspector takes a sample of a cosmetic for the purpose of test or analysis, he will intimate such purpose in writing in Form-17 to the person from whom he takes it.

Form of receipt of samples of cosmetics where fair price tendered is refused.—where the fair price, for the samples of cosmetics taken for the purpose of test or analysis, tendered under sub-section (1) of section 23 has been refused, the Inspector shall tender a receipt there for to the person from whom the said samples have been taken as specified in Form-17A.

Form of receipt for seized cosmetics.—A receipt by an Inspector for the stock of any cosmetics seized under clause (c) of sub-section 22 of the Act, shall be in Form 16.

Manner of certifying copies of seized documents.—The Drug Inspector shall return the documents, seized by him under clause (cc), or produced before him under clause (cca), of sub-section (1) of section 22 of the Act, within a period of twenty days of the date of such seizure or production, to the person from whom they were seized or, as the case may be, the person who produced them, after copies thereof or extracts therefrom have been signed by the concerned Drug Inspector and the person from whom they were seized, or as the case may be, who produced such records.

Form of order not to dispose of stocks of cosmetics.—An order in writing by an Inspector under clause (c) of sub-section 22 of the Act requiring a person not to dispose of any stock of cosmetics in the possession shall be in Form-15.

Prohibition of manufacture of cosmetic containing Mercury compounds.—No cosmetic containing Mercury compounds shall be manufactured.

LABELLING. PACKING AND STANDARDS OF COSMETICS

Prohibition of sale or distribution.— Subject to the other provisions of these rules, no person shall sell or distribute any cosmetic unless the cosmetic, if of Indian origin, is manufacturing by a licensed manufacturer and labeled and packed in accordance with these rules.

Exemption of Cosmetics not manufactured for consumption or sale in India from the provision of this part.—Labels on packages: or containers of cosmetics not manufactured for consumption or sale in

India shall be adapted to meet the specific requirements, if any, of the consignee:

Provided [hat where a cosmetic is required by the consignee to be not labeled with the name and address of the manufacturer, the labels on packages or containers shall bear a code number as approved by the licensing authority mentioned in rule 21.

Manner of labeling.— Subject to other provisions of the rules, a cosmetic shall carry—

(1) on both the inner and outer labels:

(a) The name of the cosmetics,

(b) The name of the manufacturer and complete address of the premises of the manufacturer where the cosmetic has been manufactured Provided that if the cosmetic is contained in a very small size container where the address of the manufacturer cannot be given, the name of the manufacturer and his principal place of manufacture shall be along with pin code.

(2) On the outer iabel:

A declaration of the net contents expressed in term of weight for solids, fluid measure for liquids, weight for semi-solids, combined with numerical count if the content is sub-divided:

Provided that this statement need not appear in case of a package of perfume, toilet water or the like, the net content of which does not exceed 60 ml or any package of solid or semi-solid cosmetic the net content of which does not exceed 30 grams.

(3) On the inner label; where a hazard exists:

(a) Adequate direction for sale use,

(b) Any warning, caution or special direction required to be observed by the consumer,

(c) A statement of the names and quantities of the ingredient that are hazardous or poisonous.

(4) A distinctive batch number, that is to say, the number by reference to which details of manufacture of the particular batch from which the substance in the container is taken are recorded and are available for inspection, the figures representing the batch number being preceded by the letter B:'

Provided that this clause shall not apply to any cosmetic containing 10 grams or less if the cosmetic is in solid or semi-solid state, and 25 milliliters or less if the cosmetic is in a liquid state. Provided further that in the case of soaps, instead of the batch number, the month and year of manufacture of soap shall be given on the label.

Provided further that in the case of soaps, instead of the batch number, the month and the year of manufacture of the soap shall be given on the label.

(5) Manufacturing license number, the number being preceded By the letter M.

(6) Where a package of cosmetic has only one label such label shall contain all the information required to be shown on the both the inner and the outer labels under these rules.

Prohibition against altering inscription on containers, labels or wrappers of cosmetic.—No person shall alter, obliterate or deface any inscription or mark made or recorded by the manufacturer on the container, label or wrapper of any cosmetic:

Provided that nothing in this rule shall apply to any alteration, inscription to made on the container, label or wrapper of any cosmetic at the instance or direction or with the permission of the licensing authority.

Labeling of hair dyes containing dyes, colors and pigments.— Hair dyes (containing) Para-Phenylenediamine or other dyes, colors and pigments) shall be labeled with the following legend in English and local languages and these shall appear on both the inner and the outer labels.

"Caution.— This product contains ingredients which may cause skin irritation in certain cases and so a preliminary test according to the accompanying direction should first be made. This product shall not be used for dyeing the eyelashes or eyebrow; as such a use may cause blindness."

Each package shall also contain instruction in English and local languages on the following lines for carrying out the test:— "This preparation may cause serious inflammation of the skin in some cases and so a preliminary test should always be carried out to determine whether or not special sensitivity exists. To make the test, cleanse a small area of skin behind the ear or upon the inner surface of the forearm, using either soap and water or alcohol. Apply a small quantity of the hair dye as prepared for use to the area and allow it to dry. After twenty-four hours, wash the area gently with soap and water. If no irritation or inflammation is apparent, it may be assumed that no hypersensitivity to the dye exists. The test should however, be carried out before each and every application. This preparation should on no account be used for dyeing eyebrow or eyelashes as severe inflammation of the eye or even blindness may result."

Special provisions relating to toothpaste containing fluoride.—

(i) Fluoride content in toothpaste shall not be more than 1000 ppm and the content of fluoride in terms of ppm shall be mentioned on the tube and carton.

(ii) Date of expiry should be mentioned on tube and carton.

Report of result of test or analysis of cosmetics.— Test reports on samples of cosmetics taken for test or analysis under these rules shall be supplied in Form-34

Standards for cosmetics.— Subject to the provisions of these rules, the standards for cosmetics shall be such as may be prescribed in schedule S.

FORM-31

Application for grant or renewal of a [license to manufacture cosmetics for sale or for distribution]

1. I/We, ... of .... hereby apply for the grant/renewal of license to manufacture on the premises situated at .... the following cosmetics:-
2. Name of cosmetics ....
3. Name, qualifications and experience of technical staff employed for manufacture and testing ....
4. A fee of rupees .... has been credited to Government under the head of account ....

   Date ....   Signature ....

   Note.— The application should be accompanied by a plan of the premises.

FORM-35

Form in which the Inspection Book shall be maintained

(A) The cover of the inspection Book shall contain the following particulars, namely:—

1. The name and address of the license
2. License number and the date up to which the license is valid ....

(B) (i) The pages of the !nspection Book shall be serially numbered and duty stamped by the licensing authority. The pages, other than the first and the fast and the last pages, shall have the following particulars:—

Name and designation of the Inspector who inspects the premises of the license ....

Date of Inspection ....

Observations of the Inspector ......

Signature of the Inspector

(ii) The first and last pages of the Inspection Book shall be endorsed by the licensing authority with the following words, namely:-

'Inspection Book maintained by M/s .... situated at ...... for license number ....

in Form .... under Drugs and Cosmetics Rules, 1945.

Seal and Signature of the licensing authority

Notes :— (i) Printed copy of the inspection Book may be obtained by the license from the licensing authority on payment,

(ii) The Inspection Book shall be maintained at the premises of the licensee.

(iii) The observations made by the Drug Inspector shall be in triplicate. The original copy shall be retained in the Inspection Book to be maintained in the premises of the license. The duplicate copy shall be sent to the licensing authority. The triplicate copy shall be taken as record by the Inspector.

52

Regulatory Provisions Relating to Manufacture of Cosmetics

A licence is required under the Drugs & Cosmetics Rules for manufacture of cosmetics for sale / distribution. This licence is issued by the state regulatory authorities (State Drugs Control Department or State Food and Drug Administration).

How to Obtain Licence

An application in prescribed form (Form 31) along with fee together with following documents is made to the office of the State Drugs Controller or Commissioner, Food & Drug Administration (FDA):

Layout plan of the factory premises;

A list of equipment and machinery installed;

A document about the constitution of the firm i.e., and affidavit of proprietorship in case of sole-proprietorship, a copy of partnership deed, in case of partnership firm, a copy of memorandum and articles of association in case of a private limited or public limited company;

A document showing possession of the applicant on the proposed premises for factory e.g. rent agreement, rent receipt etc.

Usually the application forms are got printed by the State Drugs Control Dept./ FDA and are available from their office. Apart from the documents mentioned above State Drugs Control Department / FDA may also require certain affidavits or some other relevant information. Before grant of licence (which is issued in Form 32) the factory premises are inspected by the officer(s) of the State regulatory agency. During inspection, the officer finds out whether:

The applicant has provided adequate space for manufacturing operations, quality control and storage of raw materials, packaging materials and finished products.

The applicant has provided adequate equipment and machinery for manufacture of cosmetics which he intends to manufacture.

The applicant has provided adequate testing facilities for raw materials & finished form of cosmetics or has made arrangements for testing with an approved testing laboratory. State regulatory agency together with federal agency approves testing laboratories where manufacturers of drugs and or cosmetics can get their products and raw materials tested.

The applicant has whole time services of a person who has either of the qualifications :

Diploma in Pharmacy (D. Pharm.),

Registered Pharmacist,

Intermediate in science with chemistry as one of the subjects.

Minimum requirements of space, equipment and machinery for manufacture of cosmetics have been prescribed under Schedule M-II to the Drugs & Cosmetics Rules.

53

Requirements of Factory Premisses for Manufactore of Cosmetics

1. General Requirements

(A) Location and Surroundings - The factory shall be located in a sanitary place and hygienic conditions shall be maintained in the premises. Premises shall not be used for residence or be interconnected with residential areas.

(B) Buildings - The buildings used for the factory shall be constructed so as to permit production under hygienic conditions and not to permit entry of insects, rodents, flies etc.

The walls of the room in which manufacturing operation are carried out, shall be up to a height of six feet from the floor, be smooth, even and washable and shall be such as not to permit retention or accumulation of dust.

(C) Water Supply - The water used in manufacture shall be of potable quality.

(D) Disposal of Water - Suitable arrangement shall be made for disposal of waste water.

(E) Health, clothing and sanitary requirement of the staff - All workers shall be free from contagious or infectious diseases. They shall be provided with clean uniforms, masks, headgears and gloves wherever required. Washing facilities shall also be provided.

(F) Medical Services - Adequate facilities for first-aid shall be provided.

(G) Working benches shall be provided for carrying out operations such as filling, labeling, packing etc. Such benches shall be fitted smooth, impervious tops capable of being washed.

CONDITIONS OF LICENCE:

Licenced cosmetics manufacturer has to comply with certain conditions. These conditions in brief are :

Manufacturer should continue to provide and maintain the premises, equipment and staff as at the time of grant of licence.

Manufacturer should test each batch or lot of raw materials before its use in the manufacture of cosmetics.

Manufacturer should test each batch of finished cosmetics. Cosmetics appearing under Schedule S should conform to the Indian Standards framed by the Bureau of Indian Standards.

Manufacturer should maintain records of raw materials, manufacture of each batch of cosmetic(s) and their testing. In the raw material and manufacturing record, atleast the particulars those given under Schedule U (I) to the Drugs and Cosmetics Rules should be shown. For convenience of the readers Schedule U (I) is reproduced here.

Suppliers of Raw Materials, Machineries and Packaging Materials

ORCHID CHEMICALS

4/28A, 1st & 2nd Floor, Kirti Nagar Industrial Area, New Delhi - 110015
Ph. : 91-11-25420785,
Mobile : 9811253331,
Telefax : 91-11-25460705,
Complete Range of Personal Care and Pharmaceutical Chemicals: Stockist:

ALKON INTERNATIONAL

Mr. sachin M. Doshl 11, Bombay Talkies Compound Malad (W), Mumbai-400064
Ph.:022-32948713,28820626
Fax.:022-28820626
E-Mail : sachln2483@redlffmail.com
Deals In: Importer & Supplier Of Cosmetics Chemicals, Pharmaceutical Raw materials & Speciality Chemicals F.om Taiwan, USA, Korea, China, German, France, Spain, i.e. Carbopol, Food Colors, Cocobetain, SLES, Microcrystalline Cellulose Powder, Lab Chemical. Aloe Vera Juice/Gel / Powder.

CHEMSPARK INDIA PVT. LTD.

A-301, 3rd Floor, Arjun Centre, B.S.Devshi Marg, Govandi - East, Mumbai 400 088.
Tel. : 022-2555 2832, 3951 1495
Fax : 022-2556 9171
E-mail address : spark2@mtnl.net.in
available cosmetics ingredients From SHANGHAI UCHEM CO. LTD., CHINA Skin Care and Lightening Agents, Disinfectants, UV Absorbers, Hair Care

DISHMAN

Pharmaceuticals & Chemicals Limited
401, Sangeet Plaza Marol Maroshi Road Andheri (E)
Mumbai - 400059 Maharashtra, India
Ph. 022-28592120,56964055
Fax. 022-28528758,56964054
E-Mail : mumbai® dishmangroup.com
Web :www.dishmangroup.com

COSPHA CARE CHEMICALS PVT. LTD.

455, Kalbadevi Road, Chikal House 1st Floor, Mumbai-400002, India.
Tel: (91- 022) 22014494, 22089210, 22036733
Fax :(91-022)22084998
Email : info@cosphacare.com
: bsinternational@vsnl.com
Deals in: Cosmetics Chemicals

GUJARAT ORGANICS LTD.

Mr./Ms.:HasitA. Dani 3A, Barodawala Mansion 81 Dr. A B Road Worli Mumbai-400018 MAHARASHTRA, India
Ph.91-22-24938687
Fax. 91-22-24974886
E-Mail : gujorg@vsnl.com
Web: www.organics.com
Deals In: Basic Products: Para Hydroxy Benzoic Acid,Para Hydroxy Benzoic AcidfElectronic Grade),Salicylic Acid Tech.,Salicylic Acid I.P., Salicylic Acid B.P.,Salicylic Acid U.S.P., Sodium Salicylate, Sodium Salicylate I.P. Sodium Salicylate B.P.Sodium Salicylate U.S.P.

H. K. CHEMICALS & PHARMACETICALS

Mr.Piyush Doshi
Post Box No.27698, Shop No.4 Indraprastha I-A Opp Ashoka Hospital Jitendra Road Malad(East),
Mumbai - 400097 Maharashtra, India
Ph. 91-22-28775829, 28774445
Fax. 91-22-28773079, 28728835

E-Mailnkc@vsnl.com
Web: www.hkoverseas.com
Deals In: cosmetic chemical:-

N.R. SHAH FRAGRANCE & FLAVOURS PVT. LTD.

Mr. Anup Shah
Ran Vir Building, 70. Princess Street, Mumbai - 400002
Maharashtra, India
Ph. 91 -22-22052745/56310618
Fax. 91-22-22018054
E-Mailanuo7shah@hotmail.com
Deals In: Fragrance, Flavours, Essential Oils, Aroma Chemicals & Colors For all Cosmetics products.

PREMIER CHEM CORPORATION

Mr. Pankaj A. Hemanl
203, Himalaya House
79 Palton Road, Mumbal-400001
Ph.:91 -22-22615578, 22615589
Fax..-91 -22-22615538
E-Mall:premierchem@vsnl.net
Web:www.premierchemcorp.com
Deals In-.dealers, exporters & importers of cosmetics chemicals

RUPAL CHEMICALS

Mr. Ashvin Goradia/Saurabh Goradia
1, Aidun Building 'B', 1st Dhobi Talao Lane, Mumbai-400002
Ph.:022-22017700, 22051520, 31075612
Fax.:022-22064014,
E-Mail: rupalchemicals@indiatimes.com
Deals In:Chemicals, Colour and pigments, Speciality Chemicals for Cosmetics Industries

S. ZHAVERI & CO.

Mr/Ms. Sonali Seth
109, Shivsmruti Chambers 49 Dr. A.B.Road Worli Mumbai-400018
Ph.:91-22-56607756/57
Fax. :91-22-56607758
E-Mail:zhaveris@vsnl.com
Web:www.szhaveri.com
Deals In : Oleochemicals and Surfactants, Emulsifiers, Co-emulsifi-ers, Fatty Alcohols, Emollients, Solublizers, Refatting / Wetting / Mositurising Agents, Viscosity Improver, Lubricants, Hard Fats, Oleogel, Fats and oils / Esters, Fatty Alcohols, Isocarboxylic Acids, Polyethylene Glycols, Surfactants, Self-Emulsifying Waxes.

TRADEWEL CORPORATION

111, Sterling Chamber, 56-Mogra Village, Andheri (E), Mumbai-400069 (India)
Tel: 022-28391197
Mob : 9322240935
Fax:022-28391197
E-mail: dealwel@vsnl.com
Deals In: AMantoin. Bronopol BP, Carbopol, Carbomer, Hydroquinone, TItanium Dioxide-Imported, Herbal Ext, P-Chloro M-Cresol, Stains, Dimethyl Isosorbide (Solubilizer), Azaleic Acid, Petroleum Jelly,Dimethyl Polysiloxane. Sodium Fluoro Phosphate, Perfumes/ Fragrances, Kokam Oil, Calcium Stearate, Organo Silicons-For Clear Shampoo, Resorcinol Etc.
Since 1984: COLOURS # HERBAL EXTRACTS. # PRESERVATIVES # EMULSIFIERS #SILICONES

VENUS PETROCHEMICALS (BOMBAY) PVT. LTD.

Mr. Atul M. Thakkar 27,1st Floor, Minerva Compound Sewree Bunder Road Sewree (East), Mumbai-400015
Ph.:+91-22-24163182
Fax.:+91 -22-24163193,14116263
E-Mail : info@venuspetrochem.com
Web:www.venuspetrochem.com
Deals In:Mosstanol L (IPA Substitute) Mosstanol 120 (Butano' Substitute) Mosstanol P (Pentanols/Hexanols) Ecoflow 200 (Drilling-Fluid) Eco-Diesel (Automotive Application) ASH-M ASH-H Mosspar M Mosspar H

YASHO INDUSTRIES PVT. LTD.

Nimish Apartment, Juhu Scheme, N.S. Road No. 5 Vile Parle (W), Mumbai-400056
Ph.:022-26186533,26186538,26146893
Fax.:022-26112014
E-Mail:yasho@bom3.vsnl.net.in
Web:www.gatewaytoindia.com/ yasho
Deals In : Isopropyl Myristate, Isopropyl Palmitate, Octyl Salicylate, Homosalate, Myristyl Myristate, Methyl Salicylate, Cetyl

Palmitate, Clove Leaf Oil, Eucalyptus Oil, Methyl EU-Genol, Eucalyptol, Orange Oil, Cinnamon Oil, Tertiary Butyl Hydroquinone. See Our Ad Through Advertiser Index

WARKEM

A-403, Bhaveshwar Plaza, LBS Marg, Mumbai - 400 086, India.
Tel, : 2500 0746, 2500 3747
Fax : 022-2500 2468, 022-2500 5764
Pharmaceuticais
Protein Hydrolysate Liquid / Powder form from milk protein (Casein), Soyabean, Peptone (meat protein) Liver Extract, Yeast Extract (Paste and Powder)
Calcium caseinate / Sodium caseinate, Whey Protein Hydrolysate
Cosmetics
Milk Protein Hydrolysate, Collagen Hydrolysate
Food Industries
Egg Albumin Hydrolysate, Groundnut Hydrolysate, Milk Protein, H.V.P. (Hydrolyzed Vegetable Protein) Inactivated Yeast
Fermentations
Peptones refined and technical series of various protein hydrolysates derived from meat, plant proteins.

L. S. AROMA INTERNATIONAL

3-A. Pollock Street, Keshowjee Chamber 3rd Floor, Kolkata-700001, West Bengal
Ph: 033-22358618,22343167
Fax: 033-22358618,22361422
E-mail: essen
E-mail: sify.com
Deals In : Sole Representative For Lothar Streek Fragrances & Flavours, Hamburg, Germany. See Our Ad Through Advertiser

ADVANCE IN-ORGANICS

Mr./ Ms.:Abhinav Gupta
2223,1st Floor, Gali Hinga Beg Tilak Bazar, Delhi-110006
Ph.:011-23968750,23935333
Mob: 9811026303,9899799723
E-Mail:abhinavdoit@sify.com
Web:www.indiamart.com/aio
Deals In:Industrial & Cosmetics Chemicals : Avobenzonc, Bees Wax, Benzophenone 3 & 4, Carbopols 934, 940, Caustic Potash, Ceto Stearyl Alcohol, Cetyl Alcohol, Cithrol GMS, Citric Acid, Cocobetaine, Coconut Oil, Emulsifying Wax, Liquid Paraffin, Microcrystaline Wax, Multani Mini. Olive Oil, P.E.G 400 & 4000, Paraffin Wax, Pola wax GP 200, Propylene Glycol, Silicons Oil, Sodium Citrate etc

YASHO INDUSTRIES PVT. LTD.

31 H, Laxmi Indl. Estate New Link Road, Andheri (w), Mumbai-400053 (India)
Tel : 91-252-56929152/56929153
Fax : 91-22-56929154
E-mail: yasho@bom3.vsnl.net.in
Website: www.yashoindustries.com

AMAN CHEMICALS

Mr. Aman Gupta
2263/67, First Floor, Naiwala Karol Bagh, New Delhi-110005
Ph.:91 -11 -25817515,25817516/17
Mob:9811027816 Fax.:91-11-25816382
E-Mail:amanchem@bol.net.in
Deals In:dealers & traders of various cosmetics chemicals and other chemicals

BAJAJ CHEMICALS

Mr./ Ms.:Anil Kumar Bajaj
5, Kamruddin Nagar (Near Govt. Primary School) Nangloi, Delhi-110041
Ph.:9811504312,25471453,25943872
E-Mail : baja chemicals59erediffmail.com
Deals in:Acid Slurry & Cosmetic Chemicals

ARUN COLOUR CHEM

Head Off.: J-92, IInd Floor, Rajouri Garden, New Delhi-110027, (India)
Phone: 91-11-55466700, 55466800
Fax:91-11-25170120
E-mail : aruncolours@indiatimes.com
Deals In : "Sun" & "Arun" Brand Primary Food Colours, Blended Food Colours, Lake Colours, Caramel Colours, Drinking Chocolate, Vanilla Powder, Custard Powder, Baking Powder, Essence and Flavours.

CONTINENTAL CHEMICALS

Mr.GK. Sawhney
M-67, Street-4, Shastri Nagar,
New Delhi-110052

Ph.:91-11-23642111,23655346
Fax.:91-11-23649176
E-Mail:coschem@ndf.vsnl.net.in
Deals In:cosmetics chemicals,essential oils, preservatives and others

GOGIA CHEMICAL INDUSTRIES PVT. LTD.

Mr. Rohit Gogia
A-127, Okhla Industrial Area, Phase-II.
New Delhi-110020
Ph.:91-11 -26385194,26383329, 26385664 Fax.:91-11-26386485
E-Mail:gcipl@ vsnl.com
Web:www.gogia.com
Deals In:natural essential oils, aromatic chemicals, fragrances, essential oils

ADVANCE IN-ORGANICS

2223,1st Floor, Gali Hinga Beg, Tilak Bazar, Delhi-110006
Ph : (O) 91-11-23968750, 23935333
Cell : 9811026303, 9899799723
E-mail: abhinavdoit@sify.com
Website : www.indiamart.com /aio
Deals in: Industrial S Cosmetics Chemicals Avobenzone Bees Wax Benzophenone 3 & 4 Carbopols 934, 940 Caustic Potash Ceto Stearyl Alcohol Cetyl Alcohol Cithrol GMS Citric Acid Cocobetaine Coconut Oil Emulsifying Wax (Anionic/ Non-Ionic G.M.S. (SE/NSE/AS) Glycerine Guar Gum Iso Propyl Alcohol Iso Propyl Myristate lanolin Alcohol Liquid Paraffin Microcrystaline Wax Multani Mitti Olive Oil P.E.G. 400 & 4000 Paraffin Wax Pola Wax GP 200 Propylene Glycol Silicone Oil Sodium Citrate Span 20/40/60/80 Stearic Acid Titanium Dioxide Tri Sodium Phosphate Tween 20/40/60/80 Ultrez 10 Wheat Germ Oil White Petroleum Jelly Zinc Oxide

KENT CHEMICALS PVT. LTD.

Corporate Office : 52, LGF World Trade Centre, Babar Lane, Connaught Place, New Delhi-110001.
Tel: 91-11-51528661/62
Fax:91-11-51528661
Works: 91-11-55451019/1020
E-mail: info@kentchem.com
Web: www.kentchem.com Deals In : Liquid Paraffin HLP, LLP & White Oil for application in Hair Oils, Creams, Lotions etc. See Our Ad Through Advertiser Index

KRISHANA ENTERPRISES

Mr./ Ms.:Vijay Sethi 503, Amber Tower Azadpur Commercial Complex (Behind Akash Cinema) Delhi-110053
Ph.:+91-11-55276150
Mobile : 9811039483
Fax. :+91-11-27866824
E-Mail:vsethi67@yahoo.com
Deals In:Pearl Powder,Waxes, Colours, Cosmetics Chemicals, Glitter Powder, Fine Chemicals, & Complete Laboratory Furnishers

AIN DYE CHEM CORPORATION

Mr./ Ms.: Prateek Jain 100, Tilak Bazar, 1st Floor, Delhi-110006
Ph. +91-11-55353690
Mob : 9810234169
Fax.+91-11-23940675
E-Mail: prateek@jaindyechem.com
Web: www.jaindyechem.com
Deals In : Pigments and Dyes.

MOUNT FRAGRANCES

Mr./ Ms.:Gaurav Mittal
G I.- 19, Lawrence Road Industrial Area, Delhi- 110035
Ph.:011-27105028
Mob: 9810141762
E-Mail: mountfragrances@yahoo.com
Web:www.mountfragrances.com
Deals In: Manufacturers & Exporters of : Menthol Bold Crystal, BP/USP, Menthol Flakes BP/USP, Mentha Oil I.P., Peppermint Oil & Other Essential Oils

PIONEER IN-ORGANICS

Mr./ Ms.:Hemendra Gupta
313-314, Tilak Bazar Delhi-110006
Ph.:23932737
Fax.:23984518
E-Mail: pioneerchem@hotmail.com
Deals In:Chemicals All For Cosmetics

RMA CHEMICAL CO.

Mr. Rajesh Jalota
1362/5, Ist floor pan mandi sadar bazar
Delhi-110006
Ph.:23610754,30933507
Mob : 9810135563
Deals In:dealer & trader of :- cosmetics chemicals and raw materials

SAROJ SYNTHETICS

Mr. Rohit Datta
25-A, Pocket-E, Mayur Vihar, Phase-II, Delhi-110091
Tel: 91-11-27726511/4811
Fax:91-11-22726511
E-mail: sarojsynthetics@rediffmail.com
Deals In : PPD, 2 Nitro PPD, PAP, SLS,

AMAR JYOTI INDUSTRIES

Fact.: A-94/6, Wazirpur Industrial Area, Delhi-52
Off.: 6307, Naya Bans, Delhi-110006 (India)
Ph : 011-27371557, 27371665, 23926652, 33121085
Fax : 011-27211067,27371665
E-mail: rajpals@nda.vsnl.net.in

ORCHID CHEMICALS

Mr. Ramesh Kumar
4/28A, 1st & IInd Floor Kirti Nagar Industrial Area New Delhi-110015
Ph.:011-25420785, 254607O5
Fax.:011-25440208
E-Mail: orchemin_rk95@rediffmail.com
Deals In:Dealers of all Cosmetics Chemicals

PURECHEM PRODUCTS

Mr./ Ms.:Naresh Kapoor
432, Mathura Road New Delhi-110014
Ph.:+91-11-24311475, 24319257, 24322092, 51616505
Fax.:+91-11-24313623
E-Mail: ajesh kapoor@yanoomail.com
Deals In: Mehandi(Henna), Amla, Reetha, Cosmetics, Chemicals, Minerals

R.S. AGENCIES

Mr./ Ms.:Smt. Kanak R. Mehta
A-38, Gujrat Appts. Pitam Pura, New Delhi-110034
Ph.:91 -11 -2258113, 22591578
Mb:9810033774
E-Mail:rsagencs@yahoo.com
Web:www.rd-singa!.com

SHRI RAM SONS WAX (P) LTD

Mr. Ram Avtar Bansal
181, Tilak Bazar, Delhi-110006
Ph.:91-11-23942451,
Mob:9811076830
Fax.:91-11-23927312
E-Mail:srs@del3.vsnl.net.in
Deals In:dealer/trader of cosmetic waxes,Parafin Wax, Shellac Wax, Bees Wax, Carnauba Wax, Candellila Wax, Montan Wax, Microcrystalline Wax & other chemicals

SWATI TRADERS

Mr. SudhirArora
12/232, RoopNagar Opp 4/56 Roop Nagar Gali No.7 Near Roshanara Paints, Delhi-110007
Ph.:91-11-23842465,23842832
Mob:9818806093
Deals In:dealers & traders of cosmetic chemicals, PPD(paraphenylene Diamine), Barium Peroxide, Sodium Perborate, Citric Acid & Others.

CONTINENTAL CHEMICALS

M-67, Street no. 4, Shastri Nagar, Delhi-110052.
PH.:23642111, 23655346, 23644486
FAX : 011-23649176
E-MAIL : coschem@ndf.vsnl.net.in

ICI INDIA LTD. UNIQEMA INDIA GLYCOLS LTD.
MOHINI ORGANICS (P) LTD.
ALPHA CHEMICALS (P) LTD
CELANSE SOLUTIONS.
NATIONAL STARCH & CHEMICALS
GUJARAT ORGANICS LTD. NEBULA PHARMA (P) LTD.
AURA SPECIALITY CHEM. PVT LTD.
GOLDFIELD FRAGRANCES LTD.

Allantoin Arlamolm812 Bio white Carbopol-etc 2020 H.E.C. Myrj-52,59 P.V.P.K.-30 Structure-2001-Plus Veegum arlacel-165 Arlaton Dioic DCA Brij-35,96,72,721 Carbopol Ultrez 10 Celquat Sc 240C

Forestall H.P.M.C. Pemulin Tr-1 Acnibio-lpm Aloe Vera carbopol 940 Cresmer-rh.40 Benzophenone-3,4 Squaleneimid Urea P.E.G.-400,1500,4000,6000 Z.P.T.O. Tea Tree Oil Metapearl

MAYUR CHEMICALS

Mr. N. Ethiraj
98, Nyniappa Naicken Street
Chennai-600003
Ph.:+91-44-25357616,25353765
Mob : 9841073044
Fax.:+91-44-25357587
Deals In:Deals in Chemicals & Solvents Required for cosmetics and herbal cosmetics industries (Preservatives, Humectants,gelling Agents)

TRISHUL CHEMICALS

Mr. /Ms.: Maulik Gandhi
B/48, Ishwarshanti Society Near Water Tank Karelibaug Vadodara -390018,
Ph. 2485761, Mob : 9898264504
E-Mail : trishulchemicals@yahoo.co.in, maulikgandhi_7®yahoo.com
Deals In: Sun Screen Agents & Ultra Violet Stabilizers (Benzophenon-1), (Benzophenon- 3), (Benzophenon-4)

KRISHANA ENTERPRISES

Contact: Mr. Vijay Sethi
Office : 503, Amber Tower, Azad Pur Commercial Complex, Behind Akash Cinema, Azad Pur, Delhi-110033
Ph.: +91-11-55276150, 9811039483
Fax:+91-11-27866824
E-mail: vsethi67@yahoo.com
Deafer & Supplier of : Pearl Powder, Waxes, Colours, Glitter Powder, Fine Chemicals, Cosmetics Raw Materials, Herbal Extracts, Essential Oils & Other Ingredients

KENT CHEMICALS PVT. LTD.

Corporate Office: 52 LGP World trade Center, Babar Lane, Connaught Place, New Delhi -110001. INDIA.
Tell: 91-11-5152 8661/62;
Fax: 91-11*5152 8661
Works: 91-11-5545 1019/1020,.
E-mail:info@kentchem.com;
URL: www.kentchem.com

Deals in: various grade of Liquid Paraffin HLP, LLP, & White Oil for application in hair oils, creams, lotions etc.

NEW BHARAT CHEMICAL WORKS

4908, Phoota Road, Sadar Bazar,
Delhil - 110006
Tel. (O) 23613307, 23538310 (R) 25437208
(M) 9810410703
Fax: 23523602
Email: nbcworks@hotmail.com
We specialized in meeting your requirements for all kinds of Waxes, Gel-Waxes, Colors Castor Oil and other Oils, Parabenes, Rosin, Pearl Powder, Stearic Acid, Glycerin, OleicAcid, A.O.S Powders & Liquids, HLP LLP, Petroleum Products, Conditioners, Emulsifiers, PPD and Hair Dye chemicals, Carbopols all grades, Lanolin, Fatty Acids Fragrances for manufacturing Toilet Soaps, Detergents, Cosmetic Products, Aerosol, Perfumes, Zarda, Guthka, Tobacco, Pan Masala, Dhoop & Agarbatti etc.
Stockists:
GODREJ INDUSTRIES LTD. SURU CHEM. & PHARMACEUTICALS (P) LTD. NEELKANTH MINE CHEM SAMIR TECH SACHEE AROMETICS LTD. V E L C O PETRO CHEMICALS (P) LTD.

TEX CHEM

4788/23, 'ASHIRWAD', Ansari Road,
Darya Ganj, New Delhi-110002
Tel: 91-11-23271239, 23277272
Fax -.91-11-23263456
E-mail: shethpankaj@hotmail.com
Deals in: Textile Auxifiaries Sugar Chemicals Cosmetics Chemicals Surfactants

SHANKAR DYES & CHEMICALS

We Solve all Critical Problems in Dyes and Chemicals
Head Office: 1209, Shankar Building, Gali No.11, Sadar Bazar, Delhi-110006
Ph. : 23673462, 23558239, 23616830,
Mb. 9810355592,
Fax. 23558239
Unit Office : 649, Gali No. 11, Sadar Bazar, Delhi-110006 (Mb. 9811577752) Branch Office: 119, Tilak Bazar, Delhi-110006.
Ph. : 23959574, 23912061

E-mail: shankardyes@rediffmail.com
www.shankardyesandchemicals.com
Complete Solution for Colour Cosmetics and Industrial Chemicals
Wholesale Dealers Stockist Deals In Specialist In Printing Auxailiries as binders, Fixer, D.A.P. Emulsifiers; Full Range of Ranipals, Golden Pigment Paste Emulsion Also I.D.I., S.C.I., Colourchem & P.D.I. All kinds of Colours, Chemicals, Pigments & Dyes Plastic Colours, Plastic Brightening Agents, D.O.P., D.B.P., D.M.P., C.P.W. Waxes, Resins, Titanium Dioxide, All Grades P.V.C. Medium, Epoxy Resins, Hardners, All Stabilizers, Fluoroscent & Pigments Colours, Pearl Powder & Paste, Foaming & Defoaming Agents
All kinds of Glitters Jari, Export Quality Plain & Rainbow DJ Dance
We Deal in Rare Items All over India Distributorship : Gilitron Products • Luxmi Brand Colours & Intermediates • Luxmi Gold Bronze Powder • Luxmi Pigments Emulsion

R.R ENTERPRISES

2202, Gali Hinga Beg Tilak Bazar,
Delhi 110006
Ph.: 011-23920730, 23977337
Fax: 011-23929312
Email,: rregroup@vsnl.com
We are pleased to offer following products: Citric Acid, Acetic Acid, Silica Gel, Boric Acid Borax, Titanium di-oxide Zinc Oxide, Caustic Potash - Flakes, Caustic Soda - Flakes, Stearic Acid, Glycerine Trisodium Phosphate
(Distributor-Indian Rare Earths Ltd.)
Potassium Hydroxide -Pellets (Pharma Grade)
Sodium Hydroxide -Pellets (Pharma Grade) (Authorised Seller - Caliron Chemicals)
Sodium Benzoate Benzoic Acid
(Ganesh Benzoplast Ltd.)
Sodium Citrate
Always Use Pure Chemicals
for better Efficiency of your Unit
excise Benefits Available.

SHREE GANESH DYE CHEM

Mr. N.H. Parikh
Plot No. 71/13, Phase-1 GIDC Estate Vatva
Ahmedabad-382445
Ph.: 079-5896563, 5890334, 30918109
Fax.:91-79-5890803, 5890334
E-Mail:kayen@wilnetonline.net;
kayenad1@sancharnet.in
Web:www.india-chemicals.com
Deals In:dealer & trader of :- hair dyes & cosmetic intermediate chemicals

UNIFINE

Mr. K.A. Valiulla
4A, 2nd Floor Shalimar Complex Mahalaxmi five Roads Paldi Ahmedabad - 380007
Ph. 079-6630741 Fax. 079-6621775
E-Mailunifine@sancharnet.in
Deals In : Chemicals and Other.

RMA CHEMICAL CO.

1362/5, First Floor, Pan Mandi, Sadar Bazar, Delhi-110006
Ph.: 23610754, 30933507
Fax.:0129-2417350 (Cell).: 9810135563
Deals in : (Foam, Carpet, Industrial & Cosmetics Chemicals) S.L.E.S., S.L.S. (L/P/N), Cocobetaine, Shampoo Base, E.G.M.S., E.G.D.S., Ceto Stearyl Alcohol, Cetyl Alcohol, P.E.G 400, GM.S.(SE/NSE/AS), Glycerine Propylene Glycol, P.G.M.S., Span 20/40/60/80, Tween 20/40/60/80, Silicone Oil, Titanium Dioxide, Sodium Citrate,Butyl Stearate,Liquid Paraffin Bees Wax, Emulsifying Wax, (Anionic/Non-Ionic), Microcrystaline Wax, Paraffin WAx, P.E.G. 4000, Zinc Oxide,Guar Gum,Coconut Oil, White Oil, Iso Propyl Alcohol, Iso Propyl Myristate, Tri Sodium Phosphate, B.H.T, White Petroleum Jelly, Stearic Acid, Caustic Potash, Citric Acid, T.E.A., L.L.P./ H.L.P

R. S. AGENCIES

Ph. : Off.- 22581133, 22591578 Cell : 98100 33774 - 310 80407
E-mail : rsagencs@yahoo.com
Deals in : Tapiaco Starch, Maize Starch, Calcium Chloride (Fuse), Zinc Chloride, Soda Ash, Light, Borax Granular, Dextrine (Yellow & White), (High Strength for

Papertubes/Cones.), Glycerine, SLES Liquid, SLS Powder, Adhesives for Corrugated Boxes Etc.

BHIMANI CHEMICALS PVT. LTD.

Mr. Jignesh Bhimani
510, Mahakant, Opp. V.S. Hospital Ellisbridge Ahmedabad-380006
Ph. 079-26575474 Fax. 079-26577318
E-Mail : pmbhimani@rediffmail.com
Web : bhimaniSbhimanigroup.com
Deals In: Authorized Dealer for Ciba Specialty Chemicals (India) Limited for their Home and Personal Care, Textile Care, Toiletries and allied products.

HINDUSTAN GUM & CHEMICALS LTD.

Mr./Ms.:V.C. Maheshwari/Vipul
Birla Colony, Bhlwani-127021
Ph.:91 (01664)-243891, 243892, 243894, 243811,243214 Fax.:91(01664)-243813
E-Mail:hichem@vsnl.com
Deals In Hair and Personal (skin) care Raw material.

R. R. INDUSTRIES

Mr. Rajinder Bansal
House No.: 1566, Sector-28, Faridabad-121003, Haryana
Ph.:91-0129-2274201 Mob.: 9312436069
Deals In : Barium Peroxide, Barium Hydroxide

SHREE ADDITIVES PHARMA & FOODS LTD.

Mr. /Ms.: Vijay Podar
A-707, Wall Street-2, Opposite Orient Club Ellies Bridge.
Ahmedabad, Gujarat, India
Ph. 91-79-26426224, 9898087950
Fax.+91-79-26560699
E-Mail: vijay@shreeaddltives.com
Web: www.shreeadditives.com
Deals In: Raw Materials to Pharma, Food & Cosmetics

SUNSHINE CHEMICALS

Mr. K.K. Jalota
13, Tikona Park market,
NIT Faridabad-121001, Haryana
Ph.:0129-2417330,2417350
Mobile: 9818163513 Fax.:0129-2417350
Deals In:consignment agent, dealer & trader of: cosmetics, chemicals and raw materials

TRADEWEL CORPORATION

111, Sterling Chamber 56-Mogra Village Andheri (E) Mumbai-400069
Ph.:022-31040935 Fax.:022-28391197
E-Mail:dealwel@vsnl.com
Deals In:Allantoin,Bronopol, BP.Carbopou, Carbomer, Hydroquinone, Titanium Dioxide- Imported,Herbal ext, p-Chloro m-CBESOL.Stains.Dimethyl, Isosorbide (Solubilizer),Azaleic Acid.Petroleum Jelly.Dimethyl, Polysiloxane.Sodium Gluoro, Phosph ate.Perfumes/Fragrances, Kokam Oil.Calcium, Stearate, Organo Silicons-For Clear Shampoo. Resorcinol etc

AMIT FINE CHEM

Mr. Amit M Shah
A-32, Siddhi Apartment Off. A.C. Road, Ashok nagar Kandivali (E),
Mumbai -400101 Maharashtra, India
Ph. 022-28870920
Fax. 022-28871551
E-Mailamit170erediffmail.com
Deals In: dlrs. of raw materials for cosmetics & ayurveda

N.R. SHAH FRAGRANCE & FLAVOURS PVT. LTD.

Mr. AnupShah
RanVir Building, 70. Princess, Street, Mumbai -400002 Maharashtra, India
Ph. 91 -22-22052745/56310618
Fax. 91-22-22018054
E-Mailanuo7shah@hotmail.com
Deals In: Fragrance, Flavours, Essential Oils, Aroma Chemicals & Colours For all Cosmetics products.

RISHABH OILS PVT. LTD.

3,Tiljala Road.Near Bundel Gate,
Kolkata-700039,
Ph: 91 - 33- 2242 5739 / 9279
Fax:91-33-2242 6087
Email: rishabhoils@vsnl.net
Web: www.indiamart.com/jojoba
Manufacturer of: 100% Pure Jojoba Oil, Jojoba Seed Powder

S.V. ENTERPRISES

Mr. / Ms.: Mahesli Kadakia
205, Khajurwala Chambers
Mumbai-400009 Maharashtra, India
Ph. +91-22-23455973,56318437
Fax. 56312565
E-Mail: kadakiam@vsni.com
Web: www.sventerprises-india.com
Deals In : Aloe vera Gel for Drinking, Health Tonic, Aloe vera for Cosmetics Use.

VISION INDIA TECHNOLOGY

B/15, GaneshSadan
Nava-Pada Shubash Rd. Domblvli (West)
Maharashtra. Dombivli -421202
Maharashtra, India
Ph.+91-09819115511
E-Mail : visionindiatech@yahoo.co.in, vision indiatech
Deals In: Supplier of Aloe vera Gel & Powder (100X, 200X & whole leaf Powder) Cosmetic & Pharma Grade.

WAY-LINK INTERNATIONAL

Mr. Arun Kumar Baid
71, B.r.b Basu Road, B-411
Kalkota - 700001 West Bengal, India
Ph. 91-33-22358933/9092
Fax. 91-33-25212082
E-Mailwaylink@vsnl.net
Deals In : Herbal Products, Cosmetics & others.

L.S. AROMA INTERNATIONAL

3-A, Pollock Street, Keshowjee Chamber
3rd Floor, Kolkata -700001
Ph. 91 -33-22358618,22343167
Fax. 91 -33-22358618,22361422
E-Mail: essen@sify.com
Deals In: Sole Representatitive For Lothar Streeek Fragrances & Flavours, Hamburg, Germany

ALBATROSS HERBALS

A-1/58, Mahipalpur Extn. New Delhi-110037
Ph.91-11-26783326
Fax. 91-11-26783326
E-Mail: herbalba@hotmail.com
Deals In: Herbal Havan Samagri/ Poojan Samagri/ Agarbatti

GYAN FLAVOURS EXPORT

Harichand Melaram Farm, East Gokul Pur, New Delhi -110094
PH.-11-22814681 Fax-11-22811745
E-Mail: gyanaroebol.net.in
Web: www.gyanflavoursexport.com
Deals In : Essential Oils, Aromatic Chemicals and Herbal Extract.

GOGIA CHEMICAL INDUSTRIES PVT. LTD.

A-127, Okhla Industrial Area, Phase-II, New Delhi -110020
Ph.-11-26385194, 26383329, 26385664
Fax. 91-11-26386485
E-Mail: gcipl@vsnl.com
Web: www.gogia.com
Deals In: Natural Essential Oils, Aromatic Chemicals, Fragrances, Essential Oils

BABA ENTERPRISES

Mr./ Ms.: Sandeep Singhal
M-25, Sector-5 Bawana Industrial Area
New Delhi-110088
Ph. 011-27483298 Fax. 011-27486872
E-Mail: baba_arom@yahoo.co.in
Deals In: Essential Oils And Aromatic Chemicals

LUHADIA EXPORTS (P) LTD.

Mr./Ms.:SanjayJaln
D-55, Gulmohar Park New Delhi-110049
Ph.-11-26853685,51013651,51740247
Fax.+91-11-51740247
E-Mail: sanjayjain87nehotmail.com
Deals In: Essential Oils, (Rose Oil And Others)

MOUNT FRAGRANCES

Mr./ Ms.: Gaurav Mittal
G.I.-19. Lawrence Road Industrial Area, Delhi-110035
Ph. 011-27105028 Mob: 9810141762
E-Mail: mountfragrances@yahoo.com
Web: www.mountfragrances.com
Deals In: Manufacturers & Exporters Of: Menthol Bold Crystal, BP/USP, Menthol Flakes BP/USP, Mentha Oil I.P., Peppermint Oil & Other Essential Oils

NUCLEAIRE

125, Priya Enclave, Road No. 72,
New Delhi-110 092
Ph.+(91)-(11)-22374311
Fax. +(91)-(11)-22374311
Deals In: Exporters Of Eucalyptus Oil, Citronella Oil, Neem Oil.

SIGMA FRAGRANCES EXPORTS (P) LTD.

Mr/Ms: Sanjay Jain
Works:Station Road, Sasni-202139 (Hathras) Up.India Corp Off: D-55, Gulmohar Park New Delhi-110049,
PH: 09412277256/ 011-26853685/ 51013651
Deals In : 100% Rose Oil, Rose Attar, Henna and Essential Oils etc.

NEHA ENTERPRISES

Mr. Vikas
K-3, Kewal Park Extension Azadpur,
New Delhi -110033
Ph.91-11-27671039, Mb:9810034231
Deals In: Neha Herbal Mehandi, Rachani Mehandi

SHIV SALES CORPORATION

P-103, Pandav Nagar Near Alkon Public School, Mayur Vihar Phase-I
New Delhi-110091, India
Ph. 011 -22790282,22792916,
Mob: 9811213799 Fax. 011-22790282
E-Mail:shivorganics@yahoo.co.in, spaorganics@yahoo.co.in
Web: www.shivorganics.com
Deals In: Natural Oils, Essential Oils, Mentha Oil, Peppermint Oil For Pan Masala, Dhoop. Hair Oil, Agarbatti Compound And Other Herbal Products And Chemicals.

VISION INDIA TECHNOLOGY

B/15,GANESHSADAN, NAVA- PAD A, SHUBHASH RD, DOMBIVLI(WEST) MAHARASHTRA:- 421202
Mob:-+91-09819115511
E-Mail:- visionindiatech@yahoo.co.in, visionindiatech@indiatimes.com
Activity :- Supplier of Aloe vera Gel & Powder (100X, 200X & whole leaf Powder) Cosmetic & Pharma Grade.

TEXTRON TECNICA

DDA MIG123, Pocket-B East Of Loni Road
New Delhi-110093
Ph.91-11-22813657, Mb:9810017563
Fax. 91-11-22813657
E-Mail: sadhnasood@satyam.net.in
S.L..EUROPE VEGETATABLE OIL, S.L. (Plimon Group-Spain)
Deals In: Importer Of Natural Oils, Essential Oils And Otherchemicals For Cosmetics Applications

A.K.AROMATICS

Mr. / Ms.: R.H. Afzal Khan
New No. 27, Maroof Street Mount Road
Chennai-600002
Tamil Nadu, India
Ph. 044-28600516 Mob: 9382302936
Deals In: manufacturer of Spray Perfumes, Attars, Agar Bathis, sambrani and sandal sticks, sticks, coils, A/C perfumes, Car Shampoo, Carpet Shampoo, Paper Soaps, Scented bags, Face Tissue paper, Perfumed Chaik, Inks, Greeting Cards, Letter Pads Flower Dust For Synthetic Flower etc.

BABA ENTERPRISES

Factory Cum
M-25, Sector-5,
Sates Office
Bawana Industrial Area, Delhi
Resi. Cum Con. Afld.
BM-30(West), Shalimar Bagh,
New Delhi-110088
Ph: Oil -27483298
Mob.: 9811379777
Fax : 011 - 27486872
9818710999
Mfr. & Dealer of : Essential Oils, Aromatic Chemicals, Herbal Extracts & Gels Facial Gel (100% Herbal) (Papaya, Cucumber, Aloe Vera, Neem, Daru-Haldi, Turmeric, Shimul Bark with Rose or Sandal) Hair Gel (100% Herbal) (Amla, Shikakai, Brahmi, Bhringraj, Heena, Neem, Jatamansi, Aloe Vera, Shankh Pushpi) Aloe Vera Brahmi Heena Turmeric Neem Papaya Shimul Bark Shankri-Pushpi & Many More Amla Cucumber Daru-Haldi Reetha Jatamansi Rose Watermelon Bhringraj Grape Orange Shikakai Tomato

GRV MERCHANDIZING

Mr. Mohan
14/3,3rd Floor HRB Chambers Andree Road Shantinagar, Bangalore - 56002
Ph.08022122885
Fax. 08051125288
E-Mail: info@ herbalmerchandizing.com
Web : www.herbalmerchandizing.com
Deals In : Cultivator and Supplier of all kinds of Herbs, Extracts and Essential Oils.

HARI CHAND MELA RAM FARM

Main Wazirabad Road, East Gokulpur, New Delhi-110 094 [INDIA]
TEL. : 91-11-22814681
Fax : +91-11-22811745
E-MAIL : gyanaro@bol,net.in
info@gyanflavoursexport.com
WEBSITE : www.gyanflavoursexport.com

S.S. HERBALS

485/2, Katra Ishwar Bhavan, Khari Baoli, Delhi-06
Off. 23954531, 23910274
Mob: 9810631790, 9810977161
Fax : 91-11-23964221
E-mail : ssherval@bol.net.in
Deals in: Medicinal Herbs, Essential Oils, Herbal Extracts ,Spices, Dried Fruits, Phyto Chemicals, Vegetable Seeds.

HIMALAYAN HERBAL PRODUCTS

Mr. / Ms.: ISH GUPTA
7km., Ludhiana Road, Village Bhoglwal, Malerkotla -148023, Punjab, India
Ph. 91 -1675-274940,250857
Cell: 9317776340
E-Mail : Himalayan. herbal@yahoo.co.in
Web : www.himalayanherbal.8k.com
Deals In : Manufacturer of Aloe Vera Gel / Powder and other products from other Plants.

RAJ & COMPANY

Behind Katju Market, Near Parsi Mandir Neemuch -458441, Madhya Pradesh, India
Ph. 91-7423-221600
Fax. 91-7423-225341
E-Mail: rajspice@sancharnet.in
Web: www.rajnco.com
Deals In: Dealer/Trader/Exporter Of Herbs & Spices.Herbal Extracts, Medicinal Plant Seeds Etc.

N.R. SHAH FRAGRANCE & FLAVOURS PVT. LTD.

Mr. AnupShah
RanVir Building, 70. Princess Street, Mumbai -400002 Maharashtra, India
Ph 91 -22-22052745/56310618
Fax. 91-22-22018054
E-Mailanuo7shah@hotmail.com
Deals In: Fragrance, Flavours, Essential Oils, Aroma Chemicals & Colors For all Cosmetics products.

GROVER & COMPANY

Mr. Ravinder Grover
13, Royd Street Kolkata-700016
Ph.033-22291176
Deals In: A Leading Producer Of Spray Perfumes, Roll-On & Raw Perfumes.

L.S. AROMA INTERNATIONAL

3-A, Pollock Street Keshowjee Chamber 3rd Floor Kolkata -700001,
Ph. 91 -33-22358618,22343167
Fax. 91 -33-22358618,22361422
E-Mail: essen@slfy.com
Deals In: Sole Representatitlve For Lothar Streeek Fragrances & Flavours, Hamburg, Germany

GOGIA CHEMICAL INDUSTRIES PVT. LTD.

A-127, Okhla Industrial Area Phase-II, New Delhi -110020
Ph. -11 -26385194, 26383329, 26385664
Fax. 91-11-26386485
E-Mail: gcipl@vsnl.com
Web: www.gogia.com
Deals In: Natural Essential Oils, Aromatic Chemicals, Fragrances, Essential Oils

GYAN FLAVOURS EXPORT

Harichand Melaram Farm, East Gokul Pur, New Delhi -110094
Ph.91-11-22814681
Fax. 91-11-22811745
E-Mail: gyanaro@bol.net.in
Web: www.gyanflavoursexport.com
Deals In: Essential Oils, Aromatic Chemicals and Herbal Extract.

JBJ PERFUMES PVT. LTD.

815, Aggarwal Millenium Tower Netaji Subhash Place Opp. T.V. Tower Pitam Pura New Delhi-110034]
Ph. 011 -27155599,30905915
Fax. 011-27193399
E-Mail : schibber@jbjperfumes.com
Web: www.jbjperfumes.com
Deals In: "JBJ" Brand:-Perfumes, Spray Perfumes, Colonges

LUHADIA EXPORTS (P) LTD.

Mr./Ms.:SanjayJaln
D-55, Gulmohar Park,
New Delhi-110049, India
Ph.-11-26853685,51013651,51740247
Fax.+91-11-51740247
E-Mail : sanjayjain87n@hotmail.com
Deals In: Essential Oils, (Rose Oil And Others)

MONET MARKETING (INDIA) PVT LTD

1202.1209A Vikram Tower 16 Rajendra Place New Delhi -110008
Ph. 91 -11 -55303296,25860183
Fax. 91-11-25720250
E-Mail : monet@mantraonline.com
Web: www.monetperfumes.com
Deals In: Marketing Of:- PASSPORT & LADY DIANA Brand Spray Perfumes And Body Perfumes

MOUNT FRAGRANCES

Mr./Ms.: Gaurav Mittal
G.I.-19, Lawrence Road Industrial Area, Delhi-110035
Ph. 011-27105028 Mob: 9810141762
E-Mail : mountfragrances@yahoo.com
Web: www.mountfragrances.com
Deals In: Manufacturers & Exporters Of : Menthol Bold Crystal, BP/USP, Menthol Flakes BP/USP, Mentha Oil I.P., Peppermint Oil & Other Essential Oils

N.R. SHAH FRAGRANCE & FLAVOURS P. LTD.

Mr, Anup Shah (Director)
Regd. Office: Ranvir Building, 70, Princess Street, Mumbai-400 002
(Maharashtra) India.
Ph.: +91-22-56310618, 22052745
Fax:+91-22-22018054
Mobile: 9821152210
E-mail: anup7shah@hotmail.com
Manufacturer, Dealer & Exporter of: Fragrances, Flavours, Essential Oils & Colours *for all Cosmetics & other Industries. We also import*

NIMMA INTERNATIONAL

C-85, Okhla Indl Area Phase-1
New Delhi-110 020
Ph.+(91)-(11)-26813190/26816449/ 9810032521/56004243
Fax. +(91)-(11)-27052595
Web: http://www.indiamart.com/nimson
Deals In: Manufacturer And Exporter Of Herbal Cosmetics Like Shampoo, Hair Oil, Talc, Cream, Sunscreen Lotion, White Petroleum Jelly And Detergents.

NUCLEAIRE

Mr./ Ms.: Navneet a Malhotra
125, Priya Enclave, Road No-72
Delhi-110092
Ph. 9810385808 Fax. 91-11-22374311
E-Mail: admin@nucle-aire.com
Web: www.nucle-aire.com
Deals In: Perfumery Chemicals, Essential Oils, Aromatic Chemicals

SHIV SALES CORPORATION

P-103, Pandav Nagar, Near Alkon Public School, Mayur Vihar Phase-I,
New Delhi -110091
Ph. 011 -22790282,22792916,
Mob: 9811213799 Fax. 011-22790282
E-Mail: shivorganics@yahoo.co.In,
spaorganics@yahoo.co.in
Web: www.shivorganics.com
Deals In: Natural Oils, Essential Oils, Mentha Oil, Peppermint Oil For Pan Masala, Dhoop, Hair Oil, Agarbatti Compound And Other Herbal Products And Chemicals.

TEXTRON TECNICA S.L, EUROPE VEGETATABLE OIL.S.L.

(Plimon Group-Spain)
DDAMIG123. Pocket-B East Of Loni Road
New Delhi-110093

Ph.91-11-22813657, Mb:9810017563
Fax. 91-11-22813657
E-Mail : sadhnasood@satyam.net.in
Deals In: Importer Of Natural Oils, Essential Oils And Otherchemicals For Cosmetics Applications

A.K. AROMATICS

Mr. /Ms.iR.H. AfzalKhan
New No. 27, Maroof Street Mount Road Chennai-600002 Cliennai -600002, Tamil Nadu, India
Ph. 044-28600516, Mob: 9382302936
Deals In: manufacturer of Spray Perfumes, Attars, Agar Bathis, sambrani and sandal sticks, sticks, coils, A/C perfumes, Car Shampoo, Carpet Shampoo, Paper Soaps, Scented bags, Face Tissue paper, Perfumed Chalk, Inks, Greeting Cards, Letter Pads Flower Dust For Synthetic Flower etc.

GRV MERCHANDIZING

Mr. Mohan
14/3, 3rd Floor HRB Chambers Andree Road Shantinagar, Bangalore - 56002 Karnataka, India
Ph.08022122885
Fax. 08051125288
E-Mail: infoeherbalmerchandizlng.com
Web : www. herbalmerchandizing.com
Deals In : Cultivator and Supplier of all kinds of Herbs, Extracts and Essential Oils.

SIGMA FRAGRANCES EXPORTS (P) LTD.

Contact: SanjayJain
Works: Station Road, Sasni-202139, (Hathras) UP, India.
Mobile: 9412277256
E-mail: sigmafragrances@hotmail.com
Corporate Office; D-55, Gulmohar Park, New Delhi-110049, India
Manufacturer of : rose oils and others

TEXTRON TECHNICA S.L. PLIMON GROUP

Girona,34, 5th and 6th floor 08400 Granollers, (BARCELONA)
SPAIN
Tel; +34 93 860 4500, Fax +34 93 870 7462
Email: textron@pilmon.com, ehernandiz@plimon.com
DDA MIG 123, Pocket B East of Loni Road, Delhi -110093
Tel : +91.11.22813657
Mob : 9810017563
Fax +91.11.22813657
E mail : sadhanasood@satyam.net.in
Natural Vegetable Oils:- Sweet Almond Oil, Apricot Kernel Oil, Hazelnut Oil, Olive Oils, Jojoba Oil, (Clear and Virgin), Walnut Oil, Evening Primrose Oil, Avocado Oil, Macadaminut Oil, Pumpkin Seed Oil, Grape Seed Oil, Peach Oil, Wheat Germ Oil, Sunflower Oil, Sesame Oil, Corn Oil, Borage Oil, Rose Hip, and other Oils

JAIN DYE CHEM CORPORATION

Mr./Ms.:PrateekJain
100, Tilak Bazar, 1 st Floor Delhi-110006
Ph. +91 -11 -55353690,9810234169
Fax. +91-11-23940675
E-Mail: prateek@jaindyechem.com
Web: www.jaindyechem.com
Deals In : Pigments and Dyes.

ARUN COLOUR CHEM

AN ISO 9001:2000 CERTIFIED COMPANY
Head Off. : J-92, IInd Floor, Rajouri Garden, New Delhi-110027, (India)
Phone : 91 -11 -55466700, 55466800
Fax:91-11-25170120
E-mail : aruncolours@indiatimes.com
Manufacturer of : Primary Food Colours, Blended Food Colours, Lake Colours, Caramel Colours, Drinking Chocolate, Vanilla Powder, Custard Powder, Baking Powder, Essence and Flavours

ALKON INTERNATIONAL

Mr. sachin M. Doshi
11, Bombay Talkies Compound Malad (W), Mumbai-400064
Ph.:022-32948713,28820626
Fax.:022-28820626
E-Mail: sachin2483@mdiffmail.com
Deals In: Importer & Supplier of CosmeticsChemicals, Pharmaceutical Raw materials & Speciality Chemicals From Taiwan, USA, Korea, China, German, France, Spain, i.e. Carbopol, Food Colors, Cocobetain, SLES, Microcrystalline

Cellulose Powder, Lab Chemical. Aloe Vera Juice/Gel/Powder.

AMITFINE CHEM

Mr. Amit M Shah
A-32, Siddhi Apartment Off. A.C. Road, Ashok nagar Kandivali (E) Mumbai -400101
Ph. 022-28870920
Fax. 022-28871551
E-Mailamit170@rediffmail.com
Deals In: dlrs. of raw materials for cosmetics & ayurveda

CHEMSPARK INDIA PVT. LTD.

Mr./ Ms.: Sanjay Tawakley
A-301,3rd Floor Arjun Centre B. S. Devshi Marg Govandi-East, Mumbai - 400088
Ph. 25552832, 39511495
Fax. 25569171
E-Mailspark2@mtnl.net.in
Deals In: cosmetic ingredients

COMMODITY TRADE INTERNATIONAL

4/86, Bharat Mahal, Marine Drive
Mumbai -400002
Ph. 022-22811264,22815218,22815372
Fax. 022-22813200
E-Mail: c6@bol netin Sbaker@vsnl.com

COSMIC INTERNATIONAL

D-904, Usha Nagar, Bhandup (W)
Mumbai -400078
Ph. 22-25665943/55552090/25667632
Fax. +(91)-(22)-55552090
Web:www.indiamart.com/cosmicinternational
Deals In: Exporter Of Anti Wrinkle Massage Creams, Anti Aging Creams, Skin Rejuvenating Creams, Beauty Cream, Vitamin Rich Moisturizer, Sunscreen Lotion, Moisturizing Body Lotion, Royal Touch Nail Lustre, Skin Care, Hair Care And Personal Care Cosmetics.

DISHMAN PHARMACEUTICALS & CHEMICALS LIMITED

401, Sangeet Plaza, Marol Maroshi Road Andheri(E), Mumbai -400059
Ph. 022-28592120,56964055
Fax. 022-28528758,56964054
E-Mail: mumbai@dishmangroup.com
Web :www.dishmangroup.com

GUJARAT ORGANICS LTD.

Mr./Ms.: Hasit A. Dani
3A, Barodawala Mansion, 81 Dr. A B Road Worli, Mumbai -400018
Ph.91-22-24938687
Fax. 91-22-24974886
E-Mail : gujorg@vsnl.com
Web: www.gujaratorganics.com
Deals In: Basic Products: Para Hydroxy Benzoic Acid,Para Hydroxy Benzoic Acid(Electronic Grade),Salicylic Acid Tech.,Salicylic Acid I.P., Salicylic Acid B.P.,Salicylic Acid U.S.P., Sodium Salicylate, Sodium Salicylate I.R.Sodium Salicylate B.R.Sodium Salicylate U.S.P.

H. K. CHEMICALS & PHARMACETICALS

Mr.Piyush Doshi
Post Box No.27698, Shop No.4 Indraprastha I-A Opp Ashoka Hospital Jitendra Road Malad(East),
Mumbai - 400097
Ph. 91 -22-28775829,28774445
Fax. 91 -22-28773079,28728835
E-Mailnkc@vsnl.com
Web: www.hkoverseas.com
Deals In: cosmetic chemical:- tRICLOSAN

YASHO INDUSTRIES PVT. LTD.

Nimish Apartment, Juhu Scheme
N.S. Road No. 5 Vile Parle (W)
Mumbai-400056
Ph.:022-26186533,26186538,26146893
Fax.:022-26112014
E-Mail:yasho@bom3.vsnl.net.in
Web:www.gatewaytoindia.com/yasho
Deals In: Isopropyl Myristate, Isopropyl Palmitate, Octyl Salicylate, Homosalate, Myristyl Myristate, Methyl Salicylate, Cetyl Palmitate, Clove Leaf Oil, Eucalyptus Oil, Methyl Eu-Genol, Eucalyptol, Orange Oil, Eucalyptus Oil, Methyl Eu-Genol, Eucalyptol, Orange Oil, Eucalyptus Oil, Methyl Eu-Genol, Eucalyptol, Orange Oil, Cinnamon Oil, Tertiary Butyl Hydrouinone.

EUROPE VEGETABLE OILS, S. L

DDA MIG 123, Pocket B East Of Loni Road
New Delhi-110093
Ph.22813657 Fax. 22813657
E-Mail : sadhanasood@satyam.net.in
Deals In: Sweet Almond Oil, Olive Oil, Jojoba Oil, Essential Oil

KENT CHEMICALS PVT. LTD.

Corporate Office:
52, LGF World Trade Centre, Babar Lane, Connaught Place, New Delhi-110001
Tel: 91-11-51528661/62
Fax:91-11-51528661
Works : 91 -11 -55451019 /1020
E-mail: info@kentchem.com
Web: www.kentchem.com
Deals In : Liquid Paraffin HLP, LLP & White Oil for application in Hair Oils, Creams, Lotions etc.

KLJ ORGANIC LTD.

Klj House, 63, Rama Marg Najafgarh Road, New Delhi-110015
Fax. 25459709

KRISHANA ENTERPRISES

Mr./Ms.: Vijay Sethi
503, Amber Tower, Azadpur Commercial Complex (Behind Akash Cinema), Delhi -110053
Ph.+91-11-55276150
Mobile: 9811039483
Fax.+91-11-27866824
E-Mail: vsethi67@yahoo.com
Deals In: Pearl Powder, Waxes, Colours, Cosmetics Chemicals, Glitter Powder, Fine Chemicals, & Complete Laboratory Furnishers

NEW BHARAT CHEMICAL WORKS

Mr. Paramjeet Singh
4901, Phoota Road Sadar Bazar, Delhi-110006, India
Ph.:91 -11 -23613307,23538310
Mb: 9810410703
Fax.: 91-11-23523602
E-Mail:nbcworks@hotmail.com
Deals In:deals in:chemicals, waxes,oils, perfumes, fatty acids, petroleum products, sLS.SLES and others

ORCHID CHEMICALS

Mr. Ramesh Kumar
4/28A, 1st & IInd Floor Kirti Nagar Industrial Area New Delhi-110015, India
Ph.:011 -25420785,25460705
Fax. :011-25440208
E-Mail: orchemin_rk95@ rediffmail.com
Deals In:Dealers of all Cosmetics Chemicals

PIONEER IN-ORGANICS

Mr. / Ms.: Hemendra Gupta
313-314,Tilak Bazar, Delhi-110006
Ph. 23932737
Fax. 23984518
E-Mail: pioneerchem@hotmail.com
Deals In: Chemicals All For Cosmetics

R. R. ENTERPRISES

Mr. Sunesh Bajaj
2202, Gali Hinga Beg Tilak Bazar Khari Baoli Delhi-110006
Ph.:91 -11 -23920730,23977337
Fax. :91-11-23929312
E-Mail :rregroup@ vsnl.com
Web: www.business, vsnl.com/rregroup
Deals In:dealer & trader of cosmetics chemicals

R.S. AGENCIES

Mr./ Ms.:Smt. Kanak R. Mehta
A-38, Gujrat Appts. Pitam Pura
New Delhi-110034
Ph. :91 -11 -2258113,22591578
Mb.: 9810033774
E-Mail:rsagencs@yahoo.com
Web:www.rd-singal.com

RMA CHEMICAL CO.

Mr. Rajesh Jalota
1362/5,1st Floor, Pan Mandi Sadar Bazar, Delhi-110006, India
Ph.:23610754, 30933507 Mb: 9810135563
Deals In:dealer & trader of :- cosmetics chemicals and raw materials

GUJARAT ORGANICS LTD.

SHANKAR DYES & CHEMICALS

Mr. Dilip Kumar
1209, Shankar Building, Gali no.-11, Sadar Bazar, Delhi-110006
Ph.:91-11-23673462, 23558239
Mb:9810355592
Fax.:91 -11 -23970589
E-Mail: shankardyes@redrffmail.com
WetawAMSlailaclyesaiclcliaiiicalscorn
Deals In:mfrs., dealears & traders of all types of pigments & dyes for colour cosmetics

SHRI RAM SONS WAX (P) LTD

Mr. Ram Avtar Bansal
181, Tilak Bazar, Delhi-110006
Ph.:91-11-23942451
Mb: 9811076830
Fax.: 91-11-23927312
E-Mail:srsgdel3.vsnl.net.in
Deals In:dealer/trader of cosmetic waxes,Parafin Wax, Shellac Wax, Bees Wax, Camauba Wax, Candellila Wax, Montan Wax, Microcrystalline Wax & other chemicals

BHIMANI CHEMICALS PVT. LTD.

Mr. Jignesh Bhimani
510. Mahakant Opp. VS. Hospital Ellisbridge Ahmedabad-380006 Gujarat, India
Ph. 079-26575474
Fax. 079-26577318
E-Mail: pmbhimani@rediffmail.com
Web : bhimani@bhimanigroup.com
Deals In: Authorized Dealer for Ciba Specialty Chemicals (India) Limited for their Home and Personal Care, Textile Care, Toiletries and allied products

TEXCHEM

Mr. P.V. Sheth
788/23, "Ashirwad", Ansari Road Darya Ganj New Delhi-110002, India
Ph.:+11-23271239, 23277272, 23263456
Fax.:23265356
E-Mail:shethpankaj@hotmail.com
Deals In:Chemicals, Speciality Chemicals, Textile Auxiliaries, Sugar Chemicals, Cosmetics Chemicals, Surfactants

TEXTRON TECNICA

Mr. Avninder K. Sood
DDAMIG123, Pocket-B East Of Loni Road New Delhi-110093
Ph,:91-11-22813657
Mb:9810017563
Fax.:91-11-22813657
E-Mail: sadhnasood@satyam.net.in
Deals In: NATURAL OILS, ESSENTIAL OILS AND OTHER CHEMICALS FOR COSMETICS APPLICATIONS

MAYUR CHEMICALS

98, Nyniappa Naicken Street
Chennai-600003
Ph.44-25357616, 25353765, 9841073044
Fax.+91-44-25357587
Deals In: Deals In Chemicals & Solvents Required For Cosmetics And Herbal Cosmetics Industries (Preservatives, Humectants, Gelling Agents)

TRISHUL CHEMICALS

Mr. / Ms.: Maulik Gandhi
B/48, Ishwarshanti Society Near Water Tank Karelibaug Vadodara -390018 Gujarat, India
Ph. 2485761 Mob:9898264504
E-Mail : trishulchemicals@yahoo.co.in. maulikgandhi_7@yahoo.com
Deals In: Sun Screen Agents & Ultra Violet Stabilizers (Benzophenon-1), (Benzophenon-3),(Benzophenon-4)

UNIFINE

Mr. K.A.Valiulla
4A, 2nd Floor, Shalimar Complex Mahalaxmi five Roads Paldi
Ahmedabad - 380007 Gujarat, India
Ph. 079-6630741 Fax. 079-6621775
E-Mailunifine@sancharnet.in
Deals In : Chemicals and Other.

HINDUSTAN GUM & CHEMICALS LTD.

Mr./ Ms.:V.C. Maheshwari / Vipul
Birla Colony, Bhiwani-127021,(Hr.)
Ph.:(01664)-243891, 243892, 243894, 243811, 243214

Fax.:91(01664)-243813
E-Mail:hichem@ vsnl.com
Deals In:Halr and Personal (skin) care Raw material.

R. R. INDUSTRIES

Mr. Rajinder Bansal
House No.: 1566, Sector-28,
Faridabad-121003, Haryana, India
Ph.:91-0129-2274201
Mob.: 9312436069
Deals In: Barium Peroxide, Barium Hydroxide

SHREE ADDITIVES PHARMA & FOODS LTD.

Mr. /Ms.:VijayPodar
A-707, Wall Street-2 Opposite Orient Club
Ellies Bridge Ahmedabad, Gujurat, India
Ph. +91-79-26426224,
Mob : 9898087950
Fax.+91-79-26560699
E-Mail: vijayeshreeadditives.com
Web: www.shreeadditives.com
Deals In: Raw Materials to Pharma, Food & Cosmetics

SUNSHINE CHEMICALS

Mr. K.K. Jalota
13, Tikona Park market, NIT
Faridabad-121001, Haryana, India
Ph.:0129-2417330,2417350
Mobile: 9818163513 Fax.:0129-2417350
Deals In:consignment agent, dealer & trader of: cosmetics chemicals and raw materials

KADYAN OVERSEAS

Near Govt. Girls School, Village Sewah, Panipat-132108, India
Tel.: 0180-2575350, Resi: 2575418
Mb. 9416019350, 9811940548
Telefax: 0180-2575418
Manufacturer & Exporter:
Flip Top Caps for Shampoo/ Hair Oil Bottles,

PRINCE POLY-PLAST

Mr Manmohan Singh
102, New Sonal Link Industrial Estate No.1, Link Road, Ma l ad (W), Mumbai: 400064, Maharashtra (India)
Tel..: 91-22-28807087
Telefax No.: 91-22-56992822
E-mail:m sohal@vsnl.net,princepolypaint® redHfmail.com
We specialize in : Spray Painting on Plastic Articles, Perfume Bottle Caps, Cosmetic Jar Caps, Cosmetic Bottle Caps, Lipstick Container, Nail Polish Bottle Caps and other plastic Products Viz. Pearls, Cubic Coating, Metallic & Lacquer Finish in different colours.

A.G. ENTERPRISES

Mr./Ms.: Gaurav Daga
C-4/1, Rajiv Nagar Industrial Area, Opp. Shri Ram Bal Bharti School Sewadham Marg, Opp. Nand Nagri Bus Depot. Mandoli Delhi-110093
Ph. +91 -11 -55256713,22343740
Fax.+91-11-22343740
E-Mail: a_g. enterprises@yahoo.com
Deals In: Plastic Packaging Material

GARGEXIMP. LTD.

42, DLF Industrial Area Kirti Nagar
New Delhi, India
Ph. 011-25417831, 25195721, 25758284
Deals In: Pvc Shrinks Films See Our Ad Through Advertiser Index

AUTO PLASTS (INDIA)

Mr./Ms.: Ajay Gupta
C-113, Gali No.-7, Majlis Park Azadpu Delhi-110052 Delhi-110052
Ph--11-27682937, 27374604, 20063969
Deals In: Plastic Bottles & Jars Based On HDPE/LDPE/PP On Fully Automatics Blow Moulding Machines For Use In Cosmetics Pharma, Chemicals, Pesticides Food Items, Pickles, Adhesives Ind. Elc.

J. K. SHRINK PACKAGING

P. S. Nagi
Flat No. 4, Block E2/5, Sector-15, Rohin Delhi-85(India)
Ph.: 011-27295655,55172744

Mobile: 9810239835
E-mail: nagijkshrink@yahoo.com
Manufacturer & Specialist of :-Cosmetics Packaging, Shrink Wraps, PVC Shrinkable Sleeve, Shrink Label, Design Maker, Shrink Packaging, Shrink Tunnels, Printed & Plain Shrink L.D., P.P., H.D.P.E, Bags etc.

MAHENDER PET INDUSTRIES

Mr. Martender P. Garg
A-94/2, Industrial Area, Wazirpur
NewDelhi-110052
Ph. 011-27375551, 27371467
Mob : 9868117623
Web : www. mahenderpetindustries.com
Deals In: Bottles & Jars, Pet preforms, P. P. Caps.

RAHUL INDUSTRIES

mit Aggarwal
-57/2 Wazir pur Industrial Area,
elhi-110052
h. 27374199, 52473031,
obile: 9810444666, 9810071555
-Mail: mlsinghal@satyam.net.in
eals In: Plastic (HDPE/LDPE/ PP/PET/ VC) Bottles

.P. PLASTICS

ohit Narang
135, DDA Sheds Okhla Industrial Area-
New Delhi-110020
.+91-11-26385400,9811324272
Mail : mohit narang@hotmail.com
eals In: Pvc Shrink Films, LDPE Shopping gs & Other All Items

NIQUE MARKETING CO.

shil Jain
90, Ashok Vihar,Phase-I
lhi-110052, India
.+91-11-31042735,9810156675
Marl: uniquesj@softhome.net
als In: Heat Shrink Films, All Kinds Of ly Bags & Pouches, Strapping Rolls & etch Films, AN Packing Machines

RINCE PDLY- PLAST

Manmohan Singh
, New Sonal Link Industrial Estate No.1,
k Road, Malad (W), Mumbai: 400064,
harashtra (India)
Tel. No. : 91-22-28807087
Telefax No.: 91-22-56992822
E-mail: msohal@vsnl.net,
princepolypaint@rediffmail.com
specialize in: Spray Painting on Plastic Articles, Perfume Bottle Caps, Cosmetic Jar Caps, Cosmetic Bottle Caps, Lipstick Container, Nail Polish Bottle Caps and other plastic Products Viz. Pea/is, Cubic Coating, Metallic & Lacquer Finish in different colours.

M/S. AUTO PLASTS (INDIA)

Mr Ajnij Gupta
Off. C-113, Street Mo.7. Majlis Park
Azadpur, Delhi-33
Works . C-36/1 Wazirpur Industrial Area,
DeHi-110052
Ph.; (O) + 91-11-27632937,
(Fac.) 27374604 (M) 20063969,
Plastic Bottles & Jars : -Based on HDPE/ LDPE/PP on Fully Automatic Blow-Mould ing Machines for use in Cosmetic .Pharma, Chemicals, Pesticides, Food items. Pickles,Adhesives Ind. Etc- With Flip-Top Caps 19mm, 25mm & 28mm Leak Proof S Quality Screen-Printing on Round & Flat Surface in Solvent Resistant Ink, that is non erosive.

A.G. AUTO PLASTICS (INDIA)

Mr. Gaurav Daga
C-4/1, Rajiv Nagar Industrial Area, Opp. Shri Ram Bal Bharti School, Sewadhain Marg, Mandoli, Delhi- 110093
Ph.:+91-11-55256713
Mob. : 9811832327
Telefax:+91-11-22343740
E-mail: agenterprises@yahoo.com
Mfrs. and Supplier of:- PET/Plastic Packaging Material For Cosmetics Packaging

KADYAN OVERSEAS

Near Govt. Girls School, Village Panlpat, Panipat - 133106, Haryana, India
Ph. 9416019350, 9811940548
Fax. 0180-2575418
Deals In: Mfrs. Of:Plastic Flip Top Caps, Wonderful Result Oriented Homoeo Tincture For Sugar, Kidney Fail,White Spot And Asthma

MINSU TRADING CORPORATION

Mr. Sumeet Naarayan Gupta
FCA-160, C-Block, Behind Ex-Army Public School, S. G. ML Nagar, Faridabad-121001
Ph.: 0129-5056628,
Mob. - 9810214691, 9312836989
Telefax - 5050628
E-mail: minstutc@mantraonline.com
Mfr.& Supplier of :- Plastic Caps, Fliptop Caps, Plastic Bottles, with Printing options, Stickers & Labels

GARG EXIM PRIVATE LIMITED.

42, DLF Industrial Area, Kirti Nagar, New Delhi-110015
Tel. : 011-51424831, 25417831
Mobile : 9212013690
E-mail : pawan@shrinkpacks.com, gargexim@hotmail.com
Website : www.shrinkpacks.com
Manufacturer & Exporter of: PVC Shrink Films, Shrink Pouches, Shrink Packing Machinery.

J. K. SHRINK PACKAGING

P. S. Magi
Flat No. 4, Block E2/5, Sector-15, Rohini, Del hi-85
Ph.: 011-27295655, 55172744
Mobile: 9810239835
E-mail: nagi_jkshrink@yahoo.com
Manufacturer & Specialist of :-Cosmetics Packaging, Shrink Wraps, PVC Shrinkable Sleeve, Shrink Label, Design Maker, Shrink Packaging, Shrink Tunnels, Printed & Plain Shrink L.D., P.P., H.D.P.E. Bags etc.

S.P. PLASTICS

Mohit Narang
A-135.DDA Sheds Okhla Industrial Area-New Delhi -110020
Ph. +91 -11 -26385400,9811324272
E-Mail : mohit narang@hotmail.com
Deals In: Pvc Shrink Films, LDPE Shoppin Bags & Other All Items

UNIQUE MARKETING CO.

Sushil Jain
C-90, Ashok Vihar, Phase-I Delhi-11005
Ph.+91-11-31C42735,9810156675
E-Mail: uniquesj@softhome.net
Deals In: Heat Shrink Films, All Kinds C Poly Bags & Pouches, Strapping Rolls Stretch Films, All Packing Machines

A.G. ENTERPRISES

Mr./Ms.: Gaurav Daga
C-4/1, Rajiv Nagar Industrial Area, Op Shri Ram Bal Bharti School Sewadha Marg Opp. Nand Nagri Bus Depot. Mand Delhi -110093, India
Ph. +91 -11 -55256713,22343740
Fax. +91-11-22343740
E-Mail: a_g_ente rprises @ y a hoo. co
Deals In: Plastic Packaging Material

SARTHAK PRINT SOFT PVT. LT

C-146/147, F. F. C, Okhla Industri Area,Phase-III, NewDelhi-110020
Ph. : 011-26315604, Telefax : 2631135
E-mail: 146sarthak@hotmail.com
Deals In : Graphic Designing, Scan ing, Services, Offset & Digital Printing

PASHUPATI MARKETING PVT. LTD.

K-94, Udyog Nagar indd Area, Rohtak Road, Delhi-110041, India
Tef. : 91-11-25483561-64
Mob : 9811034410
Fax : 91-11-25483565
E-maif: pashupatimail@vsnl.net
Import & Deals In : - Kraft Paper, Polycoa Paper, Laminated Boards

SARTHAK PRINT SOFT PVT. LTD.

C-146/147.F.F. C.Okhla Industrial Area, Phase-III, New Delhi-110020
Ph.:011-26315604
Telefax: 26311357
E-mail: 146sarthak@hotmail.com
Deals In : Graphic Designing, Scarring, IT Services, Offset & Digital Printing

ALUMINIUM FOIL LIDS, SHRINK LABELS

FCA-3580, Street No.10, A-Block, SGM Nagar, NIT, Faridabad-121001 (Haryana)
Tel,; 0129-2429184, 2429186
E-mail: vansh_foils@yahoo,com
Mfr of:- Aluminium / Blister Foil Lids Heat Sealing Machines Shrink Sleeves & Tubes Shrink Wrapping Machines Vad / Inner / Shrink Labels For Packaging of Cosmetics/ Ayurvedic / Food Products

GIRDHAR FOILS

Mr. Manish Girdhar
FCA-3580, Street No.10, A-Block, S.G.M. Nagar, NIT, Faridabad-121001 (Haryana)
Tel.: 0129-2429184, 2429186
Moblle:09811769733
E-mail: van sh_fo Us ©yahoo.com
Deals In : Aluminium / Blister Foil Lids, Heat Sealing Machines, Shrink Sleeves & Tubes, Shrink Wrapping Machines, Vad / Inner / Shrink Labels, For Packaging of Cosmetics/ Ayurvedic / Food Products

KAMAL (E) INDUSTRIES

Mr. Anand Ratna
Dutta Bhuvan, Kashinath Dhuru Road, Dadar Mumbai -400028 Maharashtra, India
Ph. 91-22-24221555, 24321555
Fax. 91-22-24373474
E-Mail: kei@vsnl.com
Web: www, ke imachines.com
Deals In: Processing & Packaging Machines for Chemicals, Pharma, Cosmetics and Food,

RIDDHIPHARMA MACHINERY LIMITED

Om Shivam
2 Tarun Bharat, Chakala, Sahar Road, Andheri(East), Mumbai - 400 069 India
Ph.91-22-28321332, 25389432,
Mobile: 09821018579
Fax. 91-22-28382479
E-Mailhitenks@vsnl.com
Web: www.riddhipharma.com
Deals Jn: Manufacturers And Exporters Of Pharmaceutical Machineries Including Tableting Machine, Hand Capsule Filling Machine With Automatic Loader, Tube Filling Machine, Ointment Mixer, Fluid Bed Dryer, Colloid Mill And Blister Packing Machines.

SHIVSHAKTI PROCESS EQUIPMENT PVT. LTD.

Mr, D.V. Vishwakarma
shrv Shakti, Opposite Subhasti Estate, Oshiwara Bridge Jogeshwari (W), Mumbai -400102, Maharashtra, India
Ph. 91-22-26788440/26790554
Mobile-9821633589
Fax. 91-22-26798284
E-Mail;-
office @ sh r vs hatarequ ipments.com
Web: www.shivshakti equipmentscom
Deals In: Manufacturer & Exporter Of : Centrifuge Machine, Fluid Bed Dryer, Tray/ Vacuum Tray Dryer, Double Cone/Rotary Vacuum Dryer, Multimill, Blenders, Reaction Vessel, Heat Exchangers, Also Undertaking Turnkey Projects for Cosmetics, Pharma, chemical, Bulk Drugs & Allied Industries

DANYAL ENGG. CO.

Mr. Aftab Ahmad
3022, Gali Hal Bandan Chowk Shahganj Ajmeri Gate Delhi-110006
Ph. 011-23212102,23217244
Mob: 9811174961,9899840233
Deals In: Plant & Machineries, Lipstick, Nail Polish, All Cosmetics, Pharmaceutical & Chemicals Machinery

KAMAL (E) INDUSTRIES

Mr./ Ms.: mr. Anand Ratna
Dutta Bhuvan, Kashinath Dhuru Road, Dadar Mumbai -400028 Maharashtra, India
Ph. 91-22-24221555,24321555
Fax. 91-22-24373474
E-Mail: kei@vsnl.com
Web www. keimachines.com
Deals In: -
Processing & Packaging Machines

DANYALENGGCO.

Mr. Aftab Ahmad
3022, Gali Nal Bandan Chowk Shahganj
Ajmeri Gate Delhi-110006
Ph. 011-23212102, 23217244
Mob: 9811174981, 9899840233
Deals In: Plant & Machineries for Lipstick, Nail Polish, All Cosmetics, Pharmaceutical & Chemicals Machinery

T. R. SHARMA ENGINEERING WORKS

A-156, HariNagar Clock Tower,
New Delhi-64 (India)
Ph: 91-11 -28123729, 25494571
Mobile: 9818125123
E-mail: paintmachinery@yahoo.com
Deals In : Manufacturer & Fabricator of Complete Plant & MachineriesFor Nail Polish / Enamel, Machineries of All kinds of Paints, Inks, Cosmetics, Ceramics and Chemical Plants i.e. Reaction Kettle, Attritors, Ball Mills, Sand Mills, Hy-Speed Mixer, Ribbon Mixer, Multi Speed Mixer and Fabrication etc.

DANYAL ENGINEERING CO.

Mr. Aftab Ahmad
3022, Gali Nal San dan, Chowk Shahganj,
Ajmeri Gate Delhi-110006
Ph. 011-23212102, 23217244
Mob: 9811174981, 9899840233
Deals In: Plant & Machineries for Lipstick, Nail Polish, All Cosmetics, Pharmaceutical & Chemicals Machinery

BABA PACKAGING

Mr. B.C. Sharma
14, Krishna Palace, Neelam Fly Ove
Faridabad-121007 Haryana, India
Ph. 0129-2291107, 2235284, 2240189
Fax. 0129-2240741
E-Mail :baba@ ndb.vsnl.net.in
Web: w ww. babapac ka g ing. com
Deals In: Mineral Water Pouch Packagin Machines, Standard FFS Machines, Zippe Pouch Machine, Augur Base FFS Machine For Packing Of Powders, Shrink Wrappin Machine, Biscuit Packaging,Machine, Computerised Weighmetric Machine

S. S. PHARMA EQUIPMENTS

Mr. Suresh Panchai
Off. : 103, Veena Industrial Estate, L.B.S Marg, Vikhroli (W), Mumbai-400083
Ph. : 91-22-25789111/25789110
Fax:91-22-25789110
E-mail: sspharmaeqp@vsnl.net
Website : www.sspharma.com

NUCON ENGINEERS

Mr. Ashok k. Manchanda
S-18,Okhlalndl,Area Phase-II,
New Delhi -110020
Ph. 011-263840133383818, 26383604
Fax. 011-26383440
Deals In: India's Leading Manufacturer Gas Analysers, Gas Chro-matographs

SHIVASCIENTIFIC GLASS PVT. LTD.

Mr./Ms.:C.S. Nair
Shiva House, Rz-84 Syed Nangloi Paschi Vihar NewDelhi-110087
Ph. 011 -25261137,25253509
Fax. 011-25258558
E-Mail: ssgpl@vsnl.net
Web: www.shivascientific.com
Deals In: Laboratory Equipments.

CITIZEN SCALES (I) PVT. LTD.

Mr, Sajith Soman
3, Pushpanjali Bldg. Gaushala Lane Ma lad (E) Mumbar -400097
Ph.022-26305170-75
Fax. 022-26305176
E-Mail: channal@citi2enscales.com
Web www. citizen *sea* les.com
Deals In: Manufacturers of electronic weighing balances & scales

KRISHNA CORPORATES

Room no. 614, Cotton exchange Building, Kalbadevi Road, Mumbai -400002
Maharashtra, India
Ph.: 22404975, 22408733
Deals In : Grey Mesh Fabrics used in filtration of various cosmetics and herbal cosmetics.

DARSHAN MOULD MAKER

487/47, Peeragarhi Near Pooja Dairy New Delhi-110087
Mob. 9810749497, 9811867676
E-Mail: darshanmoultJs@hoimail.com
Web: www.darshanmoulds.com
Deals In: Mfr. & Distributer Of :- Plastic Moulds For Various Size Blow Moulded Bottles

CENTRAL COUNCIL FOR RESEARCH IN AYURVEDA & SIDDHA

Jawahar Lai Nehru Bhartiya Chikitsa Avum Homoeopathy Anusandhan Bhawan N0.61-65, Institutional Area, Opp.'D' Block Janak Puri,
New Delhi -110058 Ph. 011-25624457
Fax. 011-25528748
E-Mail: ccras@ndi.vsnl.net.in
Web: www.ccras.org
Deals In: Ayush-64 An Anti-Malarial Drug,777 Oil An Effective Siddha Drug For Psoriasis,Ayush-56 An Anti-Epileptic Drug,Guggulu An Anli-Hyper-Lipidemic Drug, Pushkar Gugguluan Effective Formulation For Ischaemic Heart Diseases,Ayush Ghutti & Bal Rasayanafor General Health And Immunity In Children Etc.

BENEDICT'S LABORATORY

Govind Mitra Road, Patna-800004
Ph : 0612-2670806, 3955806
Fax:0612-2674652
Mobile : 09334115655, 09835042441
E-Mail; -
benedicts_Laboratory@rediffmail.com
Super Distributor : Monozyme, Qualigen Fine Chemicals,
Manufacturers of ; Stain, Reagents, Qualitative, Quantitative.
Authenticated Suppliers to : Beauty, Cosmetic Surgeons, Homoeopathic, Pathologist, Research Institute, Laboratory Testing.

PRINCE POLY-PLAST

Mr Manmohan Singh
102, New Sona! Link Industrial Estate No.1, Link Road, Ma lad (W), Mumbai-400064, Maharashtra (India)
Tel. No.: 91-22-28807087
Telefax No.: 91-22-56992822
E-mail :-m_sohal @ vsnl.net, princepotypaint® redirfmail.com
We specialize in: Spray Painting on Plastic Articles, Perfume Bottle Caps, Cosmetic Jar Caps, Cosmetic Bottle Caps, Lipstick Container, Nail Polish Bottle Caps and other plastic Products Viz. Pearls, Cubic Coating, Metallic & Lacquer Finish in different colours.

S. S. PHARMA EQUIPMENTS

Mr. Suresh Panchal
Off.: 103, Veena Industrial Estate, L.B.S. Marg, Vikhroli (W), Mumbai-400083
Ph.: 91-22-25789111/25789110
Fax:91-22-25789110
E-mail: ssph a rmaeqp@vsnl.net
Website: www.sspharma.com
Deals In : Pharmaceutical and laboratory equipments

BENEDICT'S LABORATORY

Govind Mitra Road, Patna-800004
Ph : 0612-2670806, 3955806
Fax:0612-2674652
Mobile: 09334115655, 09835042441
E-Mail: benedicts_Laboratory @ redrffmail.com

Deals In : Super Distributor: Monozyme, Oualigen Fine Chemicals, Manufacturers of: Stain, Reagents, Qualitative, Quantitative. Authenticated Suppliers to: Beauty, Cosmetic Surgeons, Homoeopathic, Pathologist, Research Institute, Laboratory Testing.

DARSHAN MOULD MAKER

487/47, Peeragarhi Near Pooja Dairy
New Delhi-110087
Mob.: 9810749497, 9811867676
E-Mail:darshanmoulds@hotmail.com
Web: www.darshanmoulds.com
Deals In: Mfr. & Distributer Of :-
Plastic Moulds For Various Size Blow Moulded Bottles

MAHENDER PET INDUSTRIES

Mr. Mahender P. Garg
A-94/2, Industrial Area, Wazirpur
New Delhi-1100S2
Ph. 011 -27375551,27371467, 9868117623
Web : www. mahenderpetindustries.com
Deals In: Bottles & Jars, Pet Preforms, P. P. Caps.

GIRDHAR FOILS

Mr. Manish Girdhar
FCA-3580, Street No.10, A-Block, SGM Nagar, NIT, Faridabad-121001 (Haryana)
Tel.: 0129-2429184, 2429186
Mobile: 09811769733
E-mail: vansh_foils@yahoo.com
Deals In : Aluminium / Blister Foil Lids, Heat Sealing Machines, Shrink Sleeves & Tubes, Shrink Wrapping Machines, Vad/ Inner/ Shrink Labels, For Packaging of Cosmetics/ Ayurvedic / Food Products See Our Ad Through Advertiser Index

KADYAN OVERSEAS

Near Govt. Girls School,
Village Panipat -132108, Haryana, India
Mob : 9416019350, 9811940548
Fax. 0180-2575418
Deals In: Mfrs. Of ;Plastic Flip Top Caps, Wonderful Result Oriented Homoeo Tincture For Sugar, Kidney Fail,White Spot And Asthma

MINSU TRADING CORPORATION

Mr./Ms.: S.N.Gupta
FCA-160, C-Block S.G.M Nagar Bandh Road (Behind Ex-Army School)
Faridabad-121001 Hariyana, India
Ph.+91-129-5050628
Mob : 9810214691
E-Mail: vc47@vsnl.com
Deals In: Plastic Bottles & Caps Including Fliptop With Printing & Stickers

PATEL ENTERPRISES

Mr. B. K. Patel
Flat #465,466 Nyay Khand-II Indrapuram
Ghaziabad-201010
(Factory Address: G-9 Sector-XI Noida-201301) Ghaziabad - 201010, U.P., India
Mob : 9312545871/9810214951
E-Mail : patel_enterprise2004@yahoo.com
Deals In: Art & Cosmetics Brush machinery Manutacturer

SIGMA ENTERPRISES

Mr. Ashwini Sharma / Vishal Sethi
1573,Sector-8
Faridabad-121006, Haryana
Ph. 0129-2311118
Mb: 9810290845/73
Fax. 0129-2311118
Deals In ; Dealers And Distributers Of Oils & Chemicals Transfering Pumps.

117. MANUFACTURE OF TIN CONTAINERS
118. MANUFACTURE OF STORAGE TANKS, PRESSURE VESSELS, HEAT EXCHANGERS
119. MARK II HAND PUMPS
120. MARUTI WORKSHOP CUM - SERVICE STATION
121. MECHANICAL JACKS
122. METAL CUTTING DIE DESIGN
123. METAL CUTTING OF AND GRINDING WHEELS (ABBRASIVE CUTTING WHEELS)
124. METAL HOOKS & CLIPS
125. METAL SEPARATION (COPP-ER , TIN, LEAD) FROM SPENT WASH ACID
126. METALLIC RING JOINTS
127. METALLIC GASKET (SPIRAL WOUND)
128. MICROVEE & ABSOLUTE FILTER
129. MICROWAVE OVEN
130. MILD STEEL INGOTS
131. MINI STEEL PLANT
132. MODERN VEHICLE WORKSHOP
133. MOPED
134. M.S.HINGES
135. M.S.INGOT AND HR. STEEL STRUCTURALS
136. M.S.INGOT BY INDUCTION FURNACES
137. M.S.PIPES
138. M.S. WELDING ELECTRODE
139. MUFFLERS & SILENCERS FOR THREE WHEELERS
140. NAIL CUTTER WITH FILER & MANICURE
141. NICHROME WIRE
142. NICKEL LINED SCREENS
143. NON-FERROUS ALLOY ROLLING
144. NON-FERROUS FORGING
145. NON-FERROUS FOUNDRY
146. NON PRESSURE
147. INCANDESCENT LAMP
148. NUMBER COMBINATION LOCKS FOR LUGGAGES
149. NUTS & BOLTS
150. PAPER COATED ALUMINIUM AND COPPER WIRE
151. PETROMAX CONTAINER
152. PHOTO ETCHING OF STAINLESS STEEL PLATES
153. PIPE GALVANIZING PLANT
154. PISTON RING-AUTOMOBILE
155. PLANT PROTECTION EQUIPMENTS
156. PLATINUM LABORATORY APPARATUS
157. PRESSURE COOKER & ALUMINIUM UTENSILS
158. PRESSURE COOKER (ALUMINIUM)
159. PRESSURE DIE CASTING
160. PRINTED ALUMINIUM COLLAPSIBLE TUBES
161. PRINTED TIN CONTAINERS
162. PRINTING PRESS (CYLINDER MACHINE)
163. PUMPS FOR CHEMICAL INDUSTRY (SPECIAL)
164. RAILWAY SLEEPERS (M.S.)
165. RAZOR TWIN BLADE
166. R.C.C SPUN PIPES
167. RECONDITIONING OF M.S. DRUMS/BARRELS
168. RE-ROLLING COPPER AND BRASS SHEET AND RODS
169. RE-ROLLING MILLS
170. RESIN COATED SAND
171. RESIN CORED SOFT SOLDER WIRES
172. ROLLING MILL (BY INDUCTION FURNACE) & MANUFACTURE OF BARS, ANGLES, SQUARES, TUBES AND OTHERS
173. ROLLER BEARING & FORGING
174. ROLLING OF STAINLESS STEEL PATTA
175. RUBBER INSULATED PLIERS (HAND TOOLS)
176. RUBBING COMPOUND FOR AUTOMOBILES
177. SCIENTIFIC LABORATORY EQUIPMENTS
178. SCOOTER ASSEMBLING
179. SECONDARY LEAD EXTRAC -TION BY SCRAP BATTERY PLATES,PIPES & SHEET
180. SEAMLESS M.S. TUBES & PIPES
181. SELF TAPPING STEEL SCREW
182. SEWING NEEDLES
183. S.G. IRON & ALLOY STEEL
184. SHEET METAL PRODUCTS, (FERROUS/NON-FERROUS)
185. SHIP/MARINE CONTAINER
186. SHOCK ABSORBERS
187. SHOE EYELETS
188. SHOT AND GRITS BY AUTOMIZATION PROCESS
189. SHOVELS
190. SILICO MANGANESE ALLOYS
191. SILENCERS (MUFFLERS) EXHAUST & TAIL PIPE FOR ALL TYPES OF VEHICLES
192. SINTERED BEARING
193. SINTERED BUSHES
194. SINTERED METAL PRODUCTS
195. SOFT AND HARD FERRITES
196. SPANNERS
197. SPARK PLUGS
198. STEEL PLANT (ELECTRIC ARC FURNACE BASED- EAF)
199. SPHERIODAL GRAPHITE CAST IRON
200. SPRAY DRYER
201. STAINLESS STEEL HINGES
202. STAINLESS STEEL SHEET ROLLING TO PRODUCE STAINLESS STEEL UTENSILS
203. STAINLESS STEEL UTENSILS
204. STAPLE PINS,PAPER PIN , GEM CLIPS ETC.
205. STEEL CASTINGS
206. STEEL CHAIN
207. STEEL FOUNDRY
208. STEEL FURNITURES AND ELECTRICAL APPLIANCES
209. STEEL PLANT (MINI)
210. STEEL RODS AND COILS FROM SCRAPS
211. STEEL ROLLING MILL
212. STEEL STRIPS (COLD ROLLED) SILICON WITH GRAIN RIENTED FOR ELECTRIC USE
213. STEEL TRANSMISSION LINE TOWERS & ROLLING MILL TO PRODUCE STEEL SECTION
214. STEEL FURNITURES AND ELECTRICAL APPLIANCES
215. STEEL WIRE DRAWING AND GALVANIZING
216. STEEL WOOL
217. SUBMERGED ARC WELDED PIPES
218. SUBMERSIBLE PUMP MANUFACTURING
219. SUPER ENAMELLED COPPER WIRE
220. THREE WHEELERS
221. TIE-ROD ENDS
222. TIN CONTAINERS
223. TOOLROOM AND SHEET METAL PRODUCTS
224. TRACTOR TRAILERS
225. TRANSMISSION POWER FITTING
226. TUBULAR POLES
227. SUPER ENAMELLED COPPER WIRES
228. TUBULAR POLES FOR ELECTRICAL TRANSMISSION (BY FABRICATION PROCESS)
229. TUBULAR POLES OF M.S. & HIGH TENSILE STEEL
230. VACUUM CLEANERS
231. VACUUM FLASK (STAINLESS STEEL)
232. VALVES FOR REFRIGERA TION AND AIR-CONDITION
233. VEHICLE WELDING & PAINTING
234. VENETION BLIND
235. WASHING MACHINES (AUTOMATIC & COMPUTERISED)
236. WATER CONTROLLER (AUTOMATIC)
237. WATCH STRAPS/CHAINS/ BRACELETS/BELT BRASS & STAINLESS STEEL
238. WATER COOLERS
239. WELDED WIRE MESH
240. WELDING ELECTRODES
241. WICK STOVES
242. WIND MILL WINDOW FRAME (FERROUS & NON-FERROUS)
243. WRIST WATCH

359. DI ETHYL OXALATE
360. DI METHYL ORTHOPHTHALATE
361. DI-METHYL PHTHALATE
362. DICLOFENAC GEL
363. DIOCTYL PHTHALATE (DOP)
364. DI PHENYL GLYCERINE
365. DI PHENYL OXIDE
366. DINITRO-CHLORO BENZENE
367. DISTILLED WATER
368. DODECYL BENZENE SULPHONATE
369. DUSTLESS CHALK
370. EDTA & ITS SALTS
371. ELECTROLESS NICKEL PLATING ON PLASTICS
372. ENDOSULFAN
373. EPOXY RESIN BASED COMPOUND
374. ETHYL ACETATE
375. EHTYL ETHER
376. ETHYL ALCOHOL (POTABLE LIQUOR)
377. ETHYL HEXANOL
378. EXTRACTION OF ESSENTIAL OILS BY SUGAR CRITICAL FLUID (CARBON DIOXIDE) METHOD FROM FLOWERS, HERBAL & SPICES
379. FERRIC ALUM
380. FERRO CHROME LIGNO SULPHONATE
381. FERRO MANGANESE
382. FERRO SILICONE
383. FERRO VANADIUM FROM VANADIUM SLUDGE
384. FERROUS SILICATE
385. FERROUS SULPHATE
386. FERTILIZER FROM ANIMAL BLOOD & LEATHER WASTE
387. FLUORESCENT TUBE LIGHT POWDER
388. FOAMED PVC COMPOUNDING & ITS PRODUCTS
389. FORMALDEHYDE
390. FRACTIONAL DISTILLATION OF D.M.O (DEMENTHOLIZED OIL)
391. FRACTIONAL DISTILLATION OF ESSENTIAL OIL & MEDICINAL PLANT EXTRACT
392. FRICTION DUST (LIQUID & POWDER) FROM CNSL
393. FRUIT FLAVOURS
394. FURFURAL FROM RICE HUSK
395. GARLIC ACID
396. GASKET SHELLAC COMPOUND
397. GEAR OIL
398. GIBBERELLIC ACID
399. GLASS PUTTY
400. GLYCERINE
401. GOSSYPOL (POLY PHENOL) FROM COTTON SEED OIL
402. GUAR GUM POWDER
403. HAIR FIXER (HAIR GEL TYPE)
404. H - ACID
405. HENNA PASTE MAKING
406. HEPTAL DEHYDE
407. HIGH CARBON FERRO CHROME
408. HYDRATED CALCIUM SILICATE BRICK
409. HYDRATED LIME FROM SEA SHELL
410. HYDROCHLORIC ACID
411. HYDRO FLUORIC ACID
412. HYDROGEN PEROXIDE (BY AUTO-OXIDATION PROCESS)
413. ICE PACKS (SOLUTIONS TYPE, WHITE GEL TYPE, VIOLET SEMI SOLID POLYMER TYPE)
414. IMPROVING DROP POINT PARAFFIN WAX FROM 45-50°C TO 75-80°C
415. INDUSTRIAL ALCOHOL
416. INTEGERATED COMPLEX OF EASTER & ALLIED PRODUCTS (D.O.P, D.B.P, ETHYL ACETATE WIRE ENAMEL & CABLE JELLY)
417. IMFL (WHISKY) & COUNTRY LIQUOR
418. IRON OXIDE FOR MAKING FERITTE
419. IRON SULPHIDE
420. JUTE BATCHING OIL
421. KESH KALA TEL (HAIR DYE LOTION) (VASMOL 33, BLACK NITE TYPE)
422. L-LYSINE MONOHYDROCHLORIDE
423. LACTIC ACID FROM WHITE SUGAR BY FERMENTATION PROCESS
424. LDPE GRANULES FROM VIRGIN (LDPE RESIN)
425. LEAD EXTRACTION FROM BATTERY SCRAP
426. LEAD OXIDE (A) LEAD MONOXIDE (B) LEAD TETRA OXIDE (C) GREYLEAD OXIDE
427. LIQUID GLUCOSE & ITS BY PRODUCTS
428. LIQUID OXYGEN BOTTLING PLANT
429. LIQUID SHOE POLISH
430. LIQUID FLOOR POLISH
431. LUBE OIL VISCOSITY IMPROVED FOR P.P.G/P.E.G
432. LUBRICANTS ASHLESS 100% COMBUSTION
433. MAGNESIUM CARBONATE AND MAGNESIUM BICARMONATE
434. MAGNESIUM HYDROXIDE POWDER
435. MAGNESIUM SILICATE
436. MAGNESIUM SULPHATE
437. MALACHITE GREEN
438. MALEIC ANHYDRIDE
439. MANGANESE SULPHATE
440. MANUFACTURING OF CARBON MONO-OXIDE WATER GAS
441. MENTHOL BOLD CRYSTALS FROM FLAKES
442. MENTHOL CRYSTAL & MENTHA OIL
443. MERCURIC OXIDE
444. METAL PRE-TREATMENT CHEMICALS
445. METHANE GAS BY SODIUM ACETATE & SODA LIME
446. METHYL ACETYL RICINOLATE
447. METOL
448. METOL FROM HYDROQUINONE & METHYLAMINE
449. MICANITE
450. MICRO NUTRIENT MIXTURE
451. MINERAL WATER
452. MINERAL WATER AND PET BOTTILNG PLANT
453. MINERAL WATER IN BOTTLES, GLASS AND POUCHES
454. MINI CEMENT PLANT (BY ROTARY KILN PROCESS)
455. MIXED FERTILIZER
456. MOSQUITO & FLIES REPELLENT AGARBATTI (INCENSE STICKS)
457. MONO CHLORO ACETIC ACID
458. MONOCROTOPHOS (TECHNICAL)
459. MOSQUITO COIL
460. MOSQUITO COIL & MAT
461. MOSQUITO MAT
462. MOTHER TINCTURE & BIO CHEMIC MEDICINES
463. NAPHTHALENE & PHENYL (INTEGRATED UNIT)
464. NATURAL MINERAL WATER BY REVERSE OSMOSIS PROCESS
465. NICKEL PLATING BRIGHTNER (PRIMARY OR CARRIER BRIGHTNER & SECONDARY BRIGHTNER)
466. NICKEL SULPHATE
467. NICOTINE FROM TOBACCO WASTE
468. NICOTINE SULPHATE FROM TOBACCO WASTE
469. NITRO BENZENE
470. NITRO CELLULOSE SANDING SEALER/LACQUER
471. NITRO MUSK
472. NITROGEN & OXYGEN GAS PLANT
473. NON-IONIC SURFACTANT (WETTING AGENT)
474. NO-CARB PASTE
475. OCTANOL
476. ORTHO NITRO PHENOL
477. OXALIC ACID FROM MOLASSES
478. OXALIC ACID FROMRICE HUSK
479. OXALIC ACID FROM TREE BARK
470. OXALIC ACID FROM WASTE VEGETABLES
471. OXYGEN GAS PLANT
472. OXYGEN GAS PLANT (AIR SEPERATION METHOD)
473. PARA-AMINO BENZOIC ACID
474. PARA-AMINO PHENOL
475. PARA TOLUENE SULPHONIC ACID
476. PECTIN FROM RAW PAPAYA
477. PERFUME (LEMON & OTHERS)

CRUDE NAPHTHA
570. TRIMETHYL AMMONIUM CHLORIDE
571. TRIPHENYL PHOSPHITE (T.P.P)
572. ULTRAMARINE BLUE (LIQUID)
573. UREA FORMALDEHYDE & MELAMINE FORMALDEHYDE POWDER
574. UNDECYLINIC ACID
575. VINYL ACETATE MONOMER
576. VITAMIN C
577. VITAMIN E
578. WASTE WATER TREATMENT PLANT FOR INDUSTRIAL SECTOR IN INDIA (ONLY MARKER SURVEY)
579. WIRE DRAWING LUBRICANT
580. WIRE ENAMEL
581. XANTHATES
582. YELLOW DEXTRIN
583. ZINC CHLORIDE
584. ZINC OXIDE
585. ZINC PHOSPHATING BY COLD PROCESS
586. ZINC SILICATE
587. ZINC STEARATE
588. ZINC SULPHATE
589. ZINC SULPHATE MONOHYDRATE
590. ACID BLACK
591. AURAMINE'O'
592. AZO DYES STUFF
593. DYE & DYE INTERMEDIATE
594. DYE INTERMEDIATES
595. MALACHITE GREEN
596. METHYLENE BLUE
597. PHTHALOCYANINE BLUE
598. PHTHALOCYANINE BLUE & GREEN
599. REACTIVE DYES
600. SULPHUR BLACK DYE
601. VAT DYES
602. WATER CHILLING PLANT
603. WADDING OIL (100%) FOR WADDING OF COTTON HOSIERY CLOTH IN THE DYEING PROCESS
604. WHITE OIL
605. WAX FLOOR POLISH

ELECTRICAL, ELECTONICS, COMPUTERS AND INFOTECH/IT PROJECTS

606. AIR CONDITIONING
607. ALUMINIUM ALLOY CONDUCTOR
608. ALUMINIUM CABLE
609. ALUMINIUM ELECTROYTIC CAPACITORS
610. AUDIO CASSETTE ASSEMBLING & RECORDING
611. AUDIO CASSETTES DUPLICATING RECORDING
612. AUDIO CASSETTES & AUDIO STUDIO
613. AUDIO CASSETTES PLANE & RECORDED
614. AUDIO MAGNETIC HEADS
615. AUDIO MAGNETIC TAPE
616. AUDIO/VIDEO CASSETTES
617. AUTO BULB/LAMPS
618. AUTOMATIC VOLTAGE STABILIZER
619. BATTERY PLATES
620. BACK OFFICE (Rs. 5000/-)
621. B/W TV & COMPUTER MONITOR PICTURE TUBE
622. BREAD BOARDS
623. CALL CENTRE
624. CAMERA (35 MM)
625. CAPACITORS
626. CARBON ELECTRODE USED FOR BATTERY CELL
627. CARBON POTETIOMETERS
628. CEILING FAN
629. CERAMIC INSULATOR
630. CHILDREN INFOTECH TRAINING INSTITUTE (Rs. 5000/-)
631. CHOKE AND PATTI
632. CHOKE AND STARTER
633. CHOKE USED FOR FLUORESCENT LAMPS
634. COLOUR TELEVISION
635. COLOUR AND BLACK & WHITE TELEVISION
636. COMPACT DISC
637. COMPACT DISC PLAYER (AUDIO/VIDEO)
638. COMPUTER EDUCATION INSTITUTE
639. COMPUTER ASSEMBLY
640. COMPUTER HARDWARE
641. COMPUTER KEYBOARD
642. COMPUTER PERIPHERALS
643. COMPUTER PRINTERS
644. COMPUTER RIBBON
645. COMPUTER RIBBON REINKING OR REFILLING
646. COMPUTER STATIONERY
647. COMPUTER STATIONERY &

IMPORTED HARDWARE PARTS
648. COMPUTER TERMINALS
649. COMPUTERISED WASHING MACHINE (AUTOMATIC)
650. COMPUTER SOFTWARE
651. CONDENSER FOR MOTOR USING MPP FILM
652. CONTENT DEVELOPMENT CENTRE (EOU) (Rs. 5000/-)
653. CONTROL PANEL BOARD
654. COOLING COIL FOR AIR CONDITIONERS
655. COPPER STRIP COIL FROM SCRAP
656. CORDLESS TELEPHONES
657. CYBER CAFE
658. CYBERKIOSK (Rs. 5000/-)
659. DATA PROCESSING CENTRE (Rs. 5000/-)
660. D.C. MICRO MOTORS
661. D.G.SETS
662. DISH ANTENNA AND CABLE T.V. NETWORK EQUIPMENT
663. DISTRIBUTION TRANSFORMERS & REPAIRS
664. DOMESTIC ELECTRICAL APPLIANCES- ROOM COOLER, WASHING MACHINE, WATER HEATER, ELECTRIC ROOM HEATER
665. E-SCHOOL
666. E-COMMERCE/BUSINESS
667. ELECTRIC ENERGY METER
668. ELECTRIC FANS
669. ELECTRIC HORN FOR AUTOMOBILE
670. ELECTRIC LAMP/GLS (INCANDESCENT LAMP)
671. ELECTRIC MIXER
672. ELECTRIC MOTORS UP TO 10 HP. REWINDING OF ALL TYPES OF MOTORS WATER PUMPS
673. ELECTRIC MOTOR WINDING (FOR FAN, MIXIES, ETC.)
674. ELECTRIC STEAM IRON
675. ELECTRICAL APPLIANCES
676. ELECTRICAL FIXTURES
677. ELECTRICAL STAMPING
678. ELECTROLYTIC CAPACITORS
679. ELECTROMAGNETIC RELAY
680. ELECTRONIC BALAST/CHOK
681. ELECTRICAL CHOKE
682. ELECTRONIC DIGITAL WATCHES
683. ELECTRONIC DIGITAL WEIGHING MACHINE
684. ELECTRONIC FIRE ALARM
685. ELECTRONIC GAS STOVE LIGHTERS
686. ELECTRONIC PRESSURE INDICATORS, ELECTRICALS, ELECTRONIC LIQUID LEVEL INDICATORS, ELECTRONIC TEMPERATURE INDICATOR, DIGITAL TACHOMETER
687. ELECTRONIC TELEPHONE INSTRUMENTS
688. ELECTRONIC TOYS
689. ELECTRONIC WATCHES & CLOCKS
690. FAX MACHINES
691. F.H.P MOTORS
692. FLOPPY DISKETTES
693. FLUORESCENT LAMP STARTER
694. FLUORESCENT TUBULAR

"Detailed Project Report" Payable in advance through Draft/Cash/M.O. in favour of *"ENGINEERS INDIA RESEARCH INSTITUTE"*. 4449, Nai Sarak (D), Main Road Delhi - 110 006 (INDIA) ● Ph : 23918117, 2391 6431, 2384 0361 ● Mob : 098114 37895 ●Fax : 91-11- 2391 6431 ●E-Mail : eirisidi@bol.net.in ● WebSite : www.eiriindia.org

LAMPS WITH INTRODUCTION TO MERCURY VAPOUR LAMP
695. FRANCHISEE COMPUTER EDUCATION CENTRE (Rs. 5000)
696. GAS DETECTOR (L.P.G)
697. GENERATOR SET & PUMP SETS
698. GENERATOR (BATTERY OPERATED)
699. GIS SERVICE CENTRE (GEOGRAPHICAL INFORMATION SYSTEMS)
700. HARDWARE FITTING FOR TRANSMISSION LINE OVERHEAD LINE MATERIAL
701. HEADERS FOR TRANSISTOR ICS SEMI CONDUCTOR
702. H.T & L.T INSULATORS
703. H.T & M.V INDUSTRIAL CUBICAL SWITCH BOARD
704. INFORMATION MOVING DISPLAY (L.E.D TYPE)
705. INSURANCE CLAIM PROCESSING CENTRE (EOU) (Rs. 5000/-)
706. INTEGRATED CIRCUITS
707. INTERNET BASED STOCK TRADING (Rs. 5000/-)
708. INTERNET SERVICE PROVIDER (I.S.P.)
709. JELLY FILLED TELEPHONE CABLES
710. LAP TOP COMPUTERS
711. LEAD ACID BATTERIES
712. LEAD ACID BATTERY PLATES AND ASSEMBLING OF BATTERY
713. LEGAL TRANSCRIPTION & SECRETARIAL SERVICES CENTER (EOU)(Rs. 5000/-)
714. LIGHT EMITTING DIODES (L.E.D)
715. LINEAR ICS TRAINER KIT
716. LOUD SPEAKER
717. L.T TRANSFORMER REPAIRING
718. MEDICAL TRANSCRIPTION CENTRE
719. METAL FILM RESISTORS
720. METALLISED POLYPROPYLENE, POLYESTER FILM CAPACITOR
721. MICA BASE ELECTRONIC COMPONENTS
722. MICA PAPER WASTE PAPER FROM MICA WASTE
723. MICRO PROCESSORS TRAINER KITS BASED ON MICRO PROCESSORS
724. MINI COMPUTER (PERSONAL COMPUTER)
725. MINIATURE CIRCUIT BREAKER (M.C.B)
726. MINIATURE WATCH BATTERIES (BUTTON CELL)
727. MIXER/GRINDER (MIXI)
728. MONO CHROME COMPUTER MONITOR
729. MOTOR START ELECTROLYTIC CAPACITOR
730. MULTI LAYER P.C.B
731. MULTIPLE RELAY FOR LOW VOLTAGE
732. NEON INDICATOR
733. NEON SIGN MANUFACTURE
734. OPTICAL FIBRE CABLES
735. ON LINE SHOPPING MALL (Rs. 5000/-)
736. OPTO MECHANICAL & ELECTRICAL EQUIPMENTS
737. PHOTO COLOUR LAB
738. PICTURE TUBE (B/W)
739. PLAIN PAPER COPIER
740. PLASTIC FILM CAPACITORS
741. POLYESTER CAPACITORS
742. PORTABLE GENERATOR SET
743. PORTAL
744. PORTABLE TELEVISION(TV)
745. POWER CAPACITORS
746. POWER INVERTERS
747. POWER PLANT
748. POWER TRANSFORMERS UP TO 600 KVA
749. PRINTED CIRCUIT BOARD
750. PVC WIRES & CABLES
751. RE-CONDITIONING OF PICTURE TUBE
752. RESIN CAST CT & PT (1 KV)
753. SEMI CONDUCTOR DEVICE
754. SEMI CONDUCTORS FOR TRANSISTORS & DIODES
755. SETTING UP OF A VIDEO STUDIO
756. SMOKE DETECTORS
757. SOLAR CELLS
758. SOLAR MODULES
759. SOLAR PHOTO VOLTAIC SYSTEM
760. SOLDER FLUXES
761. SOLAR WATER HEATING PANELS
762. STEEL FURNITURE & ELECTRICAL APPLIANCES
763. STEREO AMPLIFIERS
764. STEREO CASSETTE RECORDERS/PLAYERS
765. STREET LIGHT FITTINGS SURGE SUPPRESSOR
766. TANTALUM CAPACITORS
767. TEFLON COATED ELECTRIC CABLE
768. TELEMEDICINE (DISTANCE HEALTH CARE) (Rs. 5000/-)
769. TELEPHONE CORD/CABLE
770. TELEPHONE (PUSH BUTTON TYPE)
771. TELEPHONE (PUSH BUTTON & CORDLESS)
772. TELEVISION (CTV & B/W)
773. TELEVISION (3-D)
774. TELEVISION DEFLECTION COMPONENTS
775. TELEVISION SIGNAL BOOSTERS
776. TELEVISION TUNERS
777. TRACTION BATTERIES
778. TRAINING INSTITUTE OF MEDICAL TRANSCRIPTION
779. TRANSFORMER FOR B/W TV
780. TRANSFORMER FOR VOLTAGE STABILIZER & E.H.T
781. TRANSMISSION POWER LINE FITTING
782. TRANSMISSION TOWER FITTING
783. TV AUDIO EQUIPMENT CABINETS & THEIR ASSEMBLING UNIT
784. UN-INTERRUPTED POWER SUPPLY (U.P.S)
785. VARIABLE FREQUENCY
786. VARIABLE VOLTAGE A.C. DRIVE
787. VIDEO CASSETTES (COMPLETE MANUFACTURING & ASSEMBLING)
788. VIDEO CASSETTES RECORDER (V.C.R)
789. VIDEO FILM STUDIO
790. VOLTAGE REGULATOR FOR AUTOMOBILES
791. VOLTAGE STABILIZERS
792. VOLTAGE STABLIZER & T.V. GAIN BOOSTER
793. WAX AND CHEMICAL COATED, BRAIDED TINSEL WIRE
794. WEBSITE DESIGN & E-MAIL REGISTERING
795. WELDING ELECTRODES
796. WIND ENERGY POWER PROJECT (10 MW) WIRE WOUND POTENTIOMETERS

FOOD, AGRO FOOD, PROCESSED FOOD, AGRO PLANTATION, CULTIVATION, FARMING, DAIRY/MILK, TOBACCO/PAN MASALA, BREWERY & DISTILLERY, EDIBLE OILS, EOU FOOD PRODUCTS AND ALLIED PRODUCTS

797. ALCOHOLIC BEVERAGES & VENEGAR FROM COCONUT WATER
798. ALCOHOL DRINKS FROM ETHYL ALCOHOL BY MIXING OF VARIOUS FLAVOURS
799. ANTI SCALE COMPOUND FOR ADDING INTO SUGAR JUICE BOILING
800. APPLE JUICE CONCENTRATED & DEHYDRATED FRUIT & VEGETABLES
801. ARTIFICIAL FISH MEAL FOR POULTRY FEED
802. AUTOMATIC BISCUIT PLANT
803. BABY CEREAL FOOD AND MILK POWDER
804. BACTERIA FOR CANE JUICE
805. BAKER'S YEAST
806. BAKERY INDUSTRY
807. BANANA PUREE
808. BEER & WINE
809. BEER PLANT (BREWERY)
810. BIDI
811. BIDI & CIGARETTE
812. BISCUIT PLANT

813. BREAD (AUTOMATIC PLANT)
814. BLACK PEPPER (SPICES)
815. BREAD AND BISCUITS
816. BREEDING FARM
817. BROILER CHICKEN
819. BUTTON MUSHROOM CULTIVATION & PROCESSING
820. CANNING OF RASAGULLAS IN METAL CANS
821. CAFFEIN FROM TEA WASTE
822. CANNING OF FRUITS & VEGETABLES
823. CASEIN AND BY-PRODUCTS
824. CASHEW FRUIT JUICE FROM CASHEW FRUIT APPLE
825. CASHEWNUT KERNEL EXTRACTION FROM CASHEWNUT FRUIT
826. CASHEWNUT SHELL LIQUID & KERNEL PROCESSING
827. CASHEW FENI
828. CATECHEU (BY CHEMICAL PROCESS)
829. CATTLE FEED FROM TAPIOCA
830. CHEWING & BUBBLE GUM
831. CHICKEN/SHEEP MEAT PROCESSING
832. CHOCOLATE (MILK)
833. CIGARETTE AND BEEDIES
834. COCOA BUTTER FROM COCOA MASS
835. COCONUT PRODUCTS & BY PRODUCTS PROCESS COMPLEX
836. COLD/SOFT DRINKS
837. COLLECTION OF MILK AND MILK MAKING POWDER
838. COLLECTION OF MILK AND PACKING IN POLYTHENE POUCH (1/2 KG.1 KG. & 2 KG.)
839. CONDENSED MILK (SWEETNED)
840. CONFECTIONERY INDUSTRY (TOFFEE & CANDY, SEMI-AUTOMATIC PLANT)
841. COUNTRY LIQUOR FROM MOLASSES
842. CIGARETTE
843. DAIRY FARM AND DAIRY (MILK) PRODUCTS (PASTEURISED MILK, BUTTER, GHEE, PANEER)
844. DAIRY FARM TO PRODUCE MILK & PACKING IN POUCHES (50%) & CAN(50%)
845. DAIRY FOR MILK PROCESSING
846. DAIRY FARM (BUFALO)
847. DAL (PULSE) MILL UNIT
848. DEHYDRATION OF CARROT & GARLIC
849. DEHYDRATION & CANNING OF FRUITS & VEGETABLES
850. DEHYDRATION OF FIGS
851. DEHYDRATION OF FRUITS AND VEGETABLES
852. DEHYDRATED ONIONS AND ONION POWDER
853. DRY ICE BY BREAKING OF AIR
854. DRYING OF RED CHILLIES, HALDI, DHANIA, AND GREEN PEAS
855. EGG POWDER (40,000 EGGS PROCESSING PER DAY)
856. EXPORT OF PROCESSED FOODS AND MARINE PRODUCTS
857. FISH CANNING & POUCHING
859. FISH FARMING (PRAWN & OTHER MARINE PRODUCTS)
860. FISH MEAL
861. FLOUR MILL AND MUSTARD OIL
862. FOOD COLOUR & ORASTED GROUNDNUT GRAM PEAS, ETC IN POUCHES
863. FROG LEGS PROCESSING
864. FROZEN MEATS PROCESSING
865. FOOD FLAVOURS (WHISKY) VODKA, GRAPE, BUTTER SCOTCH)
866. FOOD PRODUCTS COMPLEX (DEHYDRATED ONIONS, GARLIC POWDER & FLAKES, CATTLE FEED, TOMATO POWDER, TOMATO PRODUCTS, CANNED FRUITS & VEGETABLES, TOMATO PURE, GROUN NUT OIL, REFIND OIL, DEHYDRATED GRAPES, BANANA POWDER & WAFFERS)
867. FRUIT JUICE, JAM, JELLIES & ALLIED PRODUCTS
868. FRUIT JUICE, PICKLES PROCESSING AND CANNING
869. FRUIT JUICE MAKING & PACKING IN PLASTIC CONTAINER/POUCHES
870. FRUIT PROCESSING (JAM & JELLIES)
871. FRUIT PULP & JUICE CONCENTRATES
872. FRUIT & VEGETABLE DRYING (FREEZE DRYING METHOD)
873. GOAT & SHEEP FARMING
874. GRAM DALL/PULSE MILL
875. GRAPE DEHYDRATION
876. HARD BOILED CANDY (TOFFEE & CANDY)
877. HERBAL CIGARETTES
878. HONEY PROCESSING & PACKAGING
879. ICE CREAM OF DIFFERENT FLAVOURS
880. ICE CREAM STABILIZER
881. ICE MAKING PLANT
882. INDIAN MADE FOREIGN LIQUOR (I.M.F.L)
883. INSTANT FOOD (IDLI MIX, DOSA MIX, GULAB JAMUN MIX)
884. INSTANT FOOD (INSTANT FOOD & FAST FOOD PARLOUR)
885. INSTANT NOODLES
886. INSTANT TEA
887. INSTANT TEA FROM BLACK TEA
888. INTEGERATED STARCH BAKING POWDER/YEAST INDUSTRY
889. IODIZED SALT
890. IODIZED SALT (ORDINARY MOISTURE-LESS/FREE FLOWING IN PLASTIC BAGS AND CONTAINERS)
891. JAM, JELLIES, FRUIT JUICE & ALLIED PRODUCTS
892. KATHA AND CUTCH
893. KHANDSARI SUGAR
894. KHANDSARI SUGAR & IMFL
895. LACTIC ACID FROM WHITE SUGAR BY FERMENTATION PROCESS
896. LACTOSE & BY PRODUCTS PROCESSING FROM MILK
897. LIQUID GLUCOSE AND ITS BYE PRODUCTS
898. MACRONI AND VERMICILLI
899. MALT EXTRACTION FROM BARLEY
900. MANGO PROCESSING (MANGO PULP, JUICE & SLICES)
901. MAYUR BRAND TYPE CHEWING TOBACCO
902. MINERAL WATER
903. MILK PRESERVATION & MARKETING TO WHOLE SELLERS (INPOUCH PACKING BY UHT TECHNOLOGY)
904. MILK PROCESSING AND PACKAGING OF MILK PRODUCTS
905. MILK PRODUCTS (CASEIN, LACTOSE, GHEE & WHEY POWDER)
906. MILK TOFFEE
907. MINI FLOUR MILL
908. MINI SUGAR PLANT
909. MISRI (PEARL SUGAR CANDIES)
910. MODERN RICE MILL
911. MURABBA
912. MUSTARD OIL EXTRACTION & REFINING
913. MUTTON TALLOW
914. NAMKEEN INDUSTRY (BHUJIA, CHANA CHUR ETC.)
915. NAMKEEN & SWEETS
916. NON-BASMATI RICE FROM PADDY
917. OLEORESIN, ESSENTIAL OIL, DYES & POWDER OF SPICES
918. OLEORESIN EXTRACTION FROM DIPTERO-CARPUT TURMINATUS AND PINUS KHASYANA
919. OLECRESIN EXTRACTION FROM CHILLI
920. PAN MASALA AND POUCH

1059. BUFFALO HORN TIP, HOOF
1060. BANQUET HALL
1061. BUTTON
1062. CALCINED PETROLEUM (C.P) COKE
1063. CANVAS SHOES
1064. CANVAS SHOES, JUNGLE BOOTS
1065. CARBON BRUSH, BRUSH HOLDER & SLIP RING
1066. CEMENT SHEETS WITH COIR FIBRE & OTHER SEGMENTS
1067. CERAMIC TILES (GLAZED) BY DOUBLE FIRING/HEATING
1068. CHILDREN RECREATION CENTRE
1069. COAL BRIQUETTES
1070. COLD STORAGE & ICE
1071. COLD STORAGE FOR FRUITS AND VEGETABLES
1072. COMPRESSOR (HERMETIC) FOR AIR CONDITIONER
1073. COSTUME JEWELLERY/ IMITATION JEWELLERY
1074. DECORATIVE LAMINATED SHEET (SUNMICA)
1075. DIAMOND CUTTING & EXPORTS
1076. DRINKING STRAW FROM PROPYLENE
1077. ENGINEERING COLLEGE
1078. ENTERTAINMENT CLUB
1079. FASHION TECHNOLOGY INSTITUTE
1080. FAST FOOD PARLOUR
1081. FAST FOOD (INSTANT FOOD & FAST FOOD PARLOUR)
1082. FIRE EXTINGUISHERS (SODA ACID TYPE)
1083. FISH NET
1084. FLORICULTURE (CUT FLOWER ROSE) WITH GREEN HOUSE
1085. FLOOR COVERING SHEET
1086. FILM STUDIO (VIDEO)
1087. FLUSH DOOR, CHIP BOARD, WOOD WOOL & OTHER INSULATING BOARDS
1088. GAS DETECTORS OF L.P.G
1089. GEMS MANUFACTURING
1090. GLASS BOTTLE BY SCRAP
1092. GOAT & SHEEP FARMING
1093. GOLD ELECTROPLATING
1094. GOLD JEWELLERY (E.O.U)
1095. GOLD PLATED SILVER JEWELLERY & CUTLERY
1096. GRANITE SLAB AND TILES
1097. GREEN HOUSE
1098. HARD CHROMIUM PLATING
1099. HEALTH CLUB AND BEAUTY PARLOUR CUM HAIR SALOON WITH SONA BATH
1100. HEALTH CLUB CUM BEAUTY PARLOUR TRAININGINSTITUTE
1101. HORN TIP, HOOVE BUTTON
1102. HOSPITAL
1103. HOSPITAL (100 BEDS)
1104. HOSPITAL (200 BEDS)
1105. ICE MAKING PLANT
1106. IMITATION AND COSTUME
1107. JEWELLERY (NECKLACE, EARRINGS EAR TOP ETC.)
1108. INITMATE SCENT CHEMICALS FROM ALL TYPES OF FLAVOUR
1109. INVESTMENT CASTING
1110. JUTE, COIR, GLASS ROPE/ SUTLI
1111. JUTE TWINE
1112. L.P.G BOTTLING PLANT
1113. L.P.G REGULATOR (DOMESTIC PURPOSE)
1114. LAMINATED PARTICLE BOARD & HARD BOARD
1115. LAMINATED SAFETY AND TOUGHENED GLASS
1116. LEASING & HIRE PURCHASE
1117. LICHEN (CHARILA)
1118. MANILA ROPES
1119. MEDICAL COLLEGE
1120. MATCH UNIT FROM WAXED PAPER
1121. MEDIUM DENSITY FIBRE BOARD
1122. MELAMINE CROCKERY
1123. MINERAL WATER
1124. MINI CEMENT PLANT
1125. MIRROR SILVER, GOLDEN, PINK, BLACK & SMOKES
1126. MODERN ADVERTISING AGENCY WITH DTP & FILM STUDIO
1127. MOTEL/SMALL HOTEL
1128. MULTI COLOUR PRINTING
1129. MULTI STOREY COMMERCIAL COMPLEX ALONGWITH RESIDENTIAL AND DELUX FLATS FOR FOREIGN TOURISTS & REVOLVING RESTAURENT AT THE TOP
1130. MULTIPLE LAMINATION INDUSTRY
1131. MUSHROOM GROWING AND PROCESSING (BY DEEP FREEZING METHOD)
1132. NEWS PAPER PRINTING
1133. NICKEL LINED INDUSTRIAL SCREEN
1134. OFFSET COLOUR PRINTING PRESS (SIX COLOUR)
1135. OFFSET PRINTING PRESS
1136. P.C.C ELECTRIC POLES
1137. PHOTOGRAPHIC DEVELOPER & FIXER
1138. PVC EXTRUSION PROFILE (DOOR & WINDOWS)
1139. POP-CORN
1140. PHOTO ETCHING OF S.S.
1141. PRE STRESSED CEMENT CONCRETE PIPES
1142. PILFER PROOF CAPS
1143. PILFER PROOF CAPS AND CROWN CAP
1144. POUCH MAKING & GRAVURE PRINTING (ROTO PRINTING)
1145. POULTRY & FISH FARMING (INTEGERATED UNIT)
1146. PRINTING OF TIN SHEETS
1147. READYMADE GARMENTS
1148. RESTAURANT
1149. ROSE PLANTATION AND ROSE OIL EXTRACTION
1150. ROTOGRAVURE PRINTING
1151. SAFETY BELTS
1152. SAFETY MATCHES
1153. SHOE LACES
1154. SILK COCOON CULTIVATION (GROWING OF SILK COCOON WARM)
1155. SILK SCREEN PRINTING FORMULATIONS FOR PLASTIC, PAPER & CLOTH
1156. SPIKENARD (JATAMANSI)
1157. STENCIL COATING SOLUTION
1158. SUGAR CANDY (MISRI)
1159. SUGAR CANE PLANTATION
1160. SUGAR CANE JUICE PRESERVATION
1161. SURAT ZARI
1162. SYNTHETIC SHOES & SOLES
1163. TEA PACKAGING INDUSTRY
1164. TENNIS BALLS
1165. THREE STAR HOTEL
1166. TRAVELLING AGENCY
1167. TRAYS, TROLLEYS FOR HOSPITAL WITH SCRATCHLESS COATING
1168. WAX EXTRACTS (TANNING POWDER)
1169. WIRE ROPE SLINGS
1170. WOOD WOOL SLAB
1171. WOODEN CANE FURNITURE WITH EXPORT POTENTIAL
1172. WOODEN FURNITURE
1173. WOODEN PANEL INCLUDING KILN SEASONING
1174. WOODEN FURNITURE
1175. WATCH CASE BUFFING
1176. WATCH DIAL
1177. WRIST WATCHES
1178. WATCHES (ELECTRONIC)
1179. ZEDOARY (KACHUR)

EDIBLE OILS, ESSENTIAL OILS LURICATIING OILS, GREASES, VEGETABLE OILS, WAXES, CAMPHOR, PERFUMES & PERFUMERY COMPOUNDS AND REFINED OILS ETC.

1180. AROMATIC PERFUMERY COMPOUND
1181. AEROSOL
1182. AGARBATTI PERFUMERY COMPOUND
1183. BEES WAX MANUFACTURE
1184. CAMPHOR
1185. CARDANOL FROM CASHEW NUT SHELL LIQUID
1186. CASTOR OIL
1187. CASTOR OIL DERIVATIVE OLEORESINS
1188. CHILLI OIL
1189. CITRONELLA OILS
1190. CLOVE OIL
1191. CONCENTRATE OF ROSE JASMINE & LILY ETC.
1192. COLOURED FLAME CANDLE

1193. CANDLES (SEMI-AUTOMATIC)
1194. CORN OIL (MAIZE OIL)
1195. DEHYDRATED CASTOR OIL
1196. EUGENOL FROM CINNAMON LEAF OIL
1197. EXTRACTION OF ESSENTIAL OIL (CARDAMON, JEERA, AJOWAN, GINGER OILS ETC. & PACKAGING OF GROUND SPICES)
1198. EXTRACTION OF JASMINE ESSENCE
1199. EXTRACTION OF ESSENTIAL OILS BY SUPER CRITICAL FLUID METHOD FROM FLOWERS, HERBS & SPICES
1200. EUCALYPTUS OIL
1201. EXTRACTION OF OIL FROM OIL SEED EXPANDEREXTRUSION TECHNOLOGY)
1202. FAT LIQUOR SULPHATED OIL
1203. FLAVOURS FOR FOOD
1204. GARLIC OIL & POWDER
1205. GINGER OIL, SANDALWOOD OIL AND NAGARMOTHA OIL
1206. GINGER OIL
1207. GINGER OIL & GINGER DUST
1208. INTEGERATED WAX COMPLEX
1209. IONONE FROM LEMON GRASS OIL
1210. JASMINE & LILLY FLOWER OIL
1211. LEMON GRASS OIL
1212. LIQUID PARAFFIN
1213. LUBE OIL & GREASE
1214. LUBRICATING OIL
1215. MENTHOL CRYSTALS
1216. MENTHOL OIL & CRYSTAL
1217. MICRO CRYSTALLINE WAX
1218. MUSTARD OIL (EDIBLE OIL)
1219. OIL FROM ARTEMISIA HERBS
1220. PALM OIL CRUSHING UNIT
1221. PAN MASALA
1222. PARAFFIN WAX
1223. PARAFFIN WAX FROM SLACK WAX
1224. REFINED OIL-SUN FLOWER OIL, GROUNDNUT OIL, STAFF FLOWER OIL & COTTON SEED OIL
1225. REFINED VEGETABLE OIL
1226. RECLAMATION OF USED ENGINE OIL
1227. RICE BRAN OIL (R.B.O)
1228. ROSE OIL EXTRACTION
1229. SMOKE LESS CANDLE
1230. SPICE OIL & OLEORESINS
1231. SOLVENT EXTRACTION PLANT (OIL CAKE BASED)
1232. SYNTHETIC ALMOND OIL
1233. SYNTHETIC TALLOW
1234. SYNTHETIC GHEE
1235. VEGETABLE OIL EXTRACTION & REFINING
1236. WADDING OIL (100%) FOR WADDING OF COTTON HOSIERY CLOTH IN DYEING PROCESS
1237. WAX EMULSION FOR TEXTILE
1238. WAX FLOOR POLISH

PAINT, ENAMEL, SOLVENTS, THINNERS, INKS & VARNISH

1239. ACRYLIC EMULSION PAINTS
1240. ALUMINIUM PAINT
1241. AUTOMOBILE PAINTS
1242. BALL POINT PEN REFILL INK
1243. BITUMINIOUS ROAD EMULSION
1244. BITUMEN
1245. BITUMINIOUS FELTS FOR WATER & DAMP PROOFING
1246. BITUMINIOUS ROAD EMULSION RAPID MEDIUM & SLOW SETTING
1247. BUFFING & POLISHING
1248. CEMENT PAINT FOR WHITE & GREY CEMENT

1249. DISPERSANT
1250. DRY DISTEMPER
1251. DRY DISTEMPER & CEMENT PAINT
1252. DUPLICATING INK BLACK FOR GESTNER DUPLICATOR
1255. EMULSION PAINTS (WATER BASED)
1256. HAMMERTONE PAINT
1257. INSULATING VARNISH & WIRE ENAMEL
1258. IRON OXIDE PIGMENTS
1259. INSULATING VARNISH (POLY VINYL BUTYRAL BASED, FFC GRADE)
1260. LIME COLOUR (CEMENT COLOUR)
1261. SYNTHETIC RED OXIDE FOR FLOORINGS
1262. SOLVENT & THINNERS
1263. MARKING INKS (WATER PROOF)
1264. METAL NAPHTHANATE (AS DRIER FOR PAINTS)
1265. N.C.PUTTY
1266. OFFSET PRINTING INK
1267. OIL BOUND DISTEMPER PAINT
1268. PAINT BRUSHES
1269. PAINT REMOVERS
1270. PAINT INDUSTRY
1271. PAINT & VARNISH
1272. PICTURE VARNISH
1273. POWDER COATING PAINT
1274. PRINTING INKS (OFFSET, FLEXO & ROTO GRAVURE)
1275. PRIMER PAINT & ENAMEL PAINT
1276. PUTTY & WATER PROOFING PAINT
1277. PRINTING INKS (FLEXO-GRAPHIC INK)
1278. PUTTY (METAL CASEMENT)
1279. RED OXIDE PRIMER (ANTI CORROSIVE)
1280. REFRECTORY PAINT (GRAPHITE BASED)
1281. SCREEN PRINTING INKS
1282. SILK SCREEN PRINTING INK FORMULATION FOR PLASTIC, PAPER, CLOTH
1283. STAMP & PAD INK
1284. STOVING PAINT
1285. SPIRIT SOLUBLE MALEIC RESIN
1286. TEXTURE PAINT
1287. THINNERS AND ITS ALLIED PRODUCTS
1288. TONER INK
1289. VARNISH THINNER (SOLVENT)
1290. VACUUM METALLIZING LACQUERS
1291. WOOD PRIMER

PHARMACEUTICAL, DRUGS, AYURVEDIC/HERBAL COSMETICS & MEDICINES, HOMOEOPATHIC MEDICINES, DISPOSABLE SYRINGE, DENTAL COLLEGE & FINE CHEMICALS ETC.

1292. AROMATIC PILLS
1293. ASPIRIN
1294. AYURVEDIC PAIN BALM OINTMENTS
1295. AYURVEDIC CHURAN AND TABLETS
1296. AYURVEDIC TABLETS (HAJMOLA TYPE)
1297. AYURVEDIC/HERBAL PHARMACY
1298. AYURVEDIC SHERBATS
1299. AYURVEDIC PRODUCTS
1300. BULK DRUGS (E.O.U)
1301. BLOOD BAGS
1302. CALCIUM GLUCONATE
1303. CAPSULE, TABLET & INJECTION WITH MODERN INSTRUMENTS
1304. CASHEW FENI
1305. CHLOROQUINONE PHOSPHATE (BULK DRUGS)
1306. CLINICAL THERMOMETER
1307. DENTAL CLINIC

"Detailed Project Report" Payable in advance through Draft/Cash/M.O. in favour of *"ENGINEERS INDIA RESEARCH INSTITUTE"*. 4449, Nai Sarak (D), Main Road Delhi - 110 006 (INDIA) ● Ph : 23918117, 2391 6431, 2384 0361 ● Mob : 098114 37895 ●Fax : 91-11- 2391 6431 ●E-Mail : eirisidi@bol.net.in ● WebSite : www.eiriindia.org

1308. DENTAL COLLEGE
1309. DENTAL GRADE EUGENOL
1310. DEXTROSE MONOHYDRATE, LIQUID GLUCOSE
1311. DEHYDRATED ONION & ONION POWDER
1312. DEXTROSE POWDER (ANHYDROUS FROM STARCH)
1314. DEXTROSE SALINE SOLUTION
1315. DISTILLERY (I.M.F.L)
1316. DISPOSABLE NEEDLES FOR SYRINGES
1317. DISPRIN
1318. DISTILLED WATER
1319. EMPTY HARD GELATINE CAPSULES
1320. FILLING & PACKING OF CAPSULES
1321. GLUCOSE - D - POWDER
1322. GLYCERINE
1323. HERBAL COSMETICS
1324. HERBAL SHAMPOO
1325. HERBAL HAIR OILS (AYURVEDIC)
1326. HOMOE & BIO-MEDICINES WITH MOTHER TINCTURE
1327. HOMOEPATHIC MEDICINES
1328. HYPODERMIC NEEDLES
1329. I.V. FLUIDS
1330. IBUPROFEN
1331. INFUSION & TRANSFUSION SETS (I.V. SET)
1332. INJECTABLE FOR PHARMACEUTICALS
1333. INJECTION AMPOULES PACKAGING BOX
1334. INTEGERATED SURGICAL COTTON
1335. ICE MAKING PLANT
1336. ICE & COLD STORAGE
1337. LACTOSE & BY PRODUCTS PROCESSING FROM MILK
1338. LICHEN (JATAMANSI CHARILA)
1339. LIQUID GLUCOSE AND ITS BY-PRODUCTS
340. L-LYSINE MONOHYDRO CHLORIDE
341. LIQUID GLUCOSE FROM POTATOES
342. MEDICAL COLLEGE
343. NICOTINE FROM TOBACCO WASTE
344. OINTMENT-AYURVEDIC (YELLOW & WHITE)
345. PHARMACEUTICAL AND FOOD GRADE GELATINE
346. PHARMACEUTICAL INDUSTRY (TABLETS, CAPSULES, LIQUID, GEL, OINTMENT POWDER INJECTABLE)
347. PHARMACEUTICAL UNIT (EOU) WITH FORMULA TIONS, INJECTABLES, ETC. PYRIDINE & DERIVATIVES
348. SALT (IODIZED SALT)
349. SALINE & INJECTION WATER
350. SALINE WATER & DEXTROSE SOLUTION (I.V.FLUID IN PLASTIC BOTTLES)
1351. SORBITOL
1352. STARCH (MAIZE)
1353. SURGICAL ADHESIVE PLASTER
1354. SURGICAL BANDAGES
1355. SURGICAL GLOVES
1357. SURGICAL COTTON
1358. SURGICAL COTTON AND BANDAGE
1359. SYNTHETIC CAMPHOR POWDER
1360. TABLETS & CAPSULES
1361. TISSUE CULTURE
1362. TINCTURE FROM RECTIFIED SPIRIT
1363. TRIMETHOPIME
1364. VETERENARY MEDICINES (ONLY FORMULATIONS)
1365. VITAMIN 'C', SORBITOL' ANHYDROUS DEXTROSE, STARCH

PULP, PAPER, STRAW/GREY BOARD, KRAFT PAPER, PACKAGING, PAPER CARRY BAGE, PAPER FROM AGRO WASTE & STATIONERY ETC.

1366. AMMONIA PAPER
1367. AUTOMATIC BOOK BINDING
1368. ADHESIVE (FEVICOL TYPE)
1369. ALL PIN & GEM CLIPS
1370. CARBON PAPER
1371. CARD BOARD
1372. CARBON LESS PAPER
1373. CELLPHANE PAPER
1374. COMPUTER FORMS & SECURITY PRINTING PRESS
1375. CORRUGATED BOARD & BOX (PRINTED & LAMINATED)
1376. CORRUGATED BOARD AND BOXES FROM FROM CARD BOARDS
1377. CORRUGATED CARTONS FROM PLAIN PAPERS
1378. CORRUGATRED PACKING & MATERIAL (BULB & TUBES PACKING)
1379. DESK TOP PUBLISHING
1380. DEFOAMING AGENT FOR PAPER PLANT
1381. DRINKING STRAW PAPER
1382. D.T.P CUM OFFSET PRESS
1383. EGG TRAYS
1384. EXERCISE NOTE BOOK, REGISTER AND PAD
1385. FLEXOGRAPHIC INK
1386. GREETING CARD BY OFFSET PRESS
1387. HAND MADE PAPER FILTER PAPER
1388. HARD BOARD
1389. INJECTION AMPOULES PACKAGING BOXES
1390. INSULATIING PAPER
1391. KRAFT PAPER
1392. KRAFT PAPER FROM BAGASSE
1393. LAMINATED PACKAGING PAPER WITH PRINTING
1394. LAMINATION & COATING ON PAPER
1395. M.G. PAPER FROM WASTE PAPER
1396. MILL PAPER FROM WASTE PAPER
1397. MILL BOARD FROM RICE & WHEAT STRAWS
1398. MILL BOARD FROM WASTE PAPER
1399. MINI PAPER PLANT FROM SISAL
1400. MINI PAPER PLANT
1401. MULTI WALL PAPER SACKS
1402. NEWS PAPER FOR CHILDREN
1403. NEWS PRINT PAPER FROM RICE STRAW BAGASSE
1404. NEWS PAPER CHILDRENS
1405. NEWS PRINT PAPER
1406. OFFSET AND TREADLE TYPE PRINTING PRESS
1407. MILL BOARD BASED ON RICE STRAW
1408. PAPER AND BOARD FROM STRAW
1409. PAPER & PAPER PRODUCTS
1410. PAPER ENVELOPES
1411. PAPER CARRY BAGS
1412. PAPER BOARD CARTON
1413. PAPER CONES FOR LOUD SPEAKERS
1414. PAPER FROM AKRA
1415. PAPER FROM BAGASSE WITH CORRUGATED BOARD & BOXES
1416. PAPER FROM BAMBOO
1417. PAPER GLASSES FOR BEVERAGES
1418. PAPER FROM RICE HUSK & WHEAT HUSK
1419. PAPER FROM TREE BARK, EUCALYPRUS WOOD
1420. PAPER PRODUCTS
1421. PAPER PLANT (WHITE WRITING & NEWS PAPER FOR PULP & WASTE PAPER)
1422. PAPER PLATES, PAPER GLASS
1423. PAPER CONES & TUBES
1425. PAPER PLANT WITH DTP & PRINTING & PUBLISHING UNIT
1426. PAPER BASED PHENOLIC SHEET
1427. PAPER CUP FOR ICE CREAM
1428. PAPER TUBES SPIRAL WINDING COMPOSIT CONTAINER
1429. PAPER LABLE FOR BEER BOTTLES
1430. PARTICLE BOARD & BLACK BOARD WITH SANDING & LAMINATION OF PARTICLE BOARD
1431. PARTICLE BOARD FROM RICE HUSK
1432. POUCH FILLING & MAKING FOR TOMATO SAUCE
1433. POUCH MAKING &

GRAVURE PRINTING
1434. PROCESSING OF PAPER FOR FEEDING IN COMPUTER
1435. PULP FROM BAMBOO & WOOD
1436. PAPER FILES
1437. PLAYING CARDS
1438. ROSIN SIZING AGENT (FOR PAPER PLANT)
1439. SAND PAPER
1440. SANITRY NAPKINS
1441. SILICON COATED PAPER
1442. STENCIL PAPER
1443. STRAW BOARD AND GREY BOARD
1444. STRAW BOARD & MILL BOARD
1445. STRAW BOARD AND PAPER BOARD
1446. TISSUE PAPER FACIAL
1447. TISSUE MOIST TOILETERY CLEANSING TISSUE AND RELATED PRODUCTS
1448. TISSUE PAPER ROLLS
1449. TETRA PACK FOR MILK PACKAGING, GHEE & OTHER LIQUIDS
1450. TOILET PAPER ROLLS
1451. TOILET PAPER & NAPKINS
1452. WAX COATED PRINTED PAPER
1453. WET FACE FRESHNER TISSUE
1454. WHITE WRITING & PRINTING PAPER
1455. WRITING & PRINTING PAPER (PAPER MILLS)

PLASTIC, B.O.P.P, ACRYLIC, DISPOSABLE PLASTIC PRODUCTS, PET PRODUCTS, P.V.C, H.D.P.E, P.P, L.D.P.E., P.U, A.B.S, THERMOFOARMING, MASTER BATCHES, & POLYMER AND RUBBER PRODUCTS, TYRE, TUBE, ADHESIVE, SHEET, COIR & MANY OTHERS

1456. ABS GRANULES FROM ABS SCRAPS FROM OLD T.V. CABINETS, WHITE GOODS ETC.
1457. ACRYLIC BEADS
1458. ACRYLIC COPOLYMER EMULSION
1459. ACRYLIC LATEX
1460. ACRYLIC SHEET
1461. ACRYLIC SHEET & MOULDED PRODUCTS
1462. ACRYLIC TEETH
1463. AUTO TUBES
1464. AUTO FLAPS FOR TRUCKS & BUSES
1465. AUTO TYRES & TUBES
1466. BABY BOTTLES (PLASTIC) WITH WHITESILICON RUBBER NIPPLES
1467. B.O.P.P. FILM
1468. B.O.P.P. PRESSURE SENSITIVE SELF ADHESIVE TAPE
1469. BABY NIPPLE (SILICON)
1470. BABY NIPPLE (BIG SIZE)
1471. BALLOON PLASTIC ADVERTISING
1472. BLISTER FILM PVC
1473. BLISTER PACKAGING & POUCH PAKAGING
1474. BLOW MOULDING PLASTIC CONTAINER
1475. COATING ON METALIZED POLYESTER FILM/METALISED PAPER/ ALIMINIUM FOIL
1476. COATING ON PLASTIC (ELECTROLYSIS) & GLASS
1477. COIR FOAM (RUBBERISED)
1478. COLOUR COATING ON PLASTICS
1479. COLOUR MASTER BATCHES FOR VARIOUS PLASTICS
1480. CYCLE TYRES AND TUBES
1481. DISPOSABLE PLASTIC CUPS GLASSES, ETC.
1482. DISPOSABLE PLASTIC SYRINGES & NEEDLES
1483. DISPOSABLE PLASTIC SYRINGES
1484. DOUGH MOULDING COMPOUND (D.M.C)
1485. EPOXY RESIN
1486. EXPANDED POLYESTRENE MOULDING (THERMOCOLE)
1487. F.R.P AUTO, SCOOTER ROOFS & CEILINGS
1488. F.R.P PRODUCTS (HELMET, WASHBASIN SHEETS, ROOFING SHEETS)
1489. FIBRE REINFORCED PLASTIC (HIGH PRESSURE MOULDING WITH SMC BMC AND DMC)
1490. FIELD RUBBER CONVERTED TO THE 60% LATEX RUBBER
1491. FLEXIBLE P.U. FOAM
1492. FORMALDEHYDE CROCKERY & OTHER ITEMS
1493. FORMALDEHYDE RESIN (UREA, PHENOL, MELEMINE)
1494. GASKET SHEET
1495. GUM BOTTLE (PVC)
1496. GLASS BEADS
1497. HDPE COATED PAPER SACK
1498. H.D.P.E. BAGS
1499. H.D.P.E. CONTAINERS (BLOW MOULDING)
1500. H.D.P.E. CONTAINER, POLY JARS BY INJECTION MOULDING (FOOD GRADE)
1501. H.D.P.E. JERRY CANS
1502. HDPE MANUFACTURING FROM ETHYLALCOHOL
1503. H.D.P.E PIPE AND FITTINGS
1504. H.D.P.E. PIPES
1505. H.D.P.E PRINTED BAGS
1506. H.D.P.E TWINES AND ROPES
1507. H.D.P.E. & L.D.P.E PIPES AND FITTINGS
1508. H.D.P.E/PP BOX STRAPPING
1509. H.D.P.E/PP WOVEN SACKS USING PLAIN LOOMS
1510. HOLOGRAM STICKERS-3D
1511. H.M BAG PLANT WITH PRINTING UNIT
1512. HAWAI CHAPPALS (RUBBER)
1513. I.V PLASTIC BOTTLE
1514. ICE CREAM CUP (PLASTIC)
1515. INJECTION MOULDED AUTO COMPONENTS
1516. INJECTION & BLOW MOULDED PLASTIC PRODUCTS
1517. INJECTION MOULDED PLASTIC PRODUCTS
1518. INTEGRATED COMPLEX ESTER'S & ALLIED PRODUCTS (D.O.P, D.B.P, & ETHYL ACETATE, BUYTL ACETATE, WIRE ENAMELS, JELLY CABLE COMPOUND)
1519. L.D.P.E. (LOW DENSITY POLY ETHYLENE) GRANULES FROM VIRGIN (L.D.P.E. RESIN)
1520. INTEGERATED SURGICAL RUBBER GOODS INDUSTRY
1521. INJECTION MOULDED PLASTIC BALLS
1522. L.D.P.E FROM ETHYL ALCOHOL
1523. LDPE MOULDED PRODUCTS
1524. LAMINATION OF COEXTRUSION MULTILAYER FILM IN ROLL FORM
1525. LATEX RUBBER
1526. LATEX RUBBER CONDOM
1527. MASTER BATCHES (COLOURED, P.V.C, L.D.P.E, H.D.P.E, ETC.)
1528. MELAMINE FORMALHYDE RESIN
1529. MOULDED LUGGAGE
1530. MULTI-LAYER (3 LAYER BAGS)
1531. MULTI-LAYER (3 LAYER) FILM WITH LAMINATION & PRINTING
1532. OIL SEAL
1533. PET BOTTLE/CONTAINERS
1534. PET BOTTLES FROM PRE FORM
1535. PET BOTTLE & MINERAL WATER
1536. PET PRE-FORM FROM PET RESIN
1537. PET PRE-FORM CUM PET BOTTLES
1538. PET PRE-FORM PET BOTTLES CUM MINERAL WATERS
1539. POLY CARBONATE RESIN
1540. PTFE COMPONENTS
1541. PU/PVC SOLE FOR SPORT SHOE BY IMPORTED M/C.
1542. PVC BATTERY SEPARATOR
1543. P.V.C COMPOUNDS (FRESH)
1544. P.V.C COMPOUNDS (SCRAP)
1545. P.V.C ELECTRICAL INSULATING TAPE
1546. P.V.C. EXTRUSION PROFILES
1547. P.V.C FITTINGS
1548. P.V.C FLEXIBLE FUSIBLE POWDER HEAT FUSIBLE POWDER
1549. P.V.C GRANULES (FOR

INSULATION & SHEETS GRADES)
1550. P.V.C GRANULES FROM PVC SCRAPS (WITH POLLUTION CONTROL)
1551. P.V.C HOSES
1552. P.V.C LEATHER CLOTH
1553. P.V.C FLEXIBLE PIPES
1554. P.V.C PIPES AND FITTINGS
1555. POLYTHENE BAGS (PRINTED)
1556. PVC PLASTICS FILM SHEET SOFT/RIGID
1557. PVC RESIN AND COMPOUND
1558. PVC RULAR
1559. PVC STABLIZERS (SINGLE PACK SYSTEM)
1560. PVC WIRE AND CABLES
1561. PAPER BASED PHENOLIC SHEET FOR ELECTRICAL
1562. PHENOL FORMALDEHYDE RESIN
1563. PHENOLIC RESIN
1564. PLASTIC BEADS FROM PLASTIC SCRAPS
1565. PLASTIC BUTTONS
1566. PLASTIC CANS
1567. PLASTIC COLLAPSIBLE TUBE
1568. PLASTIC CORRUGATED SHEET & BOXES
1569. PLASTIC FILM AND SHEETS WITH PRINTING FLEXO & ROTO/LDPE/HDPE/PP/HM/PVC
1570. PLASTIC FILTER MASTER BATCH & OTHER MASTER BATCHES FOR VARIOUS PLASTICS
1571. PLASTIC JERRY CANS
1572. PLASTIC GRANULES OR POWDER FROM PLASTIC SCRAP
1573. PLASTIC INJECTION MOULDED T.V. CABINETS
1574. PLASTIC ITEMS MANUFAC TURE FROM POWDER MELAMINE
1575. PLASTIC GOODS
1576. PLASTIC PIPES & TARPAULINES
1577. PLASTIC SHEET FROM SCRAP
1578. PLASTIC PLANT (BLOW MOULDING & INJECTION MOULDING)
1579. PLASTIC PRODUCTS (GOLD, SILVER, NICKEL)
1580. PLASTIC TOYS
1581. POLYESTER BEADING
1582. POLYESTER FILM
1583. POLYTHENE BAGS & AUTOMATIC PRINTING
1584. POLYTHENE PRINTED BAGS
1585. POLYURETHANE FOAM AND ITS PRODUCTS
1586. PROPYLENE FILM (PRINTED) & BAG MANUFACTURING
1587. PLASTIC MATS
1588. RAINBOW COLOUR ON PVC FILM & SHEET
1589. RED MUD PVC PIPES AND FITTINGS
1590. RE-RUBBERISED OF SOLID TYPE
1591. RESIN COATED SAND REXINE
1592. REXINE CLOTH & ALLIED PRODUCTS
1593. RUBBER ADHESIVE
1594. RUBBER AUTO PARTS
1595. RUBBER BELTING
1596. RUBBER MOULDING UNIT INCLUDING LINING RUBBER SHEETING
1597. RUBBER RECLAIMING
1598. RUBBER ROLLERS FOR TEXTILE MILLS & PAPER INDUSTRIES
1599. RUBBER & PLASTIC SHEETS, MATS & FLAPS
1600. RUBBER SHEET AND ALLIED HOSPITAL RUBBER GOODS
1601. RUBBERIZED PVC GASKET
1602. RUBBERISED COIR
1603. RUBBER COMPOUND FOR AUTOMOBILES
1604. SAFETY BELTS
1605. SILVER AND GOLD PLATING ON PVC AND NYLON-6
1606. SILICONE RUBBER NIPPLES/ TEATS
1607. SPECTACLE FRAMES (PLASTIC)
1608. SPUNGE RUBBER
1609. SURGICAL EXAMINATION GLOVES
1610. SYNTHETIC PEARL COATING ON POLYSTYRENE BEADS
1611. SYNTHETIC RUBBER ADHESIVE
1612. TEFLON MANUFACTURING
1613. TEFLON TAPE
1614. TEFLON TAPES & CABLES
1615. THERMOCOLE SHEET AND MOULDED PRODUCTS EXPANDED POLYESTERENE EXTRUSION PROFILES
1616. THERMOFORMED PACKAGING (BLISTER PACKAGING & POUCH PACKAGING)
1617. THERMOPLASTIC POLYURETHANE
1618. THERMOFORMED CUPS, PLATES & GLASS WITH HIPS SHEET
1619. THERMOCOLE
1620. THERMOCOLE BASED DISPOSABLE GLASS, CUPS & PLATES
1621. TOOTH BRUSHES
1622. TOY BALLOON, DECORA TIVE & INDUSTRIAL BALLOONS
1623. TREAD RUBBER
1624. TYRE RETREADING (HOT)
1625. TYRE RETREADING BY COLD PROCESS
1626. TYRE TUBES & FLAPS
1627. TYRE & TUBES
1628. UNSATURATED POLYESTER FOR REXINE
1629. V-BELT AND FAN BELT
1630. VINYL ASBESTOS AND PVC WALL PAPER
1631. VITON (FLUORO ELASTOMER)

SOAP, COSMETICS & PERFUMES

1632. ACID SLURRY, SYNTHETIC DETERGENT POWDER
1632. ACID SLURRY
1633. AGARBATTI SYNTHETIC, PERFUMERY COMPOUND
1634. AFTER SHAVE LOTION
1635. ANTISEPTIC CREAM
1636. BETA IONONE
1637. BLEACHING POWDER
1638. BLUE DETERGENT POWDER
1639. CLEANING POWDER (VIMTYPE)
1640. COLD CREAM
1641. COLOURED FLAME & PERFUMED CANDLES (RED, BLUE, GREEN FLAME)
1642. COSMETIC INDUSTRY (MODERN)
1643. COSMETIC INDUSTRY (SHAMPOO, SPRAY PERFUME, TALCUM POWDER
1644. DETERGENT POWDER (ARIEL TYPE)
1645. DETERGENT POWDER (NIRMA TYPE) FULLY AUTOMATIC PLANT
1646. DETERGENT WASHING POWDER
1647. FISH OIL SOAP
1648. GLYCERINE TRANSPARENT SOAP
1649. HAIR REMOVING CREAM
1650. HERBAL COSMETICS
1651. HERBAL SHAMPO & CREAM
1652. HERBAL/AYURVEDIC COSMETICS
1653. INCENSE POWDER, INCENSE STICKS & INCENSE CAKE
1654. OPTICAL WHITENERS
1655. ROSE OIL EXTRACTION
1656. SHAMPOOS (COCONUT OIL BASED COLD PROCESS)
1657. SHAVING CREAM
1658. SINDUR (KUMKUM)
1659. SOAP COATED PAPER
1660. SPRAY DRIED DETERGENT POWDER
1661. STAIN REMOVER
1662. TALCUM POWDER (FACE & TOILET POWDER)
1663. TOILET AND HERBAL SOAP
1664. TOOTH PASTE & POWDER
1665. WASHING DETERGENT POWDER AND WASHING SOAP
1666. WASHING POWDER LIQUID DETERGENTS, LOTION & SHAMPOO

ENTERTAINMENT CLUB WITH 4 STAR HOTEL
1779. HOSPITALS
1780. ICE CREAM PARLOUR
1781. INTERNET SERVICE PROVIDER (I.S.P.)
1782. MEDICAL COLLEGE
1783. MEDICAL COLLEGE, HOSPITAL & RESEARCH INSTITUTE
1784. MEDICAL TRANSCRIPTION CENTRE
1785. MENTAL RETARDATION HOSPITAL & CEREBRAL PALSY
1786. MOTEL/SMALL HOTEL
1787. MULTISTOREY COMMERCIAL COMPLEX
1788. MULTISTOREY RESIDENTIAL COMPLEX
1789. NURSERY SCHOOL
1790. NATURE CARE CENTRE
1791. NURSING HOME
1792. ONLINE SHOPPING MALL (RS. 5000/- REPORT)
1793. PORTAL
1794. REHABILITATION CENTRE FOR AGED & NEEDY PERSONS
1795. RESIDENTIAL CUM COMMERCIAL COMPLEX
1796. RESTAURANT
1797. RESTAURANT WITH PUB
1798. SCHOOL (PRIMARY)
1799. SCHOOL (HIGHER SECONDARY)
1800. THREE STAR HOTEL
1801. TOURIST CLUB
1802. TRAINING INSTITUTE FOR MEDICAL TRANSCRIPTION
1803. VIDEO FILM STUDIO
1804. WARE HOUSE
1805. WEBSITE DESIGN & E-MAIL REGISTERING

AGRO BASED INDUSTRIES

1806. COAL BRIQUETTES FROM AGROWASTE
1807. FURFURALFROM RICEHULL
1808. MUSHROOM CULTIVATION & PROCESSING (BUTTON)
1809. MUSHROOM GROWING & PROCESSING WITH AIR CONDITIONING
1810. MUSHROOM CULTIVATION & PROCESSING UNIT DEHYDRATION & PACKAGING OF OYSTER & PADDY STRAW MUSHROOMS
1811. ORGANIC MANURE
1812. PAPAYA CULTIVATION
1813. PAPAYA & TOMATO CULTIVATION
1814. PROCESSING & UTILISATION OF COCONUT
1815. PROCESSING OF SHEEP HAIR TO PRODUCE WOOL

BAKERY, CONFECTIONERY & FOOD PRODUCTS

1816. AGROLACTOR SOYA MILK
1817. APPLE FRUIT JUICE WITH CANNING BOTTLING
1818. AYURVEDIC SHARBAT
1819. BAKERY UNIT (PASTRIES, BREAD, BUNS, CAKE, TOFFEE ETC.)
1820. BAKING POWDER
1821. BANANA & ITS BY PRODUCTS
1822. BANANA POWDER
1823. BANANA WAFERS
1824. BANANA CULTIVATION
1825. BEER INDUSTRY
1826. DEHULLING OF JAUN FOR BEER
1827. BEER & WINE
1828. BEER, ALCOHOL, IMFL
1829. BESEN PLANT
1830. BISCUIT PLANT
1831. BREAD & BISCUIT PLANT
1832. BOTTLING PLANT COUNTRY LIQUOR FROM RECTIFIED SPIRIT
1833. BRANDY
1834. BREAD RUSKS
1835. CANNED FRUITS & VEGETABLES
1836. CANNING & PRESERVATION OF MEAT
1837. CANNING & PRESERVATION OF VEGETABLES
1838. CANNING OF MANGO PULP & MANGO SLICES
1839. CARBONATED BEVERAGS
1840. CASHEW FENI
1841. CASHEW NUT (DRIED & FRIED)
1842. CATTLE BREEDING
1843. CATTLE BREEDING & DAIRY FARM TO PRODUCE MILK
1844. CATTLE FEED FROM TAPIOCA
1845. CHEWING GINGER & AMLOKI
1846. CHEWING GUM
1847. CHILLI SAUCE
1848. CHILLI POWDER
1849. CHOCOLATE
1850. CIDER PLANT
1851. COCOA POWDER
1852. COCOA BUTTER & COCOA POWDER
1853. COCONUT SHELL POWDER
1854. COCONUT WATER
1855. COCONUT SWEET (WATERY)
1856. COCONUT MILK POWDER (DEHYDRATED)
1857. COCONUT PRODUCTS & BY PRODUCTS (INTEGRATED PLANT)
1858. COLD DRINK
1859. CURRY POWDER
1860. DAIRY FOR MILK PROCESSING (GHEE, BUTTER & PANEER)
1861. DAIRY PRODUCTS
1862. DAIRY PRODUCTS MILK PACKAGING IN POUCH (GHEE, BUTTER, ETC.
1863. DAIRY FARM TO PRDUCE MILK WITH PACKAGING (COW)
1864. DAIRY FARM TO PRDUCE MILK WITH PACKAGING (BUFALLOE)
1865. DAIRY FARM & MILK PRODUCTS
1866. DAL MOTH, CHANACHUR & BHUJIYA
1867. DEHYDRATION OF FRUITS & VEGETABLE
1868. DESICCATED COCONUT POWDER FROM COCONUTS
1869. DEHYDRATION & CANNING OF FRUITS & VEGETABLES
1870. DRY FRUIT ROASTING & PACKAGING
1871. DRYING OF RED CHILLIES, HALDI, DHANIYA, PEAS & GROUND NUT
1872. EGG POWDER
1873. FISH CANNING IN TIN & POUCHES
1874. FISH DEHYRATION (DRYING OF FISH)
1875. FISH MEAL
1876. FISH PROCESSING (BEAST FREEZING PROCESSES)
1877. FLAVOURS FOR FOOD INDUSTRIES
1878. FLOUR MILL (ROLLER)
1879. FROZEN MEAT
1880. FOOD DEHYDRATION (FRUITS & VEGETABLES)
1881. FRIED & ROASTED GROUND NUT, GRAMS, PEAR ETC.
1882. FRUIT JUICE MAKING & PACKAGING IN PLASTIC CONTAINER
1883. FRUIT JUICE IN TETRA PACK (DRINKS)
1884. FRUIT JUICE, SQUASHES, SAUCE & KETCHUP, JAM, JELLY, VINEGAR ETC.
1885. GARLIC FLAKES
1886. GARLIC POWDER
1887. GHEE & BUTTER
1888. GINGER (PULVERISED)
1889. GINGER GLAZING & PRESERVATION
1890. GINGER STORAGE
1891. GINGER PROCESSING
1892. GINGER OIL & GINGER DUST
1893. GINGER POWDER (DRY) & OLEORESIN
1894. GRAPE DEHYDRATION
1895. GRAPE CULTIVATION
1896. GRAPE JUICE
1897. HONEY PROCESSING & PACKAGING
1898. ICE CREAM & ICE CANDY
1899. ICE CUBE
1900. INVERT SUGAR
1901. IDLI MIX, DOSA MIX SAMBHAR MIX, VADA MIX, GULAB JAMUN MIX
1902. INSTANT COFFEE & INSTANT TEA

1903. INSTANT NOODLES
1904. INSTANT SOUPS
1905. IODIZED SALT FROM CRUDE SALT
1906. JAM CHUTNEY PICKLES & SQUASHES
1907. KATHA MANUFACTURING
1908. LECITHIN (SOYA BASED)
1909. LEMON & ITS PRODUCTS
1910. MACARONI MANUFACTURING
1911. MACARONI, SPAGHETTI, VERMICELLI & NOODLES
1912. MAIZE & ITS BY PRODUCTS MALTING PLANT
1913. MANGO PAPPAD (AAM PAPPAD)
1914. MANGO POWDER RIPE
1915. MANGO POWDER
1916. MANGO PROCESSING & CANNING (MANGO PULP)
1917. MEAT PROCESSING (CHICKEN MUTTON)
1918. MEAT PROCESSING (BUFFALO)
1919. MENTHOL BOLD FROM MENTHOL FLAKES
1020. MILK POWDER
1921. MILK POWDER & GHEE
1922. MILK POWDER, GHEE & SPICES
1923. MILK PRESERVATION & MARKETING TO WHOLE SELLERS
1924. MILK PRESERVATION & MARKETING TO WHOLE SELLERS (IN POUCHES)
1925. MILK TOFFEE MANUFACTURES
1926. MINERAL WATER
1927. MINERAL WATER IN POUCHES
1928. MINI FLOUR MILL ATTA MAIDA, SUJI & WHEAT BRAN
1929. MITHAI/HALWAI (SWEET & NAMKEEN)
1930. MUTTON PROCESSING
1931. PAN MASALA (MEETHA, SADA, ZARDA) MAKING & PACKING
1932. PAN MASALA AND POUCH MAKING
1933. PANEER (CHEESE)
1934. PAPAD & BARIYAN
1935. PAPAD PLANT
1936. PEPSICOLA IN POLYTUBES
1937. PETHA PACKAGING
1938. PICKLES
1939. PIGGERY/MEAT/CHICKEN PROCESSING
1940. PINE APPLE JUICE CANNING
1941. POTATO & ONION POWDER
1942. POTATO & ONION FLAKES
1943. POTATO CHIPS
1944. POTATO GRANULES
1945. POUCH FILLING FOR SAUNF SUPARI ILAICHI ETC.
1946. PRESERVATION OF RAWS MANGO JUICE
1947. PROCESSED CHEESE & MARINE PDTS.
1948. PULP FROM TARMARIND
1949. READYMATE PROCESSED FOOD
1950. RICE & CORN FLAKES
1951. RICE BASMATI (TRADING)
1952. RICE POLISHING & PACKAGING IN POUCH
1953. ROASTED/SALTED/MASALA/ CASHEW NUTS ALMONDS & PEA NUT
1954. ROLLER FLOUR MILL

INFOTECH/IT PROJECTS

1955. MEDICAL TRANSCRIPTION
1956. E-COMMERCE
1957. CYBERCAFE
1958. INTERNET SERVICE PROVIDER (ISP)
1959. COMPUTER EDUCATION CENTRE
1960. PORTAL (WEBSITE DESIGN)
1961. CALL CENTRE

TERMS AND CONDITIONS

FOR INDIA

1. Please ask for Quotations/ Proforma Invoice for Each *Market Survey Cum Detailed Techno Economic Feasibility Report.* Payable in advance through Draft/M.O./Cash in favour of 'ENGINEERS INDIA RESEARCH INSTITUTE', Delhi. Delivery by Regd.Post/Courier within 2 Days. (Postage Free)

2. Ask for a Hi Tech Projects, monthly magazine. Each issue covers approx. 75 project profiles.

FOR OVERSEAS

1. Please ask for Quotations/ Proforma Invoice in US $ for Each *Market Survey Cum Detailed Techno Economic Feasibility Report.* Payable in advance through Bank Draft in favour of 'ENGINEERS INDIA RESEARCH INSTITUTE', Delhi. (Payable in India). Delivery by Regd. Air Mail Post/Courier within 3 Days. (Postage Free)

2. Ask for a Hi Tech Projects, monthly magazine. Each issue covers approx. 75 project profiles.

ENGINEERS INDIA RESEARCH INSTITUTE

4449, Nai Sarak (D), Main Road, Delhi - 110 006 (India)
Phones: 91-11- 2391 8117, 2391 6431, 2384 0361
Fax: 91-11- 2391 6431 E-Mail : eirisidi@bol.net.in Website:www.eiriindia.org
Also at : 4/54, Roop Nagar, Delhi - 110 007 (India)
Ph:. 23840361 Mob: 098114 37895

PATRON: YOU CAN ALSO DEPOSIT THE AMOUNT IN "EIRI" ACCOUNT WITH UTI BANK LTD. CA-054010200006248 OR ICICI BANK LTD. CA-022705000598 OR UNION BANK OF INDIA CA-307201010015149 AND JUST SMS US ON PH. 09811437895

PHARMACEUTICALS & DRUGS TECHNOLOGY WITH FORMULATIONS

ISBN. 81-86732-52-7 # Rs. 950/-

Tablet & Capsules, Lubricants & Disintegrants, Pan Coating, Oral Preparations Mixtures, External Preparations, Ear Drops, Mouth Washes, Nasal Drops, Ointments, Creams & Eye Preparations, Antibiotics, Formulations, Packaging, Tablets including Amoxycillin, Analgin, Ibuprofen, Injectables, Liquid Orals, Capsules & Dry Syrups, Eye & Ear Preparations etc.

MODERN PACKAGING TECHNOLOGY FOR PROCESSED FOOD, BAKERY, SNACK FOOD, SPICES & ALLIED FOOD PRODUCTS

ISBN. 81-86732-28-4 # Rs. 600/-

Latest methods of Packaging Technology of fruits/veg. growers ,Spices mfrs., Snack food mfrs., Bakery Mfrs., and Edible oil mfrs. etc. Suppliers of Plant and Machinery have also been incorporated.

BOOKS ON SYNTHETIC DETERGENTS, SOAPS & DETERGENTS

HAND BOOK OF SYNTHETIC DETERGENTS WITH FORMULATIONS

ISBN. 81-86732-43-8 # Rs. 900/-

Group of Synthetic Detergents, Synthesis of Detergents, Manufacture of Synthetic Detergents with Formulae, Testing of Detergents and Soaps, Project Profiles, Suppliers of Machinery and Raw Materials, Acid Slurry, Sirf Excel Type Detergent, Ariel Type Detergent, Dry Mix Process, Dry Clean Unit and much more others etc.

MANUFACTURE OF HOUSEHOLD SOAPS, TOILET SOAPS & OTHER SOAPS WITH FORMULATIONS

ISBN. 81-86732-53-5 # Rs. 750/-

Soap base manufacture, Solid, household and toilet soaps manufacture, Production of soap base, Perfuming, Manufacturing process & formulations, Miscellaneous formulae, Scourig bar, Detergent cake & powder, Toilet & herbal soap, Laundry soap, Liquid soap, Complete plant Suppliers, Suppliers of chemicals, Present manufacturers etc.

BOOKS ON ESSENTIAL OILS, PERFUMES & FLAVOURS

MODERN TECHNOLOGY OF ESSENTIAL OILS

ISBN 81-86732-71-3 # Rs. 850/-

Essential Oils Technology, Essential Oils and Flavours, Production of Essential Oils & Oleoresins, Herb & Oil Yield in Different Ocimum Species, Kewda Essential Oil and Attar, Mint Oil, Lemongrass, Palmarosa Oil, Musk, Java Citronella, Bio-Chemical Studies, Patchouli Oil, Rose-Scented Geranium, Basil Oil etc.

ESSENTIAL OILS PROCESSES & FORMULATIONS HAND BOOK

ISBN. 81-86732-39-X # Rs. 650/-

Essential Oils by Steam Distillation, GC-MS studies, Essential Oil from Cinnamomum, Kewda flower distillation, Composition of essential oil frombottle brush, Composition of essential oil from flowers of Keora, Manufacturers/ Exporters of Essential oils & Aromatic Chemicals with Machinery.

HAND BOOK OF ESSENTIAL OILS MANUFACTURING & AROMATIC PLANTS

ISBN. 81-86732-27-6 # Rs. 450/-

Rose oildistillation, extraction of essential oils, Uses of indigenous aromatic plants, essential oil bearing plants status,fractionation of essential oil, essential oil of hyptis suaveolens poit, super critical fluid extraction, ginger oil, Jasmine, rose etc..

HAND BOOK OF PERFUMES WITH FORMULATIONS

ISBN. 81-86732-42-X # Rs. 750/-

Creating a Perfume, Flower Perfumes, Colognes, Raw Materials, Classification, Packaging of Perfumes, Testing of Perfumes, Aromatic Perfumery Compounds, Scent & Perfume, Spray Perfume, Suppliers of Raw Materials .

HAND BOOK OF PERFUMES & FLAVOURS

ISBN. 81-86732-30-6 # Rs. 600/-

Perfume, Formulary of Perfume & Flavour, Natural Odours Simulated with Aromatic Chemicals, Simulated Flower Scents, Simulated Marine Scents (Algae), Plant & Equipment Suppliers, Suppliers of Raw Materials, Suppliers of Perfumes. Project profiles etc.

HAND BOOK OF FLAVOURS TECHNOLOGY

ISBN 81-86732-98-5
Rs. 750/- or US $ 100/-

The book cover flavour analysis, Chemistry of flavours, Off-flavours in foods, Manufacturing processes of flavours, Plant materials used in flavouring, Principal Essential Oils used in Flavourings, Application of flavourings in food processing, Quality control, Non-Alcoholic Flavours, Flavours fruit (whiskey, vodka, Grape, Butter Scotch & Rum), Terpeneles Menthol Crystals.

ENGINEERS INDIA RESEARCH INSTITUTE Mobile : 9811437895
4449, Nai Sarak, Main Road, Delhi - 110 006 (INDIA) Ph./Fax : 91-11- 23918117, 23916431, 23840361

FLORICULTURE HAND BOOK

(Hand book of flowers growing technology)

ISBN 81-86732-72-1

Rs. 1000/- or US $ 110/-

Carnation, ChinaAster, Dahlia, Gladiolus, Gerbera, Gloriosa, Jasmine, Lilium, Lotus, Marigold, Orchids, Rose, Tuberose, Other flowers, Gypsophila, Statice, Zantedeschia, Gaillardia, Sweet Sultan, Solidago, Plant Economics of various floriculture projects etc.

HAND BOOK OF ICE CREAM TECHNOLOGY & FORMULAE

ISBN. 81-86732-70-5 ★ Rs. 525/-

Composition of Ice Cream Mixes, Manufacturing Process, Ice Cream Freezing, Ice Cream Mix Calculations, Packaging of Ice Cream, Frozen Dairy Products and Formulations, Laboratory Tests, Project Profiles, Suppliers of Machineries etc.

BOOKS ON RUBBER CHEMICALS & RUBBER GOODS

TECHNOLOGY OF RUBBER & RUBBER GOODS INDUSTRIES

ISBN. 81-86732-59-4 ★ Rs. 900/-

The book cover natural rubber , Classification, Properties, Uses and Manufacture, Latex processing and applications, Chemical aspects of rubber technology, Physical aspects of rubber technology, Styrene Butadiene Rubber (SBR), Processing and curing of Polybutadiene and Polyisoprene, Manufacture and Processing of EPDM, Butyl and Halobutyl Rubbers, Nitrile & Polyacrylic Rubber, Neoprene (Polychloroprene) & Hypalon Rubber, Silocone Rubber, Reclaimed Rubber, Latex & Foam Rubber, Vulcanisation, Manufacturing Techniques of Rubber Products, Recycling of Wastes from Rubber & Plastic, Quality control in Rubber Industry etc.

RUBBER CHEMICALS & PROCESSING INDUSTRIES

ISBN. 81-86732-15-2

 # Rs. 400/- *US$50*

The book covers Technology of Rubber Chemicals and Manufacturing of Rubber Products/Goods. Various Project Profiles are given, Suppliers of Raw Materials and Machinery, Natural Rubber, Synthetic & Acrylic Rubber, Butyl Rubber, Silicon & Nitrile Rubber, Rubber Powder etc.

BOOKS ON PAINT VARNISH LACQUER SOLVENTS, COATING, RESINS & INKS INDUSTRIES

PAINT VARNISH SOLVENTS AND COATING TECHNOLOGY

ISBN. 81-86732-44-6

 # Rs. 750/- or US$ 75/-

Introduction, General Pigments Physical Properties, Pigments Processing, Plasticizers and Solvents, Synthetic Resins, Varnishes, Pigmentation, Paints (Decorative & Building), Coatings, Industrial Paints & Coatings, Industrial Finishes, Miscellaneous Coatings and Ancillary Materials, Testing and Evaluation, Miscellaneous Formulae, Project Profiles, Suppliers of Raw Materials & Plant and Machinery, Present Manufacturers etc.

PAINT PIGMENT VARNISH & LACQUER MANUFACTURING

ISBN. 81-86732-16-0

 # Rs. 450/- or US$ 50/-

The Book covers Process, Formulations, Technology, Project Profiles on various Paint, Varnish, Lacquer manufacturing industries. Suppliers of Plant, Equipments and Machinery with Raw Materials have also been incorporated etc.

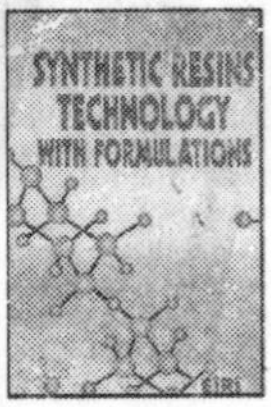

SYNTHETIC RESINS TECHNOLOGY WITH FORMULATIONS

ISBN. 81-86732-40-3

 # Rs. 800/- or US$ 80/-

Latest technology to manufacture various Synthetic Resins with formulae including epoxy resin, alkyd resins, acrylics, ion-exchange resin, melamine formaldehyde resin, phenol formaldehyde resin, polyester resin, polyvinyl acetate, polyvinyl alcohol, pvc resin & plastisol, silicones, urea formaldehyde resins etc. Suppliers of Machinery and Raw Materials etc.

TECHNOLOGY OF COATINGS, RESINS, PIGMENTS AND INKS INDUSTRIES

ISBN. 81-86732-64-0

 # Rs. 975/- or US$ 100/-

Introduction, PU Coatings, Powder Coatings, Antifouling Coatings, UV Curable Powder Coatings, Polyurethane Coating, Colour of Pigments, Caprolactone Modification of Polyester Resins, Acrylics, Additives in Paints, Polyester- based Water- borne and Solvent-borne Coil Coatings, Zinc Dust Pigment, Alkyd Manufacturing, Calcium Carbonate Extenders, Pigments for Paints Inks & Plastics, Design of Paint Formulations, Polyester Resin etc.

MODERN INKS FORMULAES & MANUFACTURING INDUSTRIES

ISBN. 81-86732-17-9

 # Rs. 325/- or US$50/-

Colour Matching, Raw Materials, Waxes & Additives, Typographic Inks, Formuations, Photogravure Inks Screen Process Inks, Ball Point Pen Inks, Testing of Finished Inks, Formulae, Toner Inks, Printing Inks, Screen & Offset Printing Inks, Stamp Pad Inks,

PROFITABLE SMALL SCALE MANUFACTURE OF SOAPS & DETERGENTS

ISBN. 81-86732-25-X # Rs. 375/-

Raw materials, soap manufacture, soap from non edible oil, soap from soap stock, Medicated soap, Shaving soap, shaving creams, synthetic detergent powder, detergent cake and powder, Enzyme detergent powder, Project Profiles on various Soap and Detergent projects, Suppliers of Plant and Machinery and raw materials etc.

ENGINEERS INDIA RESEARCH INSTITUTE Mobile : 9811437895

4449, Nai Sarak, Main Road, Delhi - 110 006 (INDIA) Ph./Fax : 91-11- 23918117, 23916431, 23840361